ECONOMIC INSECURITY AND SOCIAL SECURITY

RISK AND INSURANCE SERIES

Edited by Kenneth Black, Jr.
Georgia State College

Athearn   *Risk and Insurance*

Brinker   *Economic Insecurity and Social Security*

Huebner   *The Economics of Life Insurance*

Huebner & Black   *Life Insurance*

Huebner, Black, & Cline   *Property and Liability Insurance*

ECONOMIC INSECURITY AND SOCIAL SECURITY

Paul A. Brinker

University of Oklahoma

 New York

APPLETON-CENTURY-CROFTS

Division of Meredith Corporation

TO MY WIFE

PREFACE

Economics textbooks on insecurity in the late 1930's concentrated on the problem of unemployment and the three major sections of the Social Security Act: unemployment insurance, old-age insurance, and public assistance. Patterns of economic insecurity changed with World War II and the postwar prosperity, but economics texts on insecurity did not change accordingly. Little work was done by economists on problems of low-wage industries or minority groups. Some have contended that until several years ago many economists were oblivious to the fact that there was widespread poverty in the United States. It is the purpose of this book to include information on low-wage industries and minority groups. Accordingly there is a chapter on the low-wage industry of agriculture and a discussion of such minority groups as Negroes, Mexican-Americans, Puerto Ricans, and American Indians. Also there has been little discussion in textbooks on economic insecurity on how education and improved housing may help in the battle with insecurity. These topics are also discussed in this book. In short, the major thrust of this book is to provide more breadth to economics courses dealing with the problem of economic insecurity.

This book is divided into five main parts. Part I on Historical Perspectives, Aging, and Public Assistance includes the first six chapters. After a historical introduction in Chapter one, Chapters two through six deal with the problems of aging, premature death, and public assistance. Part II, Chapters seven through eleven, is concerned with economic problems arising from occupational disability and poor health. Part III, Chapters twelve through sixteen, deals with the problem of unemployment. Part IV, Chapters seventeen through twenty-one, discusses problems of low-income groups and other special groups in our society. Part V, Chapters twenty-two through twenty-four, deals with solutions to the insecurity problem. A bibliography is included after Chapter one and at the end of each of the five parts of the book.

I wish to thank Professor Arthur H. Reede of Pennsylvania State University for encouraging my interest in problems of economic insecurity, and for his review of the chapters on occupational disability and workmen's compensation. Appreciation is also expressed to Professor William Burgett of the University of Oklahoma's School of Architecture for reviewing the material on housing. Many thanks go to Professor John Paul Duncan of the Political Science department at the University of Oklahoma for making a number of valuable suggestions on the last chapter. I am indebted to Professor Joseph Klos of Oklahoma State University for his review. I also wish particularly to thank the following persons who reviewed the manuscript in its entirety: Professor Charles Schottland of Brandeis University; Professor Kenneth Black, Jr., of Georgia State College in Atlanta; Professor William Nelson Peach, Research Professor of Economics at the University of Oklahoma; and

Professor C. Stanley Clifton, Director of the School of Social Work at the University of Oklahoma. For the many aids given by my wife during the preparation of this manuscript, I wish to express my thanks.

P. A. B.

CONTENTS

HISTORICAL PERSPECTIVES, AGING, AND PUBLIC ASSISTANCE

HISTORICAL PERSPECTIVES

In attempting to earn a living, man has always been faced with a large number of economic problems. In most of the world today, per capita income is so low that many people are unable to provide adequate food, clothing, and shelter for themselves. Fortunately, income is much higher in the United States than elsewhere. The median family income in the United States in 1964 was $6,569.[1] Many millions of Americans, however, live on much less than this amount. In this book we will be studying these economically insecure people. Some of these people had an adequate income at one time, but have fallen into a lower income group because of a death, illness, an industrial accident, old age, or unemployment. Others in the poverty group never attained sufficient income to live well. Some in this group may be employed in low-wage industries or occupations. Many members of minority groups, such as Negroes, Spanish-Americans, and American Indians, fall into this group.

MEASUREMENT OF ADEQUATE INCOME IN THE UNITED STATES

Economists have been interested for a number of years in the concept of adequacy of income. Some have attempted to measure the concept statistically. Budgets are prepared to determine necessary income for families and individuals. Welfare agencies use such budgets regularly to determine eligibility for aid. An example of this type of budget is one prepared by the Budget Standard Service of the Community Council of Greater New York. Their budget provided that a family live on an adequate but modest level of living. A family of four—a husband, a wife, a boy of 13, and a girl of 8— would live in a house consisting of four rooms, kitchen, and bath. The husband was allocated either a topcoat or overcoat every three years; a suit nearly every year; two pairs of trousers, four or five shirts, two pairs of shoes, and 12 pairs of socks annually. Medical costs included visiting a doctor four or five times a year and a dentist twice a year for each member of the family

---

[1] *Consumer Income*, Washington, D.C., U.S. Department of Commerce, Bureau of the Census, Series P-60, No. 47 (September, 1965), Table E, p. 5.

plus drug and Blue Cross costs. The adults were permitted sufficient recreational spending to attend a movie once every three weeks, to buy a newspaper every day, and a magazine once a month. No automobile was provided for, but allowances were made for fares to and from work and school. On the basis of these costs, Table 1-1 was compiled. As shown in this table, the

TABLE 1–1. WEEKLY COSTS FOR THE FAMILY OF FOUR PERSONS (EMPLOYED MAN, HOUSEWIFE, BOY 13, GIRL 8); NEW YORK CITY, OCTOBER, 1965

Goods, Services, and Taxes	*Costs*
Food	$ 42.09
Food at home	36.59
Lunches at work	5.50
Clothing	10.70
Housing	28.89
Heat and rent	20.12
Utilities	2.51
House furnishings	3.80
Household supplies	.86
Laundry service	1.60
Transportation (non–car owner)	4.69
To and from work	3.00
Other	1.69
Medical care	6.26
Personal care	2.96
Other goods and services	17.41
Recreation, education, communications, tobacco, reading	9.73
Life insurance	2.06
Union dues	.85
Gifts, contributions, miscellaneous	3.28
Telephone	1.49
Total, all goods and services	113.00
FICA and Disability Insurance	3.64
New York State Income Tax	1.56
Federal Income Tax	10.73
Total, including taxes: week	128.93
Total, including taxes: year	6,704.00

Source: Annual Price Survey and Family Budget Cost, October, 1965, Community Council of Greater New York, Budget Standard Service Research Department, Table 1-A, p. 5.

four-person family of the ages specified needed an income of $6,704 in 1965 to live in New York City. Additional data were provided for families of various sizes and ages. For example, a single working woman, aged 45 and living alone, needed an income of $3,523. An elderly retired couple needed $3,343, compared with $5,671 for a young couple both employed. The budget prepared by the Community Council of Greater New York is somewhat similar to the "City Workers Family Budget" prepared by the U.S. Bureau of Labor Statistics. The B.L.S. figure for a family of the same size for a few years earlier in New York City was $5,970.[2] Budgets measuring poverty rather than a modest level of living show much lower income figures. Table 1-2 summarizes the various estimates of poverty income along with the number of people living in poverty in the United States.

Although the statistical methods for computing poverty differed, and the estimates of amounts of poverty varied, all analysts concluded that widespread poverty exists in the United States.

IDENTIFICATION OF THOSE LIVING IN POVERTY

Using an income of $3,130 for a nonfarm family of four, below which they would be living in poverty, the Social Security Administration found that in 1964 over 34 million persons, or 17.9 percent of our population, were living in poverty. Of all those living in poverty, 10.8 million persons were in families headed by women (46 percent of all families headed by women were living in poverty). Although the figures for poverty income were lowered by 30 percent for farm families, 4.2 million of the poor had a farm residence (33 percent of all those with a farm residence were living in poverty). Forty-eight percent of all nonwhites, comprising 10.4 million, were in the poverty group.[3] A total of 5.4 million persons 65 or over were living in poverty, or 31 percent of all the aged.[4]

Using data for poor families rather than persons, families with a large number of children tended to be poor. Of the 6.8 million poor families in America in 1964, 1.2 million of these poor families had seven or more children. Thirty-five percent of all families with seven or more children were poor. Poverty was heavily concentrated in the South. Of the 6.8 million families living in poverty, 3.3 million, or almost half, were located in the South.

Concerning the work experience of the poor, of the 6.8 million poor families, only 2.1 million had a wage earner who worked 50-52 weeks during the year. Another million poor families had a wage earner who had a full-time job but worked fewer than 50 weeks. Almost a million poor families had only a part-time worker in the family, and 2.4 million poor families had

[2] Helen Lamale and Margaret Stotz, "City Workers Family Budget," *Monthly Labor Review*, Vol. 83 (1960), Table 1, p. 787.

[3] Mollie Orshansky, "Recounting the Poor—A Five-Year Review," *Social Security Bulletin*, Vol. 29, No. 4 (April, 1966), Table 3, p. 25.

[4] Mollie Orshansky, "More About the Poor," *Social Security Bulletin*, Vol. 29, No. 5 (May, 1966), Table 1, p. 4.

TABLE 1-2. ESTIMATES OF POVERTY IN THE UNITED STATES

Author	Maximum Income for a Poverty Family of Four[a]	Number of People Living in Poverty (in Millions)	Date of Income Statistics
Lampman	$2,500	32.2	1957
AFL-CIO	$3,000[c]	41.2	1958
Social Security Administration	$3,130	34.1	1964
Council of Economic Advisors	$3,200	32.7	1965
Harrington	$3,000-$3,500	50.0	1959
David	$3,696	48.0	1956
Conference on Economic Progress[b]	$4,000[c]	38.0	1960
Survey Research Center	$4,186	28% of Adult Units 20% of Families	1960
Ornati	$4,350	46	1960

[a] An employed husband, a housewife, a boy aged 13, and a girl 8. These figures are adjusted upward for larger families and older children and downward for smaller families or younger children.

[b] In addition to 38 million living in poverty, 39 million were living in deprivation. Deprivation family income was listed from $4,000 to $5,999 and unattached individual income from $2,000 to $2,999.

[c] Multi-Person Families rather than 4 members families.

Sources: Robert J. Lampman, *The Low Income Population and Economic Growth*, U.S. Congress Joint Committee Print, No. 12 (1959), p.r. AFL-CIO, *Labor's Economic Review*, Vol. 5, No. 8 (August, 1960), p. 7. Mollie Orshansky, "Recounting the Poor— A Five-Year Review," *Social Security Bulletin*, Vol. 29 (April, 1966), Table 1, p. 23 and Table 3, p. 25. Council of Economic Advisors: *Economic Report of the President* (1967), p. 138. Michael Harrington, *The Other America* (New York, Macmillan, 1962), p. 182. Martin David, "Welfare, Income, and Budget Needs," *Review of Economics and Statistics*, Vol. 41 (1959), calculated from Table 1, p. 395 and Table 3, p. 399. Conference of Economic Progress, *Poverty and Deprivation in the United States*, Washington, D.C., Conference on Economic Progress (1962), pp. 19-22. James Morgan, Martin David, Wilbur Cohen, and Harvey Brazer, *Income and Welfare in the United States*, Survey Research Center (New York, McGraw-Hill, 1962), calculated from Table 16-1, p. 189 and Table 16-2, p. 190. Oscar Ornati, *Poverty Amid Affluence* (New York, Twentieth Century Fund, 1966), pp. 157-158.

no worker. Within this group, illness or disability was the cause of not working in 740,000 poor families.

Several occupations paid such low wages or provided so little work that poverty was experienced by large numbers. Fifty-seven percent of all private household workers were in families living in poverty, as were 29 percent of all those engaged as unskilled laborers.[5]

[5] *Ibid.*, Table 2, p. 5.

A comprehensive analysis of poverty was also made by the Survey Research Center of the University of Michigan.[6] Their researchers found that those who were poor were likely to remain poor. The heads of poor families reported an average of $2,949 as the highest income they had ever earned. About a third of all poor families reported that they never had earned more than $1,949 in any one year. The poor had few resources to fall back on. Only 10 percent of the poor had $1,000 or more in savings and none had more than $5,000. The mean equity that this group had in a home or farm amounted to $3,800. Sixty-two percent of this group had no hospitalization insurance of any kind. In analyzing transmission of poverty between generations, the Survey Research Center found that the fathers of heads of poor families were more likely to have been farmers or unskilled laborers than were the fathers of all family heads. Although 45 percent of the children in poor families completed high school, this figure compared unfavorably with a national average of 65 percent. Furthermore, 34 percent of the children of the poor completed only from 1 to 8 grades and another 21 percent completed from 9 to 11 grades.

DECLINE IN POVERTY

Lampman has made a valuable contribution in tracing the decline in poverty over time. In 1947 he found that 26 percent lived in low-income status, as compared with 19 percent in 1957. Three factors made possible the fall in the percentage of those in the low-income group during the decade. One was that the number of rural farm families declined. The second was that workers shifted into higher-paid occupations. Third, workers moved into higher-paying industries. The improvement in income of the poor came from increasing the total income in the United States rather than redistributing income. In 1957 the lowest fifth of income receivers obtained 5 percent of all income. This was the same percentage that they received in the 1930's and in 1947. However, Garvy and Denison point out that some redistribution may have occurred. Older families formerly living together with other spending units now maintain separate households. Their income is lower since they have separated, and this pulls down the average of the bottom quartile.[7]

Those not showing much improvement from 1947 to 1957 were the aged and families headed by women. The best gains were made by nonwhites. Sixty-two percent of Negro families earned below $2,500 in 1947, but only 36 percent were below this figure in 1957. Fifty-three percent of

[6] James Morgan, et al., Income and Welfare in the United States (New York, McGraw-Hill, 1962), pp. 187-217.

[7] George Garvy, "Functional and Size Distribution of Income and Their Meaning," Papers and Proceedings of the 66th Annual Meeting of the American Economic Association, American Economic Review, Vol. XLIV (May, 1954), pp. 236-253. See also E. F. Denison, "Income Types and the Size Distribution: Relation to Functional Distribution and Factor Compensation," ibid., pp. 254-269.

aged families fell into the low-income group in 1947 and this figure was reduced only to 50 percent in 1957. The corresponding figures for families headed by women were respectively 46 and 38 percent, a smaller drop than the average for all families.

Lampman forecast that about 10 percent of our population will be in the poverty class by 1977–1987, but the figure will be reduced to this percentage only if appropriate government action is taken. A later study from 1959 through 1964 showed that although the numbers living in poverty decreased from 38.9 million to 34.1 million, absolute increases in the number living in poverty were recorded for unrelated women, families with a female head with four or more children under age 18, and unrelated individuals 65 and over. Those groups showing less improvement than others from 1959 to 1964 in addition to the above were unrelated individuals 25 and over and non-whites.[8]

POVERTY AND GOVERNMENT

The activity of government will play an important role in determining whether the lower-income groups will be able to raise their income in the future. From 1948 to 1954, the lowest fifth of all consumer units paid relatively high taxes—25 percent of their income. This figure rose from 19 percent in 1938–1939. To offset the loss of tax income, transfer payments to lower-income groups have been increasing substantially in recent years. Transfer payments are made to those who are rendering no current services. They are mainly government payments for such things as old-age and unemployment insurance benefits, relief payments, military bonuses, and the like. During the last thirty years, transfer payments have increased from 1 to 5 percent of personal income. About 40 percent of all income of the lowest 20 percent are transfer payments. Obviously, decreasing the tax load of the lower-income group or increasing transfer payments will increase their income.[9]

A CASE STUDY

The Subcommittee on Low Income Families of the Joint Committee on the Economic Report has submitted a report on case studies of 100 families earning less than $2,000 a year. As a common denominator, they found low wages, intermittent work, high vulnerability to sickness, and broken homes.

[8] Orshansky, "Recounting the Poor—A Five Year Review," op. cit., p. 27.
[9] Robert J. Lampman, The Low Income Population and Economic Growth, U.S. Joint Committee Print, No. 12 (1959), pp. 13-32.

Income was insufficient to provide for adequate food, shelter, or the other necessaries of life.[10] The following is a case history of one of the families:

Case No. 22—Little Family, Houston, Texas

Members of household—father, age 47; mother, age 40; children: three girls, ages 15, 12, and 6; one boy, age 19.

Total cash income, 1949—$960. Chief earner: father. Occupation: sawmill worker.

The Little family are transients. They lived in one town for almost 12 months and then moved to another community when Mrs. Little was admitted to the State tuberculosis hospital there. The family wanted to be near her and Mr. Little was able to get a job. When Mrs. Little was released four months later, they returned to their former home, but neither Mr. Little nor John, age 19, could find work. They then moved to an eastern Texas town where the father was able to get a job with a sawmill company. They stayed there until the work gave out and then they moved to their present residence, where Mr. Little and John work for another sawmill company. When the family moves, Mr. Little and John hitchhike and Mrs. Little and the girls go in the truck that carries their household furnishings. In this way they were able to make their four moves at a total cost of only $21.62.

Both Mr. and Mrs. Little had been married before and the children are a combination of their previous marriages. There are no children by this marriage. John and Mary, 19 and 15, respectively, and Minnie May, aged 6, are Mrs. Little's children; however, they are apparently devoted to Mr. Little and refer to him as father. John works with his father at the sawmill and Mary takes care of the house and attends school when the household duties and her mother's health permit. Betty, aged 12, is Mr. Little's child.

The Littles live in a three-room "company" house which consists of a living room—bedroom combination, a kitchen, and a bedroom. There is an outdoor toilet. There are no bathing facilities, nor do they have electricity. Although they have an icebox, they only get ice for it when they go to town for groceries. Their household furnishings are scant, consisting of one table, four straight chairs, one armchair, an icebox, a double bed, and pallets on the floor upon which the children sleep.

When Mr. Little was younger, he did tenant farming with little or no success and went from farm to farm with the hope that "next year's crop would pay." It never seemed to, so when a sawmill moved into his community he gave up farming, and began to work for the mill. Sawmill companies lease a tract of timber, move in the mill equipment, erect "shotgun houses" which they rent to the millworkers, and work the tract until it is cleared. The company then moves on to the next lease. Sawmill work is seasonal. The amount of work to be had depends on the demand for lumber, the weather, and the length of time necessary to cut over the tract. The rate of daily earnings depends on "the amount a man

[10] *Making Ends Meet on Less Than $2,000 a Year,* Washington, D.C., U.S. Congress, Subcommittee on Low Income Families, Joint Committee on the Economic Report (1955), p. 4.

can log." Mr. Little and John each earn about $15 a week. Their average employment has been around 8 months of the year and their combined yearly income usually amounts to approximately $960.

The Littles spend all they make for food. The children catch rides into town to make their purchases. What they buy is filling, but not well balanced. They say that they would get more milk if they had more money. As it is, they get one quart a day. What little clothing they have has been given to them "by folks."

Mrs. Little needs a great deal of rest in bed. The household duties and the care of the younger children are left mostly to the children themselves. School is not a "must" for them. Mary takes care of the house when her mother is having bad days. If it is berry season, the children go berry-picking. Sometimes they go fishing. They aren't interested in school and they all plan to quit just as soon as they can.

The family has been in this community for around 5 months. The timber is almost through and soon they will move on.[11]

HISTORICAL APPROACH TO THE PROBLEM OF INSECURITY

Modern anthropologists have pointed out that the purpose of the formation of primitive societies was not only to dominate weaker beings but also to provide for mutual protection and promote the feeling of belongingness. Mutual aid helped to promote security although in some primitive societies the aged, the ill, or the otherwise handicapped were killed or abandoned as being too great a burden on the tribe. As tribes developed, a priesthood group arose, and this group assumed leadership in protecting the helpless. Religion became a powerful force in dictating that charity be practiced. Practically all ancient religions preached charity either for the purpose of obtaining the grace of God or out of a genuine feeling of pity.[12] From Vendidad, a book of the ancient Zoroaster religion, we read: "The riches of the infinite God will be bestowed upon him who relieves the poor." A Hindu epic has it that "He who giveth without stint food to a fatigued wayfarer, never seen before, obtaineth merit that is great." [13]

THE HEBREWS

The Hebrews have exerted a tremendous impact on the thinking of the human race. Faced with a niggardliness of nature and oppression by captors, one of their major themes was that of social justice. Moses' anger and

11 *Ibid.*, pp. 50-51.
12 Walter A. Friedlander, *Introduction to Social Welfare* (Englewood Cliffs, N.J., Prentice-Hall, 1955), pp. 9-10.
13 Amos Warner, Mary Coolidge, and George Howard, *American Charities* (New York, Thomas Crowell Co., 1919), p. 5.

slaying of an Egyptian for oppressing a Hebrew [14] demonstrated his attitude toward injustice, although his action was taken in a fit of anger. Later during the life of Moses, a rule was laid down that if money were loaned to the poor, no interest should be charged.[15] Every seven years creditors released borrowers from all debts. At the same time a command was given: "Thou shalt surely open thy hand unto thy brother, to the needy, and to thy poor, in thy land." [16] Even more stringent was the rule that every fifty years, the year of jubilee, the land had to be returned by creditors to their original owners. Any person who became poor and had to sell himself was permitted to do so only as a hired servant rather than a slave. He became free during the year of jubilee.[17] In the book of Job we have an example of how the wealthy patriarch should behave to those less fortunate than himself:

If I have withheld the poor from their desire, or have caused the eyes of the widow to fail, or have eaten my morsel alone, and the fatherless hath not eaten thereof; . . . If I have seen any perish for want of clothing, or that the needy had no clothing . . . then let my shoulder fall from the shoulder blade and mine arm be broken from the bone.[18]

THE GREEKS [19]

The putting to death of Socrates and the failure of the rulers of that time to govern wisely led Plato to propose an ideal society. Because of the small-scale economic organization of his time, he proposed communities of 5,040 families. There were to be three classes of people in his society: the rulers, the soldiers, and the workers. Plato advocated various classes in society, because his aristocratic leanings led him to believe that most of the people were incapable of profiting from higher education. In order that the rulers of the society would not become avaricious, he advocated communal living for this group. Only a fixed salary with limited expenses would be paid this group. He also felt that wives and children should be common property to keep the rulers from pressing for material gain. Plato contended that both extremes of wealth and poverty were harmful to a community. Wealth leads to luxury and indolence, whereas poverty leads to meanness and viciousness.

Aristotle, a pupil of Plato, rejected communism on grounds that communal property is not cared for properly. Furthermore, people enjoy products more if they are their own. Aristotle felt that communism would lead to

[14] Exodus, 2:11-12.
[15] *Ibid.*, 22:25.
[16] Deuteronomy, 15:7.
[17] Leviticus, 25:23, 39.
[18] Job, 31:16-22.
[19] The material on Grecian and Roman thought is taken mainly from Emory S. Bogardus, *The Development of Social Thought* (New York, Longmans, 1950), Chaps. 8-10.

much quarreling since those who worked hard would resent the more slothful. Communism in wives and children was dismissed as weakening friend-
ship and destroying love. Aristotle did agree with Plato's class society.
Aristotle was disdainful of manual labor, and like practically all other
thinkers of his time, upheld the institution of slavery. He maintained that
slaves were unable to guide themselves by reason. At the height of Athenian
society, there were 25,000 free Athenians compared to 300,000 slaves. He,
too, agreed that great wealth or poverty was harmful; therefore, he put his
faith in the middle class. Poverty, according to him, led to revolution and
crime, whereas the desire for wealth caused even greater crimes in order to
gratify passion or satisfy the desire for excess.

THE ROMANS

Emperor Marcus Aurelius (A.D. 161–180) reduced taxes of the poor and
opposed some brutalities in punishment. He advocated the social injunction
"love mankind." The Romans developed no independent philosophy of their
own, but were primarily noted for their contributions to legal philosophy.
The rights of contract and private property were stressed by them. The governments of Rome were autocratic, and little was done to help the lower
classes. What little discussion was devoted to slavery was to the effect that
it should be profitable to slaveowners. Varro, for example, suggested that in
unhealthful climates it might be more profitable to hire free workers since
capital investment in slaves might be lost through early death. He suggested
that generous treatment be accorded slaves to get more work from them.

CHRISTIANITY

The teachings of Jesus obviously have had an important impact on civilization. The basic tenet of early Christian thought was that people should
believe in a benevolent God who will grant them everlasting life in the
hereafter. Also "Thou shalt love thy neighbor as thyself." [20] Jesus himself
practiced compassion by healing the sick, giving encouragement to those
who were weary and heavy laden, and in feeding hungry multitudes. In
His preaching He suggested that mercy be practiced. As good practices He
specifically cited giving food to the hungry, water to the thirsty, lodging to
strangers, clothing to the naked, and visitations to those who were sick or
in prison. In relationships with other people, He suggested love for enemies,
and reconciliation between those who have quarreled. If evil is done, Jesus
recommended not retribution but a turning of the cheek. He added that if
a person takes away your coat through a lawsuit you should give him your
cloak also. If a person compels you to go a mile with him, Jesus suggested

[20] Matthew, 22:37-39.

that you go two miles. He added that you should give to those who ask or would borrow from you. This philosophy of love and the brotherhood of man may be summarized by what has come to be known as the Golden Rule: "And as ye would that men should do to you, do ye also to them likewise." [21]

After the passage of centuries, Christian attitudes toward social welfare have followed two contradictory points of view. A deviation from the welfare teachings of Jesus was made by St. Augustine (A.D. 354–430). St. Augustine put so much emphasis on the first commandment mentioned above, belief in God, that no corollaries on welfare were worked out for this life.[22] The status quo was looked upon as ordained by God, and therefore nothing should be done to change society or alleviate the sufferings of the unfortunate. The sufferings were temporary anyway, and were not viewed as being particularly important in relation to the problem of eternal salvation. In the Middle Ages, the class system and subjugation of the serfs by nobles was not challenged effectively by the church. Although some charity was practiced by the church, one student questions whether it contributed as much as lay society in proportion to its resources.[23] Fratricidal wars were engaged in by unoccupied barons at the expense of the peasants with little criticism from the church. Several churchmen attempted to return Christianity to the original concepts of Jesus. St. Francis of Assisi (1182–1226) moved from a monastery in an attempt to regenerate society and alleviate the conditions of the poor. One scholar maintains that the church had become so corrupt that it was saved from extinction only by the work of St. Francis.[24] Later, even though some felt that the church had a contribution to make on insecurity in this world, the voice of the church as a whole was muted. The fact that the world turned its back on the original Christian solutions to welfare problems indicates that the church made little contribution in this field for centuries.

WELFARE IN ENGLAND

Under the feudal system, security of the serfs was assured by the lords. Unemployment, old age, sickness, and the other vicissitudes of life were taken care of by the lords of the manor. The serfs, however, had to pay an extremely high price for their security—namely the loss of their freedom. With the breakdown of the feudal system and the growth of free citizens, more and more people moved into cities. This caused a number of new problems

21 Luke, 6:31.

22 Bogardus, op. cit., pp. 170-171.

23 James W. Thompson, An Economic and Social History of the Middle Ages (New York, Appleton-Century-Crofts, 1928), p. 684.

24 Ibid., p. 694.

to arise, such as maintaining income when unemployed, aged, ill, or otherwise disabled. Early social legislation was punitive in nature. When the employer class was faced with a shortage of laborers due to the Black Death, the Statute of Laborers were passed in 1349. This Act outlawed begging and required that dependent employees be forced to work for masters at the lower wages existing before the onslaught of the Death.

LAWS UNDER HENRY VIII (1509–1547)

In the year 1531 the first positive steps were taken by government to help the poor. Legislation was passed because of increased urbanization and the inability of the Church and private philanthropy to cope with the enlarging problem. The aged poor and impotent were required to register and thereafter were permitted to beg for a living. No mercy, on the other hand, was to be shown the able-bodied unemployed. In fact, idle persons were "to be tied to the end of a cart naked and be beaten with whips through the same market-town or other place until his body be bloody by reason of such whipping."[25] After five years of experience with this law, it was decided the penalties against idleness should be made even more stringent. For the second offense, the upper part of the right ear was to be cut off, and the death penalty was assessed for continuing idleness. A later law in 1547 provided that idlers should be marked with a hot iron on the breast and enslaved for two years. If the person enslaved attempted to escape, he was to be branded on the forehead or cheek with the letter "S" and enslaved forever.[26]

ELIZABETHAN POOR LAWS

Failure to secure enough money by voluntary contributions resulted in enactment of several laws during the reign of Queen Elizabeth (1558–1603), the first of which was passed in 1572. This legislation provided that the justices of the peace and other local officials assess taxes for the support of the infirm. Almshouses were to be erected to care for the needy, but all types of needy people were to be housed there together—the ill, the aged, the mentally deranged, criminals, orphans, and all others unable to support themselves. Overseers of the poor were to see to it that rogues and vagabonds were put to work. Failure to work would result in a person being put into a House of Correction, where work was provided along with punishment. Because poverty was to be taken care of locally, an attempt was made to reduce the mobility of workers so that they would not become a burden on a new community. The Law of Settlement of 1662 provided that churchwardens or overseers could complain to justices of the peace to have anyone removed

[25] Karl De Schweinitz, *England's Road to Social Security* (Philadelphia, University of Pennsylvania Press, 1943), p. 21.
[26] *Ibid.*, pp. 1-24.

who might become indigent if they rented a tenement for less than a yearly value of ten pounds. Such a law brought all sorts of abuses. It did not have to be proved that the new arrivals were actually in need, only that they might become needy. In some cases, local residents complained and had people returned to their old district so as to avoid competition in their type of work.

EIGHTEENTH- AND NINETEENTH-CENTURY LEGISLATION

In 1722 Parliament passed a law which permitted the churchwardens and overseers to contract out employment in workhouses to those who thought they could make a profit on this type of employment. Any who refused lodging and employment in such workhouses were to be denied any type of relief. The costs of relief were cut greatly by this act, for most of the poor attempted to remain out of the workhouses at all costs. The death rate in such workshops was exceptionally high both for children and the aged because the surroundings were crowded and unhealthful, and only a minimum of food was provided. The parishes in contracting out the workhouses attempted to pay as little money as possible, and the contractor attempted to make as much money as possible by providing little care for the poor.[27]

The Napoleonic Wars brought steep rises in the cost of living, but wages did not rise nearly as fast. To offset the drop in the standard of living a number of parishes devised supplemental relief payments to the poor. Such payments were completely disassociated with employment in workhouses and were paid to the poor in their own homes. The new approach to relief began in 1795 and was called the "Speenhamland system" after the town, now a part of Newbury, in which it originated. Payments under this system did help the poor, but low payments and frequently no payments gradually resulted in its demise.[28] The system was also criticized as taking away the incentive of employers to pay higher wages and the incentive of employees to seek higher wages. A Poor Commission appointed in 1832 was quite critical of the system of allowances. The Speenhamland system was replaced by a return to the older system of workhouses. The Reform Act of 1834 outlawed all forms of outdoor relief. This Act reiterated that employment in workhouses should be made so onerous that few would apply.[29] Less was paid in wages than could be earned in private industry. This principle of paying lower relief payments is still used in the United States today.[30]

[27] *Ibid.*, pp. 46-48.

[28] Mark Blaug, "The Poor Law Report Reexamined," *Journal of Economic History,*" XXIV (June, 1964), pp. 231-232. For an analysis of a number of students on Speenhamland, see Milton D. Speizman, "Speenhamland: An Experiment in Guaranteed Income," *Social Service Review,* Vol. 40, No. 1 (March, 1966), pp. 44-55.

[29] De Schweinitz, *op. cit.,* pp. 69-140.

[30] Valdemar Carlson, *Economic Security in the United States* (New York, McGraw-Hill, 1962), p. 36.

ATTITUDES TOWARD WELFARE—EIGHTEENTH-
AND NINETEENTH-CENTURIES

John Wesley (1703–1791) had some influence on welfare by preaching about the brotherhood of man and caring for one's neighbor. However, most of the thought of this period was highly individualistic in orientation. Thomas R. Malthus (1766–1834) developed his now famous Malthusian doctrine that population would outrun the food supply. His theory was used to oppose any sort of reform or care for the poor. Any amelioration of the conditions of the poor would only be temporary, for the poor would simply beget more children. No solution to the problem of poverty was worthwhile other than restricting the growth of population. Later Darwin's theory of evolution was carried over into the social field into what became known as social Darwinism. Just as the species that remain on earth were due to the "survival of the fittest," so man would progress by having the strong destroy the weak. With such a theory, little consideration or care was provided for the weak. One of the main groups who criticized the philosophy of individualism was the socialists. Karl Marx held that poverty was not due to overpopulation but to the institution of capitalism. The poor were so because they were exploited by the rich. His solution was to revise our institutions radically by a system of communism.

TWENTIETH-CENTURY LEGISLATION

The system of workhouses and the crowding of all types of indigents together in unwholesome surroundings never provided an adequate solution to the problem of age or poverty. The main impetus to the elimination of the archaic system of social legislation came with the creation of a Royal Commission on the Poor Laws and Relief of Distress in 1905. Its report was published in 1909. Although sharply divergent viewpoints were expressed by the majority, who represented local relief officers and members of private charitable organizations, and the minority, composed of Fabians and Labor, the two groups were united on some important issues. Treatment was recommended over repression. Such new approaches as the creation of labor exchanges and abolition of child labor were recommended along with unemployment and invalidity insurance. Since the Liberals had returned to power in 1906, the time was ripe for sweeping changes in social legislation.[31] An Old Age Pensions Act was passed in 1909, along with an unemployment insurance system and a national health insurance program in 1911.

Since 1945 welfare services have been expanded. In 1945 a family allowance system was introduced. In 1946 the health insurance system was radically revamped to provide medical care for all residents (compulsory

[31] De Schweinitz, *op. cit.*, pp. 184-198.

health insurance). A modernized system of child welfare services was introduced by the Children's Act of 1948. The premises of the welfare state were and are accepted by most members of British society. The term "welfare state" is used here in the narrow sense of denoting advocacy of social security and welfare programs rather than nationalization of industry.

WELFARE IN GERMANY

Attitudes and care of the aged and the poor have been more progressive in Germany than in England. In 1520 Martin Luther urged the abolition of begging. Instead he recommended that a "Common Chest" be created to provide food and money for the needy. Voluntary contributions were solicited to provide for the chest, but mandatory payments were also required. In addition to providing for the poor, the chest was used to pay the clergy, teachers, and other church officials. A number of towns adopted Luther's plan.[32] Later Frederick the Great, who ruled Prussia from 1740 to 1786, showed much concern for the welfare of his subjects. He said, "It is the business of a Sovereign, a great or small, to alleviate human misery." During his reign, he carried out many acts to help the unfortunate.[33]

WELFARE IN HAMBURG

In the town of Hamburg in 1788 a plan was adopted and copied elsewhere in Germany that was far ahead of welfare programs elsewhere. Funds were obtained by having each adult make weekly rounds in rotation among all the inhabitants. Physicians attended all who applied for relief to determine whether they could work. Those women and children who could were employed in the spinning of flax. Men and boys were employed in such occupations as making rope, cleaning the streets, and repairing roads. A hospital was organized for the indigent aged and ill, and a number of doctors were recruited to provide treatment for those who could remain at home. Nurseries were arranged to care for children if the mothers were required to work, and allowances were provided to needy families. Children were not only paid for work, but an allowance was permitted for attendance at school.[34]

NINETEENTH CENTURY

Before there were Parliaments, a royal decree in Prussia in 1839 restricted the employment of children, and another decree in 1845 regulated excessive

---

[32] *Ibid.,* pp. 36-38.
[33] W. Harbutt Dawson, *Social Insurance in Germany, 1883–1911* (London, T. Fisher Unwin, 1912), p. 2.
[34] De Schweinitz, *op. cit.,* pp. 91-94.

hours of work. Also many labor unions and benefit societies provided protection for their own members so that by 1876 some 12,000 groups were giving protection to more than two million members. More protection was provided for sickness and accidents than for old age. The modern Germany drew upon the prior progressive policies. Bismarck, for example, said, "It is the tradition of the dynasty which I serve that it takes the part of the weaker ones in the economic struggle." [35] Expediency also played a part in the formation of the legislation that was passed. Bismarck wanted to win the support of the working classes, and he favored doing this by passing social legislation. He also wished to contradict the socialist viewpoint that the state was merely an agency to suppress the masses and maintain capitalists in power. Accordingly, bills for old-age pensions were presented in the Reichstag in 1878 and for sickness and accident insurance in 1881. A sickness insurance bill was passed in 1883, an accident bill in 1884, and an old-age pension law in 1889.[36]

WELFARE IN THE UNITED STATES

Since most of our immigrants came from England, American ideas and programs for the aged and indigent followed the English system closely. Relief was handled on a local basis, and the conditions for obtaining assistance were made harsh to discourage any possibility of malingering. Whippings of beggars and driving them to other towns was practiced here as well as in England. In some cases, new immigrants lost their freedom when they became indentured servants to pay for their passage to America. Workhouses and almshouses in which all types of indigents were housed together became the main methods of caring for the aged and the poor.

Individualism became the dominant force in America, and little was done about the problem of insecurity. Fear of centralized authority has always been strong in the United States. It originated with the criticism against the English monarchy at the time of the American Revolution, and has been with us ever since. The abundance of resources in the United States and the successful working of our political democracy gave to our rural society the feeling that progress was automatic. All that people had to do to succeed was to work hard. Few security measures were needed, because people lived on farms and could provide security for their own relatives. Our thinking was also molded by the doctrine of predestination, which held that God had selected some for heaven and the remaining for hell. This doctrine left little room for charity toward unfortunates. Social legislation was not advocated, since eternal principles of justice were already in effect.

35 Dawson, *op. cit.*, pp. 1-2.
36 *Ibid.*, pp. 12-21.

Gradually here in America, as in England, it was recognized that the almshouse system had many disadvantages. Instead of housing together such diverse groups as the handicapped, disabled, insane, sick, aged, orphans, criminals, and the deaf, dumb, and crippled, separate types of programs and care for each of the groups gradually became the practice. Virginia in 1769 founded an institution for the insane, and Kentucky in 1822 founded two new institutions concurrently, one for the insane and another for the deaf and dumb.[37]

A system of outdoor relief began in 1883 in California when subsidies of $100 per year were provided for those living in public and private institutions and for the needy outside of institutions. The depressed condition of the State treasury following the panic of 1894 caused a suspension of payments in 1895, and they were not revived when good times returned. Gradually, however, our attitudes toward insecurity changed as we moved from a rural to an urban society. Urbanization brought with it a whole host of new problems such as unemployment, slums, and others which a *laissez-faire* doctrine was ill equipped to deal with. The fact that our people lived through two World Wars and a Great Depression shook the faith of those who maintained that progress would automatically come about. Instead, many people came to the realization that although progress was possible, it was something that had to be worked for. Perhaps legislation of some kind would promote progress.[38]

Prior to the 1930's, the main social welfare legislation in the United States was workmen's compensation. This was solely state legislation that came into existence during the second decade of this century. Later, the basic federal legislation passed was the Social Security Act of 1935. This act has three major programs: (1) unemployment insurance, (2) old-age insurance, and (3) assistance for the needy. Since the 1930's there has been a trend toward providing for more welfare. In 1950 the permanently totally disabled were covered under the Social Security Act. In 1960 medical payments for the aged who were in need was also provided, and later extended to all the aged. In the 1960's an attack has been made upon distress in depressed areas. A Manpower and Development Training Act has also been passed to upgrade the skills of the unemployed and poor. More federal aid has been granted for education purposes. A "War on Poverty" program has been instituted, and minority groups have received the protection of civil rights legislation.

The United States, over the past years, has tended to introduce welfare legislation later than most European countries. Even with the growth of welfare in the United States, we still have fewer security programs than West-

[37] Josephine Chapin Brown, *Public Relief 1929–1939* (New York, Holt, Rinehart & Winston, 1940), pp. 6-41.

[38] John Hogan and Francis Ianni, *American Social Insurance* (New York, Harper & Row, 1956), Chap. 4.

ern Europe. The International Labour Office found that the United States spent 6 percent of its gross national product on social security in 1960, compared with 11 percent for the median of 19 European countries. The top five in Western Europe spent 14 percent or more. The largest expenditure was 16 percent by Germany (Federal Republic).[39] Although different percentages are quoted by the Organization of European Economic Cooperation, it typically found higher expenditures in Western Europe.

Today it is no longer held by most students of social welfare that poverty is mainly the fault of personal inadequacy. This is not to deny that some instances of personal inadequacy exist. Persons with low IQ's have an extremely difficult time in attempting to earn a living in our society. The President's Panel on Mental Retardation estimates that 3 percent of our population have IQ's of less than 70. In 1960 this meant that 5.4 million in the United States were mentally retarded. This figure is expected to grow to 6.4 million by 1970.[40] Also slothfulness exists, but it sometimes is caused by a poor environment. Some personal inadequacies may be the fault of a poor environment. An inadequate diet and lack of medical care, for example, may cause slothfulness. Identification of the poor goes a long way in an understanding of the poverty problem. If it is found that many are poor because of aging, illness, injury, unemployment, lack of education, or discrimination, then environmental changes may possibly reduce poverty.

About one-fourth of those living in poverty in the United States are not in the work force.[41] They are people handicapped either by age, injuries, or ill health. Better medical care and rehabilitation could remove some of these people from the indigent class and return them to the work force. Others will be unable to earn a livelihood. For those not in the work force a major policy question is to determine how much reliance should be placed on individuals or families as contrasted to government in caring for them. If all individuals could take care of themselves or if they received sufficient aid from their families or friends, there would be little necessity for social legislation. Even with some governmental support, many of the aged, injured, and ill remain in poverty. An important question to be considered is whether government programs should be expanded or contracted.

Most of the people living in poverty in the United States are in the work force. Some of them, particularly with few skills, cannot find jobs. Recently, new methods of attacking the unemployment problem have been tried. Aid to depressed areas and retraining laws are examples. New methods of fiscal policy are also being tried to reduce the number of unemployed. Those still unable to find jobs may draw unemployment insurance.

[39] *The Cost of Social Security, 1958–1960* (Geneva, International Labor Organization, 1964), Table 3, pp. 243-248. *See also: Statistics and Sources and Uses of Finances, 1948–1958* (Paris, Organization for European Economic Cooperation, 1960).

[40] *Mental Retardation,* Washington, D.C., U.S. Department of Health, Education, and Welfare, President's Panel on Mental Retardation, October, 1962, p. 7.

[41] Morgan, *et al., op. cit.,* Table 16.5, p. 196.

Many of those living in poverty in the United States are employed either in low-wage industries or in low-wage occupations. About a fourth of all the poor have a farm residence, and many of this group attempt to earn a living in agriculture. Migratory and nonmigratory hired farm laborers earn a particularly low wage, and the income of subsistence or low-income farmers is insufficient to provide a satisfactory standard of living. Minority groups such as Negroes, Spanish-Americans, and American Indians have large proportions of their population living in poverty.

Several remedies to specifically aid low-income groups suggest themselves. Improvement of the quantity and quality of education is particularly important. Slum clearance, urban renewal, and low-cost public housing may also aid lower-income groups. Minimum wage laws may also act as a solution to poverty. Conflicting views exist in the United States as to the best ways to attack the problem of economic insecurity. The various causes of economic insecurity and possible solutions are discussed in the remaining chapters of the book.

Bibliography

Bornet, Vaughan D., *Welfare in America* (Norman, University of Oklahoma Press, 1960).

Carlson, Valdemar, *Economic Security in the United States* (New York, McGraw-Hill, 1962).

Gordon, Margaret S., ed., *Poverty in America* (San Francisco, Chandler, 1965).

Harrington, Michael, *The Other America* (New York, Macmillan, 1962).

Kolko, Gabriel, *Wealth and Power in America* (New York, Praeger, 1962).

Miller, Herman P., *Rich Man, Poor Man* (New York, Crowell, 1964).

Morgan, James, and others, *Income and Welfare in the United States* (New York, McGraw-Hill, 1962).

Myers, Robert J., *Social Insurance and Allied Government Programs* (Homewood, Ill., Irwin, 1965).

Ornati, Oscar, *Poverty Amid Affluence* (New York, Twentieth Century Fund, 1966).

Schottland, Charles I., *The Social Security Program in the United States* (New York, Appleton-Century-Crofts, 1963).

Turnbull, John G., *The Changing Faces of Economic Insecurity* (Minneapolis, University of Minnesota Press, 1966).

——, C. Arthur Williams and Earl Cheit, *Economic and Social Security*, 3rd ed. (New York, Ronald, 1967).

AGING IN OUR SOCIETY

AGED POPULATION

The number of those 65 and older in the United States has been increasing at a rate faster than that of an increasing total population. Consequently the percentage of persons over 65 has been increasing. Table 2-1 compares the growth of total population with the population of those over 65.

Table 2-1 shows that the number of people over 65 will grow much larger in the near future. In 1940 more than 9 million of the population were 65 years of age or older, but by 1975 more than twice that number will be 65 or older. The projection for the number of aged in 1975 is fairly

TABLE 2–1. POPULATION GROWTH, 1870–1975

Year	Total Population	Population 65 Years of Age and Over	Percentage of Population Over 65
1870 [a]	38,553,210	1,153,649	3
1900 [a]	75,793,991	3,080,498	4
1940	131,669,275	9,019,314	7
1950 [b]	151,132,000	12,269,000	8
1960 [b]	179,935,391	16,207,237	9
Projections:			
1975 [b,c]	227,929,000	21,159,000	9
1975 [b,d]	215,367,000	21,159,000	10

[a] Excluding persons of unknown age.
[b] Including armed forces overseas.
[c] Assumes 1950–1963 fertility level continues to 1975.
[d] Assumes fertility level of the early forties continues to 1975.
Sources: Henry Sheldon, "Future Trends in Our Older Population," from Wilma Donahue and Clark Tibbitts, eds., *The New Frontiers of Aging,* Ann Arbor: University of Michigan Press, 1957, Table IV, p. 74. Reprinted by permission. *U.S. Census of Population, 1960,* United States Summary, General Social and Economic Characteristics, PC(1)ICU.S., U.S. Department of Commerce, Bureau of the Census, Table 65, p. 1-199. *Current Population Reports,* Series P-25, No. 359, U.S. Department of Commerce, Bureau of the Census, Table A, p. 2 and Table 4, p. 14.

accurate, because those who will reach the age of 65 have already been born.

A number of factors have contributed to the percentage increase of the aged.[1] For one thing, life expectancy has increased 18 years since 1900. Most of the gain in life expectancy has come because more young people remain alive, but older people do live several years longer than they formerly did. A second cause of an increased percentage of aged is the declining birthrate. In 1950 only 1 person out of 4 was under 15 years of age whereas in 1900 1 out of 3 was under 15. A third factor causing an increased percentage of the aged is that fewer immigrants are now coming to the United States. Since the immigrant group was predominantly a younger group, the decline in their coming has resulted in a larger percentage of those over 65.

DEPENDENCY RATIOS

The increasing percentage of aged in the United States may alter American society in a number of ways. Cultural values, attitudes toward religion, politics, consumption patterns, and many other factors may be affected. Society will have to support more aged people in the future. In 1900 for every 100 workers we had 167 nonworkers. By 1950 the same number of workers had to support only 142 nonworkers.[2] The reasons for this decline were the decreasing birthrate and the increasing number of persons entering the work force, particularly women. However, the trend toward a decreasing number of dependents has been reversed. Table 2-2 is a projection of the nonworking groups that must be supported in the approaching decades. It shows that the number of dependents is primarily a function of the number of children under 20 years of age. Dependency ratios for the aged will increase over the next few years, but no great economic burden should be expected from the increasing number of aged, for national income should be much higher in the future than it is today.

ATTITUDES TOWARD THE AGED

ATTITUDES IN PRIMITIVE TRIBES

Professor Leo W. Simmons has studied the role of the aged among 71 primitive tribes.[3] He found that, almost without exception, primitive tribes granted a great deal of prestige to the aged. Factors contributing to high

---

[1] John J. Corson and John W. McConnell, *Economic Needs of Older People* (New York, Twentieth Century Fund, 1956), pp. 4-6.

[2] *Ibid.*, p. 10.

[3] Leo W. Simmons, *The Role of the Aged in Primitive Society* (New Haven, Yale, 1945), pp. 50-81.

TABLE 2–2.   DEPENDENCY RATIOS FOR THE UNITED STATES, 1870–1975

Year	Dependent Population, Under 20 Years[a]	Dependent Population, 65 Years and Over[a]	Total Dependent Population[a]
1870[b]	1,050	63	1,113
1900	863	79	942
1940	586	117	702
1950[c]	584	140	724
1960[c]	734	172	906
Projections:			
1975[c,d]	774	182	956
1975[c,e]	667	182	849

[a] Ratio of dependents to 1,000 nondependents (20-to-64 age group).
[b] Excluding persons of unknown age.
[c] Including armed forces overseas.
[d] Assumes 1963 fertility level continues to 1975.
[e] Assumes fertility level of the early forties continues to 1975.
Sources: Wilma Donahue and Clark Tibbitts, eds., *The New Frontiers of Aging,* Ann Arbor: University of Michigan Press, 1957, Table IV, p. 74. Reprinted by permission. *Current Population Reports,* Series P-25, No. 359, U.S. Department of Commerce, Bureau of Census, Table 4, pp. 15-16.

prestige were much private property, concentration of political power in restricted councils, the use of money, and the like. In matrilineal societies older women obtained a great deal of respect. Patrilineal societies, on the other hand, gave more prestige to men. Several factors tended to reduce the favor bestowed upon the aged. In more severe climates, where the aged might become more of a burden, less prestige was granted them. Also, when impermanency of residence caused a burden in moving the aged, less prestige was granted.

Other attitudes toward the aged may be revealed by reactions toward death. In some tribes, the dying were treated to good food, and their last wishes were promptly observed. In other tribes, relatives gathered respectfully about the dying to obtain special favors, disposition of property, and pronouncement of blessings. In still other tribes, the dying might be neglected, abandoned, or even killed. The latter practice was more prevalent where the climate was severe, food in short supply, and residence impermanent.[4]

OLDER, RURAL ATTITUDES IN THE UNITED STATES

In the rural nineteenth century, aged grandparents usually enjoyed an honored and central position in our society. Usually the boys stayed on the

[4] *Ibid.,* pp. 217-244.

family farm until they became 21 years old. Then fathers would attempt to help their sons establish a farm of their own nearby. Lack of modern transportation facilities prevented children from moving far away. On Sunday all of the children would congregate for a day of social visit with their parents. Cultural differences between the younger and older generations were small, and the tempo of social change was slow. The aged were honored, respected, and esteemed. Furthermore, the extended family unit tended to be a self-sufficient social unit. Whenever the aged became enfeebled, shelter was provided for them by relatives, and the problem of feeding them was not a particularly pressing problem on the farm.[5]

ATTITUDES TODAY

The shift from rural to urban living has considerably changed the cultural values attached to aging. At the turn of the century when American society was becoming urbanized, it became evident that the costs of rearing and educating children imposed an economic burden upon the family rather than an economic advantage. Consequently the birth rate began falling. Fewer children were available to support parents. Also improved educational facilities tended to give the younger generations cultural advantages that the older generation did not have. The result was that the younger group tended to look down upon their parents. One cultural goal of American society is that a young man should elevate himself above the social and economic position of his father. The son who surpasses his father then grants him less respect. Whereas in rural society the care of an aged parent was no great economic burden on children, the burden becomes increasingly great in urban society. Food cannot be grown, but must be purchased. Housing may not be available for the aged.[6] Because of the high costs of support, the aged today tend to expect less and less support from children. A Cornell University study of 3,515 people aged 63 and 64 revealed that 89 percent of them did not expect to receive any financial support from relatives, friends, or anyone else when they stopped working.[7] Another study in California found that only 29 percent of aged people receiving governmental old-age assistance felt that children should be required by law to support their parents.[8]

Other cultural values of American society are success in work and independence from others. Those not working or dependent on others are

[5] Ernest W. Burgess, "The Older Generation and the Family," in Wilma T. Donahue and Clark Tibbitts, *The New Frontiers of Aging* (Ann Arbor, Mich., University of Michigan Press, 1957), pp. 158-171.

[6] *Ibid.*

[7] *The Study of Occupational Retirement, First Progress Report,* Cornell University (Ithaca, Cornell University Press, 1953), p. 20.

[8] Floyd Bond *et al., Our Needy Aged* (New York, Holt, Rinehart and Winston, 1954), p. 299.

given less status. The problem is particularly acute among the aged, since youngsters may look forward to a period of independence and perhaps success whereas most of the aged have passed their prime. Our society may be particularly harsh on the aged, because it keeps accurate records of chronological ages. In less developed societies, where no such records are kept, the aged person retires when physiological factors require. In our society retirement may be mandatory even though the aged person can perform his job capably and wishes to continue working.[9]

Most of our urban cultural values today accord low prestige to the aged, and cause their adjustment in life temporarily to be difficult. The fact that the proportion of elderly people admitted to state mental hospitals is increasing twice as fast as that of the general public indicates that many of the aged are unable to adjust properly.[10] Although different studies have arrived at different conclusions on adjustment to retirement, several recent studies have concluded that most aged adjust successfully.[11] One study of 279 older persons in Kansas City of healthy and middle-class aged [12] showed that men had a more difficult adjustment than women. Retirement and widowhood for women means less of a change in their life than retirement for men. Women generally have more close relations with children and siblings than men have. Because women's major function is socio-emotional, they do not regret the loss of responsibility about domestic or working world tasks the way men do about their work. Even with a difficult task of adjustment, the findings of this study showed that both men and women have higher morale when they are totally disengaged from their prior life of working and raising children. Immediately after retiring from employment and after losing loved ones, the aged experience a drop in morale, but gradually they adapt to the process of disengagement until finally they have higher morale than when they were younger. Although men face the three problems of loss of membership in a group, loss of work, and loss of status identity, most succeed in solving these problems by enjoying the freedom of release from work and the opportunity to engage in recreation and other activities. Preoccupation with inner states and eventually the self-love (narcissism) of the very old aid in their adjustment. To disengage successfully,

[9] Otto Pollak, *Social Adjustment in Old Age*, Bulletin No. 59 (New York, Social Science Research Council, 1948), pp. 4-5.

[10] Bettag, Slight, Weinig, and Sorenson, *The Aged and Aging in Illinois*, Part I: *The Mentally Ill*, Research Study 68-1 (Springfield, Illinois Department of Public Welfare, 1954).

[11] G. F. Streib, W. E. Thompson, and E. A. Suchman, "The Cornell Study of Occupational Retirement," *Journal of Social Issues*, Vol. XIV (1958), p. 3; and J. Tyhurst, Lee Salk, and Miriam Kennedy, "Morbidity, Mortality, and Retirement," paper read to the 23rd Meeting of the A.A.A.S., New York (1956). For the contrary view that workers view retirement with dread, *see* I. Lorge and J. Tuckman, *Retirement and the Industrial Worker* (New York, Columbia, 1953), pp. 20-37.

[12] Elaine Cumming and William E. Henry, *Growing Old* (New York, Basic Books, 1961).

however, the aged must have sufficient health care and economic independence. They must also have the availability of siblings or substitutes.

INCOME OF THE AGED

SOURCES OF INCOME

Table 2-3 shows from what sources the aged receive their income. Over one-half the aged families and almost one-fourth of single persons over 65 receive income from earnings. Most aged couples and single persons receive some kind of retirement benefits. The major program here is old-age, survivors, disability, and health insurance (OASDHI), first formulated under the Social Security Act of 1935. This program is financed by payroll taxes levied on both employers and employees. Those not covered under the insurance program may receive public assistance. To qualify for old-age assistance (OAA), the aged must prove need and not receive a sufficiently large income from OASDHI or other sources. This program is financed out of general federal revenues and is matched with state funds. Much larger numbers of the aged are now covered than formerly under the OASDHI program, and fewer are covered under OAA. The drop in OAA has been mainly due to the increased coverage of people under the OASDHI program of the Social Security Act.

AMOUNT OF INCOME

A detailed breakdown of income of the aged is shown in Table 2-4.

The earnings of those working full time are much higher than those not working, but only a minority of the aged are engaged in full-time work. Even with government assistance, the income of the aged is quite low. Attention is particularly invited to the large percentages of both men and women with less than $1,000 income. Studies show that income of the aged is particularly low among the nonwhite and farm aged. One study showed that in 1963, 33 percent of all nonwhite families with the head over 65 had an income of less than $1,500 per year. The corresponding percentage for whites was 14 percent. Thirty percent of farmers aged 65 and over had an income of less than $1,500.[13] Income also varies quite radically from state to state. Income of husband-wife families with head aged 65 and over varied from a low of $1,606 in Mississippi to a high of $5,636 in the District of Columbia.[14]

[13] *Current Population Reports: Consumer Income,* Series P-60, No. 46, Washington, D.C., U.S. Department of Commerce, Bureau of the Census (June, 1965), Table 1, p. 10, and Table 3, p. 12.
[14] Lenore Epstein, "State Variations in Income of the Aged," *Social Security Bulletin,* Vol. 26, No. 1. (January, 1963), Table 1, p. 4.

TABLE 2–3. SOURCES OF MONEY INCOME FOR UNITS AGED 65 AND
OVER, 1962

Source of Money Income	Married Couples[a]	Nonmarried Men	Nonmarried Women	Total Nonmarried Persons
Earnings	55%	28%	23%	24%
Retirement benefits	84%	72%	64%	67%
OASDI	79%	68%	60%	62%
Other public	12%	8%	7%	7%
Private group pensions	16%	10%	3%	5%
Veterans' benefits	14%	11%	6%	8%
Interest, dividends, and rents	63%	45%	50%	48%
Private individual annuities	4%	1%	3%	3%
Unemployment insurance	3%	1%	1%	1%
Public assistance	8%	18%	17%	17%
Contributions by relatives[b]	3%	1%	6%	5%
Payments under any public program	89%	87%	78%	80%
Number of units (in thousands):				
Total	5,445	2,402	6,329	8,731
Reporting on sources	5,443	2,345	6,267	8,612

a With at least one member aged 65 or over.
b Relatives or friends not in households.
Source: "Income of the Aged in 1962: First Findings of the 1963 Survey of the Aged," Social Security Bulletin, Vol. 27, No. 3 (March, 1964), Table 1, p. 6.

ADEQUACY OF INCOME

Adequacy of income for the aged has been analyzed by the U.S. Bureau of Labor Statistics. Budgets for a retired couple have been prepared irregularly since March, 1946, for a number of larger cities in the United States. The budget calls for renting a two- or three-room unfurnished dwelling. The couple is assumed to be in reasonably good health. The budget provides for an amount of goods and services necessary for a healthful, self-respecting mode of living, and allows normal participation in community life. It provides for a modest but adequate level of living rather than a luxurious one or one providing only the basic essentials of consumption. The latest statistics available were for 20 large cities in the autumn of 1959. The budgets ranged from a low of $2,641 in Houston to a high of $3,366 in Chicago.[15]

15 Margaret S. Stotz, "The BLS Interim Budget for a Retired Couple," Monthly Labor Review, Vol. 83 (1960), pp. 1141-1157.

TABLE 2–4. SIZE OF MONEY INCOME BY OASDI BENEFICIARY STATUS FOR UNITS AGED 65 AND OVER, 1962 [a]

Total Money Income	Married Couples[b]		Nonmarried Men		Nonmarried Women		
	OASDI Beneficiaries	Nonbeneficiaries	OASDI Beneficiaries	Nonbeneficiaries	OASDI Beneficiaries[c]		Nonbeneficiaries
					Retired	Widowed	
Less than $1,000	4%	10%	26%	46%	36%	44%	65%
$1,000 to $1,499	9%	12%	32%	13%	23%	27%	14%
$1,500 to $1,999	15%	11%	14%	10%	17%	16%	7%
$2,000 to $2,499	16%	5%	13%	6%	9%	6%	4%
$2,500 to $2,999	14%	6%	6%	3%	5%	2%	2%
$3,000 to $3,999	16%	12%	5%	4%	4%	2%	3%
$4,000 to $4,999	11%	10%	2%	4%	2%	1%	1%
$5,000 to $9,999	12%	24%	2%	12%	4%	2%	2%
$10,000 and over	3%	11%	d	1%	d	1%	d
Total	100%	100%	100%	100%	100%	100%	100%
Number of units (in thousands):							
Total	3,743	1,120	1,490	803	1,912	1,502	2,543
Reporting on income	3,289	932	1,384	685	1,690	1,325	2,192
Median income	$2,710	$3,580	$1,375	$1,135	$1,300	$1,105	$755

[a] Excludes beneficiaries who received their first benefit in February, 1962, or later.

[b] With at least one member aged 65 or over.

[c] Retired women received benefits based on their own wage record, regardless of eligibility as widows; widowed women receive benefits based on the husband's wage record.

[d] Less than 0.5 percent.

Source: "Income of the Aged in 1962: First Findings of the 1963 Survey of the Aged," Social Security Bulletin, Vol. 27, No. 3 (March, 1964), Table 3, p. 9.

It is obvious from Table 2-4 that even with government payments, many of our aged are coming nowhere near obtaining the required income of this modest budget. Other data demonstrating the meager economic resources of the aged show that many of those over 65 held no liquid assets of any kind.[16]

LIVING ACCOMMODATIONS FOR THE AGED

HOUSING AND LIVING ARRANGEMENTS

If both aged members of a married couple remain alive, the problem of housing may not be an acute one, especially if the couple owns and has paid off the mortgage on their house. However, the couple may possibly desire smaller quarters. Space that had formerly been required for rearing a family is no longer necessary. When one member of the family dies, the problem of living quarters must be reconsidered. Six alternatives are available to the surviving member of the family.[17] The aged person could maintain a separate residence. The advantage of this type of arrangement is that it may prevent family friction with children or other relatives, and remaining in the same house would give continuity to the life that had been led before. A disadvantage of separate living accommodations is that it is expensive. Also, loneliness may become more of a problem, and eventually advanced old age may require some kind of care. If the aged parent moves in with the adult children, expenses and loneliness are reduced. However, a number of problems arise. Not only may the children feel that there has been an intrusion in their lives, but the aged parent may also resent a lack of privacy. Housing arrangements may be congested. If the children have received more education than their parents, social distance between the two may cause less amicable living arrangements. Also, the high status of parenthood may be forfeited when it is necessary for an aged parent to live with children. A third alternative is to move into an old-age colony, possibly in an area with a pleasant climate. Since moving to better oneself has become an accepted norm in our society, some of the aged do just this. Hotels catering to the aged also provide an alternate mode of living; however, little research has been done to evaluate the satisfactions and dissatisfactions of such a method of living. Yet another possibility is that two old people could live together. Such an arrangement would save on housing costs, and might

[16] In 1962, 10 percent of married couples had zero assets as did 28 percent of nonmarried men and 26 percent of nonmarried women. If the assets of a home are deducted, then the respective percentages having zero assets become 23, 37, and 37 percent. See L. D. Platky, "Assets of the Aged in 1962," *Social Security Bulletin*, Vol. 27, No. 11 (November, 1964), Table 1, p. 4.

[17] Otto Pollak, *The Social Aspects of Retirement* (Homewood, Ill., Irwin, 1956), pp. 10-14.

possibly eliminate the loneliness of single living. Lastly, the aged could move into old folks' homes.

Most older people do not live with their children. Seventy-two percent of married couples, 55 percent of nonmarried men, and 47 percent of nonmarried women either live alone or with nonrelatives.[18] In a study of the period from 1952 to 1960, fewer older people were found to be living with children in 1960 than at the earlier date. The respective figures for 1952 were 69, 51, and 41 percent. In general, the higher the income of the aged, the less likely they are to live with children. Forty-seven percent of aged men with an income of less than $1,000 lived alone or with nonrelatives compared with 58 percent for those with an income above $3,000. The respective figures for women were 39 and 62 percent.[19]

In cases in which an aged married couple lives with children, the aged parents are more typically the head of the household rather than the children. Of married couples living with relatives in 1960, 93 percent were heads of the family compared with 7 percent who were not.[20] In comparison with married couples, a larger percentage of aged nonmarried men and women live with relatives. Aged nonmarried women are more apt to live with relatives than men, particularly if their income is low. Since there are many more aged women living than aged men, over three times as many aged women than aged men are living with children.

ADEQUACY OF HOUSING

According to the 1960 census, a larger percentage of those over 60 years of age owned their homes than did younger people—72 to 62 percent respectively. The aged, of course, have had more years to accumulate such durable assets. On the other hand, the value of their homes ($10,000) was less than the average value of the homes of the total population ($12,600). Census data on housing reveals many inadequacies in housing in the United States. In general, houses of the aged are slightly less adequate for the aged than those for the rest of the population. The 1960 statistics show that 81 percent of those 60 and over had nondilapidated houses with private toilet, bath, and hot running water, compared with 87 percent of those under 65 years of age.[21] Also, some of the aged live in houses which are probably too large for their needs. Almost a third had more than five rooms.[22]

[18] Lenore Epstein, "Living Arrangements and Income of the Aged, 1959," *Social Security Bulletin*, Vol. 26, No. 9 (September, 1963), Table 5, p. 6.

[19] *Ibid.*, p. 5.

[20] *Ibid.*, Table 5, p. 6.

[21] *Census of Housing, 1960*, Vol. 7, *Housing of Senior Citizens*, Washington, D.C., U.S. Department of Commerce, Bureau of the Census, Table J, p. xv.

[22] Geneva Mathiason, ed., *Criteria for Retirement* (New York, Putnam, 1953), pp. 22-23.

INSTITUTIONAL CARE

Only a small percentage of the aged live in institutions, hotels, or large rooming houses. Prior to this century in the United States, the aged without means of support were sent to almshouses or poorhouses supported by public charity. Such institutions also housed orphans, the feeble-minded, the insane, the ill, and other indigents.

Painful social stigma was attached to being sent to one of these institutions, so that the aged attempted to remain out of them at all costs. Only those whose resources were totally exhausted resided there. Gradually, as understanding developed for our unfortunate citizens, methods of care improved. The feeble-minded were removed to specialized institutions and other hospitals were provided for the insane and the ill. Children were removed to separate institutions.[23] The passage of the Social Security Act in 1935 radically changed housing for the aged. Monthly pensions were received by the aged so that many could take care of their own housing needs rather than go to almshouses. One study made six months after Social Security payments began in March of 1937 showed that in 16 states there was a noticeable reduction in almshouse population. For example, Alabama closed 45 of its 65 almshouses. In Colorado 4 of 25 were closed, and the institutional population was reduced from 640 to 382.[24] A number of studies have been made to point out the deficiencies of such homes. For example, in Maryland in 1940, their Department of Public Welfare found that 96 out of 510 residents could have been placed in the care of relatives or in boarding homes. Ninety-five others needed mental hospital care. Of the remaining 319 inmates, half were bedridden. These needed specialized institutional care that they were unable to get in almshouses.[25]

Even today, findings are reported of the need for improved living for those institutionalized. In a recent study in Minnesota of 1,700 elderly citizens,[26] comparisons were made between older people living in institutions as contrasted to those living in the community. The institutionalized group were more often older, single, divorced, separated, or widowed than married and living with spouse. They were likely to have fewer children and have less contacts with relatives. They were twice as likely to say that they wished their family would pay more attention to them and to disagree with the statement that they were satisfied with the way their families treat them.

---

23 "Homes for the Aged in the United States," Bulletin No. 677, Washington, D.C., U.S. Department of Labor, Bureau of Labor Statistics, 1940, p. 1.

24 "Effects of Social Security Program on Almshouses," *Monthly Labor Review*, Vol. 47 (1938), pp. 518-526.

25 *Report on Almshouses in Maryland*, Maryland State Department of Public Welfare (Baltimore, Maryland Legislative Council, 1940), mimeographed.

26 Arnold Rose, ed., *Aging in Minnesota* (Minneapolis, University of Minnesota Press, 1963), p. 132.

In order to improve institutional living, it has been suggested that programs be organized so that those living in institutional settings are aided in establishing strong friendships with other men and women. Visits to these people were suggested along with the formation of recreational clubs and day centers for the aged. The hiring of more experienced employees for institutional work who have been trained in recreational and social activities would help.

MOBILITY

The aged are less mobile than younger people. One study showed that the aged moved less than other groups from house to house, and from counties and states to other counties and states.[27] According to the 1960 census, the proportion of aged living in urban areas was the same percentage as that of the entire population living in urban areas—69 percent.[28] The aged generally do not migrate to large cities, although certain exceptions may be noted such as Atlantic City, New Jersey, and Tampa-St. Petersburg, Florida. State capitals and university towns also tend to attract the aged. Other aged people have attracted some aged persons to a limited number of counties and small towns in Southern California, Florida, and eastern Texas. That the migration has not swamped these states may be shown by the figures that the percentage of aged who live in Florida and California, 11.2 and 8.8 percent respectively, is not far different from the national average of 9.2. In 1960, Iowa had the largest percentage of old people (12 percent) and Maine, New Hampshire, Vermont, Massachusetts, Missouri, Nebraska, Kansas, and Florida had more than 11 percent.[29] One other trend may be noted. Some of the aged move from farms to small rural towns when they become old.

RETIREMENT VILLAGES

A few experiments have been tried in the United States to improve living accommodations for the aged. In New York City, an apartment house called Tompkins Square House was built by a philanthropist in the twenties. Later the building was acquired by the Community Service Society, which offers low rent to the aged and provides resident nursing for those who need it. J. C. Penney founded a Memorial Home Community in Florida. His community has 92 two-room apartments and 116 one-room kitchenette-and-bath

[27] Mathiason, op. cit., p. 23.

[28] Census of Population, 1960, United States Summary, General Population Characteristics, Washington, D.C., U.S. Department of Commerce, Bureau of the Census (1960), PC(1)IBUS, Table 46, pp. 1-148.

[29] Ibid., Table 60, pp. 1-173. For an earlier study see T. Lynn Smith, "The Migration of the Aged," in Problems of America's Aging Population (Gainesville, University of Florida Institute of Gerontology, 1951), pp. 15-16.

units for retired ministers and other religious workers. Recreational and health services are provided at nominal fees.[30]

A number of other retirement villages such as Ryderwood, Moorehaven, and Youngstown have aroused the enthusiastic support of their sponsors, residents, and visitors.[31] There has been some argument among gerontologists as to whether the aged prefer to live in an integrated neighborhood or in separate aged villages. It is highly likely that the aged would be successfully integrated into their own neighborhood if they have lived there a long time, if the neighborhood is relatively stable and unchanging, if the neighborhood is socially homogeneous with regard to social class and racial, religious, and ethnic minorities, and if their primary friends are still living. If these conditions are not met, it may be that a retirement village would be more satisfactory for the aged. Rosow maintains that the retirement village has many advantages. Such a village provides insulation against a youth-oriented culture that rejects the aged. A retirement community also enables the aged to form many more friendships than they could in their former integrated neighborhood. Opportunities for remarriage are also maximized. If the residents of a retirement village have broadly similar life experiences and are of the same social class and if the context of segregation is insulating rather than invidious or stigmatized, Rosow hypothesizes that segregated neighborhoods will more effectively integrate older persons socially than integrated neighborhoods.[32]

PUBLIC HOUSING

The United States has constructed substantially fewer low-rent public housing units than most of Western Europe. In the United States in the few projects that have been completed, little consideration has been given to the needs of the aged. Few of the projects have permitted construction of small apartments for one inhabitant although this type of housing is desired by some of the aged who have lost their spouse. Also, some of our public housing projects specifically refuse to permit aged people to occupy them. Fortunately, there has been a growing trend toward more low-rental public housing projects for the aged. To cite a few examples, the Toledo Metropolitan Housing Authority houses people 65 years and older who have a small retirement income and no more than $5,000 in total assets. The Cleveland Metropolitan Housing Authority has a Golden Age Center which houses aged families and single persons. The maximum income limit for families with no minor dependents is $3,000. Rents are set at 23 percent of income, with a minimum of $30 per month.[33]

[30] Corson and McConnell, op. cit., p. 34.

[31] Irving Rosow, "Retirement Housing and Social Integration," The Gerontologist, Vol. 1 (June, 1961), pp. 85-91.

[32] Ibid.

[33] Fessenden S. Blanchard, Make the Most of Your Retirement (Garden City, N.Y., Doubleday, 1963), pp. 95-96.

Abroad, especially in Europe, much more has been done to house the aged. In Denmark, for example, 20 percent of all housing for aged pensioners is provided by public housing. In most countries of Europe, the public housing developments are part of planned improvement for the whole community. Many different types of public housing for the aged have been constructed abroad. Nursing homes exist everywhere, as do boarding homes. Some of the plans call for residence clubs with light housekeeping privileges. Others provide for low-rent cottage colonies. These may be one-family buildings or the duplex type or both. Large and small apartments exist for the aged, and in these a variety of nursing and recreational facilities are provided.[34] Quite clearly, most of the countries in Europe have spent considerably more thought and money than the United States in providing more adequate living accommodations for the aged.

EMPLOYMENT OF THE AGED

In December of 1966, there were over 2 million men and almost 1 million women aged 65 and over who were in the labor force. This group constituted 26 percent of all men aged 65 and over and almost 10 percent of the women.[35] Many of the aged work less than full time.

A study in 1963 showed that of workers laid off since 1957, retirement was the worker's own decision in 63 percent of the cases and the employer's decision in the remaining 37 percent.[36] Where the decision was the worker's own, retirement was due to poor health in over half the cases. However, over the years, more and more workers are retiring simply because they prefer more leisure.

INVOLUNTARY FACTORS REDUCING EMPLOYMENT OF THE AGED

There are many older people in the United States who are now idle and would prefer to work. A number of factors reduce employment of the aged. One impediment is the use of 40 or 45 years of age as a hiring deadline. A number of studies have been made to determine what percentage of companies specifically limit the hiring of new employees to younger people. Although the studies show different amounts of discrimination against older workers, all are in agreement that substantial numbers of employers limit hiring to younger people. A Bureau of Employment Security survey of 13,000

34 Hertha Kraus, "Housing Our Older Citizens," *The Annals of the American Academy of Political and Social Science,* Vol. 279 (January, 1952), pp. 126-138.

35 *Employment and Earnings,* U.S. Department of Labor, Vol. 13, No. 7 (January, 1967), Table A-14, p. 30.

36 Erdmore Palmore, "Retirement Patterns Among Aged Men: Findings of the 1963 Survey of the Aged," *Social Security Bulletin,* Vol. 27, No. 8 (August, 1964), Table 4, p. 5. For contradictory evidence on this point, see footnote 45 in this chapter.

job openings in five states in 1950 showed that 60 to 70 percent carried maximum age limitations. The restrictions were particularly stringent with regard to women. For them a majority of employers specified a maximum age of below 35.[37] Another study conducted jointly by the National Association of Manufacturers and the United States Chamber of Commerce found that 26 percent of the 279 firms studied did not hire workers over 45.[38]

Research by the New York State Joint Legislative Council uncovered the fact that hiring maximums were more prevalent in the Depression. In the thirties, 80 percent of the employers studied admitted to hiring deadlines compared with 19 percent in 1948.[39] A Minnesota survey revealed that 90 percent of employers generally used 50 as a maximum hiring deadline for men and 40 for women.[40] A Department of Labor study in April, 1956, showed that in five of seven cities, more than half of all jobs filed with employment offices contained maximum hiring ages. In three of the cities, from 73 to 79 percent of the openings contained such age limitations. The most frequently mentioned maximum age in all seven cities was 45, but 20 percent of all openings listed an age of 35 or below as the maximum.[41]

The aged experience less full-time employment than do younger workers. A survey published by the Federal Reserve Board showed that more than twice the percentage of younger workers as older workers were employed for 50 or more weeks. Most of the short-time work of the older workers was attributed to job-connected reasons rather than personal ones.[42] Other studies indicate that the duration of unemployment is longer for the aged. In February of 1966, 28 percent of the unemployed of 45 years of age and over were unemployed for 15 or more weeks compared with 19 percent in the 20 to 24 age bracket.[43] Although the aged do look for jobs, they find them more difficult to obtain. The Minnesota State Employment Security Department found that older workers comprised 32 percent of the job applicants, but only 15 percent of the hires. The same finding of much fewer hires was found in a U.S. Department of Labor study in seven cities. In that study older workers comprised

[37] "Employment and Economic Status of Older Men and Women," Bulletin No. 1092, Washington, D.C., Department of Labor, Bureau of Labor Statistics, 1952, pp. 53-54.

[38] Employment of Physically Handicapped and Older Workers, Washington, D.C., National Association of Manufacturers and U.S. Chamber of Commerce (1950), p. 23.

[39] Report of the Joint Legislative Committee on Unemployment, Legislative Document No. 66, Albany, State Legislature (1933), pp. 206 ff.; and Birthdays Don't Count, New York State Joint Legislative Document No. 61, Albany, State Legislature (1948), pp. 152-153.

[40] Older People and the Industrial Community, National Social Welfare Assembly, National Committee on the Aging, 1957 Spring Meeting (New York, John B. Watkins, 1957), p. 15.

[41] Ibid., p. 32.

[42] "1959 Survey of Consumer Finances," Federal Reserve Bulletin, Vol. 45 (1959), Supplementary Table 21, p. 723.

[43] Employment and Earnings, Washington, D.C., U.S. Department of Labor, Vol. 12, No. 9 (March, 1966), Table A-12, p. 29.

40 percent of the applicants for jobs, but received only 22 percent of the hires.[44]

Not only are the aged handicapped in finding employment by maximum age limits on hiring, but many of the aged are required to retire because of age even though they would prefer to continue working. A number of studies, but not all, show that over half of our retirements are due to mandatory company policy.[45] Another study shows that larger firms employ fewer older workers than smaller companies. In finance, insurance, and real estate, 13 percent of all employees were older than 65 for firms employing less than five employees. For firms employing 500 or more workers the corresponding percentage was 2 percent. The disparity was not so great in other industries, but smaller firms in all industries employed more older workers than large companies.[46]

In the past few years much research has been conducted to measure the contribution and costs of keeping the aged employed. The consensus of these studies is that productivity of the aged is not far below that of younger workers except for heavy manual labor. A Temple University study of 97 companies employing more than 1,000 people reported that 60 percent of their older workers were average or above in quantity of production, and of these 21 percent were rated somewhat or considerably above average in the amount produced. The figures on quality of production showed an even better record for the aged. Dr. Leonard Breen of the University of Chicago matched 100 persons in the 40 to 45 age group with the same number of people in the 60 to 65 age group. He found that the productivity of both were the same. However, the foreman in this plant had expected a difference in production in favor of the younger workers. Such expectations may be an important factor in unconsciously causing the older workers to slow down, for generally people in our society conform to the norms that are expected of them. A Bureau of Labor Statistics research study of 2,000 piece workers in eight clothing and shoe factories found that the average output per manhour remained stable through age 54, then declined. However, the output of the 55 to 64 age group was at least 90 percent as large as that of the younger workers.[47]

Tending to offset any drop in production, the older workers have a better absentee and turnover record than younger workers, and most studies show that they have a better industrial accident record although the severity

---

[44] *Older People and the Industrial Community*, pp. 15, 32.

[45] Gordon Streib and Wayne E. Thompson, "Personal and Social Adjustment in Retirement," in Donahue and Tibbitts, eds., *op. cit.*, p. 182.

[46] Sebastian Svolos, "Employment of Older Workers and Size of Employing Units," *Social Security Bulletin*, Vol. 28, No. 9 (September, 1965), pp. 25-29, 37-38.

[47] Leonard Z. Breen, "Measuring Ability of Older Workers," in *Older People and the Industrial Community*, pp. 4-5; Charles Odell, "Studies from the United States Department of Labor," in *ibid.*, p. 32. For a summary of other studies, *see* Geneva Mathiason, ed., *Flexible Retirement* (New York, Putnam, 1957), pp. 43-45, 49-50.

of their accidents is greater.[48] Pension costs may rise if older workers are hired, but these costs may be minimized if short-service employees receive no pension or a smaller one. Costs of group life, health, and accident insurance do not increase appreciably for firms hiring older workers provided a reasonable balance is maintained in the age of the work force.[49]

SOLUTIONS TO EMPLOYMENT PROBLEMS: ANTIDISCRIMINATION LAWS

Professor Sumner Slichter estimated that about 960,000 more aged people want to work in our society, and that these people would produce about $3.8 billion worth of goods. This amount of money is the loss our economy must sustain by not employing the aged.[50] An estimate by Robert Dorfman showed a much smaller number who could be added to our work force— 278,000. Dorfman's group showed an exceptionally large number who retired for health reasons—57 percent. Other studies do not show nearly as large a percentage retiring because of ill health. A Twentieth Century Fund study found that 25 percent of the aged had retired because of ill health, and the figure from a Bureau of Old Age and Survivors' Insurance report was 33 percent.[51]

The fact that many aged would like to work and that this work would materially aid the support of the aged has caused many people to search for solutions to the problem. On the government level, several states forbid discrimination in hiring, firing, and other conditions of employment solely on the basis of age. Of the 28 states that now have fair employment practice laws outlawing discrimination because of race, creed, or color, ten have added age. Eight other states have laws solely to outlaw discrimination based on age. Such laws do not require that the older worker be given preference in jobs, but if sufficient ability is shown an older worker must not be discriminated against because of age.

IMPROVED COUNSELING AND PLACEMENT

The United States Department of Labor made a comprehensive study of counseling and placement of older workers with seven state employment agencies. The major conclusion arrived at was that improved placement of

[48] Mathiason, *Flexible Retirement*, pp. 46-48.
[49] Charles Odell, *op. cit.*, p. 33.
[50] Sumner Slichter, "Economic Problems of the Support of Retired Persons," in Mathiason, *Criteria for Retirement*, p. 153.
[51] Robert Dorfman, "Economic Implications of an Aging Population," *American Economic Review*, Vol. 44, Supplement (May, 1954), p. 644; John W. McConnell, "Retirement from Industry," paper delivered at the Second Gerontological Congress, St. Louis, September, 1951; and Edna C. Wentworth, "Why Beneficiaries Retire," *Social Security Bulletin*, Vol. 8, No. 1 (January, 1945), pp. 16-20.

older workers was possible. Additional staff was recommended for the state offices. The new personnel could concentrate on breaking down the prejudice of employers against hiring older people. Also, more intensive interviewing of the aged was recommended so that more of their talents could be uncovered and more realistic employment goals adopted by them. Of a sample of 4,000 unemployed persons interviewed, most of whom were over 45 years of age, Sobel and Folk found that older unemployed persons' wage demands were unrealistic when viewed against the fact that from a third to over a half of those 50 years of age and over had to take a cut in pay of 25 cents an hour or more when reemployed. They concluded that the Employment Service probably could contribute effectively to the reemployment of older workers by encouraging them to reduce unrealistic high wage and job demands.[52]

Staff increases to counsel the aged have been authorized in the Employment Service. This step, coupled with better counseling, should help in the placement of the aged. Other suggested governmental aids are tax rebates if older workers are hired, and additions to government pensions if the aged work beyond 65 years of age. Also, the federal government passed an Older Americans Act in 1965 to promote employment of the aged and to research more fully the problems of the aged.

FLEXIBLE RETIREMENT PLANS

Some corporations have aided the employment of the aged by changing from a mandatory age retirement to a more flexible program. A study of 300 pension plans by the Bureau of Labor Statistics found that only 61 had a mandatory retirement age that was not subject to some type of flexibility. Retirement depended on the option of the company in 114 plans, but there was no automatic retirement age. Management decided according to definite procedures whether to retain workers. The other 125 plans had no compulsory retirement of any kind.[53] At the Consolidated Edison Company in New York, company policy provides for retaining workers as long as they can perform efficiently for the company. The department head makes recommendations of the retention of workers over 65 before a panel of other department heads. Other companies place a heavy emphasis on medical examinations to determine the fitness of workers. Still other companies make an effort to place older workers on easier jobs. Some labor unions have been instrumental in negotiating flexible retirement plans. In the automobile industry the worker may elect to retire at 65 and must retire at 68. The Steel Workers union is particularly opposed to any type of compulsory retirement.

[52] Irvin Sobel and Hugh Folk, "Labor Market Adjustments by Unemployed Older Workers," in A. M. Ross, ed., *Employment Policy and the Labor Market* (Berkeley, University of California Press, 1965), pp. 333-357.

[53] Mathiason, *Flexible Retirement,* pp. 23-31.

Their pension plans negotiated with the steel companies call for possible retirement at 65 if the employee so desires but with no compulsory age retirement.

Retiring workers automatically have certain advantages as well as disadvantages. In favor of automatic retirement, people can look forward to a period of leisure as a reward for work when they are still able to enjoy it. Furthermore, definite knowledge that they must retire will start workers thinking more about methods of adjusting to it. Automatic retirement is simple to administer and causes companies fewer headaches about whom to keep or retire. Under flexible retirement plans those workers who are not kept may react adversely to the fact that others are retained while they are not. The argument that retirement causes poor health has not been borne out by the facts. In a study made on this point, almost the same percentage of those retiring showed worsened health as did those who remained on the job.[54] Finally, a compulsory retirement system enables younger men to be promoted faster.

Weighty arguments may be presented in opposition to automatic retirement. Studies have shown that chronological age does not necessarily coincide with functional age. Many workers may be quite able to continue work for many years. Furthermore, society is that much wealthier in goods and services when the older workers are actively engaged in production. Third, our culture places much stress on the importance of work, and many workers, finances aside, have built their lives around the personal satisfactions obtained at work.[55] All in all, it appears that the aged should be given more opportunity to work if they so desire. At least the trend today is toward more flexible retirement systems.

GRADUAL RETIREMENT

Recently a number of companies have been experimenting with gradual retirement programs.[56] A 1955 study of the National Industrial Conference Board showed that 14 of 327 companies had a tapering-off program, although mainly for persons whose health was poor. One life insurance company in Newark, New Jersey, permits its older employees to take ten weeks of vacation prior to the year of retirement. The workers are encouraged to take five weeks during the first six months of the last year and the other five weeks during the last six months. The main purpose of the longer vacation is to aid the employee to develop plans for retirement and to permit him to explore places to which he or she may want to retire. A chewing gum manufacturer requires its employees who reach 65 years of age to take off one month a year without pay in addition to their regular vacation. In the second year he must take off two months, in the third, three months, and so on. By

[54] Streib and Thompson, *op. cit.*, p. 185.

[55] Pollak, *The Social Aspects of Retirement*, pp. 3-6.

[56] "Gradual Retirement—Latest Idea for Older Workers," *U.S. News and World Report*, Vol. 44 (September 26, 1958), pp. 88-90.

the fifth year (69 years of age), the worker would earn more income by retiring than working. Another life insurance company limits its employees to a four-day week the last year before retirement. A sterilizing equipment company permits their employees to rotate a month on and a month off. This program is voluntary, and most employees rarely ask for the rotation schedule.

NEW EMPLOYMENT OPPORTUNITIES

In a few localities private citizens or groups have attempted to find employ-ment for the aged. One group, called American Geriatric Enterprises (AGE), was formed by a doctor who was impressed by the fact that he diagnosed the main disorder of a large number of his aged patients as "unemployment." Psychosomatic disorder had followed from being unable to obtain work. The doctor found that many of the older unemployed had lost their jobs because of bankruptcy of their firms, consolidations with other companies, and dis-continuance of certain operations due to obsolescence of their product.

To help in the program, a committee of 30 industrial leaders was formed in St. Paul, Minnesota. They found that there were 1,500 unemployed aged 50 to 65 in the St. Paul area exclusive of Minneapolis. A corporation was formed with a capitalization of $25,000 by selling stock at $10 a share. Seven proj-ects were carefully evaluated, an empty garage rented, and several workers hired along with a retired 72-year-old garment manufacturer as general man-ager. The first contract called for stenciling cases for soft drink bottles. The original contracts came from industrialists who were on the board of direc-tors of AGE, but it was hoped that other outside business could be obtained later. Within a short time, 8 contracts had been obtained from 7 companies, and 14 more were being studied for economic feasibility. Ten employees had been hired, all within the ages of 50 to 65, who had been out of work an average of nine months before starting with AGE. Eventually the company not only hoped to hire more workers, and save on costs of the support of the aged, but make a profit for its stockholders as well. On a somewhat larger scale, Senior Achievement in Chicago employed 100 workers, all of whom had been retired.[57]

HEALTH OF THE AGED [58]

A decline in physical vitality in later years causes a number of problems for the aged. General deterioration means that the regenerative powers are re-duced whenever a crippling disease or accident occurs. Unfortunately, the

[57] Kenneth R. Larson, "American Geriatric Enterprises," and Frank H. Cassell, "Senior Achievement," in *Older People and the Industrial Community,* pp. 18-20, 24-25.

[58] For a more detailed analysis of health problems of the aged and solutions to such problems, *see* Chapters 9 and 10.

economic resources of the aged are less than those of other groups in the population. A particularly chronic illness may wipe out all the resources that the aged person has accumulated. Furthermore, the aged owned less health insurance than others prior to Medicare, and therefore were forced to meet costs from their own limited resources. So far as medical care goes, the failure to practice sufficient preventive medicine in the United States is a distinct liability. Cancer and other diseases may be controlled if caught early enough, but too few of our aged have regular periodic examinations. The number of aged admitted to mental hospitals has been increasing quite rapidly in recent years. A study of first admissions to state and licensed hospitals for mental disease in New York State showed an increase of 4 percent from 1921 to 1941 for males aged 15 to 19. During the same period increases in admittances for males over 75 was 46 percent. For females the increases over the same period for the same ages were respectively 31 and 60 percent.[59] Unfortunately too many of those suffering from senile psychoses have had poor social integration in their life. One study showed that only 15 percent of those suffering from senile psychoses had good social integration. The authors concluded that senile psychoses occurred most frequently whenever the aged were financially or socially unable to provide for themselves.[60] Other studies have shown that poorer classes and minority races tend to have a higher percentage of psychoses. Faris and Dunham, for example, found that in Chicago the highest rates of psychoses occurred in the rooming house and Negro sections, which were characterized by poor economic conditions, loose and disorganized family life, and a high mobility rate.[61]

REHABILITATION

A number of studies have shown that too few of our medical resources are directed to rehabilitation of the chronically ill. The possible improvements that can be made are shown in a study financed by Allegheny County, Pittsburgh, Pennsylvania. In a five-year period, rehabilitation was attempted for 608 people, most of whom were over 40. Of the total of 608 people referred to the physical medicine rehabilitation service, 207 were discharged to their homes and/or gainful occupations, 232 were improved and made ambulatory within the institution, and 122 showed no tangible improvement.

Of the 100 arthritics, 43 were discharged to their homes and another 17 were able to resume work. Only 40 remained institutionalized. Of the

[59] Benjamin Malzberg, "A Statistical Review of Mental Disorders in Later Life," in Oscar Kaplan, ed., *Mental Disorders in Later Life* (Stanford, Stanford University Press, 1956), Table 7, p. 14. *See also* Bettag *et al., op. cit.*

[60] H. W. Williams *et al.,* "Studies in Senile and Arteriosclerotic Psychoses, I— Relative Significance of Extrinsic Factors in Their Development," *American Journal of Psychiatry,* Vol. 98 (1942), pp. 712-715.

[61] R. E. L. Faris and H. W. Dunham, *Mental Disorders in Urban Areas* (Chicago, University of Chicago Press, 1939), pp. 134-142.

hemiplegics, 74 of 196 were able to go home. No further check was made to learn whether they had obtained gainful employment. Among the lower-extremity amputees, 47 in number, artificial limbs were provided to 15 and others were aided in other ways. Of the 47, 20 were discharged to their homes and 12 others found jobs; only 15 remained institutionalized. Of the 101 fracture patients, 45 were discharged to their homes and 15 found work.[62]

IMPROVED MEDICAL FACILITIES HERE AND ABROAD

A beginning has been made in the United States to provide better facilities for the aged who are ill. Under the 1954 amendments to the Hill-Burton Act, the states may receive four types of grants to assist in the construction of four special types of facilities: chronic disease hospitals; nursing homes providing skilled nursing care and related medical services; rehabilitation facilities providing an integrated program of medical, psychological, social, and vocational services; and outpatient diagnostic and treatment centers. Other countries have provided many more medical facilities for the aged than we have. In Denmark, facilities are available to house many of their aged plus additional combinational housing and hospital facilities. The largest hospital and nursing home is in Copenhagen. It has 1,600 beds, 500 of which are hospital beds, 300 nursing beds, and facilities for 800 other aged who may either be well or sick. The new sections provide for one-room flats for single people and two rooms for married couples. The home has a large library, a concert hall, an exercise yard, and lounges on each floor where guests may be entertained. In short, both housing and medical facilities are provided under this type of arrangement.[63]

ACTIVITIES OF THE AGED

To determine how well the aged used their time, one study analyzed the extent to which the aged engaged in planned activities. The various categories of activities included: activities concerned with the family, church, social, or political organizations; professional study; intellectual pursuits not related to previous professional work; physical activity; handicrafts; artistic pursuits; and collecting. Also, such purely passive activities as listening to the radio or watching television, motion pictures, dramatics, and the like

[62] Murray Ferderber, Alfred Kraft, and Gerard Hamill, "Physical Restoration of the Chronically Ill and Aged," *Geriatrics*, Vol. 8 (1953), pp. 186-197. For a summary of other studies, see Howard A. Rusk and Eugene J. Taylor, "Rehabilitation of the Chronically Ill and Aged," in Albert I. Lansing, ed., *Cowdry's Problems of Aging* (Baltimore, The Williams and Wilkins Co., 1952), pp. 942-949.

[63] Herman E. Hilleboe, "A Modern Pattern for Meeting the Health Needs of the Aging," in Donahue and Tibbitts, eds., *op. cit.*, pp. 53-55.

were included. The people were divided into several groups. Group A was composed of 100 unemployed men and women who were indigent or semi-indigent. They were recruited as volunteers from a university clinic. Their average age was 71. Group B was a retired group who had made a satis-factory adjustment to old age and had a higher financial status than group A. There were 50 people in this sample with an average age of 72. If a per-son had less than four hours of his day in planned activities as defined above, this person was classified in the doubtful category. In group A, only 20 per-cent reached a satisfactory level of planned activities; 67 percent were con-sidered doubtful; and 13 percent seemed to have nothing to do to occupy their time. The corresponding figures for group B were respectively 24, 63, and 10 percent.[64]

OLD-AGE CLUBS

A number of communities have formed social clubs, sometimes called Golden Age clubs, for the benefit of the aged. As an example of what a community may do, the activities of the MORA club of Bethlehem, Pennsylvania, are described. MORA stands for Men of Retirement Age. It was organized by the Senior Citizens Committee of the Bethlehem Community Council in consultation with the YMCA. The group is a YMCA club and meets at the YMCA building although no dues are collected nor is membership in the YMCA required. An offering box is placed at the door of the meeting room, and the men contribute as they wish. The purpose of the club is to provide fellowship, exchange of ideas, entertainment, education programs, social ac-tivities, and service functions for the community. The standing committees of the group are program, membership, ways and means, sick visitation, music, and transportation. The latter committee arranges that transportation to and from the meeting be provided for all those who do not have any. Meetings are held at 2 P.M. on Wednesday, the year round. At each meet-ing, songs are sung after the invocation. Birthdays are also recognized. In all there are 379 members with an average age of 73.8 years. To describe a typical meeting, 177 were present. Six birthdays were honored and a mo-ment of silence recorded for one of the members who had passed away that week. After a chorus of 15 had sung, color slides of the Mediterranean were shown by one of the members who had just completed a six-week cruise in that area. Other activities include pool, bridge, pinochle, and shuffleboard in which the members participate after the regular meetings and perhaps also on Friday afternoon. The club prides itself on supplying services to their town. Such diverse activities have been engaged in as repairing toys to dis-

[64] E. Busse et al., "Studies in the Process of Aging: X—The Strengths and Weak-nesses of Psychic Functioning in the Aged," American Journal of Psychiatry, Vol. 11 (1955), pp. 896-899.

tribute at Christmas for the needy and preparing workers' kits for the Community Chest campaign.[65] In a more critical vein, Irving Rosow has found in a study of 1,200 older Cleveland residents that there may be no effective substitutes for the loss of any major social role. He contends that such devices as Golden Age clubs or retirement hobbies are fundamentally bankrupt.[66]

COMMUNITY SERVICES

Although few communities have provided for comprehensive services for the aged in the United States, several of them have made a beginning with a few services. Trained social workers may be in charge of an information and referral center. Family and personal counseling may be provided, as also may be vocational and employment guidance. Adult educational facilities are sometimes available, along with a library pony service. In some communities, the Boy and Girl Scouts provide shopping and errand services for the aged. Multiphase screening health examinations and rehabilitation centers may be provided. Nursing and housekeeping services and even meals on wheels may be supplied. Foster home placement is also possible. Many facilities may be made available once a community organizes to aid the aged.[67]

PROBLEMS OF PREMATURE DEATH

Statistics show that a surprisingly larger percentage of males die rather early in life. Table 2-5 shows that 32 percent of white males aged 20 will not live to age 65. White females live somewhat longer. Nonwhites live less long than whites, again with males living less long than females.

Depending on when death occurs, a number of problems are created. If the prematurely deceased male has young children, the mother is faced with the dual task of not only supporting the children but taking care of them as well. Generally women earn less income than men, and probably the death of the male breadwinner will result in a lower standard of living for the family. If the surviving wife comes from a working-class family, very probably she will not be prepared even for a secretarial occupation. She is then forced into unskilled work at extremely low pay. Private life insurance may help appreciably. Also under the Social Security Act, survivors insurance is now made available along with aid to dependent children benefits. Even

[65] George D. Turner, "Mora Club," in *Older People and the Industrial Community*, pp. 22-24.

[66] Irving Rosow, "The Aged Family and Friends," *Social Security Bulletin*, Vol. 28, No. 11 (November, 1965), pp. 18-20.

[67] Mathiason, *Criteria for Retirement*, pp. 24-25.

TABLE 2–5. PERCENTAGE SURVIVING TO AGE 65 AND AVERAGE LIFE
EXPECTANCY, AT SPECIFIED AGES FOR WHITE MALES, 1963

Present Age	Percentage Surviving to Age 65	Average Life Expectancy (in Years)	Average Life Expectancy Beyond Age 65 (in Years)
20	68	50.1	5.1
30	69	40.8	5.8
40	71	31.6	6.6
50	75	23.0	8.0
60	87	15.8	10.8

Source: Vital Statistics of the United States, 1963, Vol. II, U.S. Department of
Health, Education, and Welfare, Part A, Table 5–2, p. 5-4.

with those aids, the death of the breadwinner generally causes a decided drop
in the standard of living of the remaining members of the family.

Summary

Statistics on population show that the number of aged in the United States
will grow very rapidly in the future. Fortunately, gross national product is
also rising rapidly so that economic support of the aged should not be an
undue burden on the economy. Various societies have taken divergent attitudes toward the aged. In our own society, our cultural values stress work,
success, and independence. The aged do not hold a particularly high place
in our value system. They also have less income than others in our society
either because of forced or voluntary retirement or inability to do heavy
work they were once able to do. The income of the aged in general is substantially below what has been ascertained as an adequate income. Most of
the aged now rely on the OASDHI program to provide them with an income.
    Low income has complicated the problem of living accommodations for
the aged. The aged are not a particularly mobile group. They tend to prefer
to remain in their own community and not to live with their children. Their
housing is less adequate than the general population. For the minority who
live in old people's homes, the care has been improving over the years. No
longer are all the insane, feeble-minded, ill, and orphans housed with the
aged. Even today, though, many nursing homes are inadequate, and hospital
facilities for the chronically ill and the senile are in short supply. In the
United States little has been done to provide low-rent public housing for the

aged, whereas in other advanced Western countries much more has been provided for the aged.

Many of our older families have at least one person who is actively engaged in work. Even more would work if hiring deadlines were reduced or eliminated and automatic retirement ages made more flexible. Both industry and government have been active in making more jobs available for the aged although still not to the degree that would be considered ideal. Health creates many problems for the aged, especially since the incidence of illness increases at the very time that income decreases. More medical care for the aged is necessary. Other countries are ahead of the United States in providing for health care and facilities. Some communities have made a beginning in providing various services for the aged, but a listing of possible services clearly indicates that few communities have made more than a small beginning.

Lastly, premature death strikes many more people than is normally suspected. Such an unfortunate event leaves many mothers and children in a destitute condition, particularly if they are from the lower classes.

OLD-AGE INSURANCE: HISTORY, ADMINISTRATION, COVERAGE, AND ELIGIBILITY

OLD-AGE PENSIONS ABROAD

GERMANY

One of the first industrial countries to pass an old-age pension plan for its citizens was Germany. Its law, passed in 1889, divided workers into five wage groups. Higher absolute taxes to finance the program were assessed the higher wage groups, who paid over twice as much as the lowest group. In percentage terms, however, the highest wage group paid a lower tax than the lowest wage group. The tax was assessed against both employees and employers. In 1911 employers paid a 3.8 percent tax, which financed not only the old-age pension and disability program but payments for sickness and accidents as well.[1] Employees paid somewhat less, since they were not taxed at all for accident insurance.[2] The government also contributed to the fund out of general revenues.

Under the original law of 1899, old-age pensions were claimable at age 70 even if the worker continued working. Later the age limit was lowered to 65 and pensions could be received even at 60 provided the worker had been unemployed for at least a year.[3] In 1899 the benefits were set at 72 reichsmarks plus an increment varying with the amount of contributions made to the fund. The highest wage group received more than twice as large benefits as the lowest wage group. In 1911 the basic amount was raised to 360 reichsmarks plus increments. Survivors' benefits to widows and dependent children were added by 1911 amendments. The social insurance schemes were extremely hard hit by the inflation of the early 1920's. Benefits became less and less adequate as the cost of living rose. Furthermore, the value of the assets of the programs were destroyed by inflation. The depression of the thirties also caused difficulties. Because of reduced contributions, benefits

---

[1] W. Harbutt Dawson, *Social Insurance in Germany, 1883–1911* (London, T. Fisher Unwin, 1912), p. 212.

[2] C. A. Kulp, *Social Insurance Coordination: An Analysis of German and British Organization* (Washington, Social Science Research Council, 1938), p. 212.

[3] Sakman *et al.*, "An Outline of Foreign Social Insurance and Assistance Laws," Bureau Report No. 5, Washington, D.C., Federal Security Agency, Social Security Board, Bureau of Research and Statistics (1940), pp. 10-11.

had to be reduced, and the government had to increase its share of the cost.[4] In 1938 the government paid about 40 percent of the old-age–invalidity pensions from general revenues.[5]

Extensive revisions were made in the law for West Germany in 1957. At the present time all are covered by the law except salaried persons who earn more than 15,000 marks per year. The tax rate is 7 percent of payrolls on both employees and employers unless the worker earns so little that no tax is assessed on him. In this case the tax rate on the employer is 14 percent. Government contributions average about one-third of the payments of wage earners and somewhat less for salaried personnel. Benefits are based on past wages plus years of coverage.[6]

ENGLAND

In 1772 a bill providing for annuities paid by local government passed the House of Commons but was defeated in the House of Lords. As early as 1786 a plan for nationwide compulsory old-age and disability insurance had been advocated. Later, around the 1870's the campaign began in earnest to provide some sort of compulsory governmental insurance to protect against the exigencies of life. The campaign was initiated by a clergyman of the Church of England, the Reverend William Lewery Blackley. Proponents of such proposals were finally successful in getting an old-age pension act passed in 1909. In 1911 unemployment and health insurance were added. The Old Age Pension Act of 1909 provided pensions financed solely by the government for both the aged and the disabled. The government paid 5 shillings weekly to all persons 70 years of age and over provided their income did not exceed 8 shillings a week. In addition, a candidate was disqualified if he failed to work regularly during his prime of life. The courts decided whether habitual drunkards and the shiftless had worked sufficiently to merit a pension. This section was removed in 1919. Because of rapidly rising living costs during World War I, pension benefits were raised at that time.

During the first third of the present century, the number of persons over 65 more than doubled. With the rising number of aged and the increasing level of benefits, between 1914 and 1924 the cost of the program nearly doubled. In order to lower the age of eligibility to 65 but not impose too heavy a drain on the treasury, a contributory pension system was passed in 1925. Then, at age 70, the original noncontributory system became applicable. Equal benefits were paid at 65 to those contributing to the system regardless of earnings, but the means test was kept in the noncontributory

[4] Kulp, op. cit., p. 71.
[5] Ibid., p. 119.
[6] Social Security Programs Throughout the World, 1961, Washington, D.C.: U.S. Department of Health, Education, and Welfare, Social Security Administration (1961), pp. 190-191.

system for those aged 70 or more. Under the contributory system, pensions were also paid to widows, dependent children, and orphans of those who had paid into the fund.[7]

The Beveridge Report was issued in 1943 with suggestions for wholesale improvement of social security. After the war a number of improvements were made in the system. In 1957 the Labour Party formally advanced a detailed program that called for substantial changes in the system. The Conservative Party in 1958 came forth with its own proposals. These proposals were later introduced into Parliament and with certain changes became law in July of 1959. The system of all workers paying the same tax and receiving the same benefit was abandoned. The flat rate of benefits was so low that pensions were especially inadequate for those who had been earning higher incomes. A study by the government actuary had uncovered the fact that the inadequate government program had resulted in more than one-third of the working population being covered under other pension programs, either public or private. Many were receiving a larger pension than the government was paying.

At the present time a flat benefit is paid to all employees who earn £9 a week or less. For higher-paid workers benefits are graduated according to past earnings and length of service. Higher-paid workers pay a larger amount in taxes but a smaller percentage than lower-paid employees. Employers pay about the same amount in taxes as employees. Government contributions equal about a fourth of the flat taxes and a slightly higher amount for the self-employed. The employer is now permitted to provide his own pension system for his workers provided that payments are as large as the government's, that the system is an irrevocable trust, and rights of workers are preserved if the worker leaves his employer.[8]

OTHER COUNTRIES

All of the European countries and all North American countries now have old-age pension programs. Almost all of South America has such programs, but there are fewer in Central America, the Middle East, Asia, and Africa, though several of these countries are now introducing a number of welfare programs. In Africa, for example, old-age programs were introduced on the Ivory Coast in 1960 and the Congo and Guinea in 1961.[9]

Many countries preceded the United States in providing old-age pensions as seen by scanning the dates when these countries adopted an old-age program: Germany, 1889; Great Britain, 1909; Luxemburg, 1911; Rumania,

---

[7] Kulp, op. cit., pp. 145-156.

[8] "New Graduated Retirement Benefits in Great Britain," Social Security Bulletin, Vol. 22 (September, 1959), pp. 4-9.

[9] 1963 Report on the World Social Situation (New York, The United Nations, 1963), pp. 94-104.

1912; Sweden, 1913; Italy, 1919; Netherlands, 1919; Spain, 1919; Uruguay, 1919; Denmark, 1921; U.S.S.R., 1922; Belgium, 1924; Bulgaria, 1924; Chile, 1924; Czechoslovakia, 1924; France, 1928; Hungary, 1928; Greece, 1932; and Poland, 1933.[10]

HISTORY OF OLD-AGE PENSIONS IN THE UNITED STATES

EARLY HISTORY

As indicated in Chapter 1, in colonial America the indigent aged were required to live with all other groups who were unable to take care of themselves. During and following this period, care for the aged, as for other groups, was provided by local communities. Almshouses were the accepted method of care, although on occasion some groups experimented with "outdoor" relief. It was not until the twentieth century that more comprehensive plans for the aged were introduced. The initiative and referendum served the needs of the indigent in Arizona in 1914 when an old-age pension act was passed, but it was declared unconstitutional. The first act to remain on the books was that in Alaska (1915), which provided for $12.50 monthly payments to aged pioneers in lieu of care in the Alaska Pioneers Home. State laws providing for old-age pensions were passed in 1923 in Montana, Nevada, and Pennsylvania. None of these laws, however, effectively provided for the aged. Although the law in Montana nominally was a mandatory one, payments were left to the option of the counties, few of which provided pensions. Nevada's law depended entirely upon county financing, which was not forthcoming in large amounts. Pennsylvania's law was declared unconstitutional. Prior to 1935 six other states passed laws that provided for county financing of old-age pensions. In general, these laws were ineffectual in obtaining old-age pensions, for the counties simply did not appropriate funds. A more workable type of law was passed in California in 1929. This law was mandatory, and required that both the state and the county contribute money for pensions for the aged. Before 1935, seven other states adopted laws similar to California's.[11]

One major group who received old-age pensions were our soldiers and sailors. By 1910, all but six states had granted old-age pensions to Civil War veterans and after World War I, thirty states made provision for aged veterans of that war.[12] For many years the federal government also has had a

---

[10] Sakman *et al., op. cit.,* pp. 6-20.

[11] Harvey Lebrun, "Evolution of the American Pension System," *Sociology and Social Research,* Vol. 20 (1935–1936), pp. 453-462.

[12] Anne H. Geddes, *Trends in Relief Expenditures, 1910–1935,* Research Monograph X, Washington, D.C., Works Progress Administration (1937), p. 3.

pension program for veterans. Patriotism and the voting power of veterans groups were sufficient to provide security for at least one group in America.

STATE LEGISLATION IN THE 1930'S

Before the passage of the federal Social Security Act, state old-age pensions were not effective. Pensions were low. They averaged about $14.53 per month per person in 1934. The states that had adequately financed pension laws required such rigid residence requirements that few of the aged could qualify. Arizona, for example, stipulated that applicants had to reside there 35 years to be eligible for a pension, and most of the others required 15 to 20 years.[13] Of the 7.5 million aged in 1934, about 180,000 received state pensions, another 165,000 received industrial pensions,[14] and about 15,000 workers were recipients of old-age pensions through labor unions. The only unions of any size to have a pension system were the Locomotive Engineers, Typographers, Carpenters, and Bricklayers.[15]

In 1933, whereas $25 million was spent in the United States for old-age pensions, Great Britain spent nearly $400 million with a population of only about one-third of ours. If their figure is multiplied by three to account for our larger population, we would have spent $1.2 billion instead of $25 million to match their figure.[16]

The main impetus to the passage of federal old-age pensions and other social legislation came from the Great Depression of the 1930's. Local charities were swamped with additional people applying for relief for the first time. Local communities, our first line of defense for relief, were faced with decreasing revenues, for many people were forced to default in payment of their property taxes. Although a few states attempted to step into the breach, their taxing abilities were limited also. It appeared that borrowing from banks would be necessary, but neither local nor state governments had sufficient resources to borrow on any large scale. Furthermore, many such governments had already borrowed up to their statutory or constitutional limits. Some state constitutions did not permit them to handle the problem of relief at all.[17] As the depression deepened and more and more were thrown out of work, the only government capable of preventing starvation and hunger on a mass basis was the federal government.

---

[13] Maxwell Stewart, *Social Security* (New York, Norton, 1937), p. 113.

[14] Joseph P. Harris, "The Social Security Program of the United States," *American Political Science Review*, Vol. 30, No. 3 (June, 1936), pp. 470-477.

[15] Stewart, *op. cit.*, pp. 51-52.

[16] *Social Security in America*, Washington, D.C., Social Security Board (1937), p. 347.

[17] Lewis Meriam, *Relief and Social Security* (Washington, Brookings Institution, 1946), pp. 10-11.

FEDERAL ACTION PRIOR TO 1935

The first bill introduced in Congress to provide for old-age pensions for all elderly people in need of assistance was introduced by Congressman William B. Wilson in 1907. Four years later Congressman Victor L. Berger, a Socialist, introduced a bill which called for $4 a week pensions for all those over 60 years of age who had an income of less than $10 a week. It was not until 21 years later, after the onslaught of the Depression, that the federal government took any action. In July of 1932, Congress granted the Reconstruction Finance Corporation $300 million to lend to the states and localities for relief purposes. When Franklin D. Roosevelt assumed office in March of 1933, practically all of this money had been lent out. In that year the Federal Emergency Relief Administration was created. Instead of lending money to the states, outright grants were made provided that the states added $3 for every $1 of the federal grant. Two hundred fifty million dollars was provided on a matching basis along with another $250 million to be given to states that were financially unable to match the federal grants. Then, in the winter of 1933, the federal government employed 4 million people under its Civil Works Administration program in work at reasonably adequate wages. Other federal public works programs followed, such as the Public Works Administration, Works Progress Administration, Civilian Conservation Corps, and the National Youth Administration. It was the feeling, though, that in addition to providing work relief a federal insurance program should be instituted.[18]

COMMITTEE ON ECONOMIC SECURITY

After several bills on old-age pensions and unemployment insurance had been introduced in Congress, President Franklin D. Roosevelt appointed the Committee on Economic Security on June 29, 1934, by executive order. This committee was composed of the Secretary of Labor as chairman, the Secretaries of the Treasury and Agriculture, the Attorney General, and the Federal Emergency Relief Administration. In the same executive order President Roosevelt created an Advisory Council to the Committee on Economic Security. This council was composed of 23 experts on social insurance from the fields of industry, labor, and social work. An executive Director (Edwin E. Witte of the University of Wisconsin) was chosen to implement the executive order, and a Technical Board was also created to help with the program.[19] The completed reports of the staff members comprised more than

[18] Stewart, op. cit., pp. 89-90, 111.
[19] Edwin E. Witte, The Development of the Social Security Act (Madison, Wisc., University of Wisconsin Press, 1962), p. 9.

a dozen large volumes of typewritten material.[20] The Advisory Council submitted its report on December 18, 1934, and the Committee on Economic Security its report on January 15, 1935.[21] After a hearing in both houses of Congress, the Social Security Bill was introduced.

Supporting data for an old-age pension program showed that many of our aged were without economic resources. In Connecticut, for example, it was found in 1932 that 49 percent of the aged there had income of less than $300 per year, and that more than 33 percent had no income of any kind. Other studies in New York and Massachusetts revealed that from 23 to 65 percent of the aged had incomes of less than $300 annually and less than $5000 in property.[22] Almshouses were rejected as a solution to the problems of the aged. Shocking deficiencies were found in this type of care. Such houses still suffered from having too many diverse groups of disabled all thrown together with too little financial resources to provide adequate care.

The Committee on Economic Security formulated a plan which provided for two programs for the aged. One, an insurance program, would provide payments as a matter of right to wage-earners who would contribute to the system. The other was an old age assistance program, which would cover only those in need and be financed from general tax revenues.

OPPOSITION TO THE SOCIAL SECURITY BILL

At the Congressional hearings on the bill, few appearances were made by employers. Representatives of the United States Chamber of Commerce and the National Retail Dry Goods Association spoke in favor of the program although some amendments were suggested by the former. The bill was attacked by the National Association of Manufacturers, the Illinois Manufacturers' Association, and the Ohio Manufacturers' Association. The latter organization violently attacked the bill. At the time of the Congressional hearings, employer groups in general knew so little about the bill that no decisive stand was taken upon it. Later such groups were aroused by opponents of the measure and sent many letters and telegrams of protest to their Congressmen.[23] The National Metal Trades Association opposed all parts of the bill on the ground that it would supply the lazy a vehicle to secure a release from work. The support of the shiftless and unemployable, it was alleged, was placed upon the thrifty and industrious. The costs were considered too high, especially since they would be imposed on the industrious employers and employees of our society. The association further maintained that pooled funds like the old-age and unemployment insurance funds impaired confidence in public finance. The existence of reserve funds also

[20] Ibid., p. 40.
[21] Grace Abbott, From Relief to Social Security (Chicago, University of Chicago Press, 1941), pp. 199-200.
[22] Social Security in America, pp. 149-199.
[23] Witte, op. cit., pp. 88-91.

would invite labor and other groups to increase benefits, extend coverage, and provide for longer periods of protection. Not only would the employers' administrative expenses be higher in keeping all the additional records and deductions, but government administrative expenses would be higher. In short, the National Metal Trades Association could see little good in the Social Security bill.[24]

The bill went first to the Ways and Means Committee in the House of Representatives. Few members of the Committee were sympathetic to the bill. Members of this group went to the President with the advice that the old-age insurance provisions of the bill could not be passed. The President insisted that the insurance program was an important part of the bill, and that the essential features must remain intact. Edwin Witte maintained that the firm stand taken by the President saved the old-age insurance program.[25] Consideration in the executive session of the Ways and Means Committee dragged on indefinitely. The Townsendites opposed the bill because they felt that coverage of the act was not extensive enough nor benefits high enough. They themselves proposed pensions of $200 a month for all the aged without applying a means test of any kind. The Townsendites suggested financing their program by a gross transactions tax. Estimates by economists showed that the income from the tax would come nowhere near paying $200-a-month pensions. Furthermore, the $200-a-month benefit seemed unduly high in relation to the relative poverty at that time.

Business groups did not like the taxes proposed in the bill. The impression of serious opposition to the bill and no real support was counteracted by Secretary of Labor Perkins, who secured the signature of 50 prominent people in favor of the bill. This support of the bill, plus that of President Roosevelt, enabled the bill to be passed by a 371 to 33 vote in the House. In the Senate the conference committee deadlocked for an entire month on the Clark amendment, which would have exempted private retirement systems from the plan provided that the annuities paid were as high as that to be paid by the federal government. The Roosevelt administration vigorously opposed the Clark amendment on the ground that industry would insure the better risks and leave an adverse selection for the government.[26] The conference committee finally agreed to strike the amendment, and the Social Security Act passed the Senate by a vote of 76 to 7.

ADMINISTRATION

Of the three major sections of the Social Security Act, unemployment insurance, public assistance, and old age insurance, the first two programs are

[24] Statement of J. F. Kolb, Director of Industrial Relations, National Metal Trades Association, Hearings before the Committee on Finance, U.S. Senate, 74th Congress, 1st Session, on S1130, Part X (February 13-15, 1935), pp. 857-861.

[25] Witte, op. cit., pp. 91-95.

[26] Harris, op. cit., pp. 456-482.

administered by the states whereas the third is entirely federal. A purely federal system for old-age insurance was favored because it would be easier to administer. Actuarially, the federal system is more sound since estimates of total population can be made more easily. Population mobility from one state to another would have caused difficulties in estimating costs of an old-age insurance program at the state level. Also, the states might have gotten into a competitive war on tax rates. Furthermore, similar procedures for all the states should make for lower administrative costs. In addition, some states in other fields of social legislation have failed to provide adequate laws. A state administered program was adopted for unemployment insurance on the ground, among others, that the various jurisdictions could experiment with the best type of program. For the aged, however, it would be necessary for a period of 50 to 75 years to elapse to test the program through one complete life cycle. Experimentation, then, would be less valuable than insuring that the one program adopted be adequate.[27]

The old-age insurance program is administered by the Social Security Administration, which is part of the Department of Health, Education, and Welfare. The Social Security Administration has offices throughout the country. The purposes of these offices are to supply information on the program and to process claims. Each worker has a social security number which is used to keep a record of earnings upon which benefits are based. These records are kept at the central office of the Social Security Administration in Baltimore, Maryland. A beneficiary has the right to challenge a decision on his pension. A referee hears and makes a decision on the case. Further appeal is made to the Appeals Council of the Social Security Administration, and then to the federal courts. The consensus is that the OASDHI program has been administered efficiently. The expenses in 1966 (preliminary estimates) were 2 percent of benefits.[28] Little criticism has been heard about the administration of this program.

COVERAGE UNDER THE OLD-AGE INSURANCE PROGRAM

The Social Security Act of 1935 covered about 60 percent of the civilian work force in the United States.[29] The largest excluded group was the self-employed, who numbered between 10 and 11 million people in 1940. This figure included farm operators and farm tenants. The next largest excluded group was 4 to 5 million hired farm laborers, followed by about 3.5 million

27 Social Security Board, *Social Security in America*, Washington, D.C., Government Printing Office (1937), pp. 200-201.

28 Robert J. Myers and Francisco Bayo, "Old Age, Survivors and Disability Expenses," *Social Security Bulletin*, Vol. 29, No. 7 (July, 1966), Table 1, p. 4.

29 "A Report to the Secretary of Health, Education, and Welfare on Extension of Old Age and Survivors Insurance to Additional Groups of Current Workers," Washington, D.C., Consultants on Social Security (1953), p. 2.

state and local government employees and a smaller number of federal employees. The other two large exempted groups were domestic workers (about 2.5 million) and about 800,000 employees working for nonprofit organizations.[30] A major reason for excluding these groups was the fear that the administrative problems of covering them would be insurmountable.

Since such a large percentage of the aged were not covered under the insurance program, Congress created a second program, called old-age assistance (OAA), to provide pensions for those in need and drawing little or nothing under the insurance system. Until 1953 more old people obtained pensions from the old-age assistance program than from the old-age insurance program. As more and more people were covered under the insurance program, it became the larger program.

In 1939 a minor change was made to cover those working people who had already reached the age of 65. Under the original act of 1935, workers already over 65 were not taxed and could not qualify for benefits. Major increases in coverage came in amendments to the Social Security Act in 1950, 1954, and 1957.

SELF-EMPLOYED

The largest excluded group, the self-employed, had been excluded for administrative reasons. Experience under the act had shown that records for many millions of small employers could be kept accurately. Since this was so, it was reasoned that the self-employed could be covered also, and they were in 1950. In 1954, self-employed farmers were covered, in 1956 dentists and lawyers were covered, and in 1965 medical doctors were also covered. Today the only group of self-employed who are not covered are those who have net earnings of less than $400 a year.

A higher tax was placed on the self-employed than on employees, because the system was not able to collect an additional amount from a nonexistent employer. In 1968 the tax on employees was 4.4 percent and 6.4 percent for the self-employed. By 1987 the tax on employees will rise to 5.9 percent and 7.9 percent for the self-employed. The 1965 Advisory Council on Social Security recommended that the tax rate on the self-employed be no more than 1 percent more than the tax on employees on the grounds that some self-employed will be "overcharged" in relation to the benefits they receive, but this suggestion was not implemented in the 1967 amendments.

HIRED FARM LABOR

By 1950 a number of arguments were presented for covering farm employees. The problem of administering the system to small employers had been suc-

[30] *Social Security Yearbook, 1942*, Washington, D.C., p. 115.

cessfully solved. Also, at least 16 other countries had successfully covered farm workers in government old-age pension programs.[31] In addition, it was found that the poorer states had much more of a burden of welfare since farm hands were not covered under the insurance program. In Mississippi, for example, only 2 out of 10 workers in 1940 were in covered employment compared with 7 out of 10 in Rhode Island.[32] Also, it was found that agricultural workers from time to time were employed in covered employment, but earned too little to qualify for benefits. Thus, even though hired farm laborers have been one of the poorest groups in the nation, they had to pay social security taxes from which they received no benefit. For example, 46 percent of a sample of migratory workers in the five states of New Jersey, Michigan, Virginia, North Carolina, and Kentucky had earned wages in covered employment and thus paid social security taxes. Yet only 10 to 15 percent of these workers were eligible to draw social security benefits.[33] Lastly, it was argued that hired farm laborers were so poor *and* had so little annuity protection that they should be covered under the OASDHI program.

The arguments for hired farm labor coverage proved persuasive, and regularly employed farm laborers were covered under the OASDHI program in 1950. Coverage was further broadened in 1954 and changed in 1956. As of the latter date all hired farm laborers are covered who earn $150 or more a year from one employer or work for one employer on 20 or more days for cash pay computed on a time rather than piece-rate basis. The amendments also provide that a crew leader may be considered an employer. At the present time almost all farm workers are covered except those working for only short periods of time.

GOVERNMENT EMPLOYEES

In 1950, federal employees not covered under other retirement systems were included under OASDHI. State and local government employees had originally been excluded under the Social Security Act because of the constitutional difficulty of the federal authority taxing state and local governments. In 1950, state and local government employees who were not under a retirement system of their own were covered provided the state or local governments gave their consent. Under the 1954 amendments, state and local government employees already covered under retirement systems were given the option of federal coverage provided that the state or local government and the employees both approved. In 1965 about 7 out of 10 state, county,

[31] Wilbur J. Cohen, "Foreign Experience in Social Insurance Countries for Agricultural and Domestic Workers," *Social Security Bulletin,* Vol. 8 (February, 1945), p. 5.

[32] "Equality of Rights to Social Security," *Social Security Bulletin,* Vol. 10 (November, 1947), p. 20.

[33] Fred Safier, Walter Quinn, and Edward I. Fitzgerald, "The Agricultural Worker in Employment Covered by Federal Old-Age and Survivors Insurance," *Social Security Bulletin,* Vol. 4 (July, 1941), pp. 11-14.

and local employees were covered under the OASDHI program.[34] Several anomalous situations now exist concerning state coverage.[35] In all but 20 states, coverage is available only by means of a referendum among any retirement system group. The remaining 20 states, which are named in the law, may use the referendum or an alternative system whereby coverage is extended to only those members of a retirement system or group who desire such coverage, but only provided that all employees who later become employed will automatically be covered under OASDHI. The 1965 Advisory Council on Social Security recommended that the alternative option be given to all states. Until 1967, all but 19 states, specifically named by law, were prohibited from providing coverage for groups covered under a policemen or firemen retirement system. The 1967 amendments provided that firemen in the remaining states could be covered if the governor of the state certified that the overall benefit protection of the firemen would be improved by the coverage. In addition, a favorable referendum by firemen is required.

DOMESTIC WORKERS

Domestic workers had been covered under the 1935 act if they were employed by hotels, restaurants, or other business establishments, but household domestic employees were excluded from coverage. Since it had been found that the OASDHI program could successfully be applied to small employers, in 1950 it was decided to cover about 1 million of the 1.8 million household workers who were more regularly employed.[36] Coverage was slightly broadened in 1954 to include 100,000 to 200,000 more domestic workers.[37] To qualify for coverage today, a domestic employee must earn $50 in a quarter from a single employer.

NONPROFIT ORGANIZATIONS

Originally, nonprofit organizations had been excluded because such organizations had not been subject to taxation. In 1950 it was provided that if a nonprofit organization wished to be covered, and if two-thirds of the employees voted for coverage, those voting for coverage plus all new employees would be covered under the act. Since the votes were overwhelmingly in favor of coverage, Congress deleted the two-thirds vote requirement in 1960.

34 "Report of the Advisory Council on Social Security: The Status of the Social Security Program and Recommendations for Its Improvement," *Social Security Bulletin*, Vol. 28 (March, 1965), p. 37.

35 *Ibid.*

36 George H. Liebowitz, "Old Age and Survivors Insurance Coverage under the 1950 Amendments," *Social Security Bulletin*, Vol. 13 (December, 1950), p. 7.

37 "A Report to the Secretary of Health, Education, and Welfare on Extension of Old Age and Survivors Insurance to Additional Groups of Current Workers," p. 14.

The problem of separation of church and state created a knotty problem on coverage of clergymen and members of religious orders. This problem was solved in 1954 when this group was given the option on an individual basis to join the program or not. However, to elect coverage, a clergyman was required to file a waiver certificate within the second year in which he had earnings of $400 or more after 1954. Congress extended the date on several occasions because a number of clergymen who had originally rejected coverage requested another opportunity to be covered. This section of the law was improved in 1967 when it was provided that all clergymen would be covered unless they specifically rejected coverage for religious reasons. Members of religious orders who have taken a poverty vow are still compulsorily excluded.

PRESENT COVERAGE

Table 3-1 shows the increase in coverage from 1940 through 1960. More than 90 percent of those now working in paid employment are covered under the OASDHI program. Over half the persons not covered under the OASDHI program are federal, state, and local employees, almost all of whom are covered under separate retirement programs. Most of the remaining persons not covered are persons who work irregularly and who do not meet the relatively low-earnings test required for coverage. Part-time domestic workers and part-time farm laborers are in this group. Coverage was extended in 1965 to include medical doctors, medical interns, and those earning a living through tips rather than wages. As of 1966, for those who became 65 the previous year, 92 percent of all persons were eligible for social security insurance and 97 percent were eligible for either social security, civil-service retirement, or railroad retirement.[38] The 1967 amendments added some clergymen and a few more state employees.

ELIGIBILITY

In 1935 rather severe work requirements had to be met for eligibility in the OASDHI program. Not only had a worker to earn $2,000 in wages but he also had to be employed in five separate calendar years. The 1939 amendments substantially lessened the requirements for coverage. Even with the more lenient eligibility requirements, the Advisory Council to the Social Security Board in 1948 pointed out that standards were still so stringent that only about 20 percent of the population aged 65 and over were either insured or receiving benefits. The eligibility requirements have been amended a number of times since then. Eligibility now depends on whether the applicant has "fully insured" or "currently insured" status.

[38] Robert M. Ball, "Policy Issues in Social Security," *Social Security Bulletin,* Vol. 29, No. 6 (June, 1966), p. 4.

TABLE 3–1. PERSONS IN PAID EMPLOYMENT, BY OASDI COVERAGE STATUS, FOR SELECTED PERIODS AFTER ENACTMENT OF MAJOR SOCIAL SECURITY LEGISLATION

Period	Persons Employed (in Millions)	Persons Covered (in Millions)	Percentage Covered	Persons Not Covered (in Millions)	Persons Added to Coverage by Legislation (in Millions)
June 1940 (after 1935 act and 1939 legislation)	47.0	25.5	54	21.4	25.5
June 1951 (after 1950 and 1951 legislation)	62.7	46.3	74	16.4	10.2
June 1955 (after 1954 legislation)	64.6	54.9	85	9.7	7.4
June 1957 (after 1956 legislation)	66.7	60.1	90	6.6	3.3
June 1960 (after 1957–1959 legislation)	68.8	62.4	91	6.4	0.1
December 1960 (after 1960 legislation)	67.1	61.0	91	6.1	...

ᵃ Excludes 8.7 million covered under the Railroad Retirement Act.
Source: Saul Waldman, "Coverage Extension Under Old-Age, Survivors, and Disability Insurance," Social Security Bulletin, Vol. 24, No. 6 (June, 1961), Table 3, p. 7.

FULLY INSURED

A worker has "fully insured" status if he earns $50 or more in one calendar quarter (a three months period) for each calendar year elapsing after 1950. A man retiring in 1957 would have needed six quarters for "fully insured" status, where a worker retiring in 1959 would have needed eight quarters. Those reaching age 21 after 1950 need count only the period after they have reached 21. A worker must have a minimum of six quarters of coverage to qualify (in addition to the other requirements for qualification). The minimum requirement of six quarters which now exists is much less than the five years requirement of the original 1935 Act. The maximum number of quarters needed for "fully insured" status is 40. After this number is reached, the worker no longer has to earn $50 in one quarter in following years.

In 1965, a "transitional insured status" section provided payments to those 72 years of age and older with as little as three-quarters of coverage under special circumstances.[39] This is a transitional program only, and those reaching 72 years of age on or after 1964 will have the same requirements for eligibility as those with fully insured status.[40] A 1966 law provided that payments be made to retirees aged 72 and over who attained that age before 1968 even though they had no quarters of coverage. The amount paid is $40 per month for a single person and $60 for a couple (1967 amendments). This too is a transitional program, and those men who reach age 72 during 1972 and after will have the same eligibility requirements as those required for fully insured status. The payments are not automatic, but are made only in lieu of certain other types of income.[41] Since persons covered under this program contributed little if anything to the OASI trust fund, payments to this group are financed mainly out of general revenues from the treasury.

CURRENTLY INSURED

To be currently insured a worker has to be employed in 6 of the last 13 quarters, including the quarter of death or retirement. Certain periods of disability may be excluded to make the eligibility requirements more liberal. In general it is easier to obtain currently insured status than fully insured status since the worker is not required to have worked 40 quarters. It is possible, though, to be fully insured and not currently insured. If a worker

[39] For the specific circumstances, see Wilbur J. Cohen and Robert M. Ball, "Social Security Amendments of 1965: Summary and Legislative History," *Social Security Bulletin*, Vol. 28, No. 9 (September, 1965), p. 15.

[40] Wilbur J. Cohen, Robert M. Ball, and Robert J. Myers, "Social Security Payments to Noninsured Persons," *Social Security Bulletin*, Vol. 29, No. 9 (September, 1966), Table 1, p. 6.

[41] *Ibid.*, pp. 7-8.

had worked his 40 quarters to give him fully insured status, he would not be currently insured if he has not worked 6 of the last 13 quarters.

To qualify for Social Security benefits, either fully insured status or currently insured status, or both, are required to qualify for certain types of benefits. The requirements are shown in Table 3-2.

TABLE 3–2. CURRENT REQUIREMENTS FOR INSURANCE STATUS UNDER OLD-AGE, SURVIVORS, AND DISABILITY INSURANCE, BY BENEFICIARY CATEGORY

Beneficiary Category	Insured-Status Requirement for Worker
Retired worker (old-age)	Fully
Disabled worker	Fully and for disability determination
Dependents of retired worker (for old-age and disability):	
Wife	Fully
Husband	Fully
Child	Fully
Survivors of worker:	
Widow	Fully
Widower	Fully
Widowed mother	Fully or currently
Parent	Fully
Child	Fully or currently
Lump-sum payment beneficiary	Fully or currently
"Disability freeze" beneficiary	Fully and for disability determination

Source: Social Security Bulletin, Vol. 22, No. 1 (January, 1959), Table 3, p. 20, and 1967 amendments.

THE AGE REQUIREMENT

In 1935 it was provided that pensions would be paid to those covered workers who retired at age 65. In 1956 women workers were permitted to receive benefits if they retired at age 62 rather than 65 but at permanently lower benefits than they would receive if they had retired at age 65. The same provision was made applicable to men by amendments in 1961. Those who favored reducing the retirement age to 62 argued that people who lose their jobs at a higher age have a more difficult time finding a new one. Although it is true that seniority rights and other considerations cause less elderly people to be laid off, once unemployment is experienced it tends to be of a long duration. The reduction in age did not cost the system any additional expense, for the reduction in benefit was sufficient to offset the age reduction.

A study from 1962 through 1965 showed that about half the men and two-thirds of the women workers awarded retirement benefits under the social security program were under age 65. A study of the early retirees showed that a majority of those claiming benefits at age 62 were prompted to do so either by unemployment or the need to supplement earnings that were characteristically low or had dropped off substantially. The Advisory Council on Social Security in 1965 expressed concern over the low pensions of this group since they are actuarially reduced.[42]

Some countries—for example, England—provide that workers who do not retire at age 65 will receive a larger pension when they do retire. It has been estimated that if the same provision were in existence in the United States, workers who would continue to work until age 70 could receive an increase in benefits of 61 percent and still draw no more than if they had retired at 65 on a smaller pension.[43] At the present time in the United States no increases in benefits are paid for late retirement.

THE RETIREMENT TEST

All governmental pension programs must designate whether pensions will automatically be paid whenever age 65 or some other age is reached, or whether a pension should be received only when income decreases due to retirement from the work force. A few countries grant pensions regardless of retirement, but most countries, including the United States, have a retirement test. The original provisions of the Social Security Act prohibited an old-age recipient from earning any money in regular employment. The law has been modified a number of times since 1935 to permit more and more earnings. At the present time, a person aged 72 and over may earn any amount he wishes and still draw OASDHI benefits. For those below that age, a person may earn up to $1,680. Above that amount $1 in benefits will be withheld for each $2 of earnings up to $2,800. Above $2,800, $1 in benefits will be withheld for each $1 of earnings.

An amendment of 1954 eliminated counting only earnings in covered employment. Prior to 1954 older workers sought employment only in non-covered industry, for employment in covered industry resulted in a loss of Social Security benefits. Earnings from dividends and other property are permitted without limitation. From a standpoint that pensions are to make up for low incomes at retirement, such payments to property holders cannot be justified. However, since employees and the self-employed have been taxed and thus contributed to the system, Congress felt that the system should be viewed more as an annuity and that benefits be paid regardless of the amount of property income. Furthermore, people would be less likely

[42] Lenore A. Epstein, "Early Retirement and Work-Life Experience," *Social Security Bulletin*, Vol. 29, No. 3 (March, 1966), pp. 3-10.

[43] Henry W. Steinhaus, *Financing Old Age*, National Industrial Conference Board, Studies in Individual and Collective Security, No. 4 (1948), p. 35.

to save if their dividend or interest income would disqualify them from Social Security.

Several arguments may be cited in favor of paying pensions regardless of whether the worker retires. Private annuities are paid under this type of arrangement. Also, some production is lost if recipients are forced to retire from the work force. Some of the aged may wish to continue working, and perhaps their desires should be given due consideration. Lastly, although paying pensions at 65 regardless of earnings would cost more, wealthier nations may be able to afford such payments.

Weighty arguments can be mustered for maintaining the retirement test. If pensions were paid regardless of retirement, perhaps some persons would be less likely to retire. In depression times, the failure to retire may cause unemployment problems for younger people who should have replaced the aged. If the earnings test were eliminated entirely, the payroll taxes would have to rise 1 percent, according to a recent estimate of the chief actuary of the Social Security Administration.[44] If it were decided that it was possible to increase the payroll tax by 1 percent, there might be more justification for raising benefits in general rather than abolishing the retirement test. Also, if a major goal of the program is to aid in replacing income lost through retirement, the retirement test should be continued.[45]

Summary

Other countries adopted a system of old-age pensions much earlier than the United States. Germany passed such a law in 1889, and England followed in 1909. Although pension programs abroad have had to weather the severe stresses of inflation and depression, they have been gradually improved and strengthened. Such laws have become integral parts of Western civilization. Changes in legislation over the years have been to broaden and strengthen the social security system rather than weaken or abolish it.

The OASDHI program is one of the few security programs in the United States that is administered solely by the federal government. Administrative expenses of the program are quite low, and the administration of the program has been efficient.

In the United States, prior to the twentieth century, the English practice was followed of dispensing relief on a local basis and providing a harsh

[44] Robert J. Myers, "Earnings Test Under Old-Age, Survivors, and Disability Insurance, Basis, Background, and Experience," *Social Security Bulletin*, Vol. 27, No. 5 (May, 1964), p. 12.

[45] For a more comprehensive treatment of applying a retirement test, *see* Eveline Burns, *Social Security and Public Policy* (New York, McGraw-Hill, 1956), Chap. 6.

system so as to discourage malingering. Prior to the Social Security Act of 1935 several states provided a system of old-age pensions, but few of the programs were adequately financed, and pensions were quite low. The Great Depression hastened passage of a national social security system in the United States. Our basic law was passed in 1935. Opposition to an old-age insurance system was quite widespread, but strong support from President Roosevelt and leading citizens was sufficient to ensure passage of the act.

When the Social Security Act was first passed, about 60 percent of the civilian work force was covered under it. The major exclusions were the self-employed, agricultural workers, government employees, domestic employees, and employees of nonprofit organizations. Since 1935 the trend has been to cover most of the excluded groups so that today more than 90 percent of the work force is covered under the insurance program of the Social Security Act.

Eligibility under the OASDHI program is determined on the basis of past earnings. Over the years eligibility requirements have been eased to permit more coverage under the program. The age of retirement was set at 65 years of age in 1935 and has remained at that age, although persons may now retire on a reduced benefit at age 62. Some debate has arisen over whether persons should be required to retire to receive an old-age insurance benefit. Those 72 years of age and older do not have to retire. Others below this age must retire, but over the years they have been permitted to earn an increasingly larger income.

OLD-AGE INSURANCE: BENEFITS AND TAXATION

BENEFITS

In 1935 three types of money payments were provided for by law. The first went to any retired worker 65 years of age in covered industry. Second, at the death of a covered worker, a lump-sum payment was made. Third, for those who paid some taxes but were not eligible for old-age benefits, the worker was to receive a refund. The types of benefits paid have changed considerably since the original act.

LUMP-SUM PAYMENTS

Over the years lump-sum payments have been substantially curtailed. Originally, lump-sum payments equaled six times the primary insurance amount. This figure was cut to three times the primary insurance amount in 1950. A further restriction came in 1954, when the maximum lump-sum payment was limited to $255. Cuts in the lump-sum payment are in contrast to the increase in monthly benefits for retired workers. Such cuts are anomalous in view of increasing burial costs. If lump-sum payments are looked upon as an aid in burial expenses, then perhaps they should increase in line with the increased costs experienced at death. On the other hand, insurance companies are particularly opposed to increases in lump-sum benefits. They would prefer that people buy more private insurance. The influence of this group, among others, has been able to keep lump-sum benefits at a minimum.

VESTED RIGHTS IN BENEFITS

The original Social Security Act provided that workers who had been taxed under the program but had failed to qualify for benefits would be reimbursed an amount equal to 3.5 percent of wages earned in covered employment. In 1939, these sections were deleted, and no reimbursements were forthcoming. Some people protested this change on grounds that persons paying into the fund had a legal right to reimbursement. However, the Social Security Act expressly states that the act may be repealed, altered, or amended in any of its provisions at any time. Thus there is no valid contract as there is in private insurance, nor do workers have a vested right to receive benefits. One argument against guaranteeing vested rights is that future generations should be free to distribute pensions in the way that they think most desirable. Furthermore, under a vested program the government would be unable to grant larger benefits, since they would be irrevocably bound not to change the program in any way.[1] Even though these arguments are sound, there was some question at the time whether the lump-sum payments should have been taken away from those not qualifying. Probably such workers were badly in need of income. The justification given was that most recipients would receive the further advantages of dependents' and survivors' benefits, added in 1939. Obviously, though, those who could not qualify would not receive such benefits although others would.

DEPENDENTS' BENEFITS

A major change in type of benefits came in 1939 when it was decided to pay pensions not only to those 65 and over but to other dependents as well. A wife over 65 was eligible to receive an additional benefit above that received by the retired worker, as were children under 18 years of age if they were attending school. The school requirement was dropped later. The amendments obviously make the program less like private insurance. In 1950 it was reasoned that a wife under 65 years of age needed just as much income to live on as a wife over 65. Therefore, additional payments were made for a wife under 65 but only provided that she had a child under 18. In the same year, Congress recognized a complaint by women that they were discriminated against. Prior to that year dependent husbands were not given additional benefits on the basis of their wife's coverage at retirement, whereas wives did receive additional benefits when their husbands were covered. Since women paid the same tax rate as men, and since some women were in the work force because their husbands were dependent upon them as breadwinners, it was felt that the same benefits should be received regardless of sex.[2]

In 1956 an amendment provided that a retired worker's wife could receive dependents' benefits at age 62 instead of 65, but only on condition that the benefit would be permanently reduced. The major argument for reducing the age limit was that wives are generally younger than husbands, and that a hardship was created on retired workers who had to retire on their own pension without receiving additional benefits for their wives. The United States Chamber of Commerce opposed this amendment on grounds that it would add to the costs of the program. Men would be encouraged to

---

[1] Elmer F. Wollenberg, "Vested Rights in Social Security Benefits," *Oregon Law Review*, Vol. 37 (1958), pp. 313, 359.

[2] Naomi Riches, "Women Workers and Their Dependents Under the 1950 Amendments," *Social Security Bulletin*, Vol. 14 (August, 1951), p. 11.

retire earlier because additional benefits could be obtained by men with younger wives.[3]

Beginning in 1956 any disabled child over 18 could receive dependent benefits provided that he had been disabled prior to age 18. Again the type of benefit was extended to provide income to cover additional costs of supporting dependents. In 1965 it was realized that some pensioners were experiencing difficulties in sending children to college, particularly since the dependent's benefit stopped at age 18. The age limit was raised to 22 in 1965, but only provided that the dependent was continuing as a full-time student. Also aided by 1965 amendments were divorced women. A divorced woman may now receive benefits on her former husband's account at age 62 if he is alive or at age 60 if he is deceased provided that she had been married to him at least 20 years before the divorce and provided the husband was contributing or obligated by court to contribute support when he became entitled to social security benefits or died.

SURVIVORS' BENEFITS

Another important addition in type of benefit came in 1939 with the payment of survivors' benefits. The theory behind such benefits was that many survivors of covered workers had inadequate incomes of their own. The following groups were made eligible for survivors' benefits in 1939: widows over 65, children under 18, widows under 65 provided that there were children under 18 present, and dependent parents over 65 provided that the deceased worker was not survived by a widow or child who was eligible for benefits. Since 1939, amendments in the law have liberalized eligibility for survivors' benefits. The requirement that children in the 16-and-17-age category had to be attending school to receive benefits was eliminated. In the 1950 act, dependent widowers over 65 were made eligible for survivors' benefits for the first time. Here again Congress felt that widowers over 65 without sufficient earnings could be just as much in need of income as widows. Divorced wives were made eligible in the same year provided that an eligible child was present in the home. A more recent change in survivors' benefits came in 1956 when widows or parents were made eligible for payments at age 62 instead of 65. In the same year, disabled children over 18 were granted survivors' benefits provided that they had become disabled before 18.

A later change in survivors' benefits came in 1958 when it was decided to pay dependent parents even though additional benefits were paid to the widow or children under 18. The reasoning behind this change was

[3] Statement of A. D. Marshall, Chairman, Committee on Economic Security, U.S. Chamber of Commerce, *Social Security Amendments of 1955,* Hearings before the Committee on Finance, U.S. Senate, 84th Congress, 2nd Session, Part II (February 14-23, 1956), pp. 645-649.

that if parents were dependent on a deceased worker for income, then some sort of pension would be needed regardless of whether the deceased worker's wife or child were receiving a pension. No dependents' benefits are paid to support aged parents while the retired pensioner is alive; the worker must die in order that his dependent parent receive a pension. Another change in survivors' benefits came in 1965. In that year a widow became entitled to benefits at age 60 rather than 62, but at reduced amounts. Furthermore, if a widow could have qualified for benefits and remarried after reaching age 60, she will be eligible for whichever benefit is larger: either one-half the retirement benefit of her former husband or a wife's benefit based on the earnings of her present husband. The latest change in survivors' benefits came in 1967 when disabled widows and widowers were permitted to obtain benefits at age 50, but in reduced amounts.

The magnitude of survivors' benefits was so large that when these benefits were added in 1939, the face value of such benefits was estimated to be equal to the face value of all private life insurance written in the United States. This is still true today.[4]

FLAT VERSUS GRADUATED BENEFITS

The federal government in 1935 had to decide whether to pay the same benefits to all recipients or to graduate payments according to wages earned. A few countries have adopted the flat grant system, but most countries vary benefits according to past wages. The flat grant system has a distinct advantage in being simple to administer, but it has serious disadvantages as well.[5] The flat grant system might work reasonably well in a small country or in one where the cost of living and wages are fairly uniform throughout the country. Neither condition is true in the United States. Basing benefits on past earnings has the advantage of maintaining higher incomes for those who have earned more. High-wage recipients lose more income when they retire, and therefore it is felt that more benefits should be provided for them, especially since these groups have paid more taxes into the program. Some justify a differential in benefits on the ground that higher benefits will provide an incentive for people to work harder. There is some doubt as to how much more incentive higher old-age benefits stimulate. Old-age benefits probably provide less of an incentive than higher wages during the working life of an individual. After weighing all the arguments, Congress decided in 1935 to vary benefits according to past earnings.

Once it had been agreed that benefits should be based on past earnings, a number of problems arose. A problem at the beginning of the program was what to do about those who were about to retire in the near future. The

---

[4] Arthur Altmeyer, *Formative Years of Social Security* (Madison, Wisc., University of Wisconsin Press, 1966), p. 102.

[5] Eveline Burns, *Social Security and Public Policy* (New York, McGraw-Hill, 1956), pp. 38-39.

1935 act provided that benefits would be based on total earnings over the years, so that larger and larger benefits would be received the longer the recipient paid into the system. However, the benefits at first would have been so small that Congress in 1939 changed the benefit formula to base benefits on average annual wages rather than total wages over the years. Since average annual wages would not grow as fast as total wages, future benefits would not be as large. The savings from future benefits were placed into higher immediate benefits.

Another problem of basing benefits on past earnings is that low-income workers earn so little that a pension based on their earnings would be totally inadequate. For this reason the benefit formula adopted favored low-income recipients in two ways. Not only was the formula itself weighted in favor of low-wage earners, but minimum benefits were prescribed also. The benefit formula adopted in 1939 provided that the beneficiary receive 40 percent of the first $50 of his average wage plus 10 percent of the next $200 earned. The award derived from this formula was called the "primary insurance amount," upon which additional survivors' and dependents' benefits were based. As can be easily ascertained, the formula was weighted in favor of the lower-income groups. For those earning only $50 per month, a pension of $20 (40 percent of this amount) would be paid. A higher-waged employee earning $250 a month would receive a pension of $40 a month, or 16 percent of his former pay. He would receive 40 percent of the first $50 in wages ($20) plus 10 percent of his additional $200 earnings ($20).

MINIMUM BENEFITS

Low-income groups were benefited also by having minimum benefits written into the law. In 1935, the minimum benefit was $10 per month, and by 1968 this figure had been raised to $55 a month. Even the $55 figure is quite small in relation to needed income for the aged. Some of the aged have had to apply for old-age assistance benefits in addition to their old-age and survivors pension. In February of 1963, 816,100 persons were receiving both OASDI and OAA payments. The percentage of recipients receiving benefits under both OASDI and OAA dropped from 10 to more than 6 percent from June, 1948, to February, 1963, but in absolute numbers the numbers increased from 146,000 to 816,100.[6] If workers are going to receive additional OAA benefits anyway, there may be more merit in accomplishing this result through raising the minimums under the OASDHI program. Present trends indicate that more and more reliance will be placed on OASDHI and less on OAA, and raising the minimum under OASDHI would simply accelerate the trend.

[6] "Aged Persons Receiving Both OASDI and PA, Early 1963," *Social Security Bulletin*, Vol. 27 (October, 1964), Table 1, p. 28.

MAXIMUM BENEFITS

The limitation of maximum benefits was a corollary of weighting the formula in favor of low-income groups. The low-income groups received more; so the higher-income groups obtained less. Another reason for the maximum benefit was that the method of financing limited the payroll tax originally to the first $3,000 of income. Since the tax rate was limited for the high-income receivers, it was felt that their benefits should be limited also. The maximum primary insurance amount in the original act was $85 a month, and this figure has been raised several times to $218 per month in 1967. For a number of years, the maximum was not raised or raised so slowly that larger and larger numbers were drawing the maximum benefit. In 1938, only 6 percent of the covered male full-time workers were earning more than $3,000, which would have entitled them to the maximum benefit. By 1953, 49 percent of the recently retired workers drew within $10 of the maximum benefit.[7] Such a large percentage receiving the maximum amount tended to make the system more nearly like a flat grant program although the maximums have been raised considerably since then.

ADEQUACY OF BENEFITS: 1940–1949

Old-age pensioners are hurt by inflation. Although benefits from 1940 to 1949 tended to increase since benefits were geared to earnings, the cost of living rose faster than benefits. Table 4-1 shows that the consumers price index rose much faster than benefits from 1940 through 1949.

Several countries—for example, Sweden—provide for an automatic rise in benefits whenever the cost of living increases. The automatic device could be used not only in computing the benefits of future recipients but also the benefits of those already retired. Additional costs would obviously be involved under such an arrangement, but it would be possible to increase social security taxes as the cost of living and benefits rose.

The inadequacy of old-age insurance was highlighted even more when comparisons were made with old-age assistance benefits. Even though Congress did not change the formula to increase OASDI benefits from 1939 to 1950, it twice provided for increases in old-age assistance during this period. The result was that by June of 1948, a single male under the OASDI program received $18.94 monthly compared with $35.46 under OAA. For couples the amounts received were respectively $26.39 and $53.15.[8] Anomalously, those who were being taxed under the OASDI program were receiving about half of the benefits of old-age assistance beneficiaries who were

[7] Burns, op. cit., p. 53.
[8] Bureau of Old Age and Survivors Insurance, "Public Assistance Supplementation of the Income of Old-Age and Survivors Insurance Beneficiaries," Social Security Bulletin, Vol. 12 (October, 1949), pp. 10-13.

TABLE 4–1. MONTHLY OASDI BENEFIT AND THE CONSUMER PRICE INDEX, 1940–1949

Year	Average Monthly Benefit	Consumer Price Index
1940	$22.60	59.9
1941	22.70	62.9
1942	23.02	69.7
1943	23.42	74.0
1944	23.73	75.2
1945	24.19	76.9
1946	24.55	83.4
1947	24.90	95.5
1948	25.35	102.8
1949	26.00	101.8

Sources: Average monthly benefit: *Social Security Bulletin,* Annual Statistical Supplement, 1960, Table 53, p. 48. Consumer price index: *Monthly Labor Review,* various issues.

paying no direct social security tax. The need for larger pensions became so urgent that a number of labor unions in 1949 and 1950 concentrated on obtaining larger pensions as their number one issue in bargaining negotiations. The success of many unions in obtaining pensions financed solely by corporations influenced business groups finally to support larger social security benefits. The old-age insurance program financed by both employers and employees was less expensive to corporations than private pension plans financed solely by them.

FORMULA CHANGES

The formula in computing benefits has been changed a number of times since the passage of the Social Security Act in 1935. At the present time (1968), the formula provides for the following payments:

a. 71.16% of the first $110 of average monthly wages, plus
b. 25.88% of the next $290 " " " " "
c. 24.18% of the next $150 " " " " "
d. 29.43% of the next $100 " " " " "

From Table 4–2 it can be seen that the change in benefits in 1950 benefited the $80 a week worker substantially more than the $20 a week worker. The most recent increase in benefits in 1967 provided an across-the-board increase of 13 percent to all workers. However, since the maximum subject to benefits was raised, those earning the maximum income of $650 monthly will now be entitled to $218 a month as the primary insurance amount, or over 30 percent more than the former $168 a month based on the $550

TABLE 4–2.   HYPOTHETICAL MONTHLY BENEFITS OF SINGLE WORKERS

Year	Based on $20 Average Weekly Wage Before Retirement	Based on $80 Average Weekly Wage Before Retirement
1939	$41.47[a]	$48.00[a]
1950	43.33	80.00
1952	47.67	80.50
1954	47.67	102.50
1958	51.00	109.67
1966	54.58	123.36
1968	61.67	139.67

[a] Assumes 20 years of coverage.

monthly income subject to the social security tax. It must be remembered, though, that it will take a number of years before a beneficiary will reach the average wage of $650 a month since higher amounts earned will not be considered prior to the 1967 amendments.

The recent concern over the problem of poverty has brought suggestions that the minimum benefit be raised to $100 or more a month, but the figure was raised from $44 to only $55 in 1967, a 25 percent increase. Even though lower-wage earners' benefits have not been raised to $100 a month, it should be noted that some lower-wage workers receive 95 percent or even over 100 percent of their wages in benefits whereas higher-income workers draw a much smaller percentage. A single person earning an average of $650 a month, the largest amount subject to the payroll tax, would draw the maximum monthly benefit of $218 a month, or slightly over 33 percent of his wages in benefits. A person earning more than an average of $650 a month, would draw an even smaller percentage in benefits.

Several other problems of basing benefits on past wages may be noted. The fact that many workers experienced heavy amounts of unemployment in the 1930's meant that their average wages were low. For this reason, workers were given the option of beginning the computation of their average wage after the year 1950 instead of 1936. Even here large spells of unemployment or illness might unduly reduce the average wage and thus benefits. Therefore in 1956 workers were permitted to omit the lowest five years in computing their average wage. An even better method of handling this problem would be to adopt the British system of disregarding all periods of unemployment and sickness in computing the average wage.[9]

In 1939, when survivors' and dependents' benefits were first adopted, the formula provided that supplementary benefits would be based on a percentage of the retired workers' pension, called the primary insurance amount. An eligible wife would receive an amount equal to 50 percent of the primary insurance amount. If the retired husband were due a pension of $40 per

[9] Burns, *op. cit.*, p. 46.

month on his own right (the primary insurance amount), then the couple would receive 50 percent more or $60 per month. The following were the percentages of the primary insurance amount permitted for each additional type of benefit: wife (or husband of retired worker), 50 percent; child of retired worker, 50 percent; child of deceased worker, 50 percent; widow or widower, 75 percent; and parents, 50 percent. The 1950 amendments raised several of these figures. The first child was permitted an amount equal to 75 percent of the primary insurance amount and the remaining children were entitled to 50 percent. Parents' benefits were raised to 75 percent of the primary insurance benefit also. Minimum and maximum family benefits were inserted into the law. The minimum family benefit is now $55 a month, the same figure as for a retired worker himself. Clearly a family needs a larger income than a single worker, but Congress has been reluctant to provide higher minimums for low-income families. The maximum family benefit today is $434.40. Amendments in 1961 raised aged widows' benefits from 75 percent to 82½ percent of the workers' primary insurance amount. Benefits were also raised for widowers. Surviving dependent parents also received larger benefits provided that only one parent was entitled to benefits.

ADEQUACY OF BENEFITS TODAY

The average OASDI benefit for a retired couple in September-December 1965 came to $151.22 per month or $1814.64 per year. The figures for a single individual were $105.89 per month or $1270.68 per year.[10] Benefits were then raised 13 percent more in 1967. Fortunately, about 20 percent of the retired workers also draw income from private pension plans.[11] The aged may also earn some income and some of them have income producing assets. Data for 1962 showed that the median OASDI beneficiary had assets of $2,935, excluding the equity in a home.[12] If this amount had been invested at 4, 5, or even 6 percent or higher, it can easily be ascertained that most of the aged do not appreciably increase their income through invested assets.

Sometimes increases in OASDHI benefits are compared with increases in the cost of living. Since the inception of the program, OASDHI benefits have outstripped the cost of living. However, if 1954 is used as the base year, OASDHI benefits in early December of 1967 had 10 percent less purchasing power than in 1954. Increases in OASDHI benefits of 13 percent in late December of 1967 have resulted in benefits rising slightly faster than the cost of living since 1954.

Using a poverty budget of $1,500 for an aged person and $1,890 for an aged couple, the Social Security Administration found as of July 1, 1967 that 7.5 million persons aged 65 and over, or 39 percent of the total, were

[10] *Social Security Bulletin, Annual Statistical Supplement, 1965*, Table 56, p. 51.

[11] Ida Merriam, "Overlap of Benefits Under OASDI and Other Programs," *Social Security Bulletin*, Vol. 28 (April, 1965), p. 22.

[12] L. D. Platky, "Assets of the Aged in 1962: Findings of the 1963 Survey of the Aged," *Social Security Bulletin*, Vol. 27 (November, 1964), Table 1, p. 4.

poor. Of the 15.9 million persons aged 65 and over receiving social security benefits, about 6.2 million are poor. Almost the same number—5.7 million were kept out of poverty by OASDHI benefits. It was estimated by the Social Security Administration that a 15 percent increase in OASDHI benefits would move about 1.6 million aged beneficiaries and about .5 million younger beneficiaries out of poverty.[13] Since the increase in OASDHI benefits in 1967 was 13 percent, it can be seen that large numbers of the aged still live in poverty. This fact is one of the major arguments for increasing OASDHI benefits.[14]

Those who oppose an increase maintain that OASDHI benefits should meet only a small, subsistence standard. This group feels that people should save enough out of their income while working to provide additional income when they retire. Under a voluntary system, people can decide for themselves whether they wish to spend more today or save for the future. Furthermore, annuities and private pension funds have the advantage that reserves are accumulated and invested in a productive capacity.

TAXATION

Old-age pensions obviously cost billions of dollars. In 1966, the OASI program paid out over $13.4 billion to aged workers and their dependents plus survivors, disability, medical, and other benefits. The federal government is, thus faced with the important problem of financing such a program. Any type of tax, whether income, sales, payroll, property, or any other, could be used to finance a Social Security program. Most countries in the world have relied on payroll taxes upon both employees and employers plus additional supplements out of the general revenues of the government. In a study of the costs of Social Security in 24 countries, mostly in Western Europe, it was found that 10 of the countries placed a larger tax on the employee than the employer, whereas 10 others placed a higher levy upon the employer. In 4 the tax was about equal on both. In only 4 countries was more revenue obtained through general government revenues than from payroll taxes.[15]

THE TAX ON EMPLOYEES

A number of advantages exist for placing a payroll tax on an employee's pay. A major advantage is that the worker then feels that he is entitled to a pension as a matter of right since he is being taxed. There is protection also

---

[13] Statement of Robert M. Ball, Commissioner of Social Security, *Social Security Amendments of 1967*, Hearings before the Committee on Finance, U.S. Senate, 90th Congress, 1st Session on H.R. 12080, Part 1 (August 22-24, 1967).

[14] *The Status of the Social Security Program and Recommendations for Its Improvement*, Washington, D.C., Advisory Council on Social Security.

[15] "The Cost of Social Security," *International Labour Review*, Vol. 65 (1952), pp. 726-791.

against excessive liberalization of benefits since the worker realizes that any increase in benefits must be paid for out of the increased taxes he pays. In 1935 only certain workers were to be covered under the act, and this fact was used as an argument for a payroll tax on those covered rather than taxation out of general revenues. It was felt that it would be unfair to tax the general public when only specific groups would receive benefits.

A payroll tax on employees has some disadvantages as well as advantages. Unlike the personal income tax, taxes must be paid on the first $650 earned (1968) and no deductions are permitted for dependents, medical costs, and the like. Failure to lower the tax by these exemptions means that low-income earners must bear a heavy burden. The payroll tax is clearly regressive, because the present (1968) 4.4 percent tax rate is imposed only on the first $7,800 of annual earnings. A person earning below this amount pays a tax of 4.4 percent on his income, whereas a person earning, say, $15,600 pays a tax of only 2.2 percent on his income. Offsetting the disadvantage of the higher tax to low wage earners is the fact that the benefit formula is weighted in favor of the lower-income groups. The fact that the payroll tax does hit the low-income families with such force was one of the reasons why the tax on employees was used only for the old-age insurance part of the Social Security but was not imposed to pay for unemployment insurance. In the latter program, only the employer pays a payroll tax.

THE TAX ON EMPLOYERS

Since the payroll tax is imposed not only upon employees but employers as well, the tax on employers must be evaluated also. Here complications arise, because economists do not know for certain the incidence of the tax on employers. The incidence of the payroll tax on employees was not discussed since it is generally agreed that the employee must pay the tax himself. It may be argued that the workers will attempt to force the employer to pay higher wages to pay for the tax, but if workers had such strong bargaining power they would have attempted to get higher wages previously.[16] There is some question as to whether employers pay the tax out of profits, whether they pass it along to consumers in the form of higher prices, or whether they pass the tax back on the workers by withholding wage increases that they would otherwise have obtained if the payroll tax had not been imposed. So many variables are involved that economists cannot give an unequivocal answer on the incidence of the tax. In an expanding period of the business cycle, employers are better able to pass the added costs along to the consumer in price increases. In a recession, price increases are less likely. If wages are a small part of total costs, the employer is more apt to absorb the cost in-

[16] Ida C. Merriam, *Social Security Financing*, Bureau Report No. 17, Washington, D.C., Social Security Administration, Division of Research and Statistics, 1953, pp. 16-17.

crease than when labor costs are higher. If machinery is easily substituted for labor, one effect of the payroll tax may be to throw people out of work. If the firm or industry is strongly unionized, the employer is less apt to withhold wage increases. In such an instance, the employer may be unable to shift the tax backward on the workers. The incidence will depend also on the elasticity of the demand for the product. If price increases cause little or no decrease in demand, then price rises will be more general than if demand falls off sharply. With all these variables influencing the shiftability of the payroll tax, about all that can be concluded is that possibly all groups, the workers, consumers, and employers, ultimately pay part of the payroll tax, although most of the burden falls on the first two groups.[17]

Those favoring the imposition of a payroll tax on the employer point out that superannuation is a cost of production, and that just as employers set aside depreciation charges for the wearing out of machinery, so such costs should be imposed to take care of human depreciation. Also to the extent that the employer is better able to bear the added cost than workers, such a tax may be deemed advisable. These arguments lose their validity to the extent that the employer is able to shift the tax to others. In New Zealand, where it was also decided that the employer should be taxed, a tax on business profits was used instead of a payroll tax, because the profits tax is less easily shifted.

Another argument in favor of the payroll tax on employers is that some employers already have assumed the burden of paying private pensions, and the imposition of a tax on all employers would make the burden more uniform on all. Disadvantages of the payroll tax on employers are that it tends to increase labor costs and thus tends to cause a substitution of machinery for labor. Also, to the extent that the tax is shifted to consumers and workers it becomes another regressive tax.

EVALUATION OF THE PAYROLL TAX

In an evaluation of the payroll tax, the fact that it does give the workers a feeling that they have paid for the program and the fact that the tax has been able to bring in large amounts of revenue probably are sufficient arguments to retain it. On the other hand, the fact that the tax is regressive must not be glossed over lightly. Some experts, including officials of the Social Security Administration, the Advisory Council on Social Security, and others, have recommended that the government should bear part of the cost of the OASDHI program out of general revenues. One Advisory Council, for example, recommended obtaining one-third from a payroll tax on employees, one-third from a payroll tax on employers, and one-third from the general revenues of the government.[18]

    [17] Burns, *op. cit.*, pp. 161-162.
    [18] J. S. Parker, "Financial Policy in Old-Age and Survivors Insurance, 1935–50," *Social Security Bulletin*, Vol. 14 (June, 1951), p. 4.

TAXATION IN 1967

In order to finance the 13 percent increase in benefits in 1967, additional tax revenue was needed. Aside from a recommendation by George Meany, President of the AFL-CIO, that Congress begin to tap general revenues to finance part of the increase in costs, consideration was also given to raising additional revenue only from the payroll tax. The administration bill called for raising the taxable wage base from $6,600 to $10,800 and to eventually raise the tax rate 0.15 percent. Congressmen Wilbur Mills, Chairman of the House Ways and Means Committee, introduced a bill providing for raising the taxable wage base from $6,600 to $7,600 and increasing the tax rate 0.25 percent. Congress eventually adopted a taxable wage base of $7,800 and a tax increase of 0.25 percent. Proponents of raising the taxable wage base to $10,800 pointed out that higher-income employees would pay a larger percent of the tax increase if the higher base were used and the tax rate on lower-income employees would not have to be raised as high. Furthermore, using the $10,800 base would cover 82 percent of the full wages of regularly employed men in 1974 as contrasted to about 50 percent by using the $7,600 figure of the Mills bill.[19] When the Social Security Act was first passed in 1935, the taxable wage base of $3,000 covered 94 percent of the full earnings of those regularly employed.

Opponents of raising the taxable wage base pointed out that little additional benefits would go to those having to pay the higher taxes. Mr. Raymond King, Jr., Chairman of the Social Security Committee of the National Association of Life Underwriters, stated that increases in taxes under the administration bill ($10,800 base) would cause an increase in taxes of $315 per year for those at the maximum benefit level. Their increase in benefits would come only to $120 per year whereas if they had invested the $315 per year from age 21 in private insurance, an annuity of from $257 to $278 could be paid (depending on the company). King's computations excluded the tax increases necessary to pay for disability and survivors' benefits. The use of the $120 may not be quite fair, for undoubtedly the person aged 21 will receive larger benefits than this since Social Security benefits have been increasing over the years. On the other hand, in the above comparison it should be pointed out that under private insurance the worker will automatically receive his annuity benefits at age 65 whereas under Social Security the worker would have to retire. A cash surrender value is also attached to private insurance although no death benefit is paid after the person reaches 65.[20] The tax base finally settled on in 1967 was $7,800, and consequently the tax rate had to be raised higher than the administration bill called for with a tax base of $10,800.

[19] Statement of Senator Frank Moss, *Social Security Amendments of 1967*, Hearings before the Committee on Finance, U.S. Senate, 90th Congress, 1st Session on H.R. 12080, Part 2 (August 28–September 19, 1967), pp. 892-893.

[20] Statement of Raymond King, *op. cit.*, Part 3, pp. 1911-1912.

Some concern recently has been expressed that younger workers are being charged to pay for larger benefits to older workers who have contributed relatively little to the program. Under the 1967 administration bill ($10,800 base), a worker who entered the program at age 18 in 1974 when the maximum rate and tax base go into effect would contribute $68,080 to the system. The present value of monthly benefits for a man at age 65 with a wife the same age would be $51,860.[21] However, this computation did not consider the survivor and disability protection given. With coverage becoming more universal, there will be less of a problem of paying for newly covered workers who have contributed little to the system. Also younger workers today will benefit when they retire and benefits are raised without them having to pay higher taxes.

LARGE RESERVE VERSUS "PAY-AS-YOU-GO"

In the first years of the OASDI program, few people qualified for pensions and received relatively small benefits. Consequently, costs of the program were quite small. In 1940, the first year that benefits were paid, a total of only $14.8 million was paid to OASDI recipients. As more and more people became eligible and drew larger benefits, costs rose. During 1966, statistics show that over $13.4 billion were paid to the aged and their dependents in addition to survivors, disability, medical, and other benefits. The question was raised whether reserves should be accumulated to finance the large costs. Few questions in social security have aroused more controversy. Three major types of plans were recommended. On the one hand, a large reserve was advocated. In order to obtain such a reserve, taxes in the present and immediate future would have to be higher. The reserve money would be invested in United States government bonds, and draw interest. In the more distant future, part of the revenue for social security benefits could be obtained from the interest on the bonds. If the costs in the future could be estimated with a sufficient degree of accuracy, a payroll tax could be assessed and be supplemented with sufficient interest that the payroll tax could be kept level.

Under a large reserve plan, the reserve should be considered sufficient if enough revenue were obtained from the payroll taxes plus interest on the government bonds to balance expenditures. A reserve fund of this amount would not be large enough to meet all accrued liabilities incurred if the plan were terminated. To meet such accrued liabilities continuation of payments of all those receiving benefits plus payments to all others who had made contributions would be required. The accrued liability of the system at the end of 1953 was $200 billion, whereas the reserve in the fund at that time was only $18.7 billion. Insurance companies must obtain sufficient reserves to meet accrued liability, for future sales might not provide sufficient revenues to pay beneficiaries. Since the government can obtain income from

[21] Statement of Robert J. Myers, *ibid.*, p. 2007.

compulsory taxes, the government does not need as large a reserve as would be required to meet accrued liability.[22]

The opposite of the large reserve plan is the "pay-as-you-go" plan, which would tax only sufficiently to pay for benefits as they are needed. No reserve except for contingencies would be accumulated. Under the "pay-as-you-go" program, the taxes would be quite small in the beginning years of the program and then would have to be raised as benefits increased. Another alternative would be a compromise between the large reserve plan and the "pay-as-you-go" plan.

ADVANTAGES OF A LARGE RESERVE PLAN

An unquestionable advantage of the large reserve is that it would aid in assuring that payments would be made in the future.[23] It is highly probable that future citizens will honor the payment of interest on their bonds, and thus sufficient income will be assured. Those favoring the large reserve point out that if no reserve is available, pressure will arise to reduce benefits or incur government deficits, neither of which would be desirable. The large reserve plan also has the advantage of providing for a more stable payroll tax over time. An early estimate of cost, for example, showed that with a large reserve the tax would need to be somewhere between 6 and 10 percent of payrolls plus interest charges. Under the pay-as-you-go plan, payroll taxes would have to rise later to as high as 12 to 15 percent.[24] Some have been critical of the idea of forcing people in the future to pay a higher percentage tax than they themselves could accrue in benefits. Furthermore, it has been contended that the large reserve plan would provide a more honest system of bookkeeping in that monies would be collected in order to meet costs that are bound to arise. Failure to collect this money results, it is asserted, in huge hidden deficits, and the possible failure of the government to meet the rising costs.

Several arguments for the large reserve have not stood the test of time. One was that under a large reserve taxpayers would save money in that interest charges could be paid to old-age pensioners rather than to others holding the debt. However, in order to accumulate a large reserve, taxes originally would have to be higher, and this loss must be offset against the later gain. It had also been argued that the burden on future generations could be made lighter if the surplus income of Social Security had been invested in productive resources. Since much of the present debt has been incurred in military expenditures, this argument loses most of its force. Furthermore,

---

[22] Burns, *op. cit.*, p. 201.

[23] The following are some of the references on social security reserves: Seymour Harris, *The Economics of Social Security* (New York, McGraw-Hill, 1941), Chaps. 1-12; J. S. Parker, *Social Security Reserves* (Washington, D.C., American Council on Public Affairs, 1942); Burns, *op. cit.*, Chap. 10; Raymond H. Manning, *Financing Social Security* (Washington, D.C., Library of Congress, Legislative Reference Service, 1946), pp. 41-61; and Merriam, *op. cit.*, pp. 30-45.

[24] Harris, *op. cit.*, p. 97.

the tax money used in building the reserve could possibly have been invested by individuals if they had not been taxed.

DISADVANTAGES OF A LARGE RESERVE

The argument that the reserve fund tends to be deflationary is a weighty one. If the money were set aside, and not spent, the danger of deflation would be quite evident. The fact that the money is spent by the government does relieve the deflationary force. The reserve fund is only one small part of economic forces making either for inflation or deflation, and these other forces must be analyzed as well. If, for example, while the government was accumulating a reserve of $2 billion for Social Security, it was at the same time going into debt $4 billion, less criticism could be directed to the deflationary aspects of the reserve. The deflationary aspects of a large reserve weigh heavily in a recent analysis by Margaret Gordon, who argues against the larger reserve. She adds that the differences in the percentage of tax either under a reserve or pay-as-you-go is no longer as important as when the program was first inaugurated.[25] The 1965 Advisory Council on Social Security also feared the deflationary aspect of too large a reserve.

Another argument against the reserve is that a rising price level would cause reserves to be less valuable. An extreme inflation would, of course, completely wipe out the value of reserves. We do not expect such an inflation in the United States, but to the extent that the price level rises, the reserve becomes less valuable. Another argument against the reserve is that income and productivity should become larger in the future. With the added income, the future generations should be more able to pay taxes than the present generation. Also, if the government would agree to pay for part of the costs of Social Security, say one third, out of general revenues, then there would be less necessity for a large reserve. General revenues instead of higher payroll taxes would carry part of the burden.

The argument that a large reserve would tend to cause Congress to liberalize benefits unduly may have some merit. Defenders of the large reserve reply that the large reserve plan requires that the payroll tax be increased whenever benefits are further liberalized. Since people are immediately faced with an increase in payroll taxes whenever benefits are increased, they are less apt to raise benefits indiscriminately. Supporters of the large reserve have argued that the low tax at the beginning of the program has given people a false notion of the actual costs of financing such a program, and more pressure for increased benefits may be generated from an unduly low payroll tax than from a large reserve.

Although the consensus today is against the large reserve, one of the early fallacious arguments against the large reserve should be pointed out. When Social Security taxes were first levied before benefits were paid, the money was put into government bonds and spent by the government. Critics

[25] Margaret Gordon, *The Economics of Welfare Policies* (New York, Columbia, 1963), pp. 72-75.

maintained that the whole Social Security program was a hoax, and that a spending of the money proved the bankruptcy of it. Amounts such as $50 to $250 billion, the proposed size of a large reserve, cannot be withdrawn from the economy and frozen. The fact that the money was spent by the government did not mean that future old-age pensioners would be unable to obtain pensions. Barring extreme catastrophe, the credit of the government should be good. Other institutions such as banks, insurance companies, and other groups invest in government bonds, and the government spends the money received in exchange for the bonds. Little criticism is heard that the government will default to these creditors.

THE RESERVE

In 1935 four financial plans were considered. These were: (1) a vast reserve of $70 billion by 1980, although even this large amount would not have provided for the full actuarial reserve estimated by Professor Edwin Witte at $88 billion; (2) a moderate reserve of $15 billion and government subsidies of $1.4 billion a year after 1960; (3) a reserve fund of $50 billion; and (4) a compromise between plans 2 and 3. Plan 3 was the one finally adopted in 1935.[26] The Social Security Act of 1935 provided that tax collection begin in 1937 but that benefits not be paid until 1942 so that a reserve could be accumulated. In 1939, Secretary of the Treasury Morgenthau was quite worried about the deflationary aspects of a large reserve fund, and it was largely due to his influence that the large reserve plan was abandoned. Defenders of the large reserve were critical of its abandonment. They doubted that the Social Security program caused any troublesome deflation in view of other government fiscal policies of the time. From 1937 to 1940, the government collected $5.3 billion in Social Security taxes, but at the same time $2.6 billion was paid out under the program along with $10.8 billion for recovery and relief and $2.3 billion for veterans' payments.[27] In 1940 the tax on both employers and employees was kept at 1 percent instead of being raised to accumulate a large reserve. It was not raised to 1.5 percent until 1950. Benefits were raised under the 1939 act, although the increases were granted mostly to those drawing benefits in the near future. Future benefits were to be reduced so that the overall cost in the long run would be the same. In place of the large reserve, Secretary Morgenthau suggested that the system only accumulate sufficient reserves to be three times as large as annual benefits. Actually the increased earnings during the war increased Social Security income much faster than outgo, so that the reserve became much larger than three times the benefits.

Table 4-3 shows income from the OASI payroll tax, benefits paid, and the reserve that has been accumulated over the years.

26 Harris, *op. cit.*, pp. 161-163.
27 *Ibid.*, p. 42.

TABLE 4–3.　FEDERAL OLD-AGE AND SURVIVORS INSURANCE TRUST FUND
(IN MILLIONS)

Year	Receipts	Expenditures	Assets
1940	$ 368	$ 62	$ 2,031
1945	1,420	304	7,121
1950	2,928	1,022	13,721
1955	6,174	5,087	21,663
1960	11,382	11,198	20,324
1965	16,610	17,501	19,125

Sources: Social Security Bulletin, Annual Statistical Supplement, 1963, Table 12,
pp. 10-11; Vol. 28 (October, 1965), Table 5, p. 22.

FISCAL ADEQUACY

The present tax rate (1968) for the OASI program is 3.325 percent for both
employers and employees on the first $7,800 of the employees' earnings. This
figure excludes both the disability and medicare tax. The OASI tax will
gradually rise until it reaches a rate of 4.525 percent on both employers and
employees (on $7,800 earnings). The social security actuary estimates that
sufficient revenues plus interest on the surplus will result in actuarial balance
of the OASI program.[28] Using the intermediate cost estimate for a number
of years into the future, the actuary estimates that the OASI fund should
have assets of almost $160 billion by the year 2000. Even his high-cost estimate
shows a balance of $72 billion. The interest rate used for his intermediate-
cost estimate is 3¾ per cent, which is slightly below the average yield of
investments of the trust funds at the end of June, 1967 (about 3.79 percent) and considerably below the rate currently obtained for new investments
(5¼ percent).

　　One critic of the actuarial methods points out that current earnings are
used to estimate income and benefits. Since the secular trend of earnings
has been upward, this critic feels that higher earnings figures should be
used. The fact that higher earnings tend to increase the income of the
system much more than benefits led to the charge that using present earnings
results in large underestimates of income and thus in large overestimates of
the amount of taxation needed to finance the program.[29] The Social Security actuary has defended himself by taking the position that benefits will
probably be raised in the future, and that higher benefits will offset the use
of higher earnings.

[28] Robert J. Myers, Actuarial Cost Estimates for the Old-Age, Survivors, Disability,
and Health Insurance System as Modified by the Social Security Amendments of 1967,
Washington, D.C., Committee on Ways and Means, U.S. House of Representatives
(December 11, 1967), pp. 6-11.
　　[29] For this and other criticisms of actuarial methods, see Charles C. Killingsworth
and Gertrude Schroeder, "Long Range Cost Estimates of Old Age Insurance," Quarterly
Journal of Economics, Vol. 65 (1951), pp. 201-209.

Congress has vacillated between the large reserve plan and the pay-as-you-go plan. In 1956, the Social Security trust fund reached a peak of $22.6 billion and then declined to $18.2 billion in 1965. An increase of $2.3 billion was recorded for 1966, and, as stated above, the fund is expected to grow much larger in the future.

IS SOCIAL SECURITY "INSURANCE"?

Private insurance companies have set certain guidelines on eligibility, premiums, and benefits in their own programs. When the Social Security Act was passed, its proponents made every effort to sell the nation on the idea that it was "insurance." Not only was the program called "insurance," but such terms as "fully insured," "currently insured" and others found their way into the act. The purpose of stressing the insurance concept was to impress upon people that their pensions were something that they could count on receiving, for almost all private insurance companies had been able to continue payments through the worst of the Great Depression.

In spite of labeling the government program as "insurance," certain dissimilarities with private insurance must be noted. Legally, private insurance is a contractual obligation that must be fulfilled. The government program, on the other hand, is not contractually guaranteed. Congress may either add to or take away benefits at its discretion. Since it is highly improbable that Congress will take away benefits, the people in the United States have almost absolute assurance that benefits will be paid. According to Arthur Altmeyer, former administrator of Social Security, it is important not that the government program convey a contractual right but a statutory right, which is enforceable by law and not subject to the whim or caprice of administrators of the program.[30]

Under private insurance older people who take out insurance must pay much larger premiums than younger people, because they will probably make many fewer payments, but under the social insurance program, the aged were not assessed more. Moreover, under the Social Security system, but unlike private insurance, lower income persons receive larger benefits than higher income recipients in relation to the taxes they pay. Furthermore, the government program, unlike private insurance, provides larger payments for dependents and survivors of the insured without additional cost. Need of recipients for income is considered paramount over equity to the individual. Another difference between Social Security and private insurance is that the government has raised benefits to help compensate for the higher cost of living. Private insurance, on the other hand, provides only for the payment called for in the policy.

Whether the government program may be called insurance becomes largely a matter of definition. If all that is meant by the term "insurance" is that the government is pooling a number of risks to be paid by many, then

[30] Altmeyer, *op. cit.*, p. 228.

the program is insurance. To the extent that the government program provides some benefits to individuals without corresponding costs and without contractual obligation, then it differs from private insurance. Furthermore, the goals of private insurance are somewhat different from the goals of the government program. Private insurance companies of necessity must provide as much equity as possible between their various customers. They could not charge the same premiums and yet pay larger benefits to some than to others. Yet the government program does just this. Although the government must also consider equity between individuals, it must also protect against certain social hazards. Elderly workers who only recently have been covered under the Social Security program are in just as great a need for a pension as younger people who will pay into the program for many years. Because of need, newly covered elderly people will receive much more in benefits than they pay into the program.[31]

In view of the fact that too strict an application of private insurance principles may result in less adequate benefits and eligibility, Professor Eveline Burns suggested that perhaps the term "insurance" has outlived its usefulness in its applicability to the OASDHI program.[32] On the other hand, Social Security has been considered as social insurance for years, and it is probable that the term "insurance" will continue to apply to the program into the future.

Summary

Types of benefits paid have changed radically since inception of the program in 1935. Lump-sum payments at death have been reduced to a small amount. Furthermore, those not qualifying for benefits were not entitled to a refund of their contributions after 1939. Offsetting these restrictions, new types of benefits were paid to dependents and survivors of those in the program. The trend has been to cover more people and to pay higher benefits although benefits today still do not provide an adequate level of living.

Payroll taxes on both employers and employees have been used to finance the program since its inception. These taxes have stood the test of time, and probably will be kept indefinitely into the future. Actuaries estimate that the assets of the old-age and survivors insurance trust fund will grow for a number of years into the future. Unlike private insurance, it is not necessary for the OASI program to be able to pay off all accrued liability. To be actuarially sound, the program merely has to have sufficient income to meet expenses. Intermediate-cost estimates show that the OASI program is in actuarial balance.

[31] Reinhard A. Hohaus, "Equity, Adequacy, and Related Factors in Old Age Security," *The Record*, American Institute of Actuaries, June, 1938, pp. 82, 84.

[32] For a fuller discussion of applying the insurance concept to the governmental program, *see* Burns, *op. cit.*, Chap. 2.

ASSISTANCE PROGRAMS UNDER THE SOCIAL SECURITY ACT

When Congress debated passage of the Social Security Bill in 1935, much stronger support was given to old-age assistance than to old-age insurance. Two major differences exist between old-age assistance and old-age insurance. In the case of OAA, need must be shown to qualify for benefits whereas OASDHI benefits are paid as a matter of right to eligible workers who retire. Second, OAA is financed from general federal revenues on a matching basis with state funds whereas the OASDHI program is financed by a payroll tax on both employers and employees.

When Congress passed the Social Security Act, old-age assistance was considered the basic part of the assistance sections. The aid to dependent children's program and aid to the blind were added only as an incidental part of OAA. In 1950 another assistance program was added to the assistance section of the law, namely, aid to the permanently and totally disabled (APTD). Table 5-1 shows the following number of people covered under the assistance programs and the expenditures for it in the United States. As can be seen from Table 5-1, the largest public assistance expenditures in the United States go to the AFDC program, about 43 percent of all payments. Following closely behind in amounts expended is the OAA program, which accounts for about 38 percent of assistance payments. The AFDC program reaches over twice as many people as the OAA program but in smaller amounts per person. Other smaller programs are Aid to the Blind (AB) and General Assistance (GA), the only public assistance program not subsidized by the federal government.

OLD-AGE ASSISTANCE (OAA)

During the first years of Social Security, more old people received OAA payments than OASDHI benefits. Gradually over the years coverage of OASDHI has increased until it has become the much larger program. Gradually the number on the rolls of OAA has been decreasing. Whereas the OASDHI is entirely federally financed, the public assistance programs under the Social Security Act call for the states to match federal funds, which come from the general treasury rather than through an earmarked payroll tax. This method of financing public assistance places a much more severe burden on

TABLE 5-1. PUBLIC ASSISTANCE: RECEIPTS AND TOTAL PAYMENTS

Period	Total	Old-Age Assistance[a]	Aid to Blind[a,b]	Aid to the Permanently and Totally Disabled[a]	Aid to Families With Dependent Children[c]	General Assistance[d]
			Number of recipients (in thousands)			
1961		2,229	102.7	389	3,566	1,069
1962		2,183	98.7	428	3,789	900
1963		2,152	96.9	464	3,930	872
1964		2,120	95.5	509	4,219	779
1965		2,087	85.1	557	4,396	677
1966		2,073	83.7	588	4,666	663
			Amount of assistance (in thousands)			
1961	$3,410,316	$1,568,985	$84,506	$255,646	$1,148,838	$352,341
1962	3,510,353	1,566,121	83,856	281,117	1,289,824	289,435
1963	3,646,058	1,610,310	85,122	317,656	1,355,538	277,432
1964	3,815,178	1,606,429	86,189	355,643	1,496,525	270,392
1965	3,992,964	1,594,183	77,308	416,765	1,644,096	260,612
1966	4,335,131	1,633,675	85,614	487,300	1,864,614	263,925

[a] Represents data for payment to recipients of the specified type of assistance under separate programs and under the combined state adult assistance programs.

[b] Beginning September 1965, excludes state blind pension in Pennsylvania administered under state law without federal participation.

[c] Includes as recipients the children and 1 or both parents or 1 caretaker relative other than a parent in families in which the requirements of such adults were considered in determining the amount of assistance.

[d] Partly estimated. Excludes Idaho, Indiana, and Nebraska; data not available.

Source: Social Security Bulletin, Vol. 30 (May, 1967), Table M-18, p. 35.

the poorer states of the country, for these states are less industrialized and have fewer persons covered under the OASDHI program and more on OAA than the wealthier states. Over the years and even today the poor states have much larger OAA rolls than do the wealthier states. The result is that even with increased federal financing, the poorer states must still expend large sums for public assistance. Table 5-2 shows that the proportion of the aged receiving OAA payments per 1,000 population aged 65 and over varies considerably from state to state. The numbers on public assistance vary not only because of differences in state coverage under OASDHI but also because of varying state eligibility requirements.

Payments to OAA recipients are made in cash.[1] It was decided in 1935 that a cash program would best promote the dignity of the individual. The aged themselves, then, spend their income in any way they wish and in a manner in which they consider most advantageous to themselves. The amount of payment is determined by the basic subsistence requirements of the individual or family as determined by the administering agency. Any income earned was originally subtracted from this amount. For a number of years it had been suggested that the aged be permitted to earn some money without deducting it from the assistance payment. This suggestion was implemented in the 1965 amendments to the Social Security Act by providing that for OAA recipients of the first $80 earned per month, the state agency may disregard the first $20 plus one-half of the remainder.

When the Social Security Act was first passed in 1935, the OAA program was financed by federal government contributions of 50 percent of the funds and the state and local agencies the other 50 percent. The maximum federal contribution in 1935 was $30. Both the percent paid by the federal government and the maximum amounts have been raised over the years (see Table 5-3). For all assistance programs, the federal government now makes 53 percent of the payments compared with 35 percent for states and 12 percent by local governments.

Since the federal government has raised its contribution over the years, monthly OAA payments have increased. To measure the adequacy of OAA benefits accurately, statistics are needed on what the individual states pay in benefits. Table 5-4 shows benefits by states.

The disparity in payments between the states is much greater for OAA than for OASDHI. In the latter program the payments vary only from a low of $57.71 in Mississippi to a high of $85.93 in Connecticut (December 31, 1963). The differences in assistance payments are much larger than differences in the cost of living. Most of the low-benefit states are located in the South. The old-age recipient there must attempt to survive on much less than OAA recipients in some of our wealthier states. In attempting to analyze the adequacy of OAA payments, a Bureau of Public Assistance study found that OAA payments were 94.6 percent of state standards. They were

---

[1] One exception has been vendor payments for medical care. For an analysis of medical aid under assistance programs *see* Chapter 10.

TABLE 5–2. PROPORTION OF AGED POPULATION RECEIVING OLD-AGE ASSISTANCE (RECIPIENT RATE), BY STATE, DECEMBER, 1964 [a]

State	Recipient Rate [b]	State	Recipient Rate [b]
Alabama	394	Nebraska	72
Alaska	196	Nevada	125
Arizona	117	New Hampshire	62
Arkansas	285	New Jersey	22
California	176	New Mexico	176
Colorado	240	New York	31
Connecticut	27	North Carolina	123
Delaware	37	North Dakota	86
District of Columbia	32	Ohio	87
Florida	105	Oklahoma	313
Georgia	291	Oregon	52
Guam	106	Pennsylvania	39
Hawaii	33	Puerto Rico	213
Idaho	71	Rhode Island	62
Illinois	54	South Carolina	154
Indiana	49	South Dakota	93
Iowa	81	Tennessee	136
Kansas	86	Texas	275
Kentucky	188	Utah	72
Louisiana	499	Vermont	121
Maine	100	Virgin Islands	172
Maryland	40	Virginia	42
Massachusetts	89	Washington	111
Michigan	71	West Virginia	78
Minnesota	84	Wisconsin	67
Mississippi	364	Wyoming	84
Missouri	196	U. S. average	119
Montana	79		

[a] Based on civilian population as of January 1, 1965, as estimated by the Bureau of the Census.

[b] Recipients of old-age assistance per 1,000 population aged 65 and over.

Source: Social Security Bulletin, Annual Statistical Supplement, 1964, Table 112, p. 100.

lowest in the South, where they were only 88.6 percent of standard. The report pointed out that this method of determining adequacy had deficiencies. Some of the state standards were inadequate. Some of the states have not priced standards recently nor do all states include all currently accepted and validated essentials of living.[2] If the figure of $1,500 annually is accepted as that amount of income necessary for an elderly person to live on a modest scale, then the average payment under OAA is quite inadequate.

More than simply providing money is necessary for the proper assimilation of the aged in our society. One specialist, in dealing with the problems

[2] Ellen J. Perkins, "Unmet Need in Public Assistance," Social Security Bulletin, Vol. 23, No. 4 (April, 1960), p. 6.

TABLE 5–3. FORMULAS FOR DETERMINING FEDERAL CONTRIBUTIONS TO STATE OLD-AGE ASSISTANCE PROGRAMS, 1935–1965

Year	Maximum Monthly Benefit Subject to Federal Participation	Fraction of Average Benefit Paid by Federal Government
1935	$30	1/2.
1939	40	1/2.
1946	45	2/3 of first $15; 1/2 of balance.
1948	50	3/4 of first $20; 1/2 of balance.
1952	55	4/5 of first $25; 1/2 of balance.
1956	60	4/5 of first $30; 1/2 of balance.
1958	No limit	4/5 of first $30; 50–65% of next $35, depending on per capita income of state.
1961	No limit	4/5 of first $31; 50–65% of next $35, depending on per capita income of state.
1962	No limit	29/35 of first $35; 50–65% of next $35, depending on per capita income of state. Maximum federal contribution is $85, which includes vendor payments.
1965	No limit	31/37 of first $37; 50–65% of next $38, depending on per capita income of state. Maximum federal contribution is $90, which includes vendor payments.

Sources: Social Security Bulletin, Annual Statistical Supplement, 1960, pp. 116-17. Public Laws 87-543 (1962) and 89-97 (1965).

TABLE 5–4. AVERAGE OAA BENEFIT AMOUNTS PAID BY STATES, NOVEMBER, 1965

Monthly Benefit Amount[a]	Number of States	Monthly Benefit Amount[a]	Number of States
$30 to $39.99	1	$ 80 to $ 89.99	9
40 to 49.99	0	90 to 99.99	18
50 to 59.99	4	100 to 109.99	1
60 to 69.99	10	110 to 120.99	3
70 to 79.99	5		

[a] Includes vendor payments for medical care and cases receiving only such payments.
Source: Social Security Bulletin, Vol. 29, No. 3 (March, 1966), Table M–16, p. 32.

of the aged, described the aged who are under agency or institutional care as being "predominantly physically sick, brain-damaged, 'kinwrecked,' poverty-stricken, often uneducated aged individuals."[3] Their needs were pointed out as being medical care, psychiatric help, a supportive social milieu, an income, guidance, and protection. Too frequently only the goal of financial support has been recognized, and social caseworkers infrequently visit the aged after this matter has been taken care of. Specially trained caseworkers who understand the particular problems of the aged plus improved medical care were recommended.[4]

AID TO FAMILIES WITH DEPENDENT CHILDREN (AFDC)

In November of 1965, 1,056,510 families, which included 4,392,934 persons, were aided under the Aid to Families with Dependent Children program. To the surprise of many, over the years more rather than fewer families are being served under this program. Some critics have complained about the increasing numbers covered by the program. Their thinking is that relief was provided mainly to alleviate the results of the Great Depression of the thirties. Since we now have prosperity, the program should serve fewer and fewer families or perhaps be abolished altogether. However, poverty will be with us for a number of years. Therefore, it is not expected that assistance programs under the Social Security Act will be abolished in the near future. There are a number of explanations why AFDC roles have grown.[5] First, there has been a rapid increase in the child population and a substantial increase in the total number of families in the population. Second, there has been a slight increase in the proportion of families headed by women and in the rate of illegitimacy. Changes in eligibility under AFDC in permitting families with an unemployed father to qualify have also expanded the rolls. Mr. Edward V. Sparer, in a joint statement on behalf of the Columbia University School of Social Work, Mobilization for Youth, and Project on Social Welfare Law of New York University School of Law, pointed out that the rise in numbers on AFDC has been much faster than the increase in number of families headed by women and the rate of illegitimacy. He attributes the large increase in AFDC rolls mainly to the large migration from the South to the North, where welfare programs are more accessible.[6]

The major objective of the AFDC program is to develop the maximum potentialities of the children under its care. The method by which the pro-

[3] Helen Turner, "A Critique of Social Casework with Aged Individuals Receiving Public Assistance," in *Training for Service in Public Assistance*, Washington, D.C., U.S. Department of Health, Education, and Welfare, Bureau of Public Assistance (1961), p. 128.

[4] *Ibid.*, pp. 125-137.

[5] *Illegitimacy and Its Impact on the Aid to Dependent Children Program*, Washington, D.C., U.S. Department of Health, Education, and Welfare, Bureau of Public Assistance (1960), p. 31.

[6] Statement of Edward V. Sparer, *Social Security Amendments of 1967*, Hearings before the Committee on Finance, U.S. Senate, 90th Congress, 1st Session on H.R. 12080, Part 3 (Sept. 20-26, 1967), pp. 1769-1771.

gram has attempted to achieve this goal has been altered over the years. Originally it was felt that the cash award should be for the purpose of enabling the mother to remain in the home. The formulation of this program was made in the 1930's when fewer women worked outside the home. With more and more women working of their own choice, it was later felt that perhaps the homes of AFDC beneficiaries would be better off if some mothers were able to work in outside employment. More income can be earned from employment than AFDC grants would give. The new orientation of AFDC, as reflected in the 1962 Social Security amendments, is to encourage mothers to seek gainful employment and to aid in the training of those whose education and technical skills are insufficient to enable them to earn an adequate living. The cash payments of AFDC amounting to $35.10 per child (November, 1965) provide an inadequate standard of living.

One 1956 study of AFDC families in Cleveland County, Oklahoma, showed that 35 percent of the boys and 26 percent of the girls had no winter coats even though the temperature may drop below zero on occasion. Seven percent of both boys and girls had no underwear and 5 percent of the boys and 16 percent of the girls had no socks or anklets. Expenditures for food were substantially below national averages, and most of the homes were in need of major repair. Toilet facilities were lacking in many instances, and in a few there were no facilities whatever for water. Medical and dental care was insufficient. Furniture was also lacking. There were two families with six members each who owned only one bed. An average of three persons per bed was reported for all families. Two families with seven members each had no sheets of any kind. In a majority of families who had received AFDC for five years or more, the children dropped out of school by the time they were 15 and completed no more than the seventh grade. In fact it was not unusual for the children to have completed no more than the fourth or fifth grade. Quite obviously the potentialities for the good life were not being developed to a maximum for these children.[7]

The failure of cash benefits to provide an adequate living resulted in important changes in the AFDC program in 1962. By amendments to the Social Security Act, much more emphasis was placed on rehabilitation and service rather than on cash payments. A number of studies have been made to demonstrate the importance of increased social work service in the AFDC program. Ten of these studies were summarized by Winifred Bell.[8] In these projects the average case load per worker was reduced from the national average of 147 to from 35 to 50. Although added costs were necessary for more intensive social work, aid in solving the families' problems removed

---

[7] Paul A. Brinker and Harry E. Rainbolt, "Adequacy of the Aid-to-Dependent Children Program," *Southwestern Social Science Quarterly,* Vol. 39 (1958), pp. 28-32.

[8] Winifred Bell, "The Practical Value of Social Work Services: Preliminary Report on 10 Demonstration Projects in Public Assistance," reported in *Public Welfare Amendments of 1962,* Hearings before the Committee on Ways and Means, House of Representatives, 87th Congress, 2nd Session, on H.R. 10032 (February 7-13, 1962), pp. 410-415.

sufficient numbers from the rolls so that money was actually saved. In one of the projects, for example, the added costs came to $124,000 and the savings from removing families from the rolls was $256,000. In a follow-up in 16 of 37 cases where the families could be located, the earnings of all these families was $114,500, which almost equaled the cost of the project.

The 1967 amendments to the Social Security Act provided that all states would be required to set up work and training programs for welfare recipients by July 1, 1969. State welfare agencies will determine which people are appropriate for referral to the programs, but they may not include (1) children who are under age 16 or going to school; (2) any person with illness, incapacity, advanced age, or remoteness from a project that precludes effective participation in work or training; or (3) persons whose substantially continuous presence in the home is required because of the illness or incapacity of another member of the household. The state welfare agencies will refer all other available welfare recipients to the Department of Labor which will handle them under three priorities. Under priority I, the Secretary of Labor, through over 2,000 U.S. employment offices, will make arrangements for as many as possible to move into regular employment and will establish an employability plan for each person. Under priority II, all those found suitable will receive training appropriate to their needs. As an incentive to engage in training, payments of up to $30 a month will be made above the regular welfare benefits. After training as many as possible will be referred to regular employment. Under priority III, the employment office will make arrangements for special work projects to employ those who are not able to obtain jobs and are not suitable for training. These special projects will be set up by agreement between the employment office and public agencies or non-profit private agencies organized for a public service purpose. If an employee receives wages which are insufficient to raise his income to a level equal to the grant he would have received had he not been on the project plus 20 percent of his wages, a welfare check equal to the difference will be paid. In order to partially pay for the special work projects, the state welfare agency will make payments to the employment office equal to: (1) the welfare benefit the family would have been entitled to, or, if smaller, (2) a portion of the welfare benefit equal to 80 percent of the rates which the individual receives on the special project.

In the 1967 Social Security hearings, there was much heated discussion over whether this program should be mandatory or voluntary for welfare recipients. Proponents of the voluntary method maintained that the program would be more successful if welfare recipients were given the choice to participate or not. The mandatory method was viewed as a retrogression to the punitive Elizabethan poor laws. Opponents of the mandatory system pointed out that a number of states had administered their work and training programs poorly. For example, in Sutter, Imperial, and Yuba counties in rural sections of California, the "training" consists exclusively of work in building and ground maintenance, carrying slops in hospitals, county road work, and other tasks which displace regular workers without training welfare recip-

ients in any usable skills. In Madera County, Cal., work trainees are traditionally assigned to prune vines on the property of a certain agribusiness
proprietor who is paid $5 per hour to "teach" vine pruning despite the fact
that most of the welfare recipients are Mexican farm laborers who have been
pruning vines all their lives. In Tulare County, Cal., welfare recipients doing
county jobs are not provided with necessary protective clothing as are county
employees doing the same work.[9] In Georgia, job offers must be accepted by
welfare beneficiaries able to work. If the job pays less than the AFDC payment, Georgia will not supplement the income to bring it up to the level of
those receiving payments. Also in Georgia, County Boards are permitted
to terminate all employable mothers from AFDC when a picking season
opens. Thus, when a County Board announces that the okra season has
begun, mothers are cut off from AFDC even though they can not find employment.[10] Opponents of the mandatory requirement also point out that
even though protective and vendor payments are provided children whose
parents refuse work, the payments going to the family will decrease, and thus
the children will suffer.

Those favoring the mandatory employment and training requirements
have included special provisions to help make them workable. All the states
will be required to provide day-care facilities so that the mother may work.
As of 1964, only 18 states had planned to operate day-care by public welfare
agencies, 34 states had planned to provide family day-care for children, and
28 states had planned to purchase day-care in already existing centers. The
Community Action Programs under the War on Poverty also have channeled money into day-care nurseries, but even with these additional funds,
as of September 30, 1965, only 310,400 children were being taken care of in
day-care nurseries or family day-care homes. It is estimated that about 2.7
million children need such services.[11] Under the 1967 Social Security amendments, the federal government will provide a large share of the money for day-
care facilities. In all it is expected that the day-care and training program will
cost about $1 billion. Eventually, it is expected that costs will decrease when
sufficient welfare recipients become employable and begin paying taxes. Other
safeguards are written into the law such as paying for work at rates not less
than the federal and state minimums, but a section requiring that prevailing
wages be paid was deleted from the amendments.

In order to encourage welfare recipients to earn more money it was
provided by the 1967 amendments that the earned income of each child recipient who is a full-time or a part-time student not working full-time, will be

[9] Statement of Carol Ruth Silver, California Rural Legal Assistance, *Social Security
Amendments of 1967, op. cit.,* pp. 1928-1929.

[10] Statement of Leroy D. Clark, Attorney for the National Office of the Rights of
Indigents and the NAACP Legal Defense Fund, *ibid.,* Part II, pp. 1385-1386.

[11] Report of the Advisory Council on Welfare, Washington, D.C., U.S. Department of Health, Education, and Welfare, Welfare Administration (June, 1966), p. 58.
For a summary of the first seven months' operation of coverage of unemployed fathers
under AFDC, *see* "Aid to Dependent Children of Unemployed Parents, The First
Seven Months of Operation," *Social Security Bulletin,* Vol. 25 (August, 1962), pp.
7-9, 16.

excluded in determining need for assistance. In the case of any other child or an adult relative, the first $30 of earned income plus 1/3 of the remainder is also exempt. These earnings exemptions are substantially more liberal than prior Social Security exemptions.

Much criticism against AFDC has been directed at requiring the government to subsidize a family in which the father deserts. In some states elaborate efforts have been made to find deserting fathers and force them to support their families, but efforts of this type have been found to be quite expensive in terms of the small results they often accomplish. Part of the problem of desertion may be due to the organization of the AFDC program itself. To be eligible for AFDC, it was required originally that the father either not be present or be ill. Under such an arrangement a premium was placed upon the father deserting. Much criticism has been directed at circumstances in which the father supposedly separates from the mother but continues to remain at home or comes home at odd hours when the social worker will not find him. If aid could be given to families in which the father is unemployed or earns only small amounts, there would be less of a tendency to desert. In May, 1961, the Social Security Act was amended to provide that families with unemployed fathers could become eligible for AFDC payments. Unfortunately, as of 1967, only 22 states had implemented this amendment. The failure of all the states to provide coverage has resulted in the suggestion that it be made mandatory. Such a provision was not included in the 1967 amendments. Even for those states covering unemployed fathers, state definitions of unemployment have varied so much that coverage has varied also. To provide more uniformity in coverage, the 1967 amendments gave a more precise definition of unemployment which, in several respects, narrowed coverage considerably. An unemployed father may not be covered under AFDC in any month in which unemployment compensation is received, regardless of whether the unemployment compensation is substantially less than the AFDC payment. Also, the unemployed father must have worked in at least 6 of 13 calendar quarters ending within one year before the application for aid. It is estimated that about one-half the fathers in New York State will be removed from AFDC rolls by this definition. Since coverage of unemployed fathers under AFDC is so small, we may conclude that the welfare laws still place a premium on the desertion of the father. In addition, some fathers, even though employed, earn so little that they too can increase their family income via AFDC benefits through desertion. Until broader coverage of those on welfare is provided, there will be a premium to desert.

Many widows who formerly applied for AFDC benefits need no longer do so because they are now covered under survivors' benefits of the OASDHI program. Similarly, some families now receive permanent and disability benefits rather than AFDC payments. The reduction of these two types of beneficiaries under AFDC has resulted in a larger percentage of families headed by unmarried mothers or families in which fathers have deserted. Table 5-5 shows the status of fathers under the AFDC program.

So much criticism had been directed at government relief to mothers with illegitimate children that the Senate Appropriations Committee directed the Department of Health, Education, and Welfare to study and report on these problems. Some of their findings were as follows.[12] Illegitimate births have increased from 89,500 in 1940 to 201,700 in 1957. This was an increase from 3.8 to 4.7 percent of all live births. Although the rate of illegitimacy of teen-agers was 15.6 per 1,000 unmarried females, the figures were much higher for those in the 20–24, 25–29, and 30–34 year age groups—respectively, 36.6, 37.8, and 26.1 per thousand. Per 1,000 live births, the ratio of illegitimacy among nonwhites was more than 10 times that of white illegitimacy. Since a larger percentage of nonwhites live in the South, the percentage of illegitimacy was higher there. The rates for illegitimacy were much higher in larger cities than elsewhere. This study listed four causes for increased illegitimacy: (1) failure to integrate nonwhite and other groups into the accepted American culture pattern; (2) increasing premarital relations; (3) changing patterns of family life due to threat of war and annihilation, the practice of going steady, more employment of women, and the increasing mobility in life; and (4) improvement in health which permits more women to bear children. Of all illegitimate babies, about 95,000 (almost half) were adopted. Almost all of these (91 percent) were white babies.

The evidence arrived at by the Department of Health, Education, and Welfare threw doubt on the proposition that women have illegitimate children simply to draw AFDC benefits. For one thing, 87 percent of the illegitimate children were not drawing AFDC checks—only 13 percent were. Second, many of the AFDC mothers were also working. At least this would indicate that they did not have illegitimate children simply to withdraw from the work force. Third, most families did not remain on AFDC rolls for long periods of time. The average was less than 2.1 years. Lastly, about one-half of the AFDC families with illegitimate children (48 percent) had only one child born out of wedlock and another one-fourth had only two such children. In view of the relatively small AFDC benefits and the added responsibility of more children that results in many instances in spreading income a little thinner, the study concluded that it was highly doubtful that the AFDC program encouraged women to have illegitimate children. Later data showed that among families on AFDC and during the time they are on AFDC, the incidence of illegitimacy is less than that of the general public.

A number of suggestions for state action concerning AFDC clients with illegitimate children were reviewed by the investigating committee. One suggestion was that the mother be required to request sterilization in order to receive aid. This suggestion was dismissed as being cruel and inhumane and probably unconstitutional. Another suggestion was to exclude some illegitimate children from the program particularly if they were the second or additional illegitimate children on AFDC rolls. Some states have passed

[12] *Illegitimacy and Its Impact on the Aid to Dependent Children Program, op. cit.,* pp. 1-82.

TABLE 5–5. STATUS OF FATHER IN AFDC CASES, NOVEMBER–DECEMBER, 1961

Status of Father	Percentage of Families[a]
Dead	7.7
Incapacitated	17.8
Absent[b]	67.2
Divorced or legally separated	14.3
Separated without court decree	8.3
Deserted	18.4
Not married to mother	21.2
Imprisoned	4.2
Absent for other reasons	0.6
Unemployed	5.1
Other status	2.2
Total	100.0

[a] Total number of families is 910,000.
[b] Components do not add to total due to rounding.
Source: Robert H. Mugge, "Aid to Families with Dependent Children, Initial findings of the 1961 Report on the Characteristics of Recipients," Social Security Bulletin, Vol. 26, No. 3 (March, 1963), p. 9.

such laws, but they have either been vetoed by the governor or declared unconstitutional. The Social Security Administration has threatened loss of federal financial participation in the program if states adopt such a law. The Social Security Administration claims that such a law would contravene the rights of persons to equal protection of the law under the Fourteenth Amendment to the Constitution. The federal government by such a position is not condoning immorality; it is simply insisting that children in need be provided for regardless of whether they are born in or out of wedlock. Penalizing an already disadvantaged child further through withholding financial support would simply be punishing a child for the shortcomings of his parents. A third suggestion is that aid be denied on the basis of the "unsuitability" of the home. Such a criteria is not used in the Social Security Act, but in 24 states some reference is made to the requirement of the home being suitable. Six of these states simply deny assistance without any assurance that a plan is being worked out for a suitable upbringing of the child. There is grave doubt whether these states are complying with the intent of the Social Security Act. In the other states attempts are made to improve the home, and as a last resort some provide for court authority to remove the child from the home. A special commission in one state that was studying the effect of withdrawal of aid reported the following case:

Viola is in dreadful circumstances. The house is the nearest to nothing the interviewer has ever seen human beings live in. Holes were all in it, planks were off, and windows were out. For a bed, Viola has a rusted bunk-bed with fertilizer sacks sewed together and filled with a thin layer of cotton for a mattress. She had

no bed linen. The children wore rags and no shoes. Viola herself wore a corduroy skirt which was in tatters and a badly worn corduroy man's shirt.

She said she had not been able to get any work to do in 4 months. They
have existed on what "one and another" gave them. She said they haven't enough
to eat, and they possess no shoes at all. She gave her child, born Dec. 16, 1955,
to her cousin who lives in Chicago. The last clothes they have gotten were sent
last year from a friend in Chicago. This is the most wretched family this interviewer has ever seen. Viola did not complain or beg, she seemed to accept her
condition as a matter of course.[13]

A fourth suggestion—to take all illegitimate children away from their mothers—would be extremely expensive to implement. Lack of sufficient adoption
parents for nonwhite groups would make the construction of a larger number of institutions for nonwhite children necessary. The fifth and endorsed
recommendation was that intensive casework be engaged in to help such
families. The group favored rehabilitation projects to aid such mothers.
Such projects have included training in nutrition and better living standards
and training for employment.

A suggestion not discussed by the committee has aroused much controversy in Illinois and elsewhere. This suggestion was that public aid funds
be used to pay for birth control information and devices desired by clients.
Proponents of this suggestion hope that its implementation would result
in fewer illegitimate children. Opponents, on the other hand, contend that
such a proposal would promote promiscuity. One opponent stated, "I don't
see why we should pay for subsidizing the illegal activities of women on
relief." [14] Catholic groups have opposed the measure on the ground that it
results in a deviation of governmental policy of neutrality on birth control.
A compromise bill was passed in Illinois whereby birth control services were
made available to mothers over 15 years of age, whether married or unmarried, but not to others. An even broader program was implemented in
Chicago in 1965, when the Chicago Board of Health provided for a free
birth control program that was open to all residents regardless of marital status
or income. Other states also have recently inaugurated birth control programs.
An important step forward came with the 1967 Social Security amendments
which require states to offer family planning services to all appropriate AFDC
recipients.

Another control over the AFDC program came in the 1962 amendments to the Social Security Act in requiring that each state ensure that
the monetary payments under AFDC be used to the children's best interest. In
cases where the relative-payee is not providing adequate care, the administrative agency is given authority to provide counseling and guidance services.
If the relative-payee continues to misuse the money, the administrative agency
may authorize a reliable person within the community to accept the money
as payee and expend the payment for the benefit of the family. The administrative agency may also seek the appointment of a guardian. It may also

[13] *Illegitimacy and Its Impact on the Aid to Dependent Children Program,* pp.
56-57.
[14] Steiner, *op. cit.,* p. 226.

refer the case to local law-enforcement authorities, for the law now provides that continued misuse of AFDC money may result in criminal or civil penalties. As of 1967, only seven states had plans for protective payments, and in the entire nation, less than fifty assistance recipients were affected.[15]

The problem of abuse in welfare is covered in detail in the last chapter. Suffice it to say here that most people on OAA (average age 75), APTD, and many AB beneficiaries are unable to work. There are few unemployed fathers on AFDC, so this leaves mainly AFDC mothers who might be made eligible for work. The fact that the AFDC rolls have been growing prompted Congress in the 1967 amendments to limit the federal matching in the AFDC program. Federal financial participation will not be available for any excess above the percentage of absent parents who received aid to the child population under age 18 in the state as of January 1, 1968. This limitation of AFDC rolls aroused much controversy when it was being considered. Some state officials maintained that they could not legitimately limit those who could qualify, and without federal aid, the burdens on some states would become much greater. Congressman Mills, however, maintained that the "freeze" on AFDC rolls was necessary in order to put pressure on the states to undertake the work and training program rather than merely continuing in handing out welfare checks.

Another abuse of welfare is harassment of welfare beneficiaries. Some students of social welfare contend that arbitrary rules of doubtful legality pervade the public assistance system. A number of these have been listed by Edward V. Sparer as follows:

'Substitute father' rules—which deny eligibility to an AFDC mother because she engages in sexual intercourse with a man (as in Alabama and other states). Other such rules which assume nonexistent income from the man still operate despite HEW prohibitions.

The 'unmarried minor mother' rule (unique to Louisiana) which results in an eligibility requirement that both the child's father and the mother's father be absent from the home.

'Best interest' residence laws—which disqualify some newcomers who need welfare but not others, depending on the local welfare department's view of where the newcomer should live.

Non-supplementation rules, as in Georgia which require mothers to work full-time and then disqualifies them from AFDC supplementation, no matter how little they earn.

Six-month separation rules, requiring that a six-month period pass after the desertion or separation of a father before aid will be given to the children, regardless of how clear it is that the father has deserted and regardless of how needy the children are.

Search and interrogation procedures which assume welfare clients have no Fourth and Fifth Amendment rights. One type was recently declared unconstitutional by the California Supreme Court in Parrish v. Alameda County. Many other types exist.

[15] Statement of Wilbur J. Cohen, Undersecretary of Health, Education and Welfare, Social Security Amendments of 1967, op. cit., Part 1 (Aug. 22-24, 1967), p. 269.

No retroactive payment rules are followed in some states, so that rejected welfare applicants who are later adjudicated to have been wrongfully rejected, cannot obtain any of the wrongfully withheld grant money—no matter what debts, pain, and harm they suffered as a result of the wrongful denial.[16]

Another problem with AFDC is low payments, particularly in the South.[17] In Mississippi the average payment was $7.87 per child (May, 1966). Gilbert Steiner has suggested that the federal government take over the program entirely in states which refuse to pay adequate benefits.[18]

AID TO THE BLIND

Estimates of the number of blind in the world vary from 6.6 million to 14 million. The estimates vary greatly because in many parts of the world no census has been taken. The number of blind, may also vary according to the definition of blindness used. The United States is one of the few countries to use a technical definition—"central visual acuity of 20/200 or less in the better eye, with correcting glasses; or central visual acuity of more than 20/200 if there is a field defect in which the peripheral field is contracted to such an extent that the widest diameter of visual field subtends an angular distance no greater than 20 degrees." A visual acuity of 20/200 means that a person can recognize symbols and objects at 20 feet which a person with normal vision can recognize at 200 feet. In the United States, as of July 1, 1959, an estimate of the number of blind was 355,000 or an average of almost two persons per 1,000 population.[19] The number of blind in the Middle and Far East and Africa is much higher than elsewhere in the world. In these areas certain infectious diseases that cause blindness have not as yet been eradicated. These are ophthalmia neonatorum, venereal diseases, smallpox, and tuberculosis, along with trachoma and onchocerciasis. In the United States diseases associated with aging, such as cataract and glaucoma, are more prevalent as a cause of blindness.

Custodial care of the blind had begun as early as the fourth century when St. Basil at Caesaria in Cappadocia established a hospice for the blind. The first school for the blind was opened in Paris in 1784. Of many types of alphabets, the braille system of raised dots is the system used practically universally today. It was devised by Louis Braille, a blind teacher of the blind. In 1959 over 13,000 blind children were attending school in the United States. About half were in one of 50 special schools located in 41 states and Puerto Rico, and the other half were being educated with seeing children. Resource teachers or special class teachers are available if the blind are taught with seeing children. In 1858 Kentucky chartered the American

[16] Statement of Edward V. Sparer, *op. cit.,* Part 3, p. 1767.
[17] Perkins, *op. cit.,* p. 6.
[18] Steiner, *op. cit.,* p. 248.
[19] Samuel Finestone *et al., Social Casework and Blindness* (New York, American Foundation for the Blind, 1960), p. 147.

Printing House for the Blind,[20] and since 1879 federal funds have been made available to this publishing company to provide books and apparatus for the education of the blind.[21] A volunteer organization, Service for the Blind, Inc., stands ready to provide any textbooks that are needed for blind students attending college.[22] The American Foundation for the Blind has developed "Talking Books," which records reading material on long-playing phonograph discs. The government of the United States contributes to the recording of such books, because the process is quite expensive. For those blind who are unable to pay their own way, federal and state funds are available for the payment of tuition, books, supplies, and reader service. The first three are paid in full if necessary and a stipulated amount is designated for reader service. Under the reader service, the money may be used either for the rental of records or payment for a sighted person to read nonrecorded books in the home of the blind person.

Attempts are made to aid the blind in a number of other ways. For federal income tax purposes the blind receive a double exemption. In 1927 the Interstate Commerce Act was amended to permit common carriers to allow the blind to be accompanied by a guide without having to pay an extra fare. Most railroads and bus companies now provide this service. Dog guides are also provided free transportation. Other aids to the blind are eye banks, which are maintained mainly through the Lion's Club in the United States. The primary purpose of an eye bank is to obtain, preserve, and transport eyes to a qualified surgeon who performs corneal grafts. By transplanting the eye, sight may be restored for persons suffering from a particular kind of blindness or impaired vision.

Seeing-eye dogs are provided to persons who request and qualify for one. The idea was originally developed after a dog guide school had been opened in Germany to aid blind World War I veterans. As an experiment, a blind person in the United States had been trained to use a dog guide at a dog-breeding and research station in Switzerland. After the success of the experiment, the owner of the Swiss kennels opened the first American school of such a kind in Morristown, New Jersey, in 1929. The school proved successful. The school is operated by a philanthropic organization called The Seeing Eye, Inc. Modern kennels can accommodate 240 dogs a year. The costs to the blind are $150 for the first dog and $50 for any replacement. The purpose of the fee is to dispel the feeling of charity. The fee may not be paid by charitable contributions, but only by the blind person or his immediate family. People from 16 to 55 years of age may obtain a dog. Below 16, it is felt that the person may be too immature to assume responsibility of a good working partnership with a dog, and over 55 is considered too advanced in years to undergo the strenuous exercise required for the month's

[20] *Literature for the Blind* (Louisville, American Printing House for the Blind, 1957), pp. 1-2.

[21] Finestone *et al.*, *op. cit.*, pp. 150-151.

[22] Harry E. Simmons, *National Conference Library Service for the Blind*, Washington, D.C. (1952), pp. 44-45.

training course. In exceptional cases these age limits may be waived. Although employment at the time of applying for a dog is not essential, the applicant should have a plan for employment or other activity which indicates a need for a dog. About three months are needed to train a dog properly, most often a German shepherd, and another month is needed in having the dog adjust to the individual.[23]

In spite of the many aids for the blind, a recent study showed that relatively little use had been made of aids. Of all those receiving AB payments, only 10 percent had finished high school, and 65 percent had finished fewer than eight grades of school. Only 11 percent of all AB recipients had a Talking Book Machine, and only 9 percent were able to read braille. Only 1 percent of all AB recipients had the help of a guide dog.[24]

The major program for the blind that covers more blind people than any other program is the assistance program under the Social Security Act. Like the other assistance programs under this act, it is financed by matching federal with state money. In November of 1965, 94,646 recipients were receiving Aid to the Blind assistance payments. This figure constitutes more than one-fourth of all the blind persons in the United States. When the program first began in 1936, 45,000 received assistance payments. Coverage gradually increased until it reached a peak of 110,000 in 1958, and has declined since then. The average payment in November, 1965, was $89.56. As is true of other state-administered programs, the payments varied considerably from state to state. The figures are shown in Table 5-6.

Payments for additional dependents are made under the program. The blind have been aided by amendments since 1962 exempting certain income of the blind in determining eligibility. The 1965 amendments require that a state must disregard the first $85 per month earned income plus one-half of all the rest. Additional amounts may be disregarded if the blind person has a plan for achieving self-support, of which the income he receives is necessary for the fulfillment of the plan. In spite of this amendment, only 11 percent of the men drawing AB and 3.5 percent of the women had any income from working.

Another program fostered by the federal government trains the blind for industrial employment. In 1920, Congress passed the Bankhead Act, which provided for training and rehabilitation of persons disabled in industry and the blind. In 1943 the program was liberalized and expanded. A complete medical examination is given along with necessary medical and surgical services, transportation, maintenance during rehabilitation, hospitalization up to 90 days in any one case, and the supplying of occupational tools and equipment. The federal government pays all the costs for administration, vocational guidance, and placement costs, and one-half the costs of equipment, tools, and maintenance while the individual is undergoing voca-

[23] *The Road to Freedom* (Morristown, N.J., Seeing Eye, Inc., 1957).
[24] Robert H. Mugge, "Recipients of Aid to the Blind," *Welfare in Review*, Vol. 3 (April, 1965), p. 5.

TABLE 5–6. MONTHLY PAYMENTS, AID TO THE BLIND ASSISTANCE,
NOVEMBER, 1965

Monthly Payments[a]	Number of States	Monthly Payments[a]	Number of States
$150 to $159.99	1	$90 to $99.99	5
140 to 149.99	1	80 to 89.99	6
130 to 139.99	1	70 to 79.99	9
120 to 129.99	6	60 to 69.99	6
110 to 119.99	4	50 to 59.99	6
100 to 109.99	3	40 to 49.99	2

[a] Average monthly payment in November, 1965, was $89.56. All payments include vendor payments for medical care.

Source: Social Security Bulletin, Vol. 29 (March, 1966), Table M–16, p. 32.

tional rehabilitation. Only a small number receive such training in relation to those drawing Aid to the Blind payments. According to rehabilitation experts it would be possible to greatly expand the program.

Thanks to the Randolph-Sheppard Act of 1936, as amended in 1954, several thousand blind persons operate vending stands in federal and other buildings. Some states also require that vending stands in state buildings be operated by blind persons, but in other states it is not mandatory. In evaluating the economic security of the blind, the assistance payments are so small that strengthening the rehabilitation program and improving employment opportunities for the blind will be an absolute necessity if they are to be removed from the poverty group in America.

MATERNAL AND CHILD HEALTH SERVICES

Unlike the OAA, AFDC, AB, and APTD programs, which provide for open-ended grants depending on how much the state appropriates, the maternal and child programs provide for fixed annual grants from the federal government. About $160 million of federal funds were appropriated for such services in 1967 and slightly more than this amount came from state and local funds. The federal appropriations were substantially expanded by the 1967 Social Security amendments, and will reach $350 million by fiscal year 1973. Part of the increased money will be spent for family planning services.

During 1967, 287,000 mothers received medical, prenatal, and post-partum care. The largest program for needy mothers provides public health nursing services. Medical clinic services, hospital in-patient care, and dental services may also be provided. Expectant parents may also attend classes to increase their understanding of problems with babies. The unfavorable death rate among mothers and babies compared with other countries would indicate that better medical care could be provided, particularly among lower-income groups. Only 27 out of 56 counties with the highest infant mortality rate in the country had maternal and child health programs.

Services provided children include immunizations, school health examinations, and nursing services. A special program for crippled children provided care for 453,000 children in 1967. Most of these children receive clinical care, but some hospital service is provided along with treatment by physicians either in the home or at the office. The program has been expanding to include a larger percentage of nonorthopedic cases. Advances in surgery for congenital malformations have resulted in a much larger number of children taking advantage of the new surgery. As is typical of other state administered programs, some of the states provide excellent services whereas others provide little or no care.

CHILD WELFARE

A major part of money for child welfare (71 percent) provides foster home care for children. Other functions are as follows: [25]

1. Social services to a child or youth in his own home—including casework (counseling) with him or his parents or relatives, dealing with problems of behavior, emotional, and social adjustment, parent-child relationships, a physical or mental handicap, delinquent behavior or conflict with the law.

2. Social services to neglected, abused, or exploited children—frequently called "protective service."

3. Social services to unmarried mothers and their babies.

4. Homemaker service—homemakers help a family to stay together by providing a trained and supervised worker to help during an illness or incapacity of the mother.

5. Adoption service.

6. Day-care services—part-time care of children in family day-care homes or in group situations during daytime periods, usually when parents are absent from the home because of employment.

Other services of child welfare are to license and regulate institutions, foster homes, and day-care centers and to coordinate and cooperate with other community groups in community planning and the development of services.

About two-thirds of child welfare work is carried on by public agencies and the remainder by private agencies. Almost twice as many children receive child welfare services in foster homes as compared with institutions. In fiscal year 1967 a total of $451.7 million of public funds was spent for child welfare services. Of this amount the federal government contributed only $45 million (10 percent), the states provided 50 percent, and cities the

[25] *Report of the Advisory Council on Child Welfare Services,* in Hearings before the Committee on Ways and Means, House of Representatives, 87th Congress, 2nd Session, on H.R. 10032 (February 7-13, 1962), p. 247.

remaining 40 percent. There was a greater disparity in state funds in this program than most others. For every child under 21 the State of Texas spent $0.31 on child welfare services compared with $10.56 in New York State. In Texas only 6 children per 10,000 children were aided compared with a figure of 197 for the District of Columbia. Of a total of 265 counties in Texas, 226 counties, representing 36 percent of the state's child population, have no child welfare services of any kind.[26] Child welfare work has been handicapped by having too few workers. In June of 1960 there were 5,689 public child welfare caseworkers. At that time there was a shortage of 771 public professional child welfare workers and an additional 104 clerks were needed. A shortage of workers makes for extremely high case loads and insufficient services. Michigan, for example, had a load of 23 children per caseworker compared with 52 for the median state and a high of 144 for both Alabama and Mississippi.[27] About half of the counties in the United States containing one-fourth the nation's children, mostly in rural areas, have no full time public child welfare worker.[28] Some of the services of a child welfare program simply cannot be provided because of a lack of money. Homemaking services, for example, are only offered in about 150 of the 3,187 counties in the United States.[29]

An Advisory Council on Child Welfare Services suggested a number of changes in child welfare work. As was pointed out above, the federal government pays only a small share of total child welfare costs. The federal government's share has gone toward establishing and improving services rather than paying for part of the total cost of a state's program. The Advisory Council suggested that the federal government pay part of the total cost of such services. It was recommended that the federal government contribute by the use of an open-end grant as is done in OAA, AFDC, AB, and APTD rather than the flat grant system which it has been using. Federal grants for research funds in this field were suggested, as were grants for training of personnel in child welfare. It also recommended that a permanent Advisory Council on Child Welfare Services be established to provide a continuing guide for the program. Lastly it suggested that the Children's Bureau within the U.S. Department of Health, Education, and Welfare be expanded to provide more adequate services for children.[30]

Although federal matching has not occurred, federal appropriations for child welfare have been increasing over the years. The 1967 amendments to the Social Security Act increased authorizations for expenditures from $60 million to $110 million from fiscal year 1970 on. Earlier amendments in the

[26] Gladys Kammerer, *British and American Child Welfare Services* (Detroit, Wayne University Press, 1963), pp. 185-186.

[27] "Child Welfare Statistics, 1960," Statistical Series No. 64, Washington, D.C., U.S. Department of Health, Education, and Welfare, Children's Bureau, Table 10, p. 16.

[28] *Report of the Advisory Council on Child Welfare Services, op. cit.,* p. 249.

[29] *Ibid.,* p. 250.

[30] *Ibid.,* pp. 229-278.

decade stipulated that welfare plans must be coordinated with services provided under the AFDC program. AFDC payments were given for foster home care if these payments were received in the month the child was placed in a foster home. Amendments in 1967 liberalized these payments by providing that AFDC payments could be made in foster homes if in the six months before proceedings started in the court the child would have been eligible for AFDC if he had lived in the home of a relative. The 1962 amendments required that state child welfare plans must provide for coordination with services provided under the AFDC program, and such plans must show that they are working toward making child welfare services available by July 1, 1975, to all children in the state who need them. Grants were also made to institutions of higher learning to aid in the training of child welfare workers.

COMMON PROBLEMS OF ASSISTANCE PROGRAMS

ELIGIBILITY

The question of eligibility has remained one of the major problems of assistance programs. Admittedly payments should not be paid to wealthy persons, but only to the needy. In order to certify only those in need, a "means" or "needs" test is required in all states. The income of the applicant and sometimes the amount of his property must be investigated. This requirement means that much more investigation into individual affairs is necessary than with a program like OASDHI, where payments are automatically received at a certain age provided the aged person retires. The assistance applicant in essence must "take a pauper's oath" that he has insufficient income or property to support himself. A "means" test is looked upon as demeaning but necessary to properly administer the assistance program. The weaknesses of such a test have been one of the main reasons why the federal government has been covering more and more aged under OASDHI rather than OAA. Similarly more of the disabled are being covered under the OASDHI rather than under the APTD assistance program. In 1965 the insurance program covered medical care for the aged for the first time rather than having persons protected solely by the assistance section of the Act.

In determining eligibility under the assistance programs, the income of the recipient must be insufficient to live on. In order to encourage recipients to work, amendments to the Social Security Act provided that certain amounts of income may be disregarded when determining need. For the AFDC program, not only may the earned income be permitted to be set aside for future identifiable needs of a dependent child but the first $5 of monthly family income may be disregarded plus $50 of each child's earnings up to a maximum of $150 on the children's earnings. Other income limits were provided for the other assistance programs. Most of the state laws, as contrasted to the federal law, do not specify the exact amount that may be earned, but allow the administering agency to determine it.[31]

Property limits vary greatly among the states. The following statistics apply to property requirements for the OAA program. A minimum number of states (21) permit ownership of a home without limit to its value. The remaining majority restrict home ownership by one method or another.[32] In addition all states place a limit either on personal property, real property, or both.[33] Twenty-three states also limit the amount of life insurance that may be possessed by the recipient.[34] Practically all states disqualify applicants who transfer property in order to qualify for assistance.

One of the most controversial issues in assistance programs is whether property liens shall be placed on the property of all those receiving assistance. If they are, the state may recover the amount of its assistance payments at death. Under the OAA program, almost twice as many states (33) have property liens as those that do not have such a lien (18). The basic reason for such a tax is that since state aid is given to those who have property, the state should recover the amount paid at death. The major criticism of property liens is that they result in an extremely heavy inheritance or estate tax on lower-income groups in our society. A wealthy individual may pass on rather substantial sums to his heirs, thanks to generous federal and state exemptions on amounts that may be bequeathed tax-free. In addition, our tax laws permit every other generation to be omitted from the estate tax if the heir is willing to transfer his inheritance automatically to his children's children. Low-income families, however, must pay an extremely high inheritance tax, possibly 100 percent, on property inherited from an OAA recipient if they happen to reside in a state with property liens on assistance payments.

RELATIVES' RESPONSIBILITY

Another controversial issue under the assistance programs revolves around how much responsibility relatives should have for the care of dependents. In our former, predominantly rural society, care of the aged was less of a burden. In urban society, however, costs of rent and food and medical care for aged and other dependents may be quite costly. More and more our society is coming to the conclusion that society itself should bear the costs of the aged and other dependent groups. Since some economic demands on chil-

[31] The administering agency is either a county department of welfare or a local or district office of a state public welfare agency.

[32] Three states provide that the home may only be a modest one. Eight states permit the administering agency to decide whether the value of the home is too large to qualify a person for assistance. Twelve states limit the market value from $3,000 to $12,000. Six other states limit the assessed value from $2,500 to $10,000. See U.S. Department of Health, Education, and Welfare, *Characteristics of State Public Assistance Plans,* Public Assistance Report No. 50 (1964).

[33] Seven states have a limitation on real property ranging from $100 to $8,000, 23 states have limits on personal property ranging from zero to $1,450, and 21 states have limits on both real and personal property combined from $500 to $5,000.

[34] Some of the states limit the cash value and others the face value. The limits range from $300 to $10,000.

dren are primarily a matter of chance, some have reasoned that the government should support the aged rather than have relatives support them. Furthermore many families have insufficient income to support aged relatives. For these and other reasons the 1961 White House Conference on Aging recommended abolition of relatives' responsibility.[35]

About one-third of our states have no relatives' responsibility requirement in their public assistance programs. Slightly less than a third require support from relatives, and they reduce welfare payments even though relatives refuse to support the needy. The remaining states provide for relatives' responsibility, but will make payments if they are not forthcoming from relatives.[36]

Some states have both property liens and relatives' responsibility, other states may have one of these requirements but not the other, while others may have neither. Having both such requirements reduces the number of people applying for assistance, whereas many more people apply if the state has only one or none of these requirements. For the country as a whole in December of 1964 there were 119 recipients of old-age assistance per 1,000 population aged 65 and over. Eight states, however, had more than twice that number drawing OAA, with 499 per 1,000 aged on the rolls in Louisiana. Louisiana has neither property liens nor relatives' responsibility and is not as heavily industrialized as some other states. Only recently have farm families been covered on OASDHI, so that many of the aged farm families have never contributed to OASDHI and thus are not eligible for it. They must still apply for OAA payments.

CITIZENSHIP REQUIREMENTS

Before assistance payments are made, 13 states require that the person be a citizen of the United States, although eight of these states do provide that if the person has resided in the United States for a certain period, varying from 10 to 25 years, the person is then eligible. In a study of the California law, which had prohibited all noncitizens from obtaining OAA, six California professors, two economists, two political scientists, and two sociologists concluded that this section of the law should not be amended. Their reasoning was that another 5 percent would be added to the OAA rolls (45,000 people, mostly Mexicans), and that the additional cost would come to $35 million per year in addition to the then current bill of $226 million per year. California was already paying out twice as much as any other state for their OAA program. The professors feared that many Mexican nationals would be induced to bring their elder relatives into the state on the promise of support, but with the intention of later placing them on OAA rolls.[37] The

[35] For a more detailed analysis, see Alvin L. Schorr, "Filial Responsibility and the Aging, or Beyond Pluck and Luck," *Social Security Bulletin*, Vol. 25 (May, 1962), pp. 4-9.

[36] Alvin L. Schorr, *Filial Responsibility in the Modern American Family*, Washington, D.C., Government Printing Office (1960), pp. 23-24.

[37] Floyd Bond *et al., Our Needy Aged* (New York, Holt, Rinehart & Winston, 1954), pp. 347-349.

State of California took a slightly more sympathetic attitude toward their noncitizen aged and now provides that the citizenship requirement may be waived if the person has lived in the United States for 25 years and was not eligible for citizenship prior to December 24, 1952.

RESIDENCE REQUIREMENTS

Residence requirements have presented another important eligibility problem in the assistance program. Many states feared an influx of needy people, and therefore protected themselves by requiring that people reside within their borders a certain period of time before becoming eligible for assistance. The residence requirements imposed by states in 1959 for OAA benefits are shown in Table 5-7.

Most of the states that require that the person reside within the state in five of the last nine years also require that they have been in residence for the last year prior to their application. Some of the states with only one year of residence provided that this requirement would be waived if reciprocal arrangements were agreed upon with other states. The long residence requirements place a distinct hardship upon families who move to a new state and then become unemployed or ill or experience some other economic hardship. These people are precluded from obtaining governmental aid simply because they have not resided in a state long enough. Although 10 million people move from their county each year and 6 million move from their state, many are not eligible for assistance when economic disaster strikes after the family has moved. Since the federal government pays for a large share of the assistance program, the American Public Welfare Association and others have recommended that residence requirements be waived entirely. Their recommendation was based on the fact that states with minimum residence requirements have not experienced higher costs. Some states making higher monthly payments than others, however, have opposed abolition of residence requirements on the ground that their higher payments may attract too many needy. Recently in Delaware and Connecticut there have been court cases in which residence requirements have been declared unconstitutional because, according to the court, there was no rational reason for basing a person's need for public assistance on whether he had lived in the state for a long or a short period of time.

COVERAGE AND MINIMUM STANDARDS

Another problem of assistance programs is whether those on "general" relief should receive federal aid. In 1935 it was decided that federal grants should only be made available for specific groups of needy in our society such as the aged, children, and the blind. "General" relief was not covered under the Social Security Act, and the states were required to finance "general" relief from their own resources. Coverage of all needy families would require that the Social Security Act be amended not only to cover special types of dependency but "general" relief as well. The fact that the states must

TABLE 5–7.   RESIDENCE REQUIREMENTS IMPOSED BY STATES FOR OAA
BENEFITS, 1964

Residence Requirements	Number of States
None	5
One year	23
Two of the last six years	1
Three of the last nine years	2
Three of the last five years or five of the last nine years	1
Five of the last nine years	19

Source: *Characteristics of State Public Assistance Plans,* Public Assistance Report
No. 50, Bureau of Family Services, 1964.

finance their "general" relief program without federal aid has resulted in
even less ample funds than under the assistance program of the Social Security Act. Payments under OAA increased from $18.79 in 1936 to $77.03 in
December of 1963; yet at the same time general assistance payments increased only from $24.13 to $68.01. Some states have been particularly deficient in providing general assistance. In November of 1965, Arkansas paid
only $3.87 per recipient per month and North Carolina paid only $9.71.[38]

During the past few years, a number of students of welfare have been
critical of the categorical relief program, that is providing welfare only for
those who fit in specific categories such as blind, permanently disabled, etc.
Amendments to the Social Security Act in 1962 did permit states to combine a number of assistance programs, but those on general relief were still
excluded. The latest Advisory Council on Public Welfare has recommended
that categorical relief be abolished and that a single criterion be used for
welfare eligibility—that of need. This Advisory Council pointed out that in
1964 of the 34 million persons living in poverty, only 7.4 million were receiving public assistance. The 1967 amendments to the Social Security Act
took only a minor step toward increasing coverage by providing that federal
assistance would be forthcoming for emergency assistance to certain needy
families with children for thirty days in a twelve month period.

The lack of coverage of many people and the widely divergent state
standards influenced the council to recommend that the federal government
establish minimum standards for public assistance below which no state
may fall. The council pointed out that the average welfare payment provides
little more than half the amount required by a family for subsistence, and
in some low-income states it is less than a quarter of that amount. The council contended that low public assistance payments contribute to the perpetua-
tion of poverty and deprivation that extends into future generations.[39]

[38] *Social Security Bulletin,* Vol. 29 (March, 1966), Table M-16, p. 32, and Table
25, p. 44.
[39] *Report of the Advisory Council on Public Welfare,* U.S. Department of Health,
Education, and Welfare Administration (June, 1966), pp. 15-22.

FINANCING

A major problem of assistance programs is how they should be financed. When the program was first started in 1935, the federal government provided 50 percent of the funds of OAA, AB, and one-third of the AFDC payments. The state and local governments were required to match the federal grants. The result of this method of financing was to place a much heavier burden of relief on poor states than on wealthier ones. The more urbanized states had more people covered under OASDHI and therefore had to pay out less money under OAA. The poorer, rural states, however, were forced to raise large sums of money to match the federal grants. The unfairness of this formula has resulted in its being amended several times. At first the proportion of federal funds was raised and that of states and counties lowered. In 1946, for example, under OAA and AB the federal government paid two-thirds of the first $15 and one-half of the balance. At the present writing, for OAA the federal government pays $31/37$'s of the first $37 plus 50 to 65 percent of the balance, varying inversely with the state per capita income. The last part of the formula does tend to give greater relief to the poorer states. Still, the remaining part of the formula gives only equal treatment to the poorer states, and less than equal treatment if their heavier case load is considered. Some have suggested that the present type of formula be abandoned entirely, and replaced by one similar to that used in the Hill-Burton Act, which gives still greater weight to per capita income.

To determine relative state effort in all public services, the state-local payments may be compared per $1,000 of income payments in the state. Table 5-8 shows the result. The lowest-income states are paying out a larger amount per $1,000 of their income than the wealthiest states. This table would indicate that those wealthier states having below-average assistance payments clearly have the resources to do better. The table would also indicate that an improved federal formula could be devised to give further relief to the lowest-income states. Other types of assistance could also be provided in the form of improved education, health, and other services.

The Advisory Council on Public Welfare in 1966 was quite critical of the present formulas, and they recommended that they be replaced by an entirely new system.[40] The Advisory Council cited four criticisms of the present formulas. First, the formulas do not take sufficient account of state fiscal ability and effort to finance adequate and comprehensive programs. Average payments in Mississippi in August of 1966, compared with the national averages in parentheses, were as follows: OAA–$39.93 ($74.02); AB–$46.94 ($88.80); APTD–$45.41 ($80.04); AFDC–$7.90 ($35.38); and GA–$16.61 ($36.88). Even with the low payments in Mississippi, this state was paying out $1.52 per $1,000 of 1964 personal income on state and local expenditures for assistance payments. This figure was higher than that of 27 other states.

[40] *Ibid.*, p. 33.

TABLE 5–8. STATE FISCAL EFFORT FOR ALL PUBLIC SERVICES, PER $1,000 INCOME [a]

Region	All States in Region	States in Highest-Income Group[b]	States in Middle-Income Group[b]	States in Lowest-Income Group[b]
Northeast	$ 96.68	$ 92.26	$100.22	. . . .
North Central	106.34	89.64	102.41	$145.14
South	102.98	77.48	106.84	109.09
West	120.23	115.28	121.33	. . . .
United States	106.50	92.58	108.70	115.10

[a] The amount shown is the unweighted average for the specified group.

[b] The 49 states are classified by per capita income as follows: Highest income, 12; middle income, 25; lowest income, 12.

Source: Social Security Bulletin, Vol. 23, No. 4 (April, 1960), Table 5, p. 11.

A second criticism of the formulas was that they favored more federal financial support for some than for other groups of needy people. Children are the most disadvantaged, for the maximum amount subject to federal sharing for children and parents under AFDC is $32, compared with a $75 maximum for the aged, blind, and disabled. Third, the Advisory Council was critical of the fact that the categorical grants resulted in better payments for some programs than others. The federal formulas encouraged states to exert considerable effort to obtain maximum federal funds to the detriment of balanced program development. Higher federal shares are provided for medical care and social services than for basic maintenance needs. Food, clothing, and shelter are particularly neglected areas. Lastly the Advisory Council felt that the formulas are unnecessarily complex and thus complicate both public understanding and program administration.

To replace the present system, the Advisory Council recommended a uniform and simple plan, which would provide for equitable and reasonable fiscal effort among states. The state share would be expressed as a percentage of total personal income, with the wealthier states paying a larger percentage than the poorer states. The federal government would then specify national standards for an adequate program and assume the full financial responsibility for the difference in cost between the state share and the total cost of the comprehensive program in each state.

ADMINISTRATION

The public assistance programs are a joint federal-state and sometimes local governmental operation. The federal government contributes sizable amounts of money, which are administered by state or local groups. For such programs as OAA, AB, AFDC, and APTD, several federal requirements must be complied with to obtain federal money. Some of these are as follows: (1) The plan must be in effect in all political subdivisions of the state and must be mandatory upon them; (2) state participation and financing is mandatory; (3) a single state agency must administer or supervise the plan; (4) fair hearing procedure is required; (5) the plan must provide for such methods of administration as are found to be necessary for efficient operation; (6) the state agency must make all necessary reports to the federal office; (7) maximum limits are established on residence requirements; and (8) no citizen of the United States can be excluded from receiving aid if in need. A 1939 amendment required that selection of personnel must be done under a merit system. The federal agency administering this section of the Social Security Act is the Bureau of Family Services of the Social Security Administration, which is a part of the Department of Health, Education, and Welfare. The recent emphasis of the U.S. Department of Health, Education and Welfare to achieve self-support for welfare recipients may or may not be implemented by the states administering the program. Some of the states have large case loads and inadequate programs. In these instances most of the work of the State Department of Public Welfare is devoted to the routine function of certifying clients rather than engaging in extensive casework. The more progressive states have or are cutting their case loads and provide more services to clients. Federal controls are lacking at the present time to require proper case loads.

Summary

A number of assistance programs are included in the Social Security Act of 1935. Older people drawing insufficient or no OASDHI benefits and who are without adequate income or property may obtain OAA benefits. Some states are able to pay adequate OAA benefits, but others pay very small amounts. The AFDC program was inaugurated for dependent children. Because of inadequacies of monthly payments, social workers now are attempting to place as many women heading such families in gainful employment as possible. Recent developments now make families headed by unemployed fathers eligible for AFDC payments. The program now also permits a closer evaluation of the way family heads spend the AFDC money. Many of the blind receive AB payments. Here, too, emphasis has been placed on social casework to provide gainful employment for those able to engage in it. The federal government contributes only small sums to maternal and child health services and child welfare, but these programs are expanding.

In determining eligibility for assistance programs, the states vary considerably in their requirements. Those which require both relatives' responsibility and property liens have much less coverage than states with neither requirement. A major controversial issue today is whether general relief should be subsidized by the federal government. Without federal aid, many of the states provide extremely small amounts.

PRIVATE METHODS OF PROTECTION AGAINST OLD AGE AND DEATH

INDIVIDUAL LIFE INSURANCE

At the end of 1964, Social Security records show that the average amount of payments received by a widowed mother and three or more children was $197.12 monthly. Since many men prefer that their families have a larger income than this amount, many have turned to private insurance companies to provide additional security against premature death.

Mortality tables have been constructed to predict with reasonable accuracy the number who will die in each age group. Since only a relatively few young wage earners will die during the year, the insurance principle can effectively be used to spread the risk of premature death among a large group of people. Many can pay a small sum to protect against the risk of premature death. These small sums from the many then go to make up larger sums paid to the beneficiaries of the few who die.

Life insurance has been used since ancient times as a protection against premature death. Following its use by the Chinese and Babylonians, it existed in both the Grecian and Roman civilizations. Medieval guilds owe their origin partly to an attempt by artisans to band together to protect against the risks of life. Following the collapse of the guild systems, Friendly Societies were formed to give security to their members. In the United States the first commercial company to write life insurance was the Insurance Company of North America, founded in 1794. This company later withdrew from writing life insurance, but is still in existence today as one of the outstanding fire, marine, and casualty insurance companies.[1] The sales of life insurance companies have grown gradually over the years until the industry has become one of the largest in the country. During the past century life insurance in force in the United States has grown from a little more than $130 million to more than $900 billion (1965). Although there was a slight drop in the volume of life insurance in force during the Great Depression, growth since then has been especially rapid. The volume has substantially more than doubled during the past decade. Table 6-1 shows the growth of the various types of insurance from 1950 to 1965.

[1] R. W. Osler and C. C. Robinson, *Guide to Life Insurance* (Indianapolis, The Rough Notes Co., 1954), pp. 182-190.

TABLE 6–1.   LIFE INSURANCE IN FORCE IN THE UNITED STATES
(IN MILLIONS)

Plan of Insurance	1950	1965
Ordinary life	$149,071	$497,630
Group life	47,793	306,113
Industrial life	33,415	39,818
Credit life (term)	3,889	56,993
Total	234,168	900,554

Source: 1966 Life Insurance Fact Book (New York: Institute of Life Insurance, 1966), p. 19. Reprinted by permission.

There are two major types of life insurance companies—stock and mutual companies. Stock insurance companies are organized the same way that most other corporations are in this country. The stockholders put capital into the organization, vote for the board of directors, and receive the profits earned by the company. Generally, stock insurance companies sell insurance at a fixed premium. Those that do permit the policyholders to participate in dividends charge a premium that will be the maximum cost of the insurance. Then they return dividends to the insured if sufficient income is earned. Mutual companies are owned by the policyholders, who vote for the board of directors and share the profits among themselves. Since there is no capital stock outstanding, mutual companies sometimes have a difficult time when first organized. To remedy this weakness, some companies have originally incorporated as private stock companies and later changed into mutuals. For most types of insurance, stock companies do the largest share of business. Only in life insurance do mutual sales exceed that of stock companies. Mutual companies do about 70 percent of the life insurance business in the country.[2]

TYPES OF INDIVIDUAL LIFE INSURANCE

TERM INSURANCE

Life insurance companies sell four main types of policies to individuals. These are term, straight life, limited payment life, and endowment insurance. Term insurance provides protection for a limited period of time only, most frequently one to five years. If the insured does not die within this period, the policy terminates, and no cash value or other payments are made

[2] Ibid., p. 120.

by the insurance company. Since insurance companies are insuring for only a relatively short period of time during periods of relatively low death rates, they are able to sell this type of insurance at a lower cost per dollar of insurance than any other type of life insurance. Because of the low costs of this type of insurance, many insurance analysts advocate that some term insurance be bought. The purpose of life insurance is to provide income for widows and children. A widow will need more income when she is rearing children than she will afterward. Term insurance can be purchased to protect during the years when the children are being reared. Part of the widow's income needs are temporary when the children are young, and it is suggested that the temporary type of insurance (term) be used under these circumstances. Another use of term insurance is to provide for a more adequate amount of protection until the insurer earns sufficient income to pay for other types of insurance.

Since insurance companies face a greater risk of the insured person dying as he grows older, term insurance becomes more and more expensive at higher ages. The fact that premiums become so high in later years is one of the reasons why other types of insurance are bought rather than just term insurance. In fact, most insurance companies will not sell term insurance after the age of 60 or 65, so that some other type of insurance must be resorted to. Some companies permit convertibility to other types of insurance without another physical examination. If additional insurance is needed when the term insurance expires, the convertible clause is a valuable one, although term rates are slightly higher with the convertible provision.

ORDINARY OR STRAIGHT LIFE INSURANCE

The type of insurance sold most frequently is ordinary or straight life insurance. Under this type of insurance, payments are regularly made throughout the life of the insured, and at death the beneficiaries collect. Ordinary life insurance has several advantages to commend it. For one thing, premiums are stable throughout the lifetime, whereas under term insurance they keep rising at each renewal. Second, the straight life policy has a nonforfeiture or cash surrender value. If at any time the payments become too heavy, it is possible to convert the ordinary life policy into a smaller paid-up policy, term insurance, or cash. Another advantage is that the insurance is permanent whereas term insurance is only temporary. Beneficiaries always collect from a straight life insurance policy but they may not under term insurance. Last, ordinary life insurance provides a source of loanable funds to those insured. Life insurance companies will lend to policyholders. Interest is charged on these loans. Whether the loan privilege is of value to policyholders depends on whether loans could be obtained elsewhere at a lower rate of interest.

LIMITED PAYMENT LIFE INSURANCE

A third type of insurance frequently sold is limited payment life. This type of insurance limits payments to a designated number of years. Usually the number of years is 20, but it may be 30 or some other number of years. Thereafter the policy is paid up and no further premiums are required. One obvious advantage of this type of insurance is that payments are terminated after premiums have been paid for the designated number of years. Payments may be completed at retirement age when a person has less income with which to pay insurance. Also there is little doubt that a person feels quite secure when he knows that he has a paid-up policy in his possession. The main disadvantage to 20-payment life policies is that premiums are higher than under ordinary life insurance. Quite naturally more has to be charged if premiums are paid for a limited number of years rather than for the entire life of an individual. It may be that the higher payments required may restrict the amount of insurance that can be bought. If the amount of insurance purchased is limited because of the higher premiums, there may be some question about the wisdom of purchasing the higher-priced policy.

ENDOWMENT INSURANCE

Endowment insurance provides that the beneficiaries receive the face value of the policy if the insured dies before a specified length of time. If the insured does not die within this length of time, then he receives the face value of the policy. Since the insurance company must part with cash earlier under endowments and is unable to earn money on this cash, endowments are the most expensive type of insurance. Generally they are bought in order to provide money for paying off mortgages, providing education for children, and the like. If one wishes to stress investment more and protection against dying less, endowments would be the logical choice of the type of insurance to buy. More criticism has been directed against endowments than the other three types of insurance. Critics point out that if investment is wanted, then other media of investment such as common stocks will provide a larger return. Some people, though, do find it difficult to save unless a systematic plan like endowments are presented to them, and for these people endowment policies may be a good buy.

COSTS OF INSURANCE

Table 6-2 shows the difference in prices for the main types of insurance. Rates charged by insurance companies vary considerably. In comparing the payments of straight life $1000 policies of 62 companies taken out at age 25,

TABLE 6–2. COMPARATIVE TABLE OF RATES FOR NONPARTICIPATING LIFE INSURANCE [a] (ANNUAL PREMIUM PER $1,000 INSURANCE FOR MALES) [b]

Age of Insured	Form of Contract				
	10-Year Term[c]	Ordinary Life	20-Payment Life	Paid up at 65	20-Year Endowment
25	$ 4.33	$12.76	$22.14	$14.98	$43.18
35	6.23	18.02	28.23	22.17	24.09
45	11.88	26.99	36.85	36.85	47.06
55	25.75	40.98	49.47	79.41	54.44

[a] This table does not show that the higher-priced types of insurance have a cash surrender value, which term insurance does not have.

[b] These rates are for standard risks. Substandard risks take higher rates, depending on the degree to which the insured is substandard.

[c] Minimum amount of $5,000, nonrenewable but convertible within 8 years.

Source: Unique Manual, 1966, The National Underwriter Company, p. 10. Reprinted by permission.

the net cost of the highest-priced company was almost 80 percent higher than the lowest-cost company. Twenty-payment life costs varied even more.[3]

INSURANCE PROGRAMMING

Many years ago, insurance was bought in a haphazard manner. An agent would approach a customer, and suggest that insurance be bought without regard to the individual needs of the client. Today, private insurance having become a big business, more scientific methods of analysis are being used. Insurance agents have now become well trained, and have been taught to analyze the individual needs of their clients. First of all, the income needs of the family must be estimated after their breadwinner has deceased. The income needs are highly individual and will vary greatly from family to family. A family with a mortgage on a house will need a larger income than one that has already completed payments on a house. To complete house payments some families take out mortgage insurance. This insurance is decreasing term insurance; that is, it provides for decreasing amounts to be paid over a period of years. Since principal payments are being made each year on the mortgage, over a period of years less insurance is needed to pay off the mortgage. The family may be buying furniture, and have other debts. Expenses during the last illness and burial costs must be met also. Since such expenses are not recurring, they may be covered by term insurance. The more regular expenses of the family will vary according to how many chil-

[3] William J. Matteson and H. C. Harwood, *Life Insurance and Annuities from the Buyer's Point of View* (Pittsfield, The Ben Franklin Press, 1958), pp. 59, 62.

dren there are in the family, and their ages. As children grow older, more income is needed to provide for them. The peak costs come during the late teens and early twenties if a college education is provided. Thereafter the children probably will be independent, and the income needs of the widow should be much less.

In insurance programming the income potentiality of the family must be considered. Some families are able to accumulate sufficient savings to make investments. Income should be available from these investments. The addition of survivors benefits under the Social Security program will provide an additional income. Here it must be remembered that payments are made to young widows only if they have children under 18 years of age or 22 years of age if they remain in school. The widow qualifies for a benefit when she reaches the age of 60, but there may be a period when no Social Security payments will be received. This "dead period" occurs after the children have reached 18 but before the widow has reached 60.

GROUP LIFE INSURANCE

Group life insurance originated much later than individual life insurance. Insurance was carried on the lives of slaves in the slave trade, but this type of insurance more closely resembled marine insurance on cargoes than life insurance. Several plans were written early in the twentieth century. The date usually given for the beginning of large-scale group life insurance was 1912, when Montgomery Ward signed a contract with the Equitable Life Assurance Society. This contract covered 2,912 employees for $5.9 million of insurance. Group life insurance has grown by leaps and bounds since its inception. The growth of group insurance has been particularly fast since 1950. Over four times as much group insurance has been written since 1950 than was in existence in that year.

Under the typical group life insurance contract, all members of a group are covered without a medical examination. If the employees pay for part of the insurance, they generally are given the option of whether to join. Here the insurance company faces the problem of adverse selection, that is, the poor insurance prospects are apt to take insurance and the good risks may not. The insurance companies protect themselves against adverse selection by requiring that 75 percent of eligible employees must agree to take the insurance. The minimum size of an eligible group has been reduced from 50 to 10. The maximum amount of insurance permitted per individual is limited by most companies according to the total amount of insurance in force. A contract of from $1 to $1½ million may permit a maximum policy of $15,000, whereas a $2.5 to $5 million policy may allow a maximum of $25,000.[4]

4 Davis W. Gregg, An Analysis of Group Life Insurance, 3rd ed. (Philadelphia, University of Pennsylvania Press, 1962), p. 30.

Group insurance has a number of advantages that account for its pro-digious growth.[5] The fact that eligibility is automatic is quite clearly an advantage to those who are unable to pass a physical examination. Also, insurance companies refuse to sell term insurance to individuals if certain occupations are engaged in. The Prudential Company, for example, lists over 600 occupations in some 200 industries which are ineligible for term insurance, yet in almost all of these industries group insurance is sold.[6] The insurance company is protected to some degree against poor risks since many plants require that a prospective employee take a physical examination be-fore being hired. Even if no physical examination is required, the fact that the employee is working is some indication of a reasonable amount of good health. If a person terminates his employment because of illness, the group life insurance policy does not cover the employee unless a special contractual provision calls for coverage. The fact that young people are entering employ-ment and old people leaving it helps the cost record if retired personnel are not covered under the plan. For all these reasons, mortality experience has demonstrated that the costs of death are no higher in group policies than they are for death under individual life insurance policies.

A second advantage of group insurance is that it is low-cost insurance. The fact that one policy is sold covering many people cuts selling costs. Administrative costs are also lower. Expenses of medical examinations are saved, along with the costs of individual inspection reports. Another reason for the low cost is that almost all group life insurance is issued on a renew-able term basis. As was already pointed out above, term insurance is the lowest-cost type of insurance. Since no cash values exist under this type of insurance, premiums can be lower. Group term insurance is even cheaper than individual term insurance since fewer selling costs and the other costs mentioned above are incurred. A third advantage of group life insurance is that it should tend to improve plant morale. The fact that the employer has agreed to undertake the purchase of insurance either at his own expense or even at some cost to the employees demonstrates that the welfare of the workers is being looked after.

Several disadvantages of group life insurance may be noted.[7] The first is that many workers complain about the temporary nature of the insurance. The fact that they do not obtain any benefits if they retire because of illness or old age has resulted in serious complaints about group insurance. It is true that group insurance does carry a conversion privilege, which permits the insured to convert to any other type of insurance except term insurance, without a physical examination. However, the cost of insurance is then computed from the present age of the insured rather than from when the group insurance was first taken out. Few workers exercise the conversion privilege. One study

[5] *Ibid.*, pp. 18-19.
[6] Philip Gordis, *How to Buy Insurance* (New York, Norton, 1947), p. 192.
[7] Gregg, *op. cit.*, pp. 22-23.

showed that only about 1.25 percent of the policies are converted into other types of insurance. The reasons for this low rate of conversion are not known. Perhaps the higher rates of converting are discouraging to the worker or perhaps the advantages of conversion or even the possibility of converting have not been explained. Since most workers do not convert, the objection still remains that group insurance provides temporary protection only. Many workers never receive any benefits from the temporary insurance. Some employers have attempted to meet this problem by covering workers even after retirement from the work force. Obviously, cost of the insurance rises if retired workers are covered. One actuarial study has shown that the net costs per month per $1,000 would increase from $0.60 to $1.42. Even though the costs are higher there has been a trend toward covering workers after retirement.

Another criticism of group insurance has come from insurance agents, who fear that group insurance may do away with their function. Many group contracts are negotiated by home office personnel of insurance companies, and thus the use of agents and their fees are eliminated. However, group insurance may make workers more insurance conscious and thus promote rather than hinder the sale of life insurance. Even with the rapid growth in group insurance, the sales on individual life policies have increased rapidly. It does not appear that group insurance will curtail the work of insurance agents. A more fundamental criticism of group insurance is that it fails to consider the individual needs of the workers. Insurance programming is not practiced under group insurance, and usually the same amounts of insurance are made available to everyone or possibly graduated according to income. This disadvantage of group insurance is of such considerable importance that probably group insurance will not replace the need for individual insurance. Group insurance still has a use because of its cheapness. It is valuable as a temporary insurance to protect against such risks as the loss of life when children must be supported. Also it can be used to pay off mortgages or other debts that have been incurred.

EVALUATION OF PRIVATE LIFE INSURANCE

In 1965 the head of the family was insured in 9 out of every 10 families in the United States that include husband, wife, and children under 18. Unfortunately, the lower-income groups have little or no insurance. More than one-third of the families in the United States with a husband, wife, and children under 18 having life insurance have less than $5,000 worth of policies.[8] The large number of small policies and the fewer large policies make averages almost meaningless, but for what it is worth, life insurance per family would amount to $14,700 per family in the United States in

[8] 1966 *Life Insurance Fact Book* (New York, Institute of Life Insurance, 1966), p. 9.

1965.[9] Thus, even if insurance were held equally by all families, which it is not, insurance would not cover as much as two years of income for the average family. At the present time, survivor's benefits under Social Security plus life insurance provide some security at the death of the breadwinner, but the amounts available are particularly small for lower-income families. It may be that a third line of security should be stressed more than it has been in the past. This line would be to channel more money into education, especially education for women at all levels but particularly at the college level. Statistics for 1964 show that 3.3 million boys were enrolled in college compared with 2.0 million girls.[10] Further education would be extremely valuable to women in case of the death of the breadwinner. Since education provides good security protection against premature death, it is recommended that more of our resources be channeled into education than we are now spending. Along with additional education, survivor's benefits under the Social Security Act and private life insurance should go a long way in meeting the problem of premature death.

Several other problems may be noted with life insurance. In order to pay future beneficiaries, the insurance companies must of necessity take in large sums of money. In 1965, $24.6 billion was collected in insurance company premiums. Income from investments and other income was $8.5 billion, to make a total income of more than $33 billion. During the same year, life insurance benefits payments were only slightly over one-half of this income and expenses including taxes only 21 percent of the premium dollar. Insurance companies have for years been taking in more money than they have been paying out. Their total assets in 1965 were almost $159 billion dollars. In the four years following World War II, 20 percent of total personal savings went to private insurance organizations; this percentage was double that of 1910–1913.[11]

The insurance companies have invested their funds in the following manner: 7 percent in government securities, 6 percent in stocks, 37 percent in obligations of business and industry (mostly bonds); 38 percent in mortgages, 5 percent in loans to policyholders, 3 percent in real estate, and the rest in miscellaneous assets.[12]

Insurance companies have large sums of money to invest, and the channeling of these funds into productive resources has aided immensely in the growth of the American economy. One problem with life insurance investment is that the funds have been invested in the most conservative types of securities. Insurance companies' investment in common stock is limited by government regulation, and this means that insurance companies have not

[9] Ibid., p. 5.

[10] The World Almanac, 1966, p. 732.

[11] David McCahan, ed., Investment of Life Insurance Funds (Philadelphia, University of Pennsylvania Press, 1953), p. 54.

[12] 1966 Life Insurance Fact Book, p. 63.

been able to invest on a large scale in the type of securities that appreciate in value with inflation. Consequently, inflation is a serious problem to insurance companies. Not only are beneficiaries hurt by having the value of their policies reduced by higher prices but insurance company assets fail to appreciate in value since they are invested mainly in types of securities that rise only slowly as the cost of living rises. Recent amendments to state laws have been liberalized to permit insurance companies to invest more heavily in common stocks. As of 1965, $9 billion of their almost $159 billion of assets were invested in common stock.[13] One of the major problems of investing in common stocks is that some criticism may be made against the possible voting control of corporations by insurance companies. In their own right the insurance companies are already the largest corporations in America. Many people would look with concern on their control of productive facilities.

Another problem of life insurance concerns the ability to invest the savings of Americans wisely. About one-fifth of all personal savings in the United States has been channeled to life insurance companies. In the past, investment of such sums in corporate bonds, mortgages, and other securities has aided immensely in the growth of the American economy. Savings are crucial to the growth of an economy, and insurance companies have been able to aid in the process of capital formation by supplying the funds collected from buyers of insurance. To date, it must be concluded that insurance companies have made a major contribution to the growth of the United States by channeling savings into productive outlets.

ANNUITIES

Annuities provide protection just opposite to that of life insurance. They protect against the risk of living too long rather than dying too soon. The term "annuity" itself means an annual payment, but as applied to insurance, it means payments after a certain age has been reached. Annuities were slow to grow in the United States. In 1866, annuity premiums were only one-tenth of 1 percent as large as life insurance premiums. In 1920, they were scarcely 1 percent. The great impetus to annuities came during the Great Depression of the 1930's. At that time, many stocks and bonds lost much of their value. The fact that few insurance companies failed and that a guaranteed return was assured in annuities made for increased purchases of annuities on a large scale. More annuity premiums were collected in 1935 than during the 62-year period from 1855 through 1927.[14] From 1935 through 1962, the income from annuities to United States life insurance

    [13] Ibid.
    [14] Michael H. Levy, Your Insurance (New York, Harcourt, Brace & World, 1953), p. 39.

companies increased almost fivefold. By 1965 annuity premiums had risen to 14 percent of life insurance premiums.[15]

INDIVIDUAL ANNUITIES

Annuities have other advantages besides the safety of investment. If a person aged 65 needs an additional $35 a month income, this amount can be obtained by the purchase of a $5,000 annuity. The same amount of money invested elsewhere at 3 percent would bring in only $12.50 per month. Another advantage is that the annuity guarantees an income for life. If a $10,000 annuity were purchased at age 65, payments from the life insurance company would total $820 a year. If the same amount of money were invested at 3.5 percent and withdrawn at a rate of $820 a year, at age 79 the reserves would be wiped out, and no further income would be available.[16] In order to have some savings left at death and to protect against inflation, one authority recommends that part of a person's assets be placed in a straight life annuity and part in common stocks.[17]

GROUP ANNUITIES AND SELF-ADMINISTERED PENSION PLANS

When it was mentioned above that the sale of annuities had increased greatly since the 1930's no breakdown was made on the type of annuities sold. Actually there has been a tapering off in the sale of individual annuities, but group annuities financed through life insurance continue to grow. Although the first group annuity policy was written as late as 1921 by the Metropolitan Life Insurance Company,[18] at the end of 1965, 5.8 million workers were covered under pension plans financed through life insurance companies.[19] Under such plans corporations agree to install a pension system for their workers by paying insurance companies for annuities. The alternative to having an insurance company administered program is to have a corporation administer a program of it own.

Although group annuity programs have grown fast, self-administered pension programs have grown even faster, so that by 1963, 18.4 million persons were covered under noninsured private pension plans.[20] The depression of the 1930's demonstrated to employers the need for some kind of retirement income for their workers. Layoffs were a necessity, and employers realized that the economic security of a sort for their older workers could

[15] *1966 Life Insurance Fact Book*, p. 50.
[16] Gordis, *op. cit.*, pp. 238-240.
[17] Matteson and Harwood, *op. cit.*, pp. 88-90.
[18] Kenneth Black, Jr., *Group Annuities* (Philadelphia, University of Pennsylvania Press, 1955), p. 9.
[19] *1966 Life Insurance Fact Book*, p. 33.
[20] Alfred M. Skolnik, "Employee-Benefit Plans: Developments, 1954–1963," *Social Security Bulletin*, Vol. 28, No. 4 (April, 1965), p. 11.

only come about with some sort of pension plan. World War II provided further impetus to annuity and pension plans when it was ruled that wages would be frozen but that certain fringe benefits such as pensions would be permitted. Also during World War II, the excess profits tax was so high that a pension system could be inaugurated out of profits at a very small net cost. After World War II, the failure to expand benefits under the OASDHI program caused labor unions to attempt to obtain larger pensions through collective bargaining. They were helped along in this respect by a National Labor Relations Board decision of 1948 in the Inland Steel Case. The National Labor Relations Board ruled that employers must bargain on pensions.

In obtaining funds to finance a pension program, either the employer may bear the entire costs himself (noncontributory) or the employees may help pay (contributory). Arguments in favor of having employees share the cost are that the additional income from the workers should enable larger pensions to be paid. Also the workers will have more of an interest in the program if they themselves participate in the financing of it. They are more apt to recognize the cost factor in increasing benefits and thus keep benefits within reasonable limits. Arguments in favor of noncontributory pensions are that workers pay for them anyway in lieu of an increase in wages. Second, the employer may have a freer hand in administering the program if he bears the entire cost. Also of importance is the fact that the employer's payments are deductible as a business cost whereas workers' payments are not.[21] Seventy-five percent of all group annuity plans were financed by joint-employer-employee contributions.[22] Later revisions of plans have found less employee contributions.[23]

About 40 life insurance companies now write group annuities although 95 percent of the premiums are received by seven large companies.[24] Table 6-3 shows types of pension plans in the United States administered by life insurance companies. As can be seen from the table, the two major types of group annuity are the deferred annuity and deposit administration. The term "deferred" is used because payments to the beneficiary are not made immediately but are delayed until the beneficiary reaches a certain age. Under this type of annuity, the insurance company purchases a unit of deferred annuity each time a premium is received. The unit purchased is equal to a percentage of the employee's salary, usually 1.5 to 2 percent. For

[21] Dan McGill, *Fundamentals of Private Pensions* (Homewood, Ill., Irwin, 1955), pp. 65-66.

[22] Weltha Van Eenam and Martha E. Penman, "Analysis of 346 Group Annuities Underwritten in 1946–1950," Actuarial Study No. 32, Washington, D.C., Federal Security Agency, Social Security Administration, Division of the Actuary (October, 1952), p. 5.

[23] Weltha Van Eenam and Martha E. Penman, "Analysis of 157 Group Annuity Plans Amended in 1950–54," Actuarial Study No. 44, Washington, D.C., U.S. Department of Health, Education, and Welfare, Social Security Administration, Division of the Actuary (July, 1956), p. 15.

[24] Black, *op. cit.*, p. 5.

example, a life insurance company would collect $80 annually in premiums on a worker earning $4,000 if a 2 percent rate is levied. Since it is known how large a premium will be received from each salary, the exact amount of pension to be paid can be computed. Generally the pension varies according to salary and length of service although a few companies pay a flat amount to each worker. Because of the uncertainty of knowing the worker's final salary, payments are generally based on the worker's average salary over the years rather than his final salary. If the worker's salary increases over the years to qualify him for a larger pension, a separate premium is computed to pay for the larger benefits. If an employee terminates his employment or dies before retirement under a contributory program, he or his beneficiaries will receive back that part he has contributed plus interest.

TABLE 6–3. PENSION PLANS IN THE UNITED STATES INSURED WITH LIFE INSURANCE COMPANIES

In Force at End of Year	Group Annuities		Individual Policy Pension Trusts	Other Plans	Total
	Deferred Annuity	Deposit Adminis- tration			
1940:					
Number of plans	770	20	440	315	1,545
Persons covered	575,000	65,000	15,000	40,000	695,000
1965:					
Number of plans	7,980	7,700	43,580	7,000	66,260
Persons covered	2,275,000	3,410,000	795,000	560,000	7,040,000

Source: 1966 Life Insurance Fact Book (New York: Institute of Life Insurance, 1966), p. 36. Reprinted by permission.

The largest type of annuity plan used in conjunction with insurance companies is called deposit administration. In 1940, almost nine times as many persons were covered under deferred annuities as under deposit administration plans, but the latter have grown quite rapidly in recent years, and today more persons are enrolled under deposit administration plans than under deferred annuities. Under a deferred annuity plan the insurance companies buy an annuity for specific employees as soon as they receive a premium. Under a deposit administration program, all the money received by insurance companies is placed in a common fund, and an annuity is not purchased for an individual worker until he retires or at the time of vesting (paying the worker the employer's contribution if the employee leaves the company). Deposit administration plans allow the employer maximum flexibility in funding the plan. The employer may suspend premium payments for a time, or he may reduce or increase contribution within the limits set by insurance companies' underwriting rules. It is admissible for insurance companies to insist on sufficient premiums to approximate future requirements. In many cases they designate maximum or minimum practicable deposits. Under deposit administration plans, the insurance company cannot guarantee an exact pension until the annuity is bought at the time of the retirement of the worker.

Deposit administration plans may help an employer with little income to start a program by providing for small payments originally. A major reason for the growth of deposit administration plans was the competition of industrial companies carrying their own insurance and using banks as trustees. Deposit administration does provide more flexibility to companies in financing their annuity program. The major disadvantage of deposit administration is that the program may be seriously underfunded. One critic of deposit administration maintains that such plans tend to undermine the good name of insurance companies. Insurance companies lend their good name to such annuities, but cannot guarantee that specific payments will be made. In case of default by the company insuring its employees, some criticism may be directed at insurance companies. It is possible that deposit administration plans can be as fully funded as deferred annuities and thus be as secure, but there is more danger of underfunding and possibly even collapse of the whole program, especially during a recession.[25]

SELF-ADMINISTERED PLANS

There are more than three times as many employees covered under self-administered plans as under plans administered by life insurance companies. The probable reason is that corporations are attempting to save money by handling pensions themselves. Thus they save selling commissions. Another saving comes from the fact that insurance companies must pay taxes on their premium income, whereas the money set aside as pension reserves by corporations is nontaxable. These are the two main expenses saved under self-administered plans. Insurance companies have other expenses of administering the program, but these are offset by expenses under the self-administered plans. If reserves are accumulated under self-administered plans, the funds are generally held by a trustee who charges fees for services rendered. If individuals outside the firm are chosen as trustees, labor unions have designated the trustees either with or without the employer in 28 percent of pension plans studied in New York in 1955. If the trustee is a bank, labor unions rarely participate in the choosing of the trustee.[26] Actuaries must also be paid to advise the companies on costs of the program. Generally companies do save some expense by self-administering their program, but the

[25] *Ibid.*, p. 215.
[26] Victor L. Andrews, "Interest at Stake in the Investment of Pension Funds," *Monthly Labor Review,* Vol. 82, No. 7 (July, 1959), p. 755.

pension may not be as safe as it would be if handled by insurance companies.

Self-administered pension plans may be classified into pattern plans and conventional plans. Under the former the same pension is paid to everyone unless modified by seniority, whereas under conventional plans the pensions vary with the past pay of workers. In a study of 201 plans employing more than 5.5 million workers it was found that 76 percent of the plans were of the conventional type. Only this type of plan will be discussed below.

The conventional type of program may be financed without reserves on a pay-as-you-go basis. As pensions become due, the company pays them as current expenses. Terminal funding is another method of financing, whereby the company sets aside enough reserves to pay for an annuity at the time the employee retires. Advance funding requires that the company set aside reserves immediately. Generally, under advance funding enough reserves are set aside to pay for benefits credited during that year plus a certain percentage of the initial past-service liability. After all past-liability reserves have been accumulated, the company would need only to accumulate reserves for benefits credited during the year.

One advantage of advance funding is that the pension fund is more secure when reserves are available. In addition, accumulation of reserves provides that the program can be vested, and certain payments made to workers that otherwise would not be available.[27] Because of these advantages, most self-administered plans provide for advance funding. Only 3 percent of pattern plans and 2 percent of conventional self-administered plans are unfunded.[28]

In 1965, the President's Committee on Corporate Pension Funds objected to underfunding of some current pension plans. It recommended that to obtain Federal tax advantages now in existence plans with stated benefits should be required to fund fully all current service liabilities and to amortise fully all accrued liabilities. Some persons, however, including George Meany, President of the AFL-CIO, fear that full funding may place heavy burdens on existing plans and discourage the spread of new plans in the future.[29]

Under a contributory self-administered plan, the worker will at least receive back his contribution if he terminates his employment before retiring. Prior to 1952, few plans called for vesting, which gives the employee the right to terminate his employment before retirement without forfeiting the accrued pension resulting from the employer's contribution. By 1965, almost all plans had some form of vesting. The most typical vesting clause provides that a worker who completes a certain number of years of service and reaches

---

[27] McGill, *op. cit.*, pp. 130-133.

[28] *A Study of Industrial Pension Plans* (New York, Bankers Trust Company, 1965), Tables 25 and 26, p. 30.

[29] President's Committee on Corporate Pension Funds and Other Private Retirement and Welfare Programs, *Public Policy and Private Pension Programs: A Report to the President on Private Employee Retirement Plans*, Washington, D.C., Government Printing Office, Appendix D (1965), pp. 12-19.

a certain age earns the right to carry all his accumulated pension benefits with him if he terminates before retirement age.[30]

EVALUATION OF PRIVATE PENSIONS PLANS

Protection of loss of income at old age is now provided from three sources: government social security payments, private pension plans, and individual savings. Our society must determine how much reliance should be placed on each one of these three. Individual savings cannot be safely relied upon, because people in all but the highest income brackets are unable to save much. The viewpoint expressed here is that government payments should be made to carry a larger share of the burden.

The major disadvantage of relying on private pensions is that not all our workers are covered under them. For those workers who happen to be represented by strong labor unions or who happen to work for employers who have pension systems, pension benefits plus social security are now approaching an adequate minimum. In early 1963, private pensions payable at age 65 to workers with average annual earnings of $4,800 averaged about $63 a month for those with 20 years of service and $89 for 30 years of service, exclusive of Social Security. But those who are not so fortunate to be under a private pension program must struggle along on inadequate Social Security benefits. If adequate pensions are to be provided for all workers, the government will have to increase benefits under Social Security.

Those opposed to raising Social Security benefits feel that such benefits weaken the individual's financial, moral, and spiritual fibers. Since the will of the American people to provide for their own old age should not be weakened, it is suggested that Social Security payments be kept at a minimum and reliance be placed upon the two private sources of pension income —either private pension plans or individual savings.[31]

A disadvantage of too heavy a reliance on private pension plans is that many workers never remain long enough with an employer to qualify for a pension. In a census study it was shown that only 51 percent of male workers and 29 percent of female workers had been with their company for 11 or more years.[32] If eligibility requirements are set at 11 years, and some are that high, then that many fewer workers can obtain pensions. To the extent that pension rights are vested or that reciprocal arrangements are made to cover workers, there is less of a disadvantage here. In order to encourage more vesting, the President's Committee on Corporate Pension Funds in

[30] The 1965 Bankers Trust Company study reported that 94 percent of pattern plans and 97 percent of conventional plans call for some kind of vesting. *Op. cit.*, pp. 19-20.

[31] McGill, *op. cit.*, p. 44.

[32] "Experience of Workers at their Current Jobs, January, 1951," Series P. 50, No. 36, Washington, D.C., U.S. Department of Commerce, Bureau of the Census (December 5, 1951), Table I.

1965 recommended that the Internal Revenue Code be amended to require vesting of a pension plan before favored tax treatment is received. Specifically, the committee recommended that vesting begin after 15 years of service on a partial basis and that full vesting be required after 20 years of service. In reviewing this recommendation, a majority of the Advisory Committee on Labor-Management Relations felt that it would be unwise to require minimum vesting requirements for tax approval. The majority of this group stated that the added costs of vesting might result in lowering benefits or reducing the coverage of workers.[33]

Some have pointed out that private pension plans may also be detrimental in slowing down the mobility of labor. The impact of pension plans on mobility cannot be easily measured since so many other factors affect mobility as well. Seniority in layoff, chances for promotion with seniority, and longer vacations with pay are factors a worker must consider before moving. Furthermore, a worker who is familiar with his job and working conditions and has home and community attachments is reluctant to leave. The fact that the mobility of our younger workers is considerable would seem to indicate that pensions and other benefits are not unduly restricting the mobility of labor. The overall turnover figure in manufacturing in this country in 1965 was 4 percent per month.[34] This average figure conceals the higher turnover of young workers and the lower turnover of older workers. Yet it does show a relatively high degree of labor turnover. However, even with this high degree of turnover, it is probably true that private pensions slow the mobility of older workers. This problem would be alleviated if pension plans were vested and if pension credits would be transferable when an employee moved from one employer to another.

Of more importance is the problem that pension plans make employers reluctant to hire older workers. Financially it would not pay employers to hire workers at 64, only to have them retire a year later on a pension. Employers do protect themselves somewhat on this score by requiring that a number of years be worked before becoming eligible for a pension. Or perhaps an age limit may be set at the time of hiring above which a worker may not qualify for a pension. Another possibility would be to reduce the old-age benefits to those hired late in life.[35] Another suggestion is to reduce the Social Security taxes on employees hired late in life.[36]

Another area in which industrial benefits do not measure up to Social Security benefits is in the paying of survivors' benefits. These are paid with much more regularity under Social Security than under private pension plans. In certain other countries, such as the Netherlands and the Scandi-

[33] *A Report to the President on Private Employee Retirement Plans,* pp. 3-6.

[34] *Monthly Labor Review,* Vol. 89 (1966), Table B-1, p. 570.

[35] Stephen Raushenbush, *Pensions in Our Economy* (Washington, D.C., The Public Affairs Institute, 1955), p. 62.

[36] Elizabeth Brandeis, "What Road Is Forward in Social Security?," in T. C. Mc-Cormick, *Problems in the Post War World* (New York, McGraw-Hill, 1945), p. 75.

navian countries, private pension plans that do not provide widows and orphans benefits are not looked upon as satisfactory plans.[37]

In 1964 the total amount of investment in private retirement funds was over $75 billion, and this figure is expected to grow to $225 billion by 1980. In 1964 about half the investment of noninsured corporate pension funds were being placed in common stock. A problem here is whether larger amounts invested in common stocks may not give increasing power to those controlling pension funds. Although labor unions have used their voting power in several instances, mainly they have been disinterested in exercising voting control on pension investments. Most of the pension money has been channeled through bank trustees. Bank trustees have been reluctant to attempt to control corporations via stock ownership since their primary task is investment rather than the management of corporations. New York banks rarely own more than 3 percent of any common stocks. Although discounting any present danger in control of common stocks, one author suggested that a federal Welfare and Pension Plans Disclosure Act might be passed to require disclosure of any funds that held more than, for example, 10 percent of the voting stock of a corporation.[38] Congress did pass a Welfare and Pension Plans Disclosure Act in 1958 to reduce the mishandling of pension funds, but the act exempted disclosure of stocks traded on the New York Stock Exchange.

Another problem with pension funds is that the reserves will be invested in high-grade bonds and stocks and thus favor more capital formation among the larger companies. However, such investment should free other funds for investment in less safe stocks and bonds. In addition, trustees of pension funds have been alert to the advantages of investing in higher-paying issues. Offsetting the possible disadvantage of too much concentration is the advantage that pension funds are now providing a source of equity capital.[39] At least to the present time, reserve funds available for investment have enabled our economy to grow.

Summary

Social Security payments provide only a $197 maximum per month to a widowed mother and three or more children. Since many men desire a larger

[37] John K. Dyer, "Comparison of American and Foreign Pension Planning," in McGill, *op. cit.*, pp. 199-200.

[38] Robert Tilove, *Pension Funds and Economic Freedom* (New York, The Fund for the Republic, 1959), p. 85.

[39] Victor L. Andrews, "Pension Funds in the Securities Markets," *Harvard Business Review*, Vol. 37, No. 6 (November-December, 1959), p. 102.

income than this for their family, many men take out life insurance policies. There are several different types of life insurance, such as term insurance, endowments, and the like. The advantages and disadvantages of each must be analyzed to determine the best buy for each individual person. In recent years insurance programming has been adopted to fit the needs of insurance to the individual person. Many corporations also provide life insurance for their employees through group life insurance policies. Although group policies are cheaper than individual life policies, they do have a major disadvantage of not tailoring the policy to the needs of the particular individual. In recent years life insurance sales have grown by leaps and bounds, but it is mostly wealthier individuals who have adequate amounts of insurance. The typical family has insufficient insurance to provide for more than a year to two of additional income. To provide adequate defense against the exigency of the death of the breadwinner, it is suggested that protection be provided along several fronts. Adequate Social Security payments plus adequate life insurance plus adequate education of the widow should provide ample protection against the danger of premature death. Unfortunately, many of our people, especially in the lower income brackets, do not have adequate protection now.

Many individuals buy private annuities, which enables them to supplement their income in their old age. The largest number of private pensions are provided in this country through self-administered corporate pension plans followed next by corporate pensions administered by life insurance companies and lastly by annuities purchased by individuals. Such pensions supplement the payments provided by Social Security. Persons having such pensions have considerably more income than those who do not have them. The result has been that some of our aged have a much larger income at retirement than others. As yet the people of the United States have been unable to devise a plan whereby all the aged have an adequate income.

Bibliography

Altmeyer, Arthur, *Formative Years of Social Security* (Madison, Wisc., University of Wisconsin Press, 1966).

Black, Kenneth, Jr., *Life Insurance*, 6th ed. (New York, Appleton-Century-Crofts, 1966).

Blanchard, Fessenden S., *Making the Most of Your Retirement* (New York, Doubleday, 1963).

Burgess, Ernest W., *Aging in Western Societies* (Chicago, University of Chicago Press, 1960).

Cumming, Elaine, and William E. Henry, *Growing Old* (New York, Basic Books, 1961).

Finestone, Samuel, and others, *Social Casework and Blindness* (New York, American Foundation for the Blind, 1960).

Gregg, Davis, W., *An Analysis of Group Life Insurance*, 3rd ed. (Philadelphia, University of Pennsylvania Press, 1962).

Kammerer, Gladys, *British and American Child Welfare Services* (Detroit, Wayne State University Press, 1963).

Kreps, Juanita, ed., *Employment, Income and Retirement Problems of the Aged* (Durham, Duke University Press, 1963).

Leads, Morton, *The Aged, Social Work, and the Community* (Cleveland, Allen, 1961).

McGill, Dan M., *Fundamentals of Private Pensions*, 2nd ed. (Homewood, Ill., Irwin, 1964).

Melone, Joseph J., *Collectively Bargained Multi-Employer Pension Plans* (Homewood, Ill., Irwin, 1963).

National Council on Aging, *Centers for Older People* (New York, National Council on Aging, 1962).

Orbach, Harold L., and Clark Tibbitts, eds., *Aging and the Economy* (Ann Arbor, Mich., University of Michigan Press, 1963).

Patterson, Edwin W., *Legal Protection of Private Pension Expectations* (Homewood, Ill., Irwin, 1960).

Pollak, Otto, *Positive Experiences in Retirement* (Homewood, Ill., Irwin, 1957).

———, *The Social Aspects of Retirement* (Homewood, Ill., Irwin, 1956).

Rose, Arnold, ed., *Aging in Minnesota* (Minneapolis, Minn., University of Minnesota Press, 1963).

Williams, Richard H., Clark Tibbitts, and Wilma Donahue, eds., *Processes of Aging* (New York, Atherton, 1963).

Witte, Edwin E., *The Development of the Social Security Act* (Madison, Wisc., University of Wisconsin Press, 1962).

PROBLEMS OF DISABILITY AND HEALTH

CHAPTER 7

THE PROBLEM OF
OCCUPATIONAL DISABILITY

NUMBER OF WORK INJURIES

The number of industrial injuries in the United States is far larger than most people would suspect. Table 7-1 shows that over 2 million workmen receive disabling injuries each year. Of these a relatively small number are of such a serious nature as to cause death or permanent disability; yet in total the more serious injuries do loom large and in many cases result in serious economic difficulties for the recipients and their families.

TABLE 7–1. ESTIMATED NUMBER OF DISABLING WORK INJURIES, ALL
INDUSTRIES, 1940–1964

Year	Temporary Total Disabilities	Permanent Disabilities	Injuries Resulting in Death	All Disabling Injuries
1940	1,782,000	89,600[a]	18,100	1,889,700
1945	1,913,900	89,900	16,500	2,020,300
1950	1,851,600	84,900	15,500	1,952,000
1955	1,834,000	81,800	14,200	1,930,000
1960	1,854,000	82,200	13,800	1,950,000
1964	1,950,000	85,800	14,200	2,050,000

[a] Partial disabilities only.
Sources: Handbook of Labor Statistics, 1950, Bulletin 1016, U.S. Department of Labor, Bureau of Labor Statistics, Table G–2, p. 178. Monthly Labor Review, Vol. 79 (1956), p. 439; Vol. 85 (1962), p. 410; Vol. 88 (1965), p. 419.

According to one student, of 62 million going to work on any one day, 62 workers will be killed, 350 more will suffer some permanent injury, and 7,600 will suffer injuries which will cause them to miss work an average of 18 days.[1] The number of industrial injuries far exceeds losses due to war.

[1] Put another way, one American worker will be killed or permanently injured every 3 minutes and another will be injured every 11 seconds. Almost twice as many injuries occur in homes as at work, and about the same number of public nonmotor vehicle accidents occur after working hours as accidents at work. Forty-three percent more occupational accidents occur than motor vehicle accidents. See Harold M. Somers and Anne R. Somers, Workmen's Compensation (New York: Wiley, 1954), pp. 1-2.

Fewer American workers were killed in World War I than lost their lives in industry during the same period of time. During the second decade of the twentieth century more loss of life and limbs occurred in industrial accidents than in all the wars to that time.[2] During World War II, more amputations occurred from occupational accidents than in the Armed Services for a comparable period.[3]

FREQUENCY AND SEVERITY RATES

A concept of "frequency rate" has been developed to determine the number of accidents per man-hour worked. The frequency rate measures the number of injuries per one million man-hours worked.[4] Table 7-2 shows that the number of injuries varies greatly depending on the industry involved. The underground coal mining industry for example had many more times as many and more severe injuries than the communications industry. Also of importance in analyzing industrial accidents is the concept of "severity rate." The severity rate is defined as the number of days lost through occupational injuries per 1,000,000 employee-hours worked.

TABLE 7–2.   INJURY RATES FOR SELECTED INDUSTRIES, 1965

Industry	Frequency Rate [a]	Severity Rate [b]
Communications	1.19	71
Textiles	4.30	340
Wood products	13.09	968
Underground coal mining	36.71	7,542
All industries	6.53	516[c]

[a] Number of injuries per one million man-hours worked.
[b] Number of days lost through injuries per one thousand man-hours worked.
[c] 1964.
Source: *Accident Facts, 1966,* National Safety Council, p. 26.

[2] E. H. Downey, *Workmen's Compensation* (New York, Macmillan, 1924), p. 1.
[3] *Building America's Health,* President's Commission on the Health Needs of the Nation, Washington, D.C., Government Printing Office, Vol. II (1952), p. 77.
[4] The following example from Turnbull, Williams, and Cheit clearly explains the concept of "frequency" rate.

$$\text{Frequency rate} = \frac{\text{Number of disabling injuries} \times 1,000,000}{\text{Employee-hours of exposure}}$$

Thus, if a small manufacturing firm that employed, say, 250 workers for a regular work year of 2,000 hours each, and had six disabling accidents, its accident frequency rate would be $\frac{6 \times 1,000,000}{500,000}$ or 12. See John Turnbull, C. Arthur Williams, and Earl F. Cheit, *Economic and Social Security,* 3rd ed. (New York, Ronald, 1967), p. 302, fn. 3.

COSTS OF INDUSTRIAL INJURIES

Accidents occur more frequently among the young and middle-aged than the aged. This means a curtailment of many years of productive labor for those injured early in life. Accidents also tend to occur more frequently among lower-income wage earners because of the type of work involved. Usually those injured tend to have a larger number of dependents than others in our society.[5]

The economic burden of industrial accidents and diseases lies partly on workers, partly on employers, and partly on society in general. Although workers are partially compensated for losses due to industrial accidents and diseases, much of the economic burden still lies directly on them. The State of Illinois estimated in 1951 that only 13 percent of gross wage loss due to accidents was compensated for. Several other studies show a loss of from $500 million to $1.2 billion, which was not compensated for.[6]

A serious accident may change the income level of the injured worker and his dependents radically over the rest of their lives. Employers, too, are faced with heavy costs due to industrial accidents. They must pay the premium costs for workmen's compensation insurance. In 1963–1964 the cash and medical benefits paid to those injured came to $1.7 billion.[7] These figures do not include the administrative costs of private insurance companies and self-insurers. Also, sums must be paid for damages under employers' liability actions. Indirect costs to employers include loss of time by experienced workers and damage to machinery and other property. Estimates show that the indirect cost is several times that of the direct cost. Lastly, society as a whole suffers from the losses both to employers and employees, and must pay some of the costs of caring for impoverished families, court costs, and costs of administering a program for the injured.[8]

OCCUPATIONAL DISEASES

Some industries are not only faced with an accident problem but must contend with occupational diseases as well. Although less than 3 percent of all compensable disabilities are due to occupational diseases, nonetheless about 60,000 such disabilities occur per year.[9] In specific industries the incidence of such disabilities may be quite high, whereas other industries have little or no problem of this nature. In the past occupational diseases took an extreme toll of lives in a few industries. Lead poisoning was particularly

---

[5] Somers and Somers, op. cit., p. 10.
[6] Ibid., pp. 11-12.
[7] Social Security Bulletin, Annual Statistical Supplement (1964), Table 6, p. 5.
[8] Somers and Somers, op. cit., pp. 9-15.
[9] For a more detailed analysis of occupational diseases, from which the material in this paragraph was obtained, see ibid., pp. 214-225.

common in the following industries: lead smelting, lead refining, white-lead production, painting, enameling sanitary ware, making and installing plumbers' ware, printing, and pottery glazing. Lead poisoning resulted in some workers' contracting "painter's colic" or "plumbism," which frequently resulted in paralysis, delirium, dementia, and blindness. Some industries no longer use lead, and in others effective means of control have been developed. In a few newer industries, lead poisoning exists, but it has been brought under fairly effective control.[10] Similarly, radium poisoning has been effectively controlled. Radium poisoning was caused from applying luminous painting on watches that resulted in pernicious anemia, cancer, and 41 deaths in one New Jersey watch factory. In the late forties, beryllium, a metallic element used in the manufacture of fluorescent, neon, and other lights, caused several hundred cases of severe lung diseases and some deaths. To remedy this occupational disease, another element was substituted for beryllium.[11] Although a number of occupational diseases have been eradicated, industrial hygiene is still attempting to control such pulmonary and bronchial disabilities as silicosis, pneumoconiosis, and other diseases caused by dust. Similarly, diseases due to repeated motion, pressure, shock, and extreme temperatures are still numerous. Some new products such as petroleum and benzene compounds used in the manufacture of synthetic rubber have caused recent occupational diseases as have powerful new insecticides like parathion. Loss of hearing from undue noise still remains an occupational hazard, and X-ray and atomic radiation have given us new occupational disease problems to solve.[12] Table 7-3 shows the types of occupational diseases recorded in Illinois in a recent year.

INDUSTRIAL SAFETY AND HYGIENE

Toward the end of the nineteenth century, the growth of large-scale business tended to depersonalize production. Entrepreneurs no longer knew workers personally nor cared as much for their well-being. The heavy immigration at that time also resulted in even more depersonalization of the work force. These factors coupled with the increased mechanization of industry, the long work day, and child labor resulted in an extremely high accident rate. In one year, ending June 30, 1907, 4,534 workers were killed in the railroad industry alone, and in the same year 2,534 men also lost their lives in the bituminous coal industry.[13] With the high cost of both industrial accidents and diseases, it was inevitable that sooner or later society would attempt to improve the wretched conditions. Both the number of accidents

10 *Ibid.*, pp. 214-215.
11 *Ibid.*, p. 215.
12 *Ibid.*, pp. 223-224.
13 *Ibid.*, p. 9.

TABLE 7–3. OCCUPATIONAL DISEASE INJURIES REPORTED IN ILLINOIS, 1963

Diseases	Number of Injuries	Number of Fatal Injuries
Diseases due to chemical agents (lead, arsenic, cadmium, etc.)	18	0
Lung diseases due to dust (asbestosis, silicosis, tuberculosis)	27	4
Respiratory disorders (except pneumoconiosis)	23	3
Infectious and parasitic diseases (brucellosis, pulmonary tuberculosis)	20	0
Disorders due to physical conditions (motion, pressure, shock)	4	0
Miscellaneous (cancer, heart, sun radiation)	3	0
Dermatoses	234	0
Other diseases	12	0
All occupational disease injuries	341	7

Source: Annual Report: Compensable Work Injuries Reported, Part 1 (1963), Illinois Department of Labor, Table 21, p. A-50.

and their severity have decreased since the early years of the twentieth century although since 1940 the number of accidents but not their severity has increased slightly.

NATIONAL SAFETY COUNCIL

Several groups have been instrumental in reducing accidents in this country. Some employers were interested in reducing the number of accidents, and out of this interest grew the field of safety engineering. The National Safety Council was formed in 1913 by 14 young safety engineers from private industry and government. The National Safety Council has since expanded to a membership of 8,200 organizations, among which are the largest corporations of the country.[14] The National Safety Council originally dealt only with industrial accidents, but in 1915 its scope was broadened to include the prevention of accidents of all kinds, on the streets and highways, among school children, as well as in the home. The council publishes six monthly magazines dealing with various aspects of safety, and turns out safety posters, rule books, and other literature on safety. Its library has the most comprehensive collection on problems of safety, and its safety engineers attempt to answer all questions on safety. Due to budget restrictions its

14 Ibid.

services are limited primarily to members.[15] After the causal factors have been found, a number of safety techniques have been recommended to reduce the number of accidents. Some of these techniques are: demonstrations, motion pictures, posters, safety competition between groups, rewards, continuous education, and strict enforcement of safety rules.

Automatic machinery has reduced the number of accidents. Automatic machinery with push-button control eliminates hazardous belts and shafts. The process of pushing materials into machines by hand has been replaced by mechanical feeds. Placing guards on machines, insuring the proper location of machines, and providing adequate lighting has also helped. The result has been that over the years, the proportion of accidents caused by machines has been reduced drastically. Newer approaches to industrial safety have been to use industrial psychology in the attempt to reduce the number of injuries occurring among accident-prone individuals.[16]

SAFETY AND LABOR UNIONS

Labor unions have been interested in industrial safety also. Several instances of a spectacular decrease in injuries have been noted where labor unions have engaged in union-management cooperation to reduce the number of accidents. In one company, for example, the Forstmann Woolen Company engaged in a joint safety program with the Textile Workers Union, and reduced the accident rate to one-sixth the industry average.[17] Problems have arisen between management and labor unions as to where the authority for safety should be, but where the two groups have cooperated, accidents have been reduced.

SAFETY AND INSURANCE COMPANIES

Insurance companies have been another group who have been interested in accident prevention. Several early workmen's laws required insurance companies to engage in safety work. Other insurance companies became interested in the safety movement on their own volition, because they profit if accidents can be reduced below forecast rates. Some insurance companies provide safety work as a regular part of their services to companies who buy their workmen's compensation insurance. One estimate showed that insurance companies spend about 3 percent of the premiums earned on factory inspection and safety.[18] As an example of what insurance companies have

[15] Roland P. Blake, *Industrial Safety*, 2nd ed. (New York, Prentice-Hall, 1953), pp. 15-16; and 3rd ed. (1963), pp. 17-18.

[16] For a more comprehensive analysis, see *ibid*.

[17] Somers and Somers, *op. cit.*, p. 207.

[18] Arthur H. Reede, *Adequacy of Workmen's Compensation* (Cambridge, Mass., Harvard, 1947), p. 357.

done, in New York State in one year those companies selling steam boiler insurance spent twice as much money on boiler inspection as on payment of claims. One of the companies, the Hartford Steam Boiler and Inspection Company, found 20,000 dangerous defects in boilers and 180,000 less serious defects.[19] Besides inspection, insurance companies have also engaged in laboratory research to improve safety devices and techniques. Such companies, in addition, have participated with other groups interested in industrial safety through consultation, participation in programs and publications, financial support, committee work, and so forth.[20]

Unfortunately some insurance companies have not been nearly as interested in safety work as others. Some companies with only a small workmen's compensation business apparently feel that their premiums are so small that they can ill afford to engage in safety work. An annual report of the New York State Insurance Company, for example, showed that 12 firms that wrote less than $100,000 of workmen's compensation insurance spent only 1 percent of their premiums on safety.[21] Another weakness of insurance companies' safety programs is that they fail to reach the small employers. Premiums received from small employers are so small that costs of inspections of such establishments are relatively high if not prohibitive.[22]

SAFETY AND GOVERNMENT

Another group that has been interested in safety has been governmental agencies, particularly at the state level.[23] As early as 1877, Massachusetts passed the first law requiring factory safeguards. In 1911, Wisconsin enacted a law which empowered its Industrial Commission to ascertain and prescribe and enforce safety devices and safeguards. Shortly thereafter a number of other states passed the same type of legislation. The various states have engaged mainly in factory inspection, and more recently have provided such safety services as lecturers, distribution of safety literature, and the like. As has been typical of most problems administered at the state level, some states have done a good job of factory inspection and safety, and others have done very little. Eleven states have no factory inspection whatever.[24] State agencies have been understaffed. They have tended to inspect small firms less frequently than larger ones even though the smaller firms are in need of safety improvement the most.[25]

---

[19] *Ibid.,* p. 355.
[20] *Ibid.,* p. 358.
[21] *Ibid.,* p. 361.
[22] *Ibid.,* p. 362.
[23] For a more detailed analysis on industrial safety work by regulatory agencies, from which most of the material in this paragraph has been drawn, see *ibid.,* Chap. XXII.
[24] *Building America's Health, op. cit.,* Vol. II, p. 77.
[25] Reede, *op. cit.,* p. 369.

EVALUATION OF THE SAFETY MOVEMENT

With employers, workers, insurance companies, and government all interested in safety to some degree, what final evaluation can be placed on the safety movement in the United States? Over a many-year period the statistics show a declining number and severity of industrial accidents even though employment has been expanding. The safety movement, then, has been somewhat successful. On the other hand, there is room for further improvement. As has been indicated, some employers, labor unions, insurance companies, and states have taken an active and worthwhile lead in promoting industrial safety, but others have done little or nothing. Further work by all of these groups would aid in reducing accidents, particularly in small firms.

REHABILITATION

In spite of the utilization of best safety practices, accidents are still bound to occur. In the early history of mankind, inhumanity to man was apparent in the treatment of the crippled. Accidents or deformities were ruled to be the curse of devils, and abandonment to beggary and ridicule was the rule rather than the exception. Eventually the more humane teachings of Christianity plus the growth of democracy resulted in improved treatment.[26] Today a number of studies like the following can be recited to tell of the wonderful accomplishments of medicine in rehabilitating injured workers, but of the difficulty such workers have in finding new jobs:

In another instance, a worker fell off a scaffold, sustaining a broken back and paraplegia. A year later he appeared before me for an evaluation of his compensation claim. I certified him as totally and permanently disabled. Six years later he appeared at the New Jersey Rehabilitation Clinic without the crutches and braces he wore when I last saw him, but shuffling awkwardly from side to side attempting to balance himself. "What are you doing here?" I asked. "I am looking for a job." "Looking for a job? I thought I had certified you as totally and permanently disabled. What can you do?" "I am a structural ironworker," he answered. "Yes, I know you *were* a structural worker." "No," he replied, "I am a structural ironworker," "Just what do you mean?" "Well, I have been working as a structural ironworker for the past two years." "Oh, I understand," I said, "you mean you are one of those who checks material as it is brought into the building that is going up." "No," he said, "I am one of those who shinny up in the air twenty stories," and with that he presented me with credentials from his employer certifying to his work record and his ability to carry on as structural iron-

26 W. Scott Allan, *Rehabilitation: A Community Challenge* (New York, Wiley, 1958), pp. 2-3.

worker. His employer had gone out of business, and wherever the ironworker presented his credentials no one would hire him because he was a cripple.[27]

VETERANS' REHABILITATION

World Wars I and II were important stimuli in formulating rehabilitation programs. At the governmental level two important rehabilitation programs have existed since 1920, one for veterans and one for civilians. For wartime veterans with service-connected disabilities, the Veterans Administration for a number of years has had a team of rehabilitation specialists composed of counseling psychologists, training specialists, physicians, psychiatrists, clinical psychologists, and social workers. Public Law 87-815 in 1962 authorized vocational rehabilitation training under specified circumstances to veterans with service-connected disabilities incurred in peacetime as well as wartime. During fiscal year 1965, a total of 6,798 disabled veterans were trained. In all a total of 619,400 World War II veterans were trained under this program plus 73,400 Korean veterans along with 11,000 peacetime soldiers.[28] Over half the Korean veterans elected to be trained in occupations in the professional, semiprofessional, and managerial fields.[29] The largest numbers in these areas elected to be teachers, followed by accountants and engineers. Smaller groups chose to be mechanics, or to engage in clerical, sales, agriculture, or service occupations.[30] After each veteran nears the completion of his training program, he is referred to public employment agencies and otherwise assisted as necessary in securing employment.

GOVERNMENT CIVILIAN REHABILITATION

The civilian rehabilitation program was begun in 1920 when the federal government began disbursing small grants to aid those states that accepted the conditions of the federal grant. Until 1943 the program was limited to vocational counseling and training, the supplying of prosthetic appliances, and placement of the disabled. Very little money was available for the program so that only 210,000 persons had been rehabilitated in the 24-year period.

Beginning with the Barden-La Follette Act of 1943, the program was broadened to give medical aid, hospital services, maintenance and transportation, and tools and equipment along with the services formerly provided. The program was further expanded in 1954 with the passage of Public Law

[27] Henry H. Kessler, *Rehabilitation of the Physically Handicapped,* 2nd ed. (New York, Columbia, 1953), p. 175.
[28] *Annual Report, 1965,* Administrator of Veterans Affairs, Washington, D.C., Veterans Administration, p. 72.
[29] *Ibid.,* 1963, p. 73.
[30] *Ibid.,* 1961, pp. 70-71.

565, which made matching grants available for state construction of rehabilitation centers rather than having the states buy rehabilitation services elsewhere.

The matching grant program also included money for research on new methods and techniques for aiding the disabled. At the end of 1964, a total of 795 research or demonstration projects had been completed or were in operation. A number of these dealt with the mentally retarded. Here the goal was to provide social and vocational training so that some of the mentally retarded may be placed in highly selective jobs. Another larger number of projects dealt with the blind and visually handicapped. Other research projects have dealt with evaluation centers for the cerebral palsied, work adjustment centers for disabled persons with emotional problems, occupational adjustment services for epileptics, industrial homework, work evaluation of older disabled workers, rehabilitation of the chronically ill, those with hearing defects, and those afflicted with alcoholism.[31]

Under the impetus of Public Law 565 and Hill-Burton grants, the total number of rehabilitation centers has expanded rapidly in recent years. The largest rehabilitation centers provide comprehensive services for the disabled. Among these are: medical evaluation; rehabilitation nursing; prosthetic or brace fitting and training; occupational therapy; recreation or group therapy; psychological and personal counseling; prevocational evaluation, testing and training; vocational counseling and job placement; speech and hearing therapy; physical therapy; and social services.[32] During or after medical treatment, specialists in the rehabilitation center attempt to prepare the injured worker for gainful work if this is physically possible. The most successful plans have been to return the worker to his former employer since the worker is already familiar with this work environment. One study has shown that most of the injured who had returned to their former employer had successfully adjusted to their problem.[33] For those unable to work in their old position, further vocational guidance, training, and placement are necessary. The U.S. Employment Service publishes interviewing guides for specific disabilities, and gives special emphasis in this publication to placement considerations.

Federal spending on rehabilitation increased from $21.5 million in 1952 to $175 million in fiscal 1965.[34] For every $3 spent by the federal government, the states spent $2. During fiscal year 1965, a total of 134,859 persons were listed as having been rehabilitated in that year under the federal-state program.[35] As has been true of most programs administered by the states,

[31] Ibid., 1960, pp. 265-268; and Ibid., 1962, pp. 370-381.

[32] W. Scott Allan, Rehabilitation: A Community Challenge, p. 50.

[33] Earl F. Cheit, Injury and Recovery in the Course of Employment (New York, Wiley, 1961), pp. 301-302.

[34] Annual Report, 1965, Washington, D.C., U.S. Department of Health, Education and Welfare, p. 372.

[35] Ibid., p. 369.

some have excellent programs and others have mediocre or poor ones. Under the matching program in fiscal year 1965, only six states acquired all the federal allotments available to them.[36] In 1965, five states operated no rehabilitation centers but the other 45 states, the District of Columbia, Guam, and Puerto Rico operated 360 state facilities which ranged all the way from large centers to small clinics.[37]

PRIVATE REHABILITATION

A number of private agencies have been in existence for years to aid rehabilitation of the disabled. Several of the more prominent of these are operated by hospitals—the Institute of Physical Medicine and Rehabilitation, for example, which is part of the New York University–Bellevue Medical Center. A number of philanthropic organizations have fostered a number of rehabilitation centers, such as the National Society for Crippled Children, Goodwill Industries, Community Chests, and the Liberty Mutual Insurance Company, the largest private writer of workmen's compensation insurance in the United States.[38] The Liberty Mutual Insurance Company operates two rehabilitation centers, one at Boston and another at Chicago. At these centers, it was found that 85 percent of all cases could be improved to the point of being able to engage in gainful employment, and 82 percent actually did return to work. The more serious the case, of course, the more unlikely the return to work, but even in a series of 86 complicated spinal cord injury cases, more than 50 percent returned to work, and only 5 percent required continued hospital care.[39]

PERFORMANCE OF HANDICAPPED WORKERS

The performance of 11,000 impaired workmen was compared with 18,000 matched unimpaired workmen in 109 plants in 20 different industries.[40] The types and numbers of disabilities (in parentheses) were as follows: leg or arm amputees (484); lost use of hands or legs or other orthopedic problems (1,038); vision problems, half totally blind (1,172); hearing deficiencies (595); hernias (3,543); heart trouble (1,840); former tuberculosis patients (513); peptic ulcers (428); diabetic (144); multiple problems (587). These workers, along with their matched unimpaired workers, were engaged primarily in processing (58 percent) although 15 percent were in maintenance. The others were either in inspection and testing, recording and control,

[36] *Ibid.*, p. 372.
[37] *Ibid.*
[38] Somers and Somers, *op. cit.*, pp. 246-248.
[39] Allan, *op. cit.*, pp. 168-169.
[40] *The Performance of Physically Impaired Workers in Manufacturing Industries,* Bulletin 923, Washington, D.C., U.S. Department of Labor, Bureau of Labor Statistics (1948).

material movement, or custodial, or were working foreman. The findings in this study were that the output of the impaired group was slightly above that of the unimpaired group (1 percent higher). The number and severity of injuries on the job were less among the impaired workers, although the absentee and quit rate was higher among impaired workers. The main conclusion of this study was that the physically impaired as a group were fully able to compete successfully with unimpaired workers.

COSTS OF REHABILITATION

In view of the fact that most workers can be rehabilitated and that their work performance in industry is satisfactory, the question remains as to the cost of rehabilitating workers. The Office of Vocational Rehabilitation has cited an average cost per person rehabilitated of $666. A California study showed that the costs of rehabilitation came to $612 but that an additional $740 was spent on vocational guidance, placement, and administrative services.[41] The Liberty Mutual average was slightly less than this, although for comprehensive rehabilitation of severe cases of spinal cord injury the cost came to more than $10,000 per patient. Against this cost must be assessed the cost of continuing relief payments for those not rehabilitated. When comparing such costs, all studies have concluded that it is much cheaper to pay for rehabilitating disabled workers than to provide relief payments for them.

One analysis of the savings of rehabilitation was made of 130 chronic neurological cases of veterans, all but two of whom had seen service in World War I and many of whom had not been out of bed in the previous ten years.[42] After nine months of intensive rehabilitation services, 25 left the hospital and were employed, and another 40 were discharged to their homes. All but ten had shown worthwhile improvement. Figuring on the basis of a savings of five years' hospital costs at over $12 per day, the savings to the taxpayers from this rehabilitation program came to $1.1 million.

Another study was made of rehabilitation of the severely disabled aided by the United Mine Workers Welfare and Retirement program.[43] Their disabilities were as follows: quadriplegia, hemiplegia, multiple sclerosis and other neuromuscular diseases, difficult amputation problems, and severely involved arthritis cases. Of 575 referred for vocational rehabilitation services, 64 percent of these were accepted for training. Of this group 169 were later

[41] Z. L. Gulledge, "Vocational Rehabilitation of Industrially Injured Workers," in Earl F. Cheit and Margaret Gordon, eds., *Occupational Disability and Public Policy* (New York, Wiley, 1963), p. 414.

[42] Howard A. Rusk and Eugene J. Taylor, "Rehabilitation," *The Annals of the American Academy of Political and Social Science,* Vol. 273 (January, 1951), p. 139.

[43] Kenneth E. Pohlmann, "Rehabilitation of the Severely Disabled: UMWA Welfare and Retirement Fund Experience," *American Journal of Public Health,* Vol. 43 (1953), pp. 445-453.

employed with a combined estimated weekly income of $6,760. During their lifetime it was expected that this group would earn $6.8 million. If this group had become public assistance cases, the total charged to society would have ranged from $2 to $6 million. Instead they produced more than this amount in goods and services.

EVALUATION OF REHABILITATION

MEDICAL CARE

In attempting to evaluate the rehabilitation program in the United States, a number of facets of the problem must be analyzed. One aspect of rehabilitation is the quality of medical care. With improvements in medical treatment, some progress has been made in the care of the disabled. Statistics show that the extent of impairment caused by given injuries has been decreasing each year. Improved drugs, better equipment in hospitals, and improved medical techniques have all aided.

On the other hand, there is still room for improvement, particularly among those needing long-term care as a result of a severe illness or injury.[44] One staff doctor of one of the leading rehabilitation centers in the country contends that 80 to 90 percent of the patients are referred to the center for secondary complications that never would have arisen had adequate medical care been given in the first place.[45] In 1960 there were only 340 physiatrists in the country, that is, physicians who have been specially trained in the new field of physical medicine. Almost three times this many specialists are needed.[46] A six-man group at New York University, which included the most highly qualified specialists in medicine, rehabilitation, and law, concluded that 40 years of investigations demonstrated that without adequate supervision of medical care by a Compensation Board, medical care for the injured "is haphazard and often dangerously inadequate and improper." [47]

Unfortunately, today only two of the United States jurisdictions dealing with workmen's compensation approach the Industrial Association of Industrial Accident Boards and Commissions' standards for agency supervision of medical care in the clinical sense.[48] According to Professor Earl Cheit, the problems of medical administration are not extremely difficult, and helpful experience has already been accumulated. In spite of this, ade-

[44] Cheit, op. cit., p. 289.
[45] Donald Covalt, ed., Rehabilitation in Industry (New York, Grune and Stratton, 1958), pp. 1-8.
[46] Cheit, op. cit., p. 296.
[47] George Armstrong et al., New York University Workmen's Compensation (New York, New York University Center for Rehabilitation Services, 1960), p. 64.
[48] IAIABC Proceedings, 1957, Bulletin 195, Washington, D.C., U.S. Department of Labor, Bureau of Labor Standards, p. 172.

quate medical administration is still lacking. Professor Cheit was particularly critical of placing the administrative responsibility of medical care in the hands of insurance companies, for he contends that they have not followed the best practices. He also did not favor giving insurance companies the final responsibility on which of the disabled should undergo rehabilitation, nor did he feel that either the insurance company or the worker's physicians were the best group to win the cooperation of the injured workman to engage in rehabilitation.[49]

REHABILITATION CENTERS

Most states now have rehabilitation centers. In these states, however, the use of them is variable. One state, for example, made only three referrals to a rehabilitation center in one year.[50] Five states in 1965 had not yet provided any facilities for rehabilitation. One study concluded from questionnaires sent to a national sample of doctors and carriers that the two major obstacles to greater use of rehabilitation facilities was ignorance on the part of physicians about rehabilitation centers and a reluctance of other physicians to send the patient to the rehabilitation center for fear of losing a patient.[51] A study by the American Medical Association of 201 companies employing 860,438 employees in 37 workmen's compensation jurisdictions found that only 30 employees were referred to agencies for vocational training and only 124 were referred for physical rehabilitation during a one-year period. Another study found that of 800 doctors in Rhode Island, only 53 had referred patients to the Rhode Island Curative Center in a period of four years.[52]

The result of too few rehabilitation centers and inadequate referrals to them is that few people attempt rehabilitation. One study found that only 3 percent of disabled adults reported that they received any help in returning to a job after they became disabled.[53] Of a sample of 1,849 permanently and totally disabled, not using rehabilitation services, 87 percent did not know of the existence of such services.[54] Also the Industrial Association of Industrial Accident Boards and Commissions has been critical of the fact that there are few statistics on what happens to workers after the workmen's compensation board refers them to a rehabilitation center. Data are not available on the number of cases rehabilitated as a percentage of all seriously disabled cases, and only three states were able to supply statistics concerning

---

[49] Cheit, *op. cit.*, pp. 313-314.

[50] *Ibid.*, p. 296.

[51] Earl F. Cheit, "Medical Rehabilitation for Injured Workers," *Monthly Labor Review*, Vol. 85 (1962), pp. 1220-1221.

[52] Cheit, *Injury and Recovery in the Course of Employment*, p. 297.

[53] James Morgan *et al.*, *Income and Welfare in the United States* (New York, McGraw-Hill, 1962), p. 237.

[54] Donald S. Frank, "Disabled Workers and Rehabilitation Services," *Social Security Bulletin*, Vol. 26, No. 6 (June, 1963), Table 4, p. 5.

the number of workers who were still without work three months after their injury.[55]

REHABILITATION AND WORKMEN'S COMPENSATION

Another barrier to adequate rehabilitation has been workmen's compensation. There is an awareness today that the end goal of workmen's compensation should be rehabilitation of injured workmen. However, the basic workmen's compensation program of cash payments to injured workmen has tended to militate against rehabilitation. Delays in rehabilitation have occurred because many state rehabilitation programs require that the physical disability must be static or fixed before a case may be accepted. Some state agencies even go so far as to require that the entire process of litigation must be completed before a case is accepted.[56] One study found that seven years elapsed on the average after the date of injury before injured workmen were referred to a rehabilitation center.[57]

Another difficulty may be that workmen's compensation benefits may cause a workman to lose all incentive to rehabilitate himself, for if he returns to work, his workmen's compensation payments may stop. On the other hand, if a workman receives workmen's compensation, his morale may be sufficiently high that an incentive will be provided to engage in rehabilitation. With this in mind, several students of workmen's compensation suggest that we go forward on both fronts. That is, adequate workmen's compensation should be made available to provide security for workers, and worthwhile rehabilitation services also should be made available to aid workers to better adapt to their handicap.[58]

Thirteen compensation jurisdictions do provide for full workmen's compensation benefits while the worker undergoes rehabilitation. Even this type of provision is not entirely adequate, for a workman may incur other costs during rehabilitation, such as travel, maintenance away from home, plus tuition and equipment costs. In 17 jurisdictions maintenance costs are provided under the workmen's compensation law, and a few of these authorize payment for travel, tuition, and other costs of rehabilitation.[59] Unfortunately, only a minority of states have such provisions. Further encouragement to rehabilitation could come from a recommendation which the International Association of Industrial Accident Boards and Commissions has long advocated—namely, that no workmen's compensation case be closed or a final award made until rehabilitation has been completed.[60] The National Insti-

[55] *IAIABC Proceedings, 1956*, Bulletin 192, p. 210.
[56] Cheit, *Injury and Recovery in the Course of Employment*, pp. 298-299.
[57] *Report to the Chairman, Manpower Policy Committee, 1952*, Washington, D.C., U.S. Office of Defense Mobilization, Task Force of the Handicapped, p. 37.
[58] Somers and Somers, *op. cit.*, pp. 261-262.
[59] Cheit, *Injury and Recovery in the Course of Employment*, pp. 299-300.
[60] *Ibid.*, p. 308.

tute on Rehabilitation and Workmen's Compensation concurred in this recommendation.[61] Several of the states have also experimented with a requirement that workmen's compensation payments be suspended if the worker, without good cause, refuses to undergo rehabilitation.

HIRING THE HANDICAPPED

Another factor deterring rehabilitation is that some employers refuse to hire handicapped workers. In a recent survey of 1,221 employers engaged in manufacturing in six states, nearly 60 percent of the employers were unwilling to hire workers with certain physical impairments.[62] Of the six types of disabilities for which the survey checked, employers were most reluctant to hire persons with epilepsy or lung and back ailments, and were least reluctant to hire persons with eye disabilities, limb or other orthopedic disabilities, or heart trouble.

The main reasons for not hiring the handicapped as stated by employers was that the work was too heavy, or dangerous, or too complicated for handicapped workers to handle. Less than one-tenth of the employers listed the higher costs of workmen's compensation as the reason for not hiring the handicapped. Here there was a misconception among a minority of employers, particularly small ones, that hiring handicapped workers would raise workmen's compensation rates. Such rates are based upon the basic work hazards of the particular industry involved and for about 25 percent of the firms the accident experience of the particular company involved. Since most firms do not qualify for experience rating and since handicapped workers do not have a higher accident rate than other workers, there is little reason why their rates should be higher.

It is true that a handicapped worker may experience a more expensive injury if reinjured, for the loss of both eyes to one man, for example, is much more costly than the loss of one eye each to two men. A solution has been found to this problem, whereby a separate or second injury fund is created to take care of this exigency. The employer's liability is limited to the specific injury itself. The second injury fund pays the difference. If, for example, a workman who had already lost the sight of one eye lost the sight of the other eye through an injury, the employer would be liable only for the injury to the one eye. The second injury fund would make up the difference to provide a payment for total blindness. Although almost all states have second injury funds, their effectiveness in many jurisdictions has been reduced by various limitations. A majority of states limit the use

[61] Monroe Berkowitz, ed., *Rehabilitating the Disabled Worker*, Washington, D.C., U.S. Department of Health, Education, and Welfare, Vocational Rehabilitation Administration (1963), p. 57.

[62] Lloyd W. Larson, "Workmen's Compensation Laws and the Employment of the Handicapped," *Monthly Labor Review*, Vol. 85 (1962), pp. 145-148.

of the second injury fund to cases in which the prior injury resulted in a specific type of loss, of an arm, foot, or the like. Other states do not use the second injury fund unless the second injury results in permanent total disability. In spite of these restrictions, second injury funds are useful. To the extent that they are beneficial, the results of such funds should be publicized so that employers will not fear to hire handicapped workers.

Summary of Evaluation of Rehabilitation

To summarize, the success of rehabilitation will depend on the quality of medical care, the adequacy of rehabilitation centers, the solving of workmen's compensation problems, and the willingness of employers to rehire injured workmen. Some progress has been made in recent years in improving the rehabilitation program in the United States, but still further progress is needed. The quality of medical care needs upgrading, and the number of rehabilitation centers needs expanding. More of the injured need to go through a rehabilitation program. Better interrelation between workmen's compensation and rehabilitation is necessary. Lastly, more employers need to get over the fear of hiring handicapped workers. In some European countries, employers are required to hire a certain percentage of their workers from a total handicapped group.[63] Here in America, it is hoped that a more voluntary system will adequately solve the problem.

OCCUPATIONAL DISABILITY AND THE LAW

When injuries occurred during the early years of the factory system, no laws existed to protect injured workmen.[64] In order to obtain damages from an employer, the employee had to sue in court and win. If the worker was killed by the accident, no remedy of any kind was available at law, because the injured workman was required to do the suing. In court an injured workman had to base his case on the common law of negligence or tort liability. The common law was based on the assumption that someone was at fault in each accident. Whoever it was had to pay the damages. If it was the employer, he paid, but if the worker was at fault, then no damages could be collected.

At law the employer had three defenses. First he could maintain that the worker himself was a contributing cause to the accident (contributory

---

[63] Allan, *op. cit.*, p. 110.

[64] For a brief history of the development of the law from which most of the material in this section was taken, *see* Somers and Somers, *op. cit.*, Chap. 2.

negligence). Second he could maintain that a fellow employee was the cause of the accident, and absolve himself from the cost (fellow-servant rule). As an example of this type of case, it was held in England in 1837 that a butcher boy's helper was not entitled to damages from his employer because the injury was due to a butcher boy overloading a van. The third defense was that if the work was somewhat dangerous, the workman should have known this when he accepted employment. Having accepted the job, he assumed the risks of any injuries that might occur (assumption of risk). In a 1924 case in New York, a girl sued because she had contracted tuberculosis when working in a damp, unsanitary, unventilated cellar of a candy manufacturer. The judge denied her damages on the ground that the girl was fully aware of the conditions under which she worked. In short, the injured workman had little redress under the common law. If he sued, he probably would lose his job to begin with. Then the case itself might cost the workman a great deal of money. The defenses available to the employer were so powerful that the workman did not stand much chance of winning his case. One student of the subject found that workers obtained no legal relief in seven out of eight cases.[65]

EMPLOYERS' LIABILITY LAWS

The failure of the common law to provide adequate protection for injured workmen resulted in a number of state statutes being passed. These were called Employers' Liability laws. Some of these laws prohibited the employer from forcing an employee to sign a contract to relieve the employer of all liability for accidents at work. By 1908, 27 states had passed such laws. Other modifications of the common law permitted the right of suit in death cases (41 jurisdictions). Other laws in almost all states restricted the defenses of the employer—particularly the fellow-servant rule.

In spite of the laws giving injured workmen more rights, employers' liability statutes did not provide adequate protection. In the first several decades of this century 40 investigatory bodies were appointed to investigate the problem of industrial accidents. Almost all the bodies recommended that the common law and employers' liability statutes be replaced by a system of workmen's compensation. Under employers' liability laws, one study from three states showed that no compensation was received at all in almost one third of the cases and that $1,000 and over was obtained in less than 10 percent of the cases.[66] Another study showed that nine of the largest liability insurance companies paid on only one claim out of eight in the period from 1906–1908.[67] Furthermore, 30 to 50 percent had to be deducted from

[65] Downey, *op. cit.*, p. 144.

[66] I. M. Rubinow, *Social Insurance* (New York, Holt, Rinehart & Winston, 1913), pp. 93-95.

[67] Somers and Somers, *op. cit.*, p. 23.

awards to pay the legal fees for injured workmen. John R. Commons found that of $1 million paid to liability insurance companies in 1911, only $300,000 of it was received by injured workmen.[68]

Several other difficulties may be noted with employers' liability laws. Court cases took quite long to settle. In Ohio an average time of three years per case elapsed before final awards were rendered. In Illinois it took the same length of time before damages were actually received. Another criticism was that the awards received varied quite inconsistently. Whereas one worker might obtain as much as $2,700 for the loss of an eye, another less fortunate worker would receive as little as $290.[69] Finally, few employers adopted safety methods, and awards were so few that they did not provide a financial incentive to do so.

With such a serious indictment of employers' liability laws, it was not long until the various states began passing workmen's compensation laws. These are discussed in the next chapter. Coverage under workmen's compensation laws has been incomplete, so that about 25 percent of our workmen must still look to employers' liability laws in case of an accident. The most recent analysis of experience under employers' liability laws made in 1961 still showed serious weaknesses in the system.[70] Data from 40 states showed that awards had been made in only 28 death cases, 1 permanent total disability case, and 93 permanent partial (major and minor) cases. There was some undercounting, for all employers are not required to report cases to the National Council on Compensation Insurance, from which this study was drawn. The figures, however, do not seriously understate the total number of cases brought under employers' liability laws. The awards tended to remain inconsistent also. For deaths they varied from $1,750 to $17,000. The fact that most employers not covered by workmen's compensation are small employers who typically have a much higher accident rate than large employers points out the very grave weaknesses of permitting one-fourth of our workers to be governed by employers' liability laws.

Summary

Many work injuries occur each year in the United States. The frequency and severity of accidents varies considerably from one industry to another. The costs of industrial accidents are enormous and are borne by the injured

[68] John R. Commons, *Labor and Administration* (New York, Macmillan, 1913), p. 395.

[69] H. A. Millis and R. E. Montgomery, *Labor's Risks and Social Insurance* (New York, McGraw-Hill, 1938), p. 193.

[70] Cheit, *Injury and Recovery in the Course of Employment*, pp. 188-190.

and by society as a cost of production. Occupational diseases cost additional sums. A number of groups have been interested in safety—private groups, labor unions, insurance companies, and governments. Such groups are also interested in the rehabilitation of injured workmen. Because handicapped workers perform well, and because rehabilitation of the injured is less expensive than welfare payments, rehabilitation programs are worthwhile. Rehabilitation has been handicapped by a lack of adequate medical care, too few rehabilitation centers, a reluctance to undertake rehabilitation because of workmen's compensation payments, and the failure of employers to hire the handicapped. Improvement in all these areas is possible.

In the early days of the factory system, workers had to sue if they were injured since no laws protected them. Certain legal defenses of the employer made it extremely difficult for workers to collect damages. At the beginning of the twentieth century, employers' liability laws were passed which restricted the defenses of employers. Because of the costs and delays under employers' liability laws, they have been superseded by workmen's compensation laws. Failure to provide adequate coverage under workmen's compensation means that large numbers of injured workers must still take their chances under less adequate employers' liability laws.

WORKMEN'S COMPENSATION

The failure of employers' liability laws resulted in the enactment of a number of workmen's compensation laws by state legislatures in the first two decades of this century. These laws attempted to correct the major deficiencies under the common law and employers' liability laws. Workmen's compensation laws were based on the premise that payment should be made to injured workmen regardless of who was at fault in causing the accident. Industrial accidents were simply a part of the cost of producing goods and services. Employers were required to assume the risks of these costs as well as any other costs of production. Another purpose of workmen's compensation was to eliminate delay and unnecessary costs of litigation. Payments were to be awarded by separate workmen's compensation boards to speed procedure. Payments for each type of injury were fixed, so that, it was thought, there would be little need to litigate, particularly since the common law defenses of employers were made inapplicable. Employers would not have an interest in delaying cases in the hope that such delays would encourage employees to settle for less. The amounts were fixed, so that there was little to gain by delay.

Drafters of workmen's compensation laws also hoped that since employers would be required to pay, strong incentives would be provided for more safety. In order to lessen the costs of insuring, it was felt that employers would make every effort to improve safety. Some of the early state laws recognized the importance of safety by including it in the title of the law. In Massachusetts, for example, the law was titled: "An Act Relative to the Payment of Employees for Personal Injuries Received in the Course of the Employment and to the Prevention of Such Injuries." [1] Although the safety movement preceded passage of workmen's compensation laws, there is no question that such laws gave a strong impetus toward promoting more and better safety. Merit rating, basing premiums on past records of accidents, gave a direct incentive to reduce accidents, and gradually employers began to see the advantages of improved safety on its own merits. Today the importance of safety is so well recognized that most large employers would adopt the best type of safety practices regardless of whether work-

---

[1] Arthur H. Reede, *Adequacy of Workmen's Compensation* (Cambridge, Mass., Harvard, 1947), p. 321.

men's compensation laws were in existence or not. There is doubt today that merit rating has any appreciable effect on industrial safety, but it will probably continue to exist as a device to lower rates for larger companies. The coverage of occupational diseases also stimulated the growth of industrial hygiene. Workmen's compensation can take part of the credit for the reduction in accidents and deaths and the elimination or reduction of the incidence of many occupational diseases.

The first workmen's compensation laws provided for little medical care for the injured, nor was the concept of rehabilitation an original part of such laws. With the development of workmen's compensation after World War I, it was realized that medical care and rehabilitation should be made an important part of the program. Medical benefits were expanded, and rehabilitation has become the keystone to the whole program, at least in theory.[2]

The first workmen's compensation law was passed to cover Prussian railroads in 1838. The first nationwide law came in Germany in 1884. Thereafter one nation after another in Europe passed such laws so that by 1909 all the nations of Europe had some type of workmen's compensation legislation. In the United States, thanks to President Theodore Roosevelt, a federal compensation law was passed in 1908 to cover Civil Service employees.

The next year Montana passed such a law for its coal miners, but it was declared unconstitutional. Between 1910 and 1915, 30 states passed workmen's compensation laws, but a number of these were declared unconstitutional. In order to make such laws constitutional some states either amended their constitutions or provided that the employer could elect to be covered under the law. By 1917 most of the legal problems had been settled by the United States Supreme Court, which ruled in three different cases that all three of the workmen's compensation laws were legal regardless of whether they were mandatory or provided for exclusive state insurance funds. Shortly after the Supreme Court decisions, nine other states passed workmen's compensation laws so that by 1920 all states but six, concentrated in the South, had such laws. The last state to pass such a law was Mississippi in 1948. Today there are 54 workmen's compensation jurisdictions—the 50 states, Puerto Rico, and two federal laws covering three groups—Civil Service employees, public employees of the District of Columbia, and longshoremen.[3]

COVERAGE

Even though coverage of workers under workmen's compensation laws has been expanding over the years, it is far from complete today. A number of

[2] Harold M. Somers and Anne R. Somers, *Workmen's Compensation* (New York, Wiley, 1954), pp. 26-28.
[3] *Ibid.*, pp. 30-34.

industries are not covered. The railroad industry and seamen are covered under two separate federal employers' liability laws. The workers in both industries feel that benefits are higher under these laws, and therefore they have opposed being covered under workmen's compensation.[4]

Only nine states cover agricultural workers the same as other workers. Nine other states cover some types of agricultural workers, particularly those engaged in mechanized or power occupations.[5] In almost all the other jurisdictions agricultural employers may elect to be covered under the workmen's compensation law, but they are not required to. In view of the fact that the accident rate in agriculture is high, and that the income of farm workers is low, this industry is in greater need of protection against injuries than most other industries. The Bureau of Labor Standards recommends coverage of agricultural workers in the same manner as other general classes of employment.

For domestic service, only two states have complete coverage for such workers although several other states provide partial coverage. Casual labor is covered in 11 jurisdictions.[6] A few states have specific exclusions for particular industries, which have lobbied effectively not to be covered under the workmen's compensation law. Several examples are logging in Maine, turpentine labor in Florida, and both of these industries plus steam laundering, rock quarrying, and other industries in South Carolina.[7] A number of workers in public employment, particularly at the state and local level, are not covered either, although all states now have at least some coverage for their public employees.

ELECTIVE VERSUS COMPULSORY LAWS

In order for their state workmen's compensation law to be declared constitutional, some states in the early history of workmen's compensation provided that their laws be made elective rather than compulsory. Since that time, compulsory laws have been declared constitutional, but few states have changed to a compulsory law. In 1960, 30 of the laws were compulsory and 24 were elective for most of the private employments covered. In those states where coverage is elective, the laws do provide some encouragement for coverage. The fact that employers lose their common law defenses has generally inclined them to cover. Another aid to coverage is that in 19 of the 24 elective laws, election is presumed unless the employer specifically notifies the state that he will not be covered under workmen's compensa-

---

[4] For an analysis of employers' liability in these two industries, *see* Earl F. Cheit, *Injury and Recovery in the Course of Employment* (New York, Wiley, 1961), Chaps. 7, 8.

[5] *State Workmen's Compensation Laws*, Bulletin 212, Washington, D.C., U.S. Department of Labor, Bureau of Labor Standards (1964), p. 6.

[6] *Ibid.*, Bulletin 161 (May, 1960), pp. 13-16.

[7] Somers and Somers, *op. cit.*, pp. 45-46.

tion.[8] With these safeguards most of the workers are covered in the elective states. One study, although dated, showed that 1,183,000 workers under Massachusetts' elective law were covered out of a total of 1,272,000 workers.[9] Fewer government employees are covered under elective laws. In some of the elective states, the common law defenses are not removed for government employees. Also during depression periods, there may be less inclination to elect coverage. In Pennsylvania in 1937, a liberalization of workmen's compensation benefits caused many employers to elect not to be covered and reduced the number of workers covered by about one-eighth, mostly in the coal-mining industry. But in 1939, the Pennsylvania legislature reduced benefits, and the industries involved decided to reelect coverage.[10]

EXEMPTION OF NONHAZARDOUS INDUSTRIES

In 12 states workmen's compensation laws apply only to hazardous or extra-hazardous industries. This provision, too, was placed in the early laws to avoid having them declared unconstitutional. Now that the constitutional barrier has been removed, there is no logical reason for keeping this limitation to coverage. That this limitation seriously reduces coverage may be shown by an earlier study of coverage by Professor A. H. Reede. He found that the 12 states covering only hazardous industries had a median coverage of 64 percent of their workers compared with 83 percent for all states.[11] Sometimes legal cases arise over whether an injury falls within the definition of a hazardous industry. In one case recently in Oklahoma, a widow sued after her husband's death, caused by an accident at work. Oklahoma is one of the states that requires that the industry be hazardous for coverage. The court deliberated over whether the industry was hazardous, and ruled that the industry did not fall within the definition of a hazardous industry. The widow received nothing instead of $13,500, which she would have received if the industry had been classified as hazardous.

EXEMPTION OF SMALL FIRMS

Another exclusion which exempts large numbers of employees concerns the size of firms. Only 24 states cover employers who have one or more employees.[12] The other 28 jurisdictions limit coverage by the size of the firm. South Carolina has the least liberal provisions. In that state, employers who have fewer than 15 employees are exempt from the law. The remainder of the states limiting coverage by size of firm require employers to have from 2

[8] *State Workmen's Compensation Laws*, Bulletin 161 (May, 1960), pp. 2-9.
[9] Reede, *op. cit.*, p. 22.
[10] *Ibid.*, pp. 19-23, 296-297.
[11] *Ibid.*, Table 4, p. 24.
[12] *State Workmen's Compensation Laws*, Bulletin 212 (1964), pp. 4-5.

to 11 employees. The original purpose of this exclusion was for administrative reasons. It was felt that it would be too difficult to process the claims of many small employers. Since states which have covered all employees for years have had little administrative difficulty in covering small employers, there is no reason why this exemption should remain.

OCCUPATIONAL DISEASE COVERAGE

Occupational disease coverage has been a continual problem in workmen's compensation. Of 22 workmen's compensation laws existing in 1915, only Massachusetts covered occupational diseases not accidentally induced. Growth of coverage of occupational diseases under workmen's compensation laws was slow to develop. By 1920, 6 states had some type of provision and the number grew to 14 in 1930 and 26 in 1940.[13] By 1964, only one jurisdiction, Wyoming, had no coverage although 19 other states did not provide full coverage. These 19 states have what is known as schedule coverage; that is, they list the specific diseases which will be covered under the law.[14] Some of the states having schedule coverage have a much longer list of diseases covered than other states. One of the states has a list of 36 covered diseases, whereas another state only has two. Other limitations to adequate coverage of occupational diseases occur by time limits which many states place on coverage. These states provide that occupational diseases are not covered if they occur within a certain period of time after the last exposure. The time limits are generally from six months to a year after exposure. Other jurisdictions exclude coverage for occupational diseases unless the victim has been exposed to such dust diseases as silicosis, asbestosis, and other diseases for a certain period of time, for example for five out of the last ten years. Owing to the heavy costs of such diseases as silicosis and asbestosis, some employer groups have lobbied successfully to provide further restrictions on coverage. Either partial disability payments are outlawed or medical benefits are reduced or entirely eliminated for these diseases in 20 states.[15]

Blanket or full coverage for occupational diseases has been restricted because of the fear that the costs of paying for all such diseases would be too expensive for the employer. Experience over the years has indicated that occupational diseases account for only about 3 percent of work injuries. So far as costs go, all occupational disease benefits paid have amounted to a little less than 1 percent of all workmen's compensation benefits in Virginia to a high of 8.4 percent in Pennsylvania, where a high incidence of pneumoconiosis has raised the cost.[16] In general the costs have been low enough

---

13 Reede, op. cit., p. 45.
14 State Workmen's Compensation Laws, Bulletin 212 (1964), p. 8.
15 Ibid., Bulletin 161 (May, 1960), pp. 17-20.
16 Somers and Somers, op. cit., pp. 50-51.

to permit blanket coverage without much additional cost. The trend is toward blanket coverage, but many jurisdictions still fail to provide for it.

MISCELLANEOUS EXCLUSIONS

Several other special cases of exclusions may be mentioned. Five states fail to cover minors injured while illegally employed. In contrast to such exclusion, 18 jurisdictions provide that compensation above the regular amounts be paid to minors illegally employed. Over half these states require double compensation. Most of the 18 jurisdictions require that the employers pay for the additional sums themselves, for they are not permitted to insure for injuries of those illegally employed. None of the workmen's compensation acts make any distinction between citizens and aliens in regard to compensation. Some differences may be noted, though, in relation to nonresident alien dependents. Four states specifically exclude them from compensation. Nineteen states provide for smaller benefits, and nine other jurisdictions provide for the same benefits except that if they are computed to a lump sum, the nonresident alien dependents receive less. In the remaining 22 jurisdictions, the same amounts are received by nonresident alien dependents either by law or legal interpretation.[17]

ELIGIBILITY REQUIREMENTS

Certain eligibility requirements tend to limit the coverage of injured workmen under certain circumstances. In order to be covered under workmen's compensation acts, the injury must occur "out of and in the course of employment." [18] Much legal debate has ensued over whether injuries have so occurred. In general, injuries occurring on the way to or from work are not covered. Sometimes coverage is provided if the workers are riding in special buses furnished by the employer.

A question has arisen as to whether workers should be compensated for injuries while dressing for work on the employer's premise. The same problem has arisen when workers are resting or refreshing themselves. Here the more liberal courts grant compensation. Horseplay has caused legal difficulties also. Normally the courts are inclined to be more lenient if the injured victim happens to be the victim rather than the aggressor. Natural causes of injuries have also created problems. A number of cases of frostbite, heat prostration, sunstroke, and lightning cases have occurred. The prevalent practice is to grant benefits only if the worker experiences unusual exposure. Under these circumstances most lightning cases would not be covered.

---

[17] *State Workmen's Compensation Laws,* Bulletin 161 (May, 1960), pp. 65-68.
[18] Reede, *op. cit.,* pp. 35-45.

If the worker has engaged in misconduct, benefits are either denied entirely or reduced. Self-inflicted injuries and injuries resulting from intoxication are generally not compensable. Some states refuse payment to workers who have failed to use safety appliances or refuse to submit to competent treatment. A few states still deny payments for recklessness or "willful" or "culpable" negligence. In these instances the common law doctrine of negligence is apparent. Most states, although not condoning such practices, feel that withholding of benefits is not the proper remedy. Complete denial of benefits for negligence has been criticized on the grounds that it would make employers less interested in industrial safety and would deny innocent dependents adequate economic security. Because of the difficulty of determining whether hernias are occupationally induced, most states limit compensation for them.

Little is known on what percentage of accidents are not covered because they do not "arise out of and in the course of employment." In a 3½-year period of deaths in Massachusetts, there were 709 insured fatalities, but only 628 awards were granted. The trend has been toward more liberal coverage for such accidents. Certainly need can be shown in almost all such cases.

EVALUATION OF COVERAGE AND ELIGIBILITY

A number of studies have been made to estimate the numbers and percentages of workers covered and excluded from workmen's compensation laws. Professor Arthur H. Reede found that coverage increased in 1915 from 41.2 percent of all eligible workers (excluding the unemployed and self-employed) to 67 percent in 1920, 75 percent in 1930, 82 percent in 1940, and 87 percent in 1945.[19] More recently, Professor Earl Cheit concluded that 1958 coverage was 77 percent of all potentially eligible employees.[20] In 1964, the Social Security Administration estimated coverage at 80.6 percent of employed wage and salary workers. In that year 17 states had less than 70 percent of their workers covered. Twelve of these states were either Southern or Southwestern states with the other five all being located west of the Mississippi River.[21] Although labor unions and other groups have lobbied for improved coverage over the years, their strength has not been sufficient to obtain full coverage, particularly in states that are not as yet heavily industrialized. Since most students conclude the workmen's compensation laws are superior to employers' liability laws, more coverage under workmen's compensation is desirable.

[19] *Ibid.,* Table 3, p. 17, and p. 381.
[20] Cheit, *op. cit.,* Table 1.2, p. 14.
[21] Alfred M. Skolnik, "Twenty-Five Years of Workmen's Compensation Statistics," *Social Security Bulletin,* Vol. 29, No. 10 (October, 1966), pp. 4-8.

BENEFITS

Benefits under workmen's compensation are of three types. Cash payments are made to aid the worker to continue to support his family while incapacitated. Secondly, medical payments are provided for the costs of medical care. Thirdly, rehabilitation payments are also made (see previous chapter). The cash payments are divided into four types of payments depending on the severity of the accident. For those killed in industry, death benefits are paid. For those permanently incapacitated, permanent total disability payments are made. For those losing limbs or suffering other permanent damage to parts of their bodies, permanent partial disability payments are made. The remaining injuries which do not result in the permanent loss of a member are called temporary total disabilities.

DEATH BENEFITS

Approximately 14,000 deaths occur each year in industry. The social loss could be computed as the total earnings that the victim would have earned minus the cost of his maintenance during this period. It would be expected, then, that death benefits would be less than permanent total disability payments since the costs of supporting the injured workmen should be subtracted. Many states, however, pay the same benefits in death cases as in permanent total disability injuries. Benefits should also vary with the number of dependents that remain to be supported.[22] Quite clearly, a widow with four minor children is in need of more economic support than a widow who has no children. In practice, compensation for death varies considerably depending on the state involved. Some states come close to approaching an adequate benefit; others fall considerably short. Sixteen of the jurisdictions do not vary the payment according to the number of dependents. Progress, though slow, is being made in having more states pay dependents' allowances. In 1940, 23 jurisdictions paid a flat rate regardless of the number of dependents compared with 16 in 1960.

Presumably need would dictate that payments be continued until death of the widow, remarriage, or children reached at least the age of 18. However, only 13 jurisdictions provide for such benefits. All the rest either limit the payments according to a number of weeks or to a total amount. The fact that only six jurisdictions had the broader provisions in 1940 does denote progress, but still a minority of jurisdictions have such protection.

FORMULA FOR DEATH BENEFITS

Most jurisdictions base payments on a percentage of wages earned by the worker before his injury. The most typical percentage provided for a widow

22 Reede, *op. cit.*, p. 66.

with children is 66⅔ percent of wages with the next most frequent percentage being 60 percent. This figure has risen from 50 percent in 1915. Many of the state laws place maximum limits on weekly payments so that many dependents do not receive nearly as large a percentage as 66⅔. Nineteen jurisdictions have a maximum weekly benefit of less than $40, the lowest of these being Georgia ($25.50). Eleven of the states providing for a maximum below $40 are either border or southern states. The maximums in other jurisdictions are much higher. The highest is Arizona, with a weekly maximum of $153.85.

Another important restriction on death benefits is absolute limits on the total amounts of money that will be paid. Twenty-nine states have such a limitation, which ranges from a high of $25,000 in Hawaii to a low of $10,000 in South Carolina. That these limits have been raised may be seen by the fact that of 23 states having such limitation in 1940, only five had a limit above $7,000, and the median was between $5,000 to $5,999.[23] In order to protect the low-wage family, all jurisdictions except five have a minimum weekly benefit. The minimums range from $5 a week in two jurisdictions to $40.25 in the most liberal state.

ADEQUACY OF DEATH BENEFITS

A number of attempts have been made to measure the adequacy of death benefits. Professor Arthur Reede concluded that the proportion of wage loss compensated for in fatal accidents in Massachusetts was 14.8 percent (1935) and 19.6 percent for North Carolina (1940).[24] The percentage compensated for was even lower if the dependents received a flat sum rather than weekly payments. Using 1960 benefits, Professor Cheit found that death benefits replaced the following percentages of wage loss (Table 8-1). He pointed out that widows have other means of support that should be assessed. A major support today is survivors' benefits under the Social Security Act (OASDHI).[25] Other economic aids to dependents are insurance, either private or job related, retirement funds not connected with OASDHI, and third-party awards where the dependents sue third parties rather than the employer for negligence. In a study of 191 fatal accidents in California in 1956, Professor Cheit found that almost half of the dependents of those killed in industrial accidents and eligible for workmen's compensation also received OASDHI payments. Almost as many had. private life insurance (47 percent). Other sources of income with the percentage receiving them were as follows: company life insurance (34 percent), California retirement pay (14 percent) and third-party awards (4 percent). Professor Cheit

[23] Reede, *op. cit.*, Table 10, p. 77; *State Workmen's Compensation Laws*, Bulletin 161, Supplement (December, 1961), Table 11, pp. 34-38.

[24] Reede, *op. cit.*, pp. 207, 213.

[25] The remaining material of this section is taken from Cheit, *op. cit.*, Chaps. 3-5.

TABLE 8–1. LOSS REPLACED BY DEATH BENEFITS, 1960

Percentage of Loss Replaced	Number of Jurisdictions	Percentage of Loss Replaced	Number of Jurisdictions
10–19	34	50–59	2
20–29	6	60–69	1
30–39	4	70–79	1
40–49	3		

Source: Earl F. Cheit, *Injury and Recovery in the Course of Employment* (New York: John Wiley and Sons, 1961), Table 4.6, pp. 108-09. Reprinted by permission.

found that although workmen's compensation only paid 15 percent of the loss in the 191 cases, when all other payments were considered the median beneficiary received $21,293, or 34 percent of lost earnings. Workmen's compensation provided less than OASDHI for those entitled to OASDHI payments. The former paid $10,639 compared with $22,180 for OASDHI (median cases).

Beneficiaries have other sources of income as well as those mentioned above. Some widows return to work. Interest, dividends, rents, and annuities are received by some, along with payments from public assistance, and income from the second husband if the widow remarries. At the end of six years after death of the injured workman, Cheit found that when other sources of income are added to workmen's compensation, the current annual income of the widow is three-fourths of the income received in the year prior to the accident. Cheit acknowledged that this figure was overstated because no allowance was made for the increase in prices during the period.

The above figures were for the median case. Professor Cheit pointed out that some dependents of those fatally injured had a much more difficult time economically than others. Widows who remarried fared much better economically than those who did not. Furthermore, widows who worked did much better, as did widows who obtained survivors' benefits under OASDHI. In general, women between the ages of 50 and 60 fared worse than the others since fewer in this age group remarried or were eligible for survivors' benefits unless they had dependent children under 18.

In evaluating the adequacy of death benefits under workmen's compensation, such benefits by themselves replace less than 20 percent of the loss in 34 of the 51 jurisdictions and less than 40 percent in 44 jurisdictions. On the other hand, some widows who receive both OASDHI and workmen's compensation have more income after the death of their husband than before. Without integrating the two systems, many inequities result. Legislators are reluctant to raise workmen's compensation benefits, because they know that OASDHI payments are available. But those who do not receive OASDHI payments are simply out of luck.

Since OASDHI has been expanding, some have made the argument that all payments for the problem of premature death could be made through OASDHI and thus abolish workmen's compensation entirely. Several arguments may be made, though, on the side of retaining workmen's compensation. Sir William Beveridge has argued for the continuation of workmen's compensation on the grounds that it provides benefits to compensate for hazardous work, along with economic incentives for improved safety. It also offers the only justification for limiting liability under the common law.[26] If both OASDHI and workmen's compensation laws are to continue in existence, some method of coordination may be attempted. In the Minnesota law for permanent total disability, after $18,000 is paid, OASDHI payments are deducted from the workmen's compensation benefit.

Professor Earl Cheit has suggested that perhaps a workmen's compensation annuity could be purchased with deductions for OASDHI payments. The cost of providing annuities would be more than states are now paying for death benefits. Yet the overall costs would not increase greatly, for death benefits are only 10 to 15 percent of the total cost of workmen's compensation. In turn, workmen's compensation costs average only 1 percent of payrolls.

The 1965 Advisory Council on Social Security discussed the issue of concurrent OASDHI and workmen's compensation payments. This group felt that since the OASDHI was a contributory one and workmen's compensation was not, deductions should be made from workmen's compensation rather than OASDHI. However, putting this recommendation into effect will require each of the states to take action. Possibly because of the administrative problem, the 1965 amendments to the Social Security Act limited disability payments so that a disabled worker may not receive more in monthly benefits from both Social Security and workmen's compensation combined than 80 percent of the average monthly earnings credited to his Social Security account before he became disabled. Amendments to the Social Security Act in 1967 stipulated that in computing average earnings, workers earning in excess of the annual amount taxable under social security could be included. No change was made which would restrict concurrent payments of survivors' benefits and death benefits under workmen's compensation.

PERMANENT TOTAL BENEFITS

The same type of formula is used in permanent total benefits as other injuries.[27] That is, percentage of wages is paid subject to certain maximum and minimum weekly amounts. Twenty-six jurisdictions permit payments

---

[26] Sir William Beveridge, *Social Insurance and Allied Services* (New York, Macmillan, 1942), pp. 39-40.
[27] Cheit, *op. cit.*, Chaps. 6, 11.

to continue until death, but the other states either limit the number of weeks' payments or the total amount to be paid.

Appraisals have been made of the adequacy of permanent total disability payments. Professor Cheit found that older workers had less loss than younger workers. Table 8-2 shows the percentages of loss replaced that he found.

TABLE 8–2. LOSS REPLACED BY PERMANENT TOTAL DISABILITY BENEFITS, 1960

Percentage of Loss Replaced	Number of Jurisdictions (Age 44)	Number of Jurisdictions (Age 52)
0–9	1	0
10–19	23	7
20–29	5	20
30–39	15	15
40–49	3	5
50–59	4	3
60–69	0	1

Source: Computed from Earl F. Cheit, op. cit., Table 6.5, pp. 172-73.

PERMANENT PARTIAL INJURIES

Permanent partial injuries are divided into what are called scheduled and nonscheduled injuries. The scheduled injuries provide for a specific amount of payment for a specific loss, such as $200 for the loss of an arm, $40 for the loss of a toe, and so forth. The nonscheduled injuries are compensated as a percentage of wages for a limited period. Vast differences and inconsistencies in payments exist between the states. For example, Montana pays $75 for the loss of both the thumb and the first finger whereas Utah pays $60 for the loss of a thumb but only $30 for the loss of the first finger. California pays a larger amount for the loss of a leg than an arm at the shoulder—$320 compared with $300; yet Connecticut pays almost 40 percent more for the loss of an arm at the shoulder—$275 compared to $208 for the loss of a leg. Most states pay more for the loss of an arm than a leg although the healing period is longer for loss of a leg and earnings are impaired more. Apparently most of the states were misled into thinking about machine operators when they granted larger benefits for the loss of an arm. In such cases, losses of arms would result in a greater loss of earning power than the loss of a leg. However, most losses of legs occur in mining, lumbering, construction, and transportation, in all of which industries the loss of a leg has tended to bar future employment.[28]

[28] Reede, op. cit., pp. 121-122.

When workmen's compensation laws were first passed, benefits were predominantly based on loss of earnings. Most of the states later adopted a flat-rate disability schedule because they feared that paying workers according to the loss of earning power would tend to discourage workers from finding better jobs. Later California experimented with a different basis for permanent partial benefits. Both occupation and age were considered in computing benefits. A worker who lost a finger in an occupation in which the use of a finger was vital to the work would suffer much more economic loss than another worker whose loss of a finger was immaterial to his occupation. Age also was considered a factor. The assumption was made that the loss of recuperative powers of an older man should call for more compensation even though an injured younger man would be handicapped for a longer period of time. Some 75 pages of schedules were needed to compare the various injuries by occupation and ages. Although some inequities have been found within the system, a number of students feel that the California system provides for more equitable permanent partial benefits than other states.[29]

Most permanent partial cases result in minor rather than major limb loss. About 87 percent of such cases are classified as minor rather than major. In California for those workers suffering from 1 to 19 percent disability, 80 percent of the workers suffered no permanent wage loss. Unfortunately, the more severe the injury, the less adequate were the workmen's compensation payments. Professor Cheit found that for those severely injured who did suffer a wage loss, the median case showed a replacement of wages by workmen's compensation of only 36 percent. Their wage loss in the median case was $46,562 during their lifetime.

Basing benefits on the amount of disability has tended to discourage rehabilitation, for the more rehabilitation that occurs, the less cash workmen's compensation benefits that will be paid. Accordingly, a number of students of workmen's compensation have worked on the problem of how to structure workmen's compensation benefits so as to best promote rehabilitation. Earl Cheit suggested that the worker receive another payment equal to the disability payment if his employer did not reemploy him. In order to provide as much incentive as possible to reemploy the injured worker, the plan called for the employer to pay this sum himself, without being permitted to insure for it. To prevent unjust charges against the employer, the administrative agency would determine whether there were adequate reasons for not rehiring the worker. Rehabilitation would be recommended, and if adequate reasons were found for not rehiring the worker, the employer would be absolved of the extra charges. Professor Cheit cited data to show that most employees are reemployable, and most hiring of injured workers is done by their former employers. Providing a financial incentive to their

[29] Ibid., pp. 125-127.

former employers to rehire them would encourage their rehirement. He felt that since workmen's compensation already provided a penalty for high accident rates, a penalty could likewise be applied for those employers who refused for no good reason to rehire their injured workmen.[30]

TEMPORARY TOTAL DISABILITY

Most industrial injuries (93 percent) result in no permanent injury to the workman but are of a temporary nature only. On the average, these injuries result in only several weeks of disability. A California sample showed that 9 percent of the temporary total injuries cause the loss of only one day of work and 44 percent do not extend beyond seven days. Almost three-fourths of the injuries are healed within 21 days, and only 6 percent of these injuries last beyond six months.[31]

Most of the states pay a percentage of wage as a benefit, usually 66⅔ percent of wages. But as of September, 1964, twenty states set a maximum weekly benefit at $43.75 or less, with the median state paying $50. When workmen's compensation benefit laws were first passed, the weekly maximums were only slightly below the average weekly wage in manufacturing of $11.22. That weekly maximums have not kept pace with averages can be seen by noting that average weekly manufacturing wages in September, 1964, were $103.94. The latest report showed that the average temporary total disability recipient was paid $76.81 for 13.8 compensable days. Most states have a waiting period of one week in which no compensation is paid. Thirty-four jurisdictions have a waiting period of seven days, 4 require five days, 14 specify three days, 1 has a two-day waiting period, and Oregon requires none. Most of the states provide for retroactive coverage during the first week if the injury lasts beyond a specified period of time.[32] Since most states have a waiting period, the percentage compensated for in temporary total disability cases was 37 percent.[33] Although this percentage is higher than for more severe injuries, it is still substantially below the relative payments that were made when compensation laws were first passed. One study in Illinois showed that maximum weekly benefits for temporary injuries were 98 percent of average weekly earnings in 1914. By 1919 this

[30] For other suggestions of structuring cash benefits to provide incentives for rehabilitation, see Monroe Berkowitz, ed., *Rehabilitating the Disabled Worker*, Washington, D.C., U.S. Department of Health, Education, and Welfare, Vocational Rehabilitation Administration (1963), pp. 59, 75.

[31] Cheit, *op. cit.*, p. 151 and Table 2.1, p. 29; Dorothy McCamman and A. M. Skolnik, "Workmen's Compensation: Measures of Accomplishment," *Social Security Bulletin*, Vol. 17, No. 3 (March, 1954), p. 8; "Workmen's Compensation Injury Table," *Proceedings of the Casualty Acturial Society*, Vol. XLII, p. 140.

[32] *State Workmen's Compensation Laws*, Bulletin 161 (May, 1960), pp. 21-23.

[33] Alfred M. Skolnik, "Trends in Workmen's Compensation: Coverage, Benefits, and Costs," *Social Security Bulletin*, Vol. 21 (August, 1958), p. 9.

figure dropped to less than 50 percent and in 1952, the last year of the study, the amount compensated was 34 percent.[34]

MEDICAL BENEFITS

When workmen's compensation laws were first passed, they provided for cash payments to compensate for loss in wages. Shortly after passage of such laws, it became apparent that more cognizance should be taken of medical care in the program. Gradually more medical benefits were introduced into the system until today 21 states provide unlimited medical benefits by law for accidents, and another two states grant the same benefits either through court interpretation or approval of the state administering agency. Seventeen other jurisdictions do have maximum medical benefits, but their administrative agencies are authorized to extend them without limit. Only 14 states limit medical benefits. Of these states the median state provides six months of medical care. One estimate has been made of the cost of providing unlimited medical benefits in those 14 states. The increase in premiums to cover such costs would have amounted to only $126,000 for the median state.[35] Seventeen states provide less liberal medical benefits for occupational diseases than for accidents.

One of the problems involved in medical care is who should choose the doctor. If the employer or insurance company has the right to choose the doctor, there is the danger that the doctor might favor the employer in determining the amount of injury. Too many favorable decisions in favor of the employee might cause the employer or insurance company to dismiss the doctor. Where the company doctor passes on the medical determination it is contended that the state agency sees only a one-sided picture. It is almost the same as granting a company the right to choose the attorney to defend the injured workman. On the other hand, permitting the workman the free choice of a doctor may be criticized also. In such cases, the physician may be inclined to report more serious damage in order that the workman may receive a larger award. Conflicting reports depending on whom the physician represents was shown in a study of court cases studied by Professor Sam Barton in Texas.

Case No. 102

Injury: Lifting hundred-pound weight; strained right shoulder.

Company doctor: X rays show calcium deposits resultant of bursitis; believes man could go to work tomorrow if case was settled; mostly functional and emotional.

[34] H. A. Katz and E. M. Wirpel, "Workmen's Compensation 1910–1952: Are Present Benefits Adequate?" *Labor Law Journal*, Vol. 4, No. 4 (March, 1953), p. 171.
[35] Cheit, *op. cit.*, Table 2.5, pp. 44-45.

Interview: Claimant's wife stated that statements by company doctor outraged her husband.

Client's doctor: Claimant has ruptured ligaments and severe bruises.

Board award: $1,144.40

Jury award: $2,400

Case No. 121

Injury: A motor vehicle was driven into a welding machine which in turn struck an elevator door and the door in turn struck the plaintiff injurying his back, hips, pelvis, and lower extremities.

Company doctor: This man shows no physical injury to his back. On the contrary, his physical findings are typical of those seen in functional back conditions and are inconsistent with organic pathology. My diagnosis is aversion hysteria, and I don't consider him to have any disability on a physical basis.

Client's doctor: From X ray and physical examination it is seen that this man has had considerable injury to his lower back. Totally incapacitated for work as a laboring man.

Board award: $250

Agreed judgment: $1,500

Case No. 76

Injury: In truck collision, thrown forward injurying right knee cap.

Company doctor: Contusion, but not serious. Another report—no objective evidence of disability or injury to the right knee.

Client's doctor: Evidence of serious tearing of the fibers of the patellar tendon and some strain of the ligaments surrounding the knee joint.

Board award: Denied—Failure to establish compensable injury

Agreed judgment: $1,250 [36]

In the early workmen's compensation laws, few states gave the worker the right to choose his own physician. Gradually this right has expanded until on January 1, 1962, 16 jurisdictions permitted the worker free choice of a physician. In 32 jurisdictions the employer or insurance carrier selects the physician, but in 25 of the 32 jurisdictions, the worker may change doctors. In six jurisdictions, the employee may choose a physician from a panel, but in five of the six jurisdictions the panel is chosen by the employer. In the sixth jurisdiction the panel is chosen by the Workmen's Compensation Board.[37] From Professor Barton's study of Texas cases and a survey of the literature, he maintains that the method of selecting a doctor is one of the

[36] Sam B. Barton, *How Texas Cares for Her Injured Workers* (Denton, Tex., North Texas State College, 1956), pp. 37-40. Reprinted by permission.

[37] *Medical Care Under Workmen's Compensation,* U.S. Department of Labor, Bureau of Labor Standards, Bulletin 244 (1962), Chapter 2.

major issues in workmen's compensation. He along with some other students favor a system of impartial medical experts as a solution to this problem.[38]

INSURANCE PROBLEMS UNDER
WORKMEN'S COMPENSATION

There are a number of different ways that employers may insure the costs of workmen's compensation. Large employers may self-insure if they satisfy all the state requirements, such as posting bond or depositing securities. Only eight jurisdictions do not permit employers to self-insure. In 18 jurisdictions the states have a state fund with whom employers may insure. Of these 18 jurisdictions six provide for exclusive state funds; that is, employers may insure only with the exclusive state fund, and may not take out private insurance. In the other 12 of 18 jurisdictions having state funds, the funds are competitive; that is, employers may either insure through the state fund or through a private insurance company. In all the other jurisdictions there is no state fund, so that employers must insure through private insurance companies or possibly self-insure.

The amount of workmen's compensation insurance sold has increased steadily over the years. In 1917, $94 million of net premiums were written. By 1927, this figure had grown to $208 million, and reached the $1 billion mark in 1952. By 1960 a total of $2.3 billion in premiums was written. Table 8-3 shows the amounts of premiums written by the different types of carriers.

Over the years, the percentage of business written by state funds has tended to remain constant although exclusive state funds have a smaller percentage of the business than they had in 1917 and competitive state funds have a larger percentage. So far as private insurance companies go, stock companies have lost business, on a percentage basis, to the mutuals.

RATE SETTING

In the making of rates, leadership is exercised by the National Council on Compensation Insurance, which is the filing agency for rates in a majority

---

[38] The system of consulting impartial medical specialists in rating, however, has been criticized on the ground that a majority of the specialists are alleged to have insurance company connections. Professor Cheit found that in California, where the employer chooses the physicians, three-fourths of the workers were satisfied with their medical treatment. Only from 9 to 16 percent were dissatisfied. The remainder felt that some of the doctors were good and others not good, and in a few cases the workers were uncertain or there was no report as to their attitude. Professor Cheit cited evidence, on the other hand, of abuse, poor medical practice, and biased medical testimony. The evidence cited was from three AMA sponsored studies, IAIABC medical committee surveys, statements of practitioners, and three recent studies of workmen's compensation in Michigan, New York, and Texas. See Cheit, op. cit., pp. 58-59.

TABLE 8–3. RELATIVE SHARES OF WORKMEN'S COMPENSATION BUSINESS AS INDICATED BY NET PREMIUMS WRITTEN, 1917–1960 (PREMIUMS IN MILLIONS)

Carrier Group[a]	1917		1926		1940		1950		1960	
	Premiums	Percent	Premiums	Percent	Premiums	Percent	Premiums	Percent	Premiums	Percent
Private carriers	$76.2	81.0	$215.0	83.2	$269.7	76.2	$711.3	81.2	$1,903.2	83.1
Stock	64.6	68.6	154.8	59.9	166.8	47.1	439.2	50.1	935.0	40.8
Mutuals	11.6	12.4	44.7	17.3	96.9	27.4	258.1	29.5	942.8	41.2
Reciprocals, etc.	b	b	15.5	6.0	6.0	1.7	14.0[c]	1.6	25.4	1.1
State funds[d]	17.9	19.0	43.3	16.8	84.5	25.8	165.0[e]	18.8	386.6	16.9
Exclusives	11.8	12.5	24.3	9.4	39.8	11.2	69.0	7.9	201.4	8.8
Competitives	6.1	6.5	19.0	7.4	44.7	12.6	96.0	10.9	185.2	8.1
Total	94.2	100.0	258.3	100.0	354.2	100.0	876.3	100.0	2,289.8	100.0

a Subtotals do not equal components because of rounding.
b Not available.
c Earned premiums.
d Fund data are not adjusted for effects of premium discounts; therefore, they are somewhat understated. Federal Employees' Compensation System is not included.
e Puerto Rico (exclusive) is not available.
Sources: 1917, 1926, 1940: A. H. Reede, op. cit., p. 263 (based on data from Spectator Insurance Yearbooks and state reports). 1950: Harold M. Somers and Anne R. Somers, Workmen's Compensation (New York, John Wiley and Sons, 1954), Table IV–B, p. 99. 1960 stocks, mutuals, and reciprocals: Best's Fire and Casualty Edition. 1960 state funds: State reports.

of states. State funds have independent rating bureaus, but the competititve funds work closely with the National Council. In setting rates a gross manual rate is computed for all occupational classifications or industrial processes. In all, there are about 600 such classifications representing all industries and occupations. Manual rates have two components. One is the pure premium, which is based on the average loss costs of a large group of broadly homogeneous risks. The other factor is expense loading, which is based on the expenses of insuring each group. Expense loading is composed of the following factors: acquisition costs, home office administrative costs, claims adjustment, safety inspection, and maintenance of rating bureaus, taxes, profits, and contingency. The National Council on Compensation Insurance estimates that expense loading constitutes about 41 percent of gross premiums. Acquisition costs were about 17.5 percent of gross premiums, home office administrative costs were computed at 7.7 percent, and claims adjustment as 8.2 percent of gross premiums. The other three costs—safety inspection, taxes, and profit and contingency—were each about 2½ percent of gross premiums.[39]

Manual rates are computed per unit of exposure. The most reliable unit of exposure is man-hours of employment, but lack of adequate statistics has necessitated the use of payrolls instead. In order to more nearly reflect man-hours, overtime rates and bonuses are excluded from payrolls. Manual rates are quoted as a certain dollar amount per each $100 of payroll. Rates vary quite markedly from one occupation to another and from state to state for the same occupations. The average manual rate in Arizona, the highest-cost state, is more than three times as high as the rate in Georgia, the lowest-cost state. Differences in state rates are due to differences in benefits and the amount of hazardous industry in a state.

MERIT RATING

In order to reward a good safety record and encourage safety, manual rates are modified by merit rating. Since merit rating is impractical for very small risks, it is not applied to employers paying premiums of less than $500. It thus excludes about 80 percent of all firms. In a few states, merit rating is based upon the amount of safety practices put into operation. In most states this system of merit rating has been superseded by prospective experience rating, in which the actual experience rating over a given period, usually one to three years, is compared with the average of the classification to which the employer belongs. Another method, more attractive to large companies, is retrospective rating, in which an employer is tentatively rated, and then the final premium is adopted after the year of experience. The particular advantage to large companies is that the broker's commission on a percentage basis is reduced the larger the premium written. It is probably true that the

[39] Somers and Somers, *op. cit.*, p. 104.

largest firms would continue to follow the best safety practices today regardless of merit rating, but they do expect that they be given a cheaper rate because of their lower accident rate.

PROFITABILITY OF WORKMEN'S COMPENSATION INSURANCE

In general, mutual companies have operated more profitably than stock companies. In 1964, for example, stock companies showed a 3.1 percent net gain ratio over premiums charged, compared with 9.7 percent for mutual companies.[40] In general, the losses incurred as a percentage of premiums have been about the same for stock and mutual companies. The greater profitability of mutual companies comes from fewer expenses incurred. In 1964 the expense ratio (expenses as a percentage of premiums earned) of stock companies was 33.4 percent, compared with 26.6 percent for mutual companies. Most of the difference in expenses was due to selling costs.[41] Stock companies generally pay a commission to agents on each policy sold, whereas mutual companies usually pay their salesmen a salary. Mutual companies have also engaged in more selective underwriting over the years. The poorer net gain experience of the stock companies explains why they have been doing a smaller percentage of the business.

STATE VERSUS PRIVATE INSURANCE

The percentage of business written by state funds has remained relatively constant since 1917 (see Table 8-3), even though the costs of state funds are lower than private insurance companies. State funds have fewer selling costs than private companies. In weighing the merits of state funds versus private insurance, services rendered must also be evaluated. In this regard some of the state funds have not rated too well. Lack of adequate personnel standards and low salaries have been typical of a number of state funds. Some state funds have also been slow in paying claims. Safety work by many states has been inferior to that of the better private carriers. On the other hand, some private insurance companies have been criticized for being unwilling to assume high risks. A problem of this kind becomes quite grave if

[40] Skolnik, "Twenty-Five Years of Workmen's Compensation Statistics," Table 9, p. 22.

[41] Ibid.; Reede, op. cit., pp. 251-260. In a later publication, Professor Reede stated that he felt that commission scales were higher than warranted. Especially was this true on renewal commissions, in which the agent's services are likely to be somewhat less valuable than when the policy was first written. See Arthur H. Reede, "Workmen's Compensation Reform," in Proceedings of a Conference on Workmen's Compensation, 2nd Annual Conference on Business Insurance, Oregon State University (June, 1964), pp. 43-53.

no state fund is available with which the employer may insure. One possible solution here is to require the companies to assume a specific proportion of the poor risks.[42] Attempting to analyze the merits of state funds versus private insurance is difficult. Perhaps the safest generalization is that some state funds have operated efficiently as have some private insurance companies. On the other hand, other state funds and other private insurance companies have operated inefficiently.[43] Self-insurance is the cheapest way of assuming compensation liability, but the fact that more and more employers take out insurance from state funds or private companies would indicate that there are substantial advantages for doing so.[44]

ADMINISTRATION OF WORKMEN'S COMPENSATION

COURT ADMINISTRATION

Five jurisdictions, Alabama, Louisiana, New Mexico, Tennessee, and Wyoming, have no separate machinery for administering the workmen's compensation program. In these states, the injured workman and the employer or his insurance carrier are expected to arrive at a settlement. If the parties fail to agree, they may go to court. Practically all studies of this type of administration have been critical of it. Formerly, 14 states used the court administration procedure. The failure of it to perform adequately resulted in its demise in nine jurisdictions.

Several major criticisms of court administration may be noted. One is that a more specialized group dealing solely with industrial accidents and diseases should be able to familiarize itself with such problems and thus administer them more efficiently than a court. Another criticism is that a specialized administrative group should be better able than a court of law to handle such administrative problems as handling of claims, administering proper medical care, and making payments. The existence of an administering agency leaves courts the more appropriate function of appeal.[45]

Without adequate machinery for processing workmen's compensation cases, delay inevitably results. In one case a logger was disabled for six months as a result of a fall from a truck. He approached his boss about compensation, but was informed that the company wasn't insured. After a trip to the state capital by the wife of the injured workman, she was advised to have an attorney-general file suit in the appropriate county. Being too busy to file suit immediately, the case finally came to court only after a delay of a year or more. In the meantime, the employer had left the state, and the

---

[42] Somers and Somers, *op. cit.*, pp. 132-134.
[43] Reede, *op. cit.*, pp. 237-238, 259-260, 304-316.
[44] Somers and Somers, *op. cit.*, p. 127.
[45] *Ibid.*, pp. 148-150.

suit was dropped. The injured workman received no compensation of any kind, and was forced to seek public assistance to feed his family.[46]

STATE ADMINISTRATIVE AGENCIES

A more acceptable method of administering workmen's compensation is through state administering agencies. Either the agencies are a part of the State Department of Labor (19 jurisdictions), or they are an independent state agency (27 jurisdictions).[47] Since workmen's compensation is one type of labor legislation, a number of jurisdictions have placed the administration of such laws under their Department of Labor. This form of administration has been criticized on the ground that the State Department of Labor may not be completely unbiased. For this reason, a majority of jurisdictions prefer to have a separate agency.

As in many phases of governmental activity, the state workmen's compensation agencies have had a difficult time of properly administering workmen's compensation because of a lack of funds. In Texas, for example, funds provided for administration are so small that they amount to only $3 on the average for each case processed.[48] In view of the reluctance of many state legislatures to appropriate sufficient money, almost half the states now impose some administrative costs upon insurance companies and self-insurers. That such a device is bringing in more money may be seen by the fact that those states making such assessments received in income an average of 3.07 per $100 of benefits disbursed compared with $1.57 per $100 for states not making such an assessment (1964).[49]

Lack of sufficient income has meant that in many states salaries have been too low to attract high quality personnel. Besides the salary problem, the lack of Civil Service regulations has resulted in a large turnover of personnel with every new administration. Fortunately, more and more states are adopting Civil Service procedures to aid in maintaining a more efficient work force.

METHODS OF PROCESSING CASES

Agreement Method

There are three main methods of processing workmen's compensation cases.[50] The *agreement method* calls for the employer or the insurance carrier to propose a settlement. If the injured workman agrees to it, an agree-

---

[46] Inez B. Gill, *Workmen's Compensation in New Mexico* (Legislative Council Service, 1955), pp. 51-52.

[47] *State Workmen's Compensation Laws,* Bulletin 161 (May, 1960), p. 69.

[48] Barton, *op. cit.,* p. 64.

[49] Skolnik, "Twenty-Five Years of Workmen's Compensation Statistics," p. 25.

[50] Somers and Somers, *op. cit.,* pp. 150-156.

ment is signed, and no further processing by the state administering agency is necessary. A majority of states use this system. One of the obvious disadvantages of this system is that too frequently workers agree to a settlement which is not to their best interest. A study was made in New Jersey in 1958 in which 2,778 settlements were analyzed by referees (10 percent of all cases). Only 37 percent of the settlements satisfied the referees on their face. Of the remaining 1,767 cases analyzed further, additional cash payments were made in 38 percent of the cases, 26 percent were still pending, in 5 percent of the cases the settlement was found adequate, in 18 percent the workers declined a hearing, and in the remaining 13 percent the worker himself appealed the case to a higher level or filed a formal petition.[51]

Hearing and Direct Payment Methods

In order to give the workers more protection, the State of New York adopted the *hearing method,* whereby a hearing is required in each case. The requirement of a hearing in each case creates the necessity for a large number of administrative personnel. Most students of workmen's compensation were critical of New York's system as being unnecessarily cumbersome, and New York has revised its system. Most accolades go to the administrative system adopted by Wisconsin, Michigan, and four other jurisdictions called the *direct payment method.* Under this system the employer or insurance carrier is expected to begin payment on their own initiative after the waiting period has transpired. The worker does not have to agree to any type of settlement, nor to sign anything. The employer or insurance carrier is required to file a report on each case and to designate what its settlement has been. The commission contacts each injured workman to brief him of his rights under the law, and analyzes each case on its merits. Either party may challenge the settlement, and cases may be reopened within six years from the date of the last payment. In spite of the obvious merits of this system, few states have adopted it.

Court Appeal

The above procedure applies to uncontested cases. If either party is dissatisfied with the decision, it may be appealed, first to commissions in those states which have such an agency, and then to the courts. Most cases are settled informally, but estimates show that from 10 to 30 percent of the cases are contested. In some instances cases may be closed prematurely so that the worker has no choice but to contest the case. The following case is an example of the problems involved in contesting a case.

A worker in a grocery chain [was] injured when three 73-pound crates fell from the top of a stack, knocking him down and injuring his lower back and

[51] Monroe Berkowitz, *Workmen's Compensation: The New Jersey Experience* (New Brunswick, N.J., Rutgers, 1960), pp. 103-104.

causing deep lacerations to his left arm and shoulder. Although he experienced severe pain in his back and left leg and was barely able to walk, his supervisor offered no medical aid but sent the injured worker home. When the pain failed to yield to hot pack and other home remedies during the afternoon and night, the worker went to the company doctor, who took X-ray pictures, diagnosed the injury as broken ribs and a pulled ligament in the lower left side, and confined him to the hospital for four days.

As his back got no better following this treatment, the injured man consulted a second doctor, who, after examining him, confined him to the hospital for eight days employing special braces and stretchers. After this treatment the patient was improved but still unable to resume the heavy work of a warehouse worker. The insurance company, which had paid medical costs up to this point, discontinued payment, and also terminated the $25 a week compensation on grounds that he "was able to work."

When his compensation stopped coming, the worker hired a lawyer and filed suit, claiming total and permanent disability. In the meantime, his wife and five children, aged 3 to 9 years, were "feeling the pinch." Even while the compensation continued coming, their income was reduced from his pre-injury wage of $57.69 to $25 per week. They had found difficulty in trying to subsist on his regular wage and with the reduced income, they were "barely able to hang on, living from one meal to the next." Their situation was so critical that the neighbors helped out with food. (The Dallas City–County Welfare Office normally withholds assistance from compensation cases under litigation.) As a result of such economic pressure, his pregnant wife went to work and suffered a miscarriage which produced more hospital and doctor bills.

With the decline of income personal belongings went to the pawn broker, the family car was repossessed, rent payments accumulated and $200 was borrowed from a friend. Under these pressures, although still unable to work, the injured man took a job doing light janitor work but found himself unable to "hold down" even this type of employment. He believes himself permanently incapacitated to do the heavy manual labor he has always done in the past.

As a result of his court suit he was able to obtain a compromise settlement of $4,000, which would indicate a reappraisal of the seriousness of his injury by the insurance company. But one-third of this went to the lawyer and a substantial portion of the remainder was absorbed by the doctors who had been treating his injury. He had no sense of feeling in his left leg. At the time of interview the court settlement money was nearly gone, but his disability was still with him.[52]

Although higher awards are received from court appeal, such appeal has the obvious disadvantage of being slow. An example of such delay is as follows:

A claimant attorney cited, from his own experience, an extreme case of court delay involving the accidental death of a Negro worker in 1950. When his common-law wife sued for $9,000 compensation, the insurance company claimed knowledge of a marriage certificate involving another man. Search of the records

[52] Barton, *op. cit.*, pp. 13-14.

in the East Texas county, where the certificate was alleged to be on file, was unsuccessful, and the County Judge testified under oath that no such certificate was in his county records. Then the insurance company produced witnesses from West Texas who testified that the woman had lived with another man during the cotton picking season. When the plaintiff won judgment in the trial court, the case was appealed and, at the time of the interview, five years after the accident, it was before the State Supreme Court. Meanwhile, during the past winter, the plaintiff had died from 'exposure and starvation' although the attorney, who doesn't believe in lending expense money to claimants, had given the claimant expense money totalling about $500.[53]

The estimated time of making payments after the injury in the United States is one month, although some of the more efficient jurisdictions are able to make payments within one or two weeks. The one-month average is an improvement over the early days of workmen's compensation, when the average time of payment was more than two months.[54] Court cases naturally take longer. In Texas, one study showed the elapsed time from the injury to settlement of a court case was ten months.[55] In Rhode Island, it commonly takes from 15 months to 2 years for hearing and trial cases. The further the case is appealed, obviously, the longer it takes to settle.

Another criticism of court handling of workmen's compensation cases applies to those jurisdictions that permit *trial de nova*. Under this arrangement, the courts are not confined to the function of settling the legal issues involved, but they redetermine the facts in the case rather than accepting them from the state administering agency. The International Association of Industrial Accident Boards and Commission (IAIABC) has passed a resolution against court determination of the facts.

In spite of the weakness of *trial de nova*, such appeal does provide additional protection to workers. In a study of 145 Texas cases chosen at random on appeal from the Industrial Accident Board of Texas, the administrative agency in Texas for workmen's compensation, Professor Sam Barton found that the Industrial Accident Board had granted a median award of $201. Upon appeal, the median award received was $1,216. From this an average of $417 in legal fees was subtracted to leave a net median settlement of $743, or more than three times the board award. In 130 of the 145 cases more was received on appeal than the board had awarded. In the other 15 cases the court awarded less than the board. Either the claimant's attorney erred in thinking more money could be obtained from a court case or the appeal had been made by the insurance company against an award which they thought was too high. From his study Professor Barton concluded that the present system of appeal was the principal safeguard of workers' rights. He did not

---

[53] *Ibid.*, p. 44.
[54] Somers and Somers, *op. cit.*, p. 155.
[55] Barton, *op. cit.*, p. 35.

advocate any changes in the appeal system until major changes were made in the workmen's compensation law and its administration.[56]

LITIGATION PROBLEMS

It had been hoped when workmen's compensation was first introduced, that litigation would be reduced considerably. It was expected that payments would be automatically determined without recourse to expensive litigation. In practice, workmen's compensation has not eliminated extensive use of attorneys. In Oklahoma, for example, labor unions specifically advise all injured workmen to hire an attorney for their own protection. On the opposing side, insurance companies and self-insurers now employ some 5,000 attorneys to work primarily on workmen's compensation cases.[57] One major issue causing litigation revolves around whether the disability is due to employment and thus covered under the law. Hernias, occupational disease, and other borderline types of cases cause much litigation. The other major litigation issue is the determination of the extent of disability.

It is generally expected that the amount of litigation will remain large. Some attempt has been made to regulate the amount of attorney's fees. They are being standardized at about 20 percent of the benefit, although some jurisdictions still allow the attorney to collect as much as $33\frac{1}{3}$ percent or more.[58] In only 29 jurisdictions can fees be effectively regulated.[59] One suggestion made by Professor Arthur Larson is that the attorney's fees be added to the statutory benefit amount since that amount is considered to be the fair price for the injury.[60] Other suggestions to reduce litigation are to improve administration of the laws and provide more adequate benefits so that workers will be satisfied with the amount granted them.[61]

LUMP-SUM PAYMENTS

In administering workmen's compensation, most states permit benefits to be paid in a lump sum rather than in the form of a weekly benefit. When such a payment is made, the employer or insurance carrier usually is released from any further payment. A number of arguments can be advanced in favor of lump-sum payments, and these account for its popularity. First of all, the case can be settled quickly without going to a hearing, and thus save legal time and expense. Workers receive cash immediately and, in general, money

---

[56] *Ibid.*, pp. 24-31, 72.

[57] Somers and Somers, *op. cit.*, p. 180.

[58] *Ibid.*, p. 184.

[59] *Attorney's Fees in Workmen's Compensation*, U.S. Department of Labor Standards, Bulletin 220 (September, 1960), p. 6.

[60] Cheit, *op. cit.*, p. 268.

[61] For a more detailed analysis of the litigation problem, *see* Berkowitz, *Rehabilitating the Disabled Worker*, Chap. 4.

today is considered more important than money received later. Some of the money may be used for investment purposes or enable the injured workman to open a business. One study has been made of the use of funds by those obtaining lump-sum benefits. The findings of this study are summarized in Table 8-4. This study would hardly support the conclusion that a majority of workers used the funds for investment or rehabilitation purposes.

TABLE 8-4. DISPOSITION OF LUMP-SUM BENEFITS BY INJURED WORKERS

Disposition	*Percentages*
Pressing debts or living expenses	38
Investments (81% successful)	14
No special use	24
Buy or improve homes	6
Purpose not listed or unknown	17

Source: Earl F. Cheit, *Injury and Recovery in the Course of Employment* (New York: John Wiley and Sons, 1961), p. 276. Reprinted by permission.

From the insurance companies' point of view, lump-sum payments do have the advantage of limiting any further liability.[62] Furthermore, they know exactly how much the injury will cost in contrast to continuing claims that may arise through unlimited medical or other benefits. Some workers prefer cash settlements since in some cases the weekly benefits are so low as not to be adequate. Some older workers prefer cash settlements, which they may pass on to heirs. Otherwise an early death may limit the amount of benefits going to them. Lastly it has been argued that lump-sum payments aid in rehabilitation. The fact that payments are made will eliminate the problem of the workman foregoing rehabilitation until a profitable settlement is made. The lump sum may also enable the injured workman to support himself more adequately while engaging in rehabilitation.

Those arguing against lump-sum payments maintain that few workers use them for rehabilitation purposes. Furthermore, proper attention is not given to restorative medicine when the worker is paid off and not provided further treatment. The waiver of further medical treatment is one of the serious disadvantages of the lump-sum payment. In general, the worker receives less under the lump-sum arrangement. It has been found that it is mainly poorer workers who avail themselves of a lump-sum payment. Many workers do not realize until too late that they have waived all rights to future workmen's compensation, and are quite bitter when they learn the truth.

In weighing the advantages and disadvantages of lump-sum payments,

[62] For an analysis of lump-sum payments, from which this material was obtained, *see* Somers and Somers, *op. cit.,* pp. 159-164, and Cheit, *op. cit.,* pp. 274-276.

most students are of the opinion that the disadvantages outweigh the advantages. The IAIABC has suggested that the lump-sum payments should be used only in cases in which they would facilitate the rehabilitation of the worker, and that they should not be used for capital enrichment or the convenience of either the claimant's lawyer or the company or insurance carrier. The IAIABC has recommended that a better alternative to lump-sum payments would be to increase weekly benefits.[63] In spite of the serious disadvantages, it is surprising to note the widespread use of the lump-sum payment. The Illinois Industrial Commission reported that one-fourth of all its cases are lump sums, and that these payments, being of larger amounts, amounted to from 80 to 85 percent of all cash benefits.[64] In California, such cases have grown from 24.5 percent of all cases in 1950 to 39 percent in 1959.[65] The IAIABC has recommended that employers or insurance carriers should not be permitted to be released from further liability. It suggests that a state should have the right at any time to reopen a case, because sometimes damage from an accident or occupational disease may not manifest itself until years later. Only a few states, however, have adopted this recommendation.

RECORD KEEPING

One criticism of workmen's compensation administration has been that the record keeping and statistical analysis in most states has been extremely poor. IAIABC has recommended standard records, but as yet few states have adopted their standards. The dearth of statistics has handicapped the successful operation of workmen's compensation. In some jurisdictions, analysis of length of time before payment has provided administrators with an incentive to maintain or improve on the average. Records of amounts paid on certain types of injuries should also prove of value for future settlements. The most recent analysis of workmen's compensation statistics in 1959 confirmed the same findings of a quarter of a century ago that record keeping in workmen's compensation needs a substantial amount of improvement.[66]

COSTS OF ADMINISTRATION

An extensive survey of costs of administering the workmen's compensation program was made in Illinois, where it was found that from 1946 to 1949 injured workmen received $49.3 million in payments, whereas operating costs of the program came to $64 million. The $64 million were broken down

[63] *Discussion of Industrial Accidents and Diseases*, Bulletin 105, Washington, D.C., U.S. Department of Labor, Bureau of Labor Standards (1949), pp. 283-284.

[64] Somers and Somers, *op. cit.*, p. 161.

[65] Cheit, *op. cit.*, Table 9.4, p. 274.

[66] *Ibid.*, p. 252.

as follows: $9.8 million of claimants' legal expenses; $16.3 million for employers' claims expenses (primarily loss adjustment expenses of insurance carriers); $2.1 million paid by the taxpayer for the costs of judges, juries, and the Industrial Commission; and $35.8 million to insurance companies to pay for underwriting costs, and profits in handling claims paid. Although medical benefits were omitted from this analysis, the operating costs still remained quite high. A study in New York found that overhead equaled at least 45 percent of total costs. In all, then, workmen's compensation costs are much higher in relation to benefits than other forms of social insurance in the United States. They are much higher than in Ontario, which reported that administrative expenses were 7.5 percent of receipts. In Ontario the fund is an exclusive state fund and court review has been outlawed.[67] In the United States there is no question that costs of administering workmen's compensation are quite high.

POSSIBLE FEDERAL ADMINISTRATION

Owing to the many weaknesses in state workmen's compensation laws, the AFL-CIO for a number of years has advocated that a federally administered law be passed covering all the states. This suggestion has received little support in Congress. Failing this, the only alternative is to improve the laws in the 54 jurisdictions. Such revisions are difficult, particularly in those states in which workers are unorganized and have a weak lobby. In such states, workmen's compensation laws probably will not be improved substantially in the near future. It is to be hoped that industrial progress and further enlightenment will eventually result in improved workmen's compensation laws. Fortunately, the total costs of workmen's compensation average only 1 percent of payrolls, so that improvements may be made without a heavy additional cost burden.

Summary

Workmen's compensation laws were passed beginning in 1908 in the United States, after it had been found that employers' liability laws had failed to solve industrial accident problems. Exclusion from coverage among such groups as agricultural workers, employees of small employers, and others has resulted in only about three of every four workers being covered under workmen's compensation laws.

Benefit payments are least adequate for those more severely injured.

[67] Somers and Somers, *op. cit.*, pp. 193-196, 309-317.

Over the years, workmen's compensation has been paying a smaller and smaller percentage of the injured worker's wage. Workmen's compensation benefits have tended to impede rehabilitation on occasion, and experts have been working on how cash payments can best promote rather than impede rehabilitation. Yet to be solved is the problem of some persons receiving payments both under OASDHI and workmen's compensation.

In general, workmen's compensation has not been administered well in the United States. The best method of paying claims is by the direct method, whereby the state agency analyzes each case to determine the award. Unfortunately, only six jurisdictions use this method. When workmen's compensation was first adopted, it was thought that cases would be settled with little or no need for attorneys and litigation. In practice, litigation continues at a high rate. The IAIABC has recommended that a state should have the right to reopen a case at any time but few states have adopted this proposal. With all these weaknesses in workmen's compensation administration, the cost of administering this program is much higher than for other security programs.

HEALTH PROBLEMS
IN THE UNITED STATES

CHRONIC ILLNESS

Sickness results in the loss of work for many people each year.[1] Concerning chronic illness only, from July, 1963 to June, 1965 there were 16½ million persons in the United States who had some limitation of their activities due to chronic illness.[2] There were 1.6 million people aged 16 to 65 who were unable to carry on a major activity and another 7.7 million in the same age group who were limited in the amount or kind of major activity in which they could engage. Such high losses in employment result in billions of dollars of lost wages each year. Hospitalization, physicians' fees, and drugs add billions more in medical costs. Some types of chronic illness place such heavy economic burdens on individuals that only the wealthy can afford to pay the costs. Thirty percent of our families spent less than $100 for medical costs in 1963, but another 30 percent spent from $300 to $999 and an unfortunate 8 percent spent $1,000 and over.[3]

No primary prevention is yet known for such chronic diseases as alcoholism, arteriosclerosis, degenerative joint diseases, diabetes mellitus, inherited epilepsy, primary hypertension, multiple sclerosis, primary glaucoma, and rheumatoid arthritis. On the other hand, primary prevention can result in a substantial reduction of the amount and impairment due to blindness resulting from retrolental fibroplasia in premature infants, from ophthalmia neonatorum, and from glaucoma, poliomyelitis, cardiovascular diseases, deafness resulting from infections and occupational exposure to noise, dental caries, and cancer.[4]

Space will permit a discussion of recent developments of only one of

---

[1] According to the U.S. National Health Service (1964), illness or injury resulted in restricted activity in 16 days annually per person on the average for the entire population in the United States. Slightly more than five of these days on the average were spent in bed.

[2] *The U.S. National Health Survey, Health Statistics,* U.S. Department of Health, Education, and Welfare, Public Health Service, National Center for Health Statistics, Series 10, No. 32 (1966), Table 22, p. 47.

[3] "Trends in Personal Health Services," *Progress in Health Services,* Vol. 14, No. 5 (November, December, 1965), Chart II, p. 2.

[4] *Chronic Illness in the United States,* Vol. I: *Prevention of Chronic Illness,* Commission on Chronic Illness (Cambridge, Harvard, 1956), p. 18.

the chronic diseases—cancer, which is the second most frequent cause of death. The lifetime probability of developing cancer is 25 percent for males and 27 percent for females. In certain industrial processes, a wide assortment of chemical and physical agents may be conducive to the contraction of cancer. Remedies here would involve changing methods of production, secondary conversion of substances to noncarcinogenic materials, and safe disposal of waste. The reports on the close connection between smoking and lung cancer suggest an avoidance of excessive smoking or removing carcinogenic substances from cigarettes. Avoidance of overexposure to the sun is important in preventing skin cancer among fair-complexioned persons. In addition to primary prevention, important advances have been made in the secondary prevention of cancer to retard progression of the disease. Early detection here is quite important. A small cancer of the lip, for example, can be treated quickly and inexpensively if caught in time. The same lesion treated six months later may involve radical and costly surgical or radiation treatment, hospital care, substantial loss of earning capacity, prolonged invalidism, or possibly even death. The President's Commission on Heart Disease, Cancer, and Stroke has a stated that one-half of all cancer patients could be cured if knowledge already accumulated through research could be fully applied to all people in the nation.[5] A 1961 New York State Department of Health program reported the detection of seven new cases of uterine cancer by 1,000 women examined.[6] The Cancer Subcommittee of the President's Commission on Heart Disease, Cancer, and Stroke recommended that the number of comprehensive cancer research centers be expanded from 4 to 20. The subcommittee further recommended grants to 200 hospitals and medical centers for the development of cancer diagnostic treatment and consultation stations on a demonstration basis.

For a number of reasons the need for long-term institutional care for chronic patients has increased. In recent years infectious diseases have been more successfully treated, and this has resulted in people living longer and being more subject to chronic illness. Today infectious diseases as a cause of death have declined, while heart disease, cancer, and other noninfectious diseases have increased. At the same time that people are living longer, the family is less able to take care of the aged than formerly. Many women who formerly cared for the aged have entered the work force. Also, more people are reaching old age without having relatives to take care of them. This has been due to a decrease in the size of families, a larger number of childless marriages, and increases in the number of single people. Small, compact apartments also militate against having sufficient space to care for aged relatives. Increase in income is another factor that tends to increase the need

[5] *A National Program to Conquer Heart Disease, Cancer, and Stroke,* Vol. II, Washington, D.C., The President's Commission on Heart Disease, Cancer, and Stroke (1965), p. 111.

[6] *Ibid.,* pp. 107-117.

for institutional care, for more people are able to buy better medical care. Improved medical care has tended to offset the increased need for expanded facilities, but with a larger population becoming older, probably some increase in institutional care will be needed.[7]

In the past much criticism was directed at the poor quality of nursing home care. Even as late as 1954 a state study in Alabama reported that most licensed private nursing homes in Alabama were of poor construction, that arrangements for continued physician supervision were nonexistent, that the homes did not measure up to current thinking in food and nutrition, and that many of the homes had no dining space available so that patients were required to eat from the edge of their beds. The investigatory body concluded that existing facilities for the care and treatment of the chronically ill were "woefully inadequate."[8] A later study of almost half the nursing homes in Florida found that 77 percent of the homes provided a substandard amount of nursing service.[9] With the large-scale growth of nursing homes, more attention has been paid to the quality of their services. By 1961, nursing homes were licensed in all the states, and a survey by the Public Health Service of that year found that 92 percent of all nursing homes were fully licensed. One problem is that the licensing requirements tend to deal primarily with physical requirements, such as fire safety, functional layout, and sanitation. In order to improve medical and other care, the American Medical Association and American Nursing Home Association jointly sponsored a national accreditation program for nursing homes in 1963. The two groups formed an accrediting agency called the National Council for the Accreditation of Nursing Homes. Within a one-year period, this organization accredited 287 homes, and denied accreditation to 17. Considerable upgrading in providing medical care will be needed, for as late as 1961 the Public Health Survey found that only 29 percent of the skilled nursing homes had a full-time registered nurse in attendance.[10]

Although facilities still lag, at least the basic research has been done to provide guidelines for proper institutional care. The Central Service for the Chronically Ill of the Institute of Medicine of Chicago has worked closely with many existing homes and institutions and has given assistance in ar-

[7] Edna E. Nicholson, *Planning New Institutional Facilities for Long-Term Care* (New York, Putnam, 1956), pp. 3-13.

[8] *Survey of Licensed Private Nursing, Rest and Convalescent Homes for Adults in Alabama, 1954,* Alabama State Department of Public Health and Public Welfare, pp. 4-6.

[9] Hobson Britt and Margaret Jacks, "Costs and Care of Aged and Infirm Residents in Florida Nursing and Boarding Houses," in *Selected Articles on Nursing Homes,* Publication No. 732, Washington, D.C., U.S. Department of Health, Education, and Welfare, Public Health Service (1960), pp. 169-174.

[10] Testimony of Dr. H. Close Hesseltine, Chairman, National Council for Accreditation of Nursing Homes, Hearings before the Joint Subcommittee on Long-Term Care, the Special Committee on Aging, U.S. Senate, 88th Congress, 2nd Session, Part 2 (May 6, 1964), p. 138.

rangements for many thousands of aged, disabled, and chronically ill people. This group found that a majority of chronically ill patients are in need of regular nursing services, although a minority need only personal attention and routine care given by aides, attendants, and matrons under the general supervision of the physician and nurse.[11] For the most efficient treatment, it was suggested that chronic-disease hospitals be integrated as part of a general hospital unit. If the hospitals are separate, duplication occurs in diagnosis, treatment, and administration. Additional moves of the patient are necessary and there is more or less a serious break in the continuity of care. Also, coordination is made more difficult.[12] It was also recommended that nursing homes for the aged should be operated in connection with general hospitals, but that separate facilities may be acceptable, provided that ready access to hospital care is available.[13]

The Federal Commission on Chronic Illness concurred that medical care for the chronically ill should be carried on as part of a general hospital unit. This group found that isolated hospitals for the chronically ill run serious risks of deteriorating the quality of medical care, both in the general and chronic hospital. Failure to coordinate the chronic hospital with general hospitals has resulted in such defective medical care as, for example, improper amputations by surgeons who are not fully aware of the recent advances in the use of prosthetic appliances. Because of problems of this nature, the Commission on Chronic Illness recommended that the chronic hospital should be associated physically and administratively as part of the operation of a general hospital.[14]

As an example of the problems that the chronically ill must face, the case history of a heart victim is included here. His testimony was given at a hearing conducted by the President's Commission on the Nation's Health.

My name is John Cunningham. I live at 109 Set Boyden Terrace, Newark, N.J. I am a member of IUE-CIO, Local 447, and am employed at the Federal Telephone and Radio Corporation, Nutley.

Although I speak as a C.I.O. member, I feel that I am speaking for the 100,000 or more people who are afflicted with the nation's greatest killer each year: heart disease.

Up to September, 1945, I had been working at the Federal Telephone and Radio Corporation as a first-class electrician earning a salary of $1.47 per hour. I had not lost a day's pay in 21 months.

On September 5, 1945, I reported to work as usual and suddenly I began to feel severe pains in the chest area. On the advice of a doctor I was sent to the hospital, which was St. Michael's of Newark. After five days, I was sent home with a doctor's advice to see a heart specialist.

11 Nicholson, *op. cit.*, p. 15.
12 *Ibid.*, pp. 42-47.
13 *Ibid.*, pp. 64, 70.
14 *Chronic Illness in the United States*, Vol. I, p. 15.

The heart specialist diagnosed my condition as a coronary thrombosis. The cost of the examination was $25 and he ordered me to bed for six weeks, during which time I spent about $20 for medicine and other necessities.

After six weeks I made another visit to the doctor at a cost of $25, at which time he advised me that I had to take a leave from my job for a period of six months. The time lost involved in that lay-off was $1,528, plus $5 every two weeks for medicines, plus $20 per month a visit to the doctor, or a total cost of $1,712.80.

After six months the company doctor advised that I would have to change my way of living and that I would not be allowed to return to my regular type of work. He was going to refuse to pass me on examination to return to work.

On the suggestion of the heart specialist he agreed to let me return on condition that I had to do light work, sitting down while working and no overtime. Through the help of my local union I was transferred to bench work and classified as a second-class machinist at a salary of $1.32 per hour, a loss of 15 cents an hour, or $6 per week, plus overtime.

From March, 1946, when I returned to work until November, 1948, when I had my second coronary thrombosis attack, I lost about 30 days because of illness, or approximately $300 in salary during that time. I made four visits to the specialist at $25 a visit, plus the $5 every two weeks for medicine, or a total cost of $440.

In November, 1948, I was laid up again with a coronary thrombosis attack and this time I lost two months' work, at a salary of $1.47 per hour or $470.40. If I had been working at my regular trade I would have been getting $1.62 per hour at this time.

During those two months I had one visit at home by the doctor at which time he gave me an electrocardiograph examination at the cost of $25, and a visit to his office at the cost of $25, which included another cardiograph. Total cost for doctor, medicines, and lost time for the second coronary was $540.40.

From the time I returned to work on January, 1949, until June 4, 1949, I had very little lost time, but on June 4, 1949, I suffered my third coronary thrombosis attack and was sent back to St. Michael's Hospital for 21 days. The cost for this stay in the hospital to me besides what the Blue Cross paid was $70 for special medications and other examinations by the doctor, which were not covered by the Blue Cross.

After being released by the hospital I was advised to take a leave of absence until August 8, 1949, a total of nine weeks at a loss of $529.20, plus medicines and visits to the doctor, at which time he charged me only $10 a visit for two visits, or $20 plus $20 for medicines. Total cost for the third coronary attack was $569.20, including lost time, doctor, and medicines.

On August 8, 1949, I returned to work and on August 11, 1949, I had a relapse and had to take another eight months' leave of absence, which cost me in lost time $2,009.60, during which time I continued to buy medicines but did not have to visit the doctor. Total cost of the third coronary attack was $2,089.60.

I again returned to work on April 15, 1950. From then until January 20, 1951, when I was operated on for coronary thrombosis, I lost an average of three to five days a month, or approximately 30 to 35 days in nine months, or from $375 to $439 approximately.

On January 16, 1951, I again entered St. Michael's hospital, and on January 20, 1951, they operated on me. For nine days I had to have three nurses a day at $10 per nurse per day or $30 a day for nine days. I paid $270 for private nurses. My total stay in the hospital the first stage of the operation was 12 days. My total cost for the 12 days was $270 for nurses, plus $113.50 which included special pharmacy, private nurses' board or $383.50, which does not include the expenses paid by the Blue Cross.

On February 25, 1951, I reentered the hospital for my second stage of the operation and was operated on February 28, 1951. This time I had three private nurses per day for 7½ days, or a total cost of $230, and I was in the hospital 24 days, for which I paid $122.20 above what the Blue Cross covered, which included special medication and private nurses' board. The total cost to me for the second stage was $352.20, besides which I had to replace six pints of blood or pay $210 extra.

Through the cooperation of the officers and members of local No. 447, I.U.E., I was able to replace the blood by volunteer donors at the rate of two pints for one.

The total cost to me besides what Blue Cross paid was $735.70 for both operations. The only way I was able to meet these expenses was through the kindness and generosity of the officers and members of Local No. 447, I.U.E.-C.I.O. and the members of the New Jersey State C.I.O. Women's League. Between the two organizations they presented me a total of $800 which they had received by volunteer donations from their respective members.

Without this assistance, I could never have met my obligations to the hospital.

I should like to point out that the relatively small doctor and medicine bills before my operation amounted to $854, while the cost to me of the operation in hospital and nursing bills was $805.70. In other words, it cost me more before the major operation than the operation itself.

To meet my medical bills before the operation, I used up all of my $300 in cash savings, cashed in about $150 in war bonds, and borrowed $200 from the I.U.E.-C.I.O. Local 447 Credit Union.

Beyond the payments made by Blue Cross or Blue Shield, the total cost of my illness to me over a six-year period has been $6,852.90. Of this amount $5,193.20 represents wages I lost. The remainder, or $1,659.70, represents direct payments, including $340 doctors' fees, $514 for medicines, $305.70 for hospital services, and $500 for private nurses.

I should mention that these figures do not include a check for $1,500 presented to the operating surgeon by my family doctor, in addition to the $500 Blue Shield paid the surgeon for the operation. I had assumed that the Blue Shield payment would be the full payment to the surgeon and was greatly surprised when I learned of the $1,500 additional, paid by my own physician apparently out of his own pocket.

In addition to my own personal doctor, medicine, and hospital bills, we had to meet dentist bills for my daughter and my wife.

In November, 1950, we had to pay $65 to have my daughter's teeth fixed up and in May, 1952, we had to pay $13 for two visits to the doctor, plus $4 for medicine because of gland condition.

In the spring of 1947, we paid $125 to have my wife's teeth taken care of, which included two plates. And while on the subject, I might add that since I have returned to work after my operation, I have paid over $50 to cover the cost of ten trips to the doctor for periodical check-ups at $5 per visit.

After four months of convalescing, I returned to work on May 5, 1952. Since then I have not lost one day from sickness and have missed only four days for other causes, plus the fact that I have been able to work overtime every week since I returned.

I have been fortunate, but there are hundreds of thousands suffering from this condition who are not as fortunate as I have been. They no doubt would be glad to go through with this operation to be cured if they could afford it, but they can't so they go on suffering, and each year there is another 200,000, according to reports, that are hit with this killer called heart disease.[15]

The above case should not be considered unusual since heart disease is rather common. This disease and others of a chronic nature place extremely severe economic burdens on those faced with these types of illnesses.

MEDICAL PROBLEMS AMONG LOW-INCOME GROUPS

Practically all studies of medical care show deficiencies of medical care among low-income groups. Negroes receive much less medical care than whites in the United States. The rate of illness is higher among Negroes, and they live 6½ to 8 years less than do whites. Other minority groups also have high rates of illness and death. In a study of Mexican-Americans living in San Jose, California, Margaret Clark made an intensive study of groups of laborers who lived on $2,000 to $3,000 a year income. Her findings were that a major illness, operation, or hospitalization can spell economic disaster for such people. Instead of being faced with medical bills which they cannot pay, they dispense with a physician's services as long as possible. They tend to rely on home remedies, folk curers, and marginal practitioners.[16] As an example of medical treatment among Mexican-Americans, one of the cases compiled by Margaret Clark is included here:

What Happened When Lupita Got Sick—When Manuela's small daughter, Lupita, was an infant, she suffered a gastrointestinal disorder. The events of illness were as follows.

First day: The child cried a great deal and took less than her accustomed quantity of formula.

Second through fourth days: Lupita continued to cry much more than usual, rejected several of her feedings, and slept for only short periods of time, crying the remainder of the night.

[15] *Building America's Health: A Report to the President,* Vol. 5, Washington, D.C., The President's Commission on the Health Needs of the Nation (1952), pp. 4-6.

[16] Margaret Clark, *Health in the Mexican-American Culture,* Berkeley: University of California Press, 1959, p. 223. Reprinted by permission.

Fifth day: The baby began to have liquid stools and continued to cry almost continuously. Her mother discovered that her abdomen was slightly distended and took the child to be examined by the baby's baptismal godmother. The madrina discovered that the child was cutting an upper tooth and attributed the child's condition to teething. She dipped a small piece of rag in some whiskey and the child was allowed to chew this. The mother thought she saw a little improvement in Lupita's condition, but the child continued to have diarrhea and cried intermittently throughout the night.

Sixth through eighth days: Lupita developed a high fever, had persistent diarrhea and began vomiting; she took none of her formula.

Ninth day: The symptoms continued, and the child still did not eat. Manuela became alarmed and once more contracted her comadre for advice. Arrangements were made to take the child the following day to the comadre's mother-in-law, a curandera (folk curer) in a neighboring barrio.

Tenth day: The infant was examined by the curandera, who made a diagnosis of empacho. The child's back and legs were rubbed with warm olive oil and then massaged for some time. She was then given a small dose of powdered chalk.

Eleventh day: There was no improvement in the child's symptoms so Manuela took her back for a second treatment.

Twelfth day: Lupita continued to have a high fever, vomiting and diarrhea; refused all feedings; and cried incessantly. Manuela was visited that day by her sister-in-law, a practical nurse, who advised her to take the baby to a doctor without delay. The child was examined and treated by a pediatrician that afternoon. An oral antibiotic was administered and continued for two days.

Thirteenth day: The child's fever abated and other symptoms were much improved. She began to take some water and formula again.

Fourteenth day: Lupita had no symptoms, stopped crying, and apparently recovered.

Manuela in recounting the story of the child's illness some time later, recalled it in this way: "When Lupita was less than a year old, she got empacho. She was pretty sick. I took her to a curandera who is mother of Lupita's godfather. She rubbed the baby with oil and gave her some medicine. She did that for two days and then the baby got well." In retrospect, Manuela attributed the child's cure not to the pediatrician's medicine (which she had forgotten completely) but to the treatment given by the curandera.[17]

In a comprehensive study of medical care in an upstate rural New York town, Earl Koos analyzed the medical care obtained by 2,500 households, over half of whom lived within the town's boundaries and the others in surrounding rural areas. Although this and the next study cited are dated, the most recent statistics for 1963–1964 quoted on the next few pages confirm the lack of medical care among low-income groups today.[18] The area chosen was neither the largest town in the area nor the smallest. It was not an exceptionally wealthy community, nor was it extremely poor. The fami-

---

[17] *Ibid.*, pp. 185-186.
[18] Earl Koos, *The Health of Regionville* (New York, Columbia, 1954).

lies were classified into three socioeconomic classes: business or professional men (Class I), skilled or semiskilled workers (Class II), and laborers (Class III). Farm laborers were placed in Class III, and farmers into Class II. When illness struck, it was found that 77 percent of the Class I group obtained medical care through to completion, whereas only 58 percent of Class III did so. Because of lack of medical care, about twice as many disabling illnesses lasting 60 days or more were noted among those of Class III as among those of Class I. Only about 30 percent of the Class III group had a family doctor, compared with more than 80 percent of the Class I group. The Class III group used nonmedical practitioners on a much larger scale than did the other two classes. Although in some types of illness chiropractors or other nonmedical personnel may be helpful, Koos concluded that the failure to use M.D.'s for heart and other diseases appeared to be "fraught with considerable danger for the patient." He added that effort and money was wasted on poor treatment by Class III people, even though this group was particularly short of money. Preventive health examinations had been obtained by 25 percent in Class I but by only 4 percent in Class III. Furthermore, more than 80 percent of those in Class I had some form of health insurance, whereas only about 20 percent of those in Class III had any. The same findings were made on the lack of dental care among Class III. More than 90 percent in Class I had a family dentist, compared with 13 percent in Class III. Most of the use of dentists by Class III was for extractions. Whereas 52 percent of all visits to the dentist in Class I were for prophylaxis, the corresponding figure for Class III was 14 percent. Class III used dentists mainly in an emergency only. In short, Koos found substantially less medical and dental care among the laboring group than he did for business and professional families.

Another medical study involved 553 families in the Lower East Side of New York, most of whom earned from $2,000 to $4,000 annually. This study showed that most of the families failed to get adequate medical treatment. Only about 3 percent of the group were covered under a comprehensive medical insurance plan. Some of the group did not obtain dental treatment. Few had preventive medical examinations, and there was no access to reasonable psychiatric care. From this study Helen Hall concluded that "these families and those in like circumstances are without easy access to that great body of medical protection which can be had for the buying." [19] As an example of the medical problems faced by this income group, the following story from Helen Hall's study is included:

Florie Minsky, age 6, fell and fractured two bones in her wrist while in play-school. Because her mother once had a bad experience in a clinic she rushed the little girl uptown to a doctor she knew. As she had no one with whom to

[19] Helen Hall, "When Sickness Strikes a Family," in Building America's Health, Vol. 4, pp. 29-38.

leave Florie's two younger sisters, age 4 and 3, they had to go along. She took a taxi with the three little girls to the doctor and he took an X ray of the fractured wrist, put on a temporary bandage, but did not want to set it, and so sent them to a surgeon whom he recommended. The surgeon wanted $150 to set the wrist, but finally said he would do it for $75, only he must have the money in advance. Mrs. Minsky said she didn't have it, but would borrow it and bring it to him the next morning at 11 o'clock.

She left little Florie in the hospital and went back home. She had been gone with the little girls—broken wrist and all—from 10 o'clock until six. However, as soon as she had fed the little girls she went out to borrow the $75 in the neighborhood. She got a little here and a little there. One neighbor came in while she was out and left $10 on the kitchen table. By the next morning she had the $75 and met her 11 o'clock appointment, money in hand.

Then at the hospital she was met with a $62 hospital bill which they told her she must pay before she could take the child home. This bill was finally vouched for by a social agency and she brought the little girl home and relieved the neighbor who had been minding the other children for her that morning. She still had to pay $10 for the X ray and $5 for the office visit to her doctor, so that all told, not counting carfare and taxi (and another X ray), the accident had cost her $152 or approximately what her husband earned in three weeks.[20]

Statistics for July, 1963–June, 1964, show that those groups with an income of $10,000 and above made 19 percent more visits to a doctor per year than did those whose family income was under $2,000.[21] Fewer visits were made in the South, the poorest part of the country, compared with the North.[22] As would be expected, lower-income groups have a higher incidence of disease than wealthier people. Those aged 45 to 64 and earning less than $2,000 have 43 days of restricted activity per person per year, compared with 16 days for those with $10,000 a year income and above.[23] Those in the same age group with an income below $2,000 had 8 percent of their group incapacitated from carrying on a major activity due to some chronic disability, compared with only 1 percent in the above $7,000 income group.[24] Lower-income groups had much less dental care than upper-income groups. Children in higher-income families showed almost three times as many visits to a dentist as did lower-income groups.[25] About 60 percent of the 5-to-14-year-olds in the income group with less than $2,000 annual income had not been to a dentist for the past five years and most of these had never been to a dentist in their entire life.[26] Again, the South showed much less dental care than more affluent sections of the country.[27]

[20] Ibid., p. 34.
[21] Volume of Physicians' Visits, Series 10, No. 18, Washington, D.C., U.S. Department of Health, Education, and Welfare, Public Health Service, National Center for Health Statistics (1965), Table 1, p. 13.
[22] Ibid.
[23] Ibid., Series 10, No. 24, Table 19, p. 29.
[24] Ibid., Series 10, No. 17, Table 15, p. 26.
[25] Ibid., Series 10, No. 23, Table 5, p. 20.
[26] Ibid., Series 10, No. 29, Table 15, p. 27.
[27] Ibid., Series 10, No. 29, Table 28, p. 45.

Lastly, in discussing medical care among low-income groups, it should be noted that fewer people in this group have health insurance than do high-income families. In 1962–1963, only 34 percent of those having less than $2,000 a year income had hospital insurance, compared with 88 percent of those with an income above $10,000.[28]

MEDICAL CARE IN RURAL AREAS

All studies of medical care in the United States show weaknesses of medical care in rural areas. Fewer farm residents visit a doctor than urban residents. Fifty-two percent of all persons in standard metropolitan areas had been to a physician within the last six months, compared with 42 percent of those living on farms.[29] Rural people are particularly deficient in obtaining prenatal and postnatal care, general checkups, and immunizations. Dental care is also lacking among rural people. Rural farm people visit a dentist less than once a year on the average compared with almost two visits for urban people.[30] In rural areas, 22 percent of the population had never seen a dentist and another 18 percent had not visited one during the past five years. The corresponding figures for urban residents were 15 and 13 percent.[31]

Since rural people obtain medical care less frequently than urban people, a higher incidence of illness would be expected. However, the more healthful rural environment has reduced the number of acute illnesses in rural areas below the national average. On the other hand, a listing of 12 chronic ailments shows higher rates per person in rural than in urban areas for most of the diseases.[32]

One of the problems in medical care in rural areas is that lower incomes there tend to inhibit doctors and dentists from locating in rural areas. In 1959, whereas there were 158 active nonfederal physicians per 100,000 population practicing in greater metropolitan areas, only 47 were active in isolated rural counties.[33] The disparity is much less when considering only general practitioners. As would be expected in larger cities, more doctors have specialized or are associated with hospitals. However, the distance to larger cities does prevent many rural people from getting medical care. Furthermore, the doctors in rural areas are much older than they are in metropolitan areas. In isolated rural counties, 28 percent of the physicians are 65 years

[28] *Ibid.*, Series 10, No. 11, Table 1, p. 12.
[29] *Ibid.*, Series 10, No. 19, Table 4, p. 18.
[30] *Ibid.*, Series 10, No. 23, Table 1, p. 16.
[31] *Ibid.*, Series 10, No. 29, Table 25, p. 42.
[32] *Ibid.*; *U.S. National Health Survey, Health Statistics*, Series C-5 (1961), Table 18, p. 18.
[33] "Physician's Age, Type of Practice and Location," in *Health Manpower Source Book*, Section 10, Washington, D.C., U.S. Department of Health, Education, and Welfare, Public Health Service (1960), p. 11.

of age and older, compared with only 13 percent of this age in greater metropolitan areas.[34]

MEDICAL PROBLEMS AMONG THE AGED

Our population aged 65 and over has increased enormously since 1900. Most of the increase in the aged population has come through a reduction in the death rate in early years, but those living at 65 will live several years longer than would those reaching the same age in 1900. The old, of course, experience more illness than those who are young. In the period July, 1963 to June, 1964, those 64 to 75 years of age experienced 34 days of restricted activity per year, compared with 11 days for those under 25.[35] Chronic illness was much more prevalent among the aged. About 48 percent of those in the 17-to-44 age group had no chronic condition of any kind; the corresponding figure for those aged 65 and over was 19 percent. Furthermore, the chronic illness was much more disabling for elderly people. It limited the amount or kind of major activity of 26 percent of those over 65. Another 16 percent in this age group were unable to carry on a major activity at all. The corresponding figure for all age groups was respectively 7 and 2 percent.[36] As may be suspected, the greater amount of chronic illness among the aged caused them to use hospital facilities with greater frequency than those in the lower-aged group. One study showed that once a patient was admitted to a general hospital, the number of days stayed by those 65 and over was 21 days, compared with 6 days for those under 14 years of age and 13 for those 14 to 64.[37] The Health Information Foundation has estimated that hospital costs of the aged are about 2½ times higher than the costs of hospitalizing those who are younger.[38]

The aged, then, are faced with heavier medical expenses than the rest of the population. Unfortunately, the aged have fewer economic resources to meet these higher costs. Their problems have been compounded because medical costs have been rising rapidly in the past few years. Some of the actual medical problems faced by the aged prior to Medicare are cited below:

[34] *Ibid.*, p. 28.

[35] *Disability Days*, Series 10, No. 24, Washington, D.C., U.S. Department of Health, Education, and Welfare, Public Health Service, National Center for Health Statistics (1965), Table 2, p. 13.

[36] *Chronic Conditions and Activity Limitations, July, 1961–June, 1963*, Series 10, No. 17, Washington, D.C., U.S. Department of Health, Education, and Welfare, Public Health Service, National Center for Health Statistics, Table 1, p. 12.

[37] A. W. Brewster, *Hospital Utilization by Persons Insured and Uninsured in September, 1956*, Research and Statistics Note 19, Washington, D.C., U.S. Department of Health, Education, and Welfare, Social Security Administration, Division of Program Research (June 23, 1958).

[38] *Bulletin*, Health Information Foundation (February, 1960).

Only yesterday I received a letter from a lady in my own district. She is 78 years of age and has been unable to work for a long time. She had a little home of her own, five-room house. She has had to borrow money on that home in order to be able to pay her medical expenses. And she sent me a list of the medical expenses she had been paying—and the medicines she had been buying in the drug stores at these exorbitant prices they are charging for drugs today and told me her home had been taken away from her. All she had left in this world was $100. She had to give up her insurance policies. She is now going on public relief and says she is praying that something along the lines of my bill would pass so it might be of some help to her, but if not for her, because she does not expect to be in this world for long, then for others who find themselves in the same predicament.

I feel that I can't afford to go to the doctor because of the great expense for my wife. (This retired worker had spent over $2,000 in 3 years since his retirement on his wife's illness.)

Need to go to the doctor more, but because of income which is only Social Security, cannot afford it.

I feel that my wife should go to the doctor, but because of the expense of her medicine and doctor bill, she hasn't gone. I've stopped using insulin because of the expense and am trying to control my condition [diabetes] by diet.

There should be an oxygen tent in the home, but because of expense we feel we cannot afford it.

I need medical care, but since my husband's death I cannot afford it. In fact, I can't even afford to pay the medical bills left over after his death.

We need to go, but we cannot afford it.

I feel that I cannot go to the doctor because my wife has to have treatment after her nervous breakdown. I am not well, but cannot afford to go to a doctor.

My wife and I don't go to the doctor unless we absolutely have to because we can't afford to on my limited income.

We both had operations 2 years ago and are supposed to be checked by our own doctor monthly. Each office call costs my wife $5 and my checkup costs $25. We cannot afford this cost, and as a result, cannot go as often as we should.

My bank account is almost depleted. Then what? I don't want charity.[39]

[39] Testimony of Hon. Aime J. Forand and Walter P. Reuther, *Health Needs of the Aged and Aging,* Hearings before the Subcommittee on Problems of the Aged and the Aging, the Committee on Labor and Public Welfare, U.S. Senate, 86th Congress, 2nd Session (April, 1960), pp. 7-8, 228.

The aged have attempted to meet the high costs of medical care in a number of ways. Voluntary health insurance has been one way that helps share the costs. During the period July, 1962, to June, 1963, 39 percent of the aged had hospital insurance.[40] This figure is, of course, substantially less than that of the entire population, but it has been growing rapidly. Several problems may be noted with voluntary health insurance. One is that some private companies will not continue to sell such insurance to aged people.

For those having group life insurance, more and more companies are permitting convertibility to individual policies, but only a minority do so. Moreover, the costs of the policies when converted are higher. Premiums go up about 80 percent. In addition, the employer's payment of these premiums is discontinued so that the retiree feels that he is faced with an exceedingly high cost. With such high costs, most of those retiring simply do not use the conversion principle.

An added problem with medical insurance is that some policies are terminated at the option of the company. Heavy medical costs then must be borne by the aged alone. Since the Blue Cross–Blue Shield plans are nonprofit, they have attempted to cover as many old people as possible. Covering the aged, however, raises their costs, and causes them to be noncompetitive with private insurance, although mutual companies are also nonprofit. In order to be as competitive as possible with private insurance companies, the Blue groups sometimes must restrict the insurance provided the aged. In 1963, 64 of 76 Blue Cross group enrollment policies had no age restrictions, whereas for their nongroup enrollment, only 15 of 76 had no age limit and no restrictions of benefits, but 34 of these write Senior Certificates, which are available continuously or at specified periods during the year, according to each plan's policy.[41]

Several examples are cited below of problems that the aged have with health insurance.

It [our insurance] was cancelled. We were all sick—my wife, my son, and I—and they said we were getting too much. They were paying too much. I felt bad because we were in it a long time and I felt badly. They are in business and can't always gain. I feel that the reason was what they gave us. They were paying out too much. As long as I was able to pay for it, the policy should have been kept in force. I think maybe they would have made up what they lost before and should have continued. If I am sick again I will need to go to a city hospital. That's all I can do and I will have to make the best of it.

This is a retired couple. The man is 79; his wife is 69. Up until recently they had been living primarily on the proceeds of their dairy farm. Their cash income last year was $1,900.

[40] Hospital Insurance Coverage July, 1962–June, 1963, Series 10, No. 11, Washington, D.C., U.S. Department of Health, Education, and Welfare, Public Health Service, National Center for Health Statistics (1964), Table 1, p. 12.

[41] Letter from Betty Gray, Research Analyst, Blue Cross Association, April 15, 1963.

Both Mr. and Mrs. B were covered by a health insurance plan until 1951. This was an insurance company plan obtained through Mr. B's place of employment. They are no longer covered by the plan because, as Mr. B put it, he retired in 1951, and "after you retire you don't belong to anything."

In the 12 months preceding the interview, this couple had medical expenses amounting to $1,141.50. In order to pay the medical expenses they withdrew $800 from their savings and sold their cows. As a result, they no longer have an income from the dairy.

I'm not old enough to collect old-age pension, nor do I get social security.

With medical expenses and the cost of living what it is, the money I have won't last long. I shudder to think what will happen when it is gone.

My hospitalization does not cover anything that comes from diabetes, which I have. Neither does it take care of my varicose veins, which I have also. My insurance company notified me they would not pay any bills for any more varicose veins, varicose ulcer, or thrombophlebitis, as you can see by the enclosed copy of the elimination endorsement. Their reason for this is, and I quote from their letter to me:

"The purpose of this amendment is to place the insured on the basis of other policyholders who are in normal health, as our medical division feels that the illness mentioned on the rider is likely to reoccur."

I was taking needles for my varicose veins at $5 each. A series of 12 needles are needed. I have not had any for over 2 years as my surgeon went up to $10 a shot. I told him that I could not afford to pay that much. He said he had talked to several doctors and they all agreed that $10 a shot was a nominal fee.

I asked, "What do I do when I need the needles, and cannot afford them?" His answer was, "That's up to you."

This doctor has been my surgeon for many years and has operated on me about six times—when I could and did pay him what he charged.

Now that I am a widow and live on a limited means, the above answer is what he gave me.

I haven't been back to him and I still need the needles for my legs.

So what are we, that cannot afford the medication we need, to do?

Hoping you and other Congressmen will be able to work out something real soon for the aged and the needy. . . .[42]

Lack of insurance coverage and income has resulted in many instances in an inability of old people to purchase the proper amount of medical care. Some evidence of the failure to obtain medical treatment may be seen by the fact that hospital utilization of the aged with health insurance is substantially greater than for those without hospital insurance.[43]

[42] *Report of the Joint Legislative Committee on Health Insurance Plans, 1957,* Legislative Document No. 49, Albany, State of New York, pp. 69, 84-85; *Health Needs of the Aged and Aging,* pp. 342-343.

[43] Mortimer Spiegelman, *Ensuring Medical Care for the Aged* (Homewood, Ill., Irwin, 1960), Table 1, p. 118.

LACK OF PREVENTIVE MEDICINE

One of the major criticisms that has been leveled against the present fee-for-service medical system is that too little preventive medicine is practiced. In the past, probably because of the fees involved, most people went to doctors only after they became ill. The major effort was on cure rather than prevention.

Preventive medicine can be practiced in a number of different ways.[44] Immunizations can be given to prevent a number of different diseases. Medical advice can be given in the field of diet so as to prevent problems of over-weight, underweight, and vitamin deficiencies. The entire area of hygiene, including mental hygiene, is devoted to promoting more healthful living. Here not only would the medical profession be involved but all of the community resources as well. Recreational facilities, good housing, and opportunities for improved culture all aid in improving health. Lastly, early diagnosis plays an important part in preventive medicine. Many diseases can be successfully cured if treatment begins early. Going to a doctor late after cancer, syphilis, and other diseases have had a chance to spread may result in an inability to cure the patient.

All screening examination studies have shown that many people have diseases of which they are unaware. For example, in cancer tests for women it is found that of every 1,000 women examined, about eight of them will have cancer, carcinoma of the cervix, either in its earlier stages or in a later stage. Other tests show that about 5½ persons per 1,000 examined will have a previously unknown diabetes.[45] A multiphasic and diagnostic test among 3,992 longshoremen showed many with diseases they had not known about. Furthermore, too little preventive medicine was being practiced by longshoremen.[46] Other studies reveal that medical examinations uncover much illness that is not being treated. If all American people would receive regular periodic medical examinations, disease would be greatly reduced. Most people as yet do not obtain periodic examinations. Until they do Americans will not be as healthy as they could be.

LACK OF FACILITIES

In the early days of the American colonies, there were no records of any hospitals being constructed. Early care of the sick was incidental to care for the poor—care for both was provided in almshouses. The first hospital con-

[44] Michael Davis, *Medical Care for Tomorrow* (New York, Harper & Row, 1954), pp. 318-319.
[45] Testimony of Dr. John Porterfield, Deputy Surgeon, Public Health Service, *Health Needs of the Aged and Aging,* p. 37.
[46] *Building America's Health,* Vol. 3, p. 7.

structed solely for the care of the sick was at Philadelphia in 1751. The number of hospitals was slow to grow, and by 1873, when the first census of hospitals was taken in the United States, only 178 hospitals were listed. Thereafter, the construction of hospitals occurred at a rapid rate so that by 1928, the total number of hospitals reached 6,852. The depression caused the failures of a number of hospitals. Some hospital construction occurred during this period as a part of the public works programs, but most of the emphasis of these programs was to provide employment for people. Although the number of hospitals increased slightly during World War II, of necessity most of our resources had to be directed to the war effort. By 1946, we had 572 fewer general hospitals than we had in 1928, although the number of hospital beds increased by 61 percent over this same period. A comprehensive study of hospital needs was made in 1944 by the Commission of Hospital Care, an organization sponsored by the American Hospital Association and the U.S. Public Health Service. Their conclusion as to the lack of adequate hospital facilities aided in obtaining federal aid for hospital construction in 1946 (the Hill-Burton Act).[47]

In spite of federal aid, we are still short of beds for all types of hospitals. The worst shortages occur in mental hospitals, chronic illness hospitals, and nursing homes. Because of the fact that the lower-income states have fewer facilities than the wealthier states, the federal aid program has channeled more money to the low income states. Even with the larger amounts of money going to these states, facilities of a specialized nature are still lacking there. The South is particularly deficient in nursing homes and in mental hospitals, where little federal aid has been forthcoming. As of January 1, 1965, the six states of Alabama, Georgia, Kentucky, South Carolina, Mississippi, and North Carolina had less than 30 percent of needed long-term care beds, compared with a national average of 50 percent. The last two named states had only 17 and 15 percent of needed facilities, respectively. Alabama, South Carolina, and Texas were deficient in providing mental hospital facilities.[48]

SHORTAGE OF MEDICAL PERSONNEL

In general, the number of people entering professions such as engineering, chemistry, and the like has been growing by leaps and bounds, and at a much larger percentage than the general growth in population. Such is not

[47] Leslie Morgan Abbe and Anna Mae Bovey, *The Nation's Health Facilities: Ten Years of the Hill-Burton Hospital and Medical Facilities Program, 1946–56*, Publication No. 616, Washington, D.C., U.S. Department of Health, Education, and Welfare, Public Health Service (1960), pp. 11-12.

[48] *Hill-Burton State Plan Data, a National Summary, as of January 1, 1965*, Washington, D.C., U.S. Department of Health, Education, and Welfare, Public Health Service, Table 11, pp. 47-48; Table 16, pp. 55-56.

the case for physicians. The number of physicians has grown in absolute numbers, but has not kept pace with the growth in population. Whereas there were 163 doctors per 100,000 in 1880, the figure dropped to 125 in 1929. Some slight improvement was made until 1950, when the figure rose to 149, and has remained constant since then.

The availability of medical personnel is to a large extent determined by the income of the area. The South as the poorest area of the country has only about 63 percent of the number of physicians that the Northeast has per 100,000 civilian population.[49] It is gratifying to see that the number of students in medical schools has been increasing, but unfortunately it is not increasing as fast as the number of college students in general. Unless some rather vigorous steps are taken to increase the number of doctors, it will probably be true that we will not be able to maintain the same ratio of doctors to population that we have had in the past. One estimate shows that more than 10,000 students, compared with 7,336 in 1963–1964, would have to be graduated each year to keep the same ratio that we have had in the past. Quite obviously, medical school facilities and staff would have to be enlarged to meet this figure. If an attempt were made to provide the poorer areas in the country with the same number of doctors as New England, a much larger expansion of medical education would be needed than simply raising the number of graduates to 10,000. One of the handicaps today is that too few states have medical schools.

The lack of sufficient physicians may have a direct bearing on the quality of medical care. It is well known that doctors work extremely long hours today. Time spent for research and new medical developments necessarily is limited because of the need to care for an overload of patients. One intensive study made of 88 general practitioners in North Carolina by the University of North Carolina Division of Health Affairs and the Rockefeller Foundation found that 39 of the physicians (44 percent) were doing relatively poor work. Their major weakness was that they lacked fundamental clinical medical knowledge and skill, as evidenced by limited history-taking, physical examination, and the use of laboratory aids to diagnose. Many of the doctors were relying mainly on digests put out by drug companies because they could not keep up with the professional study of the literature.[50] Concerning quality of surgery, one of the most distinguished surgeons in the world recently complained that about one-half of his work consisted of attempts to correct the bad results of surgery undertaken by doctors inadequately trained in this field.[51]

The history of the growth of the dentistry profession has been different

[49] *Health Manpower Source Book,* Section 18 (1964), p. 22.

[50] O. L. Peterson *et al.,* "An Analytical Study of North Carolina General Practice, 1953–54," *Journal of Medical Education* (December, 1956), Part 2, p. 47.

[51] "Quality as Well as Quantity of Medical Care," in *Group Health Institute of 1959,* Proceedings of the Group Health Association of America, p. 116.

from that of doctors. The number of dentists increased faster than population in the one hundred years from 1840 to 1940, at which time we had 62 dentists per 100,000 population. Since that time the figure has dropped to 56 in 1963.[52]

As in medicine, the number of dentists is particularly sparse in the South. Eleven states all located in the South and Southwest have less than 38 dentists per 100,000 population. Two other states, New York and Oregon, have more than twice that many dentists.[53] Only 26 states have dentistry schools. It does not appear that the supply of dentists will increase appreciably in relation to population unless additional steps are taken to increase the number entering dentistry schools.

The number of nurses has been increasing rapidly since 1900, and has increased at a much more rapid rate than population in general. Yet again, the same weaknesses of fewer nurses in the poorer section of our country are apparent. The South has only 209 professional nurses per 100,000 population, compared with 396 in the northeastern section of the country.[54] The country is particularly short of nurses with a bachelor's degree who are qualified to teach.

One of the major problems in nursing concerns the quality of nursing education. In North Carolina, for example, 34 of the 37 accredited state schools of nursing applied for temporary national accreditation by the National Nursing Accreditation Service. Only 14 were given national temporary accreditation. The national accrediting group generally finds the following conditions to exist in the poorer schools: "(1) very few full-time faculty members; (2) large faculty turnover; (3) high work load for faculty and students; (4) heavy evening and night duty for students; (5) little or no planned clinical or ward instruction; (6) low number of service hours carried by graduate staff nurses or nonprofessional workers or both; (7) high withdrawal rates; (8) low number of daily average patients in one or more clinical fields; and (9) low scores on state board examinations." Concerning the last item, in North Carolina of 116 students who failed one or more subjects on the state examinations, 104 were from schools that were not nationally accredited. Moreover, 78 percent of the total failures on the examinations came from nine schools.[55]

The country is also short of many types of paramedical workers. There is a particular shortage of physical therapists, and the need for occupational therapists is even greater. The expansion of rehabilitation will result in the need of expansion of personnel in these areas. One estimate from the U.S.

[52] "Manpower in the 1960's," in *Health Manpower Source Book*, Section 18 (1964), p. 42.
[53] *Ibid.*, Table 26, p. 45.
[54] *Ibid.*, p. 64.
[55] Statement of Mrs. Marie B. Noell, R.N., Executive Secretary of the North Carolina State Nurses Association, in "The People Speak—Excerpts from Regional Public Hearings on Health," *Building America's Health*, Vol. 5 (1952), pp. 278-279.

Department of Labor's Office of Manpower Policy showed that whereas we had 120,000 paramedical workers engaged in rehabilitative work in 1965, by 1975 185,000 would be needed. Similarly the large expansion of the use of the X ray will result in the need for almost doubling the number from 1965 to 1975 (from 30,000 to 52,000).[56]

Summary and Conclusions

This chapter has been concerned with the weaknesses of present medical care in the United States. A balanced picture of medical care should include the strengths of the American medical system as well as the weaknesses. Certainly over the past 100 years great improvements have been made in medical care. The death rate has been lowered, and people are living longer. Certain diseases, such as diphtheria, smallpox, and many others, have been controlled. Salk vaccine has greatly reduced the amount of poliomyelitis. The long hours of schooling required to enter the medical profession has insured good quality medicine.[57] Although some students of the problem highly recommend group practice as being superior to individual practice, opportunities for individual improvement are not lacking. One estimate shows that there are about 75,000 medical meetings annually in the United States, including medical association meetings, staff conferences, regional conferences, and clinical clubs.[58] High quality medical publications are also available to all doctors.

In spite of rapid advances made in medical care, weaknesses still persist. Beginnings are just being made for improved treatment of chronic illnesses. Too little medical care is being provided low income groups, the aged, and rural inhabitants. Too little preventive medicine is being practiced. There are too few hospitals and nursing homes in the United States. The quality of care in some nursing homes is not what it ought to be. There are not enough doctors, dentists, nurses, and other paramedical workers.

There is much agreement today on the weaknesses of present medical care in the United States. There is much disagreement, however, on what types of programs should be adopted to improve medical care. The various proposed solutions to improve medical care are discussed in the next two chapters.

[56] Herman M. Sturm, "Technological Developments and Their Effects Upon Health Manpower," *Monthly Labor Review*, Vol. 90, No. 1 (January, 1967), Table 3, p. 7.

[57] For certain weaknesses in the quality of medical care, *see* Carl Malmberg, *140 Million Patients* (New York, Reynal & Hitchcock, 1947), Chapter 3.

[58] W. W. Bauer, *Santa Claus, M.D.* (Indianapolis, Bobbs-Merrill, 1950), p. 59.

PROPOSED SOLUTIONS
TO HEALTH PROBLEMS

VOLUNTARY INSURANCE

The beginning of Blue Cross plans (nonprofit hospital insurance) in the United States is usually traced to an experiment tried in 1929 when school teachers in Dallas made an agreement with the Baylor University Hospital whereby the teachers were to receive three weeks of hospital care in return for paying $3 per semester. The plan proved successful. With the deepening of the depression in the early 1930's, many hospitals became hard pressed for operating funds. A number of them attempted to obtain financing by using the Baylor plan. The first city-wide plan was put into operation in Sacramento, California in July, 1932, and shortly thereafter plans were instituted in Newark, St. Paul, and elsewhere.

In 1936 a Commission on Hospital Service was created by the American Hospital Association to serve as a clearinghouse for such plans. The Blue Cross system was officially organized in 1937 when the commission, later called the Blue Cross Association, began to approve plans that met their standards. Gradually Blue Cross plans expanded until today there are almost 80 locally autonomous Blue Cross associations throughout the nation. These associations cover a state or part of a state, and with the exception of North Carolina, these plans do not compete with one another. Hospitals have been the main organizers of Blue Cross associations. Members on the boards of directors of these associations represent the hospitals, the medical profession, and the public.

Blue Shield plans specialize mainly in providing surgical benefits rather than hospital benefits, as Blue Cross does. About 76 locally autonomous Blue Shield plans have been organized, and have received approval for operation by the National Association of Blue Shield Plans, governed by 11 directors, 3 of whom are appointed by the American Medical Association. A local medical society usually has been the organizer of a local group, and most of the plans are underwritten by participating physicians.

At first, private insurance companies showed little interest in health insurance, but as the Blue plans expanded and showed consumer demand for such protection, private insurance companies began selling health insurance. Initially, the private companies sold only group insurance,[1] but later individual policies were sold also. Today over 700 insurance companies sell health insurance.

Data on health insurance has been published by the Health Insurance Council, an organization of various commercial insurance trade associations. Their data will be cited below although social security estimates are from 6 to 10 percent below that of the Health Insurance Council. The most comprehensive coverage of the various types of health insurance is that of hospital insurance, which in 1964 covered 151 million people.[2] Fewer people had surgical than hospital coverage in 1964. Over 140 million had this type of insurance.[3] The average maximum limits on benefits ranged from $285 in the South to $425 on the Pacific Coast.[4] Almost 109 million had protection to pay for regular office calls. To provide for longer or more serious illnesses, major medical expense protection was provided for 47 million persons.[5]

Interesting differences appear between the Blue plans and those of commercial insurers. One is that Blue Cross plans provide certain hospital services, such as semiprivate accommodations regardless of the cost of the services. Another difference is that Blue plans have commonly used community rates—that is, they charged everyone in the community the same rates. One estimate showed that the expenses of those over 65 were 2½ times that of those under 65; yet both groups were charged the same rates. Competition with private insurance companies has forced some Blue groups to give ground on this principle. The private companies were covering preferred groups, and selling them insurance cheaper. The larger the percentage of high-cost enrollees became in Blue Shield and Blue Cross, the higher their costs climbed. Faced with this type of competition, some Blue groups have had to make modifications in their rate charges. The nonprofit groups do have an advantage in not attempting to make a profit. In 1965, Blue Cross needed only 5 percent of subscription income for operating expenses and reserves, and Blue Shield 10 percent. Private insurance companies retained 7 percent for group policies, but for individual policies only slightly more than half the income received was paid in benefits.[6] The fact that the private companies charge less for preferred risks has enabled them to expand faster

[1] Louis S. Reed, "Private Health Insurance in the United States: An Overview," *Social Security Bulletin*, Vol. 28, No. 12 (December, 1965), pp. 3-5.

[2] Of the 151 million, about 93 million were covered by insurance companies (mostly group policies), 63 million under Blue Cross, Blue Shield and Medical Society plans, and 7 million under independent plans. Double counting has not been eliminated from the sub-groups but was for the grand total. See Health Insurance Institute, *Source Book of Health Insurance Data* (1965), p. 14.

[3] Almost 82 million were covered by insurance companies, mostly group policies; almost 52 million were enrolled by Blue Cross, Blue Shield, and Medical Society plans; and almost 9 million were covered under independent plans. *Ibid.*, p. 16.

[4] *Ibid.*, p. 30.

[5] Almost all of this was under group insurance policies. *Ibid.*, p. 21.

[6] Louis S. Reed, "Private Health Insurance: Coverage and Financial Experience, 1965," *Social Security Bulletin*, Vol. 29, No. 11 (November, 1966), Table 3, p. 12.

than the Blue groups in recent years. In 1945, 59 percent of all hospital insurance enrollees were under Blue Cross and other Medical Society non-profit plans, but by 1965 this percentage had dropped to 38 percent.[7]

ARGUMENTS FOR VOLUNTARY INSURANCE

A number of arguments may be presented to support the position that voluntary insurance provides the best solution to our medical problems. The fact that voluntary insurance has expanded so rapidly has been cited as evidence of its success in meeting the medical problems of today. In 1940 only 12 million people had health insurance in this country. By 1950 the number had climbed to 76½ million and by 1964 the figure reached 151 million. The fact that the insurance has been bought voluntarily rather than compulsorily has been extolled as providing the individual with the freedom of choice to purchase or not purchase as he sees fit. The fact that the many plans throughout the country are different has been cited as providing valuable experimentation to determine better types of protection. Recent advances in the quality of medical care is also listed by proponents of the voluntary system as one of the reasons the voluntary system should be kept in the United States. Life expectancy has been increasing under the present system, and therefore the present system should be retained.

One economist, Dr. Emerson Schmidt of the United States Chamber of Commerce, contends that the failure to meet health needs in America is due not to lack of personal financial resources but simply a reluctance of most people to spend money for medical care. He feels that there is a psychological law restraining people from spending money for medical care. People feel that they do not need much medical assistance to begin with, and that contacting a doctor may be both costly financially and time-consuming. Furthermore, people would rather spend money on things which bring more tangible and immediate gratification. For all these reasons, people simply spend little money on medical care. Schmidt cites the fact that people spend twice as much for alcohol as for medicine. Although he recognizes that all medical inadequacies can not be explained by his psychological law, he feels that it is of sufficient importance to give strong support to the voluntary rather than the compulsory system of medical care.[8]

CRITICISMS OF VOLUNTARY INSURANCE

In spite of the many advantages of voluntary health insurance, it has not been without its critics. One criticism is that the nonprofit plans have been

[7] *Ibid.*, Table 3, p. 6.

[8] Emerson P. Schmidt, "America's Capacity to Meet Existing Health Needs," in *Building America's Health*, Vol. 4, *Financing a Health Program for America*, Washington, D.C., the President's Commission on the Health Needs of the Nation (1951–1952), pp. 134-141.

unduly under the control of hospitals and doctors. In 1964, 43 percent of the governing boards of Blue Cross were hospital representatives, another 16 percent were medical personnel, and only 32 percent of the personnel were from other walks of life. On Blue Shield governing boards, 63 percent were physicians, 6 percent were hospital representatives, and the remaining were public representatives, some of whom were plan executives who were on the board of trustees of the plan.[9] Critics contend that the interests of hospitals and physicians are overrepresented and that consumer interests are underrepresented. The result is that under Blue Shield plans, for example, a majority of physicians determine how much the remuneration should be. When the program first began, physicians were reluctant to let others share in the determination of a very vital part of their profession—their income. As the program has matured and the medical profession has realized that its interests are being adequately protected, the prediction has been made that there will be more nonphysician participation at the policy-making level of Blue Shield.[10]

Another criticism of Blue Shield insurance is that it pays surgical fees only and does not pay for routine office calls. Actually only about 10 percent of physicians' services are performed in hospitals. Some claim that office calls are generally small amounts, and that the insurance principle cannot be used. A study of this problem was made by the Health Information Foundation–National Opinion Research Center. This group found that costs of out-of-hospital services are almost as unevenly distributed among families as are hospital costs. Such costs were heavier than surgery costs. More families incurred over $200 per year for physicians' services than for surgery.[11] In view of the obvious costs, some proponents of voluntary insurance suggest that voluntary insurance be sold to provide for payments of visits to the doctor's office after the second or third call. Some insurance of this type is now in existence.

It has been charged that although millions and millions of additional people have been covered by voluntary insurance in recent years, still many millions, mostly the poorer groups in our society, do not have health insurance. This group, it is contended, need some form of insurance even more than their more wealthy compatriots. Proponents of voluntary insurance, on the other hand, point to the large growth in voluntary insurance. For those who cannot afford voluntary insurance, some additional programs such as free treatment for indigent people under public health auspices have been suggested. Most of the programs recommended, however, require that the indigent person take a "means" test. Critics reject such a test as degrading to individuals.

Another criticism of voluntary insurance is that coverage is not compre-

---

[9] Reed, *op. cit.*, pp. 8, 10.

[10] Charles G. Hayden, "An Evaluation of Blue Shield Plans," in *Building America's Health*, Vol. 4, p. 54.

[11] Harold M. Somers and Anne R. Somers, *Doctors, Patients, and Health Insurance* (Washington, D.C., The Brookings Institution, 1961), p. 380.

hensive enough. Hospitalization is owned by 151 million people, but only 140 million have surgical coverage. Fewer yet, 109 million, have physicians' fees paid for services rendered at home or in doctors' offices. Only 47 million have major medical expense coverage, which provides for almost all types of medical care, both in and out of hospitals. Major medical expense coverage includes payments for special nursing care, X rays, prescriptions, and medical appliances.[12] Typical major medical plans do not pay for the first $50, $100, $200, or $500 of expenses. They pay 75 to 80 percent of the remaining bills with maximum limits frequently of $10,000, $25,000, or $50,000. Regular medical plans without major medical coverage usually provide for only 21 to 120 days of hospitalization, although the number of days covered has been expanding. Of Blue Cross plans, 6 provide for 21 days of care, 15 grant 30-31 days, the largest majority—35—provide for 70 days, 11 plans give 120 days, and only 4 provide for a longer period.[13] The policies that provide for longer coverage must be read with extreme care. In one area, a nonprofit policy that has a "catastrophic" rider excludes coverage for heart disease and cancer, two major illnesses, and does not cover mental disease, although almost half of our hospital beds are of this type. Concerning regular Blue Cross contracts, 23 of 79 do not provide payment for mental illness. Other exclusions of 79 plans are: tuberculosis, 31 plans; alcoholism, 37 plans; drug addiction, 33 plans; self-imposed injuries, 7 plans.[14] Similarly, without major medical coverage and even with it, surgical benefits are limited.

The failure to provide comprehensive coverage has resulted in additional medical expenses for those with a heavy incidence of illness. One study, for example, showed that 33 percent of Americans who had some kind of health insurance incurred additional medical expenses of $195 or more a year plus their insurance costs. If this group had purchased comprehensive insurance, large extra amounts should not have been necessary.[15] An unlucky 8 percent in the United States spent over $1,000 for medical costs in 1963.[16]

The failure to provide comprehensive care and to cover all people has resulted in insurance paying only 33 percent of all consumer medical care costs in 1964. Although 69 percent of all consumer hospital costs were paid for by insurance, only 38 percent of all doctors' bills were paid for through insurance.[17] Very few expenses for drugs, appliances, and dentists were paid for through insurance.

[12] Source Book of Health Insurance Data, op. cit., pp. 9-12.

[13] Somers and Somers, op. cit., p. 303.

[14] Ibid., p. 307.

[15] Michael M. Davis, Medical Care for Tomorrow (New York, Harper & Row, 1954), p. 245.

[16] "Trends in Personal Health Services," Progress in Health Services, Vol. 14, No. 2 (November-December, 1965), Chart II, p. 2.

[17] Louis S. Reed and Ruth Hanft, "National Health Expenditures, 1950-64," Social Security Bulletin, Vol. 29, No. 1 (January, 1966), Table 10, p. 14.

Critics of voluntary health insurance reply to the argument that local experimentation should develop superior programs by pointing out that there is no need for experimentation since it is widely known that what is needed is comprehensive care. Anything less than that is unsatisfactory and may simply result in inequality of benefits to various people.[18]

In spite of the fact that voluntary insurance has aided in preventive medicine, critics of it are not satisfied with the preventive aspects of voluntary insurance. If regular periodic examinations for the entire population may be viewed as the goal of preventive medicine, we are far from reaching this goal under the present system. If the present system actually discourages early treatment of diseases, as the critics maintain, then it would follow that there is a higher incidence of illness and thus an increase in overall medical costs under the present system.

The present voluntary plans have been criticized on a number of other grounds. The fact that many wealthy people do not bother to take out insurance means that the risks must be spread among fewer people at higher costs. Furthermore, the fact that the poor pay the same amount as the wealthy means that the poor are paying a much larger percentage of their income for medical care than are the wealthy. The present system is thus even more regressive than a payroll tax, usually used under a compulsory system. A few voluntary programs do attempt to lighten the burden of lower-income families by having a graduated rate based on income. Lastly, some labor unions have been critical of the present voluntary system because, they maintain, whenever unions negotiate for increased contributions in order to expand benefits, the hospital or doctors' fees are raised accordingly so that no additional benefits are obtained.

INDEPENDENT HEALTH INSURANCE PLANS

Independent health insurance plans are all those other than the Blue plans or commercial insurance. Such plans may provide for sick leave pay, supplement workmen's compensation benefits, or provide for medical expenses. In the latter category over five million workers are covered under self-insured, employer-employee union plans. Surgical benefits and hospital care are most frequently covered, but over 3½ million persons also have office and home visit protection.[19]

Community independent health insurance plans have grown until today

[18] Nelson Cruikshank, "Labor Looks at the Problem of Financing Health Services," in *Building America's Health*, Vol. 4 (1951–1952), pp. 116-120.

[19] Dental society plans have been slow to grow, and in 1965 about 732,000 persons were enrolled in such plans. Physicians have organized private group clinics in which almost 250,000 persons are enrolled. Medical society plans cover many fewer workers. See Louis S. Reed and Kathleen Myers, *Independent Health Insurance Plans, 1965*, Social Security Administration, Office of Research and Statistics, Note No. 9 (1966), Table 1, p. 1.

over three million persons are enrolled in such plans. The three largest groups enroll a large percentage of persons covered under such plans. These are the Kaiser Foundation Health Plans on the West Coast and Hawaii with 1.3 million persons enrolled and two New York groups—Group Health Insurance, Inc., (999,000 enrollment) and the Health Insurance Plan of Greater New York, hereafter referred to as HIP, with an enrollment of 689,000.[20] The discussion below will be limited to that of HIP.[21]

HEALTH INSURANCE PLAN OF GREATER NEW YORK

In 1943 Mayor La Guardia appointed a special committee to look into the matter of covering the employees of New York City in a health plan. After several years of investigation and planning, the program was instituted in March of 1947. About two-thirds of the members are employees of New York City; others include employees of the United Nations, several large labor unions, and a number of privately owned companies. In 1960 HIP opened its services to individuals and families who were unable to join through employee or union groups. Medical groups have agreed to accept all applicants except those with active cancer, active tuberculosis, or a chronic incapacitating illness. No health examination is required, but a health statement, subject to review, must be filled out. Aged people are limited to 10 percent of participation in any agreement. Since the enrollment of the aged is at that figure now, people 65 and older are temporarily barred from membership. During the first year that individuals were admitted, about 10,000 persons (nongroup enrollees) joined the system.[22]

The HIP is essentially a nonprofit company, and is incorporated under the insurance laws of the State of New York. For a fee HIP agrees to provide medical care to members. In order to protect itself against adverse selection, HIP requires that 75 percent of the employees of a group with over 75 employees must join the group. It also requires that the employer pay half the costs of the premiums. Charges made by HIP vary as shown in Table 10-1. These charges do not include additional fees that the employees must pay for hospital insurance. For the fees listed below, the HIP contracts with a group of doctors to provide the following services:

1. General medical, specialist, surgical, and obstetrical care

[20] Smaller community plans are those of the Group Health Cooperative in Seattle (85,000 enrollees), the Community Health Association of Detroit with 71,000 members, and the Group Health Association of Washington, D.C. with 57,000. *Ibid.,* Appendix Table C, p. 12.

[21] For a more complete discussion *see* Robert C. Rothenberg, Karl Pickard, and Joel Rothenberg, *Group Medicine and Health Insurance in Action* (New York, Crown Publishers, 1949); Commonwealth Fund, *Health Insurance Plan of Greater New York* (Cambridge, Harvard, 1957).

[22] *Annual Report, 1961,* New York, Health Insurance Plan of Greater New York, pp. 1-3.

TABLE 10–1. QUARTERLY PREMIUM RATES FOR HIP SUBSCRIBERS,
APRIL, 1966

Number of Persons	Quarterly Premium Rate
One person:	
Group	$13.50
Nongroup	14.45
Two persons:	
Group	27.00
Nongroup	28.70
Three or more persons:	
Group	40.50
Nongroup	42.95

Source: Letter from HIP, June 1, 1966.

2. Laboratory and diagnostic procedures
3. Periodic health examinations and other preventive medical care
4. Physical therapy, radiotherapy
5. Professional services for the administration of blood or plasma
6. Eye refractions
7. Visiting Nurse Service at the home of the insured, when ordered by a physician of the Group
8. Ambulance Service from the residence of the insured to the hospital when ordered by a physician of the Group.

If a workman is injured, and is entitled to treatment under a Workmen's Compensation Law, no services are provided. Similarly, if a patient is entitled to treatment by the government, no medical care is provided. Furthermore, medical services are not provided for acute alcoholism, drug addiction, tuberculosis, mental or nervous disorders, or chronic illness in an institution other than a hospital for general care. Payments are not made for dentists or drugs, nor are payments made for special duty or private nursing service.

HIP provides the services of other professional personnel in addition to physicians and nurses. On the central staff of HIP are five social workers. On referral of physicians, those social workers counsel on behavioral difficulties, marital problems, mental retardation, and custodial care.[23] Two full-time nutritionist-dietitians help physicians prepare dietary instruction sheets, discuss dietary problems with diabetic, obese, or hypersensitive patients, and serve by individual consultations on the more difficult diet problems when referred by a physician. Five specialists have been hired in the

[23] Herbert Yahraes, *Making Medical Care Better,* Public Affairs Pamphlet No. 283 (New York, Public Affairs Pamphlets, 1959), p. 27.

field of health education. This group prepares and guides discussions on any number of topics dealing with health.[24]

Premiums under this program are paid directly to HIP, which in turn reimburses the medical group. HIP keeps a small part of the premium to pay for administrative expenses of HIP and legal insurance reserves. Each medical group is autonomous, and pays its physicians and staff in any way it wishes. HIP requires that each medical group be organized so that it shall have five family physicians and a number of specialists.[25] Each insured person is primarily the patient of one physician, usually a general practitioner. The general practitioner may then refer the patient to a specialist if he deems that such services are needed.

ADVANTAGES OF PREPAID GROUP MEDICINE

Prepaid group practice has a number of advantages. On the group practice side, both general practitioners and specialists should be able to see more patients. The general practitioner sends more of the patients along to specialists and thus has more time for his remaining patients. The specialist obtains the advantage of having his case-load already worked up, studied, and diagnosed. Also when doctors work in a group, they may pool their equipment although more and more doctors in solo practice are also doing this. Patients obtain the advantage of seeing specialists more frequently and thus should receive a higher quality medical care. In 1960 in the HIP plan, 55 percent of all physicians' services were rendered by fully qualified specialists.[26] In solo practice, 75 to 80 percent of all medical services are rendered by general practitioners. The result of more frequent use of specialists is better medical care. In New York City in a three-year period, stillbirths and deaths in early infancy occurred at a rate of 35.4 per thousand deliveries. When the mothers were attended by a private physician, the rate was lowered to 27.9. The HIP record was still better, because of the use of specialists—23.1 per thousand.[27]

Another advantage of group practices is that the records of each patient are kept in a master record file. Under solo practice, the general practitioner would have one set of records and the specialist another. Another advantage of group practice is that the doctors may arrange their schedules so that they have more time off. Physicians may rotate on the weekend and take vaca-

[24] Edwin F. Daily, "What Scope Health Insurance?" *California Medicine,* Vol. 97 (August, 1962), pp. 58-60.

[25] HIP requires at least one and preferably two pediatricians and one specialist in each of the following basic categories: internal medicine, general surgery, obstetrics-gynecology, otolaryngology, orthopedics, dermatology, psychiatry-neurology, diagnostic roentgenology-therapeutic radiology, and clinical pathology-pathologic, anatomy, urology and ophthalmology.

[26] Division of Research and Statistics, Health Insurance Plan of Greater New York, *HIP Statistical Report,* 1960, p. 6.

[27] Yahraes, *op. cit.,* p. 2.

tions without any loss of patients or pay. They are also protected against illnesses of their own, for their pay continues while they are ill. The medical group arranges that a physician be available for 24 hours of the day, seven days a week. Under this type of arrangement, patients may feel less embarrassed about calling a doctor during the night or on weekends. Lastly, the physicians benefit from group practice by using the group conference technique. Frequent consultations on complicated cases redounds to the advantage of both the patient and physicians. As one student put it, "Doctors sometimes do need, and usually respond well, to the realization that their work is observable and observed." [28]

A comprehensive insurance program results in more preventive medicine being practiced. It is to the advantage of the physicians to keep their patients well in order to reduce the number of visits. HIP requires that the medical group provide one periodic health examination annually for insured persons aged 6 through 45. For those under 6 and over 45, more frequent examinations are suggested and permitted. The periodic health examination includes a urinalysis, blood smear examination, hemoglobin determination, a seriological test for syphilis, and arrangements for an X ray. Adults over 45 also receive rectal examinations and women receive vaginal speculum and pelvic examinations. A medical group may also send a bulletin to subscribers periodically with information designed to keep the insured healthy. Also a medical group may provide health lectures on pertinent topics and may provide classes for expectant mothers and seminars on child psychology for parents. The fact that members do not have to pay for each call has encouraged more medical care. About three-fourths of all HIP enrollees see a doctor at least once a year. The corresponding figure for the United States in 1957–1958 was 65 percent. In New York City in 1951 before the growth of HIP the figure was 57 percent.[29]

DISADVANTAGES OF PREPAID GROUP MEDICINE

Comprehensive insurance with group practice has not been without its critics. An insured person may have to forego the use of his former personal physician and choose a doctor whom he knows little about. To make the choice as palatable as possible, HIP has arranged that each insured person may choose to enroll in any group he wishes. Under the HIP plan there are 31 medical groups to choose from, although not all 31 operate in all of the boroughs of New York City. In some of the boroughs as few as five medical groups exist to choose from. The insured person is given the privilege of choosing any general practitioner from within the group. Privileges are ex-

[28] Alan Gregg, *Challenges to Contemporary Medicine* (New York, Columbia, 1956), p. 61.

[29] *Health and Medical Care in New York City,* Commonwealth Fund (Cambridge, Harvard, 1957), p. 49.

tended to changing both the group and the general practitioner with whom the insured is enrolled.

Proponents of fee-for-service medicine fear that the prepaid plan detracts from the personal physician-patient relationship, although those in favor of the prepaid plan contend that their plan improves physician-patient relations. Patients no longer have to fear that the physician is suggesting an operation just to make money from the patient. Proponents of group practice also point out that the general practitioner may continue his private practice during office hours along with seeing patients who are members of the group plan. Under these circumstances the doctor may not know which of his patients are private and which are members of the group plan. All patients are treated the same, and thus there is no difference in the physician-patient relationship. Lastly, the prepaid plan has been criticized on the grounds that it will result in excessive demands on physicians, since the patients pay no charges for each call. In the HIP plan it was found, however, that excessive demands were not made upon physicians. Rather interestingly, fewer house calls were recorded under HIP than for private practice. Moreover, patients were sent to hospitals less frequently. HIP subscribers entered hospitals 20 percent less frequently than those enrolled under a Blue Cross–Blue Shield plan.[30]

The medical profession in the past has been somewhat critical of comprehensive insurance–group practice plans. HIP has been specifically rejected by four of the five county medical societies of New York City, and by indirection has been disapproved by the Medical Society of the State of New York.[31] In the minutes of the Medical Society of Queens County in New York, the practice of medicine under the HIP was branded as unethical. Four reasons were given for disapproval of HIP:

1. HIP does not have the approval of the county society.
2. The governing body of HIP does not have a medical majority and its medical members are not members of and recommended by the state society.
3. The plan does not offer complete freedom of the choice of physician.
4. The plan obtains patients by solicitation.[32]

The American Medical Association has been quite critical of other group plans as well as HIP. However, in 1961 the American Medical Association withdrew all opposition to such plans. Conflict still remains in areas of New York City, where certain hospitals have refused to accept HIP physicians in their area.

[30] Yahraes, *op. cit.*, p. 20.
[31] Jules Joskow, "Organized Medicine and the HIP of Greater New York," *Social Service Review*, Vol. 29, No. 1 (March, 1955), p. 5.
[32] *Ibid.*, p. 10.

Those favoring prepaid group practice plans hail them as being the best solution to medical problems—superior compared with limited voluntary plans and compulsory health insurance. Proponents of compulsory health insurance, on the other hand, contend that while comprehensive insurance–group practice plans are an improvement over limited voluntary insurance, they still do not give the coverage of compulsory plans. It.has been found that HIP pays only 35 percent of the total medical costs of its members. Drugs and dentistry bills, not covered under the HIP plan, account for 52 percent of the medical expenditures of HIP members.[33]

COMPULSORY HEALTH INSURANCE

A system of compulsory health insurance generally requires that the government impose a levy or tax on people in order to pay for medical services. In many countries the tax used is a payroll tax although some countries simply finance the scheme from general revenues. The types of medical services provided, such as hospitalization, physicians' services, drugs, and the like must all be spelled out in the program.

In order to provide as much freedom as possible, physicians are usually given the opportunity either to enroll in the system or not as they wish. Patients, too, are given the freedom to select doctors of their choice. They may go to a doctor who is not registered in the program if they are willing to pay private fees. Since the medical costs of registered physicians are paid for by the program and charges from nonregistered physicians are not, most people prefer to go to a doctor who is registered. Since most people go only to registered doctors, most of the doctors, too, have little choice but to join the system.

A maximum number of patients is set for each doctor. Under some compulsory health insurance systems in the world, doctors are free to treat additional private patients, but other countries forbid this practice. Doctors are given the privilege of deciding whether they will accept patients who have requested their services. Payment to the doctor is generally based on a flat sum per person per year (capitation system). It would be possible to pay the doctor for each visit, and this is the way payment is made for dentists' services under the British compulsory health insurance plan. Usually, though, payment is made per person registered rather than per doctor's visit. There are several reasons for using the flat sum per person. Obviously there is less paper work involved. Furthermore, some contend that there would be a tendency under the fee-for-service system for doctors to suggest more frequent treatment than necessary since the government would be paying for

[33] O. W. Anderson and P. B. Sheatsley, *Comprehensive Medical Insurance—A Study of Costs, Use, and Attitudes Under Two Plans,* HIP Research Series 9, New York, Health Insurance Plan of Greater New York (1959), p. 6.

it. Problems would arise from doctors who would abuse the system, even though they would be in a small minority. For these and other reasons, most compulsory health insurance systems have abolished the fee-for-service system.

The fact that payments are made by the government according to the number of patients registering with the doctor makes compulsory health insurance somewhat different from a socialized medicine program. Under the latter, all doctors would be employees of the government. Under compulsory health insurance they are not employees of the government, but simply receive capitation fees.

In a survey of 101 countries in 1960, 46 gave medical benefits or some form of medical care. In 9 countries, medical care was a public service financed from general taxation.[34] European countries typically had such programs, whereas programs were less common in underdeveloped areas.

BRITISH PROGRAM

Great Britain has had a government-sponsored medical program for a number of years, beginning in 1911. Prior to the compulsory law of 1911 most of the working class had medical insurance provided to them mainly through membership in "friendly societies." The compulsory health insurance law of 1911 covered about one-half of Britain's population. Those earning above a certain wage were excluded, as were the self-employed. Approved societies, through whom the program was administered, were permitted to reject members freely. This provision resulted in the exclusion of poor risks, who were in need of more medical care than anyone else. The services of general practitioners were obtained under this program along with drugs and medicines. Small cash amounts were payable to the ill. One critic points out that the cash payments were so low (about one-fourth of wages) that they appeared to be designed for no discernible purpose at all.[35] The program was passed in spite of opposition of the medical profession. Labor unions at first were opposed to the program, for they feared that their whole program of medical insurance would be abolished. They were won over to the scheme by the concession that permitted them to administer their own programs.

Weaknesses of the British Program

Over the years after 1911, certain weaknesses of the compulsory system became evident.[36] The system was far from being universal. Although the lower-income groups benefited most from the program, only the workers themselves and not their dependents were covered. Rejected members could

[34] 1963 Report on the World Social Situation (New York, United Nations), p. 36.
[35] Harry Eckstein, The English Health Service (Cambridge, Harvard, 1958), p. 20 n.
[36] Ibid., pp. 1-163.

get only small cash benefits. Additional benefits, such as dental care, ophthalmic services, hospital and nursing care, were to be provided on a local basis if a government audit indicated that the Approved Society—an approved local group that administered the program—had a large enough surplus. Certain Approved Societies had surpluses, whereas others did not. This meant that certain workers would receive additional benefits, whereas others would not. Slightly over half the Approved Societies provided dental and ophthalmic services, less than this number made payments for convalescent homes, and hospital benefits were paid to less than 10 percent of those covered. Even those in a more favorable Approved Society, payments of this nature covered only a small amount of the costs of these services. Services of specialists were not provided, nor was treatment for tuberculosis. Orthopedic appliances or artificial limbs were not provided either.

Additional weaknesses existed under the old medical system. One survey showed that one-third more hospitals were needed. Certain areas, such as South Wales and East Midlands, had half, or fewer, beds per population than did London. In addition, most hospitals were too small to function effectively, and there was little coordination of services between hospitals. Remuneration of doctors was not particularly good, and was particularly deficient for specialists. General practitioners were unevenly distributed, as were specialists, and too many practitioners were engaged in solo practice and too few in group practice. In most other countries individual practice had been giving ground to group practice, but in Britain little change of this type had taken place.

In 1946, with the Labour Party in power and committed to socialistic principles, there was no question that the British medical system would be revamped. The problem was whether to revamp the old system by covering more people under it, or whether to provide an entirely new program. The latter course was decided upon by passage of the National Health Service Act in 1946. Under this Act, everyone in Great Britain who so elected was covered under the program. Not only were general practitioner services and specialist services to be provided without charges of any kind, but hospital services were to be provided along with drugs, glasses, and other medical appliances. The cost of the program was to be financed by a payroll tax along with general government contributions, the latter paying for about 80 percent of the program.

Hospital Nationalization

Almost all hospitals were nationalized under this program. Prior to the Act of 1946 there was little coordination between hospitals, and it was hoped by the Labour government that nationalization would result in a more rational and coordinated hospital system. Fourteen hospital regions (later 15) were created by the Minister of Health. Leading specialists were not to be attached to single hospitals but were to make their services available in a wider area. Since many of the hospitals were small, the new program provided for distributing the medical functions among the hospitals in a more rational fashion so that each group of hospitals could perform the services normally provided in a large general hospital. Although the new system was an improvement over its predecessor, a major criticism of the hospital system under the National Health Service was that no new hospital facilities were constructed. The first new hospital began functioning in 1955, nine years after the passage of the National Health Service Act of 1946, and 17 years after the last new hospital had been constructed. Sixteen more were to be built.[37] By 1960, enough new construction had taken place to cut the waiting lists for the chronic sick almost in half.[38]

Doctor-Patient Relations

In order to foster as good a doctor-patient relationship as possible, doctors were given the choice of entering the program or not. Most of them did, including 98 percent of the general practitioners. They were also given the privilege of refusing to give service to anyone whom they felt would be undesirable. Patients, too, were given the privilege of selecting any doctor they wished. In addition, patients were given the opportunity to change doctors at their convenience. When the compulsory health insurance system was first inaugurated, it would be found that some patients abused the system by immediately changing doctors whenever they failed to get a certificate of inability to work. The rule was changed to require that a patient either give a fortnight's notice or obtain written notice from the doctor who was releasing him.[39]

A number of people have contended that the elimination of the charge for each visit has made for better doctor-patient relationships. Among those who have taken this position is Dr. H. Guy Dain, the chairman of the British Medical Association Council, the negotiating group when the compulsory system was first inaugurated.[40] On the other hand, the fact that the payment has been removed has brought about a possible problem of the frivolous call. The statistical evidence indicates that the number of calls increased only slightly under the new program, and was only slightly above the number of calls made by wealthy persons under the fee-for-service system in the United States.[41]

[37] Don Cook, "Socialized Medicine, Ten Years Old," *Harper's*, Vol. 218 (1959), p. 36.

[38] Almont Lindsey, *Socialized Medicine in England and Wales* (Chapel Hill, University of North Carolina Press, 1962), p. 297.

[39] J. L. Bienvenisti, "Socialized Medicine," *Commonwealth*, Vol. 65 (1956–1957), p. 68.

[40] Cook, *op. cit.*, p. 32.

[41] Eckstein, *op. cit.*, p. 223.

Number and Location of Physicians

Before World War II, the number of applicants to medical schools did not greatly exceed the number who could be enrolled. After the inception of compulsory health insurance, medical schools had ten times more applications than places. Scholarship aid to three-fourths of the students aided in recruiting students. Medical schools began turning out graduates at a much faster rate than population growth. In fact, the growth was so large that some suggested that too many students were being trained. A committee under Sir Henry Willink investigated this problem and concluded in 1957 that the supply of students was not too large for the current demand.[42]

One criticism of the British system frequently heard in the United States is that physicians are leaving Britain in vast numbers. Here the facts show that the number of physicians emigrating declined from 1952 to 1957. There was a loss to the United States, Canada, and a few other Commonwealth countries, but this loss was partially offset by a net inward movement from South Africa, Pakistan, and India. A committee in 1960 reported that the net emigration of doctors and dentists was not higher than for the population as a whole.[43]

The weakness of having too few doctors in certain sections of Great Britain was alleviated under the new system by requiring that all new doctors register with the Medical Practices Committee. This Committee is composed of nine members, seven of whom are doctors. The Committee is appointed by the Minister of Health, but is independent of him. The Committee has divided the country into three areas, those badly in need of doctors, intermediate areas, and areas where there are many doctors (surplus areas). In general, new doctors are not permitted to enter a surplus area unless they have very special reasons. Applications for the intermediate areas are handled on an individual basis. Doctors are, of course, welcomed in the areas of shortage. The number of overdoctored areas has been cut to a third of what it was, and differences in the number of patients between overdoctored and underdoctored areas have been reduced considerably.[44]

Physicians' Pay

Specialists are paid by the Regional Boards, which direct the hospital system. Their salaries are divided into five main categories. Specialists are paid higher salaries than are general practitioners. They are paid adequately while in training for their speciality. In general, there has been little complaint from the specialists about their pay. General practitioners are paid on a capitation basis; that is, they are paid a flat amount per year for each

[42] Lindsey, *op. cit.*, pp. 174-177.
[43] *Ibid.*, pp. 178-179.
[44] *Ibid.*, pp. 200-202, 234.

patient who registers with them. The capitation amount was raised in 1952. In 1956, the general practitioners demanded a 24 percent increase in pay, based on increases in the cost of living. When the government appointed a Royal Commission to study the matter, the General Medical Services Committee of the British Medical Association recommended that general practitioners resign from the service unless their demands were met or arbitrated. In 1957, a five percent increase was granted. Although this was much less than asked for, the medical profession decided not to resign from the service. At that time, the average practitioner was earning 2,370 pounds ($6,636) if he had the average number of patients of 2,200. Less than 1 percent of the British population earned as much as 2,000 pounds per year.[45] Since 1957, additional increases have been made in the capitation amount. A review body now exists to study the remuneration of doctors and dentists on a regular basis. In 1966 the physicians were critical of a country-wide wage freeze that denied them increases that already had been approved.

Group Practice

When the compulsory health system was inaugurated it was planned that a number of Health Centers be built to allow doctors to practice in partnership along with dentists, ophthalmologists, and local health authorities. The failure to build these centers and to foster group practice was considered to be the major weakness of the British compulsory system by Professor Harry Eckstein, Harvard political scientist, who made an intensive study of the British medical system.[46] Most of the British doctors opposed the creation of Health Centers. In order to foster group practice without such centers, the government in 1954 introduced a system of interest-free loans to provide buildings for doctors who wished to practice together. Group practice has been growing, and about 67 percent of general practitioners are reported to be practicing in a group.[47] Even with this growth in group practice, a minority of general practitioners are still attempting to practice alone, some without even such basic equipment as a washbasin with water, soap, and a towel in their consulting room. Several studies have concluded that about one-fourth of British general practice is unsatisfactory and one of these concluded that about one-twentieth is so poor that it would be difficult to find excuses for.[48] The National Health Service, of course, did not bring these conditions about, but it has been slow in eradicating them.

[45] Joel B. Montague, Jr., "A Problem of Remuneration of the British National Health Service," *Sociology and Social Research,* Vol. 43 (1958–1959), pp. 205-208.

[46] Eckstein, *op. cit.,* pp. 247-248.

[47] Cook, *op. cit.,* p. 37.

[48] For a brief summary of several studies *see* Herman M. Somers and Anne R. Somers, "The Health Service: Diagnosis and Prognosis," *Political Quarterly,* Vol. 27 (1956), pp. 410-422.

Evaluation of Britain's Compulsory Health Insurance

In evaluating the British system, there is no question that compulsory health insurance has provided more medical care. Deaths due to tuberculosis were cut to about a third of what they had been. Dentures were supplied to one million people each year from 1952 to 1955 to help improve a situation where one of five adults was toothless. The number of hearing aids increased tenfold from 1948 to 1955.[49] Not only has more medical care been given, but the people overwhelmingly approve of the system. A poll in 1956, for example, showed that 90 percent favored the system, 7 percent were undecided, and 3 percent opposed it.[50]

Compulsory health insurance proved such a popular measure in Britain that when the Conservatives returned to power in 1951 they did not seriously consider abolishing the program. Instead, the Guillebaud Committee was appointed to investigate it. One complaint was that costs of the program had risen unduly. In 1948–1949, the cost of the program was 328 million pounds and by 1953–1954 had risen to 430 million pounds. The Beveridge Report and the Coalition White Paper had estimated the costs at 170 and 132 million pounds respectively. However, neither of these reports envisioned the larger type of program that was finally adopted. Also the estimates of cost were low because the demand for dentures and glasses had been vastly underestimated, as had been hospital repairs.[51]

The Guillebaud Committee appointed two British economists to investigate the cost problem of the compulsory health system. The findings of these economists were that although costs had risen, they had risen less fast than gross national product. The net cost of the program had risen to 3.75 percent of gross national product in 1949–1950 but by 1953–1954 had decreased to 3.24 percent.[52] In 1952, patients were charged minimum fees for dentures, drugs, and appliances, but even with additional charges later, the total amounted only to about 5 percent of the gross cost of the service (above that paid by payroll taxes and government contributions). Even here there were broad exemptions. Hospital inpatients, students, and all persons under 16 years of age were excluded from some or all of these charges. Those who were financially unable to pay were reimbursed by the National Assistance Service. Expectant and nursing mothers and those under 21 years of age were not assessed for dental work of a conservative nature.[53] In 1960 the total gross cost per person of the entire system came to £16 ($45). The

[49] George B. Mangold, "Social Aspects of the British National Health Service," *Sociology and Social Research*, Vol. 42 (1957–1958), p. 95.

[50] Lindsey, *op. cit.*, p. 473.

[51] Eckstein, *op. cit.*, pp. 216-218.

[52] Brian Abel-Smith and Richard M. Titmuss, *The Cost of the National Health Service* (Cambridge, Cambridge University Press, 1956), p. 60.

[53] Lindsey, *op. cit.*, p. 82.

cost has never been more than 4 percent of national income. This figure may be compared with 4.5 percent spent in the United States in 1959.[54]

The Guillebaud Committee did point out that there were administrative problems involved with the program since doctor's care, hospitals, and local health programs were directed by three different groups. The committee felt that more study was needed before a decision could be arrived at as to whether the three groups should be merged into one or whether better liaison between the groups could improve coordination. In a later analysis, Almont Lindsey suggested that tripartite administration has been the most troublesome problem in the Health Service. The tripartite system has not precluded cooperation where the groups themselves desired to work together, but even though noteworthy gains have been made in cooperation, the overall picture still leaves no room for complacency.[55]

Other advantages of the British system are that the number of hospitals and the service in hospitals has improved. The number of doctors has increased and there is a better geographic distribution of doctors. On the other hand, there is also consensus that the program could be improved further. Weaknesses were shown in lack of hospital construction, Health Centers, administration, and domiciliary services. The British have been working to eradicate some of the weaknesses of their program.

ARGUMENTS FOR COMPULSORY HEALTH INSURANCE

A number of weighty arguments can be made in favor of compulsory health insurance. Proponents of this type of medicine contend that everyone should have access to medical care regardless of income. They point out that making medical care available should result in people having more periodic examinations, which should tend to reduce the amount of illness. The emphasis of the medical profession should be to keep people well (preventive medicine) rather than attempting to cure people after they become ill. If people regularly avail themselves of periodic examinations under compulsory health insurance, or under any type of medical practice, there is little doubt that the incidence of disease would be reduced. Early detection of such diseases as tuberculosis, cancer, the social diseases, and others would reduce the incidence of these diseases considerably.

Proponents of compulsory health insurance also point out most of the modern countries of the world have such a system. In all of the countries that have introduced a compulsory health program, none of them has ever rescinded it. If the compulsory system were unworkable, it would be abolished. The fact that all the countries having it still keep it is cited as evidence of the success of compulsory health insurance.

[54] *Ibid.*, p. 472.
[55] *Ibid.*, p. 454.

Proponents of compulsory health insurance are critical of voluntary health insurance, although they would agree that it is superior to having no insurance at all. Their major objections revolve around lack of comprehensive coverage under the voluntary system. Fewer people are covered under the voluntary system than would be under compulsory health insurance. Such groups as the poor, the aged, rural people, and others are underrepresented. These are the very groups who need an insurance program more than those who have it. Then, too, the types of voluntary medical coverage are not broad enough to suit proponents of compulsory health insurance. They would prefer that doctor's calls and services of physicians be covered for everyone in the country under a compulsory system.

ARGUMENTS AGAINST COMPULSORY HEALTH INSURANCE

In spite of the weighty arguments in favor of compulsory health insurance, many people in the United States are strongly opposed to it. The American Medical Association and the medical profession in general are bitterly opposed to compulsory health insurance. These groups extol the benefits of voluntary health insurance, and point out that with more and more people voluntarily buying health insurance there is no need for a compulsory program. Granted that the lower-income groups do not have sufficient health insurance, these groups could be provided medical care under an expanded public health program. Opponents of compulsory health insurance fear that the personal relationships between doctor and patient might be severed under the compulsory system, although there is little evidence of this happening in countries that have adopted compulsory health insurance. According to opponents, placing doctors on a fixed annual fee would destroy the incentive of doctors. However, there would be some incentive remaining in that a doctor would have to be competent enough to attract people to agree to have him serve them. Opponents, however, still feel that insufficient incentive is provided under this system.

The medical profession is particularly disturbed that the compulsory system would result in the government determining the income of doctors. If, for example, the government decided that each doctor could serve a maximum of 1,000 people for an annual fee of $10 per person, the maximum income that a general practitioner could receive from the government would be $10,000 annually. If the annual fee was raised to $20, then the annual government income of doctors would be $20,000. The annual income of doctors would depend mainly on what the government would decide to pay. Since the members of the medical profession already earn high incomes, they would prefer that the present system of medical care continue and that the government have nothing to do with the amount that physicians earn.

Other arguments against compulsory health insurance are that too many people would abuse the system since there would be no cost involved. Under these circumstances too many people might avail themselves of the services of physicians and hospital care. Unlimited demands would be made on a doctor's time with only limited payment in return.[56] Britain and other countries having compulsory insurance, however, have been able to keep this problem under control. It is also alleged that too much red tape would be involved in moving to a compulsory system. Even under voluntary insurance, physicians must now fill in more forms than they had before the introduction of insurance. Still more would need filling out if everyone were under an insurance program. Offsetting the additional paper work would be the fact that doctors would no longer have to send bills to people.

COMPREHENSIVE HOSPITALIZATION COVERAGE

THE CANADIAN PROGRAM

A number of Canadian provinces now provide for comprehensive hospital insurance without covering physicians' or surgical fees. Saskatchewan has been chosen as an example of what one province has been doing.[57] In 1962 this province expanded its program to include compulsory health insurance, but only the compulsory hospital program is discussed here. In that province enabling legislation was passed in 1927 to permit municipalities to adopt comprehensive medical plans. By 1946 only two municipalities had begun a medical program. These programs were superseded by province coverage under a Saskatchewan Hospital Services Plan of 1947.

Originally only those living in the province for six months or longer were eligible. Residents from the sparsely settled far northern portion of the province were not eligible to participate. Although the program was mandatory for most residents, it was voluntary for Indians who had lived apart from Indian reserves for a period of 18 months. As in most social welfare programs, eligibility requirements over the years have permitted more people to participate. At the present time newcomers have to live in Saskatchewan only three months to be covered. Residents in the northern section of the province are now covered under the mandatory program, and Indians are also. Today about 97 percent of the inhabitants are covered under the mandatory system. Still excluded are those who have not resided in the province three months, mental patients, tubercular patients, inmates of federal penitentiaries, and members of the Armed Forces and the Royal Canadian Mounted Police.

[56] Hayden, op. cit., p. 51.

[57] G. W. Myers, "Hospitalization Experience of a Government Hospital Care Insurance Plan," Canadian Journal of Public Health, Vol. 45 (1954), Part I: pp. 372-380, and Part II: pp. 420-429. See also: Annual Report of the Saskatchewan Hospital Services Plan, 1961 (Regina, Province of Saskatchewan Department of Public Health, 1962), pp. 1-76.

Inpatient hospital services provided are unlimited ward care, nursing services, X rays, operating room facilities, most drugs, and other services. Charges are made for semiprivate or private rooms, for private day nurses, and a few of the newer and more expensive drugs. A $5 fee is charged for outpatient emergency services as a result of an injury, but no additional charges are made for subsequent changes of casts or dressing, or removal of them. A $5 fee is also charged for outpatient human tissue specimen tests. Table 10-2 shows the use of hospital facilities under this plan.

TABLE 10–2. DAYS OF HOSPITAL CARE AND LENGTH OF STAY FOR THOSE COVERED BY SASKATCHEWAN HOSPITAL SERVICES PLAN, 1947–1965

Year	Days of Care	Average Days of Stay
Adults and children:		
1947	1,309,288	10.0
1951	1,721,629	11.1
1956	1,732,456	10.4
1961	1,871,043	9.7
1964	1,994,306	9.6
1965	1,979,652	9.6
Newborns:		
1947	188,430	9.2
1951	168,644	8.6
1956	165,777	7.4
1961	159,447	6.8
1964	147,253	6.5
1965	134,626	6.5

Source: Annual Report of the Saskatchewan Hospital Services Plan, 1965, Table III, p. 6.

During the first years of the program, utilization rates of the hospitals increased annually. During these years payments were made by the government to the hospitals on a per diem basis for each patient. This is the same system used by Blue Cross and most private insurance companies in the United States. There was some evidence that hospital boards and administrators actively encouraged a high occupancy rate in order to collect more money. In order to correct this incentive toward waste, the Saskatchewan government radically changed the method of payment to the hospitals. Beginning in 1951 the hospitals were paid a flat monthly sum which was designed to pay for about 85 percent of their estimated total costs if operated on an efficient basis. The other 15 percent of costs were paid for each patient day of service provided. In 1961 the basic program of fixed payments plus per diem costs were continued with several additions.[58] Adjustments

[58] Milton I. Roemer and Max Shain, *Hospitalization Utilization Under Insurance* (Chicago, American Hospital Association, 1959), pp. 18-19.

and additional payments may be made for added costs that are considered uncontrollable.[59] The change to the new system has tended to curb hospital use in Saskatchewan. After allowance is made for increased coverage, the case load has increased less fast, and the average days of stay has decreased.

The Saskatchewan hospital program is financed by a charge of $24 annually for each self-supporting person over 18. Unmarried dependents under 21 attending educational institutions or schools of nursing and the physically and mentally handicapped are exempt. The maximum assessed for a family, which includes the head, spouse, and nontaxable dependents is $48. Welfare recipients are covered by payment from the province.

OVERUSE OF FACILITIES

One major objection to hospital insurance is that it tends to invite the overuse of facilities. Among a number of stories of abuse is one according to which a family in Tennessee regularly used a hospital as a baby-sitter for their child while they spent a weekend in Washington. They would take the child to the hospital, allege that the baby had measles or some other disease, and then pick up the baby after they had returned from their weekend.[60] A nationwide study by the Health Information Foundation found that 14 percent of insured patients in the United States go to a hospital yearly compared with 9 percent of those who are noninsured. Furthermore, the insured people tend to stay in the hospital longer—one day a year compared with 0.7 days for those not insured. Lastly, a larger percentage of insured patients had an operation than those not insured—9 percent compared with 5 percent. Of course, these figures do not supply conclusive proof of abuse of hospitalization insurance. They may indicate that hospital insurance provides an opportunity for people to obtain hospital care that noninsurees may not take advantage of because of lack of money to pay.

One study of 25 Michigan hospitals indicated that hospital insurance was abused. This study showed that 12,102 patients spent 76,238 days in the hospital, 11,172 days of which were unnecessary for the recovery, safety, or reasonable comfort of the patient. Whereas only 14 percent of those who paid their own bills came unnecessarily or stayed unnecessarily long, the corresponding figure for those with private insurance was 30 percent and for those with Blue Cross it was 36 percent. This study also found that one of eight entered the hospital for laboratory tests or X ray because the insurance paid for it even though they could have conveniently received such tests through an outpatient department of the hospital.[61]

Roemer and Shain have found that there are a multiplicity of causes

[59] *Annual Report of the Saskatchewan Hospital Services Plan, 1961,* pp. 4-5.

[60] Milton Silverman, "The Post Reports on Health Insurance, Part I," *Saturday Evening Post* (January 7, 1958), p. 127.

[61] Harry Becker, "Controlling Use and Misuse of Hospital Care," *Hospitals,* Vol. 28 (December, 1954), pp. 61-64.

affecting the amount of hospital utilization.[62] White-collar employees tend to use hospitals more than blue-collar workers, even for those under the same hospitalization plan. An insurance program providing for more comprehensive service will tend to reduce the need for going to a hospital. Thus it has been found that the Health Insurance Plan of Greater New York, which provides for prepaid office and home calls, has significantly lower hospitalization utilization rates than does Blue Cross. Marital status also affects the rate of hospital utilization. Single, widowed, and divorced people have a higher rate of hospitalization (under prepayment) than married couples living together. Where hospitalization is prepaid, people living in poorer physical circumstances tend to use a hospital more than more affluent sections of society. Hospital utilization is also determined by the number of beds available and the efficiency of bed utilization. If two or three days are needed before an X ray is taken, bed utilization will be higher than in a hospital which is operated more efficiently. As was seen above in Saskatchewan, hospital utilization was greater when the per diem method was used in paying for hospital services.

Availability of alternative bed facilities also determines the use of hospital facilities. If more nursing homes, outpatient services, and government hospitals are available, less demand is placed on the general hospital. The method of paying physicians also has a direct bearing on hospital use. The fee-for-service system results in a larger use of hospitals than when physicians are paid on a capitation or salary basis. Private solo practice causes a higher degree of hospital use than does group practice. Differences in practice among physicians also affects the amount of hospital use. Some physicians keep their patients in hospitals much longer than other physicians. In short, Roemer and Shain found a multiplicity of causes for differential use of hospitals. The corrective solutions suggested by them were given in terms of each of the causes. For example, if the causal factor was predominantly one of the physician keeping his patients in hospitals unduly long, a comparison of records with other physicians might induce him to conform more nearly to the norm.

Even if a number of suggestions of Roemer and Shain are adopted to reduce hospital use, they and others conclude that the possibilities for reducing hospital costs are limited. From 1948 to 1958, the utilization rates for all Blue Cross members in the United States increased 16 percent. Yet during this same period, overall costs for hospital care doubled or more. These figures would indicate that additional use of hospital facilities has been only a minor cause of increased hospital costs. Other reasons for the higher costs were the general inflationary trend of the period, and improved technical services provided by hospitals in the form of enlarged staff and improved equipment. Thirty years ago there was only one hospital employee per patient, today there are two. Also salaries of hospital employees, which were

[62] Roemer and Shain, *op. cit.*

extremely low in the past, have risen to some extent. All of these factors have raised hospital costs.

MEDICAL CARE FOR THE AGED

Voluntary health insurance has not solved the medical problems of the aged. Before Medicare fewer old people had insurance than younger people. Some of the aged had been forced to drop their insurance because of continued illness. Most could not convert their group medical insurance when they retired.[63] Many others who had the privilege of converting to an individual health policy did not do so either because of insufficient income, the higher cost of policies (they rise about 80 percent in cost),[64] or indifference.

INSURANCE VERSUS ASSISTANCE

In the past few years there has been little debate over whether additional government programs are needed for medical care for the aged in addition to voluntary insurance. The major controversy has been over what type of government program would be best. The two major programs vying for adoption have been the Kerr-Mills Act of 1960 (assistance) and bills which call for coverage of medical care for the aged under OASDHI. Prior to the Kerr-Mills Act, the Social Security Act was amended in 1950 to permit states to make payments to medical vendors for welfare recipients in need of medical care. The federal government allocated no money for such payments originally, but later did so on a matching basis. In February of 1965, when money payments to OAA recipients averaged $62.44, medical vendor payments raised the payments by $16.71 per month. Vendor payments for the permanently and totally disabled were slightly higher than this amount but were lower for AB and AFDC recipients.

The Kerr-Mills Act of 1960 provided for a federal-state matching scheme whereby aged persons in medical need, both on and not on OAA, could obtain hospital and surgical benefits. The sums allocated for medical care were much larger than the vendor payments and came to $184.54 in the average case in February, 1965. Proponents of coverage under OASDHI were highly critical of the Kerr-Mills Act. They objected to having a means test to determine who should receive medical aid. They were also fearful that a number of states would not appropriate sufficient money to match federal money, and as of August, 1965, eight states had not implemented the program. Coverage

[63] Statement of Frank Van Dyke, Associate Director, New York Prepayment Study, Public Health and Administrative Medicine, Columbia University, *Health Needs of the Aged and Aging,* Hearings before the Subcommittee on Problems of the Aged and Aging, the Committee on Labor and Public Welfare, U.S. Senate, 86th Congress, 2nd Session (April 4-13, 1960), p. 244.

[64] Statement of Walter M. Foody, Vice-President, Continental Casualty Co., *ibid.,* p. 180.

under the OASDHI program would have the added advantage of permitting the aged to pay for their medical costs during their working time when their earnings were higher rather than when they were old.

Strong arguments have been raised against providing medical protection for the aged under the OASDHI program, particularly by the American Medical Association. Opponents of coverage under OASDHI were concerned that the age limit might be dropped and thus result in a comprehensive system of compulsory health insurance. Furthermore, it was pointed out that many of the aged had sufficient resources to carry their own health insurance. Under Eldercare, the AMA alternative to OASDHI coverage, about half the aged would buy their own insurance and the poorest half would receive free medical care. If the poor were covered under the assistance program and the remaining aged bought their own insurance, then there would be no need for coverage under OASDHI.

MEDICARE

In 1965, amendments to the Social Security Act provided for medical care for the aged under the insurance program. Sixty days of hospital care are provided except for the first $40. For the next 30 days all but $10 is paid. After a stay of 3 or more days in a hospital, full payment is made up to 20 days in an extended-care facility, which may be either a skilled nursing home or a convalescent section of a hospital. An additional 80 days are provided in which all but $5 is paid. There is a lifetime limit of 190 days of payments for treatment in mental hospitals. Up to 100 home-health visits by nurses and other health workers are provided in the 365 days following release from a hospital or extended care facility.

To pay for the above part of the program, both employers and employees were assessed 0.6 percent on payrolls up to $7,800 (1968). The tax rate is identical for the self-employed. This tax is to rise gradually until it reaches 0.9 percent in 1987 and after. Although it is difficult to determine whether this tax will be adequate to pay for the program, the social security actuary has estimated that the tax should be sufficient. Using his intermediate cost data, he estimates that the hospital insurance trust fund will have a balance of $15.7 billion by 1990.

All persons under the OASDHI program are automatically covered under the hospital care program. In order to make this part of the program apply to a larger group, all persons not eligible under the OASDHI program were temporarily blanketed in providing that they apply. This provision only applies to those who will reach age 65 in or before 1968. Amendments in 1967 stipulated that those reaching age in 1968 could be covered if they had a minimum of three quarters of coverage instead of the regular six. The quarters of coverage will gradually increase until the regular insured status requirement is met.

Each hospital selects an administrative intermediary to act as a link between itself and the Social Security Administration. An important role of the intermediary is to review and pay hospital claims. The intermediaries pay only on the basis of reasonable cost determinations and apply safeguards against unnecessary utilization of covered services. Most frequently the intermediaries are Blue Cross-Blue Shield associations although commercial insurance companies have been chosen in a minority of instances. The Social Security Administration has dealt directly in servicing more than 100 prepaid group practice plans.

A separate section of the 1965 amendments provides for payments for doctor bills for the aged. This part of the program provides for payment of 80 percent of reasonable charges for physician and surgeon care after the first $50 in each calendar year. One hundred home-health visits are provided for as are a number of other medical and health services such as diagnostic tests, surgical dressing and splints, and rental of medical equipment. This part of the program is financed by a $3 charge to the aged person plus a matching of the same amount by the federal government. Due to rising physicians' fees and heavier utilization than anticipated, it is expected that the monthly charge will rise to $4.00 in 1968.

In the first year of the program, four million people entered hospitals for treatment and had hospital bills amounting to $2.4 billion paid by the program. Another $640 million was paid out for other medical services, primarily to physicians. About 200,000 people received home-health visits, and in the first eight months of 1967, some 200,000 people were admitted to extended-care facilities.

A major problem with the new program has been administration. To simplify the administration, a number of amendments were added to the Social Security Act in 1967. Physician certification of the medical necessity for hospital outpatient service and admissions to general hospitals is no longer required. Payments to radiologists and pathologists were transferred from the supplementary medical insurance section (payments to doctors) to the hospital insurance section, and outpatient diagnostic services were transferred to the supplementary medical insurance section. Hospitals will now be allowed to collect small charges (up to $50) for outpatient hospital services from the beneficiary without submitting a bill to Medicare. The amendments also permit payments to the aged on the basis of an itemized bill rather than a receipted bill. Payment by assignment to the physician is still continued.

The 1967 amendments authorized the Secretary of the Department of Health, Education and Welfare to experiment with various methods of reimbursement in order to keep costs down while maintaining quality of care. Some hospitals have complained about inadequate reimbursement from the government. Also, Mr. James M. Ensign, a Vice-President of the Blue Cross Association, maintains that the $50 deductible unnecessarily complicates administration, for a central record of the deductible status must be maintained and each provider must query the master record every time service is provided.[65] Some contend that the deductible features inhibit the aged from seeking needed medical care. The fact that the program provides limited benefits has been criticized by those who feel that comprehensive care should be provided. A number of persons suggested that drug costs be covered since as much as 50 percent of drug costs are paid for by 10 percent of the aged. It was also suggested that the disabled be covered under this program, but none of these suggestions have yet been implemented.

In view of the fact that the 1965 and 1967 amendments do not provide unlimited medical care for the aged, commercial insurance companies and the Blue Cross-Blue Shield associations have been active in providing supplemental policies to cover medical costs not taken care of by Medicare.

MEDICAID

As was stated above, medical care was provided to public assistance recipients by vendor payments. This program was supplemented for the aged not on welfare by the Kerr-Mills Act in 1960. The 1965 amendments substantially altered the two programs and provided that by December 31, 1969 the two plans must be combined into one. Those receiving assistance automatically qualify for medical aid, but those not on assistance who are in need of medical care and cannot pay for it are also eligible. To be eligible for federal grants, the state programs must provide for inpatient hospital services, outpatient hospital services, laboratory and X-ray services, skilled nursing home services for individuals aged 21 and over, and physician's services. The 1967 amendments maintained the requirement for the above five services for those on public assistance, but for the medically indigent not on assistance, the state could provide either the basic five, or seven out of fourteen listed services, except that if nursing home or hospital care services are selected, the state must also provide physician's services.

Medicaid is financed by federal matching grants which provide for the federal government to pay from 50 to 83 percent of the cost, depending on the per capita income of the state. This formula provides for slightly larger federal payments than the former Kerr-Mills formula. By 1967, 21 states had already implemented the program. On the basis of 12 states which had reported completely, New York State has spent about one-half the money for the entire program. New York's eligibility requirements are sufficiently lenient to permit the lowest income third of her population to qualify for aid. The average payment per recipient for the 12 states was

[65] Statement of James V. Ensign, Vice-President of the Blue Cross Association, *Social Security Amendments of 1967,* Hearings before the Committee on Finance, U.S. Senate, 90th Congress, 1st Session on H.R. 12080, Part 2 (Aug. 28–Sept. 19, 1967), pp. 916-918.

$90.31, but these varied widely from $211.40 in Oklahoma to a low of $20.62 in Ohio. New York's payment was $139.88.

In order to forestall excessive payments to certain states, the 1967 amendments stipulated that federal participation would be limited to families with an income of no more than 150 percent of AFDC payments in the second half of 1968 and gradually lowering to 133⅓ percent in 1970. Eligibility for New York would be cut from $6,000 to $3,900 for a family of four, and 14 of the 21 states that have implemented the program will have to restrict eligibility. Of those qualified for care in New York but not on public assistance, it was estimated that about 80 percent would eventually become ineligible due to the 1967 amendments. AFDC payments in Mississippi are so low, that the 133⅓ cut-off in 1970 will only permit payments in that state for those whose income is no higher than 30 percent of its own definition of minimum need.[66] It has been estimated that the 133⅓ percent cut-off will reduce federal payments for Medicaid from $3.1 billion to $1.7 billion in fiscal 1972.[67] Another restrictive amendment in 1967 permitted the states to inaugurate a deductible or cost sharing Medicaid program for those receiving aid but not on public assistance. Previously no deductible or cost sharing program was permitted in Medicaid.

Although the above 1967 amendments show reductions in Medicaid, some amendments in that year liberalized the program. States will have until January 1, 1970 (rather than January 1, 1968) to buy-in or pay for the beneficiaries' $3 monthly fee under the supplemental medical insurance program. Also, people who are eligible for Medicaid but who do not receive cash assistance may be included in the group for which the state can purchase such coverage, but there is no federal matching in this case. To provide better protection for the aged, federal aid will be given only in those licensed nursing homes which meet certain conditions. Administrators of nursing homes will have to be licensed, and skilled nursing homes will be expected to provide home-health-care service after July 1, 1970. Vendor payments will be provided for the first time on a matching basis for people who need institutional care in the intermediate range between boarding houses and skilled nursing homes. Medicaid may now also be provided for a spouse who is living with an aged, blind, or disabled public assistance recipient if the spouse, in living with the recipient, is essential or necessary to his welfare, and if the needs of the spouse are taken into account in determining the amount of his cash payment. Last, the 1967 amendments provide that direct cash payments may be made to Medicaid recipients to meet the cost of physicians' and dentists' services if the recipients are not on public assistance.

[66] Statement of Senator Robert F. Kennedy, *Social Security Amendments of 1967,* *op. cit.,* Part 2, p. 784.

[67] *Social Security Amendments of 1967, Statistical Tables,* Washington, D.C., U.S. Senate, Committee on Finance (November 17, 1967), Table 2, p. 21.

PROPOSED SOLUTIONS TO
HEALTH PROBLEMS (CONTINUED)

PERMANENT DISABILITY INSURANCE

Permanent disability may result from a number of different causes. Severe industrial, automobile, home, and other accidents may cause permanent disability. Disability may also be caused by ill health. Depending on the severity, disability may either be permanent or temporary. Illness that is so severe that it permanently deprives a worker of his job obviously creates serious economic stress. Due to the pressing need of the permanently disabled, many have suggested that some government aid be provided for these people. A minority on the Social Security Advisory Council in 1948–1949, on the other hand, opposed any type of government action for the permanently and totally disabled. Representatives of the insurance industry on this council reported that private insurance had tried to administer a disability insurance program, and had failed. Claims had become so large that some insurance companies had gone bankrupt.[1] It was feared that people would file claims and then malinger rather than work. In spite of fears of abuse, Congress in 1950 decided to provide for government Aid to the Permanently and Totally Disabled (APTD). The two major alternate programs considered were whether the permanently ill should be covered under the assistance program of the Social Security Act or under their insurance provision of the same act. The decision in 1950 was to provide payments through the assistance program. Thus a means test was required, and fewer people could qualify for payments than if they had been automatically covered by the Social Security insurance program.

DISABILITY UNDER OASDHI

The first recognition of the permanently and totally disabled under the Social Security insurance program came in 1954 with the "disability freeze" amendment to the Social Security Act. This amendment provided that in computing a worker's wage to determine his benefits, the years of permanent

[1] Insurance companies are now coming back into this field. In 1963, over 522,000 were covered by group insurance for long-term disability. Two years earlier less than half this number were covered. See *Source Book of Health Insurance Data* (New York, Health Insurance Institute, 1964), p. 14.

and total disabled could be disregarded, so that the average wage and thus the benefit would not be reduced. Some students have likened the disability freeze to a waiver of the premium in private insurance. The United States Chamber of Commerce opposed this amendment on several grounds. One, it feared that a federally controlled system of medical examinations to determine permanent disability would be an opening wedge for socialized medicine. The chamber further maintained that the Social Security program's purpose was to provide protection during old age rather than having anything to do with sickness or accidents.[2] In spite of opposition to this amendment, it was passed. One immediate result was that Social Security payments were raised for those who had become permanently disabled. This group received a monthly increase of $10.50 per month in their Social Security benefit.[3]

The problem of whether the permanently disabled should remain under the assistance program as contrasted to the insurance program was again considered by Congress in 1956. In that year, it was decided that, since the insurance program was the major program for the aged and since a means test was demeaning, the permanently and totally disabled should more properly be covered under the insurance program. Coverage was restricted to those aged 50 and over. Actuaries estimated that the cost of this program would be 0.42 percent of payrolls taxes (intermediate estimate). To provide a small surplus in case of error, the actual tax assessed was 0.25 on both the employer and employees. This was a level premium, and it was not expected to increase.

Actual experience showed that the costs of the disability program were overestimated. A revised cost estimate came to 0.35. Apparently malingerers did not attempt to cash in on this program on any large scale. The disability fund, which is kept separate from the regular Social Security fund, accumulated assets of over $2 billion at the end of 1960. Since a surplus had been accumulating from the inception of the program, and since few arguments could be advanced for keeping disabled people below age 50 out of the program, it was decided in 1960 to eliminate the age requirement entirely. The Social Security actuary computed that the total disability cost would come to 0.56 of payrolls taxes, or only slightly more than the disability tax of 0.5 percent that already existed.[4] The total assets of the disability program rose to $2.4 billion at the end of 1961 but dropped to $1.6 billion at the end of

[2] Statement of A. D. Marshall, U.S. Chamber of Commerce, Social Security Amendments of 1954, Hearings before the Committee on Finance, U.S. Senate, 83rd Congress, 2nd Session, on H.R. 9366 (June 24–July 9, 1954), pp. 492-494.

[3] Statement of Robert M. Ball, Administration of Social Security Disability Insurance Program, Hearings before the Subcommittee on the Administration of the Social Security Laws, the Committee on Ways and Means, House of Representatives, 86th Congress, 1st Session (November 4–December 7, 1959), p. 17.

[4] Robert J. Myers, "Old-Age, Survivors, and Disability Insurance: Financing Basis and Policy Under the 1961 Amendments," Social Security Bulletin, Vol. 24, No. 9 (September, 1961), Table 1, p. 13.

1965. To offset increased benefits in 1965 and 1967, the tax rate was raised in both years. Currently the tax rate is 0.475 of 1 percent on both employees and employers on the first $7,800 of payrolls. Self-employed persons pay 0.7125 of 1 percent. The Social Security actuary now estimates that the disability fund is in balance.[5]

Payments to disabled workers equal 100 percent of the primary insurance amount paid to a retired Social Security insurance beneficiary. In September-December, 1965, after the 1965 benefit increases, an unmarried male worker received a monthly payment of $97.11. A married worker received $153.28, and a married worker with children received $181.14.[6] Increases of 13 percent more were provided by the 1967 Social Security Act amendments. In order to qualify for disability insurance under the OASDHI program, a disabled worker must not only be fully insured but must have had a total of five years out of the last ten years in covered employment. The 1967 amendments lowered the eligibility for those disabled before 31 by replacing the five of the last ten years with the requirement that he had worked in one-half the quarters between the time he was 21 and he was disabled, or alternatively, that he had worked six quarters out of the last twelve.

In 1966, about 1 million persons were receiving disability pensions under the OASDHI program. For those not qualified under the insurance program or receiving too little income under it, another 600,000 received disability payments under the assistance section of the Social Security Act (APTD).[7] From a study several years ago, it was found that about two-thirds of those drawing disability payments under the OASDHI program either had heart trouble, cerebral disabilities, mental illness, or neoplasms. About 14 percent were institutionalized or hospitalized, and another 7 percent were housebound. The remaining 78 percent were ambulatory, but were unable to work.[8]

ADMINISTRATION

When the permanently and totally disabled were first covered under the OASDHI program, it was decided to permit the states to administer this phase of the program. The major reason for doing so was to encourage rehabilitation of those applying for disability payments. The State Office of Vocational Rehabilitation is the administering agency in almost all of the states, although four states have a second agency to help blind applicants. In 1965, state agencies evaluated about 631,000 disability applicants for possible rehabilitation. Of these, around 50,000 were considered to have rehabilitation potential, and about 10,900 were rehabilitated.

[5] Social Security Bulletin, Vol. 29, No. 4 (April, 1966), Table M-4, p. 51.

[6] Social Security Bulletin, Annual Statistical Supplement (1965), Table 57, p. 52.

[7] Philip Frohlich and Lawrence D. Haber, "Disability Insurance and Public Assistance: A Study of APTD Recipients," Social Security Bulletin, Vol. 29, No. 8 (August, 1966), p. 3.

[8] Social Security Bulletin, Annual Statistical Supplement (1963), Table 108, p. 89.

A number of controversial issues have arisen under the permanent disability program. The AFL-CIO has suggested that the program should be federally administered. Their recommendation received support from the federal General Accounting Office, which contended that the federal-state system was administratively inefficient. At the present time an applicant must first appear before a local Social Security office. The Social Security branch office must determine whether the applicant has sufficient quarters of work to qualify for disability. The office personnel must be sufficiently well versed in the program to answer questions of the applicant. The branch office must obtain information on the applicants' impairments and help the applicant obtain the necessary medical and other information. The application for disability is then forwarded to the state agency, which of necessity must go through much the same routine. The General Accounting Office contended that much time and effort would be saved if the federal agency had sole control of administering the program. The General Accounting Office could see no advantage to duplicating the screening of applicants.[9] The AFL-CIO further contended that the rehabilitation phase of the program would not be hurt by complete federal administration. The federal agency could just as well refer applicants to the State Rehabilitation service. Within a State Rehabilitation office, a separate group has to process claims while other personnel engage in strictly rehabilitation services. The AFL-CIO pointed out that for every 300 beneficiaries, only one was rehabilitated, and there was no reason why this figure would be reduced under complete federal control.

Another argument for federal control is that there is too much state variation in administering the program. Some states deny benefits to a much larger percentage of applicants than other states. Finally, some states take much longer to process cases than other states.

Proponents of the present federal-state administration point out that some advantage results in having state groups contact the medical profession concerning patients' disability rather than having the federal government do it. Administration by the State Office of Vocational Rehabilitation should tend to result in more rehabilitation. While it was admitted that there was considerable variation in processing of cases by states, the federal Bureau of Old Age and Survivors Insurance has attempted to point out these variations in the hope that more uniform treatment would result. The administering group has been handicapped by a continual expansion of the program. Once it becomes routinized, it is hoped that processing time can be reduced.

ELIGIBILITY

Another controversial issue revolves around the proper definition of permanent and total disability. The exact wording in the Social Security Act defined

[9] Statement of Lloyd A. Nelson, Hearings before the Subcommittee of the Committee on Ways and Means on the Administration of the Social Security Laws, House of Representatives, 86th Congress, 1st Session (November 4–13–December 7, 1959).

permanent and total disability as "inability to engage in any substantial gainful activity by reason of any medically determinable physical or mental impairment which can be expected to result in death or to be of long-continued and indefinite duration." Those having the loss of two limbs, two major joints, or one limb when complicated by a systemic disease were considered permanently and totally disabled by medical standards. Other impairments considered as permanent and total disability were loss of sight, heart failure, lung impairments, stomach and digestive ailments, loss of kidney function, hemic and lymphatic ailments (anemia), malfunctioning of the endocrine glands, and impairment of the brain and nervous system.[10] In comparing the definitions for permanent and total disability, it was found that the medical standards set for various illnesses were about the same for both the railroad program and Social Security. The latter program did have slightly stricter standards for musculoskeletal and hemic and lymphatic illnesses and a markedly greater requirement for respiratory impairments.[11]

Large numbers of people who were ill have applied for permanent and total disability benefits. About 38 percent of them have been denied benefits. This figure is for those rejected for medical reasons only, and does not include the small number rejected because of lack of enough quarters of coverage. The AFL-CIO was critical of the fact that the Social Security program had "tighter" standards than the railroad program. They favored a definition that would permit more ill people to draw benefits. Several cases are cited below in which the denied claimant felt entitled to permanent and total disability benefits.

I have before me the case of a woman who was a nurse and whose doctors ordered her to quit work. Her physician writes that she cannot walk across the room without suffering additional anginal pain. Yet she has not been able to qualify for disability benefits.[12]

I have cases where reputable physicians have testified to the applicant's coronary artery disease and angina pectoris, still the council refused his application; cases where operations for cataracts have been performed but the applicant still suffers from exceedingly high blood pressure and blood infection, and the council refused granting benefits; cases where the applicant has arthritis so severely he can hardly walk—he too was refused; clot on the brain—request refused. I could go on and on with many additional cases.[13]

The controversy involved in defining permanently and totally disabled persons and the withholding of benefits from obviously ill persons resulted in an important amendment to the disability section of the Social Security Act in 1965. This amendment provided that after six months had elapsed, a person would be eligible for disability payments provided it was medically

---

[10] For a detailed definition of each of these impairments, *see* statement by Dr. Arthur B. Price, *ibid.*, pp. 553-558.
[11] *Ibid.*, p. 553.
[12] Statement of Hon. Tom Steed, *ibid.*, p. 122.
[13] Statement of Hon. Randall S. Harmon, *ibid.*, pp. 124-125.

certified that the person would be ill for a period of one year or longer. There is still some criticism of the six-months waiting period before benefits are paid. The AFL-CIO has pointed out that payments begin almost immediately for injuries under workmen's compensation laws.

In other suggested improvements to the disability provisions of the Social Security Act, the National Rehabilitation Association has recommended that the Social Security trust fund should pay for the costs of an evaluation of the rehabilitation potential. Others, fearful of the drain on the trust fund that would result from this change, maintain that rehabilitation costs should continue to be financed by grants from the federal treasury matched by state funds rather than from the trust fund.

The 1965 amendment to the disability section has gone a long way in covering more people who are disabled for extended periods of time. Coverage was extended slightly by a 1967 amendment which eased eligibility requirements for those disabled before the age of 31. Another 1967 amendment, however, made coverage more restrictive. This amendment does not consider a disabled individual eligible for aid unless his impairment is of such severity that he is not only unable to do his previous work but can not (considering his age, education, and work experience) engage in any other kind of substantial gainful work which exists in the national economy, regardless of whether such work exists in the general area where he lives, or whether a specific job vacancy exists for him, or if he would be hired if he applied for work. "Work which exists in the national economy" was defined to mean work that exists in significant numbers in the region in which the individual lives or in several regions in the country so as to preclude denial of benefits on the basis of the presence in the economy of isolated jobs he could do.

An important controversy arose in 1967 over whether or not Medicare should be provided for the disabled under the OASDHI program. The costs of covering the disabled would be larger than for the aged. It was estimated that the cost would reach $1 billion by 1972 and, possibly, due to the high cost factor, the disabled were not granted Medicare protection in 1967. Medical payments for long-term disability and cash payments for short-term disability are two areas of remaining need for the disabled.

TEMPORARY DISABILITY INSURANCE

Temporary ill health is of a less serious nature than permanent and total disability. Nevertheless, a person who loses two or three weeks to six months or more of pay because of illness may face grave economic hardships. Many private corporations have formal as well as informal plans to pay workers while they are temporarily ill. One estimate in 1965 showed that the annual loss of income due to nonoccupational, short-term illness came to a little over $11 billion.[14]

About 48 million people in the United States are covered by some kind

[14] Saul Waldman, "Income-Loss Protection Against Short-Term Sickness, 1948–1964," *Social Security Bulletin,* Vol. 30, No. 1 (January, 1967), Table 1, p. 18.

of protection against loss of income while temporarily ill (1964).[15] An earlier estimate by Margaret Dahm showed that 60 million in our work force are protected by cash payments while temporarily ill.[16] More than 36 million of these people are covered by insurance policies, less than two-thirds of which are group policies. About 11 million others are covered by formal paid sick leave plans. The typical group insurance policy provides for a waiting period of from 3 to 14 days, with the usual period being 7 days. The maximum period of benefits is usually from 13 to 26 weeks, usually the former. Pregnancy benefits, if they exist at all, are usually limited to 6 weeks. Benefits may be a flat amount or graduated according to past earnings. The amount granted is generally from one-half to two-thirds of earnings, excluding overtime or bonuses.[17] Maximum limits on benefits for groups of more than 500 employees ranged between $35 to $54 for over 40 percent of the employees. Almost a fourth had maximum benefits of $35 a week or less, and about one-third had benefits of $55 or more.[18]

The fact that many Americans have no protection against temporary illness has resulted in four states and the railroad industry, by a federal law, covering about 12.9 million workers.[19] The first state law was passed in Rhode Island in 1942. One of the major reasons for passage of the Rhode Island law was that a flat unemployment insurance tax of 2.7 percent had been assessed employers, which could not be reduced through experience rating as in some other states. Also employees were taxed an additional 1.5 percent. With the reduction of unemployment during the war, and increasing receipts into the unemployment insurance fund as a result of increased payrolls, the Rhode Island fund was realizing a substantial surplus. It was felt that this surplus could well be used in a program of temporary disability for workers.[20] The second state law to become effective was that of California in 1946. This law came into existence only after three prior legislative attempts to pass such a law had failed.[21] In the same year, the federal government passed a law for railroad employees. New Jersey passed its law in 1948, and the last state to pass a temporary disability law was New York in 1949. The similarities and differences in these five laws will be discussed below.

COVERAGE

These laws exempt from coverage those employed in agriculture, government, domestic service, nonprofit, and family employment. Rhode Island

[15] Source Book of Health Insurance Data (1965), p. 12.

[16] Margaret Dahm, "Temporary Disability Insurance in the United States," International Labour Review, Vol. 78 (1958), p. 552.

[17] Jesse F. Pickrell, Group Disability Insurance (Homewood, Ill., Irwin, 1958), pp. 13-14, 19-25.

[18] Source Book of Health Insurance Data (1964), p. 33.

[19] Waldman, op. cit., p. 20.

[20] Dahm, op. cit., p. 553.

[21] Earl F. Cheit, "Unemployment Disability Insurance in California," Monthly Labor Review, Vol. 82, p. 564.

and the federal railway law cover all other workers except that in Rhode Island individual workers can elect out on religious grounds. The laws of California, New Jersey, and New York are more restrictive.

ELIGIBILITY

California, New Jersey, Rhode Island, and the railroad programs all require a certain amount of past employment or wages before benefits will be paid. Of the three state laws in 1953, 13, 5, and 10 percent of the claimants respectively were denied benefits because of insufficient wages earned. The New York law provides that an employee must work four consecutive weeks in covered employment.[22] Private employers are required to cover workers who have been unemployed and then become sick within the first four weeks of unemployment. After that time, disabled workers may draw benefits from a special state fund provided that they have been out of covered work less than 26 weeks and provided that they have not had more than 5 days of noncovered work since their last covered employment. The stringency of this requirement may be seen by the fact that unemployed claimants represented less than 1 percent of all claimants in New York compared with 9 percent in California, even though New York had a higher level of unemployment than California.[23]

To be eligible for disability payments, a worker must prove that he or she is unable to work due to some physical or mental illness. Medical certification is required before benefits are paid. The worker must be under the care of a physician and obtain a certificate from him. An estimate of the duration of the illness must be made by the physician. Continued claims are not permitted without an additional medical certification if the illness exceeds the normal duration of disability for that cause. The worker applying for disability must pay all medical costs involved. The government agency may employ a physician to examine a claimant, and claims examiners are sometimes sent out to verify whether the claimant's appearance and activities are consistent with the medical report.

DISQUALIFICATIONS

A number of disqualifications have been written into the five laws. Disqualification occurs if the claimant withdraws from the work force. In California, for example, if a worker has not been working for three months nor has looked for work during this period, eligibility will be denied. The other laws have similar but not identical provisions requiring attachment to the work force.

[22] *Comparison of State Unemployment Insurance Laws,* No. U-141, Washington, D.C., U.S. Department of Labor, Bureau of Employment Security (January 1, 1966), p. D-8.
[23] Margaret Dahm, "Temporary Disability Insurance—Experience Under Existing Laws," *Monthly Labor Review,* Vol. 79 (1956), p. 681.

With the exception of the federal railway law, the other four laws limit payments for disability due to pregnancy. In order to prevent duplication of payments, certain requirements are written into the law for those receiving workmen's compensation benefits. California provides that if the workmen's compensation award is less than the temporary disability payment, the worker will receive the difference. The railway law has the same provision. New Jersey provides for no disability payment if workmen's compensation is received. Rhode Island, on the other hand, permits a beneficiary to receive both payments with a maximum limit of the lesser of 85 percent of wages or $62 plus dependents' benefits. New York provides that disability payments may be made only if the illness is not work-connected.[24] This law may result in no payments of any kind for a work-connected disability if the workmen's compensation law does not cover it, but the law is administered leniently. All the laws provide for a disqualification from disability benefits if unemployment compensation is paid. All of the temporary disability laws require a waiting period of from four to seven days before compensation is paid. The waiting period results in an elimination of many small claims that would cost relatively large sums of money in the aggregate.

BENEFITS

Benefits are based on past wages subject to maximum and minimum limits. The present maximum weekly limits are $80 in California, $55 in New York, $47 in Rhode Island, and $50 in New Jersey, and $10.20 daily for the railroad program.[25] In California, the disability benefit is somewhat higher than the unemployment insurance benefit. California also pays hospital benefits for 20 days.

All of the laws have a maximum limit of payment of 26 weeks. Further limitations are provided, which restrict the number of payments according to a percentage of base weeks worked or base period wages.[26]

FINANCING

In financing the disability program, a tax of 1 percent is assessed the employee in California on wages up to $7,400 and in Rhode Island on up to $4,800. Both New York and New Jersey require the employee to pay a 0.5 percent tax. In New York the maximum paid is limited to 30 cents a week, and in New Jersey the tax is applied only to the first $3,000 of earnings. In the latter state, the employer is also required to contribute 0.25 percent of his payroll up to $3,000 of each worker's earnings, but this tax may be increased or decreased depending on the employer's experience. The maximum tax an employer may be required to pay is 0.75 percent of payrolls and the

24 *Comparison of State Unemployment Insurance Laws, op. cit.,* pp. D-9–D-11.

25 *Ibid.,* pp. D-8–9; *Annual Report, 1965,* Washington, D.C., Railroad Retirement Board, p. 48.

26 *Comparison of State Unemployment Insurance Laws, op. cit.,* pp. D-8–9.

minimum is 0.1 percent of payrolls. In New York, the employer is required to pay any of the additional costs needed above the 0.5 percent tax on employees.[27] For railroads, the tax is assessed against employees, and ranges from 0.5 percent to 4.0 percent (the current rate) of payrolls depending on the total amount in the fund. This amount is used to finance both the unemployment insurance and disability programs.

ADMINISTRATION

Some interesting differences have occurred in the methods of administering the disability programs. In Rhode Island and the railroad industry, the program is administered solely by the government under an exclusive government program. The main argument for such a program is that a wider pooling of risks should result when all employees are covered. Also administrative costs should be lower. Private insurance companies obviously do not like exclusive state funds, which deny them the right to sell insurance. Even though sales of group health and accident insurance have not decreased where there are exclusive government funds, private insurance companies still like the privilege of competing with the state for disability insurance. In California and New Jersey, the disability program may be administered either by the state or through private insurance companies. In both states, the employee is not permitted to pay to private insurance companies more than the charge assessed by the state program. In both states the insurance companies are required to provide benefits similar to or better than those provided by the state. Additional safeguards are provided in both states. In California a majority of workers must consent to the private plan, and an individual worker is free to reject the plan and enroll in the state plan. In New Jersey, no employer, union, or employee association may profit from a private plan, and a majority of workers must consent to the plan if workers' contributions are required.

In California, the private insurance companies' percentage of covered employment under the disability program increased from 19 percent in 1947 to more than 50 percent in 1951, but since then has started to decline. By 1964 payments under privately insured plans had almost vanished. The reason is that statutory increases in benefits by the government have eliminated profit margins.

In New York the disability program is administered mainly by private insurance companies, but there is a competitive state fund. In addition there is a Special State Fund to pay disability benefits for unemployed workers. The money for this fund is obtained by assessing insurance carriers in proportion to the taxable wages insured by each one.

One study which compared private with government plans concluded that the government plans provided more protection for each dollar of contributions than private plans. Thirty-seven percent of disabled workers were

[27] *Ibid.*, p. D-6.

under government plans and accounted for 39 percent of taxable wages; yet the government plans paid 43 percent of all benefits. The larger percentage of amounts were paid out by the governments even though the government accounts generally were with smaller employers whose administrative costs for servicing were higher.[28]

In all the plans except New York, the program is administered by the same agency that administers unemployment insurance. The disability programs are coordinated with unemployment insurance and are administered jointly. In New York State, the program is administered by the State Workmen's Compensation Board. The disability programs are so different from workmen's compensation that little saving is accomplished by having both programs administered together. Nevertheless, it is interesting that New York State has had lower administrative costs than the other programs. The state administrative costs in 1954 were 0.01 percent for New York, 0.04 percent for the railroad program, 0.06 percent for Rhode Island, 0.07 percent for California, and 0.09 percent for New Jersey.[29]

EVALUATION

Since the inception of the disability programs, they have been financially sound. However, in the past few years, the state funds of California, New Jersey, and Rhode Island have run deficits. The situation was so precarious in California that in 1965 hospital benefits were temporarily suspended. Emergency legislation was enacted in 1965 to raise the tax base from $5,600 to $7,400, and when this was accomplished, hospital benefits were resumed. The additional tax revenue resulted in a surplus in the California fund for the first time in five years, and actuaries now estimate that the tax revenue should be sufficient to finance benefits. Table 11-1 shows the receipts, expenditures, and the balance in the three state funds. New York has no fund, since it requires its employers to take out disability insurance. The railway fund is a joint one with their unemployment insurance program.

One problem arising under disability insurance is abuse of the system. If workers malinger unduly simply to receive sick pay, a program of this sort would not justify itself. One study in California showed that private carriers have been concerned with malingering, particularly among secondary wage earners and those not returning to work soon enough. However, the private carriers do not consider benefit abuse as a serious overall problem.[30] Other data in support of the position that there has been little abuse in the program have been that the average days of illness compensated for

[28] John M. Diggins, "Significant Temporary Disability Insurance Data, 1959," No. U-196, Washington, D.C., U.S. Department of Labor, Bureau of Employment Security (1961), p. 1.

[29] Dahm, "Temporary Disability Insurance—Experience Under Existing Laws," op. cit., p. 683.

[30] John S. Sickley, "The Impact of a State Disability Act on Insurance Companies: A Study of the California Experience," Research Monograph No. 71 (Columbus, Ohio State University, Bureau of Business Research, 1954).

TABLE 11–1.   SUMMARY BALANCE SHEET, GOVERNMENT TEMPORARY
DISABILITY INSURANCE PROGRAMS, 1965

Item	California	New Jersey	Rhode Island
Income	$243,550,000	$23,991,430	$10,661,203
Expenditures	226,126,000	27,656,487	11,497,618
Surplus or deficit	17,424,000	−3,665,054	−836,415
Balance, Dec. 31, 1965	30,868,000	90,020,054	28,660,795

Sources: Annual reports of the state agencies.

has tended to remain the same over the years.[31] The requirement that ill-nesses must be verified medically has tended to limit abuse.

In spite of the qualified success of temporary disability insurance under the five programs discussed above, it is interesting to note that no state has passed a disability program since 1949. Although there has been an extension of other types of welfare programs, this one has been narrowly circumscribed. It may be that the method of financing these programs—taxes on employees—has not been particularly popular among employees, and therefore no enthusiasm has been generated for such legislation. Even though no additional state plans have been adopted since 1949, the growth of private plans has given more protection against illness. In 1948 payments to the ill comprised only 17 percent of the loss in income compared with 30 percent in 1965.[32]

IMPROVED MEDICAL PERSONNEL AND FACILITIES

PHYSICIANS

We have about the same number of doctors today per population as we had in 1950.[33] In attempting to analyze future needs of physicians in this country, a number of factors must be considered. The fact that a larger percentage of our population is 65 and over would call for more medical care since the aged group have a higher incidence of severe illness. As per capita income has been increasing over the years, people in America are purchasing more medical care. Thirty years ago, the average person visited a doctor only twice a year; today the average is five times a year. People in urban areas tend to visit a doctor more frequently than rural inhabitants, and America is becoming more urbanized. A larger number of physicians than previously

[31] Dahm, "Temporary Disability in the United States—Experience Under Existing Laws," op. cit., 568-570.
[32] Waldman, op. cit., Table 7, p. 26.
[33] Statistical Abstract of the United States, 1966, Washington, D.C., U.S. Department of Commerce, Bureau of the Census, Table 79 (1966), p. 65.

are engaged in full-time teaching, research, public health, individual medicine, and military service. This leaves a smaller percentage of physicians available for private practice. To balance the increasing need for medical personnel, increased efficiency in medical practice has aided the average physician in seeing about twice the number of patients he did in 1930. In weighing all these factors the Surgeon General's Consultant Group on Medical Education felt that we should at least attempt to maintain the same ratio of physicians per population that we have today. However, based mainly on the fact that physicians' salaries have risen extremely fast in recent years, Elton Rayack concluded contrariwise that there is currently a shortage of physicians' services and that government recommendations aimed at maintaining current conditions are apt to yield shortages in the future.[34]

The Surgeon General's Consultant Group made several recommendations on how to assure an adequate supply of physicians. One was that additional aid should be provided for students interested in a medical career. Large sums of money are needed to finance four years of college, four years of medical school, and one to six years of internship and residency or fellowship training. The average cost of a single year in medical school for unmarried students was $2,386 and the average cost for married students was $3,271. Unmarried students obtained 22 percent of the money for their education from working mainly during vacations. This figure compared with 21 percent for married students, whose wives added another 23 percent to their support. Forty percent of medical students come from families with $10,000 and over per year, but 20 percent come from families with less than $5,000 income. The consultant group recommended increased loans and scholarships for those unable to pay for them either from private sources, state funds, or federal funds. The group pointed out that federal aid is now being made on a much larger scale to graduate students in other fields of specialization.

In 1963, 7,278 students graduated from schools of medicine (M.D. degrees only). If we expect to maintain the present physician-population ratio, much larger numbers of students will have to be graduated in the future. Present medical schools need to be expanded, and a number of new medical schools should be constructed. Larger private and governmental appropriations will be necessary to ensure an adequate supply of physicians in the future.

QUALITY OF MEDICAL CARE

One past president of the American Medical Association indicated that problems of quality of medical care are caused by the rapid advance in medical knowledge. He stated that five years after graduation, no one is competent to practice medicine on what he learned in medical school and interning.[35]

---

[34] Elton Rayack, "The Supply of Physician's Services," *Industrial and Labor Relations Review,* Vol. 17, No. 2 (January, 1964), pp. 221-237.

[35] Roger I. Lee, *A Doctor Speaks His Mind* (Boston, Little, Brown, 1958), p. 12.

To improve the quality of medical care, a number of suggestions have been made. Dr. Walter S. Wiggins, secretary of the American Medical Association's Council on Medical Education and Hospitals, suggested that there are four ways of inducing physicians to keep abreast of new developments in their field: (1) publication of the names of physicians participating in continuing medical education programs; (2) making membership in medical societies contingent on such participation; (3) making license renewal contingent on such participation; and (4) making licenses valid for a limited time only, with renewal by examination.[36] Little support has been received to implement these suggestions.

Controls and improvement in quality are more easily aided by group practice than solo work. Consultation with others aids the quality of medical care. The fact that a physician joins a group implies that he has enough self-confidence to have others review his work. In addition, most groups have formal methods for maintaining the quality of medical care.[37]

DENTISTS

In 1930, the United States had 59 dentists per 100,000 population. By 1963 the ratio had dropped to 56. In that year, 3,191 dentists were graduated. To meet only the needs of population growth, by 1970 we will have to graduate 6,180 dentists a year, or almost double the number of graduates of 1963. Both an expansion of present facilities and the creation of a number of new schools will be needed to insure an adequate number of dentists.

HEALTH PROFESSIONS EDUCATIONAL ASSISTANCE ACT (1963)

In order to encourage the training of additional medical personnel, the Health Professions Educational Assistance Act was passed in 1963. This act provided that the federal government appropriate matching grants of $105 million over a three-year period for the construction of new teaching facilities for the training of physicians, pharmacists, optometrists, podiatrists, nurses, and professional public health personnel. Also $35 million was appropriated to assist in the construction of new teaching facilities for the training of dentists, and the same amount of money was appropriated for the replacement or rehabilitation of existing facilities for the training of all the above listed medical personnel. The amount of the federal grant is determined by the Surgeon General but may not exceed 66.67 percent for new facilities, 50 percent for other facilities, and 75 percent for public health facilities. As of 1966 it was reported that as the result of this act grants have been provided to construct 6 new medical schools and to expand 18 other medical schools. About 725 additional medical school students will be enrolled for the first year of medical school as a result of this act.

[36] New York Times (January 31, 1959), p. 40.
[37] Harold M. Somers and Anne R. Somers, Doctors, Patients, and Health Insurance (Washington, D.C., Brookings Institution, 1961), pp. 113-119.

This act also authorized the Secretary of Health, Education, and Welfare to enter into an agreement for the establishment and operation of a student loan fund with any public or nonprofit medical training school. Loans may not exceed $2,000 per student for any academic year, and must be paid back at either 3 percent or the going federal rate at the time the loan is made, whichever is greater.

NURSES TRAINING ACT (1964)

In 1965, there were 1.2 million nurses in the United States. With our increased affluence and the purchase of more medical care it is estimated that 1.7 million nurses will be needed by 1975.[38] In order to encourage additional training of nurses, the federal government in 1964 passed the Nurses Training Act. This act provided matching grants of $5 million for fiscal 1966 and $10 million for the next three fiscal years to construct new facilities for collegiate schools of nursing or the replacement or rehabilitation of existing facilities. During fiscal 1966, $10 million was appropriated in matching grants plus $15 million for the next three fiscal years for the construction of new facilities or replacement or rehabilitation of existing facilities for associate degree or diploma schools of nursing. The amount of the grant is determined by the Surgeon General, but shall not exceed 66⅔ of the cost of new facilities and 50 percent of the cost of other facilities. As of 1966, as a result of this act, 2 new schools of nursing have been opened and 14 others have expanded their facilities. As a result of these additions, 788 additional nurses will be able to be trained each year. A loan fund was also created for those taking nurses training, with a limit of $1,000 per student for the academic year.

HOSPITALS

A number of studies have been made to determine the adequacy of our hospital system, both on quantitative and qualitative bases. Most researchers have based the quantitative needs on the number of beds needed per 1,000 population. The Public Health Service ratio today has set a ratio of 4.5 beds per 1,000 state population for general hospital beds. The actual requirements read as follows: "4.5 beds per 1,000 State Population (except 5.0 and 5.5 where State Population density is from 6 to 12 persons per square mile or below 6 persons per square mile) except where reduced by unassigned reserved beds."[39] If areas have more beds than this, they are not eligible for federal aid. Fig. 11-1 shows that the United States is weakest at providing sufficient long-term care and mental hospital beds. The short-

[38] Herman M. Sturm, "Technological Developments and Their Effects Upon Health Manpower," *Monthly Labor Review,* Vol. 90, No. 1 (January, 1967), Table 3, p. 7.

[39] *Hill-Burton State Plan Data,* Publication No. 930F, 1962, Washington, D.C., U.S. Department of Health, Education, and Welfare, Public Health Service, Chart 1, p. 9.

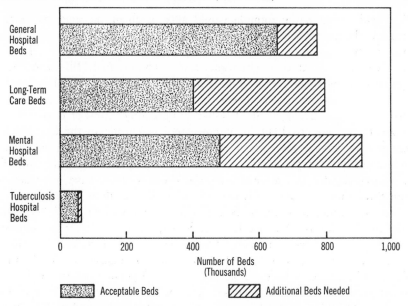

Source: Hill-Burton State Plan Data, a National Summary as of January 1, 1965, U.S. Department of Health, Education, and Welfare, Public Health Service, Table 5, p. 38; Table 11, p. 47; Table 16, p. 55; and Table 22, p. 66.

FIG. 11–1.   ACCEPTABLE HOSPITAL BEDS IN THE UNITED STATES AND ADDITIONAL BEDS NEEDED, JANUARY 1, 1965

ages of beds have been particularly acute in low-income states and in rural areas.

THE HILL-BURTON ACT

In order to help alleviate hospital shortages, Congress passed the Hill-Burton Act in 1946. The two purposes of the act were as follows: "(1) to assist the States in inventorying their existing facilities, surveying their needs for additional facilities, and developing comprehensive plans for the construction of such facilities; and (2) to provide the necessary incentive through financial assistance to the States for the construction of long-needed public and other nonprofit hospitals and public health centers." [40]

This act, as amended, appropriated $150 million annually by the federal government on a matching basis with the states. The matching formula as used in the Hill-Burton set is considered by many to be superior to the matching formula used in the Social Security Assistance programs. The Hill-Burton Act formula considers per capita income and population. With popu-

[40] *Ibid.,* p. 5.

lation held constant, the formula would allocate about six times as much income to the poorer states as to the wealthier ones.[41] However, since population has been growing much faster in the higher-income states, much less than six times is allocated to the poorer states. The original Hill-Burton Act required that the sponsor contribute two dollars for every one dollar of federal money. Even though the poorer states received larger federal appropriations, under these arrangements they had to raise larger sums of money than the wealthier states. In 1949, an improvement was made in the law which permitted the federal government to assume a larger burden, and pay from a minimum of $33\frac{1}{3}$ percent to a maximum of $66\frac{2}{3}$ percent of the cost of the project. Under this arrangement, the neediest states have constructed about three times as many beds per person as the wealthier states.

In attempting to evaluate federal government spending for hospitals under the Hill-Burton Act, one fact stands out; namely, that the percentage of needs met has been improving. The percentage of needs met is simply the number of acceptable hospital beds per 1,000 population divided by the standard of how many beds are needed per 1,000 population. In 1948, the United States had 388,144 acceptable general hospital beds, which was 59 percent of 652,972, the total number of acceptable beds needed. By 1962, the number of acceptable beds had increased to 632,444, which was 80 percent of the total beds needed. Not all of the increase in hospital beds during this period could be attributed to Hill-Burton spending. From 1948 to 1954, for example, projects constructed with Hill-Burton money comprised only 23 percent of the value of construction put in place during those years for all nonfederal general hospital facilities. Nevertheless, it may be concluded that Hill-Burton money was an aid in the construction of many hospital facilities.

Even though the number of hospitals increased and lower-income states received larger amounts of money per capita than wealthier states, a further problem is whether the states spent their money wisely. Before the Hill-Burton money is released to a state, the state must present a single comprehensive plan for hospital construction in the state. Existing facilities, population, income, and need data are used in planning a program of construction. In general, funds were allocated to areas of unmet needs, which in many states were rural areas. Care had to be taken not to locate hospitals in areas depopulating too fast, but the planning required in each state before a project was accepted aided in insuring the proper construction of facilities.

One criticism of the Hill-Burton Act was that all of the money was spent for construction of general hospitals. In 1954 some of the shortcomings of the Hill-Burton Act were remedied. The act was amended to provide specific funds for construction of nursing homes, diagnostic and treatment cen-

[41] Paul A. Brinker and Burley Walker, Jr., "The Hill-Burton Act: 1948–1954," *Review of Economics and Statistics,* Vol. 44 (1962), p. 210.

ters, rehabilitation facilities, and chronic disease hospitals. The Public Health Service was also authorized to make grants for research, experiments, and demonstrations relating to the effective utilization of hospital services, facilities, and resources. A Community Health Services and Facilities Act of 1961 expanded the research program by authorizing demonstration construction and equipment projects. In view of bed shortages, particularly in the area of long-term care beds (chronic disease and nursing home beds) and mental health facilities, it is evident that criticism of the Hill-Burton Act should be in terms of too small appropriations rather than excessive expenditures.

PUBLIC HEALTH PROGRAMS

EARLY PUBLIC HEALTH PROGRAMS

One of the best-known and widely accepted definitions of public health is that of Charles-Edward A. Winslow:

Public Health is the Science and Art of preventing disease, prolonging life, and promoting health and efficiency through organized community effort for the sanitation of the environment, the control of communicable infections, the education of the individual in personal hygiene, the organization of medical and nursing services for the early diagnosis and preventive treatment of disease, and the development of the social machinery to insure everyone a standard of living adequate for the maintenance of health, and so organizing these benefits as to enable every citizen to realize his birthright of health and longevity.[42]

Although few records are available on public health in pre-Christian times, observance of present primitive tribes demonstrates that some forms of public health have been practiced for centuries.[43] Proper rules for the disposing of excreta are almost universal. Many American Indian tribes, for example, provided that the downstream side of the camp be used for excretory purposes. Many groups have elaborate and set requirements for burial of the dead. Disease is recognized by almost all tribes, and such remedies as voodoo quarantine, tribal dancing, and smoke and noise are used. Greek civilization placed a high degree of importance on personal hygiene, but the weak, ill, and crippled were either ignored or destroyed. Roman civilization was known to have supervised public bars, houses of ill fame, and weights and measures. Many streets were paved, and a system of drainage installed. Garbage and

[42] Charles-Edward Winslow, "The Untilled Field of Public Health," *Modern Medicine*, Vol. 2 (March, 1920), p. 183.

[43] This section on the history of public health has been drawn mainly from John J. Hanlon, *Principles of Public Health Administration*, 3rd ed. (St. Louis, C. V. Mosby Co., 1960), Chap. 2.

rubbish were regularly removed. Aqueducts and tunnels were constructed to provide a relatively safe water supply.

During the Dark Ages, little public health was practiced. People seldom bathed, and were clothed in notoriously dirty garments. There was an utter disregard for sanitation, so that refuse and waste were allowed to accumulate in and around dwellings. During the 1340's the Black Death in the form of bubonic plague decimated whole countries. Thirteen million were said to have died of this disease in China, and India was practically depopulated. About 25 million died of the disease in Europe. As a first halting step to the control of disease, a number of ports banned entry of infected ships or quarantined those who were ill. The spreading of leprosy was controlled by rigid segregation of those having the disease. This method of control was so successful that the disease was largely eradicated from Europe by the sixteenth century.

Even as late as the nineteenth century, in many areas good public practices were at a minimum. One writer, Edwin Chadwick, noted that more than one-half of the children of the working classes died before their fifth birthday. Gradually improvements began. In 1837 a National Vaccination Board was established in England, and in 1848 a General Board of Health was created for the entire country. In the United States, city health departments were in evidence in Baltimore as early as 1798 and in Charlestown, South Carolina, and Philadelphia shortly thereafter. As late as the end of the nineteenth century, however, pitch was burned and cannon were fired as measures to combat yellow fever, but gradually better methods were found to attack the problem of disease. One commentator states that Jenner's discovery of vaccination for smallpox has saved as many lives as all other preventive and curative medicine combined.[44] In America, the public health movement originated as a program to meet a local and community problem. The first efforts in public health were directed at the control of such diseases as typhoid fever, cholera, smallpox, and yellow fever. Around 1870 the states began organizing state departments of public health.

FEDERAL PROGRAMS

A Marine Hospital Service Act was passed in 1798 to provide medical and hospital care for sick and disabled seamen. In 1878 the first port quarantine act was passed to prevent the spread of epidemic diseases. Gradually the number of hospitals for seamen expanded until today 12 hospitals are in existence for this group. These hospitals are administered by the United States Public Health Service, which was created in 1902, and took its present name in 1912. A leprosy hospital was constructed in 1917, and a federal venereal disease program inaugurated in 1918. In 1921 the federal govern-

[44] Hollis S. Ingraham, "Statistics and Medical Knowledge," *American Journal of Public Health*, Vol. 48 (1958), p. 1451.

ment began supporting maternal and children's health, and in 1929, three federal hospitals were constructed for drug addicts. By 1935, the total federal budget for health services, however, amounted to only $10 million annually. With the passage of the Social Security Act in 1935, federal public health services expanded, and in 1964 about $4.8 billion annually was spent for medical and health purposes. The largest single federal expenditure was $1.5 billion for support of federal hospital facilities, followed by $1.1 billion for medical research. Other large federal expenditures aid public and private hospital construction, nursing-home care, and other activities.[45]

STATE PUBLIC HEALTH PROGRAMS

At the state level, each of the states has a Department of Public Health. The main function of these departments is to promote the establishment of full-time local health departments. Financial aid is sometimes provided local health departments. Direct services are sometimes provided local areas in the form of mobile chest X rays, dental clinics, venereal disease clinics, plus activities connected with sanitary engineering, laboratory services, and statistical services. As in most other programs, some states provide relatively complete services whereas others do not. Almost all state Departments of Public Health provide for control over general communicable diseases, and control of tuberculosis, cancer, heart diseases, maternal and child health services, control over mosquitoes, rodents, occupational health services, health education, laboratory services, and vital statistics. On the other hand, many of the state Departments of Public Health exercise little or no control over arthritis, diabetes, and other diseases.[46]

LOCAL PUBLIC HEALTH PROGRAMS

On the local level, the largest single budget item is for public nursing. About half of all local public health funds are spent on public health nursing. The figure is somewhat lower for the larger local public health units. According to Dr. John Hanlon, the proportion of money allocated to various public health functions in the larger local health units are as follows: administration, 10 percent; vital statistics, 5 percent; health education, 5 percent; public health nursing, 35 percent; child hygiene, 15 percent; communicable disease control, 10 percent; sanitation, 10 percent; laboratories, 5 percent; and miscellaneous, 5 percent.[47] Public health nurses provide nursing care in homes, aid in the treatment of patients, and guide individuals with social and emotional difficulties to the appropriate community agencies. In addi-

[45] Louis S. Reed and Ruth S. Hanft, "National Health Expenditures, 1950–64," *Social Security Bulletin*, Vol. 29, No. 1 (January, 1966), Table 1, p. 4.

[46] Hanlon, *op. cit.*, pp. 346-351.

[47] Hanlon, *op. cit.* (2nd ed., 1955), p. 319.

tion, public health nurses collaborate with other professions in fostering community health programs and in educating persons in public health.[48] Today there are about 30,000 nurses practicing in the field of public health. Using the estimate of one public nurse per 2,000 people, about 85,000 public nurses would be needed. The supply of public health nurses is so short that one student maintains that only through additional federal and state aid will sufficient financing be made available to provide enough public health nurses on the local level.[49] He suggested that not only should the functions of home care nursing be provided but that such services as the following should be added: physical and occupational therapy, medical social work, X ray and laboratory service, housekeeper service, transportation, sickroom equipment, supplies, and appliances.

In the area of environmental health vast strides have been made over the years to improve the purity of our water supplies, install sewerage systems, pasteurize milk, and remove garbage and refuse. In spite of these improvements, much still remains to be done. Some communities are still without water works systems, and others without sewer systems. Adequate facilities are particularly deficient in rural areas. The goal of having all milk pasteurized has not been reached either. Attacks are just beginning on the air pollution problems in Los Angeles and other industrial areas. It is questionable whether sufficient information has been amassed to prevent such catastrophes as fog pollution, which resulted in the death of a number of people in 1948 in Donora, Pennsylvania, former home of the author of this text. Radiation problems are in need of further research also. Improvements have been made in the control of housing inspection, but again more needs to be done in this area. The development of DDT has aided greatly in control of mosquitoes, lice, and other disease vectors. However, we are still short of sanitary engineers, sanitarians, and veterinarians.

One of the earliest functions to which most public health work has been devoted in the past has been the control of communicable diseases. For smallpox it was found that vaccination was quite effective in controlling this disease. In spite of obvious merits of compulsory vaccination, only 16 states require it, although 21 others either permit local jurisdictions to enact compulsory provisions or require vaccination in case of a threatened epidemic or exposure to smallpox. Strangely, 7 states have laws prohibiting or restricting the use of compulsory vaccination. All 7 of these states have a higher incidence of smallpox than most of the other states of the country. These states are Arizona, California, Minnesota, North Dakota, South Dakota, Utah, and Washington.[50] The recent success of the polio vaccine

[48] Hanlon, op. cit. (3rd ed., 1960), Chap. 18.

[49] Milton Terris, "The Changing Face of Public Health," American Journal of Public Health, Vol. 49 (1959), p. 1115.

[50] Hanlon, op. cit. (3rd ed., 1960), pp. 551-553.

has resulted in mass immunization against this disease. Yet even here, only slightly more than 80 percent of those under age 20 have had all three doses of polio vaccine (1965). In spite of less than complete success with this disease, the incidence has been decreasing, as is also true of a number of other diseases. Certain diseases, such as typhoid and yellow fever, have been successfully eradicated or reduced to minimum proportions in the United States and elsewhere.

With the reduction in importance of the communicable diseases, public health groups have been turning their attention to chronic diseases, which have been becoming relatively more important. Public Health Departments have been slow in changing to meet the major health threats of today, but they are making the transition. A few examples are cited of what progressive local public health units are doing in their attack on the chronic diseases.[51] In Washington, D.C., both a mass diabetes and a multiple screening test have been given over a period of several years. Of 96,366 screened for diabetes, it was found that 3,220 screened positive, and of these 1,111 were diagnosed as diabetic (1.17 percent of those screened). A similar type mobile multiphasic screening program in Arizona found newly discovered cases of tuberculosis, diabetes, and glaucoma.

Today about one-fourth of the counties in the United States have no local public health services, and these counties house about 10 percent of the population. In general, the counties without public health units are sparsely populated, and are located in the rural areas of the western Great Plains and the Rocky Mountains. Little progress has been made in expanding public health services since 1952. Between 1951 and 1957, the population of the United States increased by 11.5 percent, whereas additions of full-time state and local health personnel increased only by 7.5 percent. Nurses and sanitarians accounted for the greater part of the increase in personnel, and actual decreases were shown for physicians, engineers, and laboratory personnel. Most public health units spend far below the amounts necessary to provide adequate services.

Three new graduate schools have been added to the ten that already existed in 1947–1948, and the number of degrees for the Master of Public Health has almost doubled since that period. However, the student body has been largely that of public health nurses, health educators, sanitarians, and other public health personnel. The number of physicians enrolling for the degree of Doctor of Public Health has not increased during the same period.[52] From 1947 to 1960 the actual number of physicians employed in public health declined. On the other hand, increases were recorded for

[51] Paul Q. Peterson, "The Health Department's Responsibility in Chronic Disease Programs," *American Journal of Public Health*, Vol. 50 (1960), pp. 134-139.

[52] Wilson G. Smillie and Martha Luginbuhl, "Training of Public Health Personnel in the United States and Canada," *American Journal of Public Health*, Vol. 49 (1959), pp. 455-461.

nurses, sanitarians, social workers, psychologists, and physical therapists.[53]

In the past, public health programs were vigorously opposed as being socialistic and unneeded. More recently, such groups as the American Medical Association have taken a more favorable attitude toward public health. It has been realized that the indigent are unlikely to be able to obtain adequate medical care through private medicine. If these groups could obtain care through public health departments, then the American Medical Association maintains that all persons could have access to medical care. Therefore there is no need for compulsory health insurance. In spite of the changed attitude of the American Medical Association, public health groups are still short of funds and personnel to adequately carry out all their suggested functions. In realizing that public health should function on a broader scale, some state and local groups have been expanding their expenditures in this field. However, most of the increase has come in a few states—New York, California, Pennsylvania, Ohio, and New Jersey.

Summary

Many and varied solutions have been suggested to improve health care in the United States. The American Medical Association and most physicians prefer that voluntary health insurance be used as the mainstay of the American system of medicine. The enormous growth in voluntary insurance during the past few decades is evidence of its success. Due to the fact that voluntary insurance covers only a small percentage of total medical costs, other solutions to the medical problem have been suggested. Prepaid group practice plans now cover more than three million people in the United States. These plans have proved to be successful. Since they cover only a limited group of people, proponents of compulsory health insurance suggest that a more comprehensive program be instituted. Compulsory health insurance has worked successfully in many countries of the world. The intense opposition to compulsory health insurance by most of the medical profession in the United States will probably forestall its introduction in the United States. A less comprehensive insurance system covering only hospitals has been introduced in Canada. The program has worked well there. The particularly difficult health problems of the aged have called for more government intervention in this field. Today the aged are covered both under the assistance section and the insurance section of the Social Security Act.

The permanently and totally disabled have been given federal assist-

[53] Herbert Domke, "Changes in Organization and Services of Local Health Departments," *Public Health Reports,* Vol. 78 (1963), p. 387.

ance since 1950. After being covered originally only under the assistance section of the Social Security Act, the disabled now may receive payments under the insurance section of the same act. This program has worked successfully. In 1965 an important amendment provided for coverage for those ill for one year or longer. Temporary disability is provided by many private corporations in addition to four states and the railroads. Both the private and public programs have been successful. Even with this success the last state to inaugurate such a program did so in 1949.

Bibliography

Allan, W. Scott, Rehabilitation: A Community Challenge (New York, Wiley, 1958).

Berkowitz, Monroe, ed., Rehabilitating the Disabled Worker (Washington, Vocational Rehabilitation Administration, 1963).

————, Workmen's Compensation: The New Jersey Experience (New Brunswick, Rutgers University Press, 1960).

Blake, Roland P., Industrial Safety, 3rd ed. (Englewood Cliffs, N.J., Prentice-Hall, 1963).

Cheit, Earl F., Injury and Recovery in the Course of Employment (New York, Wiley, 1958).

————, and Margaret Gordon, eds., Occupational Disability and Public Policy (New York, Wiley, 1963).

Clark, Margaret, Health in the Mexican-American Culture (Berkeley, University of California Press, 1959).

Eckstein, Harry, The English Health Service (Cambridge, Harvard, 1958).

Eilers, Robert D., Regulation of Blue Cross and Blue Shield Plans (Homewood, Ill., Irwin, 1963).

Faulkner, Edwin J., Health Insurance (New York, McGraw-Hill, 1960).

Follmann, J. F., Jr., Medical Care and Health Insurance (Homewood, Ill., Irwin, 1963).

Lindsey, Almont, Socialized Medicine in England and Wales (Chapel Hill, University of North Carolina Press, 1962).

Osborn, Grant M., Compulsory Temporary Disability Insurance in the United States (Homewood, Ill., Irwin, 1958).

Somers, Harold M., and Anne R. Somers, Workmen's Compensation (New York, Wiley, 1954).

————, Doctors, Patients, and Health Insurance (Washington, Brookings Institution, 1961).

Spiegelman, Mortimer, Insuring Medical Care for the Aged (Homewood, Ill., Irwin, 1960).

THE PROBLEM OF UNEMPLOYMENT

UNEMPLOYMENT:
MEASUREMENT AND CAUSES

Prior to the Industrial Revolution, unemployment presented few problems to mankind. In economies that were primarily agrarian, workers could remain on the land all year, and at least share in the food grown there. A basic threat to security came with famines and failure to grow the necessary crops, but at least employment was had in the attempt to produce food. As more and more people moved into towns and cities, unemployment became one of the major problems faced by urban civilization. This was so because nations experienced periodic panics or reductions in business. During these periods goods could not be sold, and it became unprofitable to retain laborers. With layoffs came grave problems because workers no longer were living on farms and growing their own food. They were thrown on their own resources until rehired, but unfortunately their resources were meager. Even in the wealthiest country in the world, the United States, statistics by the Survey Research Center of the University of Michigan in 1960 showed that 39 percent of all spending units had liquid assets of less than $200. Included as liquid assets were U. S. Savings Bonds, checking accounts, savings accounts in banks, and shares in savings and loan associations and credit unions; currency was excluded.[1] The fact that workers' resources are so few has created enormous problems, especially when large numbers are unemployed.

The economic repercussions of unemployment to the individual are serious, especially if unemployment lasts a long time. The financial hardship becomes extremely burdensome if the unemployed person is head of a household with a family to support. Of necessity, food must be bought, and rent and utility bills must be paid. E. Wight Bakke has made detailed studies of the effects of unemployment on workers in both the United States and England. In the latter country, for example, one English worker, an experienced mechanic and motor-lorry driver, who had been unemployed for a considerable period of time, expressed his demoralization thus: "It isn't the hard work of tramping about so much, although that is bad enough. It's the hopelessness of every step you take when you go in search of a job you know isn't there."[2] Bakke pointed out that the unemployed go through a

---

[1] *Survey of Consumer Finances, 1960*, Survey Research Center (Ann Arbor, Braum-Brumfield, 1961), Table 4-1, p. 77.

[2] E. Wight Bakke, *The Unemployed Man* (New York, Dutton, 1934), p. 67.

number of stages, one of which he called "disorganization." Credit from the grocer and landlord gets out of hand, and debts for such things as medical care and fuel mount. Inability to find a job anywhere causes the worker to lose confidence in himself and in private industry, which is unable to provide employment. The customary purchases of food must give way to cheaper, bulk foods. The purchase of such health foods as milk and eggs must be drastically reduced. To save on fuel, house temperatures are cut below the comfort level. Medical care must be reduced or eliminated. Needed repairs of furniture cannot be made nor can worn-out clothing be replaced. Expenditures such as club dues must eventually be curtailed and thus appearances can no longer be maintained.[3]

For many years so little was known about the causes of unemployment or the effects upon people that little or no state action was taken to help the unemployed. However, with the improvement of our economic knowledge, all modern countries have adopted programs to reduce the number of unemployed and to provide unemployment insurance programs for those who remain unemployed.

THE MEASUREMENT OF UNEMPLOYMENT

One of the first steps necessary before the unemployment problem can be adequately attacked is to obtain statistics on the amount and duration of unemployment. In the United States several sources of statistics on unemployment are available, but the most frequently cited statistics are those of the Bureau of the Census. The Bureau of the Census presents monthly estimates of unemployment. It compiles its figures of the total number of unemployed in the country each month from a sample of 52,500 addresses. In this probability sample representative of the entire civilian noninstitutional population, the census divides the population into three groups: the employed, the unemployed, and those not in the work force. The census defines as employed those who are aged 14 years and over who during a specified week (1) work full or part time for pay or profit; or (2) work without pay in a family enterprise (farm or business) at least 15 hours; or (3) have a job but do not work because of illness, vacation, labor-management dispute, or bad weather. The census considers a person unemployed aged 14 years or over who is not working but is seeking a job during a specified week. Table 12-1 shows the annual statistics compiled by the Bureau of the Census since 1900.

CRITICISM OF EMPLOYMENT STATISTICS

Criticisms have been made that the official census statistics tend to both overestimate and underestimate the number of unemployed. Those main-

[3] E. Wight Bakke, *Citizens Without Work* (New Haven, Yale, 1940), pp. 162-164.

TABLE 12–1.   UNEMPLOYMENT, ANNUAL AVERAGE, PERSONS 14 YEARS
OLD AND OVER, 1900–1965

Year	Number Unemployed	Percentage of Civilian Labor Force	Percentage of Nonfarm Employees
1900	1,420,000	5.0	8.7
1905	1,000,000	3.1	5.1
1910	2,150,000	5.9	9.1
1915	3,840,000	9.7	14.3
1920	1,670,000	4.0	5.8
1925	1,800,000	4.0	5.9
1930	4,340,000	8.9	13.0
1935	10,610,000	20.1	28.4
1940	8,120,000	14.6	20.2
1945	1,040,000	1.9	2.5
1950	3,142,000	5.0	6.6
1955	2,654,000	4.0	4.7
1960	3,931,000	5.6	6.4
1965	3,456,000	4.6	5.1

Sources: 1900–1950: Stanley Lebergott, "Annual Estimates of Unemployment in the United States," in National Bureau of Economic Research, The Measurement and Behavior of Unemployment (Princeton, Princeton University Press, 1957), pp. 215-216. 1955 to date: Monthly Labor Review, various issues, Table A–1. The data are not strictly comparable due to changes in methods of measuring unemployment.

taining that the figures tend to exaggerate the problem point out that the major social problem arises only for the male unemployed group from ages 25 to 65. The problem of unemployment among women, it is alleged, can largely be forgotten about since most women are not heads of family nor primary breadwinners in the family. Unemployment to such women is not a major problem for they can always fall back on the earnings of their husbands. Similarly, unemployment among youth does not present a serious problem, for youth can depend on their parents for support. Those 65 years of age or over can draw either their old-age pension or old-age assistance. If only the male unemployed ages 25-64 are counted, the unemployment statistics would be much lower. For example, in March of 1966, at a time when the official statistics recorded unemployment at a little more than 3 million, only slightly more than 1 million of the unemployed were males between the ages of 26 and 65.

On the other hand, it must be pointed out that many women are the heads of households and the only support for their families. Similarly many males below the ages of 25 have families to support. A November 1961 figure from the U. S. Department of Labor showed that if all married women and single persons under 20 were excluded from the unemployed, the rate of unemployment would have declined only from 5.6 to 4.6 percent of the work force.[4] It should also be pointed out that in many instances the earnings of a second person in the family are essential to economic well-being. Moreover, many married women who are unemployed also have unemployed husbands. Of 929,000 married women unemployed in 1961, 171,000 or 18 percent, had husbands who were also unemployed.[5] Unemployment among secondary workers may therefore reflect a serious exhaustion of family economic resources.[6]

Those who criticize the official unemployment statistics as being too small suggest that a number of changes be made to count the number of unemployed more accurately.[7] The census classifies people as employed even though they work as little as one hour during the survey week. Among this group are many people who are desirous of working full time, but no such work is available. Some part-time workers prefer shorter hours, though, and would not accept full-time work. The hours lost by the partially employed desiring full-time work could be computed into a smaller figure of full-time employment. That is, if 40 hours is designated as the full-time work week and two workers each work 20 hours, then one worker may be considered as totally unemployed. In March, 1954, there were 2,756,000 part-time workers who preferred full-time work. The 2,756,000 were subdivided into two groups—economic part-time workers and involuntary part-time workers. The former were regular full-time workers working part time because of such part-time factors as slack work, job turnover, material shortages, and repairs to plant or equipment. The involuntary part-time workers were those whose regular job was part time only but who would have preferred full-time work. Of the 2,756,000 partially employed in March, 1954, 1,878,000 were economic part-time workers.[8] Their loss of employment was equivalent to having slightly more than 1 million more workers totally unemployed.

Some people drop out of the work force entirely after a futile search for a job. If jobs were available, this group would accept them. These people are not counted as unemployed; if they were, the unemployment figures would be higher. Unemployment of this type is frequently referred to as hidden unemployment. Bowen and Finegan have attempted to measure the amount of hidden unemployment. Working with the urban labor force only (73 percent of the work force in 1960), they found in April of 1960 that

[4] Ewan Clague, "Adequacy of Unemployment Data for Government Uses," *Monthly Labor Review*, Vol. 55 (1962), pp. 128-129.

[5] Robert L. Stein, "Married Women and the Level of Unemployment," *Monthly Labor Review*, Vol. 84 (1961), p. 870.

[6] Stanley Lebergott, "Measuring Unemployment," *Review of Economics and Statistics*, Vol. 36 (1954), pp. 397-398.

[7] Russ Nixon, "Correction of Census Bureau Estimates of Unemployment," *Review of Economics and Statistics*, Vol. 32 (1950), pp. 50-55.

[8] *The Measurement and Behavior of Unemployment*, National Bureau of Economic Research (Princeton, Princeton, 1957), Table A-10, p. 117.

there were 718,000 who were experiencing hidden unemployment. At that time the official statistics recorded a 5.1 percent rate of unemployment. If those experiencing hidden unemployment were included, the rate would have been 6.4 percent. Women constituted 415,000 of those experiencing hidden unemployment (58 percent), and males 14 to 19 another 116,000. For a number of reasons suggested by Bowen and Finegan, the amount of hidden unemployment grew from 1940 through 1950 to 1960. Whereas in 1940 an unemployment rate 1 percent above average was associated with an over-all participation rate in the labor force of about ¼ of 1 percent below average, by 1960 an unemployment rate 1 percent above average was associated with an over-all participation rate of ¾ of 1 percent below average.[9]

COMPARATIVE RATES OF UNEMPLOYMENT IN VARIOUS COUNTRIES

In the Great Depression practically all countries experienced large amounts of unemployment. Today the rate of unemployment is lower but varies among countries. Table 12-2 compares the rate of unemployment in eight countries.

No definitive study has been made of the differential rate of unemploy-

TABLE 12–2.   UNEMPLOYMENT RATES IN EIGHT COUNTRIES, 1960, AND GROWTH OF LABOR FORCE, 1951–1960

Country	Unemployment Rate, 1960[a]	Percentage Change in Labor Force, 1951–60
United States[b]	5.6	12
Canada	7.0	23
France	1.9	-2
Germany (West)	1.0	18
Great Britain	2.4	5
Italy	4.3	4
Japan	1.1	25
Sweden	1.5[c]	12

[a] Adjusted to U.S. definitions.
[b] Including Alaska and Hawaii.
[c] 1961.

Source: Robert J. Myers and John H. Chandler, "Toward Explaining International Unemployment Rates," *Monthly Labor Review,* Vol. 85 (1962), Table 1, p. 970.

[9] William G. Bowen and T. A. Finegan, "Labor Force Participation and Unemployment," *Employment Policy and the Labor Market,* A. M. Ross, ed. (Berkeley, University of California Press, 1965), pp. 115-161.

ment among countries. One study [10] that was made excluded such factors as the form of economic organization (free enterprise, socialism, etc.), the level of wages, and government action to reduce unemployment, such as training and placement programs and monetary and fiscal policy. Of the factors studied, demographic factors were discounted as an explanation of the higher unemployment rate in the United States. The United States civilian labor force did grow by eight million workers from 1951 to 1960, but percentage increases in the labor force were even larger in Canada, Germany, and Japan and as high in Sweden. It is true, though, that the labor force increased considerably less in Great Britain and Italy, and declined in France.

Unemployment was slightly higher among women than men in 1960 in the United States—5.9 percent compared with 5.4 percent. Three of the countries employed fewer women than did the United States, but the others either employed the same percentage or more. Youth under 20 also had higher rates of unemployment, but the United States had fewer of this age group in the work force than all the other countries except France, which had the same rate as the United States.

Several factors were used to explain the differential rate of unemployment. One was that the United States had fewer agricultural workers, who tend to show low degrees of unemployment but high degrees of underemployment. If the United States had the same percentages of unpaid family workers and self-employed as Japan with the same rates of unemployment, the United States unemployment figure would have been 3.7 percent instead of 5.6 percent. Nevertheless, Great Britain, Germany, and Sweden have relatively few workers in agriculture, and have less unemployment than the United States. The small percentage of agricultural workers in the United States provided only a partial explanation of our higher degree of unemployment.

Seven of the eight countries expanded gross national product at a faster rate than the United States from 1951 to 1960. Japan's rate of growth was three times that of the United States, and Western Germany's was more than twice as great. The more rapid rate of economic expansion elsewhere was a factor in the lower rates of unemployment there. Another factor explaining the higher rate of unemployment in the United States is that most of the other countries provide more legal protection for employees. In Italy, the worker's right to his job is safeguarded both by law and by union contracts. In Germany, France, and Great Britain, both private employers and the state, itself a large employer, feel a high degree of responsibility for employment, and continue to provide employment even when sales decline. In Japan, appointment to a regular job assures employment until retirement. Monthly salaries replace the hourly wage.

[10] Robert J. Myers and John H. Chandler, "Toward Explaining International Unemployment Rates," *Monthly Labor Review*, Vol. 85 (1962), pp. 969-974.

CONCENTRATIONS OF UNEMPLOYMENT

Statistics that break down employment according to sex, age, color, marital status, industry, and occupation are available.[11] Women experience more unemployment than men. From 1947 through 1965, there was only one year in which the unemployment of women was less than that of men (1947).[12] A heavy incidence of unemployment is experienced by those under 20 years of age. Unemployment then drops until age 54 is reached. The figures then show that unemployment begins rising for men but not for women. For men only in March of 1966, the unemployment rate of those 16 to 19 was 13.1 percent. This figure declined to 2.0 percent for those 35 to 54 and then began to rise. It reached 3.4 percent for those 55 to 64.[13] Statistics also show that nonwhites experience much more unemployment than whites. In March of 1966, the white rate was 3.6 percent, compared with 7.7 percent for nonwhites.[14] The higher percentage of nonwhite unemployment holds true for both men and women. When broken down by marital status, those married and living together show a much lower percentage of unemployment than single persons, the widowed, or the divorced. For males with a spouse present the rate of unemployment is 2.4 percent, compared with 12.7 percent for single persons and 6.0 percent for those widowed or divorced.[15] Certain industries also experience more unemployment than others. Generally, the following industries experience unemployment above the national average: forestry and fishing; construction; domestic service; personal services; amusement and recreation; retail trade; and manufacturing. The lowest amount of unemployment is experienced in public administration, finance, insurance, and real estate; and professional related services. Using a breakdown of occupations, the highest rates of unemployment are experienced by nonfarm laborers. Operatives (semiskilled workers) also have a higher incidence of unemployment than the average for all occupations. Much lower amounts of unemployment were experienced by professional employees and managers. In March of 1966, 8.9 percent of nonfarm laborers were unemployed, compared with 5.0 percent for operatives, and 1.2 percent for professional and technical employees. The national average was 4.0 percent.[16]

[11] For a detailed analysis, see Philip M. Hauser, "Differential Unemployment in the United States," in The Measurement and Behavior of Unemployment, pp. 243-278.

[12] Employment and Earnings, Washington, D.C., U.S. Department of Labor, Bureau of Labor Statistics, Vol. 12, No. 10 (April, 1966), Table A-2, p. 14.

[13] Ibid., Table A-5, p. 16.

[14] Ibid., Table A-3, p. 15.

[15] Ibid., Table A-8, p. 17.

[16] Ibid., Table A-7, p. 17.

DURATION OF UNEMPLOYMENT

The main casualties of unemployment are those who are unable to find jobs for a number of months or even years. The Great Depression of the 1930's caused much more long-term unemployment than the less severe postwar recessions. As late as April, 1940, two-thirds of the unemployed had been without jobs for more than three months. Fig. 12-1 shows that in cyclical downswings since 1956 a half million to almost two million were unemployed for 15 weeks or more. Chart 12-1 also shows that in the postwar recessions since 1956, only in 1958 did the long-term unemployed constitute

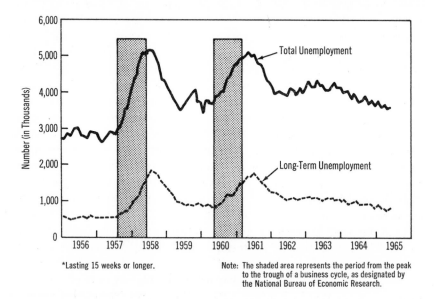

*Lasting 15 weeks or longer.

Note: The shaded area represents the period from the peak to the trough of a business cycle, as designated by the National Bureau of Economic Research.

Source: Susan B. Holland, "Long-Term Unemployment in the 1960's," *Monthly Labor Review*, Vol. 88, No. 9 (September, 1965), p. 1071.

FIG. 12–1. TOTAL AND LONG-TERM * UNEMPLOYMENT, SEASONALLY ADJUSTED, JANUARY 1956–JUNE 1965

more than one-third of the unemployed. Even in the postwar period some of the short-period unemployed may become unemployed again within the same year, so that many may have been unemployed for 15 weeks in the entire year. In 1959, for example, 39 percent of those with any unemployment had two or more spells of unemployment during the year, and 22 percent had three or more spells.

The long-term unemployed is composed of groups who generally have a difficult time finding employment—the aged, nonwhites, the less skilled and educated, and workers from declining occupations, industries, or areas. Adult men over 45 who become unemployed have a difficult time finding jobs. In March of 1966, 37 percent of men aged 45 and over were unemployed for 15 weeks or longer, compared with 20 percent of those aged 20 to 24. Nonwhites also experience more long-term unemployment than whites. In March of 1966, 24 percent of unemployed whites had been out of work 15 weeks or longer, compared with 28 percent for nonwhites. Workers in certain industries experience much longer periods of unemployment than other industries. Employees in the steel, auto, machinery, textile, mining, agriculture, and construction industries experience longer periods of unemployment than in more stable industries such as wholesale and retail trade, services, and finance. By occupation, unskilled and semiskilled workers experience long periods of unemployment. Persons with no previous work experience also remain unemployed longer than others. Persons with less than a high school education represented three-fourths of those out of work 15 weeks or more, although this group constituted only one-half of the civilian labor force.[17] Another study of the long-term unemployed showed that operatives (semiskilled workers) comprised the largest group by far. By industry the largest percentage of the long-term unemployed were in manufacturing.[18]

TYPES OF UNEMPLOYMENT

SEASONAL UNEMPLOYMENT

Changes in the seasons have been a cause of unemployment in the United States. When cold weather begins to set in during November, seasonal unemployment increases and reaches a peak in February. In this month seasonal unemployment is concentrated heavily in outdoor industries and in trade and allied industries after Christmas. With a revival of these industries in spring, unemployment declines seasonally until June. The end of the school term, with the concomitant increase in job applications, again increases seasonal unemployment. The harvests of August and the return of many to school reduces seasonal unemployment in the fall until it begins to rise again in November. It is expected that the amount of seasonal unemployment will change over the years, for each of the expanding and contracting industries has a seasonal pattern of its own, and the pattern may change within industries.

Professor David C. Smith found that in the United States seasonal un-

[17] Jane L. Meredith, "Long-Term Unemployment in the United States," *Monthly Labor Review*, Vol. 84 (1961), pp. 601-610.
[18] Nora R. Tucker, "The Challenge," *Employment Security Review*, Vol. 29, No. 12 (December, 1962), p. 3.

employment constituted slightly over 20 percent of all unemployment in 1951 in the United States but declined to 13½ percent of all unemployment in 1962. On the other hand, there has been an upward shift in the annual unemployment rate that has been relatively greater than the decline in the seasonal amplitude of unemployment. Thus there has been an increase in seasonal unemployment as a percent of the labor force from 0.67 in 1951 to 0.76 in 1962.[19]

The Bureau of Labor Statistics now computes an index of seasonal unemployment for four groups: men, 20 years of age and over; women, 20 years of age and over; boys, 14-19 years; and girls, 14-19. It then adds these to get a composite seasonal index.[20] Table 12-3 shows their figures for 1965.

TABLE 12–3. DECOMPOSITION OF TOTAL UNEMPLOYMENT, 1965

Month	Actual Unemployed (Thousands)	Seasonally Adjusted (Thousands)	Trend- Cycle (Thousands)	Implied Seasonal (Percentage)
Jan.	3,995	3,631	3,663	110.0
Feb.	4,217	3,737	3,633	112.8
Mar.	3,741	3,537	3,588	105.8
Apr.	3,552	3,614	3,550	98.3
May	3,334	3,490	3,517	95.5
June	4,287	3,566	3,471	120.2
July	3,602	3,436	3,435	104.8
Aug.	3,256	3,385	3,397	96.2
Sept.	2,876	3,314	3,324	86.8
Oct.	2,758	3,285	3,262	84.0
Nov.	2,966	3,198	3,192	92.7
Dec.	2,887	3,126	3,096	92.4

Source: Letter from Morton S. Raff, Mathematical Statistician, Bureau of Labor Statistics, September 13, 1966.

Causes of seasonal unemployment are due mainly to changes in the climate. Some crops are only marketable at certain periods of the year, and harvesting and processing of these crops are seasonal in nature. Seasonal employment and unemployment is caused also because the demand for certain products is considerably influenced by the weather. More ice cream is eaten in the summer, whereas more fuel is consumed in the winter. The demand for different types of clothing naturally changes with the seasons.

[19] David C. Smith, "Seasonal Unemployment and Economic Conditions," *Employment Policy and the Labor Market, op. cit.*, pp. 191-209.

[20] Letter from Morton S. Raff, Mathematical Statistician, Bureau of Labor Statistics (September 13, 1966). For a listing of articles on the problems of statistically computing a seasonal index see footnote 14 of the article cited in footnote 19.

Climate is also responsible for the drop in employment in the construction industry during the winter months. The fact that one such industry is affected means that other industries dependent on it also experience seasonal demand. For example, the cement industry and others heavily dependent on construction have highly seasonal demands for their products. Holiday buying of products at Christmas and Easter affects demand seasonally also. Toys and many other products enjoy much greater sales at Christmas than at any other time. Seasonal unemployment is also affected by the movement in and out of the work force when school closes in June and opens in the fall.

TECHNOLOGICAL UNEMPLOYMENT

The term "technological unemployment" was coined many years ago by Karl Marx. Marx contended that the substitution of machines for men would cause mass unemployment if production were controlled by capitalists under a system of private property. Since Marx's time, many billion dollars' worth of new equipment has been added, and yet employment has kept increasing rather than decreasing. Since 1870 output per man-hour has more than quadrupled. If the total production had remained the same today as in 1870, only one-fourth as many workers would have been needed. Yet employment increased from ten million to more than 65 million during this period. Whether the introduction of new machinery will cause unemployment or not will depend upon a number of variables. If the labor-saving device cuts costs and prices are reduced accordingly, the amount of employment will depend upon the elasticity of demand. If the reduction in prices causes large increases in purchases, then employment will increase, possibly by large amounts. If the demand for the product is more inelastic, unemployment may possibly result. If new machinery is introduced in an expanding industry, total employment in the industry may increase even though some labor has been displaced by machines. Although the invention of the automobile did cause technological displacement in the carriage industry, many more were employed in the new industry than in the old one. If machinery is introduced in a declining industry, on the other hand, unemployment will result. If machinery is introduced during a period of prosperity, there is a much better chance that the displaced workers will be absorbed elsewhere in the economy than when a depression exists. Other factors that might affect the amount of unemployment are the amount of monopoly, distribution of income, and wage policy.

In the recent past, much has been heard about "automation" and its impact upon employment. The term itself connotes the process of making production automatic. There has been some dispute as to whether automation is anything different from the mechanization that has occurred in the past. Mr. Clifton W. Phalen, President of the Michigan Bell Telephone Company, stated as follows: "To me it [automation] means general technological progress that has been taking place in our industry and in others for many years." [21] On the other hand, others have felt that automation represents something new. Walter Reuther said:

Automation is the second phase of the industrial revolution. . . . Automation makes a completely new development in the technological process because automation, in addition to substituting mechanical power for human power, begins to substitute mechanical judgment for human judgment—the machine begins to substitute the thinking process on a mechanical basis for the thinking process which heretofore was done exclusively by the human mind.[22]

Regardless of whether the recent innovations are considered as something entirely new or merely a continuation of the old process, there is no question that the trend toward mechanization has been accentuated. For example, the M.I.T. Servomechanisms Laboratory has developed a milling machine that is directed by a digital computer. The computer directs the machine how to cut according to specifications contained on a punch tape. No human intervention is necessary since the progress of the machine in cutting is recorded onto a tape, which feeds information back to the machine.[23] Output per man-hour in automatic factories should increase. Professor James R. Bright of the Harvard Business School, for example, found that output per man-hour increased by the following percentages in seven plants after automation: 20, 76, 106, 133, 180, 425, and 800 percent.[24]

Estimates of the effects of automation on employment have differed radically. Dr. Norbert Wiener, a mathematician, in 1954 claimed that the amount of unemployment caused by automation in the United States would surpass by far even that of the unemployment of the thirties.[25] Others, on the other hand, have suggested that employment will continue to increase as in the past. Professor Almarin Phillips, for example, has shown that employment has increased in four industries in which major technological changes have occurred. From 1946 through 1955 employment in the chemical and allied products industry increased 120 percent, in the petroleum and coal products industry 109 percent, in the instruments industry 127 percent, and in the electrical machinery industry 136 percent.[26] In a study of 13 firms, Pro-

[21] *Automation and Technological Change,* Hearings before the Subcommittee on Economic Stabilization, the Joint Committee on the Economic Report, 84th Congress (October, 1955), p. 516.

[22] *Ibid.,* p. 121.

[23] William Pease, "An Automatic Machine Tool," *Scientific American* (September, 1952), pp. 109-115.

[24] James R. Bright, *Automation and Management* (Cambridge, Graduate School of Business Administration, Harvard University, 1958), p. 171.

[25] Norbert Wiener, *The Human Use of Human Beings* (Boston, Houghton Mifflin, 1954), p. 189.

[26] Almarin Phillips, *Automation: Its Impact on Economic Growth and Stability* (Washington, D.C., American Enterprise Association, Inc., 1957), p. 25.

fessor James Bright found that after the firms had installed automatic machinery, employment increased in three, dropped in two firms, and remained the same in the others.[27]

A physical scientist, Richard L. Meier of the University of Chicago, listed a number of industries he believes ripe for automation: bakery products, beverages, confectionery, rayon, knit goods, paperboard containers, printing, chemical, petroleum refining, glass products, cement, agricultural machinery, miscellaneous machinery, communications, limited-price retailing, and some miscellaneous items. These industries use only about 8 percent of the work force, and Meier doubts that employment could be reduced by as much as 50 percent in these industries in a 20-year period.[28]

Diebold has pointed out that although the following types of activities will use automatic machines, they will not be automatized: agriculture, trade, service, construction, mining, the self-employed, and professional fields. These fields in 1949 accounted for 56 percent of the total labor force, excluding the armed forces.[29] More leisure time made available by automation should expand employment opportunities in some areas, such as service and recreation. Also automatic factories will still need workers. For example, although the atomic processing plant at Oak Ridge, Tennessee, is operated by a few girls at a control panel, many hundreds of maintenance men are given employment.[30] Automation will open new positions for programmers, "systems" engineers, and more highly trained managers.[31] New industries should be able to expand employment, although Walter Reuther pointed out that even automation is being automated. He quoted the Department of Labor statistics to the effect that between 1947 and 1952, output in the electronics industry increased 275 percent, but employment rose only 40 percent.[32]

In some industries, replacement of workers may not be as acute as was first thought. Secretary of Labor James P. Mitchell testified before a Congressional subcommittee on results of a Department of Labor study on the employment effects of a large insurance company that had installed an electronic computer. The planning and installation took a considerable period of time. No girls were laid off. Instead they were reassigned to and retrained on other jobs. The fact that the company was an expanding one helped solve the employment problem. New jobs of a highly skilled nature were created by the introduction of the computer. The company was still faced with a

27 Bright, *op. cit.*, p. 175.
28 John Diebold, *Automation: The Advent of the Automatic Factory* (Princeton, Van Nostrand, 1952), p. 149.
29 *Ibid.*, p. 148.
30 *Ibid.*, pp. 142-143.
31 *Automation*, London, Department of Scientific and Industrial Research (London: Her Majesty's Stationary Office, 1956), p. 75.
32 *Automation and Technological Change*, p. 109.

clerical labor shortage, and still went to employment offices for female clerical help as it had before the installation of the computer.[33] Given a well-
functioning economic system, there is every reason to expect that automation
should result in a rising standard of living for all. Not only will it be possible
to increase production, but we should accompany the increase, as in the
past, with shorter hours and longer vacation periods.

Although the long-run effects of automation should be highly beneficial,
in the short run some technological displacement will occur. Joseph Beirne,
president of the Communications Workers of America, pointed out that
between 1920 and 1954, the number of telephones in the United States
increased by 433 percent compared with a 152 percent increase in employment. Beirne fears what may happen if the number of phones and phone
calls does not continue to increase. From 1929 to 1935, for example, the
number of telephones decreased 9 percent and the number of phone calls
by 6 percent, but employment decreased 33 percent. If the telephone business
expands only at the slow pace of 1954, Mr. Beirne estimated that there
will be from 100,000 to 115,000 fewer people employed by the Bell System.[34] James B. Carey, president of the International Union of Electrical
Workers, pointed out that in 1954 sales of the Westinghouse Corporation
increased almost $50 million over 1953 and net profits after taxes increased
$10.3 million. At the same time employment dropped from 122,729 to
117,143.[35] Statistics for all nonfarm wage and salary jobs from 1953 to 1965
showed that employment on nonagricultural payrolls increased from 55.3
million to 67.6 million. During this period, however, employment decreased
in mining and transportation. Decreases here were more than offset by increases in manufacturing, construction, wholesale and retail trade, finance,
insurance, real estate, service, and government.[36]

One problem brought about by automation is highlighted by a quip
of Walter Reuther in reply to a question of an official of the Ford Motor
Company as to how the union was going to collect dues from the new
machinery. Reuther asked how the company would expect the machines to
buy Fords. Adequate purchasing power is needed. Another problem raised
by automation is its effects on small business. The efficiency of large, automated factories may become so great as to preclude competition by smaller
nonautomated firms. Labor unions quite naturally are also concerned about
the short-run employment effects. Mr. Reuther suggested that earlier retirement under the Social Security Act should be considered for those tech-
nologically displaced. He also recommended government aid to distressed
areas and communities, which might be affected by automation. In addition,

[33] *Ibid.*, p. 263.
[34] *Ibid.*, pp. 339-340.
[35] *Ibid.*, p. 226.
[36] *Employment and Earnings,* Vol. 12, No. 10 (April, 1966), Table B-1, p. 27.

he recommended the guaranteed annual wage, improved education, a raise in minimum wages, reduction of the work week, and aid to small business men.[37]

FRICTIONAL UNEMPLOYMENT

During World War II, even when there was so much excess purchasing power in relation to available goods, the official unemployment statistics recorded more than 670,000 unemployed on an annual basis in 1944. Frictional unemployment may be defined as that amount of unemployment which exists regardless of how much additional purchasing power is created. At any given time, frictional unemployment may be considered as that part of total unemployment which is equal to the number of job vacancies.[38] Unemployment above this amount would be of the cyclical or some other variety. Frictional employment is caused by a voluntary shifting of jobs and changes in demand for labor by individual companies even when the total number of job opportunities is in balance with the number of job seekers. The magnitude of job shifting is quite large in the United States. For the 12-month period ending May, 1949, there were a total of 35 million entries into the labor force and about 34 million withdrawals. With this large amount of entering and re-entering into the work force, some people will not immediately be able to find jobs. Also, each year a relatively large number of firms discontinue business. In 1948 about 350,000 businesses, or roughly 9 percent of the total number of business establishments, were discontinued. But at the same time 375,000 new businesses were opened up. It takes time before some of the workers can be shifted, and in the interim they are frictionally unemployed. Other frictions may develop in the economy to create unemployment. A strike on one location may cause shortages of materials and unemployment elsewhere. Shortage of natural gas during the winter or other types of shortages of materials may cause some unemployment also.[39]

A lively dispute has existed in the United States as to how much unemployment can be considered as frictional. The question is quite an important one from a public standpoint, for at some point corrective measures should be taken to reduce the amount of unemployment. Professor Albert Rees analyzed a number of methods of measuring full employment.[40] He pointed out that probably the most widely used method of measuring full

[37] *Automation and Technological Change,* pp. 104-114.

[38] A. J. Jaffe and Charles D. Stewart, *Manpower Resources and Utilization* (New York, Wiley, 1951), p. 85.

[39] Harold Wool and Colman Winegarden, "Recent Unemployment Trends," *Monthly Labor Review,* Vol. 70 (1950), pp. 489-492.

[40] Albert Rees, "The Meaning and Measuring of Full Employment," in *The Measurement and Behavior of Unemployment,* pp. 13-62.

employment is to consider the lowest unemployment previously reached. From 1946 through April, 1954, the minimum unemployment for any 12-month period was 2.3 percent of the civilian work force, for the 12 months ending October, 1953. If 2.3. percent is considered the frictional amount of unemployment, then in November of 1966, with a civilian work force of almost 77.9 million, the number of frictionally unemployed would be almost 1.8 million. In November of 1966, there were actually 2.8 million workers unemployed or 3.7 percent of the civilian work force. In view of the inflation in 1966 of over 3 percent, the government will probably not take steps to further increase effective demand to decrease unemployment. Under these circumstances, it is highly doubtful that a figure of 1.8 million unemployed will be reached in the near future.

STRUCTURAL UNEMPLOYMENT

Some unemployment results from long-term economic changes, such as a decline of an industry where demand has fallen off and geographic movement of industries.[41] This type of unemployment is called structural unemployment. Heavy unemployment in depressed areas results from the structural changes listed above. Such unemployment also includes that of disadvantaged groups who experience heavy unemployment even in periods of prosperity. Here the structure of our institutions has not proven sufficiently flexible to provide employment for such groups.

The Bureau of Employment Security of the United States Department of Labor regularly gathers data on unemployment from local labor market areas. The Bureau has divided the country into 150 labor market areas. The areas are classified in Table 12-4.

TABLE 12–4.   CLASSIFICATION OF THE 150 LABOR MARKET AREAS

Labor Supply Category	Percentage of Unemployment[a]	Description
Group A	Less than 1.5	Overall labor shortage
Group B	1.5 to 2.9	Low unemployment
Group C	3.0 to 5.9	Moderate unemployment
Group D	6.0 to 8.9	Substantial unemployment
Group E	9.0 to 11.9	Substantial unemployment
Group F	12.0 or more	Substantial unemployment

[a] Based on area's total work force.
Source: U.S. Department of Labor, Bureau of Employment Security.

[41] Stein, op. cit., p. 357 fn.

In February of 1966, when the national rate of unemployment was 3.3 percent, 2 of the 150 major labor market areas were classified in Group F. These were Mayaguez and Ponce in Puerto Rico. No markets were in Group E, and there were 16 in Group D. These were Fresno, San Bernardino, San Diego, Stockton, Fall River, Lawrence, Lowell, New Bedford, Duluth, Altoona, Scranton, Wilkes-Barre, Charleston, Huntington, Wheeling, and Atlantic City.[42] Several characteristics of these areas may be noted. Employment in many of them tends to be concentrated in manufacturing. The major areas tend to have been affected by stagnation in one or two industries, such as textiles in New England and coal in Pennsylvania and West Virginia.

LACK OF AGGREGATE DEMAND

The worsening of the employment picture from 1957 to 1960 led the Joint Economic Committee of the United States to study whether the deepening unemployment was due to a deficiency of aggregate demand or structural maladjustments. The Joint Committee concluded that the rising unemployment was due mainly to a deficiency of aggregate demand. Their conclusion was supported by the fact that real gross national product increased at a considerably slower pace from 1957 to 1960 than from 1948 to 1957. Furthermore, unemployment rose in every occupational and industrial group. The fact that there was no unusual concentration of unemployment in the period 1957–1960, and that both interindustry and geographical mobility of workers was rapid indicated that a higher level of demand would have solved the unemployment problem.[43] Although a lack of aggregate demand was an important cause of the increased unemployment from 1957 through 1960, this is not to say that structural maladjustments may not also cause unemployment. Both aggregate demand and structural maladjustments must be continually studied so that appropriate remedies can be provided for both of them.[44]

[42] *Area Trends in Employment and Unemployment,* January-February, 1966, Washington, D.C., Bureau of Employment Security, pp. 11-15.

[43] James W. Knowles and Edward D. Kalacheck, *Higher Unemployment Rates, 1957–1960: Structural Transformation or Inadequate Demand,* Subcommittee on Economic Statistics of the Joint Economic Committee, 87th Congress, 1st Session (1961), pp. 1-78. For a critical analysis of the aggregate demand thesis, *see* Richard G. Lipsey, "Structural and Deficient Demand Unemployment Reconsidered," *Employment Policy and the Labor Market, op. cit.,* pp. 210-255.

[44] For support of the structuralist position *see* Richard Wilcock and Walter Franke, *Unwanted Workers* (New York, Free Press, 1963), pp. 276-283; Clarence Long, *A Theory of Creeping Unemployment and Labor Force Replacement,* a paper delivered before the Catholic Economic Association, St. Louis, Mo. (December 27, 1960); C. Killingsworth on the nation's manpower revolution, Part 5, U.S. Senate, Committee on Labor and Public Welfare, 88th Congress, 1st Session (1963), pp. 1485-1511. For the position that unemployment has been due both to inadequate demand and structural change, *see* Eleanor Gilpatrick, *Structural Unemployment and Aggregate Demand* (Baltimore, Johns Hopkins, 1966).

Summary

Unemployment has become an important problem with the growth of urban society. Although methods vary on the measurement of unemployment, there is agreement that large-scale unemployment has caused serious problems in our society. The rate of unemployment in the United States has been higher than in most industrial countries in modern Europe. Unemployment becomes an especially acute problem for those unemployed for long periods of time.

Unemployment may be caused by a number of factors. Seasonal factors cause unemployment, as does technological displacement. Even when aggregate demand is quite high some unemployment, called frictional unemployment, exists because of a changing of jobs and the closing of plants. Some unemployment occurs in depressed areas owing to a drop in demand for certain products as well as a geographical shifting of industries. This type of unemployment is called structural unemployment, which also includes the disadvantaged groups in our society who experience high rates of unemployment. Lastly, insufficient aggregate demand causes unemployment.

SOLUTIONS TO THE
UNEMPLOYMENT PROBLEM

Solutions to the problem of unemployment vary according to the causes of unemployment. Different solutions have been recommended according to whether the unemployment is due to seasonal, technological, structural, or other causes.

SEASONAL UNEMPLOYMENT

Entrepreneurs have been aware for many years that the costs of seasonal production are high. Equipment cannot be fully utilized. Many other fixed expenses such as rent and salaries continue regardless of whether sales are made or not. Labor may become restless when unemployed, and permanent work may be sought elsewhere. Failure to hold a permanent, efficient work force may necessitate expensive training programs for inexperienced workers. Short employment also tends to cause workers to reduce output in order to be paid for more hours than are really necessary. For all of these reasons, many employers have taken definite steps to reduce seasonal unemployment.

Some employers have attempted to push their sales in the off season. At one time, two-thirds of the demand for Sherwin-Williams paint came in the spring of the year. The company put on a "Paint in the Fall" campaign, and was also successful in inducing consumers to refinish floors during the winter. A highly seasonal demand was replaced by year-round buying.[1] Not only may sales be pushed in the off season but also new off-season uses may be made of products. In the food industry, the movement toward frozen foods has aided in increased sales that were formerly not available in the off season.

If the storage costs are not too great, production and employment may be regularized even though demand is highly seasonal. The Gorham Silver Company, producers of wedding silver, found that most of their silverware was sold in June and October. Though they could do little to change the patterns of weddings in the United States, they simply estimated the sales

---

[1] Sam Lewisohn et al., Can Business Prevent Unemployment? (New York, Knopf, 1925), pp. 11-12.

annually, and then manufactured $\frac{1}{12}$ of the estimate each month.[2] If storage costs run too high, then perhaps the company may seek to obtain more advance ordering of its product. The Kalamazoo Sled Company, for example, persuaded buyers to order sleds immediately following the Christmas season on the ground that buyers have the best knowledge of requirements at that time.[3]

Products may sometimes be diversified in order to regularize employment. The Dennison Manufacturing Company had formerly made jewelry boxes, which were sold mainly at Christmas time. The company added other products such as crepe paper, printed labels, tags and other types of boxes, and thus was able to provide more stable employment.[4] Sometimes it is possible to sell products in foreign areas where the seasons are the reverse of ours. The Jantzen Knitting Mills Company has been active in developing the sale of bathing suits in the southern hemisphere.[5] In conclusion, it may be stated that there are a number of means that are available to reduce seasonal unemployment. However, various climatic and other factors present serious obstacles to complete elimination of the problem. It is probable that some seasonal unemployment will be experienced in the foreseeable future.

TECHNOLOGICAL UNEMPLOYMENT

Several labor unions have negotiated contracts with employers to mitigate the results of technological unemployment. The Armour Company and the Amalgamated Meat Cutters and the United Packinghouse Workers established an automation fund of $500,000. The fund was administered by a committee of nine members, four composed of management representatives—two each from two labor unions—and an impartial chairman. The committee was created for the purpose of studying the problems resulting from modernization and was to make recommendations for the solutions to such problems. The committee was permitted to authorize expenditures from the fund for training qualified workers.[6] One of the findings of the committee was that automation evidenced itself mainly in the closing of obsolescent plants rather than displacing workers in operating plants. In 1959 the Armour Company announced plans for closing six production plants—two large plants in Chicago and St. Louis and four smaller plants in Columbus, Fargo, Atlanta, and Tifton. More than 20 percent of the company's total plant capacity was

[2] Paul Douglas and Aaron Director, *The Problem of Unemployment* (New York, Macmillan, 1931), pp. 94-95.

[3] Edwin S. Smith, *Reducing Seasonal Unemployment* (New York, McGraw-Hill, 1931), p. 124.

[4] *Ibid.*, p. 102.

[5] *Ibid.*, p. 93.

[6] "Longshoring and Meatpacking Automation Settlements," *Monthly Labor Review*, Vol. 82 (1959), pp. 1108-1110.

shut down, and more than 5,000 production employees lost their jobs. In the following year the company closed its Oklahoma City plant and terminated 420 employees there.

Studies were made of those laid off in Columbus, Fargo, East St. Louis, and Oklahoma City.[7] It was found that the unemployment rate of terminated employees one year after the closedown was 56 percent in East St. Louis, and between 25 and 30 percent in Columbus and Fargo. Forty percent were still unemployed in Oklahoma City eight months after the shutdown. Older workers had a more difficult time finding jobs, as did women and Negroes. Public employment services were found to be of little help in finding new jobs for workers. Those finding new jobs were unable to earn the same income as at Armour, where they had earned $2.20 per hour compared with $1.86 in their new jobs. Severance pay was used by 50 percent of the group to pay old debts so that the pay was not available as a means of support while looking for employment.

In Oklahoma City, the fund announced that testing and counseling were available from the Oklahoma State Employment Service, and that the committee would pay for the first $60 of training plus one-half of the balance up to a maximum of $150. Of the 431 sent this information, 170 completed both the testing and interviewing. As was to be expected, many more of the unemployed participated than those who had already found jobs. The Oklahoma Employment Service reported that only 60 of the 170 showed promise of benefiting from some form of vocational training. Training was given in a variety of subjects such as typing, office methods, blueprint reading, upholstery, welding, basic electronics, beauty parlor techniques, real estate business methods, air conditioning, and auto mechanics.

The conclusions of the committee from the Oklahoma City study were that careful advance planning and contact with other employers and the Employment Service would benefit employees more than a sudden "crash" program. The committee found that public employment services in their present status were relatively ineffective in finding jobs for the unemployed. A carefully planned continuing education promoted both by the company and unions would improve workers' chances of finding jobs. Retraining on a crash basis would help only a few workers, particularly if they were older and had little formal education to start with. The general conclusions of the committee were that the country's educational programs should be studied in relation to future employment. Improvements in the Employment Service such as counseling were suggested, and loans or grants to move people were recommended. Improvements in unemployment compensation were suggested, as were studies of integrating private and public pension plans. Most important of all, a rapid rate of economic growth for the country was stressed as a major condition of employing workers displaced by automation. The

[7] "Progress Report of Armour's Tripartite Automation Committee," *Monthly Labor Review*, Vol. 84 (1961), pp. 851-857.

labor unions recommended the shorter work week as an aid, but this recommendation was opposed both by company members and the impartial chairman.

STRUCTURAL UNEMPLOYMENT

Other countries besides the United States have been faced with the problem of depressed areas. In England, for example, it was found that certain areas had many more unemployed than others.[8] These areas had a less diversified base than other areas and were dependent mainly on iron and steel, coal mining, ship building, or tin plating. In several communities, such as Jarrow in Durham and Merthyr Tydfil, South Wales, unemployment reached the extremely high percentage of 70 to 80 percent of insured workers in 1934.

England has made a direct attack on reducing unemployment in areas of high unemployment. In 1934, six areas were designated as special areas, and commissioners were appointed to attempt to facilitate economic development. With the expansion of war industries, government expenditures were channeled into these areas. After World War II, four other areas were added to the list of depressed areas, now called "development areas." The Board of Trade was given authority to pass on the location site of all new factories above a certain minimum size. To this negative control was added the positive authority to construct factories, improve sites, acquire land, and provide financial assistance to local authorities.

The new program was quite successful in channeling industry into the depressed areas. More than half of all the new factories constructed between 1945 and 1950 were located in the development areas. Whereas these areas had accounted for 38 percent of unemployment in 1932, the percentage dropped to 4 percent in February, 1950. By the end of 1955, unemployment in the eight areas then classified as development areas had fallen to 1.9 percent of the insured male labor force and 2.5 percent of the female work force. In the nation as a whole for that year, 0.9 percent of the insured male labor force were unemployed compared with 1.1 percent for females. In the United States during the same year, unemployment averaged 4 percent of the labor force.[9]

A number of bills have been introduced in the United States Congress during the past few years to aid depressed areas. Senator Douglas, in sponsoring such bills, has pointed out that certain areas in the United States have been depressed for a number of years.[10] The costs of unemployment insurance and welfare payments for those areas have been quite high. Money

---

[8] William H. Miernyk, "British and American Approaches to Structural Unemployment," *Industrial and Labor Relations Review*, Vol. 12, No. 1 (1958), pp. 3-19.

[9] *Ibid.*

[10] *Congressional Record*, Washington, D.C., 85th Congress, 2nd Session, Vol. 104, No. 73 (May 8, 1958), pp. 7435-7538.

could better be spent in revitalizing these areas than in continuing relief. If industry could be attracted there, higher income for the population could result in improved living for all. Better education could be provided children in those areas, and the children could grow up with the hope for a better life. Senator Douglas estimated that at least 70 of the larger industrial areas in 20 states had large amounts of unemployment and should be aided. These areas would include almost five million workers, or 7.2 percent of the total national labor force. Rural depressed areas should also be aided, according to Douglas. In the 300 lowest-income rural counties lived seven million persons, most of them in poverty.

Aid-to-depressed-area legislation has not been without its critics. President Eisenhower twice vetoed such bills. Although claiming to be sympathetic with the aims of the bills, he maintained that the Douglas bill went too far in diminishing local responsibility for the unemployment problem.[11] President Eisenhower felt that the loans provided for in the bill were for too long a period. He favored 25-year loans rather than the 40 years called for in the bill. Instead of the loans being for 65 percent of the total cost of the project, President Eisenhower favored a lower figure of 35 percent. He also objected to what he considered the artificially low interest rates of the bill, which called for one-fourth of 1 percent above the rate of interest which the government must pay on issues of comparable duration. He also doubted that federal loans for the construction of industrial buildings would be an appropriate remedy to the problem of surplus labor in agricultural communities. President Eisenhower stated that he favored an area assistance bill, and hoped that such a bill would be passed by Congress along the lines of his suggestions.

AID TO DEPRESSED AREAS PROGRAM

An Area Redevelopment Act became law in May of 1961. Primarily it was a loan program to private companies and public groups in areas of heavy unemployment or underemployment. In some cases, grants were provided. Today the program is administered by the Economic Development Administration, which is a part of the U. S. Department of Commerce. Before a community can receive financial aid, it must draw up an Overall Economic Development Program showing a step-by-step plan which the community feels must be followed to achieve new growth and new jobs. The economy of the area must be described, and should include topographic features, climate, land-use patterns, public utility and transportation services, and school and hospital facilities. In addition to facts on population and labor force, information should be forthcoming on employment by industry, the

---

[11] Dwight D. Eisenhower, "Memorandum of Disapproval," *The Labor Market and Employment Security* (September, 1958), pp. 3-4.

amount of unemployment or underemployment, the factors contributing to the decline of the area, and the efforts made to solve the economic problem. The potential of the area is analyzed and should include a study of mining, forestry, agricultural, recreational, industrial, human, and other resources of the area. Deterrent factors must be evaluated, such as lack of venture capital and entrepreneurial initiative, lack of transportation or poor terrain, lack of structure or parking facilities, lack of public utility services, physical deterioration of the area, and weaknesses in local government financial capabilities. Fig. 13-1 shows areas eligible for federal aid.

From 1961 to 1965, 598 areas received assistance for at least one project, and 36 areas received approval for at least ten projects. Loans to private business totaled $176 million during the four-year period in which it is expected that 67,000 jobs will be provided. Business loans were made for all major types of industries in the country. The largest number went to the lumber and wood products industry (about an eighth of all business loans), followed by recreation and the hotel and motel industry groups. A smaller number of public facility projects were approved in the four years (157), and these were to provide employment for 51,000 persons. The largest number of projects were for electricity, gas, and sanitary services.[12] At the completion of the four-year period, unemployment dropped substantially more in these depressed areas than in the rest of the country. The 1964 average unemployment rates for areas eligible in July, 1965, were 2.3 percentage points lower than the average of all areas eligible in 1961. This compares with a 1.5 percentage decline for the entire country.[13]

Several other laws have aided in the attack on unemployment. The Accelerated Public Works Act of 1962, which provided for the spending of several billions on public works on a matching basis with the states in areas of heavy unemployment and underemployment, was terminated in 1964. In 1965, an Appalachian Regional Development Act was passed to aid in the depressed areas of the Appalachian Mountains. Originally 80 percent of the funds went for development of highways, but as the program develops more funds will be channeled into other areas of development. In 1965 a Public Works and Economic Development Act was also passed. An innovation in this program was that Regional Action Planning Commissions were created to analyze the problems of regions or sections of the country that have lagged behind the rest of the country. It is planned to study the regions and their needs thoroughly before action programs are undertaken.

EVALUATION

As the Economic Development program has operated, funds are available for a loan only if private capital is not forthcoming. This requirement precludes

[12] *Annual Report, 1965,* U.S. Department of Commerce, pp. 12-13.
[13] *Ibid.,* p. 12.

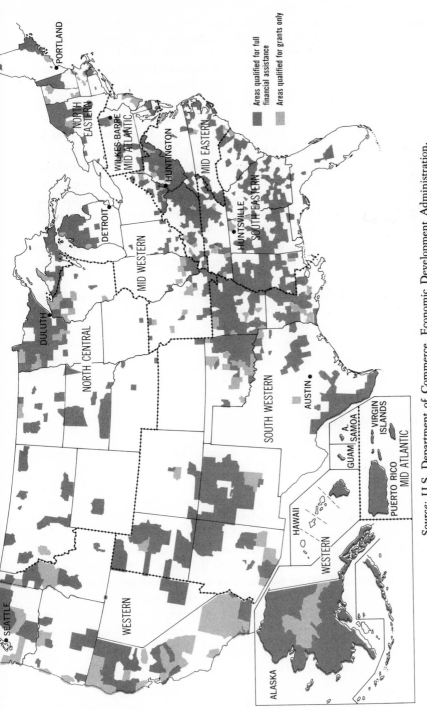

Legend:
- Areas qualified for full financial assistance
- Areas qualified for grants only

Source: U.S. Department of Commerce, Economic Development Administration.

FIG. 13–1. AREAS QUALIFIED FOR ECONOMIC ASSISTANCE, JULY 1, 1966

287

the larger corporations in the United States from participating in the program since they have access to private capital funds. Disqualifying large corporations from the program has limited its effectiveness.

According to Sar Levitan, possibly the worst mistake of the program was to make too many areas eligible.[14] More than a third of our 3,100 counties were made eligible to receive assistance. Levitan maintained that if more aid had been channeled to fewer areas, the program would have been more successful. Politically, however, it was felt that more areas had to be included in order to get Congressional support for the bill. The result, however, according to Levitan, is that more than half the larger eligible areas and one-third of the smaller areas showed population increases from 1950 to 1960, although supposedly the program was to aid declining communities. Levitan doubted that "the medicines prescribed by Congress are sufficiently potent to cure the ills of depressed areas." He suggested that consideration should be given to preferential treatment in securing government contracts and offering rapid tax amortization or other tax incentives to induce business to locate or expand in depressed areas.[15]

In addition to the specific solutions suggested above to solve the problems of technological and structural unemployment, several programs have been developed that have attempted to solve not only these types of unemployment but frictional unemployment as well. These programs are retraining workers and public employment offices. These programs will be discussed in that order.

RETRAINING WORKERS

Most countries in Western Europe have proceeded further with retraining unemployed workers than has the United States.[16] Such programs began in a number of Western European countries either immediately after World War I or during the economic crises which followed that war. A brief summary of what Sweden is doing is included here.

Training of unemployed workers has been in effect in Sweden for many years. The government policy was not only to train workers to alleviate unemployment but to train workers for skills that were in short supply. The Royal Labor Market Board in Sweden ascertains immediate training needs from current and estimated future skilled manpower requirements. A Central Board of Vocational Training considers and approves courses of training. For fiscal 1961–1962, 105 million kroner (more than $20 million) was approved for training purposes. About 70 percent of this money will cover the

---

[14] Sar Levitan, *Federal Aid to Depressed Areas* (Baltimore, Johns Hopkins, 1964), p. 250.

[15] *Ibid.*, pp. 246-254.

[16] Phyllis P. Groom, "Retraining the Unemployed, I: European Government Programs," *Monthly Labor Review*, Vol. 84 (1961), pp. 823-828.

costs of conducting the courses and the remaining for trainee living allowances. In March, 1961, 9,200 persons were undergoing training out of a total of 20,700 persons registered for unemployment compensation. Instruction was given in some 60 trades. Courses generally lasted for 1 year, although some were as short as 4 months and some as long as 22 months. Courses most frequently given in 1959 were for automotive repairmen; welders; radio, television, and radar technicians; machinists; and for those in the building trades.

TRAINING IN THE UNITED STATES

A number of states inaugurated training programs for the unemployed beginning in 1957.[17] Labor unions have also been more active recently in providing more training for their workers.[18] The federal government sponsored a small program under the Area Redevelopment Act of 1961. The program was much expanded under the Manpower Development and Training Act of 1962. The purpose of this act was to appraise the manpower requirements of the United States and to develop and apply information and methods needed to deal with the problems of unemployment resulting from automation, technological change, and other causes of persistent unemployment. The Secretary of Labor was authorized to provide a program for testing, counseling, and training for unemployed or underemployed people. Workers must have had three years of experience in gainful employment to qualify for training, but this requirement was waived if the trainee was under 21 or if the trainee was a worker in a farm family with less than $1,200 annual net family income. Before training is provided, the Secretary of Labor must determine whether there is reasonable expectation of employment in the occupation being trained for. Also the trainee must agree to accept employment outside his area of residence.

The Secretary of Labor was authorized to enter into agreements with states to train the eligible unemployed or underemployed. Payments to trainees were not to be made for more than 52 weeks. The federal government has been paying 90 percent of the cost of the program and state governments the rest. The amount of payment to workers while in training originally was not to exceed average weekly unemployment compensation payment. Those workers eligible for less than the average unemployment benefit were to receive a supplemental training allowance to bring them up to the average figure while training. No training allowance was to exceed $35 per week or $5 per day (inclusive of unemployment compensation benefit). Transportation allowances of 10 cents per mile were permitted.

[17] Phyllis P. Groom, "Retraining the Unemployed, II: Federal and State Legislation on Retraining," *Monthly Labor Review*, Vol. 84 (1961), pp. 939-943.

[18] Rennard Davis, "Retraining the Unemployed, III: Skill Improvement Training for Electricians and Plumbers," *Monthly Labor Review*, Vol. 84 (1961), pp. 1074-1080.

Several amendments were made to the law and signed by the President on December 19, 1963.[19] The eligibility requirement was lowered from three to two years. Furthermore, anyone in the houshould was permitted to receive training allowances if the head of the household is unemployed. The living allowance was increased to $10 per week above the level of unemployment compensation. The additional allowance is not across the board. Rather it is only to be used when the allowance is so low as to jeopardize the ability of the individual to enter and remain in training. Family need and duration of the training were considered in allocating the additional $10. Part-time work was also permitted without the reduction in training allowance support. The use of private training facilities was authorized along with pilot experimental programs dealing with labor mobility. For those unable to read and write, an additional 20 weeks of allowances was provided to improve skills in this area. Because of the heavy unemployment among youth, the age limit for youth training allowances was reduced from 19 years of age to 17. Instead of allocating only 5 percent of total allowances for youths, the figure was raised to 25 percent. In order that the program not encourage school dropouts, the amendments provided that every effort should be made to encourage youths to return to school rather than enter the special training program, and that youths had to be out of work a year before applying. Amendments to the law have provided for Labor Mobility Demonstration Projects, in which grants or loans may be made to help move unemployed persons who cannot reasonably be expected to secure full-time employment in their home community. Also, the length of the training has been extended to 104 weeks (plus the 20 weeks of literacy training if needed).

In 1965, 225,268 persons were approved for training. Most of the training was of the "in school" type rather than on-the-job training, but present administrators of the program wish to place more emphasis upon on-the-job training. The largest group was trained for skilled jobs, such as welding and auto mechanics. Other large groups were trained as machine operators, stenographers, and nurses aides. Generally, those with more education have been taking advantage of the training. Only 7 percent of those in training had less than eight years of schooling although this group comprised a much larger percentage of those unemployed. However, each year of the program shows progress in enrolling more of those with a minimum amount of education. Only 10 percent of the trainees were 45 years of age and older although this group constituted almost twice the percentage of those unemployed. That Negroes have not been discriminated against may be shown by the figure that 34 percent of the trainees were Negroes although they comprised only about 20 percent of the unemployed.

In attempting to evaluate the training programs, Gerald Somers used a

[19] "A Report of the Secretary of Labor on Manpower Research and Training," Washington, D.C., U.S. Department of Labor, 1964, paper transmitted to Congress (March, 1964), pp. 69-73.

number of different criteria.[20] Of 45 persons given basic literacy training, tests showed that one-third scored the same or lower after taking the training. More than half the students were borderline defectives with I.Q.'s under 80. Somers concluded that serious questions could be raised about the method of selection of trainees and the instruction they were given. The fact that 70 to 75 percent of all those who began completed their MDTA training by the end of 1963 indicated a very respectable showing to Somers, although he pointed out that a smaller percentage of older workers and those with the longest period of unemployment prior to training completed it. In West Virginia, those who completed training had a better record of employment after training than the following four control groups: those who dropped out of training, those who did not report for training after acceptance, those whose applications for training were not accepted, and a group of unemployed non-applicants. In the same West Virginia sample it was found that those who completed training earned substantially more income than a sample of non-applicant unemployed. Social gains of the training were shown by lower amounts of unemployment insurance and welfare benefits paid after training and larger income taxes paid. Those who completed training made up their loss of earnings while training in 18 months, and it took only a little longer than this in income tax revenue to pay for the entire cost of the training. From these studies, Somers concluded that the economic gains of the trainees seemed to outweigh the economic costs, and when the social-psychological benefits obtained by the trainees were added, the program very definitely was a beneficial one.

PUBLIC EMPLOYMENT OFFICES

A better marketplace where job information is available should tend to decrease the amount of unemployment and provide better job opportunities for workers. Until recent years employment offices in the United States have almost exclusively been privately owned and operated. Prior to the depression of the 1930's, Paul Douglas estimated that there were 3,000 to 4,000 private fee-charging employment agencies in the United States, or more than double the number of public offices that existed in 1937. New York City alone had 1,150 fee-charging offices in 1930, and Chicago had approximately 400 offices.[21]

Although private placement offices have provided services to workers in finding jobs, some weaknesses of private agencies were quite apparent. In some cases, employment offices had agreements with employers to fire workers

[20] Gerald G. Somers, "Retraining: An Evaluation," *Employment Policy and the Labor Market*, A. M. Ross, ed. (Berkeley, University of California Press, 1965), pp. 271-298.

[21] Douglas and Director, *op. cit.*, p. 266.

regularly so that new employees would have to be hired. Then the fee was split between the employment agency and the employer. High fees were sometimes exacted for finding jobs. In Cincinnati, for example, the average fee of private agencies for higher-paid clerical jobs amounted on the average to 60 percent of the first month's salary.[22] Other abuses were failure to make adequate refunds if jobs were not obtained, rendering of inadequate service, misrepresenting working conditions, and selling jobs to the highest bidder.[23] Since a system of public employment offices would tend to eliminate some if not most of the abuses of private employment agencies, a number of states and municipalities have at one time or another created public employment offices.

Recognition of the fact that the federal government should provide impetus for a better system of public employment offices resulted in the passage of the Wagner-Peyser Act of 1933. This act provided for a matching of federal with state funds if the states would operate public employment offices. Later, when the Social Security Act was passed in 1935, it became almost mandatory for the states to create public employment offices, for unemployment insurance could be paid only to those who registered for work at a public employment office. Funds were allocated from Social Security taxes along with Wagner-Peyser matching funds to pay for the costs of the public system. During World War II, the entire system was taken over by the federal government but was returned again to the states in November of 1946. At the same time, the matching system of the Wagner-Peyser Act came to an end, and the system was financed entirely by federal grants.[24] A United States Employment Service exists within the U. S. Department of Labor to develop and prescribe minimum standards of efficiency for the operation of the state-managed employment offices.

Under President Kennedy the scope and functions of the United States Employment Offices were expanded. In his Economic Message to Congress in 1961, President Kennedy suggested that expanded counseling and placement be provided workers in urban depressed areas and rural areas of chronic underemployment. He also suggested more services to those losing jobs through automation, older workers, and recent graduates from colleges and high schools.

The United States Employment Service performs seven major functions.[25] The first of these is to place workers into jobs for which they are suited. Interarea recruitment facilities help to improve geographical mobility of labor. About 6½ million workers were placed in jobs in 1965. Second, a system of counseling has been developed. A year-round program of coun-

22 *Ibid.*, p. 267.

23 For a more detailed analysis, *see ibid.*, pp. 266-273.

24 "The Public Employment Service System, 1933–1953," *Employment Security Review* (June, 1953), pp. 57-58.

25 William Haber and Daniel H. Kruger, *The Role of the United States Employment Service in a Changing Economy* (Kalamazoo, Upjohn Institute, 1964), pp. 41-58.

seling has been developed with students about to enter the labor market. Occupational and labor market information is supplied students. Aptitude tests are also given. In 1965 the Employment Service counseled 2.2 million persons and tested nearly 2.6 million. Third, services are provided to special groups such as veterans, young workers, older workers, and professional and technical workers. Fourth, information is compiled on trends in employment in various industries and occupations, and manpower availability in labor markets. Such information is invaluable to employers who are planning plant expansion and to other organizations and public agencies interested in manpower problems concerning economic development and public welfare. A dictionary of Occupational Titles has been compiled that identifies, describes, and classifies more than 30,000 jobs. Fifth, industrial services are provided employers and unions. The USES consults with employers on various techniques used in resolving manpower problems. The service has aided union apprenticeship training by the use of USES selection and aptitude tests. Sixth, the USES makes its services available to other government agencies and community organizations that request its services. Such groups as vocational training agencies, schools, and welfare organizations are in constant need of information from the USES. Lately, the USES cooperates with various groups interested in area redevelopment and training of workers.

A number of studies have been made of the effectiveness of public employment agencies. In general, the findings are that only a minority of workers use such services. Placements tend to be higher for personal service occupations, small retail stores, agriculture, and unskilled labor than for other occupations. Public employment offices place relatively few workers in banks and insurance agencies. Scarcely any professional workers or those employed in educational pursuits are found jobs. Labor unions placed almost all workers in the traditionally closed shop trades such as construction, printing, trucking, and the like.[26]

Professor Lloyd Reynolds, among others, has pointed out that a main way of findings jobs for blue-collar workers is through numerous friends, relatives, or other contacts. Furthermore, companies tend to hire workers who apply at the gate for jobs if their qualifications are satisfactory. It is only after attempting to fill the job themselves by their own foremen or their own employment office that a company will go to a public employment office. Since the best jobs are obtained by promotions or given to friends, the Employment Service gets an adverse selection of jobs. Also the better-paying companies have less difficulty in hiring workers, so that there is a tendency for less favorably situated employers to use the service more. The service in addition tends to get the less capable workers. Those with the best qualifications are more apt to obtain jobs on their own, and thus leave the less

[26] George B. Baldwin, "Talamuse: A Study of the Place of the Public Employment Service," *Industrial and Labor Relations Review*, Vol. 4, No. 4 (July, 1951), pp. 512-513.

efficient to apply for work through the Employment Service. In Reynold's sample, 63 percent of the unskilled workers had found the service helpful at one time or another in finding jobs, compared with 29 percent for skilled workers.[27]

Paul Jacobs also has found that the unemployed find more jobs via the grapevine than through the public employment service.[28] It is not that unemployed workers distrust the employment service or are hostile to it; it is simply that the public employment service is just something that exists outside their world.

Even though improvements have been made in the USES in recent years, further improvement is still possible. Haber and Kruger suggest that the interarea recruitment system needs strengthening. They also feel that more money should be appropriated by the federal government so that the state services can more properly perform their functions. Haber and Kruger were also critical of the federal method of allocating funds to the states. Now the formula for allocating funds is solely a quantitative one that places a premium on the number of placements, even though many are of short duration. Haber and Kruger suggest that quality of work should also be considered, and that more meaningful evaluation techniques should be applied. More sound personnel administration was also recommended. Finally, research into the various manpower problems needs expanding.[29] With all these suggestions, the USES could perform a broader function more effectively.

LACK OF AGGREGATE DEMAND

BUILT-IN STABILIZERS

Remedies for lack of aggregate demand fall into three main categories—built-in stabilizers, monetary, and fiscal policy. Built-in stabilizers are those that automatically take effect to aid the economy without waiting for decision-making of any kind when aggregate demand failure causes recessions. One of the important automatic stabilizers is unemployment insurance. Taxes are earmarked for the unemployed, and payments become larger when unemployment increases. Several studies have been made to determine what percentage of wage loss is compensated for by unemployment insurance. To quote from one, Professor Richard Lester analyzed the data from 1948 to 1959.[30] He found that all public programs for unemployment insurance compensated no more than 23 percent of the wage loss from total unemploy-

---

[27] Lloyd Reynolds, pp. 270-271.

[28] Paul Jacobs, "Unemployment as a Way of Life," *Employment Policy and the Labor Market, op. cit.,* pp. 396-397.

[29] Haber and Kruger, *op. cit.,* pp. 112-122.

[30] Richard A. Lester, "The Economic Significance of Unemployment Compensation," *Review of Economics and Statistics,* Vol. 42 (1960), pp. 349-372.

ment. If total and partial unemployment are combined, no more than 18 percent of the wage loss was compensated for. Over the 12-year period the percentage of wage loss compensated for by unemployment insurance did not rise. Although there were extensions of coverage and increases in the duration of unemployment compensation benefits, these apparently were offset by lags in the weekly benefit amount. Lester also analyzed the protection given in 16 different states. In the 1958–1959 recession, New York provided the best protection, with 23 percent of wage loss compensated for. The poorest record was compiled by South Carolina with only 6 percent of wage loss recovered through unemployment compensation.[31]

Tax reductions also aid as built-in stabilizers. Before the withholding provisions were adopted for the federal personal income tax in 1943, the income tax was paid the year after the income was earned. This meant that in a recession year, relatively high taxes might have to be paid after a downturn in business. Today the withholding provisions provide for an immediate tax reduction if income drops. Corporation income taxes also decrease if business declines. OASDHI payments may also be considered a built-in stabilizer since these payments provide a cushion in case older workers are laid off. For the two contractions of 1949 and 1953–1954, 14 and 89 percent respectively of the fall in national income was offset by the automatic stabilizers (increases in transfer payments and decreases in taxes). The larger figure in 1953–1954 may be attributed to the large decrease in government revenues during this period.[32]

Although built-in stabilizers aid in recessions, recent findings are that these stabilizers prevent the economy from expanding as rapidly as it otherwise might during an upswing. One analysis showed that in the three expansion periods of 1948, 1949–1953, and 1954–1957, the automatic stabilizers increased government income so much that 28 percent of the increase in national income was absorbed by it.[33] That is, for every increase of $1 billion in national income, increases in the automatic stabilizers absorbed $280 million of the $1 billion increase. In future expansions it may be that the government will be required to direct action to offset the deflationary aspects of the built-in stabilizers. Fortunately, however, the built-in stabilizers do provide more beneficial results in recessions, but since they compensate for only a part of the loss of income, other solutions have been advocated to go along with them.

MONETARY REMEDIES

In order to increase the gross national product and provide as large an amount of employment as possible, monetary policies have been used to curb

[31] *Ibid.*
[32] M. O. Clement, "The Quantitative Impact of Automatic Stabilizers," *Review of Economics and Statistics,* Vol. 42 (1960), pp. 56-61.
[33] *Ibid.*

both inflation and contraction. Different monetary weapons are used depending on whether it is inflation or contraction that the authorities are fighting. When the economy is faced with inflation, the monetary authorities may attempt to restrict the use of credit. They are able to restrict credit by a number of methods, such as selling government securities, raising the rediscount rate, raising reserve requirements, and tightening requirements for selective types of loans, such as brokers loans and consumer credit. The Federal Reserve Banks sell government securities to reduce net bank reserves and reduce the money supply. The liquidity of bank portfolios is reduced, and banks are less willing and able to loan money. Since the Federal Reserve Banks own more than $69 billion in government securities (December, 1963), the potential effect of such selling is quite powerful although selling on such a large scale would have the disadvantage of breaking the price of government securities.

The Federal Reserve authorities may also raise the rediscount rate. The purpose of this move is to raise the cost of borrowing to discourage it. Reserve requirements may also be raised. Such a step forces banks to keep more reserves and thus they are not able to loan as much. Raising reserve requirements has the same effect as selling government securities, but it is felt that this method is awkward and cumbersome as a control method. A small change of one-half of 1 percent in reserves would absorb a very large quantity of reserves, and particularly affect many medium-sized and small banks. For this reason, since 1951 the Federal Reserve authorities have rarely raised reserve requirements, although they have lowered them.[34] Open market operations (buying and selling of government securities) and control over the rediscount rate are the two main weapons of the Federal Reserve System.

Selective controls on particular types of credit have been used in the past, but today such controls are restricted to brokers' loans. If speculation becomes too rampant on the stock market, margin requirements on brokers' loans may be raised to discourage it. At one time, consumer credit was regulated by controlling the amount of down payment and the length of the loan. The Federal Reserve System no longer has this power. Although the banking system could aid in restricting excessive consumer credit during a boom and easing requirements in a recession, neither the Board of Governors of the Federal Reserve System nor the Committee for Economic Development's Commission on Money and Credit recommend the reinstitution of consumer controls. The latter group was almost evenly divided on the subject, and so made no recommendation except that further study should be made on how to administer consumer controls more effectively. Their main objection to it was problems of administration. It was contended that evasion was a major argument against consumer controls. In the automobile field, for exam-

---

[34] *Money and Credit: Their Influence on Jobs, Prices, and Growth,* Report of the Commission on Money and Credit (Englewood Cliffs, N.J., Prentice-Hall, 1961), pp. 66-71.

ple, charges in down payments could be evaded by changing trade-in allowances, and sometimes leasing arrangements could be used to get around credit restrictions.[35]

During a recession period, the monetary authorities reverse the processes described above. The appropriate open market policy is to buy government securities to ease credit along with lowering the rediscount rate. Reserve requirements may be lowered as may margin requirements on brokers' loans. Most economists feel that the monetary weapons in controlling a recession are not as powerful as those in controlling an expansion. To aid in fighting a recession, about the most the monetary authorities can do is to make credit more available, but they cannot guarantee that use will be made of this credit. In an expansion period, the banking system does have a more powerful weapon in restricting credit.

The use of monetary controls has varied over the years. During the 1920's, the Federal Reserve authorities began using the controls outlined above, and monetary controls were held in high regard. The advent of the Great Depression demonstrated that monetary policy alone was insufficient, and it fell into disrepute. After World War II, management of the large federal debt was so new that supporting the price of government securities was given a high priority even though this meant buying securities during an inflationary period. With the Treasury–Federal Reserve Accord in 1951, monetary policy came again into its own, and open market operations and rediscount policy has been used regularly since. Under the accord, the Federal Reserve discontinued its pegs on bond prices. The result was that the prices of long-term issues began to sag, and thus interest rates rose.

EVALUATION OF MONETARY REMEDIES

Monetary policy has not been without its critics. Professor Milton Friedman has contended that monetary policy affects economic conditions only after so long and variable a lag that discretionary policy should be abandoned.[36] Monetary controls do take time in affecting the economy, but many economists feel that they are worthwhile. Friedman, on the other hand, favors the abolition of the discretionary powers of the Federal Reserve, and replacing it with an automatic system whereby the supply of money increases by a fixed amount annually. Friedman received some support for his automatic proposal from Professor Martin Bronfenbrenner, who tested statistically the performance of the discretionary system over what would have been obtained by an automatic increase in the supply of money from 1901 to 1958. He concluded that the automatic system would have worked better than the discretionary system, although the record of the automatic system was less satis-

[35] *Ibid.*, pp. 73-74.
[36] Milton Friedman, "The Lag in Effect in Monetary Policy," *Journal of Political Economy,* Vol. 69 (1961), pp. 447-466.

factory after World War II than before.[37] Ralph Young of the Board of Governors of the Federal Reserve System pointed out, though, that the superiority of the automatic system was mainly due to its superior performance during the credit inflation between 1916 and 1921. If these years had been eliminated, the data would support discretionary monetary policy.[38] In view of the fact that the automatic system would require a radical change in our banking system, it is probable that the discretionary system will remain. It is to be expected that every attempt will be made to decrease the lag between introduction of monetary controls and their results in the business world.

Another criticism of monetary policy made by Gurley and Shaw is that the exemption of nonintermediary facilities from controls renders such controls less effective. They pointed out that the proportion of financial assets of commercial banks to the financial assets of all other financial intermediaries was cut in half from 1900 to 1949.[39] Such institutions as mutual savings banks, savings and loan associations, insurance companies, public and private pension funds, government insurance and lending agencies, credit unions, and private investment companies now do much more business than formerly. Although it is recognized that intermediary institutions provide close substitutes for cash balances, J. M. Culbertson, among others, holds that commercial banks do perform the unique function of creating money, and therefore they are the group to which monetary policy should apply.[40] The Commission on Money and Credit did not recommend extending controls to nonbank intermediaries. This group maintained that velocity effects of movements out of currency and demand deposits to claims on nonbank financial intermediaries when credit is tightened do not appear great, and therefore controls need not be applied to nonbank intermediaries.[41]

The increase in velocity has also been cited as another limitation of monetary controls.[42] Increases in velocity may offset decreases in the money supply. However, both in 1955–1957 and in 1959, monetary restriction induced a decline in residential construction of $3 to $4 billion. Business investment was also reduced. Monetary restraints seem to have an important effect on the level and rate of growth of economic activity.[43]

One other criticism of recent monetary policy is that restricting credit

[37] Martin Bronfenbrenner, "Statistical Tests of Rival Monetary Rules," *Journal of Political Economy*, Vol. 69 (1961), p. 13.

[38] Ralph A. Young, "Report of the Commission on Money and Credit: A Commentary," *American Economic Review*, Vol. 52 (Proc., 1962), p. 314.

[39] John G. Gurley and E. S. Shaw, "Financial Aspects of Economic Development," *American Economic Review*, Vol. 45 (1955), Table I, p. 522.

[40] J. M. Culbertson, "Intermediaries and Monetary Theory: A Criticism of the Gurley-Shaw Theory," *American Economic Review*, Vol. 48 (1948), p. 120.

[41] *Money and Credit: Their Influence on Jobs, Prices, and Growth*, pp. 78-81.

[42] Stephen W. Roussease, "Velocity Changes and the Effectiveness of Monetary Policy, 1951–57," *Review of Economics and Statistics*, Vol. 42 (1960), p. 31.

[43] *Money and Credit: Their Influence on Jobs, Prices, and Growth*, pp. 48-56.

tends to restrict the expansion of small companies who are in need of loans, whereas large companies can continue to expand through the use of internal financing. Galbraith maintains that our restrictive monetary policy has about as much strength in promoting monopoly as repeal of our antitrust laws would have.[44] Attempts to measure the monopoly effects of monetary policy were made by G. L. Bach and Huizenga. They found that banks having little cash to spare—"tight banks"—did not discriminate against small borrowers but rather restricted credit to all-sized borrowers. The discrimination among borrowers was largely on the traditional banking standard of creditworthiness of the borrowers.[45] Allan H. Metzler also pointed out that large companies extend large amounts of additional trade credit to smaller firms, and help finance small companies' expansion in this way.[46]

Since monetary policy does depend on the discretion of the Federal Reserve authorities, errors can be made in applying the weapons too vigorously or too slowly. Some have criticized the Federal Reserve authorities for placing a higher priority on controlling inflation than they do on eliminating unemployment. Assigning a high priority to price stability would result in a tighter money policy than some economists, with different goals in mind, might prefer. Sidney Weintraub maintained that the figure of minus $500 million in free reserves demonstrated a much too tight policy in the first half of 1957 and a causal factor for the subsequent downturn.[47] It was also asserted that after the recession occurred, the Federal Reserve authorities were too slow in reversing their tight money policy. Although the expansion came to an end in the second quarter of 1957, the tight money policy continued as late as October and November of 1957.[48] Similarly, criticism was made of letting interest rates rise so fast in 1959 that the boom may have been shortened.[49]

Finally, some criticism has been made that the controlling group of the Federal Reserve System, the Board of Governors, is completely independent of the administrative machinery of the government. In the future, it is possible that the Federal Reserve authorities will take a different viewpoint on methods of monetary control than the administration in power. In order to alleviate this problem, the Commission on Money and Credit recommended that the Federal Reserve Board Chairman and Vice-Chairman should be des-

[44] John K. Galbraith, "Market Structure and Stabilization Policy," *Review of Economics and Statistics*, Vol. 39 (1957), pp. 124-133.

[45] G. L. Bach and C. J. Huizenga, "The Differential Effects of Tight Money," *American Economic Review*, Vol. 51 (1961), pp. 52-80.

[46] Allan H. Metzler, "Mercantile Credit, Monetary Policy, and Size of Firms," *Review of Economics and Statistics*, Vol. 42 (1960), pp. 429-437.

[47] Sidney Weintraub, "Monetary Policy, 1957–59: Too Tight, Too Often," *Review of Economics and Statistics*, Vol. 42 (1960), p. 279.

[48] Paul A. Samuelson, "Reflections on Monetary Policy," *Review of Economics and Statistics*, Vol. 42 (1960), p. 264.

[49] Warren L. Smith, "Monetary Policy, 1957–1960: An Appraisal," *Review of Economics and Statistics*, Vol. 42 (1960), p. 271.

ignated by the President from among the board's membership to serve for four-year terms coterminous with the President's. The commission also suggested that the term of office be reduced from 14 to 10 years and that the number of members be reduced from 7 to 5 with overlapping terms, one expiring each odd-numbered year.[50] This recommendation would still not give the President control over the Board of Governors, but until there is overt conflict between the President and the board, probably no changes will be made in the composition of the board.

FISCAL POLICY

The lack of aggregate demand may also be attacked by government fiscal policy. Once a depression has begun, the government will automatically take in less revenue, even at the same tax rates. Since personal, corporate, and other income will have dropped, lower taxes will be paid on the reduced income. A government budget expected to be in balance will thus incur a deficit because of the drop in revenue. The Committee for Economic Development has suggested that such a deficit will provide sufficient cure for recessions.[51] In a severe recession some economists would go further and advocate either reducing taxes or increasing government expenditures, or both. Tax reductions can be either directed at increasing consumption or investment or both. If the major need is to increase consumption, the personal income tax can be lowered in such a way as to benefit low-income groups the most. If additional incentives are desired to increase investment, taxes on business groups can be reduced. Some economists have suggested that a formula should be devised that would provide for automatic tax cuts or increases in government spending whenever production drops or unemployment increases by a certain amount. Others maintain that certain erratic results might occur unless the President were given discretionary powers to decrease taxes or increase spending. Giving discretionary powers to the President has been criticized on the ground that the opposition party would contend that the President would use these weapons to obtain votes.

Public works programs do create a number of problems. The larger types of public works, sometimes called "heavy" public works, consist of such projects as dams, housing, public buildings, and river and harbor developments. These projects may take several years to complete. If a recession is of short duration, such projects might actually call for additional expenditures of government money after the corner of prosperity has already been turned. Lighter government programs comprise such projects as road building and maintenance, irrigation, soil conservation, flood control, airport improvements, and landscaping. These can be put into operation and terminated more quickly. Even on the lighter projects, though, the government

---

[50] *Money and Credit: Their Influence on Jobs, Prices, and Growth*, p. 87.
[51] *The Stabilizing Budget Policy*, Committee for Economic Development, 1950.

may be in competition with the private construction industry, and so keep construction costs higher than they otherwise might be. Recently, suggestions have been made to plan for future public capital expenditures on a five-year basis. Not only would the program deal with acquisition of physical assets, but it should include plans for growth-inducing services such as outlays for research and education. A program of this sort would also coordinate federal expenditures with that of state and local governments.[52]

Another problem that arises with a government deficit is that of enlarging the public debt. Probably future generations will not be required to pay higher taxes to pay off the debt. The government may simply refinance the debt by borrowing an identical amount that becomes due. Added taxes must be paid, though, to pay the additional interest charges on the debt. Fortunately, the increased amounts of money taken from the future generation are paid back to the interest receivers of that generation, but some redistribution of income does occur toward the creditor class. In weighing the advantages and disadvantages of the use of fiscal policy in fighting depressions, most economists agree that whether the budget is balanced in any one year is not particularly important. Some hold that even if the debt increases over a period of years, little danger is involved provided that income is increasing also. Fiscal policy is now considered as one of the most potent weapons available in fighting depressions. Monetary policy and the automatic stabilizers will be relied upon, but if unemployment still continues to rise, it is expected that fiscal weapons will be called upon.

Better governmental machinery to help fight depressions came with the passage of the Employment Act of 1946. This act encouraged governmental and private action to promote full employment. The act created a three-man Council of Economic Advisors to recommend economic policies for full employment to the President. Later a staff was also provided for a Joint Economic Committee of Congress with the same end in view. The fact that both of our political parties have endorsed policies to promote prosperity should be of some aid in insuring that unemployment will not become unduly large. Although unemployment kept increasing for a number of years since 1954, finally fiscal policy was brought to bear through the tax cut of 1964. This cut of $11 billion was responsible for substantially reducing the number of unemployed.

Summary

A number of remedies for seasonal unemployment have been attempted such as pushing off-season sales, developing new off-season uses of products, stor-

---

[52] *Money and Credit: Their Influence on Jobs, Prices, and Growth*, pp. 149-150.

ing for future sales, and a number of others. Even with such programs climatic and other factors have made it extremely difficult to substantially reduce seasonal unemployment. Technological, frictional, and structural unemployment have been attacked mainly through depressed area legislation, retraining of workers, and improved public employment services. All of these have aided in reducing the number of unemployed. Lack of aggregate demand has been fought mainly through the automatic stabilizers and monetary and fiscal policy. With these weapons employed in the attack on unemployment, some reduction in unemployment has occurred during the past few years.

UNEMPLOYMENT INSURANCE: HISTORY, COVERAGE, ELIGIBILITY, AND ADMINISTRATION

Some unemployment will probably remain, even though much of it could be alleviated. The problem analyzed in this chapter is what type of care, if any, should be provided for the unemployed. Possibly private or public charitable organizations could look after those needing care. At least this was how the problem was taken care of in the past. Unemployment was considered a personal fault, and the doctrine of individualism taught that any person could find a job if enough initiative were used. Consequently, little was done for the unemployed, who were considered shiftless and no better than tramps. As more and more social scientists studied the problem of unemployment, it became increasingly clear to them that the real causes of unemployment were economic depressions, secular decline in certain industries, bankruptcies, seasonal declines, and the like. The change in emphasis in the causes of unemployment called for better remedial methods.

Some English trade unions paid unemployment benefits early in their history, and a few American unions followed suit. In the United States, however, coverage by labor unions was small, and not many workers were protected against unemployment by labor unions. It was reported in 1930 that only 13 national or international labor unions had ever had a system of unemployment insurance, and that all but four of the plans had been discontinued. The union membership covered by the four plans in the United States was 1,320, and $13,613 was paid in benefits in 1928. Some local unions, as contrasted to nationals, formulated systems of unemployment insurance on their own, but in 1928 only about 37 local unions with a membership of 33,400 had such insurance. These locals paid only $236,000 in unemployment benefits.[1] Private employers might possibly have solved the problem by voluntarily covering their own employees, but too few employers in the United States provided unemployment benefits. Some 22 plans jointly financed by employers and employees covering 65,000 persons were in existence in 1928 along with 13 plans financed solely by the employer and covering 13,000 employees.[2] Coverage was so small that most of the students of

[1] Bryce M. Stewart, *Unemployment Benefits in the United States* (New York, Little & Ives Co., 1930), p. 201.

[2] *Ibid.*, pp. 201-202.

the problem looked elsewhere for a solution. Private unemployment insurance generally has not been advocated as an alternate solution to government insurance. Although private insurance works well for such types of risks as death, fires, accidents, and the like, the greater risks of insuring against unemployment resulted in private insurance companies not handling this type of insurance. It appeared to most students of the problem in the United States that some form of unemployment insurance adopted by the government would be superior to any other method. Experience from abroad tended to support this viewpoint.

Granted that some form of government intervention is necessary to provide unemployment insurance, the question remains whether the federal government should administer the system, or whether it should be the province of state governments. A third alternative is a mixed system of joint federal and state control. Prior to the passage of the Federal Social Security Act of 1935, few states had experimented with unemployment insurance laws. The first state law went into effect in Wisconsin in 1932. Other states were reluctant to pass such legislation for fear of putting themselves at a disadvantage taxwise compared with other states. A Washington state law was voided, and a Utah law never went into effect. Four other states had passed unemployment insurance laws prior to the federal act, but these were all passed in anticipation of the federal law. Competition between states to keep taxes low provided too great a hurdle to overcome so far as state legislation of this type was concerned.[3]

At the national level, first notice of unemployment insurance came about when a Socialist representative in Congress in 1916 introduced a resolution for a commission to draft an unemployment insurance bill. At the hearings, several persons testified in favor of such a bill, but Samuel Gompers, president of the American Federation of Labor, argued that the system should be voluntary rather than compulsory. In 1928, another Socialist, Victor Berger, introduced an unemployment insurance bill, but this bill was never reported out of the Committee of the Judiciary. The advent of the Great Depression caused more concern about unemployment, and the 1932 platform of the Democratic Party called for adoption of a compulsory federal law. The American Federation of Labor in 1932 also reversed its position to that of favoring such a law. Finally, in 1935, Congress passed the Social Security Act, which provided for a federal tax on payrolls to finance unemployment insurance but with state administration of the system.

THE SOCIAL SECURITY ACT OF 1935

The Social Security Act provided that a 1 percent tax be levied on covered employers in 1936, 2 percent in 1937, and 3 percent thereafter. In covered

[3] Eveline M. Burns, "Unemployment Compensation in the United States," *International Labour Review,* Vol. 37 (1938), p. 585.

employment, the government taxed all employers who hired eight or more employees on at least one day of 20 weeks per year. An amendment in 1939 made the tax applicable to the first $3,000 only on the ground that the tax on higher paid employees was too high in relation to possible benefits received. Another amendment in 1956 reduced the coverage from eight to four employees. If the states passed an acceptable unemployment compensation act, employers of the state were permitted to credit against what they owed the federal government any sums they had paid to their state unemployment insurance system up to 90 percent of the federal tax. The federal government receives 0.4 percent (formerly 0.3 percent), and it has used this money to reimburse the states for costs arising from administering the system. Since all employers were required to pay the federal tax, all the states found it worthwhile to pass an unemployment insurance law. Otherwise the federal government would have collected the tax without paying back any benefits to the state. In order to build an adequate fund in the states, the federal government required that no payments be made from state funds for two years.

All the funds collected by the state must be sent to the Secretary of the Treasury of the United States, who then deposits this money in the Unemployment Trust Fund. The Secretary keeps as much cash on hand as he thinks necessary to meet the costs of paying unemployment benefits, and the remainder he invests in United States bonds or in obligations which are guaranteed by the United States government. It was thought wiser to have the money invested thus than to permit the states discretion on investments, some of which may have proved to be unsafe.

A further federal requirement is that benefits must be paid through state public employment offices or such other agencies as the Social Security Board may approve. Before the passage of the Social Security Act, many states did not have such offices. The authors of the act felt that an adequate unemployment insurance system should be supplemented by adequate public employment offices so that those workers applying for unemployment insurance would at the same time be given access to information on where to find another job. In several states, the Social Security Board prevented the payment of unemployment compensation through relief offices,[4] and required that all payments be made through genuine employment offices.

COVERAGE

When the Social Security Act was passed in 1935, many groups were not covered under the Act. Major extensions of coverage came in 1954 with the coverage of smaller firms and federal civilian employees and in 1958 with the coverage of ex-servicemen. Even with an expanded coverage, today about

[4] Raymond C. Atkinson, *The Federal Role in Unemployment Compensation Administration*, Washington, D.C., Social Science Research Council, Committee on Social Security (1941), p. 37.

one-fourth of all employees are not covered under the unemployment insurance program. Fig. 14-1 shows those covered and those excluded.

The figure below shows that the largest group excluded from coverage are state and local government employees. These groups were excluded because of the constitutional problem of the federal government taxing state and local governments. The problem has been partially solved today by permitting state and local governments to be covered if they so desire. By 1964, ten states covered all state employees on a compulsory basis and four others covered some state employees. Two states mandatorily covered all local government employees and six states did likewise for some local employees. Fifteen states permitted coverage of both state and local government employees by election and ten other states provided for elective coverage of local government groups only. Statistics from covered states show that while unemployment among such government groups is small, it is substantial enough to call for some protection for these employees.[5] The low costs and the device of having the states pay only for actual costs are further reasons why such government employees should be covered.

The second largest excluded group are those engaged in domestic service. A 1939 amendment expressly excluded cooks, maids, and others working in fraternities and sororities. Domestic employees were excluded from coverage because some of them worked in a number of different households, few of which kept adequate wage records. In many instances, the duration of employment was brief. Also, complications would arise because many employees receive part of their pay in room and board, laundry, and similar wages in kind. On the other hand, the need of protection for domestic workers is great since their regular income is so low. Among the states, only New York and Hawaii cover domestics employed in the home, and they cover only those employers who have $500 and $250 respectively in quarterly payrolls. Experience in these states and other countries indicates that domestic servants can be successfully covered.

The third largest group excluded from unemployment compensation are farm and agricultural processing workers. The exclusion was originally made because of the fear of administrative difficulties in covering and keeping accurate records of many employees who worked on millions of small farms. Furthermore, many of the workers were migratory laborers. In 1939, amendments to the Social Security Act excluded those engaged in handling, processing, storage, and transportation of agricultural commodities if incidental to ordinary farming operations. These employees were excluded even though they worked in plants employing over 100 workers. A typical excluded citrus packing house is a maze of conveyor belts and machinery which cannot be distinguished from the ordinary urban factory. In 1957, Hawaii passed the first law covering agricultural workers under its unemployment insurance law.

[5] William Haber and Merrill G. Murray, *Unemployment Insurance in the American Economy* (Homewood, Ill., Irwin, 1966), pp. 165-166.

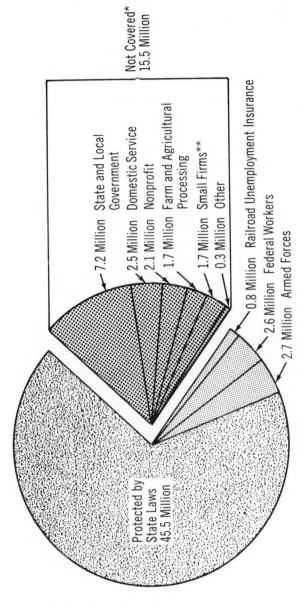

Not Covered*
15.5 Million

7.2 Million State and Local Government
2.5 Million Domestic Service
2.1 Million Nonprofit
1.7 Million Farm and Agricultural Processing
1.7 Million Small Firms**
0.3 Million Other
0.8 Million Railroad Unemployment Insurance
2.6 Million Federal Workers
2.7 Million Armed Forces

Protected by State Laws
45.5 Million

*Excludes clergymen and members of religious orders, student nurses, interns, and students employed in schools where enrolled.

**Excludes small firms added to coverage by Michigan, effective January 1, 1966.

Source: U.S. Department of Labor, *Unemployment Insurance Review*, Vol. 14, No. 1 (January, 1967), p. 12.

FIG. 14–1. UNEMPLOYMENT INSURANCE COVERAGE OF WAGE AND SALARY WORKERS, 1965

(Over 50 Million Wage Earners Are Protected by Unemployment Insurance)

The Hawaiian law was applicable only if the farm employed 20 or more workers for 20 weeks. One study on the problems and feasibility of covering farm workers was made in three states. The conclusion arrived at was that although coverage would present problems, these would not be insurmountable.[6] Also, other countries have successfully covered agricultural workers; Great Britain, for example, has included such workers since 1936.[7]

Due to fear that the administrative problems of covering small employers would be great if not insurmountable, the unemployment sections of the Social Security Act covered only those employers who hired eight or more employees in 20 different weeks. The states, however, were permitted to cover smaller employers, and a number of them did. Since experience in these states proved that such employers could be covered without difficulty, in 1954 Congress decided to cover employers of four or more employees. Twenty states now cover employers of one or more workers.[8]

Another group exempt from unemployment insurance coverage are nonprofit organizations. Only four states cover such employees, and all four exempt the clergy and members of religious orders.[9] One study made by the National Social Welfare Assembly found that employees of nonprofit organizations do experience significant unemployment although less than the labor force as a whole. The fact that nonprofit organizations could qualify for lower unemployment insurance tax rates through experience rating would be an argument to cover such a group. The costs would not be large.

A particularly knotty problem of coverage arises in the case of seasonal workers. Some seasonal workers are automatically excluded by the exemption on agricultural workers, and others are excluded because they have failed to work long enough to qualify to meet the minimum requirements for coverage. Ida C. Merriam feels that exclusions for casual labor may be justified, but she maintains that the arguments for exemptions of seasonal workers are less worthy.[10] One argument for not covering seasonal workers is that they are already compensated for unemployment by reason of higher base rates during the operating season. However, some seasonal workers receive quite low wages. Another argument against coverage is that if seasonal employment is particularly important in a state, heavy drains on the unemployment insurance fund might result. The system may be weakened so much that insufficient money would be available to protect against cyclical unemployment. Since many states do limit the benefits and duration to past

[6] A Study of the Feasibility of Covering Farm Workers Under Unemployment Compensation, Hartford, Conn., Connecticut Labor Department, Employment Security Division (1961), 239 pages.

[7] A. J. Altmeyer, "Social Security in Relation to Agriculture and Rural Areas," Social Security Bulletin, Vol. 3, No. 7 (July, 1940), p. 7.

[8] Comparison of State Unemployment Insurance Laws, No. U-141, Washington, D.C., U.S. Department of Labor, Bureau of Employment Security (January 1, 1966), p. CT-1.

[9] Ibid., p. C-9.

[10] Ida C. Merriam, "Seasonal Workers and Unemployment Compensation," Social Security Bulletin, Vol. 1, No. 9 (September, 1938), pp. 8-15.

earnings, though, there is less drain on the fund from seasonal employment than would occur if benefits and duration were not so limited. The argument that benefit payments to seasonal workers will subsidize and thus encourage seasonal operations may be countered by the argument that with a seasonal exemption employers may curtail normal operations in order to be exempt.

Fifteen states in 1966 permit payment of unemployment benefits during the normal operating season but will not pay in the off season when the industry is not operating. For states having seasonal exclusions, the federal agency administering the federal provisions of the law, the Bureau of Employment Security, recommended that seasonal workers who normally and regularly obtain off-season work each year be covered when they fail to obtain their off-season work. Similarly, they recommended that employees who normally are employed the year round in seasonal industries, such as watchmen, clerks, maintenance men, salesmen, and the like, should be covered regardless of the exemption of other workers in the industry.[11] Certain employers favor covering seasonal workers in order to supplement the wages of their workers and provide a "stand by" labor force for them.[12]

Summary on Coverage

In 1935, large numbers of employees were exempt from the unemployment insurance sections of the Social Security Act mainly because of the fear of administrative difficulties in covering small employers and other groups. Since 1935, administrative experience has demonstrated that most groups still exempt could be covered without serious difficulty. Since 1935, the trend has been toward more coverage, but today about one out of four employees are still not covered under unemployment insurance. In view of a lack of logical arguments against coverage, it would appear that coverage should be extended to more groups in the future.

ELIGIBILITY

Minimum Earnings and Employment

Before workers are eligible for unemployment compensation, all states require that the worker either shall have worked a certain length of time or that he shall have earned a certain minimum amount in wages. By such requirements, casual laborers are eliminated from coverage. The unemploy-

[11] "Standards and Procedures for the Compensation of Seasonal Unemployment," Memorandum No. 11, Washington, D.C., Federal Security Agency, Social Security Board, Bureau of Employment Security (1940), pp. 8, 9.

[12] "Seasonal Workers in California," Bulletin No. 21, State of California, Department of Employment (1947), p. 16.

ment insurance fund is also protected to the extent that at least a certain amount of money is paid into the fund before it is withdrawn in the form of benefits. Of the 52 jurisdictions having unemployment insurance (the District of Columbia, Puerto Rico, and the 50 states), 14 states have a flat amount of money which must be earned that ranges from $300 to $800. The obvious disadvantage of this eligibility requirement is that high wage workers can qualify by working only a few days. Furthermore, since wages have been rising over the years, a flat minimum becomes less effective each year unless the state legislature raises the minimum. Fourteen other states require that some multiple of weekly benefits or high-quarter wages be earned before unemployment benefits are paid. A typical requirement is that 30 times the weekly benefit amount be earned. Since the benefit amount approximates one-half of weekly earnings, a multiple of 30 is assumed to require about 15 weeks of full-time employment. This formula also has the disadvantage that higher paid workers qualify by working fewer weeks than lower paid workers. To avoid the disadvantages of the above formulas, more and more states are changing to a certain number of weeks ranging from 14 to 26, with 20 weeks the most common. Certain minimum amounts of from $15 to $20 must be earned to qualify as a week of work. The 20-week requirement has proven to be a more strict requirement than the formula of 30 times the weekly benefit amount.

The minimum earning eligibility requirement eliminates a significant number of people from unemployment compensation. California, for example, reported that from 1938 through 1952, 15 percent of all claimants for unemployment insurance were denied benefits on grounds of insufficient or no earnings.[13] In a study of the five-year period from 1956 through 1960 for all states, it was found that eligibility requirements had increased substantially. Part of the rise was due to increased wages over the period, but some states raised requirements higher than the increase in wages, primarily to tighten requirements.[14]

Waiting Period

Practically all states provide that no unemployment compensation be paid for the first week of unemployment. When the Social Security Act was first passed, a two-week waiting period was common, and this figure has gradually been reduced to one. Three states (Delaware, Maryland, and Nevada) have no waiting period. New York has only a four-day waiting period. Seven states pay for the first week of unemployment provided that the unemployment lasts a certain period of time.[15]

[13] *Sourcebook on Unemployment Compensation,* State of California, Department of Employment (1953), p. 68.

[14] "Unemployment Insurance in the USA," *Employment Security Review,* Vol. 27, No. 8 (August, 1960), pp. 11-12.

[15] *Comparison of State Unemployment Insurance Laws,* Table BT-3, p. BT-5, and p. BT-10.

Ability and Availability

The eligibility requirement on ability to work concerns physical capability of working. Nine states protect those who have become ill after they have become unemployed by paying unemployment insurance provided that no suitable work has been offered such claimants. Generally, availability to work means being "ready, willing, and able" to work. Workers engaged in training or retraining programs are generally not available for work, but 22 states now permit payment of unemployment compensation under such circumstances. All states could profitably adopt such a provision.

All state laws require registration for employment at a public employment office as a prior condition of eligibility. In theory, the law requires not only registration at the employment office but also that the applicant actively be seeking work on his own. Only Tennessee explicitly states that an individual who is able and available for work and who has registered and reported need not actively seek work or make an independent search for it. Maryland exempts those who are 60 years of age or older from actively seeking work or those who will be recalled to their old job within 30 days. Handicapped workers, such as those on crutches, may be treated more leniently than others in their search for work. On the other hand, statements by college students who contend they are looking for work after college begins tend to be suspect.[16]

DISQUALIFICATIONS FROM UNEMPLOYMENT INSURANCE

STRIKES AND LOCKOUTS

Problems of paying or refusing to pay unemployment benefits to strikers must be decided one way or the other. The Federal Emergency Relief Administration in the early 1930's paid strikers on the ground that a denial of relief would be a "particularly cruel method of strike-breaking." [17] However, the position adopted in administering unemployment insurance benefits by all states except New York and Rhode Island is the opposite one of denying benefits to strikers. In New York and Rhode Island benefits are paid only after the waiting period plus seven and six weeks respectively. The basis of the exclusion is that the strikers are not involuntarily unemployed, but have chosen of their free will to leave work. There is no question that payment of unemployment benefits would provide substantial financial security to workers while striking. Payment of such benefits during a strike could be

16 "Recent Appeal Decisions on Unemployment Benefits: Availability of College Students," *The Labor Market and Employment Security* (July, 1962), pp. 22-25.

17 James L. Myers, "Relief for Strikers' Families," *Survey*, Vol. LXX (October, 1934), p. 307.

considered as enlisting governmental aid to finance strikes. It is possible that many more strikes would be called if such governmental financing were available. An added difficulty with compensating strikes is that heavy drains on the unemployment insurance fund would occur in large strikes affecting many thousands of workers.[18]

Many problems have arisen in administering the disqualification for striking. If a strike occurs at one plant of an employer, the states must decide whether the workers at other plants of the employer who are idle because of lack of parts should receive compensation. A strike at the Ford Motor Company at Dearborn, Michigan, idled Ford workers in four other states. Three paid compensation and the other did not. A question of disqualification arises when workers walk out because of an infringement of a statutory law by the employer. Only four states specifically guarantee payment under such circumstances. Similar cases arise when workers go on strike in protest against an employer who has fired workers for union activity or otherwise violated the National Labor Relations Act. Here, four states specifically provide unemployment compensation during such strikes, but the others do not. Controversy has also arisen over whether workers who are locked out should receive unemployment compensation. In such circumstances workers do not take the initiative in leaving work, but payment to workers would throw financial support to the workers and militate against the employer. Lockouts are compensable in 12 states but not in the others. In some of these states, problems have arisen in determining whether the dispute was a strike or a lockout.

VOLUNTARILY LEAVING WORK

All states provide some sort of disqualification for workers who voluntarily leave their work without good cause. Several exceptions to this disqualification have been made by a number of states. These exceptions are important in analyzing whether all states should provide some relief from this disqualification. New Hampshire provides that a man may quit work without good cause and receive compensation if he has held the job less than four weeks and found it not to be suitable. In 28 states when a person leaves a plant voluntarily, compensation is paid if the worker has good cause, including personal reasons, for leaving. Twenty-four other jurisdictions do not recognize personal reasons for leaving but require that the good cause be connected with the work. If a worker resigned from heavy work and sought

[18] For example, the West Virginia Board of Review estimated that the coal strike of 1939, which idled over 100,000 miners in West Virginia, would have exhausted the state's unemployment insurance fund in eight weeks even if figured from the highest surplus the fund had accumulated. See K. Pribram, "Compensation for Unemployment During Industrial Disputes," *Monthly Labor Review*, Vol. 51 (1940), p. 1376.

lighter work because of health reasons, the more liberal states would pay unemployment benefits, but the less liberal states would not compensate because the leave was not work-connected.

Twenty-six states prohibit the payment of any unemployment insurance during the duration of the unemployment for those voluntarily quitting without good cause. Labor unions oppose such a long disqualification on grounds that most workers cannot afford to remain unemployed indefinitely. After a worker has sought employment elsewhere for a certain period, benefits should be paid to him because he has been actively seeking work. In line with this philosophy, a number of states disqualify workers from benefits only for a limited period of time.

In 16 states not only are benefits postponed, but any benefit rights earned on the job voluntarily left are either cancelled or reduced. If, for example, an employee was required to work for a certain time before drawing benefits, and all of his employment was with the company he had voluntarily left, then not only would he be disqualified from drawing unemployment compensation but none of the wages earned on this job could be credited to him.

Quite obviously labor groups oppose this provision, and feel that workers quitting should be penalized only to the extent of losing compensation while disqualified without any further subtraction of benefits.

MISCONDUCT

All 52 jurisdictions provide for a reduction or cancellation of benefits for those discharged because of misconduct. All states have the problem of defining "misconduct," and all must distinguish between misconduct and inefficiency. If a clerk's sales record falls off because he or she has been impolite to customers, should the impoliteness be interpreted as misconduct or simply as a personality failure or inefficiency? Quite naturally labor groups insist that the misconduct disqualification be used only for genuine cases of misconduct, and they have protested too frequent use of this disqualification by some states in the past. Management, on the other hand, would take fewer exceptions to a broader use of misconduct in disqualification. Normally inadvertent, simple, or ordinary negligence is not considered misconduct.

Eighteen states disqualify workers from compensation for misconduct for a set number of weeks ranging from 3 to 8. These states, and other states that vary the weeks of disqualification according to the severity of the misconduct, agree with the principle that disqualification should be limited. Failure to obtain unemployment for, say, a month would be sufficient penalty. Only 24 states totally cancel unemployment benefits for the duration of the unemployment for the claimant fired because of misconduct.

REFUSING OTHER SUITABLE WORK

All states provide for some sort of disqualification for refusing other suitable work. A wide difference of opinion separates students of social security on a proper definition of what constitutes other suitable work. Conservatives hold that almost any type of job should be considered suitable, especially to an unemployed worker. From this viewpoint many contend that the system of unemployment insurance is subject to a great deal of abuse by persons refusing to take other jobs, even at lower pay and in different localities. Liberals, on the other hand, maintain that wages and other labor standards would be severely threatened if workers are forced to take any job offered upon threat of disqualification for unemployment insurance. Consequently, they hold out for a definition of suitable work that will maintain workers on about the same plane that they had been on before becoming unemployed.

As with the other types of disqualifications, the states are split on whether to disqualify workers completely or simply reduce benefits for refusing other suitable work. Twenty-three states disqualify claimants for the duration of the unemployment. Several of these provide additional penalties, such as canceling wage credits earned for any future unemployment during the benefit year. On the other hand, 14 states limit the disqualification to a specific number of weeks ranging from 3 to 8, and the other states provide for a variation in the number of weeks of disqualification from 4 to 16, depending on the ruling of the administrator.

DISQUALIFICATIONS—CONCLUSIONS

Over the years administrators have been disqualifying more and more unemployment insurance claimants. In 1945, the number disqualified per 1,000 claimants was 15.9, and this figure increased to 23.5 by 1964.[19] The laws have also been amended to provide for longer periods of disqualification. In 1937, only one state disqualified for the duration of unemployment for voluntarily quitting, two states for engaging in misconduct, and six for refusing suitable work. By 1966, the respective number of states was 26, 24, and 23.[20] The purpose of the tighter administration and stricter laws is, of course, to prevent abuse of the system. As would be expected, management and labor have split over this issue, with management favoring more disqualification and labor less. Neutral observers have split over this issue also. At the very least, the cancelation of benefit rights for future spells of unemployment should be abolished since such provisions obviously are punitive in nature and as such have no place in an insurance system.[21]

[19] Haber and Murray, op. cit., Table 15-1, p. 283.
[20] Ibid., p. 302.
[21] Ibid., pp. 304-305.

ADMINISTRATION OF UNEMPLOYMENT INSURANCE

FEDERAL ADMINISTRATION

At the present time, the Bureau of Employment Security of the U.S. Department of Labor administers the unemployment insurance sections of the Social Security Act. The Bureau of Employment Security has the function of reviewing requests for funds to administer the program by state agencies. It also administers the sections of the law requiring state compliance on such matters as not denying compensation if work is less favorable, if a strike is in existence, or if the individual is required to join a company union or refrain from joining or remaining a member of a bona fide labor union. Federal control of unemployment insurance is limited to the federal tax on payrolls, control over administrative expenses of state agencies, and several restrictions on administering the law.

STATE ADMINISTRATION

Most of the administration of unemployment insurance laws in the United States is under control of state governments, and practically all personnel hired for both unemployment insurance and employment services are state employees. At the state level, a frequent type of administration is that of an independent state agency (14 states). Nineteen other states provide for an independent department that reports directly to the governor of the state. In 19 states unemployment insurance is administered under the state Department of Labor.[22]

All but 3 states have advisory councils to assist in recommending improvements in the program. The members of the advisory council are appointed either by the governor (27 states) or by the agency administering the program. The purpose of the advisory councils is to study the unemployment insurance program and the administration of it. Recommendations are made either to the governor or to the legislature. Professor Joseph Becker made an intensive study of 15 state advisory councils plus the Federal Advistory Council. He found that the prospects of effective councils varied greatly from state to state and even within states over time. He felt that the one necessary condition for success was the factor of personalities. He suggested that the most successful types of councils were those in which labor and management representatives hammered out amendments to the law by the process of bargaining and compromise.[23] A different view is that council members should think of themselves as a part of government and give serious

[22] *Comparison of State Unemployment Insurance Laws*, pp. A-3–4.
[23] Joseph M. Becker, *Shared Government in Employment Security* (New York, Columbia, 1959), pp. 472-474.

attention to the general public interest. Richard Lester was critical of "agreed bills," that is, agreement by the labor and management members of an advisory council on the ground that such bills lack any evaluation of contents of the law.[24]

To better understand the workings of the agency devoted to administering the unemployment insurance program, a summary of functions of a typical agency is given. First of all, the agency must determine which employers are covered under both the federal and the state law, and then liability for a payroll tax is placed on those employers covered. The tax rates must be computed by the agency, because these vary according to how much unemployment has been experienced in the past. Since benefits depend on past wages, wage data must also be collected from employers. Then the office accepts claims for those filing for unemployment insurance benefits. Not only must an initial claim be made, but the recipient must report to the office weekly thereafter. After receiving the claim, the office determines whether the claimant has worked long enough to qualify for insurance. The office also investigates whether the claimant has not disqualified himself by reason of quitting work voluntarily or for some other reason. If the claimant qualifies, then his benefit must be computed from past wage records, and a record of such payments must be made. Since the agency also attempts to find work for the claimant, the functions of the employment service are also administered by the same agency.

All states have had the problem of determining how many of its functions can best be handled in the central office and how many should be handled locally. Some states have found that delegating of functions to the local offices has not only saved the state money but also speeded payment of benefits.[25] Since both the state employment offices and unemployment benefits are administered by the same agency, the question arises as to whether the same personnel should perform both functions or whether more specialization should occur. No hard and fast rules can be made. In a local office containing only one or two workers, these employees will of necessity have to perform both functions. As the offices grow larger, more specialization may be permitted. A problem has arisen in most offices at one time or another of having to transfer personnel away from the employment function in order to handle an unusually large number of applications for unemployment insurance. One suggestion here is to hire temporary claims takers so that the work of the employment service will not be neglected at that time.[26]

The states are required by the federal provisions of the act to provide an appeal on those claims for which the state refuses payment. All except

[24] Richard A. Lester, *The Economics of Unemployment Compensation* (Princeton, Princeton, 1962), p. 107.

[25] Hendrick G. Nobel, "Decentralization of Benefit Claims Operations," *Employment Security Review*, Vol. 18, No. 3 (March, 1951), pp. 27-29.

[26] Robert C. Goodwin, "The Administrator's Responsibility for a Balanced Employment Security Program," *Labor Law Journal*, Vol. 1 (November, 1950), p. 1111.

four states provide for two appeal stages before cases can be appealed to state courts. The initial appeals authority is generally one person, called either an examiner or referee. For the final appeal the one-man referee is still the most common, but 22 states use a three-man appeal board.

ABUSE OF UNEMPLOYMENT INSURANCE

Fulton Lewis, Jr. asked a number of young male unemployment insurance claimants whether they would accept jobs on his Maryland farm. When they refused such work, he classified them as illegitimate claimants. Of those interviewed, he found that 96 percent should have been disqualified from receiving benefits since they refused work on his farm.[27] Those who feel that the unemployed should be required to accept only work suitable to their training and skills justify the refusal of farm work and would find no abuse. Other violations of the law are more clear cut. Sometimes persons fail to report finding a new job, and illegally draw unemployment compensation at the same time that they are working. Others permanently withdraw from the work force but draw benefits by falsely claiming that they are looking for work.

Investigations have been made on the number of people drawing benefits illegally. The number of working violators in three states varied from 1 to 12 percent, and the percent of nonworking violators was even higher.[28] A comprehensive study of abuse of unemployment compensation was made by Joseph Becker after World War II. He concluded that if the whole program is viewed from the perspective of how many persons filed claims in relation to all those covered under the system, there was little evidence to support the view that unemployment insurance promoted widespread malingering and substantially reduced potential employment. Only 13 percent of those covered under the program received any unemployment benefits at all in 1946 and only 5.9 percent of potential claimants exhausted all their benefits.[29] Furthermore, unemployment did not climb to a particularly high figure even at the peak of the reconversion period. More recent statistics show that in fiscal 1964, only 12 out of every 1,000 beneficiaries were found to have made fraudulent claims that resulted in overpayment of benefits. Of every $100 paid out in benefits, only 31 cents was an overpayment resulting in fraud and 64 percent of the overpayments due to fraud were recovered from the claimants.[30]

Fortunately, good administration can reduce the amount of abuse of

[27] Joseph M. Becker, *The Problem of Abuse in Unemployment Benefits* (New York, Columbia, 1953), p. 57.

[28] *Ibid.*, pp. 169-239.

[29] *Ibid.*, p. 358.

[30] William Haber and Merrill G. Murray, *Unemployment Insurance in the American Economy* (Homewood, Ill., Irwin, 1966), p. 137.

unemployment insurance. Audits on wages can be taken to apprehend working violators. Frequent interviews and field investigations can also be used to reduce abuse. Fraud detection is made somewhat easier from findings that fraud tends to be concentrated among those drawing unemployment benefits for extended periods of time. In Florida, for example, of all fraud detected, 77 percent involved claimants receiving five or more payments in a calendar quarter.[31] We may conclude then that fraud does exist in the unemployment program but that it is only practiced by a small minority of recipients. It is detectable by efficient administration. Good administration can remove most of the complaints about abuse of the program.

PROBLEMS OF THE JOINT FEDERAL-STATE SYSTEM

Although the Social Security Act left formulation of the program and administration of it to the states, several federal requirements are written into the law and must be observed by the states before money is released to the states either for administration or unemployment benefits. The law reads as follows:

Compensation shall not be denied in such State to any otherwise eligible individual for refusing to accept new work under any of the following conditions:

a. If the position offered is vacant due directly to a strike, lock-out, or other labor dispute;

b. If the wages, hours or other conditions of work offered are substantially less favorable to the individual than those prevailing for similar work in the locality;

c. If as a condition of being employed the individual would be required to join a company union or to resign from or refrain from joining any bona fide labor organization.

In addition, the states must meet certain administrative requirements in order to be entitled to a grant for administration. These include (1) adequate methods of administration and personnel standards; (2) payment through public employment offices or such agencies as the Secretary of Labor may approve; (3) opportunity for a fair hearing before an impartial tribunal for all individuals whose claims for benefits are denied; and (4) submission of such reports as are required by the Secretary of Labor.

The federal administrative requirements have had the salutary effect of having the states develop their personnel administration on a merit basis. Under this section of the law, the federal government required South Dakota to pay unemployment compensation through a public employment office rather than through the state public welfare office. Also, Arizona was advised

[31] William U. Norwood, "Matching Wage Records and Benefit Payment Records," *Employment Security Review*, Vol. 19, No. 2 (June, 1952), p. 11.

that its Employment Service director would have to devote full time to his duties.

A number of controversies have occurred between the federal government and the states over requirements a, b, and c listed above. In one case in which compensation had been denied, the California Appeal Board recognized that an error had been made and agreed to reopen the case. The Bureau of Employment Security was not satisfied with the report of the Appeal Board, and the Bureau proposed that California sign a statement agreeing to pay the workers. The state declined to sign on the ground that the state would be required to prejudge the case and improperly limit the correct procedure of a fair hearing before an impartial tribunal. Upon threat of losing its unemployment compensation, California paid the workers, though under protest.

In order to clarify the issue, the Knowland amendment to the Social Security Act was passed in 1950. This amendment provided that the Secretary of Labor may not make a finding of noncompliance until the question shall have been decided by the highest judicial authority given jurisdiction under the state law. Management favored the amendment as did the legislative committee of the Interstate Conference of Employment Security Agencies, a group of state officials who have been fearful of undue federal interference. Labor unions, on the other hand, strongly opposed this amendment. They feared that the states could unduly prolong the appeals procedure and thus hamstring proper enforcement of the law. In California, for example, in cases that had gone to the State Supreme Court from the appeals board, 29 months elapsed before the final decision.[32]

In view of the number of federal-state controversies,[33] the Secretary of Labor asked the Bureau of Employment Security to study the possibility of providing sanctions that stopped short of withholding funds. The Bureau was unable to suggest effective sanctions that would be less sweeping. Another possibility could be to provide for federal court review of the Secretary's findings.

FEDERAL FUNDS FOR ADMINISTRATION

Another problem of the joint federal-state system is that ever since the beginning of the Social Security system and at the present time, the federal government pays 100 percent of the money for administration of the system; yet it is the states who do the administering. One possible objection to this system is that the states may become wasteful in operating the system since it is the federal government rather than the states which must pay the bills.

[32] Arthur P. Allen, "The Knowland Amendment to the Social Security Act," *Labor Law Journal*, Vol. 2 (1951), p. 425.

[33] For a summary of these, *see* Haber and Murray, *Unemployment Insurance in the American Economy*, pp. 448-450.

The federal government, however, has kept a close rein on expenditures, and therefore waste has been kept to a minimum. Many states maintain that so little money is appropriated to them that they cannot do an adequate job of administering the system.

When the Social Security system was first inaugurated and at the present time, the federal government obtains the funds needed for administration from an earmarked part of the payroll tax used to finance the system. It was estimated that about three-tenths of 1 percent was needed for administration, and this was the amount earmarked. Experience under the act demonstrated that some states in more sparsely settled areas required more than this amount to administer the program, but most states needed less. Consequently the tax was more than sufficient to administer the program. Over a period of years, a surplus of more than a billion dollars accrued to the federal government. Since it was not stated in the law that this money should be kept in the unemployment insurance system, it was spent by the federal government to meet general expenses not connected with unemployment. Because many felt that it was unfair that a tax should be levied supposedly for unemployment insurance administration, but then spent for other things, the law was changed in 1960. The amount earmarked for administration was raised from 0.3 to 0.4 percent (effective January 1, 1961). Any administrative surplus was to be placed in an emergency reserve until the fund reached $550 million. After that the surplus is to be allocated to the states in the proportion that their covered payrolls bear to the aggregate, provided, however, that at least $250 million is maintained in the Employment Security Administration Account. The purpose of the emergency fund has been to loan funds at no interest to states whose unemployment is high. The emergency loan fund was originally created by the George Loan Fund amendment of 1944. No state became eligible for a loan during its provisions. A later Reed Loan Fund amendment was passed in 1954, and a few loans were made from it to Alaska, Michigan, and Pennsylvania. The requirements for loans were tightened by Public Law 86–778 in 1960 to provide that loans shall only be made available if a state fund becomes bankrupt.

Several alternatives to the present 100 percent administrative grant to the states suggest themselves. One is that the federal government simply return to the states the exact amount collected from it for administration. Naturally, the states with high administrative costs would not like this system for their administrative tax might have to be raised. Another suggestion is to abolish the federal collection for administration and have the states raise their own money. Both of the above suggestions have the weakness that they might eliminate some of the federal standards which now exist in the program. In view of this weakness, it is likely that the present system of 100 percent federal grants for administration will continue for some time into the future.

INTERSTATE WORKERS

Another problem created by the joint federal-state system is that of the inter-state worker. Obviously with a purely federal system, all workers would be treated uniformly regardless of whether they crossed state boundaries. Under the present system, in which the various states have many different require-ments of their own, a number of problems arise with interstate workers. Satisfactory adaptations have been made to some of these problems. For example, if a worker qualifies for unemployment insurance in one state but then moves to another state and becomes unemployed, the state to which he has moved agrees to act as an agent in processing the claim of the worker and then forwards it to the first state for payment. Reciprocal arrangements have been worked out in all but three states on the problem of the worker having insufficient eligibility in one state but where he would have sufficient eligibility if employment in a previous state had been counted. One minor problem remains of mobile workers who would be covered in one state but not in another due to different size of firm requirements. Here, 36 states permit the employer to elect coverage.[34] It is also possible for an interstate worker to draw unemployment benefits in two states for a longer period of time than he could draw insurance if he lived in one state and experienced the same amount of unemployment.[35]

ADVANTAGES OF A PURELY FEDERAL SYSTEM

The advantages of a purely federal unemployment insurance system are sub-stantial. All of the other countries of the world with two exceptions have adopted a nationwide system. Switzerland's unemployment insurance pro-gram is administered by the cantons (states) under a federal law providing for partial financing by the federal government. Norway also has a locally administered system with national grants to make up deficits in local funds.[36] The reason for predominantly national systems is that such systems do have marked advantages. In the United States, many of the states are quite small. In New England, for example, six separate systems had to be created with a director and an administrative system for each state. Had the federal gov-ernment administered the program, it would have streamlined the system more in accordance with actual need for personnel. Furthermore, personnel could more readily be transferred from place to place. The smallness of some states also militates against sound insurance principles, for a small state prob-

---

[34] *Ibid.*, pp. 462-464.

[35] Ida Merriam and Elizabeth Bliss, "Unemployment Compensation Rights of Workers Employed in One State," Report No. 11, Washington, D.C., Federal Security Agency, Social Security Board, Bureau of Research and Statistics (1941), p. 2.

[36] Atkinson, *op. cit.*, p. 3.

ably will have little diversification of industry. If industry becomes depressed, heavy drains are made on the unemployment insurance fund.

The records and tax system could be simplified if only one federal levy were provided. Furthermore, no problem of inequities in dealing with interstate workers would arise. In addition, more uniform benefits would be provided throughout the country. Tax rates would be uniform also, and the purely federal system would eliminate the present competition among states to reduce the unemployment insurance tax through experience rating. Bearing of the cost of unemployment nationally would place less burden on the states experiencing heavy unemployment. Solvency of 52 systems combined into one would be greater than for any one separate system. Also, the fact that heavy payments are concentrated in several of the states means that these states cannot afford to pay as high benefits as could the federal government, which would have an average burden that was less than that in the heavy-unemployment states. Finally, the present system of requiring the federal government to estimate needed administrative expenses in states in which coverage, benefits, disqualifications, and administrative organization differ is more difficult than if the federal government were administering a uniform system throughout the country.

ADVANTAGES OF A MIXED FEDERAL-STATE SYSTEM

The unemployment insurance system actually adopted in this country was one of joint federal and state control. The federal government provided for a 3 percent tax (in 1938 and thereafter) on all employers in the country. The states were practically forced to adopt the program unless they wanted to lose the tax money collected. Although the federal government appropriates money to administer the program and requires that certain minimum standards be met, actual administration of unemployment insurance is carried out by the states. One argument in favor of the mixed system, of major importance when the Social Security Act was passed, was that having many different jurisdictions would enable the states to experiment with various types of programs. With the passage of time, though, it could be argued that the best methods in each of the states should now be recognizable, and that one system including all the best methods should now be adopted. When the Social Security Act was first passed in 1935, there was some question that a completely federal system would be constitutional, but at the present writing there is no question that it would be. Another argument in favor of the present mixed system is that the cost of living is higher in certain parts of the country than in others and that benefits should vary accordingly. Another advantage of decentralized administration is that the program is operated by those who are more fully aware of local conditions, although offsetting this factor is the possible broader experience of federal administrators. Finally, an argument in favor of the present system is that local administration is probably more sensitive toward pressure for faster service than a purely federal system would be. The fact that there is some antifederal bias in the United States and that there is a good deal of state pride will probably result in keeping the present mixed system intact.

Summary

The failure of private enterprise, labor unions, and state governments to provide unemployment insurance in the United States resulted in the federal government providing for such a program under the Social Security Act of 1935. The United States adopted such legislation later than Western Europe.

Today more than three-fourths of American workers are covered under our unemployment insurance programs. Although coverage has been expanded since the original act of 1935, large groups are still exempt from the law. Before workers become eligible for unemployment compensation they must have earned a minimum of wages or have been employed for a minimum period of time. A waiting period of one week is required in most of the laws, but a few have reduced the waiting period below this length of time. To qualify for benefits, workers must be able and available for work. Several disqualifications are provided for striking, voluntarily leaving work, misconduct, or refusing other suitable work.

Administration of the laws is primarily the responsibility of the several states. Some states have administered the law well and others have not. Weaknesses have been noted in preventing abuse of the program. Several problems arose with federal controls, one serious enough to result in the Knowland Amendment which provides that the Secretary of Labor may not make findings of state noncompliance of the law until the question is decided by the highest judicial authority of the states. Although the mixed system has resulted in a number of deficiencies, little support is in evidence for a completely federal system.

UNEMPLOYMENT INSURANCE:
BENEFITS AND TAXATION

BENEFITS

In disbursing unemployment benefits, either all workers could be paid an equal amount or benefits could be graduated according to past wages. Most countries graduate benefits. There are several reasons for gradation of benefits. One is that higher-paid workers are used to a larger amount of income; therefore they should receive larger benefits. Higher benefits enable them to maintain a standard of living approximating their normal status. Also in countries where a payroll tax is used, the higher the wages, the more taxes are collected. The larger tax collections from higher-paid workers may justify larger benefits to them.[1]

In the United States, all states vary benefits according to past wages. Of necessity, then, some record of past wages must be kept, and some formula must be devised to correlate benefits with past wages. In most states (39) a record of quarterly earnings rather than weekly or annual wages is kept. The benefit is then paid as a fraction of the highest quarterly earnings in the base period.

The definition of "base period" is spelled out in all the laws. The base period is most frequently defined as the first four of the last five quarters preceding the benefit year (33 states). The benefit year is in turn defined most frequently as the one year or 52-week period in which unemployment first begins (42 states). An alternate definition of the base year is the last four quarters preceding the benefit year (5 states). Since wage rates generally rise rather than fall, the use of the latter formula tends to provide a higher weekly benefit than the more common formula of the first four of the last five quarters.

Choosing the highest quarter on which to base benefits was done primarily to gear benefits to full weekly wages rather than to a quarter when less than full employment was experienced. With 13 weeks in a quarter, the payment of $\frac{1}{13}$ of the highest quarter's wages would provide the worker with 100 percent of the loss of his wages. Since most students of unemployment insurance agree that less than full wages should be paid so that in-

<hr />

[1] Joseph M. Becker, *The Adequacy of the Benefit Amount in Unemployment Insurance* (Kalamazoo, Upjohn Institute, 1961), pp. 13-18.

centive to seek work is not discouraged, no state pays as high a fraction as $\frac{1}{13}$ of the high quarter wage. The use of $\frac{1}{26}$ theoretically would provide for 50 percent compensation, but even in the high quarter some part-time work may be experienced. Thus, use of the fraction $\frac{1}{26}$ would probably not compensate the workers for 50 percent of the loss of a full week's pay. For this reason the fraction usually ranges from $\frac{1}{20}$ to $\frac{1}{25}$, with $\frac{1}{25}$ being used most frequently. Most states use the same fraction for all workers, but 11 states vary the fraction according to the wages earned. In all 11 states, the fraction is adjusted so that the lower-paid workers will receive a larger percentage of benefit than higher-paid workers.

To facilitate collection of wage rate data, seven states have changed from quarterly data to the use of annual wages. Annual earnings are less than high-quarter wages because of irregular employment. In Alabama, for example, annual earnings for a sample group of claimants averaged only 2.7 times the earnings in the highest quarter.[2] Furthermore, since irregular employment tends to be concentrated among the lower-paid workers, the lower-paid workers suffer from changing to an annual wage formula. To cite Alabama again, annual earnings for claimants earning less than $50 in the highest quarter were only 1.7 times the highest quarterly earnings, whereas the ratio was 2.9 for those earning between $150 and $300 in the highest quarter.[3] Even though the percentage varies to aid the lower-paid worker, in a study of benefits both before and after the change to annual wages it was found that a larger proportion of workers drew smaller than higher amounts. Also a larger percentage were drawing minimum benefits, a smaller percentage received the maximum benefit, and state benefits as a whole dropped. In the three states where direct comparisons were possible it was found that after the change from quarterly to annual wages, average weekly benefits dropped 3, 6, and 26 percent, although in ten adjacent states not changing to annual data, there was a slight increase in average weekly benefits.[4]

MINIMUM BENEFITS

In order to provide a minimum of subsistence to unemployed workers, all states designate that regardless of full-time wages earned a worker will receive at least a minimum weekly benefit. Eleven states add dependents' allowances. Including the amounts permitted for dependents, the minimum weekly benefits for all the states are shown in Table 15-1.

[2] Thomas C. Fichandler, "The Effects of Relating Weekly Benefit Amounts to Annual Earnings," *Social Security Bulletin*, Vol. 3, No. 4 (April, 1940), p. 4.

[3] *Ibid.*, p. 5.

[4] *Ibid.*, p. 6. Haber and Murray point out that there has been a recent trend toward returning to weekly wage data. For the arguments they use in favoring this trend, *see* William Haber and Merrill G. Murray, *Unemployment Insurance in the American Economy* (Homewood, Ill., Irwin), pp. 175-178.

TABLE 15–1.   MINIMUM WEEKLY UNEMPLOYMENT INSURANCE BENEFITS (NUMBER OF STATES a WITH SPECIFIED MINIMUM), 1966

Minimum Weekly Benefit	Without Dependents	With Maximum Dependents	Minimum Weekly Benefit	Without Dependents	With Maximum Dependents
$ 3.00	1	0	$15.00	4	0
$ 5.00	1	0	$16.00	0	4
$ 7.00	2	0	$17.00	2	0
$ 8.00	2	0	$18.00	0	1
$ 9.00	2	0	$20.00	1	1
$10.00	16	1	$21.00	0	1
$11.00	1	0	$22.00	0	1
$12.00	8	0	$24.00	0	1
$13.00	1	0	$25.00	1	0
$14.00	1	2			

a No augmented benefit is shown for Illinois and Iowa because only claimants with wages above those necessary for maximum weekly benefit are eligible for augmented benefits.

Source: Comparison of State Unemployment Insurance Laws, January 1, 1966, No. U-141, U.S. Department of Labor, Bureau of Employment Security, Table BT–10, pp. BT-23-25.

Table 15-1 highlights the problem of permitting the various states to adopt their own Social Security programs. As can be seen, the eight lowest minimum-benefit states set the figure at one-half or less than the amount that the seven highest states pay. In general, the lowest-paying states are the low-income states of the South. Several of the low-paying states, however, have relatively high per capita incomes. It is true that certain areas have lower costs of living than others that might possibly justify lower benefits, but differences in the cost of living are not nearly so great as the differences in minimum benefits.

MAXIMUM BENEFITS

Although the fraction designated provides workers at least 50 percent of their full-time weekly wage loss, all states except one have maximum weekly limits on benefit payments. The weekly maximums tend to reduce the percentage obtained below the 50 percent figure. The maximum amounts, including the states paying dependents' allowances, are shown in Table 15-2.

As with minimum benefits the range in maximums is quite great. The bottom eight states have a maximum which is half or less than the top four states.

TABLE 15–2. MAXIMUM WEEKLY UNEMPLOYMENT INSURANCE BENEFITS
(NUMBER OF STATES WITH SPECIFIED MAXIMUM), 1966

Maximum Weekly Benefit	Without Dependents	With Maximum Dependents	Maximum Weekly Benefit	Without Dependents	With Maximum Dependents
$20.00	1	0	$48.00	3	0
$30.00	1	0	$50.00	3	0
$32.00	1	0	$51.00	1	0
$33.00	1	0	$53.00	0	1
$34.00	2	0	$55.00	2	1
$35.00	2	0	$57.00	1	0
$36.00	3	0	$59.00	0	1
$37.00	1	0	$60.00	0	1
$38.00	4	0	$61.00	1	1
$40.00	4	0	$62.00	1	0
$42.00	2	0	$65.00	1	0
$43.00	1	1	$67.00	0	1
$44.00	1	0	$70.00	0	2
$45.00	3	0	$72.00	0	1
$46.00	1	0	$75.00	0	1
$47.00	1	0			

Source: *Comparison of State Unemployment Insurance Laws, January 1, 1966,* No. U-141, U.S. Department of Labor, Bureau of Employment Security, Table BT–10, pp. BT-23-25.

ADEQUACY OF BENEFITS

Adequacy of unemployment benefits has been analyzed in a variety of ways. One way is to compare benefits today with those in the past. Table 15-3 traces unemployment benefits from 1939 to the present and compares benefits with the consumer's price index and average weekly earnings.

Table 15-3 shows quite clearly that average weekly benefits have outstripped the cost of living. The real income of unemployment benefit recipients has therefore increased. On the other hand, benefits as a percentage of wages are less today than they were in 1939.

ARGUMENTS FOR HIGHER BENEFITS

Proponents of higher benefits cite the evidence shown from Table 15-3 that benefits have not risen as fast as wages. More of the unemployed are precluded from drawing higher benefits, because they are already receiving the maximum. In 1939, for example, only 26 percent of all benefits were at the maximum ceiling, whereas by 1954, 62 percent were at the ceiling. Some

TABLE 15–3.   COMPARISON OF UNEMPLOYMENT BENEFITS WITH WAGES
AND COST OF LIVING, 1939–1965

Year	Average Weekly Benefits	Index of Benefits[a]	Consumer Price Index[a]	Average Weekly Wages[b]	Index of Average Weekly Wages[a]	Benefits as Percentage of Wages
1939	$10.66	100	100	$ 23.86	100	40.4
1951	21.08	198	187	64.71	271	32.6
1957	28.21	265	202	82.39	341	34.2
1965[c]	38.81	364	226	110.92	464	35.0

[a] 1939 = 100.
[b] For production workers in manufacturing.
[c] December.
Sources: *Adequacy of Benefits Under Unemployment Insurance,* U.S. Department of Labor, Bureau of Employment Security (September, 1952), Table B–13. *Monthly Labor Review,* various issues. *Social Security Bulletin,* various issues.

improvement has been made in raising maximums since 1954, but in 1961, 46 percent of all the unemployed were obtaining the same maximum benefit. In fifteen states in 1961, over 60 to as high as 81 percent of new insured claimants were eligible for maximum benefits.[5] The failure of benefits to rise in relation to earnings has caused many to press for higher benefits. A Federal Advisory Council recommended that the maximums be raised to not less than three-fifths to two-thirds of average weekly earnings. The vote, however, was not unanimous. The recommendation passed by a 12-to-5 vote, with all the negative votes being cast by employer members. Also three of the public members who cast an affirmative vote stated that they would have preferred that the maximum be set at 50 percent.[6]

Some have argued for higher benefits on the basis of need. A number of studies have shown that unemployment benefits do not pay the costs of food and shelter, let alone other amenities of life.[7] Furthermore, a number of studies have found that single workers' benefits are more adequate than married workers'. For one thing, single workers need less income. For another, married workers earn about 50 percent more than single workers so that their benefits are curtailed more by weekly benefit ceilings. One study in Michigan found that a single person was receiving more than needed to provide

[5] *Evaluation of Coverage and Benefit Provisions of State Unemployment Insurance Laws, as of December 31, 1961,* Washington, D.C., U.S. Department of Labor, Bureau of Employment Security, Table 6.

[6] Miriam Civic, "Height and Width of Unemployment Benefits," *Conference Board Business Record,* Vol. 11 (1954), p. 311.

[7] Joseph Schachter, "Unemployment Benefits, Wages, and Living Costs," *Social Security Bulletin,* Vol. 11 (1948), p. 8.

for food and shelter, whereas larger families were not receiving enough to pay for these necessities. In a sample study from six states it was found that weekly benefits for single persons equaled or exceeded nondeferrable expenditures, defined as cash outlays for food, shelter, utilities, and medical care. However, for four-person households, benefits fell short in all six states, ranging from 12 to 40 percent less than nondeferrable expenditures.[8]

One method of overcoming the loss to families is to provide dependency benefits. At the present writing 11 states now have dependents' benefits. The 11 states pay allowances that range from $1 to $9 additional weekly per dependent. Most of the 11 states pay a flat amount per dependent, but several increase benefits by designating higher maximum benefits for those with dependents. Labor in some states has opposed the variable maximum on the ground that it may tend to keep the maximums of other workers too low. The various states paying dependents' allowances set maximum limits on payments even though the family has a large number of children. Some states, for example, limit the allowances to one-half the weekly benefit amount. Most of the 11 states also limit the number of dependents eligible for payment.[9] Those arguing for higher benefits maintain that the fact that most states do not provide for dependents' allowances shows inadequacy as does the low dependency allowances and restrictions in the minority of states that do make such payments.

Another argument for higher benefits is that this would aid in alleviating recessions. Professor Richard Lester has estimated that unemployment compensation made up about 18 percent of wage and salary loss caused by unemployment from 1948 to 1961. The percentage remained about the same over the years. Increases in coverage and duration of benefits were offset by lagging benefits. A larger percentage of wages is paid in the early stages of the recession before the limit on the duration of benefits is reached. Even with a relatively small percentage of wages being compensated, in the recession of 1958 unemployment benefits rose to almost $4 billion, an increase of almost $2 billion from the previous prosperity. Increases in benefits result in larger sums being spent during recessions. Unemployment benefits, however, can do only a limited amount of good during recessions, since such benefits amount to less than 2 percent of labor income or total consumption expenditures.[10]

[8] Senator James M. Teahen, "Michigan's New Approach to Maximum Benefit Rates in Unemployment Compensation," *American Economic Security*, Vol. 11, No. 3 (June–July, 1954), p. 26; Richard A. Lester, *The Economics of Unemployment Compensation* (Princeton, Industrial Relations Section, 1962), pp. 32-33; Haber and Murray, *op. cit.*, pp. 186-192.

[9] Olga Halsey, "Dependents' Allowances under State Unemployment Insurance Laws," *Social Security Bulletin*, Vol. 14, No. 2 (February, 1951), pp. 3-9; *Comparison of State Unemployment Insurance Laws*, Washington, D.C., U.S. Department of Labor, Bureau of Employment Security (January 1, 1962), pp. 66-71.

[10] Lester, *op. cit.*, pp. 8-24, 35-39.

ARGUMENTS AGAINST HIGHER BENEFITS

Those opposed to higher benefits point out that benefits have risen faster than the cost of living (see Table 15-3). Frank Cliffe, a vice-president of the H. J. Heinz Company, who represented the United States Chamber of Commerce in a Congressional hearing on Social Security, stated that by 1954 maximum benefits had about tripled over 1937, whereas the cost of living had not even doubled.[11] The cost of living argument has not been without its critics. Professor Richard Lester pointed out that the earlier period was one of less than full employment when industrial product and income were quite low. Benefits in such a period, according to Lester, should not be compared with the economy of today with its much larger production and income.[12]

The argument for raising maximums based on the failure of such maximums to keep pace with average earnings has met with several criticisms. The figures quoted for comparative purposes are average weekly wages of all workers. These tend to be higher than the average weekly wages of unemployment beneficiaries. Average weekly wages are used because statistics on wages of unemployment beneficiaries are difficult to obtain. The Bureau of Employment Security has assumed that the wages of the beneficiaries would be understated in about the same proportion over a period of years. If such is the case, then it would be permissible to substitute the average weekly earnings of all workers to compare with trends in maximum unemployment benefits. The National Industrial Conference Board has challenged the assumption of the uniform underestimation of beneficiaries' wages over a period of years. This board found that the wages of beneficiaries would be close to that of average weekly earnings of all workers after a downturn in business but not at the peak. The board also found that the relationship between beneficiaries' weekly wages and average weekly earnings of all workers varied considerably between states, and depended on such factors as occupation, industry, age, and sex composition of covered workers, the degree of seasonality of work, and the coverage qualifications of the various states.[13]

Several other criticisms of the use of average weekly earnings have been made. Income taxes are much higher today than they were during the beginnings of social security. The suggestion has therefore been made that maximum benefits be compared with wages after taxes rather than before taxes. On the other hand, it should be pointed out that workers today receive much larger fringe benefits than during the 1930's. The fringe benefits are

[11] Testimony of Frank Cliffe, Vice President of the H. J. Heinz Co., representing the U.S. Chamber of Commerce, "Unemployment Insurance," Hearings before the Committee on Ways and Means, House of Representatives, 83rd Congress, 2nd Session, on H.R. 6546, 6539, 7054, 8857, and 8585, p. 132.

[12] Testimony of Richard Lester, ibid., p. 231.

[13] Civic, op. cit., p. 311.

not included in the statistics on average weekly wages. It may well be, then, that the additional fringe benefits would tend to offset the additional income taxes they must pay. One final criticism of the use of average weekly earnings is that it includes overtime pay, which did not exist during the 1930's. Accordingly, the average weekly earnings show an upward bias. On the other hand, it could be pointed out that such overtime earnings are actually received, and that unemployment benefits should attempt to compensate for part of the actual wage loss, which would include rather than exclude overtime wages.

The duration of benefits has been extended and in 11 states dependents' allowances have been added. A nine-state study showed that when these factors were included, maximums rose from $180–$300 in the original laws to over $900 in 1954. These states accounted for one-fifth of all covered workers.[14] Some contend that benefits are now so high that the incentive to work is being impaired. For lower-paid workers drawing minimum benefits, benefits come close to matching wages, particularly if carfare and other incidental expenses are considered. On the other hand, certain fringe benefits are lost by not working, and these should be considered as income also. Furthermore, the higher the wage, the less the possibility that benefits will approach wages.

ADEQUACY OF BENEFITS—CONCLUSIONS

When all the arguments for and against benefit increases are analyzed, several conclusions may be arrived at. First, the fact that benefits are so low as to prevent payment of nondeferrable expenses would indicate that benefits need to be raised. Second, the fact that such large proportions of workers receive the maximum benefit, which is many instances is far below 50 percent of wages, would call for a raising of maximum benefits. A number of students of unemployment insurance have pointed out that flexible maximums based on average state wages would provide more adequate benefits than a flat dollar maximum. The use of 66⅔ of average state wages would provide a great majority of claimants with at least 50 percent of wages. Last, dependents' benefits are necessary in order to provide for the greater need of the unemployed who must support a family.

DURATION OF BENEFITS

Nine states have a maximum number of weeks' payment that apply to all eligible claimants. (See Table 15-4.) The remaining states not only have a maximum number of weeks' limitation, but also limit the duration according

[14] *Ibid.*, p. 309.

to the amount of wages earned or weeks employed. Twenty-eight states limit benefits to a fraction or percentage of base-period wages. The most frequent fraction used is one-third. That is, if a claimant had earned $300 in base-period wages, his maximum benefit would be $100. If his benefits amounted to $25 per week, then he would be eligible for unemployment benefits for only four weeks.

The question of how many weeks' compensation should be paid has been debated ever since the beginning of Social Security. For those who view unemployment insurance as a restricted system for the payment of limited benefits for short temporary layoffs, both the amount and duration of benefits should be severely limited. On the other hand, if unemployment insurance is viewed as the major program to provide the main source of sustenance for the worker until reemployed, larger benefits for a longer duration are advocated. When unemployment insurance first came into existence in the United States, public works projects were still in abundance, and were used as a major line of defense against unemployment. The elimination of such projects on a large scale has meant that the unemployment insurance program must bear more of the brunt of taking care of the unemployed.

LIMITATIONS ON DURATION BY PAST WAGES OR EMPLOYMENT

When limits on duration of benefits were first placed in the state laws, experts were convinced that avoidance of heavy drains on unemployment insurance necessitated tying duration of benefits to past wages or periods of employment. Such methods of limiting duration have tended to discriminate against the worker who has been employed only a short time or earned low wages. A number of studies showed that higher-paid workers who were entitled to more weeks of benefit payments than lower-paid workers tended to exhaust benefits less frequently than the lower-paid worker. From these studies, conclusions were drawn that those who needed unemployment insurance least (the highest-paid workers) were receiving the most protection. Conversely, tying duration of benefits to past wages or employment tended to reduce the number of weeks of benefit for those least able to finance periods of unemployment.[15]

Administrative simplicity would favor a uniform number of weeks' benefits for all workers. Also if it is assumed that most unemployment is due to shortcomings of our economic system rather than laziness of individuals, then the lower-skilled workers are being penalized for the shortcomings of our economic system. Furthermore, payments tied to past wages are not really necessary for actuarial soundness. Otherwise, life insurance benefits would have to be geared to the number of payments made. Actuarial sound-

[15] "Duration of Benefits Under Unemployment Insurance," Program Letter No. 175, Washington, D.C., Federal Security Agency, Bureau of Employment Security (1949), p. 13.

TABLE 15-4. DISTRIBUTION OF STATE MAXIMUM LENGTHS OF DURATION OF UNEMPLOYMENT INSURANCE, ON SPECIFIED DATES

Distribution in Weeks	Number of States								
	Dec. 1, 1937[a]	Aug. 1, 1941[a]	June 30, 1945	Sept. 1, 1949	Dec. 1, 1953	Oct. 1, 1957	Jan. 1, 1962[b]	Jan. 1, 1964[c]	Jan. 1, 1966[c]
12–14	12	9	2	1	0	0	0	0	0
15–17	33	29	14	5	4	1	0	0	0
18–20	4	12	23	23	18	13	1	0	0
21–23	0	0	6	5	2	3	2	1	1
24–26	0	0	5	17	27	33	39	40	41
27 and over	0	0	1	0	0	1	9	10	9
Total number of states	49[a]	50[a]	51	51	51	51	51	51	51

[a] In 1937, two states based maximum duration in terms of money rather than weeks; in 1941, one state did so.
[b] Seven states provided for a longer benefit when unemployment in the state reached a specified level.
[c] Eight states provided for a longer benefit when unemployment in the state reached a specified level.

Source: Comparison of State Unemployment Insurance Laws, U.S. Department of Labor, Bureau of Employment Security, various issues.

ness requires only that benefits paid to the whole group be at most equal to or less than the amounts collected in the system. Since adequate amounts have been collected over the years, including those states which provide for a uniform duration, there appears to be no necessary reason why duration of benefits should be tied to past wages or employment.[16] Sound administration should be able to overcome the objection that workers would abuse the system if duration of benefits were not tied to past earnings.

ADEQUACY OF DURATION

Several different conclusions on duration of benefits have been drawn. Some have reasoned that those drawing benefits for the longest periods are in need of help other than unemployment insurance, and thus they argue for a relatively short duration of unemployment benefits. They would place more emphasis on retraining programs and moving people from depressed areas to places where jobs are available. Long-term unemployment benefits may merely tie workers to a depressed area when they should be seeking work elsewhere. All the experts are in agreement that unemployment benefits should not be continued indefinitely, but if they are not, how long should benefits be paid? Twenty-six weeks is now paid by most states. Eveline Burns feels that a normal benefit duration of 40 weeks may be too long both because payments may be made to those who do not want year-round employment and because an effort should be made to train workers for a different type of work after they have been unemployed for so long a period of time.[17]

Even though it is agreed that unemployment benefits should not be paid indefinitely, a case can be made for extending benefits beyond 26 weeks, particularly in recession years. The recession of 1948–1949 lasted 11 months, that of 1953–1954, 13 months, the 1957–1958 recession 10 months, and the 1960–1961 downturn 10 months.

To combat the recession of 1958, the federal government passed the Temporary Unemployment Compensation Act of 1958 (TUC).[18] This program provided for 50 percent longer individual benefit payments. In Pennsylvania, for example, where workers were entitled to 30 weeks of compensation, the TUC program provided for 45 weeks of payment. The additional payments were financed through loans from the federal government. Seventeen states participated in the program, and borrowed $446 million. These states have been faced with the problem of obtaining sufficient payroll tax income to pay back the borrowed money. The problem has been particularly acute

[16] *Ibid.*, p. 11.

[17] Eveline Burns, "New Guidelines for Unemployment Insurance," *Employment Security Review*, Vol. 29, No. 8 (August, 1962), p. 8.

[18] The information in this section is drawn from Harry Malisoff, *The Financing of Extended Unemployment Insurance Benefits in the United States* (Kalamazoo, Upjohn Institute, 1963).

for Alaska, Michigan, and Pennsylvania. Several suggestions have been made either to forgive these states the costs, reduce them, or postpone payments. The Interstate Conference of Employment Security Agencies, however, has taken a strong stand against all such proposals. This group pointed out that the question of loans versus grants had been thoroughly debated before passage of the law, and that therefore the loans should not turn into grants.

Because of the difficulties with the TUC program, a different approach was tried with extended benefits in 1961 when the Temporary Extended Unemployment Compensation Act was passed (TEUC). Under this act, an additional 0.4 percent federal payroll tax was to be collected in 1963 and 1964. An amendment in 1963 reduced the additional tax to 0.25 percent. Receipts from the tax were paid into a separate account known as the "federal extended compensation account." Grants (rather than loans) were paid between April 7, 1961, and June 30, 1962. Benefits were provided for 50 percent additional weeks; however, no payments were to exceed 39 weeks. Under the TEUC program, benefits of almost $800 million were paid. Only six states withdrew more money from the fund than the tax rate accumulated. These were Alaska, California, Kentucky, Michigan, Ohio, and Pennsylvania. Some criticism arose from the states who were net contributors to the deficit states. Doubt was also expressed that employers should be assessed to pay the entire cost of the extended benefits. Further criticism was that the program should have gone into effect only when a recession occurred rather than attempting to meet the needs of structural unemployment in depressed areas or for long-time unemployed individuals.

Haber and Murray criticized the extended benefit program on several grounds.[19] They favored an additional 26-week extended benefit period rather than 13 weeks on the ground that 58 percent of the long-term unemployed exhausted benefits that were paid for only 39 weeks. They made a case for providing extended benefits as a regular part of the unemployment insurance system rather than only when a recession occurs. Here they cited data to show that claimants for regular benefits did not differ greatly from those obtaining extended benefits. The sex, age, industrial and occupational characteristics of regular and extended benefit claimants were quite similar. To finance extended benefit programs, they favored both the federal and state governments sharing the cost with the employers.

Several states of their own volition have passed laws since 1958 to provide for extended benefits if there is a recession.

PARTIAL UNEMPLOYMENT BENEFITS

When the Social Security Act was first passed and states began formulating their own laws, the states had to decide what to do about the problem of

[19] Haber and Murray, op. cit., Chapters 12 and 13.

partial unemployment. If a worker were totally unemployed, benefits would be paid. But what about the worker who worked one day each week and received only 20 percent of his regular pay? By not working at all, he could possibly draw as much as 50 percent of his wages in employment insurance. In order to give workers an incentive to work part time, all states now provide for some form of partial benefits.

Partial unemployment insurance can be especially justified whenever states adopt experience rating, as all the states have now done. Experience rating provides for a lowered unemployment insurance tax rate if few workers are laid off. Since reporting little unemployment does provide tax advantages, an employer might cut the hours of work of his employees rather than lay them off. The payment of partial benefits would tend to forestall excessive use of cutting of hours.

Most of the states (32) classify a worker as partially unemployed if he earns less in industry than he would draw in unemployment benefits. Eighteen other states favor the unemployed somewhat more by providing that compensation may be received if earnings are less than weekly benefits plus from $2 to $22.50. Most states provide that the partial benefit shall be the normal weekly benefit amount minus earnings, with certain amounts of earnings ranging from $2 to $25 disregarded in the deduction. To cite an example, if $10 in earnings are disregarded in computing partial benefits, a worker who normally would draw $25 in benefits, but who earned $20 by working a few days, would obtain $15 in unemployment benefits.

UNEMPLOYMENT INSURANCE TAXATION

Any tax might possibly have been chosen to finance unemployment insurance. We have already discussed why a payroll tax on both the employer and employees was chosen as the most appropriate tax to finance old-age pensions. Even though our system of unemployment insurance was created by the same act as our old-age pension plan, the Social Security Act of 1935, the tax programs to finance both systems were not identical. To finance unemployment benefits, a 3 percent tax (after the first several years) was placed on payrolls of employers only. A 1939 amendment provided that the 3 percent tax shall apply only to the first $3,000 of each employee's earnings. Eighteen states now provide for a higher taxable wage base.

In requiring that both employer and employee contribute to finance old-age pensions, it was felt that employee contributions would give workers the feeling that they were earning and thus deserving their pensions. On the other hand, it was concluded that unemployment was more the responsibility of the employer. In view of the fact that the unemployment insurance program was to take care of only a minimum amount of unemployment, it was felt that the employer could finance this part himself. Public works and other governmental aid would be used for longer periods of unemployment.

SHOULD EMPLOYEES BE TAXED?

Since the passage of the Social Security Act, some have advocated that the system of taxation be changed to include the taxing of employees also.[20] Nine states at one time or another have taxed employees in addition to employers, but today only three states tax both employees and employers. Alabama has a 0.25 to 0.50 percent tax on the first $3,000, Alaska has a 0.3 to 0.9 percent tax on annual wages up to $7,000, and New Jersey has a tax of 0.25 percent on annual wages up to $3,000. An Advisory Council on Social Security once recommended the taxing of employees on grounds that it would demonstrate more clearly the right of the worker to obtain unemployment benefits. It would also convey more of an impression that the program was an insurance program rather than relief or public assistance. In addition, most other countries provide for contributions by both employers and employees. It was felt also that worker participation would arouse more interest in the program among workers. Lastly, since part of the tax on employers is shifted to consumers in the form of higher prices or back to workers in smaller pay increases, the tax on employees would simply give more recognition to the fact that the workers do pay for the unemployment insurance program. A recent analysis by Richard Lester, however, challenges the viewpoint that most of the employer's payroll tax is shifted. He points out that the differential tax rate in states makes it difficult for some employers to pass on the tax to consumers. The same reasoning applies for the differential rates within states. For these and other reasons, Lester estimates that perhaps no more than a third of the unemployment compensation tax burden is shifted to consumers in the form of higher prices.[21]

In opposing a payroll tax on employees, spokesmen for laboring groups point out that the present taxes are already high enough to pay for the program, and that the workers should not be burdened with another direct and regressive tax. This group would rather have the government bear part of the costs of the program out of general revenue, as is done in Great Britain and elsewhere. More reliance would thus be placed on the personal and corporate income taxes, which are more progressive than payroll taxes. Eveline Burns once pointed out that relatively little attention has been given to using more progressive taxes, but she suggested that if the unemployment insurance program is expanded to bear most of the brunt of unemployment more attention might possibly be paid to it.[22]

[20] "Unemployment Insurance—A Report to the Senate Committee on Finance," Senate Document No. 206, Washington, D.C., 80th Congress, 2nd Session, Advisory Council on Social Security (1948), pp. 27-29.

[21] Lester, *The Economics of Unemployment Compensation*, pp. 60-67.

[22] Eveline M. Burns, *The American Social Security System* (Boston, Houghton Mifflin, 1949), p. 155.

ADEQUACY OF THE PAYROLL TAX

When the Social Security Act was passed, so little experience with unemployment insurance had been accumulated that it was not known exactly how high a tax should be levied. In view of the fact that many millions were unemployed during the 1930's, a relatively high tax of 2.7 percent on payrolls plus 0.3 percent for administration was assessed. In order to build the fund, it was also provided that collections should be made for two years before any payments were made. Experience over the years has shown that even with increased benefits and duration of payments, many states did not need a tax of 2.7 percent. Table 15-5 shows the income and disbursements for the unemployment insurance program since its inception. The table shows that beginning in 1940, the balance in the fund began to grow by leaps and bounds. Payrolls increased to enlarge contributions while at the same time unemployment was being cut to such low levels that benefits were dropping. By 1945, the surplus had reached over $7 billion. Since that time it rose slowly until it reached $9.6 billion in 1953. The recessions of 1954, 1958, and 1960 caused decreases in the fund, but increasing prosperity since then has improved the balance.

TABLE 15–5. THE UNEMPLOYMENT INSURANCE TRUST FUND
(IN MILLIONS)

Year[a]	Receipts	Interest Earned in Fund	Expenditures	Total Assets at End of Year
1937	$ 567	$ 8	$ 2	$ 638
1940	861	59	615	1,958
1945	1,161	118	462	7,537
1950	1,190	146	1,342	7,721
1955	1,215	185	1,352	8,764
1960	2,300	195	2,748	6,653
1965	2,973	266	2,165	8,568

[a] Beginning with 1950, data are not comparable with those for earlier years because of a change in the Treasury source used.
Source: Social Security Bulletin, Annual Statistical Supplement, 1964, Table 12, pp. 10-11.

The adequacy of unemployment insurance reserves varies state by state. Congress has permitted the states to vary their tax rate by experience rating. Under this system, an employer with a record of stable employment may qualify for lower tax rates. In 1938 only one state was experimenting with such a system and by 1940 only four varied the payroll tax according to employment experience. However, the failure of Congress to permit a lowering of the tax rate except through experience rating caused state after state to adopt the system in order to keep reserves from growing too large. In 1941, 17 had adopted experience rating, and this number grew to 34 in 1942 and 45 in 1945. Finally by 1948, all the states had inaugurated experience rating into their laws. Puerto Rico does not have experience rating in its law; Alaska repealed its experience rating in 1955, but reinstituted it in 1960.

Some of the states have cut their payroll taxes quite low and so threatened the safety of their unemployment insurance system. Several other states have had a high incidence of unemployment in depressed industries and have been unable to accumulate adequate reserves even though their tax rate is 2.7 percent or higher. In the recession of 1958, Alaska, Michigan, and Pennsylvania had such heavy expenditures that they had to receive federal money to stabilize their dwindling reserves. Serious criticism has been raised against the financial methods used by some of the states. Professor Orme Phelps has gone so far as to contend that the tax and benefit formulas have been formulated in such a haphazard manner that only a pretense of an insurance system remains.[23] Others have also pointed out the poor coordination between taxes and costs.[24] To cite an example, both Iowa and Massachusetts from 1946 to 1950 were using the same tax rate of 1.3 percent. Yet Iowa had the highest reserves of any of the states, and was paying out relatively small benefits. Massachusetts, on the other hand, had the lowest reserves of any of the states at the end of 1950, and was faced with high costs due to the large amount of unemployment in the state. An analysis of other states shows the same lack of balance between taxes, benefits, and reserve. To determine the safety of a state reserve, the Bureau of Employment Security uses a criterion of 1½ times the highest 12-month benefit cost rate during the preceding ten years. On this basis the reserves of 20 states were inadequate in 1964.[25]

EXPERIENCE RATING

When unemployment insurance was first inaugurated in the United States, a majority of states had what might be called a "pooled" fund. That is, all the funds collected from each employer went into a common or pooled fund, and benefits were paid from this fund. Seven states, on the other hand, followed the system first introduced in Wisconsin of having individual reserve funds. Instead of the tax money flowing into a pooled fund, the amounts collected from each employer were duly recorded and credited to the account

[23] Orme W. Phelps, *Introduction to Labor Economics* (New York, McGraw-Hill, 1950), p. 175.
[24] E. J. Eberling, "Financial Policy in a Period of Low Unemployment Insurance Disbursements," *Employment Security Review*, Vol. 18, No. 12 (December, 1951), p. 7.
[25] Haber and Murray, *op. cit.*, p. 323.

of each employer. When a benefit was paid, the amount then was deducted from the reserve of the employer who laid off the worker. Professor John R. Commons of the University of Wisconsin was a leading advocate of the individual reserve fund. Prior to formulating plans for unemployment insurance, he had worked with problems of workmen's compensation. In this field he was quite impressed with the fact that possible reductions in rates greatly influenced employers to install safety programs and reduce the number of accidents. He then concluded that if each employer were held accountable and had to pay higher taxes for each employee that he laid off, unemployment might be considerably reduced. He therefore advocated the individual reserve fund in preference to the pooled fund. Unfortunately, however, the individual reserve fund has the fundamental weakness that when unemployment strikes, the individual employer may not have accumulated sufficient reserves to pay adequate benefits. Pooling all the money into one state fund, and spreading the risks among all employers, enables the fund to be more adequate. Consequently, over the years all of the states that began with the individual reserve fund, including Wisconsin, have changed over to the pooled fund.

Even though the pooled fund has become the predominant method of handling funds, the states have attempted to exert some influence on employers to stabilize and regularize employment by offering them the possibility of a reduced tax if few employees are laid off. The Social Security Act permits a reduction in the 2.7 percent tax for one reason only—a good record of maintaining employment. A record is kept on each employer, and if it is found that he has stabilized employment, his tax rate may be cut below 2.7 percent. The system of reducing taxes is known as experience rating, for the reduction is contingent on the employment experience of individual employers. As was stated above, all the states now use one type or another of experience rating.

RESERVE-RATIO SYSTEM

Four major types of experience rating have been developed in the United States, and each type is used by three or more states. The purpose of each type is to stimulate the employer to regularize his employment so that a tax reduction may be obtained. The earliest and most popular system, the reserve-ratio system, is now used by 32 states. Under this system, a record is kept of all the money paid into the unemployment insurance fund from each employer. A reserve is then computed for each employer by subtracting benefits paid from the contributions made. The reserve is then computed as a percentage of taxable wages in order that the ratio will be a meaningful one. A $100,000 reserve may appear quite large to an employer who has only $10,000 in taxable wages each year, but it would be much smaller for a firm having a payroll of four million dollars. To cite an example from the Michigan law, if an employer had contributed $40,000 to the unemployment insurance fund, and had paid out $6,000 in benefits, his reserve would be $34,000. If his annual payroll was $340,000, his reserve ratio would be 10 percent. The Michigan law provides that those having a 10 percent reserve ratio will pay a 0.7 percent tax. If the reserve ratio had been 12.6 percent or higher, then the lowest rate of 0.1 percent would be assessed. On the other hand, if the reserve ratio was less than 4.2 percent, the maximum rate of 2.8 percent would be paid. Other higher taxes are assessed if the fund is in a weak position.

Several criticisms have been leveled at the reserve-ratio system. For one thing, the actual number of weeks of unemployment benefits drawn is not subject to control by the employer, yet it is a vital factor in computing his tax. If an employer happens to be located in a small town with few opportunities for employment, his employees may draw benefits for the maximum number of weeks. Thus the benefits paid out will be large, and the reserve of the employer low. On the other hand, an employer in a large metropolitan area may experience the happy result of having his employees find jobs elsewhere almost immediately. There will be little drain on his reserve, and thus he will qualify for a lower tax rate. The rural employer might have attempted to regularize employment on a much broader scale than the metropolitan employer; yet he will pay a higher unemployment insurance tax.[26] Another criticism of the reserve-ratio plan is that when payrolls are reduced, the tax rate automatically drops.[27] Since the ratio is that of reserves to payrolls, the lower the payroll becomes, the higher the ratio, and the higher the ratio the lower the tax. Some states use different systems of experience rating, but all of these have weaknesses also.

EXPERIENCE RATING—EVALUATION

Proponents of experience rating have advanced two main arguments in favor of it. First of all it provides a stimulus to regularize employment. If such regularization is accomplished, then the employer is rewarded by a lower unemployment tax rate. Second, such differential taxation has the alleged advantage of allocating costs where they belong. If unstable employers are the cause of the heavy unemployment benefit costs, then they or the consumers of their products should pay for the higher costs of doing business.

In studies made of the effect of experience rating on regularizing employment, it has been found that experience rating has stimulated only a minimum number of firms to regularize employment, and once the methods of regularization had been adopted, they would be continued even though

[26] Almon R. Arnold, "Experience Rating," *Yale Law Review*, Vol. 55 (1945–1946), p. 232.

[27] Harry Weiss, "Unemployment Prevention Through Unemployment Compensation," *Political Science Quarterly*, Vol. 58 (1938), p. 18.

experience ratings were abolished. A study by Charles A. Myers of 247 firms in Wisconsin showed that 11 percent of the firms had accomplished an appreciable amount of employment regularization, 15 percent some regularization, 35 percent only negligible results, and 39 percent no regularization at all.[28] Another criticism of experience rating is that some industries are naturally more stable than others, and that employers in these industries automatically receive a lower tax rate even though they have done little or nothing to regularize employment. Furthermore, most unemployment is due to cyclical or secular changes over which the employer has little control. Also the tax rate will depend on such fortuitous circumstances as whether the employee finds a job quickly or not (under three of the four main systems of experience rating) and upon whether payrolls are increasing or decreasing.

Another criticism of experience rating is that it tends to lower taxes in good times and raise them in periods of depression. The proper fiscal policy would be to lower taxes in periods of recession and raise them in periods of prosperity. Experience rating does just the opposite. One of the major criticisms against experience rating has been that it has been abused by a number of states. These states have simply used the device to lower taxes. In the ten states taxing employers the least, the scale of benefits is quite low. Only three of the ten pay above average benefits. Had the other seven states not cut taxes so low, they would have been able to pay more adequate benefits. Furthermore, the number of states that permit a reduction of the tax rate to zero has been growing. For those employers who can qualify, 16 states (January 1, 1966) permit an employer to pay no taxes at all, and only 13 states set the minimum rate of taxation at 0.5 percent or higher. Such taxation has placed states in competition with one another to lower taxes. Certainly this type of competition was not intended by the authors of the original Social Security Act.[29]

Another criticism of experience rating is that it has resulted in much less income being collected than otherwise would have been available for unemployment compensation. Income from state and federal employment taxes increased from only $0.9 billion in 1938 to $2.6 billion in 1960. During the same period OASDHI taxes increased from $0.5 billion to $11.9 billion. All federal, state, and local taxes increased from $14.8 billion to $131.5 billion during the same period. The employer tax rate as a percentage of taxable wages for unemployment insurance decreased from 2.75 percent to 1.9 percent during the same period, and the limitation of taxing only the first $3,000 reduced the employer state tax as a percentage of total wages from 2.69 percent to 1.18 percent.[30] Lastly, the argument that the unstable indus-

---

[28] Charles A. Myers, "Employment Stabilization and the Wisconsin Act," *American Economic Review*, Vol. 29 (1939), pp. 708-723, and "Experience Rating in Unemployment Compensation," *American Economic Review*, Vol. 35 (1945), p. 353.

[29] Ruth Reticker, "The Financing of Unemployment Insurance," *Monthly Labor Review*, Vol. 70 (1950), p. 261.

[30] Lester, *The Economics of Unemployment Compensation*, Table 7, p. 58.

tries should pay for their own high unemployment is rebutted by the argument that such industries may create and support the more stable service and trades industries in an area. Furthermore, if certain unstable industries are necessary in our economy, then workers who remain and are needed in these industries should not be penalized via lower wages because of the higher taxes. If it is assumed that the incidence of taxation is on the consumer who must pay higher prices, there is more justification for the higher taxation than if the tax is shifted back on the workers.[31]

Criticisms of experience rating have called forth a number of proposed solutions. Some would eliminate experience rating entirely, and impose a standard federal rate applicable to all industries within all states. Others would merely impose a federal minimum below which none of the states could cut. Even though it is fairly well agreed that experience rating is unable to eradicate the major causes of unemployment—cyclical and secular fluctuations—some wish to keep experience rating in order to provide employers with an incentive to regularize seasonal and minor fluctuations in employment. At the very least, the abuse of experience rating should be eliminated.

RAISING THE TAX BASE

An argument has ensued in the program as to whether it would be best to obtain more revenue by raising the tax base or raising the rates. When the $3,000 limit originated in 1939, this figure included 98 percent of the total wages paid in covered employment. By 1963 the figure had dropped to 58 percent. Professor Lester has cited a number of reasons in support of raising the tax base rather than raising tax rates.[32] First, failure to raise the tax base results in a lower percentage of wages being taxed in good times than during recessions. Second, a tax on the first $3,000 results in a highly seasonal tax during the first part of the year. Third, the financial soundness of the program is weakened when maximum benefits are raised without providing additional tax revenue. In 1961, 15 states had a maximum benefit of $45 or more per week. Assuming that 50 percent of wages should be paid in benefits, the recipient's earnings would have to be $4,680 to qualify for the maximum; yet the tax base is only $3,000. Clearly the maintenance of the $3,000 tax base both undermines the financial soundness of the program and keeps benefits low. In addition, the $3,000 tax base places a relatively larger tax burden on low wage, highly competitive industries than higher wage industries. In Mississippi, where low wage industries exist, 76 percent of all wages are taxed for unemployment insurance, whereas in Michigan, which has higher-paid industries, only 56 percent of total wages are taxed. In view of these

---

[31] Myers, "Experience Rating," p. 349.
[32] Lester, *The Economics of Unemployment Compensation*, pp. 72-83.

arguments it would appear that raising the tax base would be one of the most equitable means of raising additional revenue. Eighteen states already have raised the rate above the federal $3,000 base.

Summary

In almost all countries higher unemployment benefits are granted to higher-paid employees. Basing benefits on past wages does result in the inconvenience of collecting past wage data, but most countries feel that benefits should not be uniform for all workers. In the United States minimum weekly benefits vary from $3 to $25, and maximum benefits vary from $20 to $75. Although benefits have been raised over the years even faster than the cost of living, they have not kept pace with average wages. Arguments for higher benefits have stressed the needs of beneficiaries and the inadequacy of dependents' allowances. Those opposed to increasing benefits fear that too high benefits may curtail the incentive of the unemployed to find regular jobs. The duration of benefits has been extended over the years primarily because public works projects are no longer available as a second line of relief. At the present writing most states provide for 26 weeks of benefits as the maximum. The federal government temporarily extended the period to 39 weeks, but in 1962 this part of the program was discontinued.

Unemployment insurance in the United States is financed by a payroll tax on employers. The tax has proved adequate to finance unemployment benefits of small amounts in most states, but the reserves of some of the states are so low as to invite worry. The states have been permitted to lower the original 2.7 percent federal tax by experience rating. The purpose of experience rating was to encourage employers to stabilize employment. Although experience rating may help stabilize employment for a year or two, thereafter employers recognize the advantage of stabilization even without a tax advantage. Experience rating has been abused by a number of states, which have reduced the tax rate so low as to preclude adequate benefits. Because of this abuse, some have advocated a completely federal unemployment insurance system. Others have suggested that the federal government at least impose a minimum tax rate on all employers. As an alternative to raising rates it would be possible to raise the tax base from $3,000 to some higher figure.

PRIVATE METHODS OF
ALLEVIATING UNEMPLOYMENT

THE GUARANTEED ANNUAL WAGE

As the name implies, guaranteed annual wage plans attempt to guarantee the wage of the worker for one year. Such plans could be used as an alternate system to unemployment insurance. Perhaps little unemployment insurance would be needed if workers were guaranteed a wage at least for one year. Guaranteed wages have been motivated by the quest for more security. If salaried employees and some farm employees are guaranteed wages the year around, some wage earners feel that they should obtain similar guarantees. One of the first plans was put into operation in 1894 in the wallpaper industry. A newly formed amalgamation of wallpaper producers controlled from 50 to 75 percent of the business in the industry. In 1894, as a result of economies effected by the amalgamation, the plants were closed down for a longer period than usual. Before the members of the National Association of Machine Printers and Color Mixers labor union would agree to a new contract, they demanded and won a guarantee of 11 months' employment. In 1896, the guarantee was extended to 12 months. The plan was continued in existence until 1930, when a dispute over administration of the plan, the Depression, and the rise of substitute materials all helped to cause its abandonment.[1]

The most comprehensive study of guaranteed annual wage plans was made by the Bureau of Labor Statistics from 1944 to 1947. Ninety thousand employers were contacted to determine the extent to which guarantee plans had been adopted in the United States. In their sample the bureau found that 347 plans had been instituted from before 1900 through 1945. Only three were started prior to 1900, and only 55 had been begun before 1934.[2] Three of the largest companies initiating successful plans were the Procter & Gamble Company (started in 1923), the Geo. A. Hormel and Co., meat-packers (begun in 1931), and the Nunn-Bush Shoe Company, which put its

---

[1] "Guaranteed Wage or Employment Plans," Bulletin No. 906, Washington, D.C., U.S. Department of Labor, Bureau of Labor Statistics (1947), pp. 4-6.

[2] *Ibid.*, pp. 1-5.

plan into operation in 1935. The plans of these three companies will be described briefly.[3]

PROCTER & GAMBLE PLAN

The Procter & Gamble Guarantee of Regular Employment plan originated in 1923 with William Cooper Procter, whose grandfather had started the business may years before. William Cooper Procter is also credited with introducing a half-day off on Saturday in 1886 even before he became the chief officer of the company. Other enlightened policies followed, such as profit-sharing, old-age pensions, and death and disability allowances. Mr. Procter's attitude toward employees was one of kindness tempered with firmness. One of the major reasons for instituting the guarantee was his concern for the unemployed worker who wanted and needed to work.

Procter & Gamble produces such well-known items as Ivory Soap and Crisco, along with other household products. While the purchase of such products by consumers was fairly regular, the sales of the company fluctuated widely and made for irregularity of employment. The fluctuations were caused by speculative buying of soaps and shortenings by wholesalers. This alternately slowed or speeded production and resulted in peaks and valleys in factory output.

Since final consumption of the products was relatively stable over the year, Mr. Procter sought to stabilize product sales. He instituted in 1920 a practice of selling products directly to retailers. New district sales offices were created by P & G, and these offices made estimates of yearly sales in advance. Then a production schedule was developed by the P & G manufacturing department. By 1923 the attempt to regularize sales was so successful that Mr. Procter could put the Guarantee of Regular Employment in effect. It provided a guarantee of at least 48 weeks of employment in each calendar year for eligible employees. During 1933 the company reduced the work week to 75 percent of the established amount at three factories because of the Depression. However, by the end of that year the situation had righted itself and all employees had worked their full 48 weeks or its time equivalent.

Successive revisions of the plan have increased the length-of-service eligibility requirement from one-half to two years of continuous service, and limited the guarantee to hourly-rated employees. These employees are the ones primarily affected by ups and downs in business conditions. It appears that these changes, most of which were made in 1932, 1933, and 1936, were due mainly to the depressed and uncertain business conditions existing during the thirties. The guarantee has remained much the same since then,

---

[3] Jack Chernick and George Hellickson, *Guaranteed Annual Wages* (Minneapolis, Minn., University of Minnesota Press, 1945). See also: *The Guaranteed Annual Wage* (Washington, D.C., Bureau of National Affairs, 1955).

except that employees of several plants who entered the plan on a 32-hours-a-week basis later were raised to a 40-hours-a-week basis.

The Guarantee of Regular Employment Plan was proposed and inaugurated by the company when no labor unions existed at Procter & Gamble. Although at the present time labor unions bargain with Procter & Gamble, the guarantee has not been subject to collective negotiations. The company may transfer workers to lower-paid jobs on the grounds that it is employment rather than wages that are guaranteed. Workers may also be discharged at any time, and the entire plan may be cancelled upon due notice by the company. The company has never set aside special funds to finance the plan, and it maintains that even during the poorest business years the plan did not cost more than 3 percent of its payroll.

GEO. A. HORMEL AND CO. PLAN

Although Geo. A. Hormel and Co. is not one of the largest "Big Four" meat packers, it is one of the largest family-operated organizations in the meat-packing business. When the plan was put into effect, Jay Hormel, the son of George Hormel, was managing its operations. In 1929, he was accosted by one of his laid-off employees, who informed Hormel that horses were treated better than men, that at least they were not turned out on the street by the company. This statement started Jay Hormel to thinking. A few years later (1931) a guaranteed wage plan was inaugurated in several departments on an experimental basis. Although Mr. Hormel talked to the employees about the plan and tried to enlist their support, they remained cool to the whole idea. In 1933 they organized an independent union, later affiliated with Packinghouse Workers (AFL–CIO). One of their demands they attempted to enforce by a strike was that the guaranteed annual wage be dropped, for fear that it would cause a speed-up. Later, however, when the union had to deal with layoff of workers, it suggested that the guaranteed annual wage be reconsidered. Mr. Hormel has felt that a union is indispensable to such a plan in order that the workers can more adequately express themselves about the various problems involved. Mr. Hormel contended that the hourly wage must have been started by some employer who was trying to chisel an advantage from workers. He added that even if this were not true, the hourly wage system makes the worker carry the burden of declines in business.

The Hormel Company was faced with receiving an uneven supply of livestock during different periods of the year. In some months more than two and a half times the number of livestock were received than at other times. Under such circumstances employment by the month was quite irregular, although on an annual basis it was much more stable. Under the Hormel guaranteed annual wage, 52 weekly paychecks are guaranteed each year at the employee's hourly rate times the number of hours in the standard work week. The Hormel plan is one of the few that takes advantage of a Fair Labor Standards Act provision that waives overtime pay up to 56 hours per week if an annual wage guarantee is given. In actual practice the company and union have agreed to pay for overtime in excess of 53 hours. Either side may terminate the guarantee upon 90 days' notice. In addition to the guarantee, workers may participate in both a profit-sharing and incentive wage plan.

Most students consider that the Hormel plan has been quite successful. One estimate showed that Hormel's workers were 50 percent more productive than others in the meat-packing industry. Cost of the plan from 1939 to 1945 was estimated at about 3 percent of payrolls. In the recession of 1954, the company had to pay out $650,000 for 400,000 hours of unworked time, or 1.5 percent of total wages. However, Hormel has benefited from higher productivity, from lower unemployment insurance taxes, and from the savings in not having to pay time and a half for overtime. Roughly $350,000 was saved on lowered unemployment insurance taxes alone in 1954.

NUNN-BUSH SHOE COMPANY

The Nunn-Bush Shoe Company adopted its annual wage plan in 1935 as a result of the Depression. In 1932 the company's shoe sales fell off 30 percent, and 20 percent of the regular work force were laid off. The company was unable to cut prices because of inflexible wage rates. A plan was then evolved with employee participation to tie wage payments to the price of shoes. Employees were rewarded for possible cuts in wages by guaranteeing them 52 paychecks per year. At first a certain percentage of the wholesale value of the company's products went into wage payments. Later the system was changed to provide that 36 percent of the value added to raw material costs would be set aside for payments to labor. The new system proved more accurate because raw material costs fluctuated and labor's participation was wholly in connection with added values. Conservative estimates are now made on the amounts to be paid in weekly earnings. Any surplus that accrues from the money allocated from the 36 percent of the value added is placed into a reserve fund. At the end of each 30-day period, the money from the surplus fund is paid to the workers over and above any reserve which the employees decide to maintain. If the reserve should become depleted during the course of a year, the weekly draw of the workers is cut.

The plan is jointly administered by both management and an independent labor union. Workers are divided into three classes. Only class A employees participate in the 52-paycheck guarantee and the flexible wage plan. Class B employees do not have a 52-paycheck guarantee but do participate in the flexible wage plan. Class C employees, those with fewer than two years of service, operate under neither the guarantee nor the flexible wage plan. At the end of 1954, class A and B employees comprised 70 percent of all the workers. No one in these groups has ever been laid off, so that the class B employees have experienced regular employment even though not under the 52-paycheck guarantee.

As to the effectiveness of the plan, demand has not been more stable in this shoe company, but management has made a conscious effort to stabilize production, and has succeeded to an appreciable extent. Thus employment has been appreciably stabilized also. Statistics from 1950 to 1953 show that Nunn-Bush employees have been enlarging the spread between their earnings and that of the leather and leather products industry in general. As of February, 1963, the Nunn-Bush company has issued 1,440 consecutive weekly paychecks without missing a payment to workers.[4]

SUPPORT FOR GAW PLANS

Guaranteed annual wage plans before the 1930's were fostered and supported mainly by businessmen.[5] Then during the 1930's government attempted to encourage such plans by providing for tax exemption or reduction from the unemployment insurance tax. In Wisconsin, a complete exemption from unemployment taxation was provided under state law. Ninety-six of the 347 plans studied by the Bureau of Labor Statistics were Wisconsin firms who introduced plans to obtain tax benefits. When the federal Social Security Act was passed, Wisconsin elected to be covered by it, and so the tax exemption was lost. Although the federal Social Security Act did provide tax reduction for those guaranteeing employment, no firms took advantage of this provision. All 96 Wisconsin firms abandoned their plans at this time.

Federal government encouragement of guaranteed plans has been more successful under the Fair Labor Standards Act. The 1938 provisions of this act stated that firms that guaranteed 2,000 hours of employment per year, no more nor less, were permitted to hire workers for 12 hours a day or 56 per week without paying overtime rates. Some of the rigidity of the exemption was removed in the 1949 amendments of the act, which permitted the overtime exemption for as little as 46 weeks a year and 30 hours per week. Firms can employ workers for as many as 2,240 hours per year although all employment over 2,180 hours must be paid at one and a half times the regular rate of pay. A few firms have taken advantage of waiving overtime pay by guaranteeing wages.

The main impetus in favor of such plans since 1940 has come from labor unions. Philip Murray, Walter Reuther, and others from the Congress of Industrial Organizations have come out strongly for such plans. Reuther, for example, stated at the 1953 convention of the Congress of Industrial Organi-

---

[4] Letter from Walter Fanning, Vice President, Nunn-Bush Shoe Company (February 19, 1963).

[5] For a brief history of guaranteed annual wage plans, see Don Seastone, "The History of Guaranteed Wages and Employment," *Journal of Economic History,* Vol. 15 (1955), pp. 134-150.

zations that the labor union movement would mobilize its resources in a major effort to obtain the guaranteed annual wage for workers.[6] Although the United Automobile Workers, United Steel Workers, the International Union of Electrical Workers—the "Big Three" of the Congress of Industrial Organizations—and other unions proposed plans to be worked out by collective bargaining, few such plans were sold to management. A sample study by the Bureau of Labor Statistics in 1952 found only 20 plans which guaranteed wages or employment for a substantial part of the year. Beginning in 1952 through 1955, local 688 of the Teamsters Union was able to negotiate such plans with 75 firms in the St. Louis area. The Packinghouse Workers and east-coast Longshoremen have also signed several annual wage contracts. However, as of March, 1955, only about 15,000 to 18,000 workers were covered by guaranteed annual wage plans.[7] A later Bureau of Labor Statistics study of 1,773 labor contracts under which about 7½ million workers were covered in 1962–1963 found that 139 contracts covering about 600,000 workers guaranteed employment or wages for at least a week to some or all the workers. Of these contracts, only six provided for the annual guarantee.[8]

Partisan supporters of the guaranteed annual wage picture substantial advantages arising from such plans. For one thing, the security of the worker is greatly strengthened. No longer do workers have to worry as much about being laid off, for they now have a 52-week guarantee of either wages or employment. Consumption expenditures of groups assured a stable income should be expected to increase, and this trend has been verified statistically at Austin, Minnesota, the headquarters of the Hormel Packing Co. From 1932 to 1940, the time deposits of the two banks in Austin dropped from almost $2½ million to $2 million even though population increased 50 percent and average weekly earnings increased by the same percentage. However, some increase in building and loan savings and savings in the Hormel Company credit union was noted.[9]

A major advantage of annual-wage schemes is that they tend to regularize seasonal unemployment. An American Legion study of 12 firms that adopted the annual wage showed that prior to the plan, 58 percent of their workers were fully employed, compared with 91 percent after the plan had been adopted.[10] Lessened turnover of workers, higher morale, and steadier production all should make for lowered costs for companies.[11] Although such

[6] "Guaranteed Annual Wages," *Economic Outlook*, Vol. 14, No. 10 (October, 1953), p. 75.

[7] *The Guaranteed Annual Wage*, p. 8.

[8] *Major Collective Bargaining Agreements: Supplemental Unemployment Benefit Plans and Wage-Employment Guarantees*, Bulletin No. 1425-3, Washington, D.C., U.S. Department of Labor, Bureau of Labor Statistics (1965), p. 2.

[9] Chernick and Hellickson, *op. cit.*, p. 122.

[10] *Ibid.*, p. 106.

[11] "Guaranteed Employment in 1955," *Economic Outlook*, Vol. 16, No. 4 (April, 1955), p. 29.

plans would not be a cure-all for the business cycle, they might contribute toward cyclical stability by collecting funds to pay for the guarantee during prosperity and then help to maintain consumption by paying out such funds during the recession.

WEAKNESSES OF THE GAW

Critics of the guaranteed annual wage have vigorously protested against such plans. The redistribution of income to potentially unemployed workers obviously must be paid by someone, and the critics fear that the increased costs to the businessman will deter investment. One of the more detailed estimates of costs of a plan was presented by Murray Latimer in the Steelworkers brief in 1952 before the Wage Stabilization Board.[12] On the assumption that unemployment would not be heavy in the steel industry because of large defense orders and a sizable civilian demand for steel products, Latimer estimated that gross costs would be 8.4 cents per hour.[13] Payment of part of this cost would be paid through the already existent unemployment insurance system. Subtracting this cost, the net cost would be 6.5 cents an hour. The guarantee would have gone only to those with three or more years' seniority with the company, and the guarantee would be for 30 hours for 52 weeks. Costs were figured if the guarantee were for either 20, 30, or 32 hours per week. For 30 hours, the gross cost was 8.4 cents per hour or 6.5 per hour net. Of course, costs would be substantially higher if heavy unemployment occurred or if all workers were covered 40 hours a week for the 52 weeks.

Professor Wayne Leeman feels that the adding of such costs to the employer and forcing employers to carry the added risks of possible unemployment would seriously deter business investment. Less investment will be undertaken, because any expansion of plant and work force would call for additional wage guarantees.[14] Wages change from variable to fixed costs, and this adds to the employer's risks, because fixed costs cannot be cut when business drops off. Some other authors concur on the deleterious effects on investment. A. D. H. Kaplan, for example, doubts whether the Ford Company could have shut down to change from the Model T to new models in 1927 had it been forced to pay wages to the workers while unemployed.[15]

Management's extreme reluctance to make guarantees of a nature that may possibly bankrupt companies, especially during a serious depression, has caused labor unions to formulate guaranteed plans with limited liability. As

[12] Don Seastone, "The Status of Guaranteed Wages and Employment in Collective Bargaining," American Economic Review, Vol. 44 (1954), pp. 911-913.

[13] "Guaranteed Wages and Unemployment Insurance," Business Record, Vol. 11 (1954), p. 26.

[14] Wayne Leeman, "The Guaranteed Annual Wage, Employment, and Economic Progress," Industrial and Labor Relations Review, Vol. 8 (1955), pp. 565-571.

[15] A. D. H. Kaplan, The Guarantee of Annual Wages (Washington, D.C., Brookings Institution, 1947), p. 185 n.

has been pointed out, the 1953 Steelworkers plan not only limited the number of workers covered (those with three years or more seniority), but also limited the number of hours guaranteed from 28 to 32 per week. The Steelworkers went one step further, and agreed that whenever the fund was exhausted, the companies would not be required to continue the guarantee. The company guarantee was to be limited to the cents-per-hour figure set aside to pay the 28–32-hour guarantee. Labor groups and others thought that by limiting the liability, corporations would be much more receptive to the guarantee plans. However, few corporations agreed to introduce the plans even with the limited liability.

Frank Cassell, manager of Industrial Relations for the Inland Steel Company, pointed out that once the fund money was exhausted, labor would clamor for the companies to continue paying the guarantee. He cited the case of the United Mine Workers, who originally negotiated a 5 cents per ton welfare fund for coal miners in 1946 and then because of the inadequacy of the fund kept renegotiating until by 1954 the charges were 40 cents per ton in bituminous and 50 cents per ton in anthracite.[16]

Emerson Schmidt, economist for the United States Chamber of Commerce, and others also contend that the limited liability is only a snare to employers, and that they would be under extreme pressure to make good the guarantee.[17] However, it is true that the guarantee plans in existence during the great depression of the 1930's did manage to continue without the pressure to hold fast to the 100 percent guarantee. For example, seven substantial revisions downward in the guarantee were made by Procter & Gamble in 1932–1933. Other plans were modified in a similar manner.[18] On the other hand, management spokesmen are correct in maintaining that only if the 52 weeks guarantee is to be maintained should the plans be called "guaranteed annual" wages.[19] The proposed Steelworkers plan for 30 hours guarantee for 52 weeks really only guarantees 75 percent of pay, and perhaps not even that much if the fund becomes exhausted. With such limitations of liability, the guaranteed plans are more similar to supplemental unemployment benefit plans than they are to 100 percent guaranteed wages.

Another criticism of the guaranteed annual wage is that it will tend to keep workers from attempting to find jobs elsewhere. This may be true even though the plan requires that the employees enroll at the government employment office for work. For example, the federal unemployment insurance program for World War II veterans called for payments of $20 per week for

[16] Frank H. Cassell, "Where Do We Stand with the Guaranteed Annual Wage?" *Personnel,* Vol. 30, No. 5 (March, 1954), p. 351.

[17] Emerson Schmidt, "The Guaranteed Wage—Super Unemployment Compensation," *American Economic Security,* Vol. 12 (1955), p. 14.

[18] S. Herbert Unterberger, "How the New Guaranteed Annual Wage Proposals Meet Employer Objections," *Labor Law Journal,* Vol. 6, No. 5 (May, 1955), p. 315.

[19] Thomas F. Johnson and Leonard J. Calhoun, "The Guaranteed Annual Wage in Collective Bargaining," *American Economic Security,* Vol. 11 (1954), p. 27.

52 weeks. In Puerto Rico, the $20 a week was as high or higher than average wages for those working. Consequently 62 percent of the veterans of Puerto Rico who started to draw compensation obtained payments for 52 weeks. On the other hand, in Wisconsin, where the $20 a week was below the regular rate of pay, only 2.4 percent who drew benefits did so for 52 weeks.[20]

Still another criticism revolves around the problem of who should receive the guaranteed payments. The older workers with the most seniority would retain their jobs and be paid their regular wages for working while the men with the least seniority would be drawing their pay for not working. Furthermore, even though wages are maintained, consumption may still drop because laid-off workers would be reluctant to buy such durable goods as cars, houses, and the like.[21]

SUPPLEMENTAL UNEMPLOYMENT BENEFITS

The failure to obtain the guaranteed annual wage from many firms resulted in labor unions officials' suggesting that the employer's liability be limited and that less than 100 percent of wages be guaranteed for less than one year. Almost all of the newer plans attempted to integrate them with unemployment insurance and so were called supplemental unemployment benefits. Although state legislatures have liberalized unemployment benefits since inception of the unemployment insurance program, the benefits appear quite small to those who must live on them. Failure to obtain adequate benefits from state legislatures has resulted in a number of labor unions attempting to get at the bargaining table what they have been unable to get from the state legislatures. During the past few years, the number of contracts containing supplemental unemployment benefits has grown. Statistics in 1964 showed that almost two million workers are covered under such plans.[22]

Two main types of supplemental unemployment benefits have been negotiated in the United States.[23] The most frequent type of supplement provides for payments out of earmarked funds to supplement regular unemployment insurance. The other type plan provides for crediting earmarked money to each individual worker, who then has a right to obtain this money when he leaves the company. All SUB plans have been financed solely by the employer.[24] Most frequently employers have set aside five cents an hour

---

[20] "Jobs or Jobless Pay—The Real Issue Behind the New Guaranteed Wage Proposals" (Washington, D.C., U.S. Chamber of Commerce, 1954), p. 12.

[21] Johnson and Calhoun, *op. cit.*, pp. 20-26.

[22] Alfred M. Skolnik, "Ten Years of Employee Benefit Plans," *Social Security Bulletin*, Vol. 29, No. 4 (April, 1966), Table 1, p. 6.

[23] "Supplemental Unemployment Benefits in the United States," *International Labor Review*, Vol. 74, No. 7 (November, 1956), pp. 475-479.

[24] Dorothy R. Kittner, "Supplemental Unemployment Benefit Plans in Major Agreements," *Monthly Labor Review*, Vol. 88 (1965), p. 20.

for each hour worked by an employee. The liability of the employer is limited to this cash contribution in most plans, but in some plans an additional two to five cents an hour is assessed the employer. Whenever a fund reaches a certain size, payments into the fund cease. The purposes of this provision are to limit excessive accumulation of funds and to provide an incentive to the employer to regularize employment.

Most frequently SUB plans provide for weekly unemployment insurance benefits of from 60 to 62 percent of before-tax earnings although some plans provide for as little as 55 percent and as much as 80 percent. These figures include both regular unemployment insurance and the supplement. Total weekly maximums per worker are provided in all the plans, but for about 60 percent of the employees the maximums vary according to whether regular unemployment insurance is being received or not. The duration of benefits vary according to the number of weeks worked in most plans with a limit of 52 weeks payments provided in four out of five plans and fewer weeks for the remaining. Partial supplemental benefits are also paid to almost all the workers under such plans as are separation pay and moving allowances to about half the workers.

PITTSBURGH PLATE GLASS PLAN

The other main type of supplemental unemployment benefit plans provides a type of savings fund to the indivdual workers who may draw out the money for such exigencies as unemployment, illness, or even a transfer to another company. At death, the money credited to the worker goes to the widow or nearest beneficiary. Such type contracts have been negotiated by the flat-glass unions and others. In the Pittsburgh Plate Glass Company contract, the company agrees to contribute 10 cents an hour into a trust fund, which must keep the money in cash or in United States government obligations. After the fund reaches $600 per worker, the company still pays the 10 cents per hour, but it then goes to the worker as additional vacation pay. If a worker becomes injured, ill, or unemployed, for more than two pay periods, he may draw a maximum of $30 per week from the fund or 10 percent of the money he has in the fund, whichever is less. The minimum payments are $15 per week, or the balance in the fund, whichever is less.

COMPARISON OF PLANS

In comparing the two types of supplemental benefits, several differences may be noted. In the more narrow supplemental benefit plans as contrasted to the individual savings plan (Pittsburgh Plate Glass), there is a redistribution of income from the employed workers to the unemployed. Since unemployment generally strikes the less skilled group and those with less seniority, the narrower type plan tends to favor this group. No such redistribution from the employed to the unemployed exists under the "savings" plan. In the long run, it is probably true that the savings plan will cost the employers more money. As regular unemployment benefits increase, the narrower plans provide for a reduction into the supplemental unemployment fund. Costs for supplemental benefits will thus decrease. On the other hand, in the Pittsburgh Plate Glass type contract, the 10 cents per hour must be paid continuously regardless of whether regular unemployment benefits increase or not. It is true, though, that the flat-glass contracts do provide more types of benefits with their money, such as sick pay, vacation pay, termination pay, and death along with unemployment benefits.

ELIGIBILITY FOR UNEMPLOYMENT COMPENSATION UNDER SUB PLANS

A legal problem has arisen with the negotiation of supplemental unemployment insurance contracts.[25] The problem is that supplemental benefits might possibly be considered as wages and therefore make workers ineligible for regular unemployment benefits. Four states have passed laws permitting the concurrent payment of regular and supplemental benefits. In 36 other states either officials of the unemployment compensation commission or the attorney general have ruled that it is permissible to make both payments concurrently. Four states, however, have refused to permit such concurrent payments, two by law and two by administrative ruling. In one of these states, Ohio, the labor unions filed an initiative petition to permit integration, but the people voted down the proposal. Both Ford and General Motors corporations requested a favorable vote on this proposal, but both were heavy contributors to the Ohio Information Committee, which was instrumental in defeating the Congress of Industrial Organizations petition.[26] In order to make concurrent payments legal, the unions devised a plan to draw regular benefits for several weeks, and then to disqualify workers for the regular benefits in order to draw an accumulation of supplementary benefits. But in prohibiting the integration of the two plans, three of the four states even outlawed such a system of dovetailing.[27] Two of the four states prohibiting integration of supplemental unemployment benefits with unemployment insurance are located in the South,[28] where antilabor attitudes are more prevalent than elsewhere in the country.

[25] "State Action on SUB Plans," *The Labor Market and Employment Security,* (November, 1957), pp. 21-23.

[26] Edward D. Wickersham, "Legislative Implications of Recent Unemployment Benefit Agreements," *Labor Law Journal,* Vol. 7, No. 6 (June, 1956), pp. 341-342.

[27] "Supplemental Unemployment Benefits in the United States," p. 478.

[28] Jack Chernick and Charles Naef, "Legal and Political Aspects of the Integration of Unemployment Insurance and SUB Plans," *Industrial and Labor Relations Review,* Vol. 12 (1958), pp. 28-32.

CRITICISMS OF SUB PLANS

Several criticisms of supplemental benefits have been expressed.[29] The payments have been considered "capricious" in the sense that in some states little or no supplemental payments will be made. These states already have an adequate system of regular unemployment compensation. For the employees residing in states that pay low regular unemployment benefits, the supplemental grants will be much larger. Contrariwise, it could be argued that such supplemental grants are simply correcting an inequity brought about by disparity in regular unemployment payments in the various states. Another criticism is that the higher the unemployment insurance payment, the greater the chances of malingering. It is true, though, that those administering the unemployment insurance program will still require the "ready and able to work" criterion before paying benefits. It is also true that most workers, expecially those with a family, barely obtain a minimum of health and decency standard at full pay, and they can scarcely be satisfied with receiving only 65 to 75 percent of that amount.

Professor Jules Bachman of New York University has stressed the danger of the high costs of increasing the supplements.[30] Bachman pointed out that the earlier contracts called for 65 percent of wages for the first four weeks and 60 percent for the next 22 weeks. Later contracts provided for some liberalization of these benefits. In the Allis-Chalmers–United Automobile contract, a 65 percent payment was negotiated for all 26 weeks. Then the basic steel and can industries extended benefits to 52 weeks. In calculating cost, Bachman estimated that the Ford Plan would cost the company a little over 13 percent of the basic weekly straight time wage of $72.80 if unemployment reached 1 percent of man-hours worked. If the Ford contract had called for 65 percent payments for 26 weeks rather than 65 percent for 4 weeks and 60 percent for 22 additional, the costs of the plan would have increased 36 percent over the last 22-week period. Guaranteed annual wages of 100 percent of wages would be even more expensive. The costs of providing full wages of $72.80 per week would come to 59 percent of the basic weekly straight-time wage rate or an increase of 335 percent over the original supplemental unemployment benefit plan adopted.

In spite of all the criticisms against supplemental unemployment insurance plans, the major argument for them is that they bolster weaknesses in our present unemployment insurance laws. So long as such laws continue to set maximum benefits at figures 30 to 40 percent of weekly wages, labor continues to clamor for higher benefits. What labor unions have been unable

---

[29] "Supplemental Unemployment Benefits in the United States," p. 478.

[30] Jules Bachman, "High Costs of Liberalizing SUB Plans," *Harvard Business Review*, Vol. 34, No. 6 (1956), pp. 69-74.

to obtain through the state legislatures, some have been able to obtain through collective bargaining. If and when the states liberalize their regular unemployment benefits, probably less pressure will be exerted to increase such benefits by collective bargaining.

EVALUATION OF GAW AND SUB PLANS

In attempting to evaluate the merits of the guaranteed annual wage, Professors Alvin Hansen and Paul Samuelson, although not unfavorable to such plans, point out that if they had to choose between the guaranteed annual wage and other antidepression policies, such as unemployment insurance, social security programs, or monetary and fiscal policy the guaranteed annual wage would be chosen last.[31] Very little support has been obtained in favor of legislation requiring that the guaranteed annual wage be adopted. On the other hand, if and when relatively full employment could be maintained, the guaranteed annual wage could possibly regularize employment in seasonal industries without bringing undue costs upon employers.

The fact that labor unions have made a major breakthrough with supplemental unemployment benefits in 1955 negotiations would tend to lend support to the viewpoint that those unions that do not as yet have such benefits will press for such benefits rather than the guaranteed annual wage. If any concessions are obtainable from management, it is much easier to obtain 50 to 65 percent of wages for 26 weeks under a supplemental unemployment benefit program than it is to obtain 100 percent of wages for a year under a guaranteed annual wage program. The fact that almost 2 million workers are now covered under supplemental unemployment benefits, whereas only 15,000 to 18,000 employees are under guaranteed wage plans, would indicate that labor unions have been much more successful in obtaining supplemental benefits than the guaranteed annual wage.

SEVERANCE PAY AND LAYOFF BENEFIT PLANS

Severance Pay and Layoff Benefit Plans have grown very rapidly since World War II (see Fig. 16-1). Of almost 2,000 major agreements studied, in which almost 7½ million workers were employed, such plans appeared in 30 percent of the agreements and covered about 40 percent of workers under all agreements. The plans were concentrated in manufacturing, and five labor unions were parties to almost half of the plans: Steelworkers, Auto Workers, Communication Workers, Ladies' Garment Workers, and Electri-

---

[31] Alvin Hansen and Paul Samuelson, "Economic Analysis of Guaranteed Wages," Bulletin No. 907, Washington, D.C., U.S. Department of Labor, Bureau of Labor Statistics (1947), p. 5.

cal Workers (IBEW). A number of plans provided for severance pay only
upon termination of employment (rather than layoff). Those plans with no
explicit termination statement usually provided compensation for "layoff,"
but some of these excluded short-term layoffs.

Most of the plans are unfunded, but the funded plans have continued
to grow and constitute one-fourth of all plans. The amount of benefit is
generally based on length of service, with one week's pay for one year of
service being typical for short-service employees. For those employed for a
number of years, more weeks pay was granted for each year of service, sometimes as high as four weeks pay for each year of service.[32]

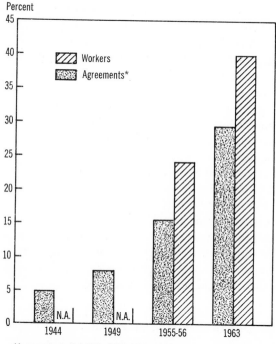

*Agreements studied: 1944—9,500; 1949—2,137;
1955-56—1,692; 1963—1,773.

Source: Leon Lunden and Ernestine Moore, "Severance Pay and Layoff Benefit
Plans," Monthly Labor Review, Vol. 88, No. 1 (January, 1965), p. 29.

FIG. 16–1.   SEVERANCE PAY AND LAYOFF BENEFIT PLANS IN
UNION AGREEMENTS, 1944–1963

[32] Leon Lunden and Ernestine Moore, "Severance Pay and Layoff Benefit Plans,"
Monthly Labor Review, Vol. 88, No. 1 (January, 1965), pp. 27-34.

Summary

Guaranteed Annual Wage Plans have been in existence for many years. A few were inaugurated before the turn of the century. Several large companies, such as Procter & Gamble and the Hormel Co., have successfully operated such plans for a number of years. Since 1940 the main impetus in support of such plans has come from labor unions. In general, management has not been enthusiastic about such plans, for they do present the threat of added costs. Labor unions have been more successful in negotiating supplemental unemployment benefit plans, which provide a half to two-thirds pay or more from 26 to 52 weeks. In recent years there has also been a rapid growth of severance pay plans for workers who are terminated or, sometimes, laid off.

Bibliography

Asbell, Bernard, The New Improved American (New York, McGraw-Hill, 1965).

Becker, Joseph M., The Adequacy of the Benefit Amount in Unemployment Insurance (Kalamazoo, Upjohn Institute, 1961).

————, ed., In Aid of the Unemployed. (Baltimore, Johns Hopkins, 1965).

————, The Problem of Abuse in Unemployment Benefits (New York, Columbia, 1953).

Bureau of National Affairs, The Guaranteed Annual Wage (Washington, Bureau of National Affairs, 1955).

Dunlop, John T., ed., Automation and Technological Change (Englewood Cliffs, N.J., Prentice-Hall, 1962).

Haber, William, and Daniel Kruger, The Role of the United States Employment Service in a Changing Economy (Kalamazoo, Upjohn Institute, 1964).

Lester, Richard A., The Economics of Unemployment Compensation (Princeton, Princeton, 1962).

Levitan, Sar, Federal Aid to Depressed Areas (Baltimore, Johns Hopkins, 1964).

Lineberry, William P., ed., The Challenge of Full Employment (New York, Wilson, 1962).

Malisoff, Harry, The Financing of Extended Unemployment Insurance Benefits (Kalamazoo, Upjohn Institute, 1963).

Mann, Floyd C., and L. Richard Hoffman, Automation and the Worker (New York, Holt, Rinehart and Winston, 1960).

Michael, Daniel N., Cybernation: The Silent Conquest (Santa Barbara, Calif., Center for Study of Democratic Institutions, 1962).

Mueller, Eva, and Jay Schmiedeskamp, *Persistent Unemployment 1957–1961* (Kalamazoo, Upjohn Institute, 1962).

National Bureau of Economic Research, *The Measurement and Behavior of Unemployment* (Princeton, Princeton, 1957).

Ross, Arthur M., ed., *Conference on Unemployment and the American Economy* (New York, Wiley, 1964).

Simon, Herbert, *The Shape of Automation for Men and Management* (New York, Harper & Row, 1965).

Wilcock, Richard C., and Walter H. Franke, *Unwanted Workers* (New York, Free Press, 1963).

Wolfbein, Seymour, *Employment and Unemployment in the United States* (Chicago, Science Research Associates, 1964).

PROBLEMS OF LOW-INCOME AND SPECIAL GROUPS

LOW-WAGE INDUSTRIES:
THE CASE OF AGRICULTURE

Certain industries in the United States pay much lower wages to workers than other industries. Table 17-1 shows the median annual earnings of families according to the industry of the head of the family.

TABLE 17–1. MEDIAN ANNUAL FAMILY INCOME, BY OCCUPATION OF HEAD OF FAMILY, MARCH, 1965

Industry	Metropolitan	Nonmetropolitan
Agriculture, forestry, and fishing	$4,603	$3,012
Mining	a	6,984
Construction	7,787	5,780
Manufacturing	8,240	6,633
Transportation, communications, and public utilities	8,058	6,883
Wholesale trade	8,425	6,057
Retail trade	7,026	5,643
Finance, insurance, and real estate	8,428	7,962
Business and repair services	7,036	6,000
Personal services	4,928	3,833
Professional and related services	8,888	7,094
Public administration	8,508	7,355

a Not available.

Source: Consumer Income, Series P-60, U.S. Department of Commerce, Bureau of the Census, No. 48 (April, 1966), Table 8, pp. 21-22.

Even within industries earnings vary considerably. In manufacturing in 1962, for example, the annual earnings in petroleum and coal products were $7,404, compared with $3,538 in apparel and other finished-fabric products. As can be seen from Table 17-1, earnings in agriculture are substantially below all other industries. In 1964 it was estimated that over 4 million of our 34 million poor had a farm residence. A third of all persons living on farms were poor.[1]

[1] Mollie Orshansky, "Recounting the Poor—A Five Year Review," *Social Security Bulletin,* Vol. 29, No. 4 (April, 1966), Table 3, p. 25.

HIRED FARM LABOR

Poverty in agriculture is concentrated among two groups—hired farm labor and low-income farm owners or renters. They will be studied in this order. Table 17-2 shows the number of workers employed as farm wage workers.

TABLE 17–2. NUMBERS OF HIRED FARM WORKERS
(IN THOUSANDS)

Year	Workers with 25 Days or More of Farm Wage Work During the Year			Workers with Less Than 25 Days of Farm Wage Work During the Year			All Farm Wage Workers		
	Male	Female	Total	Male	Female	Total	Male	Female	Total
1945	1,576	389	1,965	799	448	1,247	2,375	837	3,212
1946	1,584	369	1,953	536	281	817	2,120	650	2,770
1947	1,864	351	2,215	723	456	1,179	2,587	807	3,394
1948	2,036	466	2,502	784	466	1,250	2,820	932	3,752
1949	2,001	.509	2,510	1,020	610	1,630	3,021	1,119	4,140
1950	....	...	....	....	...	....	3,221	1,121	4,342
1951	1,718	438	2,156	674	444	1,118	2,392	882	3,274
1952	1,558	414	1,972	660	348	1,008	2,218	762	2,980
1954	1,544	364	1,908	693	408	1,101	2,237	772	3,009
1956	1,553	525	2,078	972	525	1,497	2,525	1,050	3,575
1957	1,673	527	2,200	1,092	670	1,762	2,765	1,197	3,962
1958	1,788	531	2,319	1,199	694	1,893	2,987	1,225	4,212
1959	1,690	476	2,166	880	531	1,412	2,570	1,007	3,577
1960	1,698	463	2,162	966	566	1,531	2,664	1,029	3,693
1963	1,480	382	1,862	1,135	601	1,735	2,615	983	3,597
1964	1,487	514	2,001	911	458	1,369	2,398	972	3,370

Sources: Sheridan T. Maitland and Dorothy A. Fisher, *The Hired Farm Working Force of 1957*, Bulletin No. 208, U.S. Department of Agriculture, Agricultural Marketing Service (1959), Table 1, p. 2. Louis J. Ducoff and Sheridan T. Maitland, eds., *The Hired Farm Working Force of 1960*, Agriculture Information Bulletin No. 266, U.S. Department of Agriculture (1961), Table 1, p. 29. Agricultural Economic Report No. 76, U.S. Department of Agriculture (1965), Table 4, pp. 10-12 and No. 82 (1965), Table 1, p. 8.

Underemployment constitutes one of the major problems of hired farm labor. In 1957, 1.1 million hired workers listed farm work as their chief activity. Yet in that year, only 655,000 worked at least 150 days during the year.[2] New methods of technology complicate the employment problems

[2] Sheridan T. Maitland and Dorothy A. Fisher, *The Hired Farm Working Force of 1957*, Bulletin No. 208, Washington, D.C., U.S. Department of Agriculture, Agricultural Marketing Service (1959), pp. 9, 11.

of hired farm laborers.[3] For example, mechanical sweetcorn harvesters have reduced picking costs by as much as 57 percent and bean harvestors have saved 75 percent. The trend in number of days worked has been downward, but through improved government efforts, the trend has been reversed in the last few years.

EARNINGS OF HIRED FARM LABOR

Not only are hired farm workers handicapped by underemployment, but their wage rates while working are substantially below other industries. Table 17-3 shows that although farm wage rates have increased over the years, they have not kept pace with factory wages. In 1963 the annual earnings of hired farm workers who were employed more than 250 days was $2,240, compared with $1,411 for those working 150 to 249 days and $813 for those working from 75 to 149 days.

TABLE 17–3.   AVERAGE HOURLY EARNINGS, MANUFACTURING AND AGRICULTURE, 1929–1965

Year	Manufacturing	Agriculture	Agriculture as Percentage of Manufacturing
1929	$0.57	$0.24	42
1937	0.62	0.17	27
1947	1.24	0.55	44
1959	2.22	0.80	36
1965	2.61	0.95	36

Sources: Harry S. Kantor, "A Minimum Wage for Farm Workers," Monthly Labor Review, Vol. 83 (1960), p. 677; Farm Labor (May 10, 1966), p. 3; Monthly Labor Review, Vol. 89, No. 4 (April, 1966), Table C–1, p. 455.

SOCIAL LEGISLATION FOR FARM LABORERS

Agricultural labor has been exempt from most of the labor and social legislation passed to aid practically all other segments of our society. Farm laborers are not covered under the National Labor Relations Act, which guarantees labor the right to organize free from employer interference and to bargain collectively. The failure to cover agricultural workers has made organization of farm workers exceptionally difficult. Employer groups oppose coverage of farm workers under the National Labor Relations Act on the ground that

[3] Migratory Labor Notes, No. 12, Washington, D.C., the President's Committee on Migratory Labor (1960), p. 3.

their crops must be harvested during a relatively short period of several weeks at which time a strike would be economically disastrous. As an alternative to the present system of no bargaining rights, it would be possible to confer bargaining rights on such workers, and then require compulsory arbitration in case of a dispute.[4] The income of hired farm labor is so low that such workers are in need of labor union protection more than most other workers.

In most states, hired farm laborers are exempt from workmen's compensation legislation. It has been found that the accident rate is higher in agriculture than most other industries. About one-fourth of all deaths throughout all industry occurred in agriculture, more than in all other industries.[5] In spite of the great need of accident insurance for these low-income workers, only five states—California, Hawaii, Massachusetts, New Jersey, Oregon—and the territory of Puerto Rico cover all farm workers. Sixteen other states provide partial coverage.[6] A special committee on farm coverage of the International Association of Industrial Accident Boards and Commissions recommended the same coverage for farm employees as all other employees.[7]

Practically all states fail to cover agricultural labor under their unemployment insurance laws.[8] Coverage would be quite expensive and a drain on the unemployment insurance fund, but this might be the avenue that could be used to raise farm labor income until more permanent solutions are found to the problem. Cold weather, which delays harvesting, has literally caused starvation of a number of migrants. They have little or no savings, and no means are available to tide many of them over.

Farm laborers were also exempt from the Fair Labor Standards Act covering minimum wages. Some maintain that agriculture is too poor to be covered under such legislation. Perhaps here it would be possible to use an industry board, as is used by some states. Under this type of arrangement, the board investigates conditions in a particular industry, and then issues an order as to the appropriate minimum wage. Geographical differentials may be more justified in agriculture than other industries, because hourly wages as of April 1, 1965, fluctuated from a low of 62 cents per hour in South Carolina to a high of $1.42 in Connecticut (without room and board).[9] The American Farm Bureau Federation has opposed coverage under the Fair Labor Standards Act for six reasons:

[4] Clay L. Cochran, *Hired Farm Labor and the Federal Government*, unpublished Ph.D. dissertation, University of North Carolina (1950), p. 191.

[5] Donald L. Ream, *Agricultural Workers and Workmen's Compensation*, Bulletin No. 206, Washington, D.C., U.S. Department of Labor, Bureau of Labor Standards (1959), p. 3.

[6] *Status of Agricultural Workers Under State and Federal Labor Laws*, Fact Sheet No. 2, Washington, D.C., U.S. Department of Labor, Bureau of Labor Standards (December, 1965), pp. 9-11.

[7] Ream, *op. cit.*, p. 10.

[8] For an analysis of coverage of agricultural workers under unemployment compensation, *see* Chapter 14.

[9] *Farm Labor* (April, 1966), p. 6.

1. Most farm workers are furnished perquisites of some kind—housing, meals, food, transportation, etc.
2. Most harvest labor in which migratory workers are engaged is on a piece-work basis.
3. Migratory workers often work irregular hours.
4. In any group there will be shirkers. In factory employment they can be weeded out. This is not true in seasonal harvest work.
5. There are wide variations between output of migratory workers engaged in piece work.
6. Within the limitations of economic factors, farm wages tend to rise in parallel lines with other workers.[10]

None of the problems raised by the American Farm Bureau present insurmountable barriers to coverage. Pieceworkers in many other industries are covered. Similarly, workers who do not produce could be weeded out, or a tolerance could be provided as in the Wisconsin state law or the Mexican agreement. Under the Wisconsin law, piece rates must yield .53 cents or more to 75 percent of the workers.[11]

The latest census data shows that 3 percent of all farms paid out 51 percent of all farm wages.[12] At the state level, the minimum wage laws of Hawaii and Puerto Rico specifically apply to agricultural workers. The minimum wage laws are broad enough in nine other jurisdictions to cover farm workers and in two of these specific minimum wages have been set by wage orders. At the federal level, the Fair Labor Standards Act was amended in 1966 to cover farms using 500 man-days of labor in any calendar quarter of the previous year (roughly equivalent to the use of seven full time workers). Because agriculture is a poorer industry than most others, the minimum wage for agriculture in 1967 will be only $1.00 and will rise to only $1.30 by 1971 whereas all other covered workers will be receiving $1.60 in that year.

Although farm workers were not covered originally under the old age insurance program, hired farm laborers are now covered. The major problem today in this area involves providing sufficient information to hired farm workers so that they know about the program. Otherwise, payments may not be collected from them, or deductions may be made by employers without forwarding them to the government. A number of instances have been reported of lack of knowledge of the program. Booklets, a film strip, and posters have been prepared by the Bureau of Old-Age and Survivors

[10] Testimony of Matt Triggs, Assistant Legislative Director, American Farm Bureau Federation, *Report on Farm Labor,* before the National Advisory Committee on Farm Labor, Washington, D.C. (1959), p. 24.
[11] Harry S. Kantor, "A Minimum Wage for Farm Workers," *Monthly Labor Review,* Vol. 83 (1960), pp. 679-689.
[12] Statement of the Honorable Willard Wirtz, Hearings Before the Subcommittee on Migratory Labor of the Committee on Labor and Public Welfare, U.S. Senate, 89th Congress, 1st and 2nd Sessions on S. 1864–1868 (March-July, 1965), p. 36.

Insurance for use with these workers, and church groups have been active in some areas to publicize the coverage of such workers. Still more needs to be done to make certain that all agricultural workers participate in the program.

MIGRATORY FARM WORKERS

As a part of the hired farm labor force, migratory workers are exempt from labor and social legislation the same as the nonmigratory hired farm labor force. Inclusion of farm laborers under these laws would aid both groups. Migratory workers have additional problems which should be analyzed. About 409,000 migratory farm workers were in the labor market at some time during 1960. Because of the difficulty of counting migratory workers since some of them are on the move, it is probable that the migratory labor force was actually higher. Little change in numbers of migratory workers has been noted since 1947, although the numbers have fluctuated from a low of 352,000 in 1952 to a high of 477,000 in 1959. About three-fourths of the migratory force was male, and most of the workers were young. Forty-eight percent were below the age of 25, and almost half of these had not reached eighteen. Owing to the strenuousness of the work, only 10 percent of the migratory labor force was over 55.[13] Fig. 17-1 shows that most migratory workers start from California, Texas, the Appalachian region and Florida and then journey northward in various routes. In 1963, for all workers working more than 150 days, the annual income of migratory workers was $1,361 compared with $1,938 for nonmigratory farm laborers.[14] Underemployment is even more of a problem for migratory workers than nonmigratory labor. For those working more than 25 days, the migratory male worker averaged only 141 days of employment in 1962 compared with 163 days for nonmigratory workers.[15] As can be seen by Fig. 17-2, large numbers of migratory workers are either Spanish-Americans or nonwhites.

LIVING CONDITIONS

The conditions under which such workers live has been depicted by Dr. Hector Garcia, a physician from Corpus Christi, Texas, in testimony before the National Advisory Council on Farm Labor.

The children of migrant parents are born into a world completely of their own. An anemic mother, and possibly a tubercular father—a life that will take

[13] Reed E. Friend and Robert R. Stansberry, Jr., *The Hired Farm Working Force of 1960*, Bulletin No. 266, Washington, D.C., U.S. Department of Agriculture (1962), Tables 22, 23, p. 41.
[14] *The Hired Farm Working Force of 1963*, Washington, D.C., U.S. Department of Agriculture, Economic Research Service, Table 8, p. 24.
[15] *Ibid.*, Table 21, p. 53.

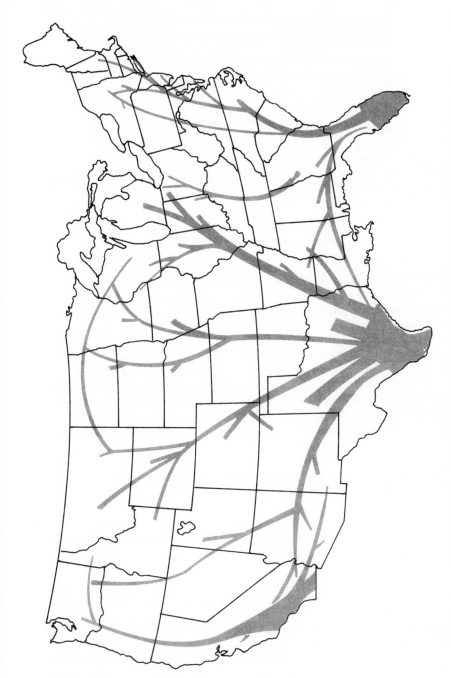

Source: *Hired Farm Workers in the United States*, U.S. Department of Labor, Bureau of Employment Security (1961), p. 31.

FIG. 17–1. TRAVEL PATTERNS OF SEASONAL MIGRATORY AGRICULTURAL WORKERS

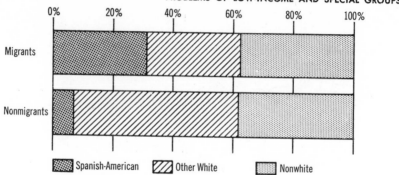

Source: Reed E. Friend and Robert R. Stansberry, Jr., *The Hired Farm Working Force of 1960*, Bulletin No. 266, Washington, D.C., U.S. Department of Agriculture (1962), p. 9.

FIG. 17–2. MIGRATORY STATUS OF WORKERS WHO DID 25 DAYS OR MORE OF FARM WORK, U.S., 1960

him into his world where he may possibly die within one year, either from diarrhea, tuberculosis or malnutrition. His infancy would be a very close association with his brothers and sisters. Their home would be [a] one or two-room shack, with no inside running water and no flushing-toilet facilities. If he lives to be of school age, he could possibly go to many schools on different occasions at different places, but will never average more than three years of schooling in his life time. . . . His future life will be one of wandering, poverty and more sickness.

As a migrant, his world will be from the Atlantic to the Pacific—from the Great Lakes to the Rio Grande. It will be his world, however, only in that the only piece of property that he will own will be his grave.

I may be here because I am still haunted by that remembrance of a day ten years ago when the little boy came to my office to ask me to go and see his mother who was sick. I went to his home—a one-room shack. I found a dead mother with six children laying in the same bed, all covered with blood from the hemorrhage of a dying tubercular mother.[16]

Another description of migratory workers' conditions comes from Rev. K. P. Thornton, Director of the Migrant Missionary Fellowship, Pompano Beach, Florida:

Most camps are dilapidated shacks with large families living in one room with no windows. The toilet facilities are the outside "privy" type that are so filthy many use the ground. The water supply is outside faucets with no water in the dwellings. Why should little children be forced to live in such filthy surroundings just because they were born in a migrant family?

There is no way to heat the dwellings and bedding is not provided. In cold weather there is much suffering and we have supplied blankets to many of them.

[16] *Report on Farm Labor*, pp. 5-6.

In our area, within 18 miles of our mission, there are 90 camps ranging from 25 to 500 workers and it is these that need your attention.

Last winter, when all the crops were frozen and there was little or no work for over three months, we had many appeal to us for medical aid. We took them to county authorities, and were sent from one agency to another until we were worn out and, in some cases, paid the bill ourselves. Finally we were told that there was a provision whereby some of the expense was paid by the state. There is no place where a migrant can go for help and know that he is going to get it.[17]

LABOR CONTRACTORS

Many migrant workers receive their employment through labor contractors. The labor contractor system has resulted in a number of abuses. Sometimes the contractors do not remit to migratory workers all of the wages paid by the employer. Instead they keep some of the money themselves. Contractors sometimes charge excessive fees for their services. At other times, they fail to report and pay the proper Social Security taxes required by law. In order to remedy such abuses, a federal law was passed in 1964 licensing labor contractors. Not only should such a licensing system prevent some of the abuses listed above, but it should also enable the government to enforce better standards of employment. The Department of Labor has issued regulations that the use of public employment facilities be denied employers who undercut wages or fail to provide adequate housing, transportation, and other working conditions, but without a licensing of labor contractors such regulations were extremely difficult to police.[18] Owing to a number of accidents involving migratory workers, the Interstate Commerce Commission in September, 1959, amended its safety regulations on interstate transportation of farm workers to provide for a removal of all trucks and buses found to be in poor condition. Here again enforcement of such regulations was extremely difficult without a federal licensing system for contractors.

HOUSING

Housing presents a particularly difficult problem for migratory workers. Since migratory workers need shelter for only a short time, employers are reluctant to spend much money on housing facilities. It is possible at a relatively low cost to provide for barracks-type facilities with indoor plumbing and a minimum of conveniences. Most migratory workers do not have these, and are forced in many instances to live in barns, shacks, tents, or any makeshift type of arrangement. The latest President's Commission on Migratory Labor reported that housing facilities for migratory workers were improving mainly through voluntary efforts of employers but that much of

17 *Ibid.*, p. 8.
18 *Ibid.*, pp. 11-12.

the housing now available does not meet the minimum standards of health and decency. Thirty-two states have laws regulating housing on labor camps, but these are not rigidly enforced.

In 1936, the Federal Resettlement Administration began the operation of two emergency housing camps, which had been constructed by the California State Relief Administration. Later the program consisted of 95 camps serving 121 cities in 16 states. At first tents were used. These were later replaced by small wooden or metal shelters that had a minimum of furniture, a stove, and bed frames. Community comfort stations contained toilets, showers, and laundry facilities. Community centers were added for recreational, governing, and nursery activities. Also the camps had health clinics. Along with federal supervision, the camps had democratically elected camp councils. The standard camp was constructed at a cost of from $200,000 to $250,000. Some mobile units were added to provide housing for migrants after they had left their home base. The American Farm Bureau Federation, the National Grange, and other employer groups were instrumental in forcing the sale of these camps in 1943. The major fear was that a concentration of laborers in one place might lead to unionization of farm workers.[19] The failure to provide adequate housing since 1943 may possibly bring a revival of public housing for migrant workers. The President's Commission on Migratory Labor under President Truman recommended construction of home-base public housing sites by the Federal Public Housing Administration. For housing needed for shorter periods, the Commission recommended the creation of labor camps by the states financed by a federal grants-in-aid program.[20]

HEALTH

The income of most migratory families is so low that vitamin and other dietary deficiencies result. Their health problems are further complicated by poor housing and a lack of sanitary facilities. Couple these deficiencies with insufficient income to purchase adequate medical treatment and the result is serious health problems for migratory workers. All past studies of health of migrant workers revealed the serious problem that existed. A Fresno County, California, study found that diarrheal disease among children from farm labor camps was significantly higher than for children in housing projects.[21] A Colorado study found that migrants' infant mortality rates were twice as high as the state average because more than a third of the births of migrant children occurred without the presence of a physician. Occasionally

[19] Cochran, op. cit., pp. 118-131.

[20] Migratory Labor in American Agriculture, Report of the President's Commission on Migratory Labor, Washington, D.C. (1951), pp. 150-151.

[21] This and the following studies were summarized in Lucile Leone and Helen Johnston, "Agricultural Migrants and Public Health," Public Health Reports, Vol. 69 (1954), p. 4.

newspapers print stories of actual starvation of migrants, particularly when poor weather prevents a harvesting of crops.

Using emergency relief funds, the federal Farm Security Administration in 1938 began operation of a number of health clinics in various parts of the United States. Nurses were employed to operate camp clinics to dispense simple medical care. Physicians were hired either by the hour or were paid a set fee per patient for visits to the doctor's offices. Operations, child deliveries, and other major operations were paid for on a fee-for-service basis. By March, 1943, the medical program in the California-Arizona area alone included 16 clinics, two mobile medical units, and three referral offices. Clinics were operated in other parts of the country, and two hospitals were opened. In 1943, with the widespread opposition to the work of the Farm Security Administration, the program was abolished.[22] With a more liberal Congress in 1962, a Migrant Health Act was passed. This act authorized the Public Health Service to make grants to public and other nonprofit agencies to pay part of the cost of establishing and operating health clinics for migratory workers. As of December, 1965, grants have been awarded for 60 health projects in 30 jurisdictions.

EDUCATION

All studies of migratory labor have reported serious educational deficiencies among children of migratory workers. In a 1958–1959 survey made by the U.S. Department of Labor, of 1,700 migrant children under 16 who were illegally employed during school hours, 66 percent were in grades below normal for their ages. The higher the age, the larger the percentages who were behind. At age 15, 87 percent of the children were in grades below normal.[23] Several states have made appropriations to help finance the education of migrant children, but too little has been done in most states to insure an adequate education for such children.

The median hired farm laborer over 45 years old (migratory and non-migratory combined) has completed only five years of schooling. Those aged 25 to 44 completed less than 8 grades. Younger farm wage workers aged 18–24 have more education—over 10 years, but this is several years less than the general population of the same age.[24]

WELFARE

Owing to the state operation of public welfare offices in the United States, migratory workers frequently are denied aid simply because they have not

[22] Cochran, op. cit., pp. 128-131.

[23] Report to the President on Domestic Migratory Farm Labor, Washington, D.C. (1960), p. 17.

[24] James D. Cowhig, Education and Earnings of the Hired Farm Working Force of 1960, Agriculture Information Bulletin No. 262, Washington, D.C., U.S. Department of Agriculture (1962), Figure 1, p. 9.

resided in a state long enough. Thus those most in need of aid are denied access to the major programs designed to alleviate distress. In order to make such workers eligible for relief, the Advisory Council on Public Assistance has recommended that federal grants-in-aid should be made available only where no residence requirements are imposed by the state concerned. The position of the Advisory Council has particular merit, because most of the funds come from the federal government.

FOREIGN CONTRACT LABOR

The migratory labor problem in the United States has been complicated by the importation of Mexican and other labor under contract with the United States. The importation of Mexican labor first began during World War II, to alleviate the war shortage of American labor. From 65,000 to 85,000 workers were admitted annually during the war years. Since the war the number of workers grew until by 1959, 464,128 foreign workers were admitted.[25] In 1965 the foreign contract system was abolished. Differences of opinion exist as to the actual need of foreign contract labor. Farm employer groups in this country who are interested in guarantees that there will be adequate labor supply to harvest the crops maintain that the foreign supply of farm workers is needed. Representatives of farm workers, on the other hand, maintain that the income of domestic farm labor is so low that the importation of foreign workers aggravates the grave plight of domestic workers. In cotton picking, for example, where foreign labor had been used extensively, the average price paid for picking 100 pounds of cotton dropped from $2.65 to $2.60 from 1947 to 1959. In Texas, the biggest user of Mexican labor for cotton picking, the price dropped from $2.75 to $2.35.[26]

The Mexican agreement did have a number of safeguards for their migratory workers that might well be applied to our own domestic migrants. All of the Mexican workers were given a physical examination to assure that they met the mental and health requirements for admission to the United States. The United States Government paid transportation expenses of the workers from the migratory stations in Mexico to reception centers in the United States. American employers agreed to pay the transportation expenses from the reception centers to the place of employment and back again to the reception centers.

American employers agreed to pay the prevailing rate of wages to Mexican nationals. Mexican nationals were guaranteed at least three-fourths of the work days contracted for in the work contract with the American employer. Mexican workers were given the right to elect their own representa-

[25] *Statistical Abstract of the United States, 1963*, Washington, D.C., U.S. Department of Commerce, Bureau of the Census, Table 128, p. 103.

[26] Statement of Jacob Clayman, Industrial Union Department, AFL-CIO, before the Subcommittee on Agriculture on Extension of Mexican Farm Labor Program (1960), pp. 13-17.

tives, who were required to be recognized by the employer in collective bargaining negotiations. The employer agreed to furnish hygienic lodgings, including blankets, when necessary, beds, and mattresses or cots. The employer agreed to provide the same guarantees for medical care and personal injury as provided for domestic workers. In the absence of a state law, the employer agreed to pay $1,000 for a death, permanent and total disability, loss of both hands, and similar injuries. Smaller amounts were paid for less serious injuries. All hospital and medical expenses had to be paid by the employer.[27]

Mexican nationals received considerably better treatment than domestic workers. The same provisions applied to domestic workers would aid in raising their standard of living. Some of these provisions were made applicable to domestic workers when recruitment was carried on by the Farm Security Administration prior to 1943. Congress eliminated such safeguards in 1943 when it passed Public Law 45, which provided that no federal funds for recruitment of domestic farm labor could be used directly or indirectly to "fix, regulate, or to impose minimum wages or housing standards, to regulate hours of work, or to impose or enforce collective-bargaining requirements." The Pace Amendment (1943) to this law required that written approval of the county agent must be obtained before recruitment of domestic farm labor could take place.[28]

More recently state Migratory Labor Committees have been created in a number of states to attempt to improve the status of migrant workers through studies, legislative action, and local aid. The War on Poverty program has also expended small sums of money for migrant workers.

LOW-INCOME FARMERS

Although gross farm income has increased slightly since 1953, production expenses have increased even more so that realized net income of farmers was somewhat lower in 1964 than it was in 1953 (see Fig. 17-3). By 1966, income was higher. Fortunately, the number of farm operators has decreased so that actual income per person has increased slightly on farms. Nonfarm income per person has increased even faster than farm income so that farm income is a smaller percentage of nonfarm income per person today than it was in 1953.

Table 17-4 shows the classification of farms used in the 1964 Census of Agriculture. The number of farms in each classification is also shown. This table shows that large numbers of farms, particularly in Class V and VI, have a low income, as do many part-time farmers.

The geographical distribution of farms with less than $2,500 of gross

[27] *Mexican Agricultural Workers*, Treaties and Other International Acts, Series 2331, Publication 4435, Washington, D.C., U.S. Department of State (1951).
[28] Cochran, *op. cit.*, pp. 154-157.

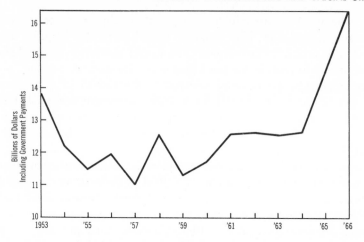

Source: Farm Income Situation, No. FIS-197, U.S. Department of Agriculture, Economic Research Service (February, 1965), p. 1.

FIG. 17–3. REALIZED NET FARM INCOME

sales is shown in Fig. 17-4. The concentration of such farms is in the South and the Appalachian Mountain region, although significant numbers of such farms exist in Washington, Oregon, and elsewhere. In general, the low-income-producing farms are smaller than high-income farms. Of all farms with less than $2,500 a year gross sales, 75 percent had fewer than 100 acres.[29] Such farms were particularly deficient of equipment. On Class VI commercial farms (less than $2,500 farm sales), only 48 percent had tractors, 58 percent had automobiles, 31 percent had telephones, and 31 percent had home freezers.[30]

CAUSES OF RURAL POVERTY

There are a number of causes of rural poverty. Improvements in technology have been so widespread that large increases in agricultural production have occurred. Over three times as much crop production is now obtained per hour of work compared with the period before World War I.[31] Put another way, each farm worker produces enough to supply himself and more than 22 other persons, or almost six times the number of persons supplied by each farm worker in 1820.[32] Couple this increased production with an in-

[29] *Census of Agriculture, 1959*, Washington, D.C., U.S. Department of Commerce, Bureau of the Census, and U.S. Department of Agriculture, Vol. II, Chapter XI, p. 1203.
[30] *Ibid.*, Table 5, pp. 1214-1215.
[31] *Changes in Farm Productivity and Efficiency*, Statistical Bulletin No. 233, Washington, D.C., U.S. Department of Agriculture (1958), p. 2.
[32] *Ibid.*, p. 3.

TABLE 17–4. NUMBER OF FARMS IN THE UNITED STATES, 1964

	Number of Farms	*Definition of Class*
Commercial:	2,165,727	
Class I	141,906	$40,000 or more farm products sold
Class II	259,894	$20,000 to $39,999 farm products sold
Class III	467,105	$10,000 to $19,999 farm products sold
Class IV	504,625	$5,000 to $9,999 farm products sold
Class V	443,928	$2,500 to $4,999 farm products sold
Class VI	348,269	$50 to $2,499 farm products sold, the operator worked less than 100 days off the farm, his income and that of his family from nonfarm sources is less than the value of all farm products sold, and the operator is under 65 years of age
Total commercial	3,157,864	
Other farms:	992,127	
Part-time	639,404	$50 to $2,499 farm products sold, operator worked more than 100 days off the farm or income of the operator and his family from non-farm sources is greater than the value of all farm products sold, farm operator under 65 years of age
Part-retirement	350,555	$50 to $2,499 farm products sold, farm operator 65 years old and over
Abnormal	2,178	Institutional farms, Indian reservations, experimental farms, grazing associations, etc.
Total other farms	992,127	
Total U. S. farms	3,157,864	

Sources: U.S. Department of Commerce, Vol. II, Chapter XI, Table 1, p. 1192. *1964 Census of Agriculture,* Preliminary Report, Series A C 64-P1, Table 1, p. 2.

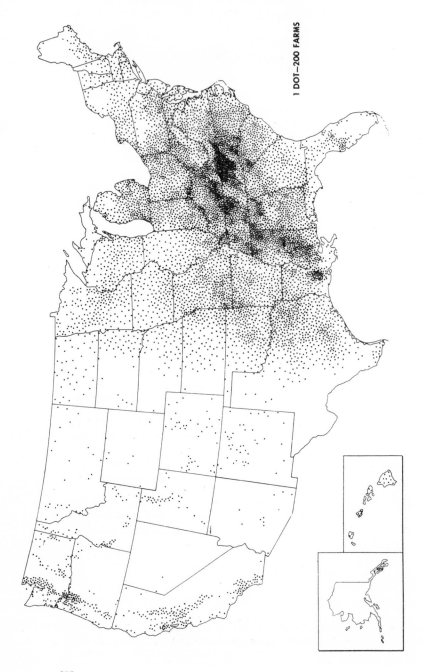

Source: Map No. A59-4A27, U.S. Department of Commerce, Bureau of the Census.

FIG. 17–4.   FARMS WITH LESS THAN $2,500 GROSS SALES, 1959

1 DOT—200 FARMS

elastic demand for most farm products, and the result is lower income. More-over, the income elasticity of farm products is quite low. Consumers simply do not allocate much of their increased income on additional food expendi-tures. To complicate matters even further, rural areas in this country have a high birthrate. Whereas the urban net reproduction rate was 1,085 (1,000 people reproducing 1,085), the rural farm reproduction rate was 1,859. Dur-ing the decade of the 1950's the replacement ratio of rural farm men was 168 for every 100 departures from death or retirement. This means that even if farm population remains constant, 68 out of 168 farmers (about 40 per-cent) would have to leave farms. In the South, the replacement ratio for rural farm males is about 200.[33] One estimate by Karl Shoemaker of the Fed-eral Extension Service showed that for rural male children becoming 20 years of age from 1954 to 1965 only one in ten can expect to become a com-mercial farm operator grossing over $5,000 a year income.[34]

For low-income farms, a main cause of poverty is that many of the farms are simply too small to eke out a decent living. Low-income farms are also hampered by a lack of equipment and capital. In addition, the educational attainment in many rural areas is so low that intelligent farming is pre-cluded.

SOLUTIONS TO RURAL POVERTY

PARITY PRICING

The major program to improve farm income for many years in the United States has been parity pricing. The underlying theory of the program is that farm income can be raised or at least sustained if a floor of parity pricing is placed under agricultural prices. In order to raise farm prices, the government has attempted to reduce agricultural production through restrictions on farm acreage. In attempting to raise income through price increases, it is quite apparent that farmers must produce first before they can obtain the benefits of high prices. It follows then that those that produce most receive the most benefits from parity pricing. The top 8 percent of our farms produced 50 percent of the value of all farm products sold (1959 Census). Thus this group received the largest amount of benefit from high farm prices. The lowest 61 percent of our farms produced only 12 percent of the value of all farm products sold.

[33] *The Tenure Status of Farmworkers in the United States*, Technical Bulletin No. 1217, Washington, D.C., U.S. Department of Agriculture, Agricultural Research Service and Agricultural Marketing Service (1960), pp. 44-45.

[34] Karl Shoemaker, "Opportunities and Limitations for Employment of Farm People Within and Outside of Farming," unpublished paper prepared for a seminar on Agricultural Resource Adjustments, organized by the Division of Agricultural Economics Program, Federal Extension Service, U.S. Department of Agriculture (1958).

Even though small farmers receive relatively little benefit from parity pricing, it would be incorrect to conclude that such farmers would be as well off without parity prices as with them. In the tobacco price support program, for example, in 1950, 565,554 farm allotments were established on a total of 1.47 million acres, or only 2.6 acres per farm. Similarly in cotton, of 1.1 million cotton allotments, over 500,000 were on farms with five acres or less. The formulas were devised to give the smaller farmer larger acreage proportionally than large farmers. Furthermore, agricultural economists at Iowa State University have estimated what would happen to farm income if the government abolished its parity and crop restriction program. These economists concluded that farm production would increase and that farm prices would drop drastically. Corn would drop from $1.05 per bushel to 66 cents and wheat would drop from $1.82 per bushel to 74 cents. With a somewhat higher production, farm income would drop drastically.[35] Parity pricing probably does provide some protection to low-income farmers. Yet production of low-income farmers is so low that parity pricing of itself will not bring an adequate income to poor farmers. Other remedies must be sought for low-income farmers.

POPULATION CONTROL

In view of our high rural birthrate, it is imperative for many people to move from farms in order to improve their income. Another suggestion is that the birthrate be reduced by better contraception practices. Friedman and his colleagues found that 80 percent of the couples with at least some high school education do something designed to limit conception, or plan to, compared with less than 60 percent of the women who have only a grammar school education. The use of contraceptives among lower-status people is less effective than for those of higher status. In one study, by the time women had reached the 30–34 age period, 48 percent of the fecund grammar school women who had used contraceptives had more children than they wished, compared with only 15 percent or less for those with more education. From these studies, Rainwater and Weinstein conclude that to properly control the birthrate not only will information be needed about proper contraceptive methods but that the knowledge must be made meaningful to the people. In their study, they report results of two Japanese experiments where physicians and their assistants discussed family planning, gave out contraceptives, and visited the couples regularly to encourage their continued use. In a three-year period, the birthrate in the villages dropped from 26.7 per 1,000 population to 14.6 and in the slum the corresponding drop was from 53.9 to 16.5.[36]

[35] "Farm Problem—One Way to Deal With It," *U. S. News and World Report* (May 30, 1960), pp. 104-105.

[36] Lee Rainwater, *And the Poor Get Children* (Chicago, Quadrangle Books, 1960).

OUTMIGRATION

Since 1920, more than 25 million people have migrated from farms to urban areas or nonfarm occupations. The annual average net outmigration is shown in Table 17-5. This table shows that the net outmigration during the depression decade of the thirties was much lower than for the more prosperous decades. Fewer jobs were available during the depression decade, and many farm people had no alternative but to stay on farms. These statistics demonstrate that a major solution to the farm problem lies not alone in agricultural policy but in expanding our urban economy at a rapid enough rate. The faster our urban economy expands, the more our surplus farm population can be absorbed into it. Evidence exists that the migration from low-income farming areas is higher than migration from high-income farming areas.[37]

TABLE 17–5. NET OUTMIGRATION FROM THE FARM POPULATION, AVERAGE ANNUAL NUMBER OF PERSONS AND RATES, SELECTED PERIODS, 1920–1959

Period[a]	Average Annual Net Outmigration[b]	Annual Rate of Net Outmigration (in Percentage)[c]
1920–1930	−630,000	−2.0
1930–1940	−383,000	−1.2
1940–1950	−952,000	−3.5
1950–1959	−805,000	−3.5

[a] Data relate to April.

[b] Includes persons who have not moved but whose residence is no longer classified as on a farm.

[c] Based on the data in the previous column and the average of the April farm populations for the period indicated.

Source: Farm Population, Estimates for 1950–59, U.S. Department of Agriculture, Agricultural Marketing Service (February, 1960), p. 4.

In spite of the large outmigration from farms, it has not been sufficient to eliminate rural poverty or increase per capita farm income relative to nonfarm income. The figures on net migration hide the fact that relatively large numbers of people move from nonfarm to farm residences. In 1950, for example, slightly more than one million people moved from nonfarm to farm residences. Generally these were young people who were married. Slightly over half took farm jobs. The median number of years schooling

[37] Farm Population, Estimates for 1950–59, Washington, D.C., U.S. Department of Agriculture, Agricultural Marketing Service, Table 1, p. 5.

for them was 8.5 years, compared to 8.2 for the farm population and 9.5 for the urban and rural nonfarm population. Although these census data give no reasons for the movement back to the farms, Professor D. Gale Johnson infers that the low educational achievement of this group may have given them insufficient training for urban life and that perhaps they had become dissatisfied with some aspect of urban life.[38]

Little has been done on the part of the government to directly facilitate the movement out of agriculture. The Wagner-Peyser Act of 1933 established a nationwide system of employment offices to be administered by the individual states. Unfortunately, there is a general lack of facilities and staff where the rural underemployed are located.[39] The employment service generally functions within an urban local labor market and does not reach out into the rural area.[40] Employment counseling has been expanded recently but only at the larger offices. Cooperative counseling programs have been worked out with the public schools, but again schools in rural towns and villages are almost entirely without such services. Only recently have attempts been made to have public employment offices service rural areas. To improve job information, D. Gale Johnson has suggested that a national labor extension service be created similar to the agricultural extension service that now exists but to apply to both urban and rural people. The purpose of this organization would be to provide information of career opportunities, earnings of jobs, training required, sources of information on job openings, how to apply for jobs, the nature of the work, and major locations of such jobs.[41] In addition to informational service, perhaps assistance should be given to facilitate migration. Job training and grants or loans to facilitate outmigration could be provided.[42] Lastly, improved education is needed in rural areas. Weaknesses of education in rural and low-income areas are the main reasons that federal aid to education is suggested. This proposal will be discussed below in Chapter 22.

FARM TENANCY LOANS

Another proposal to improve farm income is to reduce farm tenancy. Farm tenancy increased from 1880 until 1930, when more than 50 percent of all farms were operated by tenants.

Three reasons explain the increase in farm tenancy from 1880 to 1930. First, the amount of capital needed to become an owner plus the equipment and operating expenses were quite large in relation to farm income. In the

---

[38] D. Gale Johnson, "Policies to Improve the Labor Transfer Process," *American Economic Review*, Vol. 50, No. 2 (May, 1960), p. 407.

[39] *Underemployment of Rural Families*, Washington, D.C., Joint Committee on the Economic Report, 82nd Congress, 1st Session (1951), p. 63.

[40] Johnson, *op. cit.*, p. 408.

[41] *Ibid.*, p. 408.

[42] *Ibid.*, pp. 408-409.

corn belt, for example, the average cash grain farm had an investment of $97,000 in 1957 not counting the value of farm dwellings. Winter wheat farms in the Southern Plains averaged $81,000 and the average cotton farm in the Southern Piedmont averaged $17,000. Secondly, recurring business depressions have depleted the resources of farm families and kept them from becoming farm owners. Foreclosures increased spectacularly during the 1930's, and forced many owner-operators to become tenants or hired laborers. Lastly, the large birthrate on farms meant that there were more human resources than land resources available. Farm ownership was simply not a possibility for many.[43]

During the 1930's the trend toward increasing farm tenancy was reversed, and today only 19 percent of farms are operated by tenants. Four factors have been responsible for decreased tenancy. Better transportation and communication facilities made the vocational mobility of farm people greater so that they could leave the farms. World War II and the postwar prosperity provided many urban jobs for farm workers. They also gave farmers more income to become owners. Lastly, both public and private credit facilities have improved. Most of the credit facilities have been used by higher-income commercial farmers. However, the Bankhead-Jones Act of 1937 specifically provided for loans to tenants to buy farms. This program has been continued under the Farmers Home Administration program today.[44] This program provides for a 100 percent no down-payment loan.

The Farmers Home Administration requires that a county committee of three be organized, two of whom must be farmers. The county committee selects a limited number of tenants for loans. These are certified to the Farmers Home Administration, which makes the final decision. The Farmers Home Administration has attempted to approve only those loans that will place the borrower on an efficient family type unit. Too small units are ineligible for loans, as are loans for exceptionally large units. In 1946, several changes were made in the law. The low interest rate of 3½ percent on such loans was raised but may not exceed 5 percent. Secondly, loans must be refinanced through a private agency at a rate not exceeding 5 percent if a production credit association, Federal Land bank, or other responsible cooperative or private credit source is able to take over the loans. Lastly, part of the funds of this program were to go to creditors to insure mortgages. Under this type of insured loan, the highest amount loaned may not exceed 90 percent of the value of the farm. Less questionable changes in 1946 provided that loans could be used to enlarge farms to efficient family-size units or to make needed land and building improvements if the farms were already large enough.[45]

The farm ownership program, on the whole, has been a beneficial one.

[43] *The Tenure Status of Farmworkers in the United States,* p. 1.
[44] *Ibid.*
[45] *Underemployment of Rural Families,* p. 40.

A study of borrowers in 1953 showed that families who had a net worth of $2,868 before borrowing in 1946 had a net worth of $8,749 five years later. Their real income increased 15 percent. Another study of 1941 borrowers showed similar gains in net worth and income.[46] The government has not lost money on this loan program. Cumulatively from November, 1946, through June 30, 1962, $380 million has been paid on the principal of loans totaling $678 million. Interest payments totaled $142 million. Only $3 million had to be written off and accounts totaling $725,000 have been reduced to judgment. For the same period loan insurance authorization was granted for an additional $416 million.[47]

A major criticism of the farm ownership loan program has been the small-scale nature of its operations. In 1965, the Farmers Home Administration made farm ownership loans of $45 million to only 3,382 farmers and 8,804 other farmers obtained funds through private sources which were insured by the Farmers Home Administration. Considering that there are ¾ million tenants and sharecroppers in the United States, it would take considerable time to eliminate tenancy if sole reliance were placed on the Farmers Home Administration. That concentration of farm ownership is still a problem may be seen from the fact that 3 percent of the owners held 41 percent of the farm land held by individuals. In the South, concentration is even greater. There 3 percent of its owners hold 46 percent of the acreage. The same study showed that 18 percent of all owners did not live on farms, and that 35 percent were not active farmers.[48] Although ownership of farm land is concentrated, the ownership is primarily one by individuals rather than corporations. Corporations owned 6 percent of the farm land, and were most prevalent in the western states of Nevada, Arizona, Wyoming, and Texas, plus Florida.[49] The main reliance on reducing tenancy in the United States today is the movement of tenants off farms to urban areas. The movement of tenants has been quite rapid in recent years. In 1959 the number of tenants was less than a third of what they had been in 1940 (2.4 million in 1940 and 0.8 million in 1959).

PRODUCTION LOANS

Production loans to low-income farmers are administered by the Farmers Home Administration. Credit is made available only to those who are financially unable to help themselves or are unable to obtain credit on reasonable

[46] *Report of the Administrator of the Farmers Home Administration, 1953,* Washington, D.C., U.S. Department of Agriculture, p. 7.

[47] Letter from Howard Bertsch, Administrator, Farmers Home Administration (February 25, 1963).

[48] Buis T. Inman and William N. Pippin, *Farm Land Ownership in the United States,* Miscellaneous Publication No. 699, Washington, D.C., U.S. Department of Agriculture, Bureau of Agricultural Economics (1949), pp. 20, 50.

[49] *Ibid.,* p. 6.

terms through existing channels of credit. After some experience with these loans, the Farmers Home Administration concluded that it should curtail its seasonal credit of seed, feed, and fertilizer, since these of themselves would not increase farm income to any great extent. Instead of seasonal credit of this type, the Farmers Home Administration has been placing much more emphasis on supplying the farmer with equipment, stock, and enough capital to carry on an adequate farming business. Loans are from one to five years at an interest rate of 5 percent.[50] Resource guides have been developed to show the various types of farming suitable for a locality and the resources and capital necessary to provide for an adequate income. An example of what the Farmers Home Administration accomplished in Morgan County, Georgia, is recorded as follows:

Cotton farmers of Morgan County are breaking away from an inefficient farming pattern. Morgan County is typical of the Piedmont area that experienced a decline in the cotton economy many years ago. Some of the farmers abandoned their land to the boll weevil. Some moved away from the county. More farmers remained, however, than the cotton land could support.

Morgan County farmers knew they could increase their incomes and make more efficient use of their resources by adding milk production and some other enterprises to their farming system, but few could finance the cost of making these adjustments. Lack of enough collateral kept many from qualifying for loans from the local banks and cooperative credit sources.

The Farmers Home Administration has helped more than one-third of the 969 commercial farmers in Morgan County. More than 300 operating loans for livestock and equipment amounting to about $425,000 have been made since Nov. 1946. Since 1938, 94 families have been assisted in buying and developing farms with about $400,000 of farm ownership funds. Twenty-one families have received farm housing loans in the past three and a half years.

Of the 135 Morgan County families operating grade A dairies last year, 58 have received assistance from the Farmers Home Administration.

Usually these farmers started with herds of 18 to 20 cows. They built new dairy barns, commonly combining milking barn, milk room, and feed room under one roof. They installed new water systems. They bought milking machines, milk coolers, hot water heaters, cans and strainers. They developed permanent pastures, temporary winter grazing areas, and supplemental summer pastures. Their fields, previously exposed to the erosive effects of the weather, are now protected by green covers of clover, lespedeza, dallisgrass, and Bermuda Grass.

In three years after fencing their cotton fields and planting them to grass, the 58 farmers increased their average net worth about $5,000. Their gross income last year was about three times the 1949 county average of $3,422. They have developed 4,200 acres of good pasture. All 58 families now have electricity and own trucks or automobiles; most of them now have running water, and good stoves using butane gas or electricity; and about half have home freezers. More than half have built new houses or modernized their old homes.

[50] *Underemployment of Rural Families*, p. 32.

The last census showed that although the total number of farms in Morgan County declined considerably between 1935 and 1950, the number of owner-operated farms increased from 303 to 451—a gain of 148 farms. This trend reflects the work of the Farmers Home Administration. Of the 92 farm purchase loans made by the agency between 1938 and 1952, three-fourths were used to buy farms previously operated by tenants. In addition about 10 percent of the families who were aided by operating credit have been so successful that they acquired enough capital to buy farms with some financial assistance from other credit sources.

Cotton is still an important cash crop in Morgan County, but not to the extent of former years. A number of Farmers Home Administration borrowers still have some cotton along with their dairy cows. Their record books show they have learned to grow more bales on fewer acres, thus releasing more land for pasture. Financial records of borrowers who have not yet tried to shift away from cotton show incomes averaging considerably lower than for those who have taken up dairying.

In 1953 about 100 Morgan County families were assisted through the Madison office of the Farmers Home Administration, which also serves Jasper and Putnam Counties. Twenty-nine of the 40 families active in the farm-ownership program were ahead of payment schedules last spring, and only one farmer was behind schedule. Those using operating credit have paid more than has come due on their loans. About 250 operating loans and 54 farm ownership loans have been fully paid.[51]

Follow-up studies of borrowers of Farmers Home Administration production loans have shown even larger increases in income than farm ownership loans. This would be expected since these loans can increase the facilities on the farm rather than merely change the ownership arrangements. In an analysis of 25,460 families who retired their operating loans in fiscal year 1952, their net worth was $3,560 when they borrowed. Three and a half years later their net worth was $6,655. The value of their annual production increased from $2,646 to $4,521 per farm, an increase of 55.6 percent after allowance is made for price-level changes. The government has not lost money on this program. Cumulatively from November, 1946, through June 30, 1962, $1.7 billion in principal has been paid on loan advances of $2.3 billion. The principal payments represent 96 percent of the $1.8 billion matured. In interest $166 million has been earned. Only $21 million has been written off and accounts totaling $2.7 million have been reduced to judgment.[52]

In spite of the advantages provided by the Farmers Home Administration, the program has not been without its critics. In view of the relative surplus of farm products, some economists maintain that the government should not encourage increased production in farming as is done under the

[51] *Report of the Administrator of the Farmers Home Administration, 1953*, pp. 17-18.

[52] Letter from Howard Bertsch, Administrator, Farmers Home Administration (February 25, 1963).

Farmers Home Administration program. It could be argued, though, that farm enlargement and improvement loans will enable some farmers to obtain an adequate-sized acreage, and move others off the farms. Both those who remain and those who move are helped economically by such loans. To the extent that the loans go into the production of needed products, such as the example of milk in Morgan County, the program can be considered a success.

Another criticism has been that the Farmers Home Administration program is on such a small scale that it has been ineffective. In 1965, 72,597 farmers were loaned $300 million. If all of this money had been divided among all low-income farmers, the amount of money which could have been loaned per farm would have been negligible. Almost 33 percent more farmers (1965) apply for loans than get them simply because the Farmers Home Administration has insufficient sums to loan. Many others do not bother to apply, for they realize how little money the Farmers Home Administration has.[53]

In the past, another criticism of the program has been that the loans went to such small and inefficient farms that few benefits could be derived from such loans. In 1942, the Farm Security Administration reported that 52 percent of the farms receiving rehabilitation loans failed to provide minimum effective employment opportunities.[54] A more recent criticism is that many of the production loans are going to farmers who have a somewhat higher income than the low-income farmer. In a sample of Farmers Home Administration borrowers in 1954 and 1955, it was found that borrowers had an average gross farm income before borrowing of $3,300. While the net income of this group is quite low, farmers with less than a $2,500 gross income are not the group being helped by Farmers Home Administration loans.[55] Recent changes have been made to aid lower-income farmers through the War on Poverty (see Chapter 24).

After weighing all the criticisms of the production loans by the Farmers Home Administration, this author concludes the program should be continued. Farm income of those receiving loans has increased. In view of the fact that millions of our farm people are still living in poverty and that relatively few people are reached each year, the program could profitably be expanded.

RURAL COMMUNITY DEVELOPMENT SERVICE

The most recent program to help low-income farmers is the Rural Community Development program, which began on a pilot basis in 1955–1956.[56]

53 *Underemployment of Rural Families*, p. 33.

54 *Ibid.*, pp. 38-39.

55 *The Tenure Status of Farmworkers in the United States*, p. 61.

56 *Annual Report of the Secretary of Agriculture*, Washington, D.C., U.S. Department of Agriculture (1959), pp. 31-36, and (1962), pp. 39-50.

At that time projects were started in 54 counties. By 1959, 200 counties were included, and by 1962, Rural Development committees were organized in 1,800 counties with more than 50,000 members serving on committees. The basic idea behind the program is that progress will have to be made on a number of fronts to eliminate rural poverty. Not only is the program geared to more efficient farming but includes improved marketing along with industrial development, educational and vocational training, and better sanitation and health.

In order to improve farming, the U.S. Department of Agriculture, through its Federal Extension Service, hired 143 additional agents. The larger commercial farmers have generally been the ones to obtain help from the county agent. For the Rural Community Development program it was felt that additional personnel was needed primarily to help the low-income farmers. Twenty-one of the agents hired had statewide or areawide program responsibilities. Although this part of the program has been discontinued, other personnel have aided rural depressed counties. The Soil Conservation Service has supplied 75 man-years of technical assistance so that 2,573 farms now have soil survey maps and other information to help adopt better conservation practices. The U.S. Forest Service assigned a specialist in each of its regional offices to work full or part time to improve management and marketing of forestry products. The Agricultural Stabilization and Conservation Committees in 19 states increased the allocation of the Agricultural Conservation Program in Rural Development counties, and the Farmers Home Administration increased its loans in these counties as well.

Farm marketing has received attention through 60 projects in 44 counties. New packing plants have been built, and cooperative marketing associations have been formed among small farmers. The results have been that new marketing outlets have been established. The Farmer Cooperative Service has provided guidance in this area. Two special publications have been issued to acquaint the professional personnel in the program with the role of cooperatives and credit unions in stimulating rural economic growth.

The Rural Community Development counties are also attempting to stimulate industrial growth. The Department of Labor in 1959 opened demonstration projects in a few states and then expanded the program to improve employment services in rural areas. The Small Business Administration has channeled 63 loans amounting to $2½ million into these areas. At least 9,000 additional jobs were provided. New firms hired workers in the following industries: wood planing and finishing, food handling and processing, clothing manufacture, feed milling, charcoal manufacture, boat building, and others.

Educational and training programs, stay-in-school campaigns, vocational guidance, and other programs have been adopted in 145 projects to aid youth in rural depressed areas. Other groups not mentioned above who are participating in the program are the U.S. Department of Health, Education, and

Welfare, the U.S. Department of Commerce, the U.S. Department of the Interior, the Social Security Administration, the Rural Electrification Administration, and the Council of Economic Advisors. The Under Secretary of Agriculture, as Chairman of the Committee for the Rural Development Program, has responsibility for the direction of the program at the national level. To help him, a National Coordinator of the program has been appointed.

The Rural Community Development program has made only a beginning. With past experience as a guide, it should be possible to expand the program to cover practically all low-income rural counties. Although the advantages of the program outweigh the disadvantages, several shortcomings of the program may be noted.[57] The first appropriation for the Rural Community Development program was $2 million in 1957, and this figure grew only to $2.7 million in fiscal 1961, and is expected to reach $3.5 million in 1967. The yearly cost equals the daily cost of storage of surplus farm products for one day. For the 10 million rural farm people living in rural depressed areas, the federal expenditures annually for this program have totalled only 30 cents per rural inhabitant. Although the program has been enlarged from the original 54 counties, expenditures for the program have been so limited as to preclude adequate aid to poor, rural counties. Additional aid is now forthcoming from the companion Area Redevelopment program (see Chapter 13), but funds are woefully inadequate to reduce poverty effectively in many rural counties.

INCREASING CONSUMPTION OF FARM PRODUCTS

SURPLUS FOOD DISTRIBUTION TO THE NEEDY

In a seminar which the author was privileged to attend, several hours were spent on the problem of agricultural surpluses. The group was rather despairing of what to do about the problem. Two hours later, after the gloom of surpluses had deepened, one economist took the group by storm by suggesting that "We eat the stuff!" Proposals to increase farm consumption have existed for some time. As early as 1933, the Federal Emergency Relief Administration purchased food and clothing to distribute to the needy. When the emergency slaughter of surplus pigs and sows was initiated in 1933, the Department of Agriculture distributed some of the hog products to the Federal Emergency Relief Administration. The Department of Agriculture also advanced funds to the same agency to purchase dairy and beef products.

In 1935, Congress passed Public Law 320, which provided that 30 percent of the customs revenue be made available to the Department of Agri-

[57] Don Paarlberg, "Rural Development Achievements and Shortcomings as Seen at the Federal Level," *Journal of Farm Economics*, Vol. 43 (1961), pp. 1511-1517.

culture to aid in increased consumption of food products by low-income groups. Under this authority, the Department of Agriculture proceeded to buy surplus products and make them available to state welfare agencies.[58] In fiscal 1961 more than 23 million people received surplus food. Included were 15.5 million schoolchildren, 1.4 million in charitable institutions, and 6.4 million needy persons in family units. People under such welfare programs as Old-Age Assistance, Aid to Families with Dependent Children, and the like are automatically eligible for surplus food. Others may qualify after screening by county welfare offices. One problem with county administration is that a few of the counties have not bothered to come under the program. In Oklahoma, for example, 7 of 77 counties do not distribute surplus food to the needy even though the food is received free. The only expenses incurred by the county are to provide clerical help to distribute the food, plus storage costs and transportation expenses in obtaining the food from the state. One of the first moves of the Kennedy administration was to increase substantially the surplus food distribution to needy families. In addition to flour, cornmeal, nonfat dried milk, rice, lard, and butter, needy families early in 1961 began receiving canned pork and gravy, dried whole eggs, dry beans, peanut butter, and rolled oats. About 1.1 billion pounds of food, worth about $470 million, were donated by the federal government for distribution in all 50 states and the territories during 1965.[59] Surplus food is also distributed free or through subsidy to countries abroad.[60]

FOOD STAMP PROGRAMS

In 1939 a plan was conceived to provide the needy with food by giving them 50 cents' worth of blue stamps free for every dollar's worth of orange stamps purchased. The orange stamps were treated as cash, which could be spent on any food products. Blue stamps could only be used to purchase surplus foods. The plan was later adopted to dispose of surplus cotton.[61] The plan did aid in increasing the consumption of needy families.[62] The food stamp plan was discontinued in 1943. It was reinstated on a trial basis by the Kennedy administration in 1961 in eight depressed counties. Needy participants were permitted to buy coupon books in the amount that they generally spent for food. There were then given coupon books of a higher monetary value. From July through November of 1961, 138,000 persons purchased $1.7 mil-

[58] Frederick V. Waugh, "The Food Distribution Programs of the Agricultural Marketing Administration," The Annals of the American Academy of Political and Social Science, Vol. 225 (May, 1943), p. 169.

[59] Budget of the United States, fiscal year ending June 30, 1967, Washington, D.C., Bureau of the Budget, p. 136.

[60] Annual Report of the Secretary of Agriculture, 1961, p. 46.

[61] Olive T. Kephart, "The Effect of the Stamp Plan on Living Levels," Monthly Labor Review, Vol. 51 (1940), pp. 1060-1065.

[62] Don Wharton, "The Federal Food Stamp Plan," American Mercury, Vol. 49 (1940), p. 478.

lion a month of coupon books and received coupon books valued at $2.8 million. Thus the program cost the government slightly over $1 million per month. Instead of being restricted to surplus foods as in the earlier plan, the recipients could purchase any foods except a few imported items. Participants in the program preferred it to the Direct Distribution Program (distribution of surplus products), because the families had a free choice of foods. In evaluation of this program in the first six months of operation, the Agricultural Marketing Service of the U.S. Department of Agriculture concluded that the program was a success. Since then the program has been greatly enlarged so that by 1967 expenditures are expected to be $150 million.

SCHOOL LUNCHES

Another program to increase food consumption and also improve the health of children was provided in the National School Lunch Act of 1946. This act provides that the federal government match state and local funds to subsidize school lunches. Federal contributions including donated commodities and the special milk program totaled $364 million in fiscal 1962. About 35 percent of the children attending the nation's public schools participate in the National School Lunch program.[63] Participation is greatest in our largest cities and smallest in our smaller town and rural areas.[64] Figures for 1963 show that the total cost per lunch came to 48.3 cents. Of this amount 10.7 cents was a federal subsidy and 10.5 cents was the state and local subsidy. The children paid the rest.[65] About 10 percent of the children who have the least income receive free meals.[66]

The need for a school lunch program is quite apparent. Professor Lampman estimates that there are 11 million children in families that are in the bottom 19 percent of our families that do not average $2,500 for a family of four.[67] The lack of proper diet for children in the lower-income groups has been found by a number of studies. Faith Clark found that families with incomes between $2,000 and $3,000 in 1959 were getting only a little more than half the calcium believed necessary by the National Research Council. They were only getting about two-thirds the needed amount of ascorbic acid and only 87 percent of the protein. A study in a children's hospital found

[63] Budget of the United States, fiscal year ending June 30, 1967, p. 133.

[64] Kenneth E. Anderson, Urban School Systems Without Lunch Service as a Potential Market for Foods, Bulletin No. 443, Washington, D.C., U.S. Department of Agriculture, Agricultural Marketing Service (1961), p. 4.

[65] Analyses of Source of Funds, Matching Requirements and Participation in the Program, Fiscal Years 1947–63, Washington, D.C., U.S. Department of Agriculture, National School Lunch Program, mimeographed, p. 1.

[66] Statement of Mrs. Alice Radue, Legislative Committee of the National Congress of Parents and Teachers, Department of Agriculture Appropriations for 1959, Hearings before the Subcommittee of the Committee on Appropriations, House of Representatives, Part V, 85th Congress, 2nd Session, p. 130.

[67] Lampman, The Low Income Population and Economic Growth, op. cit., p. 7.

that 3 to 5 percent of the children who go through its outpatient department have nutritional anemia in severe degrees and 10 percent of the children who are hospitalized have severe anemia. A study by the Florida State Board of Health found that in one large high school, more than 40 percent of the 740 students did not have any fruit for the day. In a combined junior and senior high school 35 percent of the children who did not eat in the school lunchroom had no milk for the day.[68]

Whether school lunches can remedy such deficiencies is another matter. Professor Pauline B. Mack, in making a nine-year study of more than 200 typical school lunches, found that there were none which met the objectives of compensating fully for omission in the home diets of the great majority of children to whom they were fed. More than one-half failed to provide even one-third, or one meal's quota, of the energy and the major currently calculated nutrient allowances recommended by the food and nutrition board of the National Research Council for the sex and age composition of the respective group of children. However, Professor Mack found that children did show marked improvement provided that the lunches were planned by a trained dietitian, who also studied the diets at home so that the school lunches complemented the meals received at home, at least in major part. She pointed out the dangers involved in having lay people in charge of the program. At one school that was attended exclusively by a foreign racial group, medical examinations and nutritional tests showed that the children were receiving a diet comparatively high in carbohydrates but low in all other required nutrients. They were very poorly nourished in most respects. When a school lunch program was inaugurated, a volunteer committee of mothers was placed in charge of the program with the result that more of the same heavy carbohydrate diet was served at the school lunch.[69]

Studies in Florida, South Carolina, and elsewhere have found that school lunches have helped nutritionally.[70] The basic problem is one of financing the program. In the past several years, of 43 states replying, 32 reported that they had to increase the price of their lunches. Unfortunately, increasing prices results in less participation. Sixteen states reported that the increase in prices caused decreased participation. Two of the states reported a one-third decrease in participation.[71] As a goal for the program, lunches should be served to considerably more than the one-third of the children now receiving lunches. If all children with a family income of $2,000 per year or

---

[68] Statement of Mrs. Ada Barnett Stough, Executive Director, American Parents Committee, National School Lunch Program, *Department of Agriculture Appropriations for 1958,* Hearings before the Subcommittee of the Committee on Appropriations, Part V, 85th Congress, 1st Session, pp. 21-22.

[69] Pauline B. Mack, "A Nine-Year Study of the School Lunch," *Journal of Home Economics,* Vol. 39 (1947), pp. 73-76.

[70] Statement of Mrs. Ada Barnett Stough, pp. 21-22.

[71] Statement of Mrs. Ada Barnett Stough, p. 132.

less were given a free meal, and more participation occurred, the costs to the various governments would, of course, increase.

Summary

Of the 32 million living in poverty in the United States, about 8 million have a rural farm residence. The hired labor force in this country is composed of over 1 million workers who listed farm work as their chief activity. There is much underemployment among this group, and only slightly more than half of them work 150 or more days per year. Their annual income is far below an adequate amount. Agricultural workers are exempt from most of the social legislation passed to relieve other distressed groups. They are not given bargaining rights as most other groups are under the National Labor Relations Act. Neither are they covered in most states by workmen's compensation, unemployment insurance, minimum wage laws, or public assistance. The only coverage for hired farm labor has been under the federal minimum wage law and the OASDHI program. In the latter program administrative difficulties have kept some workers from coverage.

Our migratory farm workers have additional difficulties besides being not covered under social legislation. In migrating, their work is less steady than nonmigratory workers. Much underemployment exists among migratory workers. Abuses by labor contractors have resulted in federal licensing of contractors. Housing and health present serious problems for migratory workers. Serious educational deficiencies exist among migratory children, many of whom work in violation of our child labor laws.

We have many subsistence farmers who are living on an extremely low income. Most of these farmers are located in the South, but farm poverty exists in other parts of the country as well. Parity pricing has helped to maintain the income of low-income farmers, but most of the benefits of parity pricing have gone to the most affluent farmers who produce the most. Outmigration has helped to improve per capita farm income, but it has not been fast enough to abolish rural poverty. More could be done to increase the migration from rural areas both in the form of information, training, and placement of workers. Federal aid to education would ease the crushing burden under which low-income rural communities are attempting to educate their youth, only to see them migrate. Farm tenancy tends to handicap many farmers also. The trend is toward a reduction of farm tenancy, although the Farmers Home Administration program of farm ownership loans is so small that only a few thousand tenants are helped each year. Production loans have been on a somewhat larger scale, but even here the program is miniature in relation to the number of poor farmers. The most recent step to eliminate rural poverty has been the Rural Community Development program. Tried in some of our poorest rural counties, it has attempted not only to improve farm production and marketing but also to increase industrial development, improve educational and vocational training, and improve sanitation and health. An expansion of this program should help. Lastly, increasing farm consumption through foreign aid, distribution to the needy, and to children under the National School Lunch program should help reduce rural poverty.

MINORITY GROUPS: NEGROES
IN THE UNITED STATES

Certain minority groups comprise large numbers falling in low-wage occupations. In 1963, of 7.2 million families living in poverty 2.1 million (29 percent) were nonwhite.[1] The problem of nonwhite poverty is primarily a Negro problem since Negroes comprise about 95 percent of our nonwhite population. Other nonwhite groups such as the American Indian face grave economic problems also.

INCOME AND HOUSING

In March of 1965 the median family income of nonwhite families living in metropolitan areas was $4,671. However, over a fourth had incomes of below $3,000. Income for nonwhites living in nonmetropolitan areas was much lower—$2,308.[2] The income for vast numbers of nonwhites is so low as to cause grave economic problems among nonwhites—so low that not even the necessities of life may be purchased. The census of 1960 showed that less than half of all nonwhite houses were classified as not dilapidated and as having a private toilet, bath, and hot running water. The figure for whites was 79 percent, compared with 44 percent for nonwhites.[3] Overcrowding was also evident for a large percentage of the nonwhite population. About one-third of all nonwhite families live in houses averaging more than 1.01 persons per room.[4] Quite obviously family living becomes more complicated and frustrating when families must live in substandard and crowded housing.

MEDICAL CARE

Negroes are unable to buy as much health care as whites. This statement holds true even when it is a matter of life or death. The statistics of death

[1] Mollie Orshansky, "Counting the Poor," *Social Security Bulletin*, Vol. 28, No. 1 (January, 1965), p. 21.

[2] *Current Population Reports*, Series P-60, No. 48, Washington, D.C., U.S. Department of Commerce, Bureau of the Census (1966), Table 11, p. 26.

[3] *1960 Census of Housing*, U.S. Summary, Washington, D.C., U.S. Department of Commerce, Bureau of the Census, HC(1), No. 1, Table 22, pp. 1-210, Figure 17, p. xxxvii.

[4] *Ibid.*, Table 23, pp. 1-212.

rates for certain treatable diseases show quite clearly the lack of medical care of nonwhites. The death rates for tuberculosis, syphilis, intestinal infections, rheumatic fever, influenza, and genitourinary diseases were from two to eight times as great for nonwhites as whites.[5] Since large numbers of nonwhite women do not have a physician at childbirth, both the maternal and childbirth death rate is much higher among nonwhites than among whites. Of 638,928 births of nonwhites in 1963, a midwife rather than a physician was present at 61,908 (10 percent). The corresponding percentage for whites was 0.4 percent.[6] The failure to get adequate medical care shortens the lives of nonwhites in the United States. The nonwhite male in the United States in 1963 lived on an average 6½ years less than the white male and the nonwhite female lived 8 years less than the white female.

POPULATION

The number of nonwhites in the United States in 1900 was a little over 9 million, or 12 percent of our population. By 1950, the number of nonwhites had grown to almost 16 million, but the white population had grown faster so that the nonwhite population was only 10 percent of the population. By 1960 the nonwhite population numbered 20.5 million or 11 percent of the population.[7] Although the nonwhites have a higher death rate than whites, the marked excess in the birthrate of nonwhites has enabled the nonwhite population to grow at a faster rate than the white population since 1950.

RURAL NEGROES

Large numbers of Negroes have been moving from farms. In 1930, 40 percent of Negroes lived in a rural farm environment, but by 1960 this figure had been reduced to 8 percent. Many Negroes have moved out of the South also. Whereas about three-fourths of all Negroes lived in the South in 1940, by 1960 this figure had been reduced to a little over one half. The movement of the Negroes from farms and out of the South can be explained mainly by economic factors. Income in urban areas is much higher for Negroes than in a rural farm environment. Table 18-1 shows the income of Negroes in metropolitan and nonmetropolitan areas, and that nonmetropolitan income in general is less than metropolitan income (cities above 50,000), and this is particularly so for nonwhites. In general, the rural Negro lives in an extreme degree of poverty. Part of the problem of most Negro farmers is that

[5] *Vital Statistics in the United States, 1963*, Vol. II, Part A, Washington, D.C., U.S. Department of Health, Education, and Welfare, Table 1-20, pp. 1-39, 1-72.

[6] *Ibid.*, Vol. I, Table 1-24, pp. 1-26.

[7] *General Social and Economic Characteristics, United States Summary, 1960*, PC(1)–1C, U.S., Washington, D.C., U.S. Department of Commerce, Bureau of the Census, Table 65, pp. 1-199.

they own no land, and therefore must rent or share the crop with the white owner. The 1959 Census of Agriculture showed that there were 97,388 full Negro owners compared with 141,017 tenants. The corresponding figure for whites was 2.0 million full owners and 0.6 million tenants. The number of Negro tenants increased from 559,000 in 1900 to 710,000 in 1920, and has been decreasing ever since.[8] Even where Negroes do acquire land, they still remain poor, for their land is of a poor quality in out-of-the-way places. The value of land per acre for Negro full owners in 1959 was $105, compared with $149 for Negro tenants.[9] Farm studies show that Negro full owners have much less equipment to operate with, and that they diversify their crops much less than white owners.[10]

TABLE 18–1. INCOME OF WHITE AND NONWHITE FAMILIES AND UNRE-LATED INDIVIDUALS, METROPOLITAN AND NONMETROPOLITAN, 1964

Families or Unrelated Individuals	Metropolitan		Nonmetropolitan	
	Median Income	Percentage Below $3,000	Median Income	Percentage Below $3,000
Families:				
White	$7,603	11	$5,513	24
Nonwhite	4,671	27	2,308	63
Unrelated individuals:				
White	2,455	56	1,449	71
Nonwhite	1,722	68	851	91

Source: Current Population Reports: Consumer Income, Series P-60, U.S. Department of Commerce, Bureau of the Census, No. 48 (April, 1966), Table 1, p. 13.

The Negro farmer is typically a sharecropper, a term denoting that the tenant pays the rent in the form of a share or percentage of the crop produced rather than a cash rent. The rental charges are from a third to a half or more of the crop depending on who furnishes the machinery and seed, feed, and fertilizer. In addition the Negro frequently runs out of money, and must borrow from a white creditor for living allowances. Since with such a low income the Negro is a poor risk, the rate of interest charged is high. Part of the pitifully small income of the Negro must go to meet interest payments borrowed at high rates.

[8] Census of Agriculture, 1959, Vol. II, Washington, D.C., U.S. Department of Agriculture and U.S. Department of Commerce, Bureau of the Census, Chapter X, Table 4, p. 1832.

[9] Ibid., Chapter X, Table 9, p. 1036.

[10] Victor Perlo, The Negro in Southern Agriculture (New York, International Publishers, 1953), pp. 33-40.

The major program to help farmers in this country has been the parity pricing system. Higher prices for farm products have enabled Negro farmers to make more money than without price supports. However, the poorest 44 percent of our farms produced only 5 percent of the value of farm products sold.[11] Since parity prices help only those that produce, low income farmers receive few of the benefits of parity pricing. The protection of maintaining farm prices does help sustain Negro farm income, but most Negro farmers produce so little that the parity price has not enabled them to climb from poverty. A program geared more closely to poor farmers has been the Farmers Home Administration program, which loans money to poor farmers to buy or improve their farms. Loans must be approved first by a local county committee of three members. Usually these people are white farmers, who tend to favor white borrowers over Negro borrowers. Even if no prejudice is involved, white farmers usually have more resources than Negro farmers and are considered better risks. For this reason and also because the Farmers Home Administration has been on such a small scale, little hope for the Negro farmer can be held out in this direction. Since the United States already has a relative surplus of farm products and the Negro farmer is handicapped in so many ways, it is clear that the main hope of most Negro farmers today is for them to move off farms into urban areas.

RURAL EDUCATION

Negro education in rural schools is particularly deficient. The lack of education not only results in a poorly trained agricultural work force, but also causes serious handicaps to those Negroes who move into urban society without sufficient training. The South spends only about three-fourths as much on education per pupil as the rest of the nation. Although the South spends a larger percentage of its income for education than the rest of the country, it still fell far short of matching the per pupil expenditures for the country. Rural southern children are handicapped even more, for in the South only about 81 percent as much is spent in rural areas per child as in urban areas. The rural Negro child is handicapped even more, for less is expended on their education than on white education.[12]

Rural schools for Negroes in the South spend less than one-half as much per child as is spent on the average in the whole United States. Lower pay for teachers, higher teaching loads, and less library expenditures are typical of the Negro rural school. The 1954 Supreme Court decision outlawing segregation in education should help in the border and northern states where some schools have been integrated. The South, however, is integrating

11 *Census of Agriculture, 1959,* Vol. II, Chapter XI, p. 1206.
12 Patrick McCauley and Edward D. Ball, *Southern Schools: Progress and Problems* (Nashville, Southern Education Reporting Service, 1959), pp. 37-38, and Table 22, p. 107.

at such a slow pace that it will be some years before the force of the Supreme Court decision will have an appreciable effect on Negro education in the South.[13] The Civil Rights Act of 1964 should aid in the integration process (see page 416 below). Federal aid to education should particularly aid the low-income states of the South. This proposal is discussed in detail in Chapter 22.

URBAN NEGROES

Urban Negro income is substantially higher than rural Negro income. The income differential has caused the Negro trek from rural areas. Since urban areas in the South are closer than northern cities, some of the Negroes have moved there. Negro income in southern cities is far below that of most northern cities. For example, the median income of Negro males in Columbia, S. C., was $1,654, Nashville $1,967, Orlando $1,910, and Shreveport $1,547. These figures may be compared with the cities of Flint, $4,296; Gary, $4,173; and San Jose, $4,065. Many of the Negroes learn of the higher income potential in the North, and have moved en masse, particularly to larger northern cities. In the decade of the 1950's, more than two million nonwhites, or 10 percent of the nonwhite population, moved to 17 of the largest cities of the country, mainly located out of the South. According to the 1960 Census, 5.5 million nonwhites, or more than 25 percent, lived within the city limits of 17 large cities. Only 12 percent of the white population lived in the same cities. The assimilation of this group of Negroes will remain one of the major problems of the American people for a number of years. Although in many areas of the North integrated schooling exists, the fact that Negroes move into segregated housing areas has resulted in de facto segregation. It may be that concentrating large numbers of Negroes into a few large cities may delay integrated housing and other forms of integration for years. If Negroes had moved to smaller cities in the North, the problem of assimilation possibly would have been easier.

URBAN EDUCATION

In some slum areas half or more of the children drop out of school in grades 9, 10, and 11.[14] Many of the school drop-outs are unable to find jobs. In making a study of slum versus wealthy schools, James B. Conant concluded that a continuation of the present slum situation was "a menace to the social and political health of the large cities." In his study he found that expendi-

[13] *Survey of School Desegregation in the Southern and Border States, 1965–66,* Washington, D.C., U.S. Commission on Civil Rights, pp. 1, 27-28.

[14] The material in this section was taken from James B. Conant, *Slums and Suburbs* (New York, McGraw-Hill, 1961). Reprinted by permission.

tures per pupil in wealthy suburban schools were over twice that of slum areas. Whereas the wealthier schools were likely to be spacious, modern buildings staffed with 70 professionals per 1,000 pupils, the slum school was apt to be crowded, often dilapidated, and unattractive, and staffed by 40 or fewer professionals per 1,000 pupils.

Conant feared the mass of unemployed and frustrations of Negro youth in deteriorated slums. He compared their plight "to the piling up of inflammable material in an empty building in a city block. Potentialities for trouble —indeed possibilities of disaster—are surely there." In describing one of the large city Negro slum areas, typical of other slums, he pointed out that most of the inhabitants had come from the Deep South within the last month to the last three years. The turnover of students was so rapid that one principal remarked that a teacher absent for more than one week would have difficulty recognizing her class when she returned. About a third of the families were headed by women who move from one rented room to another month after month. The children change schools regularly. Only 33 percent of the parents had completed elementary school, and only 10 percent had graduated from high school. In some of the Negro slums, gang warfare existed among the boys, and vicious fights occurred outside of school between Negro girls. In reply to a school questionnaire on what their biggest problem was, a majority of junior high school girls replied that it was getting from the street into their apartments without being molested in the hallways of their tenements. Some of the children slept while in school. Conant attributed this to no place to sleep at home or else incredibly violent family fights and horrors through the night.

The slum conditions of Negroes, according to Conant, is in need of attack on many fronts. Employment for youth is desperately needed. So is improved housing and family relations. His prescriptions for education were more detailed since the book *Slums and Suburbs* was primarily about education in slums compared with wealthy neighborhoods. The reading problem was a major one, for so many of the pupils were slow readers. In spite of serious efforts, many ninth-grade Negro slum pupils—over half in some schools—were reading at the sixth-grade level or lower. In some schools where progress was being made to improve reading, attempts were made to interest the head of the family in newspapers, magazines, and possibly even books. Many such schools use social workers or visiting teachers to keep the parent or parents in touch with the schools.

Some have pointed out that early immigrants to America had to endure slum conditions. They had confidence that they could pull themselves out of poverty, and did so. Negroes today lack such a conviction. In addition, foreign immigrants came from a poor but stable society. Pride of family and often strong church connections aided the immigrants. Also labor shortages during the earlier period enabled most immigrants to obtain jobs. The replacement of unskilled workers by automation will make job opportunities for Negroes much more difficult to obtain. Conditions of today in terms of the kinds of people and their economic and social setting are far different from the poor city districts of 1900.

Conant recommended that school guidance officers in large cities should be given the responsibility of following the careers of youth from the time they leave school until age 21. He felt that there was too abrupt a break for students leaving school at 16. He suggested that guidance staffs should be doubled in most of our large cities to perform this function. Improved vocational and apprenticeship training were recommended. Several projects have been implemented to improve education in slum areas. Aided by the Ford Foundation, the Great Cities Gray Areas School Improvement Program has attempted to improve education in several large cities. The various projects range all the way from remedial reading clinics, special orientation centers for newly arrived migrants from the South, programs for overaged pupils, to special school-community coordinating teams, which integrate the efforts of teachers, students, parents, employers, labor organizations, and social agencies. Lastly, Conant recommended a pay differential for teachers in slum schools. Otherwise teachers with the most seniority choose to teach in more prosperous areas. The result is that slum schools are staffed with the newly hired, substitutes, and emergency teachers. Some of Conant's recommendations are:

As to the schools in the large city slums:

8. The contrast in the money spent per pupil in wealthy suburban schools and in slum schools of the large cities challenges the concept of equality of opportunity in American public education. More money is needed in slum schools.
9. Social dynamite is building up in our large cities in the form of unemployed out-of-school youth, especially in the Negro slums. We need accurate and frank information neighborhood by neighborhood.
10. The schools should be given the responsibility for educational and vocational guidance of youth after they leave school until age 21. This will require more money.
11. Increased attention ought to be paid in both slums and suburbs to developing meaningful courses for pupils with less than average abilities. To this end consideration should be given by every school and community to the expansion of work-study programs for slow students, and to the provision of at least auto mechanics shop for boys in every high school in metropolitan areas.
12. Employment opportunities in the large cities must be promptly opened on a nondiscriminatory basis. Because of the attitude of management and labor this can be done only through the use of Federal funds.
13. The answer to improving Negro education in the large Northern cities is to spend more money and to upgrade Negro schools, many of which are in

slums, rather than to effect token integration by transporting pupils across attendance lines. Fully integrated teaching staffs are a necessity as well.

14. More teachers and perhaps more pay for teachers are necessary for schools in the slums than in either the high income districts of the large cities or the wealthy suburbs. Special training programs for teachers in slum schools are needed.

15. No effort should be spared in slum areas to enlist the support of parents in the education of their children. To this end, adult education programs should be improved and expanded.

16. Big cities need decentralized administration in order to bring the schools closer to the needs of the people in each neighborhood and to make each school fit the local situation.

17. Nonpolitical, honest school boards composed of high-minded citizens who can differentiate between policy-making and administration are essential. An aroused public opinion is needed to correct the situation in those cities where such school boards do not exist.[15]

Conant reserved judgment on whether Negro children have as high a scholastic aptitude as white children. In a description of an all-white slum, the grade achievement of children in grade 4 was a full year below their grade placement—a typical achievement in any slum area. The houses in the area were old. Large homes were rented from absentee owners by single rooms or small, two- or three-room apartments to large families. The people living there were transients, the unemployed, the unskilled and unschooled, and distressed families, many of whose members were recently either admitted or released from mental or penal institutions. All sorts of evil flourished in this community, such as peddling of dope, drunkenness, diseases, accidents, truancies, physical, mental, and moral handicaps, and sex perversion, some of which involved children. This white-slum study concluded with the observation that there was no reason to believe that students in this group were inherently or genetically less capable than average students. Conant applied the same reasoning to Negroes. Only after Negroes have been placed in stable, high-income communities will comparisons between Negroes and whites have merit.

Recently a comprehensive study was made to determine the equality of educational opportunity in the United States.[16] This study analyzed the schooling of more than 645,000 students in all sections of the country of Puerto Rican, Negro, Mexican-American, American Indian, Oriental-American, and white backgrounds. Here only the schooling of Negroes and whites will be compared. Most of the Negro schools were segregated. More than 65 percent of all Negro pupils in the first grade attended schools that were be-

---

[15] *Ibid.*, pp. 145-147.

[16] James Coleman *et al.*, *Equality of Educational Opportunity*, Washington, D.C., U.S. Department of Health, Education, and Welfare, Office of Education (1966).

tween 90 and 100 percent Negro. Less segregation existed in higher grades, but even in the 12th grade, 66 percent of all Negroes attended schools that were 50 percent or more Negro. There was more segregation, of course, in the South than in the North.

In general, the facilities for Negro schools were not inferior to that of whites. Relatively recent construction in the South built to avoid integration has resulted in the Negroes' occupying newer building than whites. Since the schools were newer, a larger percentage of Negroes was attending schools with an auditorium, cafeteria, and infirmary. Negro students had more full-time librarians and free textbooks than white students, although white students more often had a sufficient number of textbooks and had libraries with a larger number of books per student. Weaknesses in facilities for Negroes were evidenced in their having fewer shops with power tools, and fewer science and language laboratories.

Negro students had less access to accelerated curricula and college preparatory curricula. Their schools were less frequently regionally accredited. They less frequently had speech impairment classes, and they used intelligence tests less frequently. They less frequently had a school band, a school newspaper, or a debating team. Negro pupils less frequently took courses in science, language, English, and mathematics. Teachers of Negroes made lower scores on verbal tests given them, and more of such teachers attended colleges not offering graduate degrees. Negro students were further handicapped by having fewer encyclopedias in the home, having fewer mothers who had graduated from high school, and by coming from larger families than whites.

In testing for achievement, it was found that the original deficiencies of Negroes worsened as they progressed through school. At grade six the average Negro was 1.6 years behind whites, but by the twelfth grade they were 3.3 years behind. Negroes were particularly disadvantaged in the South, where they scored farther below southern whites than northern Negroes scored below northern whites.

An important part of the study was to analyze the factors affecting the achievement of students. One finding was that facilities and curricula of the schools accounted for little variation in pupil achievement. The quality of teaching, however, showed a strong relation to pupil achievement. Students achieved more when their teachers scored higher on the verbal skills tests, had a high level of education, and had parents who had a high level of education. Most important of all, students did better if the aspirations of the other students in the school were high. This finding has important implications for the integration of schools. One is that little will be accomplished by integrating lower-class Negroes with lower-class white students. Much more would be accomplished educationally by integrating lower-class Negroes with either middle-class Negroes or middle-class whites.

FAMILY DISORGANIZATION

An added problem in the migration of Negroes from rural to urban areas is that the cohesiveness of families tends to break down.[17] A history of the Negro reveals several factors that have weakened family ties. Slavery broke many families. The Emancipation period also weakened family ties by destroying the authority of the slaveowners and customary ways of family life. Disorganization came about, for example, when the men left to work in turpentine or lumber camps and when the women left to work in town to supplement their income. Promiscuous sex relations and constant changing of spouses became typical among demoralized elements of the free Negroes in the South. During both World Wars I and II, millions of Negroes moved northward, many of them cutting family ties at home.

Even though urban income for nonwhites is substantially higher than nonwhite rural income, it still is not sufficient for a minimum health and decency standard of living. With weaker family traditions and all the frustrations of low income, the urban Negro family is much less stable than that of the white. The 1960 census shows that many more nonwhites live as single individuals and fewer as married couples than do whites. Although nonwhites constitute 11 percent of the population, they comprise 13 percent of all unrelated individuals and 8 percent of married couples.[18] It is common among sociologists to stress the stabilizing factor of the family on human behavior. Many Negroes lack this stabilizing force, and within urban areas tend to congregate in areas where boarding-house living predominates. Large percentages of Negro families have no male head, and the mother frequently must let the children shift for themselves while she earns a living. Out of such an environment comes much juvenile delinquency and crime. Statistics on crime show about three or four times as much on the part of Negroes as whites. Low-rent public housing is one remedy suggested for family disorganization. This remedy is discussed in detail in Chapter 22.

EMPLOYMENT PROBLEMS

When Negroes shift from rural to urban environment, they tend to be discriminated against in getting jobs. Table 18-2 shows the occupational movement of Negroes from 1940 to 1966, particularly that many Negroes moved out of agriculture. Negroes made spectacular gains in the operatives class

[17] For a more comprehensive treatment of this subject from which most of the information in this paragraph was obtained, see E. Franklin Frazier, *The Negro Family in the United States* (New York, The Dryden Press, 1951). See also Daniel P. Moynihan, *The Negro Family—the Case for National Action*, Washington, D.C., U.S. Department of Labor, Office of Policy Planning and Research (March, 1966).

[18] *General Social and Economic Characteristics, United States Summary, 1960*, Table 79, pp. 1-210.

(semiskilled or factory workmen), so that by 1950, the nonwhites had as large a percentage in this category as the whites. Yet the 1966 figures still show a heavy concentration of nonwhites as unskilled workers, service, and private household work. Whereas over a third of all white women in 1966 were in clerical and secretarial positions, less than 15 percent of nonwhite women held such jobs. The largest single woman's occupation was that of a maid. Table 18-2 also shows that fewer Negroes than whites are employed in the skilled trades. Here discrimination by labor unions has tended to keep the Negroes down. In the past, a number of labor unions excluded Negroes by constitutional provisions, but by 1963 the last AFL-CIO international union removed its race bar.[19] A number of other unions have attempted to control Negro membership through segregated locals. Although the number of such locals is decreasing, they are not likely to disappear completely for a number of years. A number of unions, such as the Machinists, Bricklayers, Longshoremen, Paper Makers, and various railroad unions have a national policy that white and colored locals should merge, but because of local autonomy they will not employ sanctions to enforce mergers.[20]

The most typical way labor unions exclude Negroes is through informal exclusion. Negroes' applications for employment may simply be ignored or rejected for any number of reasons. In general, informal exclusion is practiced more in the South than elsewhere, and is more frequently found in craft than in industrial unions. The New York City Commission on Human Rights, for example, found few Negro members in the following unions: elevator constructors, plumbers, operating engineers, sheetmetal workers, ornamental bridge workers, metallic lathers, plasterers, masons, steamfitters, and carpenters.[21] In 1962, the President's Committee on Equal Employment Opportunity represented by its chairman, Vice-President Lyndon B. Johnson, signed joint statements with 116 national AFL-CIO and 300 directly chartered local unions representing 11 million workers to eliminate discrimination. Although the President's Committee deals only with government contracts, the unions agreed to extend the program for fair practices to all employment.[22] The main job remaining is to implement the program at the local level, where discrimination still exists.

The data for 1966 showed little gain in increasing the number of manager and proprietors' jobs for Negroes. The types of businesses most frequently established by Negroes are small-scale stores such as eating and drinking establishments, grocery stores, barbershops, cleaning and pressing establishments, taverns, and filling stations.[23] Larger-scale white-owned competitors, such as chain groceries, are able to price lower than the smaller-scale

[19] F. Ray Marshall, *The Negro and Organized Labor* (New York, Wiley, 1965), p. 90.
[20] *Ibid.*, p. 104.
[21] *Ibid.*, Table 6-1, p. 123.
[22] *Monthly Labor Review*, Vol. 86 (1963), pp. 58-59.
[23] Frazier, *op. cit.*, p. 402.

TABLE 18–2. OCCUPATION GROUP OF EMPLOYED PERSONS, BY SEX, FOR THE UNITED STATES: 1940 TO 1966 (IN PERCENTAGES)

	Male				Female			
	White		Non-White		White		Non-White	
	1940	1966	1940	1966	1940	1966	1940	1966
Professional	6.6	13.0	1.9	5.7	14.8	13.8	4.3	8.6
Farmers and farm managers	14.2	4.3	21.1	2.4	1.1	0.5	3.0	0.5
Managers, officials, and proprietors	10.6	14.2	1.6	3.4	4.3	4.8	0.8	1.5
Clerical and kindred	6.5	7.1	1.2	6.6	24.5	34.8	1.0	13.4
Sales workers	6.8	6.5	1.0	1.9	8.1	7.9	0.6	1.9
Craftsmen, foremen and kindred	15.9	20.4	4.4	12.4	1.1	1.0	0.2	0.7
Operatives and kindred workers	18.7	19.9	12.4	27.2	20.3	15.4	6.6	15.8
Private household workers	0.1	0.1	2.3	0.3	10.9	5.5	58.6	28.0
Service workers	5.2	6.2	12.3	15.3	11.5	14.0	10.4	25.5
Farm laborers	7.0	2.2	20.0	5.2	1.2	2.0	12.9	3.5
Laborers	7.6	6.2	21.3	19.6	0.9	0.4	0.8	0.7
Occupation not reported	0.7	0.0	0.6	0.0	1.3	0.0	0.7	0.0
Total[a]	100	100	100	100	100	100	100	100

[a] May not add to totals due to rounding.

Sources: 1940: *Monthly Labor Review*, U.S. Department of Labor, Vol. 76 (1953), p. 599. 1966: *Employment and Earnings*, U.S. Department of Labor, Vol. 13, No. 7 (January, 1967), Table 21, p. 102.

Negro establishments. As a result Negro entrepreneurs get only a small share of the business in Negro neighborhoods. Negro banks and insurance companies have been particularly unsuccessful, and Negro entrepreneurs have not gone into manufacturing enterprises on a large scale. Several reasons may be suggested as to why Negro business remains insignificant.[24] First, the Negro is at a competitive disadvantage because of the small-scale nature of his business. Second, credit is not as available to Negroes as it is to whites. Third, Negro consumers are poorer than white consumers. Fourth, some discrimination is involved in not renting choice real estate sites to Negroes. Last, Negroes lack a business tradition. With all these handicaps, there appears little hope that the Negro middle class can provide sufficient employment for Negroes in a segregated society.

Negroes have been improving their occupational status slowly over the years. Relative to whites their income improved during and shortly after World War II. The improvement was due to the tight labor market during this period.[25] Since 1951 the relative position of the Negro deteriorated, as Table 18-3 shows. Better education of whites and discrimination in employment against nonwhites are several factors responsible for white income increasing faster than nonwhite income. Discrimination does lower income, as was shown by the State of Connecticut's Commission on Civil Rights, which found that the average income of Negro families whose members had completed high school or college was roughly equivalent to that of white families whose members had not gone beyond grade school.[26]

FAIR EMPLOYMENT PRACTICE COMMITTEE

If high-paying jobs are wanted, Negroes will have to depend upon being integrated into the white economy. Here the problem of fair employment practice legislation becomes important. In 1941, with many workers drafted into our Armed Forces and many new war jobs becoming available, it was still the practice of many employers to refuse to hire Negroes. President Randolph of the Railway Porters Union threatened to march on Washington to protest discrimination in the employment of Negroes. Although no fair employment legislation would have been possible at that time because of filibuster privileges in the U.S. Senate, President Roosevelt issued an executive order outlawing discrimination in the government and on war orders. Improvement in Negro employment in Washington, D.C., was immediate. In 1938, even though 20 percent of the population was Negro, only 8.5 percent of all government employees were Negroes, and 90 percent of these were hired in subclerical jobs. By 1942, 17 percent of all jobs in government

[24] *Ibid.*, pp. 409-413.
[25] Elton Rayack, "Discrimination and the Occupational Progress of Negroes," *Review of Economics and Statistics*, Vol. 43 (1961), p. 211.
[26] *Civil Rights: Excerpts from the 1961 United States Commission on Civil Rights Report*, Washington, D.C., U.S. Commission on Civil Rights (1961), p. 53.

TABLE 18–3. MEDIAN WAGE AND SALARY INCOME, MALES 14 YEARS
OF AGE AND OVER WITH WAGE AND SALARY INCOME, BY COLOR,
1939–1964

Year	White	Nonwhite	Nonwhite as Percentage of White
1939	$1,112	$ 460	41.4
1947	2,357	1,279	54.2
1948	2,711	1,615	59.6
1949	2,735	1,367	50.0
1950	2,982	1,878	61.3
1951	3,345	2,060	61.6
1952	3,507	2,038	58.1
1953	3,760	2,233	59.4
1954	3,754	2,131	56.8
1955	3,986	2,342	58.8
1956	4,260	2,396	56.2
1957	4,396	2,436	55.4
1958	4,569	2,652	57.7
1959	4,902	2,844	58.0
1960	5,137	3,075	59.9
1961	5,287	3,015	57.0
1962	5,462	3,023	55.3
1963	5,663	3,217	56.8
1964	5,853	3,426	58.6

Source: Current Population Reports: Consumer Income, Series P-60, U.S. Department of Commerce, Bureau of the Census, various issues.

in Washington were held by Negroes, and only 50 percent of these were subclerical.

During the five years that the Fair Employment Practice Committee was in existence, nearly 5,000 discrimination cases were settled.[27] Most of these were settled without requiring a hearing. As an example of the type of work carried on by the committee, in a midwestern war plant, Negroes were scheduled to be trained as automatic screw-machine operators. They were refused instruction by white teachers, and were transferred to common labor. Upon appeal to the committee, and with the cooperation of the War and Navy Departments, the Negroes were placed back into training. All of this was accomplished without an incident, and without the Fair Employment Practice Committee having to hold a hearing on this case.[28]

The committee was not successful in eradicating discrimination in all

[27] Final Report, Fair Employment Practice Committee, Washington, D.C. (1946), p. viii.
[28] Ibid, p. 11.

cases. On the railroads, for example, where discrimination against Negroes exists to a large degree, ten southern railroads and seven unions never did come into compliance, although six railroads and one union did integrate. The committee analyzed carefully its results in the South. There the Negroes did not file as many cases proportionally as they did in other parts of the country. Complaints were received about having a Fair Employment Practice Office in Atlanta, where Negro secretaries worked beside white secretaries. The committee reported that about 30 percent of the cases not dismissed for lack of jurisdiction or for other reasons were settled to the satisfaction of complainants in the South. Where both management and labor unions were firm in supporting the employment of Negroes, little trouble occurred.[29] Since the committee viewed its work as successful, it recommended Congressional action to outlaw employment discrimination. Such legislation was finally passed in 1964 (see below, pp. 416-417).

PRESIDENT'S COMMITTEE ON EQUAL EMPLOYMENT OPPORTUNITY

Since World War II various federal commissions have continued to eradicate discrimination in the government service and on government contracts. The most recent federal commission was called the President's Committee on Equal Employment Opportunity, created in 1961 and terminated in 1965. If a government employee felt that he had been discriminated against because of race, creed, or color, he could have filed a complaint with the agency to which he belongs, or with the President's Committee on Equal Employment Opportunity. The head of each federal department or agency had an Employment Policy Officer to handle such complaints. A complaint had to be processed within 30 days from receipt of the complaint and notification sent to the Executive Vice Chairman of the President's Committee on Equal Employment Opportunity of the disposition. The complainant was allowed to demand a hearing. If the department or agency concerned ruled against the employee, the latter was able to appeal the case to the Executive Vice Chairman of the President's Committee for review.

President Kennedy requested all federal government agencies to make a survey of their own employment patterns, and to take steps to establish or strengthen nondiscrimination policies. All federal groups were to advise their employees of their guaranteed right to equal treatment and equal opportunity. A random spot check of a number of agencies in December of 1961 found that the overall nonwhite employment was in fair proportion to the nonwhite population, but most of the nonwhite jobs were concentrated in the lower grades. From this spot check, it was determined that the major discrimination that existed in the federal government was in not promoting nonwhites to higher paying jobs. The Civil Service Commission and a number of agencies launched recruiting programs among nonwhites in order to

29 *Ibid.*, p. viii.

bring minority workers into federal employment at grade levels commensurate with their abilities and training. In addition, employment policy officers were hired in each agency to implement the equal opportunity program. Full-time personnel working on these issues should help.

In dealing with private firms with government contracts, Vice President Lyndon B. Johnson, Chairman of the President's Committee on Equal Employment Opportunity, called a meeting of the presidents of the 50 largest defense contracting firms to review a Plans for Progress program. These plans contain statements of policy of the company as well as specific steps they will take to insure equal employment opportunity. Records of employment and upgrading of nonwhites were submitted to the President's Committee. These plans have been signed by the defense contracting firms.

As of October 31, 1963, 2,243 complaints had been processed in the federal government by the President's Committee on Equal Employment Opportunity. Of these, 36 percent resulted in corrective action being taken. The largest number of cases dealt with failing to promote because of color. Other cases concerned the failure to hire minority groups, firing because of race, and a multitude of other problems such as the use of derogatory terms, lack of use of the courtesy titles of "Mr." and "Mrs.," poor supervisory-employment relations, lack of communications, inconsistent assignments, failure to train employees, and others.[30] The President's Committee also attempted to eradicate discrimination on government contracts. As an example of the results on government contracts, the following cases are cited:

> The Equal Opportunity Program has resulted in Negroes becoming production workers in a tobacco plant in North Carolina; getting into production jobs in an oil refinery in Illinois and oil and chemical plants in Louisiana; becoming seamstresses in a textile plant in South Carolina; getting metal fabricating jobs in a Missouri plant; transferring into production work in aircraft plants in Georgia and North Carolina; getting carpenter work in Florida; moving into electronic production jobs in Connecticut and Tennessee; and many other breakthroughs in other areas.[31]

EVALUATION OF THE PRE CIVIL RIGHTS ANTIDISCRIMINATORY PROGRAM

In spite of the progress made by the President's Commission on Equal Employment Opportunity, several gaps in the program may be noted. Grants-in-aid programs were not subject to the President's executive order outlawing discrimination in the federal government and on government contracts. The United States Commission on Civil Rights recommended in 1961 that

---

[30] *The First Nine Months: Report of the President's Committee on Equal Employment Opportunity*, Washington, D.C. (January 15, 1962), p. 13; *Report to the President*, Washington, D.C., President's Committee on Equal Employment Opportunity (1963), p. 4.

[31] *Report to the President*, p. 2.

discriminatory employment practices be abolished on federal grants-in-aid programs. This commission favored Congressional legislation to outlaw discrimination, because it maintained that an agency created only by a Presidential executive order was limited in budget and legal authority. The commission particularly noted that the President's Commission on Equal Employment Opportunity lacked direct jurisdiction over labor unions. Here they suggested amendment of the Labor-Management Reporting and Disclosure Act of 1959 to forbid labor unions to refuse membership, segregate, or expel any person because of race, color, religion, or national origin. Although the Armed Forces Reserves are theoretically subject to Executive Order 9981 outlawing discrimination, the United States Commission on Civil Rights pointed out that some states had segregated reserve units and others completely excluded Negroes. The same discrimination was noted for the National Guard.[32]

STATE FAIR EMPLOYMENT LAWS

Twenty-eight states have passed fair employment practice laws, all since World War II. Several of them, however, have no enforcement procedures. Most of the state laws create a state commission to process complaints of discrimination. The typical state law forbids an employer to discriminate against workers because of race, creed, or national origin when hiring, firing, or setting terms and conditions of employment. Labor unions also are forbidden to discriminate either in admission or treatment of any workers. Discriminatory pre-employment inquiries, such as requesting stenographers of a certain religion or race, is outlawed. A few states, including Rhode Island and Washington, explicitly prohibit discriminatory referrals by employment agencies.[33]

Most cases are settled by an informal investigation of the state commission. If the commission is unsuccessful in accomplishing its purposes informally, it may hold a hearing and issue a cease and desist order against the defendant. Such orders are enforceable in court. As an example of the work of one of the state agencies, the New York State Commission for Human Rights processed 8,984 cases of alleged employment discrimination from 1945 through 1964. Of these cases, 605 alleged discrimination due to age, outlawed in 1958. Almost 2,000 cases of discrimination in housing were filed along with slightly more than 1,000 cases of public accommodation discrimination and 25 cases of discrimination in education. Of the employment cases in 1964, the commission sustained the specific complaint in almost 26 percent of the cases. In another 5 percent, although no specific cause of complaint

---

[32] *Civil Rights: Excerpts from the 1961 United States Commission on Civil Rights Report*, pp. 51-62.

[33] "The Operation of State Fair Employment Practices Commissions," *Harvard Law Review*, Vol. 68 (1955–1956), pp. 687-689.

was found, other discriminatory practices were found and adjusted. In 59 percent of the cases, the specific complaint was dismissed and no other discriminatory practices were found. Another 6 percent of cases were withdrawn and 4 percent were dismissed for lack of jurisdiction.[34]

Norgren and Hill made comparisons of improvements in employment in New York State with effective administration of its FEP law and three states without such a law, Indiana, Illinois, and Missouri. Their findings were that Negro employment in many occupational categories increased substantially more in New York than the other states. They also found that New York State had been more successful in applying its law than other states with such law. They attributed the success of New York to adequate funds and a full-time salaried commission.[35]

Experience under some state antidiscrimination laws has shown that fewer cases have been filed than was expected. Some workers do not have the proper training to qualify for jobs, others do not bother to seek employment where employment is discriminatory, and others are simply unaware of the privileges extended to them by law. The limited success of most of the state laws has led to a comparison of the laws to determine what may be done to improve and strengthen them.

One suggestion is that the state commission be permitted to file complaints on its own authority rather than wait for aggrieved individuals to file them. Such a step would permit a more systematic attack on discrimination. The commission could analyze the problem throughout the state and determine the major areas and occupations in which discrimination exists. Merely processing individual complaints may result in the commission investigating a plant with few employees, whereas a large plant may go uninvestigated because no complaints have been made there. Another suggestion, explicitly adopted by Rhode Island and implicitly by New York, is that private associations organized for the purpose of curbing discrimination should be given authority to file complaints. Experience in both states has shown that such associations have not filed unwarranted complaints. Requiring back pay for violations of the law may provide a financial incentive for obeying the law. Publicity on violations and a mandatory maintenance of compliance records have also been suggested to improve state laws.[36] Adequate funds and a full-time commission should help also.

HOUSING PROBLEMS

In order for school and employment integration to work effectively, housing integration will have to be implemented. Segregated housing tends to result

[34] *Annual Report, 1964*, New York State Commission for Human Rights, Table 1, p. 11, and Table 4, p. 13.

[35] Paul H. Norgren and Samuel E. Hill, *Toward Fair Employment* (New York, Columbia, 1964), Chap. 6.

[36] "The Operation of State Fair Employment Practices Commissions," pp. 690-697.

in segregated education even if the school system follows a nondiscrimination policy. Negroes do face housing restrictions. The United States Commission on Civil Rights reported in their first housing study in 1959 that housing was "the one commodity in the American market . . . not freely available on equal terms to everyone who can afford to pay." [37] Sometimes white property owners refuse to sell to Negroes. Real estate agents may restrict sales to whites only. Loans may also be less frequently forthcoming to Negroes.

A study in seven cities on what happened to property values when Negroes began moving into a neighborhood since 1940 showed that prices most frequently rose or remained stable rather than dropped. Nonwhites were able generally to move into the area fast enough to prevent a drop in values. Even in areas of light entry of Negroes, property values tended to increase rather than decrease. Some evidence shows that there is less resistance to racially mixed neighborhoods when the nonwhite group is not numerous and is not perceived as being the dominant numerical element. Under such circumstances, there is more chance that housing desegregation will succeed.[38]

Of a nonfarm home mortgage debt of $160 billion at the end of 1960, more than $100 billion was held by financial institutions that were federally supervised. The Federal Home Loan Bank Board regulates federal savings and loan associations, and national banks are regulated by the Comptroller of the Currency, the Board of Governors of the Federal Reserve System, and the Federal Deposit Insurance Corporation. The United States Commission on Civil Rights contends that banks and savings and loan companies are a major factor in denying equal housing opportunity. Mortgage credit, the Commission claims, is frequently denied to borrowers solely on the basis of race or color.

In order to eliminate such discrimination, the United States Commission on Civil Rights recommended that the President issue an executive order to direct all federal agencies concerned with housing and home mortgage credit to shape their policies and practices so that the national objective of equal opportunity in housing will be reached. The commission further recommended that the FHA and VA loan guarantees and FNMA second-mortgage money be made available only if builders and developers agree not to discriminate on the grounds of race, creed, or color. The commission pointed out that each of these agencies has expressed itself as opposing the inclusion of race as a factor or eligibility for loans, but none of them has taken effective steps to eradicate discrimination. The commission also recommended that federal funds for urban renewal and low-cost public housing

[37] *Civil Rights: Excerpts from the 1961 United States Commission on Civil Rights Report*, p. 64.
[38] Luigi Laurente, *Property Values and Race* (Berkeley, University of California Press, 1960).

be granted only on condition that applicants for such housing not be discriminated against because of race, creed, or color. They further recommended that urban renewal loans be made only if there is a sufficiency of adequate housing for displacees. Sufficient relocation facilities were recommended if necessary.[39] Other types of housing discrimination have existed in refusal to accept Negroes in motels and hotels. Any refusal to admit Negroes on an equal basis with whites, whether it is in restaurants, amusement parks, or any other type of facility, has been degrading to Negroes, and tends to make second-class citizens of them. Additional powers have been granted the Housing and Home Finance Administrator, but many discriminatory practices are still being engaged in at the local level.

VOTING RIGHTS

Some students of underdeveloped countries maintain that voting rights are an absolute necessity for members of minority groups if job and other opportunities are to be made available to them. The same theory could be applied to Negro rights in the South. In the 11 states of the Deep South in the summer of 1964, it was reported that the percentage of voting-age Negroes registered to vote ranged from a low of 7 percent in Mississippi to a high of 67 percent in Tennessee.[40] Only two other of the southern states had as many as 40 percent registered. The Civil Rights Act of 1964 should aid in guaranteeing voting privileges. This act prohibits registrars from applying different standards to white and Negro voting applicants. Literacy tests must be in writing except for blind persons, and a sixth-grade education is made a rebuttable presumption of literacy. The problem of the law will be in its enforcement. In 1965, for example, a staff attorney of the U.S. Commission on Civil Rights reported that in Issaquena County, Mississippi, more difficult test questions were given Negroes and that incorrect interpretations of the Constitution were more readily accepted from whites than from Negroes.[41] Bills have been suggested in Congress to have federal registrars enroll applicants if they are being denied their legal voting privileges, and such a bill became law in the Voting Rights Act of 1965.

The U.S. Civil Rights Commission has reported on a study in 21 counties in the South in which Negroes are in a majority.[42] In only four of these did substantial numbers of Negroes vote. In three of the four voting counties, light industry existed, but in the other counties, agriculture was the predominant means of livelihood. In several of the nonvoting counties where

---

[39] *Civil Rights: Excerpts from the 1961 United States Commission on Civil Rights Report*, pp. 63-77.

[40] *Voting*, Vol. 1, Hearings before the U.S. Commission on Civil Rights, Jackson, Mississippi (February 16-20, 1965), p. 243.

[41] *Ibid.*, pp. 47-52.

[42] *Civil Rights: Excerpts from the 1961 United States Commission on Civil Rights Report*, pp. 25-35.

Negroes attempted to vote, they were subject to such economic reprisals as eviction from farms, cutting off of supplies and credit, and cancellation of insurance policies. The dependent economic position of the Negroes was one of the most significant factors that kept them from voting.

In two of the four voting counties, Negroes ran for office and sometimes won. In the voting counties there were several Negro justices of the peace and Negroes were called for jury duty. One advantage obtained by Negroes in the voting counties was that there was less of a gap in the quality of white versus Negro schools. Teachers in the voting counties were not harassed or intimidated about voting as they were in some of the nonvoting counties.

Although Negroes had bettered themselves when voting privileges were obtained, equality was still far from being obtained. Public schools were still segregated, as were public libraries, public transportation facilities, and other public accommodations. Public employment opportunities were still not open in the four counties. The U.S. Civil Rights Commission concluded from this study that there was some correlation between voting and other rights, but that the correlation was limited and uncertain. The right to vote did not result in quick, tangible gains in other areas. The right to vote, however, was and is an indispensable part of "just" government.

ADMINISTRATION OF JUSTICE

Although police brutality is illegal, it still is practiced by a minority of policemen in the United States.[43] From a comprehensive study of the Department of Justice files, the U.S. Civil Rights Commission concluded that Negroes bear the brunt of official brutality proportionately more than any other group in American society. The Commission was also concerned about the less widespread problem of American police officers condoning or conniving in private violence. The failure to protect "Freedom Riders" in Alabama was cited as an example. Although the Supreme Court as early as 1880 ruled that discriminatory exclusion of otherwise qualified citizens from jury panels was a violation of the equal protection clause of the Fourteenth Amendment, exclusion of Negroes from juries still exists in many parts of the South.

The U.S. Civil Rights Commission has made a number of recommendations to provide more equal administration of justice among races. This commission pointed out that there was far less criticism of violence by federal police officers than by state and local police. The reason is that the federal government has used superior methods in screening and training their officers. Psychological tests can weed out candidates prone to violence. Training in human relations and scientific police techniques should aid in reducing violence. Since the commission reasoned that preventive measures such as

43 *Ibid.*, pp. 79-87.

testing and training are more conducive to reducing violence than applying remedies once it has occurred, they recommended that Congress consider the advisability of providing grants-in-aid to those state and local police forces interested in improving the professional quality of their groups.

Federal Civil Rights Acts provide for both civil and criminal penalties against police brutality. In a recent two-year period, 42 federal civil suits were filed based on alleged police brutality. None of these was successful. In a recent 2½-year period, the Department of Justice authorized 52 criminal prosecutions, but only 6 were successful. Lack of witnesses, failure to obtain concrete evidence, and testimony of more believable police witnesses made convictions extremely difficult. Another deterrent to effective prosecution has been the 16-year-old Supreme Court decision in Screws v. United States in which the court held that to sustain a prosecution under the Federal Civil Rights Acts the government had to prove that the police officer had a "specific intent" to violate the constitutional rights of the victim. A mere criminal intent to hurt would not be sufficient for a federal conviction under the Federal Civil Rights Acts. The U.S. Civil Rights Commission recommended a change in federal law to make prosecution legally more enforceable.

The commission also recommended that governments be held jointly responsible with the police officers in case of violence. This recommendation was made to encourage more civil suits. These are not filed, because few police officers are able to satisfy a substantial money judgment. Last, the commission felt that Congress should consider permitting the Attorney General of the United States to file civil suits against those excluding minority groups from serving on juries.

CIVIL RIGHTS ACT OF 1964

The most comprehensive federal law dealing with minority groups was passed in 1964. Title I of the act prohibits registrars from applying different standards to white and Negro voting applicants. Title II prohibits discrimination or refusal of service on the basis of race in hotels, motels, restaurants, gasoline stations, and places of amusement if their operations affect interstate commerce or if their discrimination is supported by state action. Title III grants all groups equal access to public facilities, such as parks, stadiums, and swimming pools. To strengthen integration in public schools, Title IV confers upon the Attorney General the right to sue for enforcement, if private citizens are unable to sue effectively. Discrimination in any programs receiving federal aid is outlawed in Title VI. Title VII outlaws discrimination in employment by both employers and labor unions with 100 or more employees or members. In four years, the number of employees and members will be reduced to 25. Suits to enforce the various provisions of the law may be brought by individuals or the Attorney General, and varies according to the section of the law to be enforced. The Civil Rights Commission, which had been created in 1957, was given the authority to investigate allegations of denial of the right to vote, and was to serve as a national clearinghouse on discrimination based on race, color, religion or national origin in the fields of voting, education, housing, employment, the use of public facilities, transportation, administration of justice, and others. An Equal Employment Opportunity Commission was created to investigate and attempt to eliminate discriminatory employment practices. The enforcement sections of this part of the law were weakened when the Equal Employment Opportunity Commission was not given power to issue "cease and desist" orders against recalcitrant employers and labor unions. Instead, suits for court enforcement must be filed. Slow court procedure has resulted in much delay in eliminating discriminatory employment practices. The NAACP maintains that broad patterns of employment discrimination still continue to exist in major sections of the American economy such as steel, textile, pulp and paper manufacturing, shipbuilding, automotive and electrical manufacturing, the chemical industry, major carriers in the trucking and railroad industry, banking, and communications.[44]

The Civil Rights Act of 1964 has resulted in improving voting rights and reducing discriminatory practices in public accommodations and facilities. Integration in schooling is slowly being accomplished.[45] Similarly, progress is being made to reduce discriminatory practices in employment, but it is slower than necessary due to the weak enforcement provisions of the law. In 1966 legislation was introduced to require open housing for Negroes, but this legislation did not pass.

Summary

The economic plight of Negroes and other minority groups is so serious that their problems constitute one of the major economic problems of our time. A rapidly expanding economy and general prosperity has helped and will help minority races in the future. Additional attention must be directed to minority groups if further progress is to be made. An analysis of our rural economy shows that it cannot support Negroes adequately. Some outmigration is needed. The migration of Negroes is complicated by the fact that

[44] Letter from Mr. Herbert Hill, Labor Secretary, NAACP (January 9, 1967).

[45] In the South in the fall 1966 term, the number of Negroes in schools with whites more than doubled. No progress was noted for Alabama, but all the other southern states recorded gains in integration. However, none of the states of Alabama, Mississippi, Louisiana, South Carolina, and Georgia had even 10 percent of Negro pupils attending school with whites. See *United States News*, "Integration in the South—Where It Stands Now" (December 19, 1966), p. 10.

rural Negroes are so poorly educated. Rural Negro education needs improvement as does urban Negro education. Family disorganization is a problem in urban areas. Low-rent public housing would help this problem. Negroes have been discriminated against in employment opportunities. The federal government has taken steps to eradicate discrimination in government employment and on government contracts, and the Civil Rights Act of 1964 outlaws discrimination among both employers and labor unions with 100 or more employees or members. A number of states have Fair Employment Practice laws. Negroes are particularly discriminated against when it comes to housing. However, segregation in motels, hotels, eating establishments, and other public and private facilities is gradually being eliminated. Negroes in some states still lack voting privileges. Police brutality is still a problem in certain areas in the United States. Private violence is still condoned on occasion. Jury rights are also withheld from Negroes in the South. The Civil Rights Act of 1964 attempted to correct abuses in these areas. Although progress is being made, the United States still has a long way to go to provide Negroes equal opportunities with whites. Adoption of the Civil Rights Act of 1964 should improve the ecomonic position of Negroes in American society, particularly if its enforcement provisions are improved.

MINORITY GROUPS (CONTINUED): SPANISH-AMERICANS AND AMERICAN INDIANS IN THE UNITED STATES

SPANISH-AMERICANS

Over 300 years ago the first Spaniards came to New Mexico, which was then the northwestern outpost of Spain's empire in the New World. Most of the Spaniards were males, and many of them married Indian women who were natives of the region. Land grants from the Spanish crown permitted many settlers to gain permanent possession of the land. Stock-raising became the principal occupation along with subsistence farming.[1] These communities became a part of the United States after the Mexican War in 1846. Other Mexicans have come to the United States and have settled principally in the states of Texas, New Mexico, Arizona, and California. According to the 1960 Census, 1,735,992 first- and second-generation Mexicans are now living in the United States.[2] Eighty-six percent of this group live in the four states of Texas, California, Arizona, and New Mexico.[3]

PUERTO RICAN MIGRATION

Puerto Ricans are another Spanish-American group who have migrated to the United States. A few began migrating to the United States after the Spanish-American War of 1898. From 1909 to 1940 the number of individuals migrating to the United States varied between 900 to 1,900 per year. World War II speeded immigration with the result that migration rose to an annual average of 18,000.[4] By 1950, 245,880 Puerto Ricans lived in the five New York City boroughs. With the advent of cheap airline traffic from

[1] John H. Burma, *Spanish-Speaking Groups in the United States* (Durham, Duke, 1954), pp. 3-5.
[2] *General Social and Economic Characteristics, United States Summary, 1960,* PC(1)–IC, U.S., Washington, D.C., U.S. Department of Commerce, Bureau of the Census, Table 69, pp. 1-203.
[3] *Ibid.,* Table 40.
[4] Beatrice Bishop Berle, *80 Puerto Rican Families in New York City* (New York, Columbia, 1958), p. 27.

Puerto Rico to New York, the migration became much larger (49,000 annually from 1951 to 1955) so that by 1955, 538,000 Puerto Ricans lived in New York City. The migration began slowing down in 1956, but by 1960 the figure reached 612,574. In 1961 there was a small net outmigration, but this was reversed in 1962. Puerto Ricans have moved to other parts of the United States as well as New York City, but by 1950, 85 percent of all Puerto Rican migrants lived in New York City. The figure since then has declined, and has leveled off at 60 percent.[5] Within New York City, the heaviest concentration of Puerto Ricans is in East Harlem (Spanish Harlem or El Barrio), but they can be found almost continuously from Harlem down to the Chelsea District, in the twenties.[6]

REASONS FOR MIGRATING

The major reason for the migration of Spanish-Americans to the United States has been economic in nature. Income data show that Mexico has a per capita income of $233 and Puerto Rico $473, compared with $2,108 for the United States (1957).[7] Population pressure in both Puerto Rico and Mexico has induced some of the migrants to leave. With improved health and sanitation conditions in Puerto Rico, the population of the island has doubled in the past 50 years. Although the economy of Puerto Rico has been expanding rapidly, as yet full employment has not been reached. On January 1, 1966, unemployment in Mayagüez, Puerto Rico, was 14.8 percent and in Ponce the figure was 18.7 percent.[8] One of the dominant crops, sugar, does not require full-time use of workers, and such laborers experience a serious drop in income when they are not working.

In Mexico, movements of populations to the cities have been heavy. Between 1940 and 1950 population of the border towns of Mexicali increased 240 percent; Tijuana, 259 percent; Ciudad Juárez, 149 percent; Nogales, 78 percent; Nuevo Laredo, 99 percent; and Matamoros, 179 percent. These areas have been unable to assimilate all of those who have moved to the cities. For example, when 25,000 cotton pickers were needed in the Matamoros area, 60,000 were available.[9]

Economic expansion in the United States has been a major factor in attracting Spanish-Americans. From 1900 to 1930 almost 10 percent of Mexico's population came to the United States. The immigration of Mexicans

[5] Facts and Figures, 1963 (New York, Commonwealth of Puerto Rico, Migration Division, 1963), p. 16.

[6] Christopher Rand, The Puerto Ricans (New York, Oxford, 1958), pp. 3-5. Reprinted by permission.

[7] Mikoto Asuri and E. E. Hagen, World Income, 1957 (Cambridge, M.I.T., 1959), pp. 11-12.

[8] Area Trends in Employment, March 1966, Washington, D.C., U.S. Department of Labor, Bureau of Employment Security, p. 45.

[9] Burma, op. cit., p. 46.

closely coincided with the growth of a number of our industries—railroads, mining, citrus fruits, sugar beets, winter vegetables, and cotton.[10] For Puerto Ricans several correlations have been made between prosperity on the main-land and the amount of immigration from Puerto Rico. One of these studies from 1908–1909 to 1947–1948 (fiscal years) showed a correlation of .73.[11] When the mainland economy is expanding, heavy influxes of Puerto Ricans have been recorded. After Puerto Ricans became acquainted with such ma-terial goods as radios, TV sets, automobiles, and other desirable consumer goods, many have migrated in order to earn the higher mainland income with which to purchase such goods.

Although weaknesses in the Mexican and Puerto Rican economies and the higher purchasing power of the mainland United States economy have been the major factors inducing immigration, other causes should be men-tioned. In one study, family reasons were cited by Puerto Ricans as the second main reason for coming to the mainland.[12] Once some Puerto Ricans have come to the mainland, they write relatives and friends, and sometimes encourage them to come too. For example, 36 Puerto Rican men were placed in an iron foundry in Milwaukee. Today that community has expanded to 3,000, through the use of family intelligence. Similarly, one Puerto Rican in Haverstraw, New York, induced 900 others to migrate there. In Cleve-land there are about 4,000 Puerto Ricans, most of whom are related to one another.[13] Other reasons why Spanish-Americans migrate to the United States are improved schools, medical care, cultural advances, and improved welfare programs. Although few come to the mainland solely for the purpose of obtaining welfare payments, such benefits and programs are more compre-hensive and ample on the mainland than in Puerto Rico.

TYPES OF MIGRANTS

Several studies have been made of the types of Spanish-Americans coming to the United States. Mexican immigrants came primarily from towns of over 3,000 population. They were not the most backward nor primitive of the Mexican population. Most Mexicans, even those engaged in agricultural work, tended to live in groups rather than in isolated farm houses. Few of the Mexican migrants have been Indians. Rather they have been *mestizos,* a mixture of Spaniards and natives.

The Mexican revolution caused some of the displaced hacienda workers to migrate to the United States. In a study of Mexican migrants to San

[10] *Ibid.,* pp. 40-41.
[11] C. Wright Mills, Clarence Senior, and Rose Kohn Goldsen, *The Puerto Rican Journey* (New York, Harper & Row, 1950), p. 43. The other study showed an even higher correlation of .82. *See* A. J. Jaffe, ed., *Puerto Rican Population of New York City* (New York, Bureau of Applied Social Research, 1954), p. 25.
[12] Mills, Senior, and Goldsen, *op. cit.,* Table III-5, p. 50.
[13] Rand, *op. cit.,* p. 54.

Bernardino, California, more than a third of the men who were in their middle fifties to their late seventies in age had been hacienda workers, who possibly had been displaced by the revolution of 1911. Almost a third had been *arrieros*, or worked for *arrieros*, who cart or transport goods. Other occupations were woodcutters, sellers of charcoal or milk, shoemakers, stonemasons, muleteers, miners, and cattle herders. According to a sampling taken of the Mexican immigrants to San Bernardino, California, 26 percent of them had received no schooling and 19 percent had less than five years of education. Those migrating to San Bernardino were not of the lowest income group in Mexico, nor had they come from the most isolated and rural areas. Many of them possessed considerable skills in their native occupations, but these skills were not the type which were in demand in the growing industrial economy of the United States.[14]

A detailed study of 5,000 Puerto Ricans migrating to Spanish Harlem and the Morrisania area of the Bronx prior to 1950 showed that the migrants constituted a greater proportion of women than the island population, that they included a greater proportion of people in the productive age groups and fewer children and aged, and that they were more literate than the general Puerto Rican population, although their average education attainment was only six to eight years of schooling. The migration was essentially one of urban dwellers who had a slightly larger proportion of white-collar, skilled, and semiskilled workers than the Puerto Rican population. There were fewer single persons among the migrants, but there were more divorced persons than in the native population.[15]

INCOME AND EMPLOYMENT OF MEXICAN IMMIGRANTS

Income levels of Spanish-American immigrants in the United States were quite low during the Great Depression of the 1930's. Even as late as December, 1941, the Los Angeles Co-ordinating Council reported that the median Mexican family income was $790 a year, or $520 less than was the minimum necessary for decent food and housing for a family of five. World War II increased migrant income considerably. In the San Bernardino study, the average Mexican earnings were $149.60 per month in 1943 compared with $193.39 for the average factory workman in the United States. A steel and shell company paid wages to Mexicans approximating the national average, but those working for the railroad received less. About 10 percent of San Bernardino's Mexican population was employed in agriculture and received $109 monthly on the average, or as low as $80 a month for some of them. Four percent of the Mexican population received transfer payments—pensions, unemployment insurance, or welfare payments—averaging $49 a month

[14] Ruth D. Tuck, *Not With the Fist* (New York, Harcourt, Brace & World, 1946), pp. 61-71.

[15] Mills, Senior, and Goldsen, *op. cit.*, Chap. 2.

or as low as $26 a month. The wealthiest 11 percent earned over $250 a month, but except for two merchant families, the higher income was obtained by having more than one worker in the family.[16]

Large numbers of Mexican migrants have become migratory agricultural workers in the United States. A majority of migratory workers are of Mexican descent. Their problems have already been discussed in Chapter 17. The early migrants who came to New Mexico hundreds of years ago and who engaged in stock raising and subsistence agriculture have gradually experienced a decline in their incomes. The major reason has been the system of dividing the land equally among all the heirs. The result has been that the large farms have gradually been reduced in size until the average size is 10 acres, and 80 percent of the farms have less than 15 acres. Some are as small as 20 yards wide by 100 yards long. With such small farms, 90 percent of the rural families obtain less than a subsistence living from farming.

Many of the Hispanos (Mexican-Americans) have lost their land, because New Mexico has a real property tax, which if not paid results in foreclosure. Since 1854, Hispanos have lost 2 million acres of private land, 1.7 million acres of communal land, and an additional 1.8 million acres have been taken by the state for its educational fund. Additional vast areas have been given to railroads or have become national forests. It is quite obvious that the size of farms for grazing and growing crops has become so small that little economic progress can be made by remaining on such farms even though improved methods may be introduced.[17] Like most of the subsistence farmers elsewhere in the United States, the Hispanos need to migrate to urban areas, which can provide them a higher standard of living.

Most Mexicans migrating to cities have gone generally to the Southwest, where they have been hired as unskilled workers at low pay. Mexicans constituted about 60 percent of the common labor in the mines of the Southwest and constitute a majority of workers on southwestern railroad section gangs. In Los Angeles one study showed that 55 percent of the Mexicans were hired as unskilled laborers, as contrasted to 21 percent for Anglo workers. The largest concentration of Mexicans outside of the Southwest reside in Chicago, where they have found employment in the steel, meat packing, and other industries. Of Carnegie-Illinois Steel Company's 18,000 employees in this area, 4,000 are Mexicans.[18] The hourly rate of pay is, of course, high in the steel industry, but this industry has been plagued with a heavy incidence of cyclical unemployment.

Data for standard metropolitan areas from the 1960 Census show that the white population with Spanish surnames have quite a low income in some American cities. Median family income for this group in the following Texas cities was as follows: Austin, $3,289; Corpus Christi, $3,298; Laredo,

[16] Tuck, *op. cit.*, pp. 174-175.
[17] Burma, *op. cit.*, pp. 13-19.
[18] *Ibid.*, pp. 63-71.

$2,466; Lubbock, $3,263; and San Angelo, $2,707. The following percentages of families in these cities had an annual income of less than $2,000 respectively: 23, 25, 42, 20, and 33 percent.[19] In other Texas cities, income was higher. That Mexican-Americans can climb the ladder to higher income may be shown by a few statistics on their median family income in several California cities: Long Beach, $6,200; Los Angeles, $5,564; Alhambra, $6,492; and Altadena, $7,058.[20]

INCOME AND EMPLOYMENT OF PUERTO RICAN MIGRANTS

Some of the Puerto Rican immigrants own *bodegas* (grocery stores) or bars, but generally these are small, for the Italian and Jewish merchants, who have been in New York City longer, own the larger establishments. Many Puerto Ricans work in small garment factories in Harlem. Although Puerto Ricans have found jobs in practically all industries, heavy concentrations of employment occur in jewelry and plastic manufacturing shops and in the hotel and restaurant industry. The Waldorf-Astoria Hotel, for example, hires 500 Puerto Rican men and women. A study of 5,000 Puerto Rican migrants to New York City prior to 1950 showed that their income from the first job in New York City was about twice as much as their last Puerto Rican job for those who came during the 1920's and 1930's. For those coming during World War II or thereafter, their New York City income was almost three times as high as their last Puerto Rican job. The cost of living is about the same in both areas except that higher fuel bills must be paid in the winter in New York City. The earlier migrants were able to raise their income during their residence in New York, so that they were earning more than the new arrivals from Puerto Rico. This was true for men and for white women, but colored women who arrived before World War II earned only the same income as those arriving after the war.

Census data for 1960 show that median family income of Puerto Ricans in Manhattan was $3,459.[21] In one census tract, the median family income was as low as $2,564.[22] Other Puerto Ricans earned more income and have moved to higher-income neighborhoods. In Queens, median family income for Puerto Ricans is $6,665. Even though substantially higher earnings were made in New York City than in Puerto Rico, many of the Puerto Ricans had to accept positions which called for less skill than they held in Puerto Rico. Only 21 percent of the men held higher positions in New York City than in Puerto Rico, compared with 40 percent who experienced downward

[19] *Census of Population and Housing, 1960,* Final Report, PHC(1), Nos. 11, 33, 74, 85, and 133, Washington, D.C., U.S. Department of Commerce, Bureau of the Census, Table 5.
[20] *Ibid.,* No. 82, Table 5, p. 603.
[21] *Ibid.,* PHC(1)-104, Part 1, Table P-5, p. 724.
[22] *Ibid.,* p. 746.

mobility. For women the corresponding figures were 17 and 40 percent respectively. Fewer Puerto Ricans were able to obtain white-collar jobs in New York City than on the island. In Puerto Rico 24 percent of the males and 17 percent of the females were engaged in white-collar work, but on coming to the mainland, only 15 percent of the males and 9 percent of the females held white-collar jobs. On the other hand, slightly fewer Puerto Ricans were engaged in unskilled work in New York City compared with Puerto Rico. For unskilled labor, 29 percent held such jobs in Puerto Rico, compared with 25 percent having such jobs in New York City.[23]

HOUSING OF PUERTO RICAN MIGRANTS

Although Spanish-Americans are economically better off in the United States than in Latin America, some of them face severe economic hardship here in the United States. The housing in New York City is particularly dilapidated. Prior to the coming of Puerto Ricans in large numbers, some of the slums that had housed former immigrants had been boarded up. With the large numbers of Puerto Ricans crowding into the city, some of the abandoned housing was brought back into use. The following describes some of this housing:

Many dwellings were said to be infested with vermin: with rats, cockroaches, and bedbugs—or *ratas, cucarachas,* and *chinches,* as they were more familiarly known to the inhabitants. Cockroaches were the only ones of these I saw—on walls near stoves—but I heard about the others. As a rule the nurses I talked with had had direct experience with children with rat-bites—and they would advise mothers not to feed the little children in bed, as this might leave scraps to lure the rats that way. A special vermin problem was caused by the tearing down of slums, I learned, for when this happened the rats would move to nearby blocks and infest them heavily. The use of rat poison created another problem: the children might eat it and be sick. The children were also vulnerable to a poison malady called *pica,* which came from picking the plaster out of walls and eating it, to satisfy some craving.

The worst apartment I saw was on 113th Street, three flights up in an old tenement. It had one bedroom, a kitchen, a bathroom, and what might be called a large closet off the kitchen's other side. A Mrs. Rodriguez lived there with seven small children. She paid sixty dollars a month in rent, she said, and drew a hundred and twenty dollars in relief. She also had a husband living elsewhere—whether legally married or not, I cannot say—and he sent her a hundred dollars monthly. The family ate meat three times a week, she said, and when we were there she had some potato cakes and salt codfish on the stove, plus mashed potatoes for the youngest child, an infant. She owned a sewing machine and a small radio, and had a small four-burner gas stove and a double sink in the kitchen. Much of the kitchen's space was taken up with clothes hanging on

[23] Mills, Senior, and Goldsen, *op. cit.,* Chap. 4.

lines. The bedroom, which was small, had plaster off its walls in spots, one of these being at least a yard wide, with the laths laid bare. Mrs. Rodriguez said the wind came in there, and she had recently to buy four blankets because of it to keep the children warm. Elsewhere the walls were indescribably dirty— scribbled over, smeared over, and smudged over. The room had one set of double-deck bunk beds, one single bed, one crib, and one little mattress on the floor, the floor itself being uneven and covered with torn, patchy linoleum.

I asked Mrs. Rodriguez if she had any rats or mice.

"Plenty of both," she answered. "But I have a cat. I don't like cats, but it's the only thing to do here."

Then she showed me some of the children's clothes on the lines in the kitchen. They were full of little holes, which she said had been made by rats before the cat had joined the household.[24]

Suddenly he was telling me about a landlord who had made forty-five wretched pigeonholes out of five apartments. Forty-five of them, can you believe it? Renting for sixteen, eighteen, twenty-three dollars. Nine hundred dollars a week he is making. More than that. Can you imagine it? And he has put in nothing. Nothing! [25]

Our interviewers often reported spotlessly clean apartments crawling with roaches, the housewife frantic and frustrated. Leaking roofs ("We have to wear rubbers when it rains"), broken windows, and splintered steps are common. "The alleyways and streets are filthy, the garbage man never comes this way." Frequently, the Puerto Rican family must bribe the superintendent or agent in order to obtain even the worst apartment.[26]

Often it is up to Eastville tenants themselves to plaster holes in the walls to keep the rats from entering their homes. Alicia Colar, a twelve-year-old girl, was making her bed before going to school one morning. As she shook out the sheets, a rat fell from her bed. She was frightened and ran from the room screaming. Her father simply brought plaster and covered a crack in the wall through which the animal had come into the apartment. Rat extermination campaigns, however, frequently serve only to exacerbate Eastvillers' discontent, for the rodents, trying to quench the thirst produced by the poison they have consumed, go out into the streets, the corridors, and the sidewalks, and there they die. This litter remains to rot and decay.[27]

Down the hall in Apartment 2, the reporter found a very "strong case." There were holes in both the floor and the ceiling, big enough for the biggest rats. Cockroaches crawled up the kitchen wall. A curtain divided off a section of the room for a bedroom . . . the reporter walked to the kitchen to watch the cockroaches. . . .[28]

Out of 1,000 tenants interviewed in East Harlem, the following numbers

[24] Rand, op. cit., pp. 18-19.
[25] Ibid., p. 166.
[26] Mills, Senior, and Goldsen, op. cit., p. 93.
[27] Elena Padilla, Up from Puerto Rico (New York, Columbia, 1958), p. 8.
[28] Dan Wakefield, Island in the City (Boston, Houghton Mifflin, 1959), p. 226. Reprinted by permission.

of housing violations were reported: defective wiring, 721; defective plumbing, 612; windows broken, 571; rats in the building, 895; gas leaks, 696; no heat, 778; no hot water, 553; leaks in the roof, 308. . . .[29]

The 1960 Census of Housing reported that of the 156,110 units occupied by household heads of Puerto Rican births or parentage in New York City, almost all were rented rather than owned (only 7,396 were occupied by owners). Of the rented houses, only 59 percent were classified as "sound" and with "all plumbing facilities." In both rented and owned facilities, 19,867 units had only shared toilet facilities and 245 did not even have these facilities. A total of 3,755 had only cold water inside the structure, 56 had no piped water of any sort. A total of 18,259 had only shared bathtub or shower facilities, and 1,230 had no bathtub or shower facilities. Most of the units had been built before 1929. Almost 40 percent of the units housed more than one person per room.[30] The median rent paid for renter occupied housing was $62 per month.[31]

Although no fees are supposed to be charged for the privilege of renting an apartment, a number of subterfuges have been used. Old broken furniture may be sold at high charges in lieu of a rental fee. One young married couple paid $1,400 for kitchen tables and chairs in order to rent it. Of 1,000 people surveyed, 119 admitted paying $60,952 in order to rent houses.[32] One landlord made a fake sale to a dummy corporation, which then evicted its tenants and then rented them out to new tenants who had to pay a fee plus their rent. As one of the leaders of the Puerto Rican community said, "You can sell the lousiest apartment here for two hundred, three hundred dollars.[33] The following story tells of the problems that tenants have even though city inspections are provided:

Big patches of the wall were bare of plaster. "He won't fix those till he learns that the inspector is coming," the woman said. "Then do you know what he does? He puts newspaper in the holes and throws a little plaster on them. Of course it all falls out again in a few days, but meanwhile the inspector has seen it." [34]

Some tenants cannot afford to complain because they may be asked to move or the landlord may threaten to have the place condemned, in which case the tenant would fear that he would find no other housing. Furthermore, if too many tenants are living in an apartment, they cannot complain. One expert in housing, Mr. Charles Abrams, the head of the New York State

[29] *Ibid.*, p. 258.
[30] *Census of Housing, 1960*, Washington, D.C., U.S. Department of Commerce, Bureau of the Census, New York, Table 41, pp. 34-173.
[31] *Ibid.*, Table 42, pp. 24-173.
[32] Wakefield, *op. cit.*, p. 238.
[33] Rand, *op. cit.*, p. 196.
[34] *Ibid.*

Commission Against Discrimination, after circling the globe on a UN housing mission, concluded that the Puerto Rican slums in Harlem are "among the worst in the world." [35] The New York Housing Authority has now built facilities to house 93,000 families. As yet much smaller percentages of Puerto Ricans are housed in the public housing because of the recency of their migration, the reluctance of some to fill out forms, the lack of proof of marriage by some Puerto Rican couples, and the fact that some Puerto Rican families are too large to qualify for public housing.[36]

HOUSING OF MEXICAN MIGRANTS

That Mexican immigrants do not have the best housing either may be seen by the condition of housing of those with Spanish surnames according to the 1960 Census of Housing. Of 73 towns in Texas having more than 400 households headed by those with a Spanish surname, only 22 of the towns (30 percent) had 50 percent of the Spanish houses classified as "sound" and "with all plumbing facilities." The housing is only slightly better in New Mexico, but it is substantially better in Arizona and California. Only 39 percent of the New Mexican cities had 50 percent or more of their Spanish houses classified as adequate, compared with 70 percent for Arizona and 92 percent for California.[37] These figures are for urban areas only, and conceal the poorer hot ing in rural areas.

HEALTH PROBLEMS

Concentration of Puerto Rican immigrants in New York City slum areas has tended to accentuate the health problem. Both overcrowding and unsanitary conditions tend to promote disease. The incidence of tuberculosis among Puerto Ricans in New York City is higher than that of whites and Negroes. Also the rate of first admissions for dementia praecox for Puerto Ricans in New York City was almost twice as high as that of non-Puerto Ricans.[38] In a study of 80 Puerto Rican families, Dr. Beatrice Berle found that there were marked differences between families in the incidence of disease and amount of hospitalization. Her findings confirm other studies, which show that about 6 percent of the families require a very large proportion of health and adjustment assistance. Berle concurs with the findings of Dubos that not only overcrowding and unsanitary conditions make for a

[35] Charles Abrams, "How to Remedy Our 'Puerto Rican Problems,'" *Commentary*, Vol. 19 (1955), p. 121.

[36] Rand, *op. cit.*, pp. 104-105.

[37] *Census of Housing, 1960*; information on Texas, New Mexico, Arizona, and California computed from Tables 40 and 41 in respective state sections.

[38] Berle, *op. cit.*, Chap. IX.

higher disease rate but that social and psychological factors affected by moving from a rural to an industrial society may increase the susceptibility to disease. Since it is mainly multiproblem families that have the most health problems, Berle suggests that a family service center be established in the slum area. In such centers the family, not the disease or the individual alone, would be studied and treated as a unit.[39]

THE NARCOTICS PROBLEM

Slum conditions have accentuated the drug problem in Spanish Harlem. A study by Dr. Isidor Chein, Professor of Psychology at New York University, found that three-fourths of the adolescent users lived in just 15 percent of the city's census tracts. These tracts were largely Negro and Puerto Rican, and were the poorest, most crowded, and physically dilapidated in the city.[40] Violations of narcotics laws are much more numerous in New York City than elsewhere. Juvenile arrests in New York City numbered 1,209 out of a total of 1,623 in larger cities throughout the country. The knowledge of narcotics among youngsters may be shown by the answers given to a ninth-grade teacher in Spanish Harlem who asked her class to write a paper on "What I Know about Narcotics":

One day me and my friends were playing baseball in a lot, and this car pulled up and one of the men called over and asked us would we like to buy some stuff that will make us drunk and feel good for the rest of the day. He said we'll be able to play ball much better and I said no because I knew what he was talking about. In the summer early in the morning around Fifth Avenue and 110th Street a car comes by and men line up to get this injection, but when the car does not come by, the men almost go crazy.

A lot of boys on my block uses it. The kind they use comes in a little container which they call a cap. The name that they call it by is Horse (heroin). Some of them puts it on a piece of a match box cover and inhale it. But some of the boys says afterwards it makes you scratch a lot. They won't tell where they get it from but they say it cost $1 for a cap. A cap is red with a white bank in the middle of it . . . it also makes the boys throw up. You can tell when someone has been using it by looking at his eyes. He also scratches a lot.

I saw some men in a hallway one day as I was coming from school. They had a long white stick, some people call it reefers. Some call it marijuana. It had an awful smell. They would take a little puff, then smoke a cigarette behind it to make the smell go away. That was suppose to make them high. Another kind of narcotics is a cap of horse, which costs at least a dollar. The way they take it to get high is to put a little tiny batch in the top of the cap and sniff it. It doesn't have much of a smell. Another way to take Horse is pour all

[39] *Ibid.,* Chaps. XII, XIII.
[40] Wakefield, *op. cit.,* p. 103.

the powder out on a flat mirror and take a straw and you sniff it with the straw into your nose.

I see nothing, hear nothing, say nothing, know nothing.[41]

The pressures that adolescents are subjected to in the slum surrounding are shown in the following story:

Pee-Wee is one of the lucky ones and strong ones who were able to grow up on one of the hottest blocks of narcotics traffic in the world without getting hooked. He did, however, have his brush with one form of narcotics that was at the time inevitable. He learned about "snorting" (inhaling cocaine) in high school. It was extra-curricular and required.

"If I wanted to live," he once recalled, "I had to get on it. Everybody was on it, so for six months I did and was miserable. I was lucky. There were thirty-six guys in my high school class. I've lost track of some, but today there are only three I know of out doing something—me, one guy who's an air force pilot, and one who's an engineer. The rest I know of are scattered in and out of jails and hospitals from here to Lexington."

Cocaine is not a physically addicting drug, but most of the guys who went through its use moved on to heroin, which like morphine becomes almost as necessary for the body of the addict as water for the body of the ordinary person.[42]

For treatment of drug addicts, New York City has a community hospital at Riverside, which only accepts those under 21 years of age. Few other facilities are available, and sometimes people suffering from other diseases may not be admitted to a hospital because of drug addiction. Addicts may be admitted to jail, where no treatment is provided. The closest hospital is a federal one at Lexington, Kentucky. The East Harlem Protestant Parish has formed a Narcotics Committee, whose purpose is to aid addicts and provide the necessary papers for their admission to Lexington.[43]

In a follow-up study of 453 discharged patients from the Public Health Service Hospital at Lexington, it was found that 97 percent continued their addiction during the five years after treatment. However, by the fifth year only 46 percent of the study population were still addicted, but some of the others were abstinent simply by virtue of being in jail. Those patients admitted after 30 years of age showed less continued addiction than those under 30. About 70 percent of the group had arrests after leaving Lexington, about two-thirds of which involved the use of drugs—that is, possession of narcotics or hypodermic needles, forging prescriptions, selling drugs, and similar offenses. After five years, 41 percent of the group were unemployed. About the same percentage were returned to Lexington for further treatment. Few patients received psychiatric aftercare, particularly of the out-

41 *Ibid.*, p. 96.
42 *Ibid.*, pp. 104-105.
43 *Ibid.*, pp. 87-114.

patient clinical type. In view of the high relapse, unemployment, and arrest rate it was recommended that more systematic community aftercare be provided for addicts.[44] Other students of the problem point out that in England the amount of traffic in illegal narcotics is negligible. There, addiction is legally treated by physicians rather than through the police and prisons. The public in England regards addiction as an illness.[45]

CRIME

The necessity of obtaining money to buy drugs results in a greater amount of stealing than otherwise would occur. Gambling and prostitution also flourish in slum areas. A description of the disorganization of a Puerto Rican slum area in New York City by a resident follows:

"You even get used to it, man. It don't get to you unless it's someone right in the family who's the one that gets hurt. There isn't as much gang fighting now as there used to be but it still goes on, and so does the regular killing, besides the gang stuff. People think all that stuff was over in the twenties with machine guns shooting out of cars and all that, but it's still really here—it's just got more under cover. You can still get a guy killed anytime. You hire a kid who's high and you promise him a fix. For a fix, he'll do anything. Then if you want to make sure nobody knows about it afterward you give him an overdose and that does it. They call it suicide."

A mother who lives in the neighborhood agreed, and added, "Yes, there are times when you see a car pull up, and they push out a girl all beat up and her clothes torn. After a while you get used to seeing it—violence. The thing you learn, the first thing you learn is, 'I didn't see anything.' No matter where you were or what happened, you didn't see anything."

Sometimes the people who live in it call East Harlem "The Jungle," and that is its law—you didn't see anything. When you really don't see it, you hear about it later. There is always a story of violence past or the threat of violence to come. Some people make a living from it, and some make a living from its by-product—fear.[46]

Some of the younger Puerto Ricans have formed into gangs. These are formally organized clubs whose purpose is either social or fighting. In the latter the members are expected to learn to fight, train, and plan attacks upon enemy gangs, and construct and purchase weapons for their assault. They claim certain territory to be their own, and those who cross boundaries may get into trouble even though they are not members of any gang themselves.

[44] Henrietta Duvall, Ben Locke, and Leon Brill, "Followup Study of Narcotic Drug Addicts Five Years After Hospitalization," *Public Health Reports*, Vol. 78, No. 3 (March, 1963), pp. 185-193.

[45] "Contradictions in Addiction," *Public Health Reports*, Vol. 78, No. 8 (August, 1963), p. 671.

[46] Wakefield, *op. cit.*, p. 122.

Some of the gangs wear the same type of hats, pants, uniforms, or jackets to be recognized.[47] Fortunately for New York, the Puerto Rican gangs tend to disband as their members become older. There has been little evidence of the formation of or continuation of gangs by Puerto Rican men.

In order to reduce the amount of juvenile delinquency in New York, a New York City Youth Board was created in 1947 with 28 members appointed by the mayor. Fifty percent of the money comes from the State of New York and the remaining part from the city. Over half of the income is spent for recreation and special projects. Smaller amounts are spent for treatment services and projects, referral units, group work, community planning, research, and administration. Approximately 100,000 youths are reached each year, slightly over half in recreational programs and another 30,000 in referral units and treatment. Seventy-five percent of all delinquency is concentrated in 1 percent of New York City families.[48] The heaviest concentrations of juvenile delinquency are among Negroes in Central Harlem and Puerto Ricans in East Harlem. Although the city has attempted to reduce the increasing surge of delinquency, as yet the tide has not been turned. Recent statistics show that juvenile delinquency in New York is still on the increase (Fig. 19-1). Adult arrests, too, have increased.

That crime is not restricted to immigrants on the East Coast may be seen in the San Bernardino study, which showed that although Hispanos constituted only 12 percent of the population, they furnish 28 percent of the juvenile arrests.[49] In general, Hispanos, as contrasted to Anglos, committed a larger proportion of petty theft, drunkenness, and personal violence. The largest-scale riot against Mexican-Americans came in Los Angeles during World War II. A group of 11 sailors were attacked by Mexican youths when walking through a slum area. For several days thereafter several thousand sailors, soldiers, and civilians beat up every zoot-suiter and Mexican they could find. Carey McWilliams blamed most of the trouble on the Hearst Press. After the Japanese were removed, Mexicans became the major scapegoat in California. The newspapers began playing up Mexican crime and delinquency until a full-scale offensive was finally waged against the Mexicans.[50]

LABOR UNIONS

One aid to migrants in the United States has been labor unions, whose major function has been to help the working class. The International Ladies' Garment Workers' Union has been particularly active in organizing the garment

[47] Padilla, *op. cit.*, pp. 226-236.
[48] *New Direction in Delinquency Prevention, 1947–1957*, New York City Youth Board (1957), pp. 1-39.
[49] Tuck, *op. cit.*, p. 213.
[50] Carey McWilliams, *North from Mexico* (New York, Lippincott, 1949), p. 227.

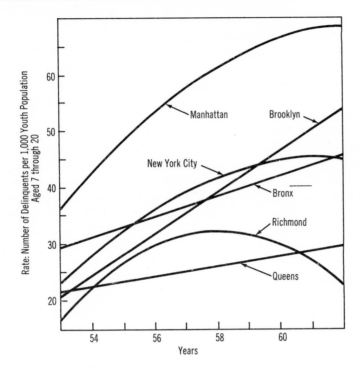

Source: Ten-Year Delinquency Trends in New York City, New York City Youth Board (March, 1964), Chart 1, p. xiv.

FIG. 19–1.   CITY AND BOROUGH DELINQUENCY TRENDS, 1953–1962

shops hiring Puerto Ricans in East Harlem. Most of them are now organized, but a minority of shops hiring Puerto Ricans are still unorganized. Some bosses bound the workers to them by granting them loans or providing a credit reference for the Puerto Ricans buying goods on time. An attempt to organize will be met by the bosses' threat to withdraw the credit rating and to have the furniture returned to the store. Puerto Ricans were acquainted with labor unions on their home island, but such unions have been relatively ineffectual there. In 1958, 10 international unions were operating in Puerto Rico, but they had succeeded in organizing only 27 of 455 new factories. Unions have been effective in raising minimum wages through the government, but when they do that, many workers feel little compulsion to join the union—they get wage increases anyway.

In New York City racketeering and preying upon Puerto Ricans has caused many of the migrants to fear and distrust unions. When the workers of Starke Design Company wrote a letter to the Association of Catholic Trade Unionists asking for an investigation, because they paid $3 a month dues without seeing an agreement of any kind, all 49 workers were discharged. At Morgan's Leather Goods and Rudee's Leather Goods the workers were given the choice of joining a Retail Clerks union or being fired. Four dollars was deducted from their pay out of their weekly pay of $42. Two workers who asked the union to see the contract were fired by their boss. The following complaints were received by the Association of Catholic Trade Unionists in a six-month period: "Contracts never seen by the workers; no union meetings; no union elections; no grievances processed by the union; lay-offs of workers just before they were due to get vacation or holiday periods with pay; seldom any seniority; seldom any welfare or sickness benefits; and workers signed up in the union under threat of firing by the boss." [51] After the Association of Catholic Trades Unions was called before the McClellan Committee, AFL-CIO president George Meany sent a special representative to New York City to help honest unionism. Some of the worst leaders and locals were expelled, but today there still lingers deep resentment against unions by many Puerto Rican migrants.[52]

EDUCATION

Schools represent a major institution for upward mobility in our society. In New York City the problem of educating the Puerto Ricans has been complicated by the language barrier. Once students fell behind, they were segregated into what are called adjustment classes. One exposé of the New York City school system found that students in such classes in the ninth and higher grades could not read or write. Overworked teachers gave "fake" lessons of copying unintelligible materials merely to keep the students occupied.[53] In one study of 80 Puerto Rican migrants, three boys were placed in the class corresponding to their chronological age. Being unable to understand English, they fell behind in their work and all three became delinquents and were sent to jail within two years after arrival.[54] Others had to stay away from school during the coldest part of the winter because they had insufficient clothing.

Building facilities in East Harlem also needed considerable improvement. Of 15 elementary schools in the area in 1956, only two had been constructed recently and eight had been built before the turn of the century. The shortage of space was so acute that all but two public schools were operating on at least a double shift. Some had three shifts. An East Harlem Citizens Committee has aided in obtaining new facilities and modernization of old ones.

A Ford Foundation grant provided funds for a study of Puerto Rican

[51] Wakefield, *op. cit.*, pp. 206-207.
[52] *Ibid.*, pp. 191-212.
[53] George H. Allen, *Undercover Teacher* (New York, Doubleday, 1960), pp. 138-139.
[54] Berle, *op. cit.*, p. 51.

education in New York City. In 1958 a new program was instituted to better assimilate Puerto Ricans in the New York school system.[55] It is to be hoped that the present practice of Puerto Ricans dropping out of school at age 16 in the long run will be reversed so that Puerto Ricans as well as all other groups in American society will be trained to the capacity of their capabilities.

The same lack of educational opportunity may be noted for Mexican immigrants. One study of 60,000 Spanish-speaking students in the Southwest showed that 55 percent of those above the first grade were two years overage for the grade they were in.[56] Another study found that in Texas only 53 percent of the children of school age of Mexican descent were actually enrolled in school and attending regularly.[57] A conclusion of Ruth Tuck in her San Bernardino study was that the "tragedy of the second generation is that it is so incompletely educated."[58] She pointed out that incomes of the Mexican families were so low that children had to drop out of school to supplement their families' meager income. Progressing beyond the eighth or ninth grade represents an almost insurmountable barrier for the child in the poorest families. Fewer still go to college. A study of 33 colleges in Texas showed that Spanish-name students formed 1.6 percent of the total enrollment, although they made up 20.4 percent of the white population of school age.[59] Legal restrictions against segregating Mexican students in school have aided in their education, but much more still remains to be done. Improved curriculum and counseling is necessary along with financial aid to induce youths to remain in school.

DISCRIMINATION

State fair employment practice laws in California and New York have helped immigrants find jobs, but most states do not have such laws. The creation of branches of the Fair Employment Practices Commission in the Southwest during World War II did aid in eliminating discriminatory practices then. In the New Mexico, Texas, and Louisiana region, 37 percent of the complaints involved discrimination against Hispanos as did 23 percent of the complaints in the California, Nevada, and Arizona area.[60] In San Bernardino, the Hispanos sued in federal court in 1943 before the civic swimming pool

[55] Wakefield, op. cit., pp. 149-187.

[56] G. I. Sanchez, Forgotten People (Albuquerque, University of New Mexico Press, 1940), pp. 30-31.

[57] Wilson Little, Spanish-Speaking Children in Texas (Austin, University of Texas Press, 1944), pp. 64-65.

[58] Tuck, op. cit., p. 189.

[59] Ruth Ann Fogarties, Texas-Born Spanish-Name Students in Texas Colleges and Universities (1945–46), Inter-American Education Occasional Papers, III (Austin, University of Texas Press, 1948).

[60] McWilliams, op. cit., p. 198.

was opened to them. Shortly thereafter the "white trade only" signs were voluntarily removed from stores, possibly for fear of another legal defeat.

The methods of discrimination are no longer overt but are more subtle. Service in a bar or café may become extremely slow for a Hispano. Anglos may be seated ahead of waiting Mexicans on the pretext that reservations have been made. Almost all the Hispanos live in one section of town in San Bernardino. Many Anglos refuse to sell houses to Mexicans. The pattern of segregated housing has resulted in segregated schooling. Under such schooling the Hispanos learn to speak an accented English, which remains with them for the rest of their lives. It also makes them ignorant of life outside their own group. The result of the various forms of discrimination is that the second generation had little nostalgia for their *colonia* (Mexican section). Bitterness is expressed toward the dominant Anglos.[61]

The fact that about a third of all Puerto Ricans are colored has resulted in discrimination against this group as against American Negroes. Those of intermediate color particularly notice discrimination that they were not used to in Puerto Rico. This group has adapted least well to New York City society.[62] Some hostility now exists between American Negroes and newer Puerto Ricans. The former dislike the influx of the backward Hispanos, and the newer Puerto Ricans seek to remain different from American Negroes because of the known discrimination against them by American society.

Summary on Spanish-Americans

Spanish-Americans in general improve their economic lot by coming to the United States. Language presents a barrier to assimilation in addition to the barriers of discrimination already existing against newcomers. C. Wright Mills found that adaptation does take place over time. To adapt, the Hispano must climb over the difficult barriers of language, poor housing, relatively low income, and discrimination. Economic security is still lacking for a majority of Spanish-American migrants. Much remains to be done now and in the future to raise the Hispanos from economic and social poverty.

AMERICAN INDIANS

According to the 1960 Census, there were 523,591 Indians residing in the United States. Some controversy exists as to the exact definition of an Indian,

---

[61] Tuck, *op. cit.*, pp. 160-161, 186-187, 197-231.
[62] Mills, Senior, and Goldsen, *op. cit.*, Table VIII-II, p. 152.

and by using a broader definition the number could be expanded by slightly more than 10 percent.[63] One estimate of Indian population before the arrival of the white man was from 800,000 to 1 million. By 1850 the Indian population in the United States dwindled to 250,000. The reduction in population was due to disease, whiskey and attendant dissipation, removals, starvations, massacres, and adverse effects of unaccustomed conditions.[64] From 1850 to 1900 the Indian population remained stable and since the latter date has begun to increase. In 1960, 82 percent of the Indians resided in 14 states, and the 5 states of Oklahoma, Arizona, New Mexico, California, and North Carolina housed 54 percent of our Indian population. More than half of present-day Indians live on reservations. With mobility from reservations it is expected that the Indian population will be less concentrated in the future.

TREATIES

From 1789 until 1850 the United States negotiated and ratified 245 treaties with the Indians. During this period the United States government secured more than 450 million acres of land for less than $90 million or 20 cents an acre.[65] The consensus is that wholesale fraud was perpetrated upon the Indians in acquiring the land. Land-hungry speculators, military defeats, and plain dishonesty robbed the Indians of much of their land. Sitting Bull, for example, stated that he would be glad to make a treaty with white men if the government would send him a white man who would tell the truth. The Cherokee tribe took a voluntary vow of poverty, because they believed that as long as they possessed anything worth taking, white men would keep after them until they got it.[66]

THE RESERVATION SYSTEM

Until the Civil War, the national policy in dealing with Indian tribes was based on treaty, with the tribes considered as independent nations. During and after the Civil War it was reasoned that Indian tribes had none of the elements of nationality. Rather they were wards of the country. Beginning in 1867 Indians were placed on reservations in the West regardless of the wishes of the Indians. An act passed in 1871 specifically denied independent nation status to Indian tribes. Although the Indians had no concept of private property rights, the Dawes act of 1887 authorized the President of the United

---

[63] J. Mixon Radley, "The Demography of the Indians," *Annals of the American Academy of Political and Social Science,* Vol. 311 (May, 1957), p. 27.

[64] James Mooney, "Population," in *Handbook of the American Indian,* Washington, D.C., Bureau of American Ethnology, Vol. 2, Bulletin 30 (1910), p. 286.

[65] Walter R. Blumenthal, *American Indians Dispossessed* (Philadelphia, G. S. MacManus Co., 1955), p. 18.

[66] Stanley Vestal, *Southwesterners Write* (Albuquerque, University of New Mexico Press, 1946), p. 337.

States to divide Indian reservations into individual holdings. The head of the family was allotted 80 acres of agricultural land until the expiration of a trust period of 25 years, or longer, if the President deemed an extension desirable. Thereafter the Indian could do with the land as he wished, subject to the laws of the state or territory in which he lived. In 1906 permission was given the Indians to sell their land immediately if they were shown to be competent. More than half of the landholders sold their land, spent the proceeds, and then became destitute.

In 1924 Indians were granted citizenship. The next significant Indian legislation came in 1934, when allotting of tribal land to individuals was abolished. Two million dollars a year was appropriated for the purchase of land for tribes. In 1946 an Indian Claims Commission was created to adjudicate claims against the United States on behalf of any Indian tribe, but not individual Indians. As of July 1, 1966, 322 claims have been acted upon. Of these, 143 have been dismissed. Payment of $208 million has been made for millions of acres of land. That the Indian Claims Commission backlog of cases is large may be seen from the figures that 279 cases are still pending, most of which were filed in 1951.[67]

Beginning in 1950, when a new Commissioner of Indian Affairs was appointed, the policy of the Bureau of Indian Affairs was changed to remove the United States government from the Indian affairs. In 1953 trusteeship of the Bureau of Indian Affairs was terminated for five specific tribes and all of the Indians living in California, Florida, New York, and Texas. Since that time termination of Bureau of Indian Affairs trusteeships has only occurred when specifically requested by tribes.[68]

In 1961, Secretary of the Interior Udall appointed a Special Task Force on Indian Affairs to report on Indian matters. The Special Task Force analyzed the aims of the Bureau of Indian Affairs, which at the time were threefold in nature:

1. To create conditions under which the Indians will advance their social, economic, and political adjustment to achieve a status comparable to that of their non-Indian neighbors.
2. To encourage Indians and Indian tribes to assume an increasing measure of self-sufficiency.
3. To terminate, at appropriate times, federal supervision and services special to Indians.

The Special Task Force concluded that so much dissension had arisen over the termination program that Indians were reluctant to support transitional

---

[67] Memorandum from William Carmack, Assistant Commissioner, Bureau of Indian Affairs (July 8, 1966).

[68] *Annual Report of the Secretary of the Interior, 1961*, Washington, D.C., U.S. Department of the Interior (1961), p. 277.

programs for fear of premature federal withdrawal. The Special Task Force recommended that termination per se no longer be listed as a major objective of the federal Indian program. It felt rather that the Indians should be assisted to advance socially, economically, and politically to the point where special services are no longer justified.[69]

CULTURAL PROBLEMS

Vernon Malan, in his study of the Kyle, South Dakota community, has classified Indian families in accordance with the degree of acculturation they have attained.[70] He points out that usually the biological and sociological full-blood families adhere to the traditional ways of Indian life, and are influenced by the Indian value system in their social reactions and behavior. A second segment of the population he calls transitional. These are Indians, usually of mixed blood, who are clinging to a part of the old Indian ways but are also accepting some of the manners and customs of Western society. A third group he calls transpositional families; these are the people who largely renounce the Indian ways and customs and have accepted wholeheartedly the values of American society. Almost invariably in such families there is a non-Indian parent. The economic well-being of those accepting Western culture is much higher than that of the traditional Indians who cling to their ancient customs. The cultural lag in this latter group of Indians accentuates their present economic poverty.

Several factors are responsible for the cultural lag of Indians. One is that Indians are not future-oriented. In our American way of life we think in terms of what the future will bring, and so we plan and prepare for it. But in Indian culture the Indian life is oriented to the present. Indians live for today; tomorrow will take care of itself. Indian culture also lacks a sense of time. Time in the sense of measuring duration by clock and days of the week is not important to the person reared in the Indian way of life. In many of the early languages of the Plains Indians, there was no word for time as we know and measure it. Anthropologists tell us that the language of a society will reflect the things that people feel are most important; and the fact that the language of the Plains Indians in many instances contains no word for time is an indication of their feeling that time is unimportant. In the simple life of the hunter and the gatherer there is not the same necessity for budgeting daily hours, and so it is only natural that Indians would have less consideration for time than industrial society has.

Indians also lack a habituation to hard work. While it was not an easy task for the hunter and the warrior to brave the dangers of the trail in ful-

[69] *Report to the Secretary of the Interior*, Washington, D.C., Task Force on Indian Affairs (1961), p. 6.

[70] The material for this section has been taken from Leslie Towle, "Poverty and the Oklahoma Indian," *Sooner* (July-August, 1964), pp. 10-13, 24.

filling his social and economic role, the work of gathering the food and keeping the camp comfortable was left to the women. The hunter and warrior could not lower his status in society by working. Indians are also unused to saving. They rarely think of accumulating a capital sum that could be invested to provide an economic opportunity. Theirs is not an acquisitive society. With all the cultural differences, many Indians find it difficult, if not impossible, to accommodate themselves to the newer white American culture.

INCOME AND EMPLOYMENT

Income of Indians is extremely low. Data in 1964 from Indian reservations showed that of 40,551 families, 19,053 have incomes of less than $2,000, and 28,066 were below $3,000.[71]

Sources of income of Indians vary from reservation to reservation. Statistics for the Navajo showed that slightly over a fifth of their income came from railroad employment off the reservation. The next largest source of income, bringing in about half as much as railroad income, was farming and stock raising on the reservation. Other large sources of income in decreasing order of importance were federal employment on the reservation, nonagricultural employment off the reservation, railroad unemployment compensation, federal employment off the reservation, public assistance and welfare, and agricultural employment off the reservation.[72] For all Indian males in the United States, 20 percent of their income comes from agriculture and for another 17 percent from unskilled labor. Indian males are particularly underrepresented in professional, managerial, clerical, and sales work.[73]

Of the land still owned by Indians, 40.5 million acres are owned as part of reservations, mostly in the semiarid Southwest, and 11.6 acres have been allotted to individual Indians.[74] More than half the allotted tracts have been sold (71,593 out of 115,130 tracts).[75] Today, passing on of land to all the children in the family has resulted in 23,462 allotments out of 115,130 to be held by six or more heirs.[76]

Because of the semiarid nature of much of the land owned by Indians, irrigation projects have been developed. Major irrigation projects in 1961 were the San Carlos Project on the Colorado River in Arizona, the Coachella Valley Project in California, the Duck Valley Project in Nevada, and

[71] Memorandum from William Carmack, see footnote 67.

[72] Robert M. Young, *Navajo Yearbook of Planning in Action*, Report No. V, Calendar Year 1955 (Window Rock, Arizona, Navajo Agency, 1956), p. 64.

[73] *Census of Population, 1960*, Vol. IV, Final Report PC(2)–IC, *Nonwhite Population by Race*, Washington, D.C., U.S. Department of Commerce, Bureau of the Census, Table 33, p. 104.

[74] *Annual Report of the Secretary of the Interior, 1961*, p. 299.

[75] Blumenthal, *op. cit.*, p. 159.

[76] *Ibid.*

two projects in New Mexico for Navajos and Pueblos. Indian agriculture has also been aided by county agents and the U.S. Soil Conservation program. Bureau of Indian Affairs specialists have pointed out that some of the Indian land has been overgrazed, particularly when drought occurs, and the Pueblos of New Mexico among others have voluntarily reduced their livestock to comply with better range management.[77]

EDUCATION

Education of Indians will have to improve considerably if Indian income is to increase. The original United States policy, beginning with a treaty in 1860, was to educate Indians in boarding schools so that the children would be freed from the language and habits of their untutored and often times savage parents.[78] Unfortunately, too few were educated. According to the 1950 Census, 21 percent of the Indians over 5 years of age have had no formal education. As late as 1953 half of the Navajo children were not in school, mostly due to lack of facilities.

Since that period of time, a determined effort has been made to increase the education of Indians. It was decided that as many Indians as possible should attend public schools near their homes rather than attend far-removed boarding schools. In fiscal year 1958, the Bureau of Indian Affairs operated 310 federal schools in the United States and by fiscal 1961 the number had dropped to 279. In order to encourage more local school attendance, roads had to be made more passable and bus transportation had to be made available. Recently, the number of Indian students has increased rapidly. In 1953 a program was put into effect to start 14,000 Navajo children in school within two years. By 1955, 13,000 of the 14,000 were attending school. Similar programs were adopted for other tribes. Although education for Indians has improved, weaknesses still exist. In the 1965 Navajo school census, there were 45,969 Navajo children aged 6 to 18. Of these, 36,839 were in school.[79]

In order to help remedy the lack of education and the illiteracy among adult Indians, 28 agencies and locations throughout the United States are now serving about 107 Indian communities. Reading, writing, civic skills, and other subjects are taught to about 5,800 adults. In addition, 600 Indian students attend college with the help of Bureau of Indian Affairs loans and grants. The bureau also helps other Indian students to secure nonfederal scholarship aid. Vocational training has aided adult Indians also. In fiscal year 1963, 2,911 Indians were being trained in schools for vocational training, and another 675 were enrolled in Area Redevelopment Administration training programs, along with 245 enrolled in on-the-job training. A survey

[77] *Annual Report of the Secretary of the Interior, 1961*, pp. 306-312.
[78] *Annual Report of the Indian Commissioner to the Secretary of the Interior, 1885*, p. 23.
[79] Memorandum from William Carmack, *see* footnote 67.

completed in 1961 showed that 81 percent of all those completing training in vocational schools were placed in suitable around-the-year jobs. The counseling given Indians during the training enabled 52 percent of those discontinuing training to find suitable employment also.[80]

HEALTH

All studies of Indians show that their economic resources have been so poor that they have experienced serious health problems. In 1950 the average life span for Indians was 36 years, compared with 61 years for non-Indians. Some of the poorer tribes averaged substantially less than the average. The average life span of the Papago Indian was 17 years and of Navajos it was 20 years.[81] Treatable diseases caused many more deaths among Indians than among whites. Infant deaths were also much higher than in the general population. In 1957 it was reported that 426.9 Indians per 100,000 had tuberculosis, compared with 51 cases per 100,000 for the rest of the population. Gastroenteric diseases caused nine times as many deaths among Indians as among the total population in the United States. Furthermore, 23 percent of all Indian deaths occurred among infants, compared with 7 percent for the population as a whole.[82]

In 1955 adequate personnel was simply not available to aid the health of Indians. Half of the Indian hospitals had only one doctor. There were insufficient pharmacists to ensure safety in the use of drugs. The environmental sanitation staff was extremely small and there were few dentists and dental assistants. Public Health nursing services were spread thin, and there was only a skeleton staff of medical social workers. There were no nutritionists nor specialists in maternal and child health.[83]

In 1955 broad responsibilities for the Indians' health was transferred from the Bureau of Indian Affairs to the Public Health Service of the U.S. Department of Health, Education, and Welfare. As of June 1965, the number of physicians and dentists more than doubled, and the following health professional groups increased three or four fold: pharmacists, sanitary engineers, sanitarians and sanitarian aides, medical social workers, health education workers, nutritionists, dietitians, and health record librarians. At the close of fiscal year 1965, the Division of Indian Health of the Public Health Service was operating 49 hospitals—47 general and two tuberculosis sana-

[80] *Annual Report of the Secretary of the Interior, 1961,* pp. 286-291, 295-296; *1963,* pp. 23-24.

[81] James R. Shaw, "Guarding the Health of Our Indian Citizens," *Journal of the American Hospital Association* (April 16, 1957).

[82] *Answers to Your Questions on American Indians,* Washington, D.C., U.S. Department of the Interior, Bureau of Indian Affairs (Lawrence, Kansas, Haskell Institute, 1959), p. 27; *Progress in Indian Health,* Washington, D.C., U.S. Department of Health, Education, and Welfare, Public Health Service (1959), p. 2.

[83] *Progress in Indian Health,* Washington, D.C., U.S. Department of Health, Education, and Welfare, Public Health Service (1959), p. 1.

toriums; 30 health centers with full-time staff, 16 health centers at the larger Bureau of Indian Affairs boarding schools, and many health stations. Through fiscal 1965, basic sanitation facilities have been made available to more than 24,000 Indian and Alaskan native families in more than 350 communities. This level of accomplishment represents 29 percent of the required effort to provide beneficiary families with essential water and waste disposal facilities.[84]

The results of the new health program have been encouraging. From fiscal year 1955 through fiscal year 1965, the number of hospital admissions almost doubled, and almost triple the amount of dental services were provided. The death rate due to tuberculosis decreased about 61 percent, although it is still higher than the national average. The Indian infant death rate declined 45 percent, but it is still 1½ times that of the general public.[85] In spite of the improvements, the fact that the death and disease rate is still much higher among Indians than the rest of the United States population would indicate that further efforts are needed to improve Indian health.

RELOCATION PROGRAM

Income on most reservations has fallen far short of the needs for a decent livelihood for Indians. Among the Navajos, for example, it has been estimated that 45,000 people could earn an adequate living on the reservation; yet the population in 1956 was 78,000. In 1959 it was reported that in at least 8 of the 17 Land Management Districts the range was seriously overgrazed, and that the number of livestock exceeded the total estimated range-carrying capacity by nearly 33 percent.[86]

One of the programs designed to aid reservation Indians is the Relocation Program. Under this program, which began in 1952, the Bureau of Indian Affairs offers financial assistance and limited social services to place reservation Indians in full time employment in industrial areas. The Bureau of Indian Affairs will pay the transportation costs from the reservation to the city of employment and subsistence expenses enroute. Up to $50 is provided for shipment of household goods. Up to four weeks of subsistence allowances are provided after arrival of the Indian at his new destination. A supplemental subsistence is also made available for those Indians who become unemployed through no fault of their own and who are not eligible for unemployment compensation. Lastly, up to $50 is provided for tools and equipment for apprentice workers. Almost 60 percent of the expenses of this program are used to pay the staff who are administering the program and

[84] *Indian Health Highlights, 1966*, Washington, D.C., U.S. Department of Health, Education, and Welfare, Public Health Service, pp. xvii-xx.

[85] *Indian Health Highlights, 1966*, p. xiii.

[86] *The Navajo Yearbook, 1961*, Washington, D.C., U.S. Department of the Interior, Bureau of Indian Affairs, p. 164.

who provide the necessary counseling for Indians. Table 19-1 shows the number of Indians who have been relocated under this program.

TABLE 19-1.   RELOCATIONS OF INDIANS, 1952–1963.

Fiscal Year	Units	Persons	Fiscal Year	Units	Persons
1952	442	868	1958	2,373	5,728
1953	697	1,470	1959	1,655	3,560
1954	1,222	2,553	1960	1,798	3,674
1955	1,500	3,459	1961	1,822	3,468
1956	1,742	4,275	1962	1,866	3,494
1957	4,184	6,964	1963	1,696	3,318

Source: Annual Reports, Secretary of the Interior.

More single persons, predominantly males, have been placed in urban jobs than families. The Bureau of Indian Affairs operates seven relocation service offices to help place Indians. Three of these are located in California— Los Angeles, Oakland, and San Jose. The other four offices are located in Chicago, Cleveland, Denver, and Dallas. These offices place Indians nation- wide. Several smaller regional placement offices are located in Minneapolis, Oklahoma City, and Tulsa. Over several years offices have been closed in Waukegan and Joliet, Illinois, Cincinnati, San Francisco, and St. Louis be- cause of their comparative unpopularity as a destination of reservation In- dians. At the reservation end, services are provided at 43 agency jurisdictions, some of which served smaller nearby agencies on an itinerant basis. One of the problems of the program has been that a relatively large percentage of Indians moved to urban areas return to the reservation. In fiscal year 1953, 32 percent of the Indians returned, and the figure is now between 20 and 24 percent. It is hoped that better vocational training and more effec- tive staff services at destination points will reduce the number of Indians returning to the reservations.

INDUSTRIAL DEVELOPMENT PROGRAM

Another major facet of raising Indian income is the attracting of industries to reservation areas. The Bureau of Indian Affairs has developed an Indus- trial Development Program whose purpose is to work with tribal leaders to explain the basic concepts of industrial development and the need to coop- erate with communities to create the proper industrial climate. Tribal and community groups are aided in organizing industrial development founda- tions to attract industries. The bureau gathers basic information on resource availability, and provides information to industries interested in locating in Indian areas. Indian tribes themselves have allocated funds for industrial development, and 10 industrial development corporations have been organized with a combined capitalization of $1,850,000.[87] Since the origination of this program in 1955, 25 factories have been opened, and employ several thousand workers in the following industries: manufacturing of fishing tackle, charcoal briquetting, basket manufacturing, quilt manufacturing, wood treatment, furniture manufacturing, moccasin manufacturing, manufacture of electronic components, knitted garments manufacturing, leather goods manufacturing, and the production of house trailers.[88]

Summary on American Indians

Indians remain one of the most economically depressed groups in the United States today. The failure to educate Indians has resulted in grinding poverty. Today attempts are being made to remedy the deficiencies in education. The economic resources of reservations are not sufficient to provide an adequate livelihood for Indians. One of two things, or both, must be done to remedy this situation. Either more Indians must leave the reservations to earn a living primarily in our urban economy, or more industry must be attracted to the reservations. Both of these are happening, but at such a relatively slow pace that poverty among Indians will continue for a number of years into the future.

[87] *Annual Report of the Secretary of the Interior, 1961,* pp. 296-297.
[88] *Annual Reports of the Secretary of the Interior,* various issues.

WOMEN AND CHILDREN

WOMEN

Of the 34.6 million people living on low incomes in 1963, Mollie Orshansky found that 45 percent were in units headed by women. Since so much poverty is concentrated among women, some analysis should be made of their problems.

WOMEN IN RURAL SOCIETY

In a rural economy before the turn of the century, especially in the West, women had to be extremely self-reliant. Professor John Ise describes the work which his mother did on coming to a western Kansas prairie farm in 1873. She helped her husband plant, harvest, and engage in all the other miscellaneous tasks of their farm such as fighting fires, grasshoppers, and the like. Later, when sons and neighbors took over the farm work, a heavy load still remained for her. Not only did food have to be cooked and processed, but clothing had to be made, along with cultivating the kitchen garden, herding the cows to pasture and back, feeding the pigs, hens, milking, and churning butter. In addition she made brooms, mattresses and floor mats, and soap. In food processing, she made molasses and vinegar and brewed browned rye grain for coffee. She did laundry for bachelors and widowers, ran the community's post office from her home, and sold butter and eggs.[1] In addition, women in the past had many more children to take care of than they have today.

INCREASING EMPLOYMENT OF WOMEN

Farming was still the way of life for a majority of Americans in 1870. However, the Census of that year listed 2 million women in the work force, or one out of every eight women over 10 years of age. The decennial census reports (Table 20-1) show an increasing participation of women in the work force. The trend toward increasing participation of women in the work force was accelerated during World War II, when manpower was scarce. Women by the millions moved into industry. After the war, many decided

[1] John Ise, *Sod and Stubble* (New York, Wilson-Erickson, 1936).

TABLE 20–1. FEMALE LABOR FORCE, 1890–1960

Year	Female Labor Force [a]	Female Labor Force as Percentage of Total Labor Force
	Gainful Workers Aged 10 and Over	
1890	4,006,000	17.4
1900	5,319,000	18.8
1910	7,445,000	21.5
1920	8,637,000	21.4
1930	10,752,000	22.0
	Labor Force Aged 14 and Over	
1930	10,396,000	23.6
1940	13,015,000	25.7
1950	16,552,000	29.0
1960	22,409,000	32.1

[a] Up to and including 1930, the Census counted "gainful workers" aged 10 and over. After 1930, it counted persons in the "labor force" aged 14 and over. Basically, gainful workers were individuals who regarded themselves as having a regular occupation producing an income, regardless of what they were doing at the time of the Census. Persons in the labor force are those who worked or sought work for pay or profit during the week preceding the Census. Under both definitions, some women who worked without pay on family farms or in family businesses were also included. The labor-force figures for 1930 were estimated by the Bureau of the Census from the gainful-worker figures.

Source: Decennial Census Reports, U.S. Department of Commerce, Bureau of the Census.

that they preferred working to remaining at home. From 1950 to 1960 an additional 5.8 million entered the work force.

The age and marital status of women in the work force has changed considerably since 1890. Then, most working women were single and about half were under 25 years of age. Today most working women in the work force are married and about half are over 40 years of age. In 1890, 7 out of 10 women were single, whereas today 3 out of 4 are married. In 1890, the percentage of women employed started to drop from age 20 on. By 1956, the drop started at age 19, but reversed itself after age 30 to reach another peak of employment at 50. At that age in 1956, 44 percent of all women were in the work force, compared with only 15 percent in 1890.[2] Part of the explanation for the larger percentage of older women working is that in 1957 the median age of the mother was only 48 when the youngest child married, compared with 55 in 1890. Women today are marrying younger

[2] *Womanpower*, National Manpower Council (New York, Columbia, 1957), pp. 10, 126.

than they did in 1890, and they are having their last child earlier. The average woman now marries at age 20, compared with 22 in 1890, and has her last child at 26, compared with 32 in 1890.[3]

New inventions have made work in the home easier, and this has induced some women to seek employment. A number of other factors are also important in determining whether women work. Single, divorced, or widowed women are much more apt to work than married women. Women of minority races, such as Negroes, work more frequently than white women out of financial necessity. Women whose husbands are unskilled workers also work more frequently. Statistics for 1950 showed that whereas 28 percent of the wives of salaried professional and managerial workers were in the work force, 38 percent of the wives of unskilled workers were.[4] In certain areas of the country larger percentages of women work than in other sections, mainly depending on whether jobs are available. Fewer women work in the steel-mill region, for example, because the work is considered too heavy for women and shift rotation in the steel mills makes working less convenient for women.

WOMEN'S OCCUPATIONS AND EARNINGS

Although the census of 1870 listed some women employed in all 338 occupations, domestic service accounted for almost half of all women employed. By adding six other occupations, agricultural laborers, seamstresses, milliners, teachers, textile mill workers, and laundresses, 93 percent of all paid work of women was accounted for. Not only have more women entered the work force since 1870, but they have entered into more types of work. By 1950, the seven leading occupations of women accounted for only 48 percent of all women's occupations and the top 20 occupations accounted for only 72 percent of all their employment. The major trend during this period has been away from low-paying jobs such as domestic service into better paying secretarial, clerical, and other white-collar and professional positions. Even with this trend, the employment of women tends to be more narrowly restricted to fewer occupations than the employment of men.

In March 1965, the average income of men living in metropolitan areas and heading a family was $7,635, compared with $3,879 for women.[5] One reason for the higher wage of men is that more of them work full time than women. Almost one-third of all working women employed were employed on a part-time rather than a full-time basis. The number of part-time women

[3] P. C. Glick, "The Life Cycle of the Family," *Marriage and Family Living* (February, 1955), p. 4.

[4] Margaret S. Carroll, "The Working Wife and Her Family's Economic Position," *Monthly Labor Review*, Vol. 85 (1962), Table 2, p. 371.

[5] *Current Population Reports*, Series P-60, No. 48, Washington, D.C., U.S. Department of Commerce, Bureau of the Census (April, 1966), Table 2, p. 14.

workers has been growing much faster than the number of full-time women workers. From 1950 to 1958, the percentage of women working full time increased by 14.5 percent, but during the same time the percentage of part-time women workers increased by 46.7 percent.[6] Since many women must also carry the duty of being the homemaker, full-time work is looked upon by many as requiring too long hours of work. Part-time work, on the other hand, is not looked upon as so onerous. A number of industries can use part-time workers in order to meet peak business periods, to relieve regular workers from excessively long hours, and to perform work which does not require a full week's work. About 5.5 million of the 6.7 million women employed part time for a salary were engaged in wholesale and retail trade, private household, and service industries.[7]

Part-time work provides only a partial explanation for the lower wages of women, for full-time women workers earn only 66 percent as much as men. This figure is for metropolitan areas, where full-time men earn $8,563, compared with $5,614 for women. In nonmetropolitan areas, full-time women earn only 61 percent of what men earn. The earnings are $6,513 for men and $3,992 for women.[8] More women tend to take jobs in low-wage industries. In 1964 the median income for women engaged in year-round full-time work in personal services was $1,809, and retail trade saleswomen received $2,899. Where women work merely to supplement their husband's income, such low pay may not be disastrous. However, where women are the sole support of their families or the chief breadwinner, poverty results. One study by the Census showed that about 20 percent of all nonfarm women workers were either the sole or chief breadwinner in their family.[9]

WORKING WIVES AND MOTHERS

In a study of working wives, it was found that the wives of low-earning husbands earned lower incomes than wives whose husbands' earning power was greater. More wives of low-income husbands worked than those who had higher income. Employed women contributed 27 percent of their families' total income. Wives working for the full year contributed 38 percent compared with 18 percent for those employed during only part of the year. The earnings of the wife were sufficient to bring the family incomes above the City Workers Family Budget (Bureau of Labor Statistics) in about half the instances where the husband's income alone was below the budget.[10]

Relatively few women with children under six who live with their hus-

[6] Part-Time Employment for Women, Bulletin No. 273, Washington, D.C., U.S. Department of Labor, Women's Bureau (1960), p. 3.

[7] Ibid., p. 19.

[8] Current Population Reports, Series P-60, No. 48 (April, 1966), Table 2, p. 14.

[9] Womanpower, p. 71.

[10] Carroll, op. cit., pp. 366-374.

bands are in the work force—16 percent. Yet there are so many women with young children that there are 2.5 million of them with children under six who are working. They constitute about one-eighth of all working women. Most of them work because their husbands' earnings are relatively low and expenses are high in furnishing a home. About a fifth of working women with young children are either widowed, divorced, or separated.[11]

The consensus appears to be that young children need the care of the mother in the home.[12] For older children, the charge has not been proved that working mothers have caused the reported rise in juvenile delinquency. Most of the prominent men in European history were raised by "nannies" or governesses rather than by their own mothers.[13] This fact would indicate that the presence of the mother in the home is not necessary at all times. Five hundred delinquents were compared with a like number of nondelinquents who had similar intelligence, ethnic background, age, and residence in underprivileged areas.[14] The delinquent group did not contain a larger percentage of mothers who regularly worked outside the home. However, the delinquent boys did have a larger percentage of mothers who sporadically worked. The mothers who were occasionally employed were found to have had a history of delinquency themselves. They tended to be married to men who were emotionally disturbed and who had poor work habits. It may have been that such factors rather than working caused the delinquent tendencies in their children. Of the housewives who remained at home and provided good supervision to their children, 32 percent of the children became delinquent compared with 84 percent delinquent who had poor supervision. Where the mother was regularly employed and had provided good supervision, only 19 percent became delinquent, compared with a 77 percent delinquency rate for those working mothers having poor supervision. Interestingly, the working mothers had a lower rate of delinquency among their children.

An important factor affecting delinquency was the quality of supervision given the children regardless of whether the mother was working. A study by Albert Bandura and R. H. Walters also found that there were fewer delinquents when mothers worked. The study dealt with middle-class delinquents. The interpretation given was that middle-class working mothers had arranged to provide for more adequate supervision for their children.[15] The statistics unfortunately showed that a majority of working mothers did not arrange that adequate supervision be provided for their children during

[11] *Womanpower*, p. 69.

[12] *Ibid.*, p. 54.

[13] Eleanor E. Maccoby, "Effects Upon Children of Their Mothers' Outside Employment," in *Work in the Lives of Married Women*, National Manpower Council (New York, Columbia, 1958), p. 151.

[14] Sheldon Glueck and Eleanor Glueck, *Unravelling Juvenile Delinquency* (New York, Commonwealth Fund, 1950).

[15] Maccoby, *op. cit.*, p. 154.

the mothers' working hours. A comprehensive study of child-care arrangements of full-time working mothers showed that one of eight children 6 to 11 years old cared for themselves.[16]

In attempting to evaluate the effect of working mothers upon children, Eleanor Maccoby cites two other studies.[17] One of these compared a group of two-year-olds in a residential nursery in England with another group the same age who attended a day-care nursery. The children in the day nursery who saw their parents every day adjusted better than the children who did not see their parents. Another study was of the "kibbutzim," the day-care nurseries in Israel where the parents see their children for only an hour or so each day. Here it was found that the children in the "kibbutzim" were quite attached to their parents, and that by age ten they had developed more mature personalities than home-reared children. From these and other studies, Maccoby was unable to generalize as to whether maternal employment was "good" or "bad" for children. She concluded that some mothers should work and others should not depending upon a number of factors. These factors she listed as: "the age of the children, the nature of the mother's motivation to work, the mother's skill in child care and that of her substitute, the composition of the family (especially whether it contains a good substitute caretaker), the stability of the husband, and the pressure of absence of tension between the husband and wife." [18] She felt that fact-finding had only just begun in evaluating the impact of these various factors on the children of working mothers.

DAY-CARE SERVICES

Some communities have provided for day-care services for working mothers. The Children's Bureau of the U.S. Department of Health, Education, and Welfare has advocated an effective licensing system for such services. The Bureau has suggested that nurseries be located in the community in which the child lives so that the time and trouble in long travel is eliminated. Other recommendations are for well-trained staffs, and caring for smaller groups of children, preferably even giving the child some time alone each day. For older children, some communities have provided for extended programs to care for the children until the mother arrives at home.[19] The State of California has made provision for child-care facilities, but few other states have followed suit. Public housing projects recognize the need for providing child-care services also. Voluntary agencies, such as churches, have provided

[16] Henry C. Lajewski, *Child Care Arrangements of Full-Time Working Mothers,* Publication No. 378, Washington, D.C., U.S. Department of Health, Education, and Welfare, Children's Bureau (1959), p. 18.

[17] Maccoby, *op. cit.,* pp. 166-168.

[18] *Ibid.,* p. 172.

[19] Katherine Brownell Oettinger, "Maternal Employment and Children," in *Work in the Lives of Married Women,* p. 147.

some services, but it is felt that the Community Chests and United Fund Campaigns have not done as much as they could possibly do in caring for the overall needs of the children of working mothers.[20] Recently the Federal government has aided in the support of day-care nurseries, but only about 310,000 children are taken care of whereas 2.7 million children need such care.

WOMEN'S EDUCATION

Part of the low income by women is a function of low educational attainment. About 40 percent of our girls today are not graduating from high school,[21] and many of these fall into low wage jobs. Formal schooling of any kind for girls was not generally accepted prior to the nineteenth century.[22] College education for women came even later. It was not until 201 years after Harvard College opened its doors that the first woman was admitted to an American college—Oberlin in 1837.[23] The arguments for depriving women of a higher education were the same as used against minority groups today. The major argument was that women were mentally inferior, and thus could not assimilate a college education. Another argument was that women were too frail physically to stand the rigors of a college education. Finally, it was held that a college education for women would reduce the birthrate. These arguments no longer carry much weight.[24] Yet the problem of advanced education for women remains with us.

Table 20-2 shows that although the absolute number of women enrolled in colleges has been increasing, women constitute a smaller percentage of college students than they did in 1920. Apparently costs and other considerations have given precedence of education to men over women. Only about one-fourth of the women who are capable of doing college work graduate from college.[25] If it is true that the greatest waste in resources in the United States is the failure to educate youth sufficiently, then it follows that the greatest waste comes in the failure to educate our women, for almost 50 percent more boys go to college than girls. Early marriages are also causing a dropout of girls from college before they are able to graduate. Comparisons of our record of college education of women with Russia shows that the percentages of women compared with men enrolled in the United States in 1959 were 35 percent and 51 percent in Russia. The percentage of women students in medicine in the United States was 5.5 percent compared with

[20] "Conference Discussion: Working Mothers and the Development of Children," in National Manpower Council, *Work in the Lives of Married Women* (New York, Columbia, 1958), pp. 191-194.

[21] National Manpower Council, *Womanpower*, p. 221.

[22] Mabel Newcomer, *A Century of Higher Education for American Women* (New York, Harper & Row, 1959), p. 6.

[23] *Ibid.*, p. 5.

[24] *Ibid.*, pp. 25-32.

[25] *Womanpower*, p. 33.

TABLE 20–2. WOMEN ENROLLED IN INSTITUTIONS OF HIGHER LEARNING,
REGULAR SESSION, 1870–1964

Year	Women Enrolled		
	Number	As Percentage of All Women 18 to 21 Years of Age	As Percentage of All Students Enrolled
1870	11,000	0.7	21.0
1880	40,000	1.9	33.4
1890	56,000	2.2	35.9
1900	85,000	2.8	36.8
1910	140,000	3.8	39.6
1920	283,000	7.6	47.3
1930	481,000	10.5	43.7
1940	601,000	12.2	40.2
1950	806,000	17.9	30.2
1958	1,148,000	23.0	35.2
1964	2,052,000	a	38.6

a Not available.

Sources: Mabel Newcomer, *A Century of Higher Education for American Women*
(New York, Harper & Row, 1959), p. 46. Reprinted by permission. *World Almanac*,
1966, p. 732.

69 percent in Russia. The percentages for engineering were 0.6 and 39 percent respectively.[26]

In order to expand the opportunities for the effective development of
womanpower, the National Manpower Council has made a number of
recommendations, such as improving education and vocational guidance for
women, increasing occupational guidance and placement services for mature
women who want to work, and increasing scholarships and financing of
women capable of doing advanced work in college and graduate schools.[27]

WOMEN'S PROTECTIVE LEGISLATION

As early as the 1870's, protective legislation was passed to protect women
workers. Most frequently, such laws deal with minimum wages, maximum
hours, meal and rest periods, and night work. Minimum wage laws have
been adopted by 35 states, the District of Columbia, and Puerto Rico.[28]
However, only a few of these have a minimum wage of as high as $1.25 an
hour. Unlike the federal law, most state laws use wage boards to determine

[26] *The Education of Women*, Commission on the Education of Women of the
American Council on Education, No. 4 (December, 1958).

[27] *Womanpower*, p. 35.

[28] *State Minimum Wage Laws*, U.S. Department of Labor, Women's Bureau,
Women's Bureau Leaflet 4 (revised April, 1966).

what the minimum wage should be in each industry. Most of the minimum wage laws cover women only, but a few states include men and minors too. Almost all states have passed laws regulating the maximum hours of work for women although in some states relatively long hours are permitted. Only slightly more than half the states limit the maximum hours per day to 8 and the maximum weekly hours to 48. A number of states require one day of rest in every 7 days of a work-week for women. A minority of states either prohibit nightwork for women in one or more occupations or have other regulations concerning nightwork. These laws should help in the protection against exploitation.

Laws requiring equal pay for equal work have been passed by almost half the states, and the federal Civil Service has followed this principle since 1923. Most of the differences in pay of fully employed men and women is probably due more to employment in different kinds of jobs, although sometimes women are paid less for the same work. A recent study of the Bureau of Labor Statistics on earnings in the machinery industry showed that women with the same job titles in the same plants were earning from 95 to 99 percent of men's earnings on an hourly basis.[29] In 1963, a federal law was passed guaranteeing equal pay for equal work. Equal pay laws should help to correct inequities in pay between the sexes.

CHILDREN

The income statistics of 1963 show that almost 11 million children out of a total number of 67 million in the United States under 18 years of age were living in families with an income of less than $3,000 annually. Thus 16 percent of the children in the United States are being raised in families with extremely meager economic resources.[30] It is generally true that as the number of children increases beyond two, total family income starts dropping.[31] Lampman's study shows that 34 percent of all families with seven or more persons fell into the low-income group. Large families, according to Lampman, accounted for 22 percent of all people living at a low-income level.[32]

A hundred or more years ago in the United States, when our economy was not nearly so productive as it is today, much more poverty existed than now. The only alternative most families thought they had was to put their

---

[29] *Womanpower*, p. 225.

[30] Mollie Orshansky, "Counting the Poor," *Social Security Bulletin*, Vol. 28, No. 1 (January, 1965), Table 1, p. 11.

[31] *Children and Youth: Their Health and Welfare*, Bulletin No. 363, Washington, D.C., U.S. Department of Health, Education, and Welfare, Children's Bureau (1958), Chart 5.

[32] Robert J. Lampman, *The Low Income Population and Economic Growth*, Washington, D.C., Joint Economic Committee, U.S. Congress, 86th Congress, 1st Session (1959), Table 1, p. 6.

children to work. As time passed, it was realized that putting children to work without educating them first was self-defeating. We now have statistics (1961) to show that persons with a high school education will earn over their lifetime $68,099 more than eighth-grade graduates and $37,659 more than high school dropouts.[33] The emphasis today is to attempt to induce all people to obtain as much education as they can profitably assimilate. Our record is improving. In 1945–1946, only 69 percent of youths aged 14 to 17 were in school. By 1964–1965, this group had risen to 93 percent. But even with this improvement, almost one-fourth of our 17-year-old youth failed to obtain a high school diploma (1963–1964). In 1964, about 44 percent of those aged 18–21 were enrolled in college,[34] but a large percentage of this group will not obtain a bachelor's degree. More will be said about the problem of education in Chapter 22.

CHILD LABOR LEGISLATION

As early as 1813 in Connecticut, legislation was passed to regulate child labor. In that year, Connecticut required that mill owners teach the children in their mills to read, write, and do arithmetic. Massachusetts in 1836 required employed children under 15 to attend school at least three months a year. Six years later, the same state limited hours for children under 12 years of age to 10 hours of work a day. The first state to ban child labor for those under 12 was Pennsylvania in 1848.[35] The law applied to employment in cotton, woolen, and silk factories. In 1906 a federal law to curb child labor was first introduced into Congress. The bill was not passed at that time, but finally was approved in 1916. This law later was declared unconstitutional. Twenty-eight states had ratified approval of an amendment to the Constitution to outlaw child labor. Such an amendment became unnecessary when Congress again passed a bill outlawing child labor as part of the Fair Labor Standards Act of 1938. The Supreme Court ruled that such a law was constitutional.[36]

Fair Labor Standards Act

The Fair Labor Standards Act sets the following minimum ages for workers:

1. A minimum age of 18 for all occupations declared hazardous by the Secretary of Labor. As of 1967, the Secretary of Labor has issued 17 orders prohibiting employment in the following industries: manufacture of ex-

---

[33] *Digest of Educational Statistics, 1965,* Washington, D.C., U.S. Department of Health, Education, and Welfare, Table 106, p. 132.

[34] *Ibid.,* Table 7, p. 14; Table 37, p. 53; Table 51, p. 76.

[35] *Self-Training Unit on Child Labor Laws for Youth,* Bulletin No. 202, Washington, D.C., U.S. Department of Labor, Bureau of Labor Standards (1959), p. 2.

[36] *Ibid.,* p. 3.

plosives; bricks, tile, and kindred products; motor-vehicle occupations; mining; logging and sawmilling; power-driven woodworking machine operations, power-driven hoisting apparatus occupations, power-driven metal forming, punching, and shearing machine occupations; power-driven paper products machine occupations; occupations involving exposure to radioactive substances; occupations in slaughtering and meat-packing establishments and rendering plants; excavating; roofing operations; and wrecking, demolition, and shipbuilding operations.

2. A minimum age of 16 for those employed during school hours. Work is prohibited outside of school hours at the same age for those engaged in manufacturing, mining, and other industries designated by the Secretary of Labor. The Secretary prohibits such employment on power-driven machinery, except office machines, public messenger service, transportation, warehousing and storage, communications, public utilities, and construction.

3. A minimum age of 14 years after school hours for all occupations not covered under the 16 or 18 age limitation. The Secretary of Labor was empowered to provide further restrictions in this category. The law now permits only three hours of work on a school day and eight hours on a nonschool day. Maximum weekly hours are set at 18 when school is in session and 40 hours a week when school is not in session. No work may be performed after 7 P.M or before 7 A.M.

Exemptions from the above three requirements are granted to children employed in agriculture provided that they work after school, to child actors and actresses, to newspaper boys who deliver to consumers, and children who work for their parents except in manufacturing, mining, or other hazardous jobs. Any goods moving in interstate commerce are covered by the child labor provisions except that retail trade is covered only when the establishment performs an operation that changes the nature or form of the goods.

State Child Labor Laws

All the states have laws regulating child labor, and whenever their laws set a higher minimum age than the Fair Labor Standards Act, the state requirement must be followed. At the present writing, 20 states have a minimum age of 16 in manufacturing both during and after school hours. Twenty-two states and Puerto Rico have a 16-year minimum for all employment during school hours, but some of these exempt agriculture and domestic service. Four additional states have the 16-year minimum during school hours for specific industries or establishments. All the remaining states set a 14- or 15-year minimum age for work during school hours in most occupations. Additional regulations cover maximum hours of work, and almost all the states have higher minimum ages for hazardous industries.[37]

[37] *State Child-Labor Standards*, Bulletin No. 158, Washington, D.C., U.S. Department of Labor, Bureau of Labor Standards (1966), pp. vii-ix.

Employment of Children

Although school enrollment statistics have shown improvement over the years, we have not yet attained 100 percent enrollment for those under 18. In addition, one study, although dated, showed that many of our youngsters still in school worked long hours after school. Of every 100 students aged 14 to 17 working after school hours in October of 1957, 27 worked 22 hours or longer per week, and of these, 14 worked 35 hours or longer. The long hours were concentrated particularly in agriculture, where 40 percent of those working put in a 35-hour, or longer, work week.[38]

An added problem is that some employers illegally hire children in violation of the child labor laws. For fiscal year 1964, 21,006 minors were employed in violation of the Fair Labor Standards Act. The following are examples of violations:

A 9-year-old boy turning logs in a lumber mill and concentration yard, a 13-year-old girl peeling tomatoes in a cannery, youngsters 8 and 11 cleaning bricks for a construction firm, a 12-year-old girl cutting peaches in a commercial dry yard, and a 13-year-old boy hanging chickens on a conveyor for a poultry-processing plant.[39]

Even though the child labor restrictions were less strict in agriculture than the rest of industry, 43 percent of the violations of the federal law involved illegal employment in this industry.[40] The government has attempted to aid in this problem by issuing certificates of eligibility for employment, but although certification is desirable, it has not eliminated illegal employment of children.

JUVENILE DELINQUENCY

Much time, effort, and money have gone into attempts to properly assimilate youth into our adult culture. About half a billion dollars was spent in 1960 on recreation by local, state, and federal governments. Even with this expenditure, gross inequalities exist in recreational facilities. Such facilities were particularly lacking among minority races, rural people, low-income, and other groups. One major hindrance to the expansion of organized recreation is lack of funds.[41] Expenditures on recreation can be viewed as a preventive measure to problems of youth. Even with such programs, cer-

38 *Highlights on Young Workers Under 18*, Washington, D.C., U.S. Department of Labor, Bureau of Labor Standards (1959), p. 2.

39 *Annual Report, Fiscal Year 1959*, Washington, D.C., U.S. Department of Labor, p. 256.

40 *Ibid.*, p. 257.

41 Harold D. Meyer and Charles K. Brightbill, *Community Recreation* (Englewood Cliffs, N.J., Prentice-Hall, 1956), pp. 68-85.

tain youths face particular problems of lack of parents, physical and mental handicaps, and other problems.

Amount of Juvenile Delinquency

Those who drop out of school while still quite young obviously are less well trained for jobs than those with more education. Since there is greater difficulty in placing unskilled workers in industry, youths have much higher rates of unemployment than those somewhat older. Unemployment for those 18 and 19 ranged from 7 to 18 percent from 1947 through 1965.[42] This group of unemployed as well as other juveniles in lower-income urban neighborhoods are more prone to become juvenile delinquents than youths in rural or wealthier communities. Rates of juvenile delinquency were about three times greater in predominantly urban than in rural areas.[43] However, the improvements in transportation and easier access of rural youths to urban areas has caused rural delinquency to grow faster than urban delinquency. Since 1949 the trend in amounts of juvenile delinquency, except for 1961, has been upward. In 1964, a total of 686,000 delinquency cases were disposed of by Juvenile Courts.[44]

Causes of Juvenile Delinquency

Rates of juvenile delinquency are five times as high for boys as for girls. The types of offenses committed are different also. For boys almost half the cases involved some form of stealing whereas over half the girls were referred for being ungovernable, running away, and sex offenses.[45] There are a number of theories as to the causes of juvenile delinquency. One theory, tied directly to economic insecurity, was propounded by Cohen, Cloward, and Ohlin, among others. Lower-class socialization does not equip boys to perform according to middle-class standards. Consequently the boys suffer status deprivation and lack self-esteem. Such a loss of status may be recouped through gang or other activity, some of which may not be legal. Other theories of juvenile delinquency stress maladjustments of adolescence, and other more psychologically oriented theories tend to stress personal inadequacies.[46]

---

[42] *Manpower Report of the President, 1966,* Washington, D.C., U.S. Department of Labor, Table A-12, p. 167.

[43] *Juvenile Court Statistics, 1964,* Statistical Series No. 83, Washington, D.C., U.S. Department of Health, Education, and Welfare, Children's Bureau (1965), Table 3, p. 9.

[44] *Ibid.,* Table 1, p. 9.

[45] *Report to Congress on Juvenile Delinquency,* Washington, D.C., Children's Bureau and National Institute of Health (1960), p. 32.

[46] For a summary of sociological theories of juvenile delinquency and their implications for eradication, see David Bordua, "Sociological Theories and Their Implication for Juvenile Delinquency," in *Juvenile Delinquency: Facts, Facets,* No. 2, Washington, D.C., U.S. Department of Health, Education, and Welfare, Children's Bureau (1960).

Juvenile Courts

The attack on juvenile delinquency has gone forward on many fronts. The first juvenile court law was enacted in Illinois in 1899, and by 1917, only three states remained without juvenile court legislation.[47] In a recent cooperative venture, the National Probation and Parole Association, the National Council of Juvenile Court Judges, and the Children's Bureau recommended a new Standard Family Court Act. Rather than recommending a new court, this group suggested that a family court division be established in the highest court of general trial jurisdiction. By tying the family court in with the present court system, the family court would obtain more status than it now has. The new arrangement possibly could take place without a major change in our present state court system and probably would avoid constitutional difficulties. Such an arrangement would combine the present juvenile court with cases involving domestic relations. In large centers of population, juvenile cases would necessarily involve separate judges simply from the problem of case load, but in less populous areas one judge could handle both types of cases.[48] Recent theory suggests that effective operation of specialized courts requires that they make use of specialized services of social workers, physicians, psychiatrists, and psychologists. Otherwise the courts cannot adequately carry on their function.[49]

Detention Facilities

While awaiting a hearing on serious charges the concept emerged almost simultaneously with the development of juvenile courts that children should not be placed in county jails. Instead, separate detention facilities should be used. In practice, separate facilities have not been provided. In over 2,500 out of 3,100 counties in the United States, the only detention home is the county jail. Over 100,000 children are detained annually in county jails.[50] The National Probation and Parole Association has determined that from $15 to $18 is needed per day per child in detention homes. A Fels Institute study on expenditures in 21 detention homes showed that much less was actually being spent. The Fels Institute estimated that 54 to 85 percent more expenditures were needed to satisfy the standard set by the National Probation and Parole Association. The institute did point out that some money

[47] *Report to Congress on Juvenile Delinquency, 1960,* Washington, D.C., U.S. Department of Health, Education, and Welfare, Children's Bureau, and National Institute of Mental Health, p. 7.

[48] Harriet L. Goldberg and William H. Sheridan, "Family Courts—An Urgent Need," in *Juvenile Delinquency: Facts, Facets,* No. 6 (1960), pp. 5-6.

[49] *Ibid.,* p. 3.

[50] *Report to Congress on Juvenile Delinquency,* p. 41.

could be saved by not sending so many children to detention homes in the first place.[51]

Probation Officers

Rather than relying more on training schools, the emphasis today is on greater use of probation officers. For one thing, costs are much less. The National Probation and Parole Association estimates that probation costs per year per child are around $200 to $250 annually compared with $3,000 for training school services.[52] Not only are costs less, but it is felt that by the use of a good probation system, rehabilitation can be effected as well or better than by sending children to training schools. The generally recognized standard of a maximum workload for a probation officer is 50 workload units. Workload units are used rather than number of youths served since five times as much time must be spent on investigation as contrasted to supervision. Using this standard, the Fels Institute found that the average workload for probation officers is 3.25 times as great as it should be.[53] Additional probation officers are needed. The quality of probation officers needs upgrading also. The recommended training is a master's degree in social work. Only 10 percent of them had such a degree, and 14 percent did not have a bachelor's degree of any kind.[54]

Training Schools

It has been recognized for some time that the purpose of training schools is not confinement but rather rehabilitation. Rehabilitation calls for a staff of workers trained professionally. A Children's Bureau study in 1957 found a serious understaffing of training schools. Not only were such schools short of psychiatrists and psychologists, but they were also short of cottage parents, sometimes called group supervisors, counselors, or house parents. The Children's Bureau estimated that 266 full-time psychiatrists and the same number of psychologists were needed in all institutions for juvenile delinquents. Actually, only 9 full-time and 54 part-time psychiatrists were employed, along with 112 full-time and 34 part-time psychologists. The Bureau also estimated a need for 10,000 cottage parents, compared with 4,679 actually employed in this occupation. The quality demanded of cottage parents also calls for accredited college with a sequence in the social sciences. At the present time, only two colleges—St. Louis University and Hunter College—offer continuing courses on a regular basis for cottage parents.[55] That a

[51] "Comparison of Expenditures and Estimated Standard Costs for Selected Juvenile Delinquency Services," Government Consulting Service, Fels Institute of Local and State Government, University of Pennsylvania, in *Juvenile Delinquency: Facts, Facets*, No. 10 (1960), pp. 4-17.

[52] *Ibid.*, p. 26.

[53] *Ibid.*, p. 43.

[54] *Ibid.*

[55] *Ibid.*, pp. 12-13.

better-trained staff gets better results may be seen from comparing the amount of recidivism among youths in different types of institutions. One experimental project with a well-trained staff reported 30 percent of former Negro inmates as recidivists compared with 70 percent at a nearby State Training School.[56]

Not only are better staffs required, but overcrowding must be avoided also. The same Fels Institute study showed that all states had need of more facilities. The amount of overcrowding ranged by states from a low of 3 percent to a high content of almost 94 percent.[57] Serious deficiencies in appropriations were found, particularly in the South, where per capita student costs averaged 38 percent of Pacific Coast costs.[58] Later national statistics (1963) showed southern expenditures for public institutions to be only 34 percent of Middle Atlantic state expenditures.[59] In 274 training schools studied, the Fels Institute estimated that an additional $32 million was needed for operating costs annually. As the population of children increases, still larger amounts of money will be needed.[60] Most of the money was needed for education and treatment rather than general administration and operation. Additional money would be necessary for construction or capital requirements.

Other Aids

Good-quality police work is also essential in attempting to deal with juvenile delinquency. Almost all cities of over 100,000 have specialists to deal with youth. Only half of the departments in cities of 25,000 to 50,000 population have such specialists, and few departments under 25,000 have them.[61] As another alleviative measure, 12 states now operate camps in order to help juvenile delinquents. Having caseworkers work with underprivileged groups is being tried also.

Evaluation of Programs

Most evaluation studies analyze the degree of recidivism of juvenile delinquents. A summary of such studies concluded that about 15 percent of juvenile delinquents "fail" during probation, more than 30 percent fail after probation, and 40 percent fail after a period in a training school.[62] The conclusion arrived at from these statistics was that recidivism rates were far too high for public complacency.

[56] *Report to Congress on Juvenile Delinquency*, p. 25.
[57] "Comparison of Expenditures and Estimated Standard Costs . . . ," p. 39.
[58] *Ibid.*, p. 21.
[59] *Statistics on Public Institutions*, Statistical Series No. 78, Washington, D.C., U.S. Department of Health, Education, and Welfare, Children's Bureau (1964), Table M, p. 37.
[60] "Comparison of Expenditures and Estimated Standard Costs . . . ," pp. 5-6.
[61] *Report to Congress on Juvenile Delinquency*, p. 26.
[62] Paul Schreiber, "How Effective Are Services for the Treatment of Delinquents?" in *Juvenile Delinquency: Facts, Facets*, No. 9 (1960), p. 13.

Serious shortcomings exist in expenditures of various sorts that should help to alleviate the problem of juvenile delinquency. These were noted above. Not only alleviative but preventive measures for juvenile delinquency are sorely needed. Here the entire resources of the community and country are needed to stem the rising tide of delinquency. One study has been made to determine the community resources in all of the 3,106 counties in the United States of community services. The ten items making up the index were as follows:

Full time local health unit

Public recreation unit

Public health nursing services

Probation service

Family counselling service

Private group work and leisure time
  agencies

General assistance program in public welfare

Child welfare service

Central fund raising for private
  agencies

Community planning organization

The findings were that certain key resources were missing from all but five counties. The median county had about a third of the necessary programs.[63] The recent poverty legislation recognizes serious weaknesses in dealing with youths in America. This act will be discussed in detail in Chapter 24. From a broader point of view, all of the programs discussed in this book will have to come into play in order to prevent and alleviate poverty and to insure a more orderly assimilation of youth into adult society.

Summary

Women are increasingly entering the work force in the United States. Some do this because their family income is particularly low. Others enter the work force even though their family income is adequate primarily because there are no children remaining at home when the average wife reaches the age of 48. Even with the increased employment of women, income of many families remains low. This is particularly so if women are the major bread-winners in the family. Part of the poverty of families headed by women may be explained by the fact that women have entered fewer occupations than men. Those that they have entered have tended to be lower paid than other occupations. Working wives have been blamed as a major cause of juvenile delinquency in the United States; however, most studies on this problem conclude that a more important cause is poor supervision of the children.

[63] *Report to Congress on Juvenile Delinquency*, p. 35.

Day-care services are particularly needed in the United States. Additional education for women would aid in solving their problems also. Legislation has been passed in a number of states to provide for minimum wages, hours regulations, and equal pay for equal work.

Many children are handicapped in the United States because they are reared in families with an extremely low income. Many of these children drop out of school to enter the work force. Although both federal and state laws regulate the employment of minors, the laws are deficient in a number of respects. Failure to provide adequate employment for youths dropping out of school has abetted the growth of juvenile delinquency. Lack of proper detention facilities, overworked probation officers, and inadequate training schools have contributed to our failure to reduce juvenile delinquency. The failure to provide adequate community resources has contributed to the problem also. The concentration on youth problems of the poverty legislation of 1964 should be a beginning to a solution of some of these problems.

SECURITY PROGRAMS
FOR SPECIAL GROUPS

Special security programs have been provided for particular groups in the United States. Such groups are veterans, employees of the railroad industry, and government employees, federal, state, and local. Programs for each of these groups will be analyzed in that order.

VETERANS' PROGRAMS

REVOLUTIONARY WAR VETERANS

The Revolutionary War period was one in which rugged individualism held sway. Few security programs existed, although in 1776 a law was passed providing for national pensions for American soldiers with service-connected disabilities. From that date to the present more security has been provided for veterans than for the rest of the population. In 1778 officers were rewarded by a bill which provided them with seven years of half pay after the war provided that they continued in service until the end of the war. In 1780 the seven-year pension was changed to a lifetime one, and in 1783 the first five years of the pension was changed from half pay to full pay. Also in 1780 survivors benefits of half pay for seven years were provided widows and orphans of officers who died or would die in service. No such provisions were made for dependents of noncommissioned officers. Other aids to Revolutionary War veterans were public land grants of from 100 acres for enlisted men to 1,100 acres for major generals, provided that the men enlisted and served until the end of the war.

NINETEENTH-CENTURY WAR VETERANS

Although the land grants were continued to veterans of the War of 1812 and the Mexican War, pensions were not provided these latter groups until many years after these wars, in the 1870's and 1880's. The first home for disabled veterans was established in 1811, a Naval Home in Philadelphia. In 1862 Civil War veterans were granted disability pensions if their disability was service-incurred. Widows and dependent children of the disabled were also granted pensions. President Cleveland in 1887 vetoed a bill providing for pensions for needy Civil War veterans or their widows, but the bill was again passed in 1890 and signed by President Harrison.

WORLD WAR I PROGRAMS

In World War I compensation was provided for those disabled in the service and their dependents, as in past wars. Several new innovations were made. Life insurance for soldiers replaced the pension system although the fact that only 10 percent of the servicemen continued it after the war made the new system relatively ineffective. Later in 1936 a pension was provided for needy, disabled veterans. Vocational rehabilitation was provided for all those with a disability of more than 10 percent, but this program was terminated in 1924. Medical and hospital care was provided for all those with a disability of more than 10 percent, and in 1924 such care was extended to all veterans regardless of the origin of their disabilities. Preference was given to those veterans in need.[1]

WORLD WAR II PROGRAMS

Instead of extending the World War I insurance system for World War II veterans, a new system was created. The National Service Life Insurance Act of 1940 provided for 5-year term insurance from $1,000 to $10,000. The policy could be renewed at its termination without a physical examination or it could be converted to a level-premium contract with a cash value. Disability payments were later added to the program. Soldiers had to buy this insurance, but the government did not charge anything extra for war risk. The numbers having such insurance dropped from 13.5 million in 1945 to 6.3 million in 1959, but the percentage drop was not nearly so great as it had been after World War I.

The Korean War resulted in a further rethinking of an insurance program for veterans. A basic change, adopted by the Servicemen's Indemnity Act of 1951, provided for a noncontributory or free insurance policy of $10,000 for every member of the Armed Services. The new program lasted only until Dec. 31, 1956.

The federal government has accumulated $6 billion in funds from servicemen's payments, and has these invested in federal securities. Surpluses from this fund enabled the federal government to pay a regular dividend. In fiscal 1963, a dividend of $435 million was paid to policyholders. In addition, $368 million was paid to beneficiaries of deceased policyholders. Since

[1] *The Historical Development of Veterans' Benefits in the United States,* A Report on Veterans' Benefits in the United States by the President's Commission on Veterans' Pensions, Staff Report No. 1, 84th Congress, 2nd Session, House Committee Print No. 244 (1956), pp. 1-46.

the inception of the program, a total of $18 billion has been paid out, 50 percent of which was for death benefits and 38 percent in policy dividends. The remaining was divided among disability benefits, matured endowments, and surrender values. Under the Korean program, servicemen were not entitled to policy dividends since they made no contribution for insurance.[2]

One of the new benefits provided for World War II veterans by the Servicemen's Readjustment Act of 1944 was a general educational program for discharged veterans. Tuition up to $500 per year was originally provided plus an allowance which varied according to the number of dependents. As will be pointed out in Chapter 22, many Americans have not obtained an education commensurate with their capabilities. War, of course, detracts from obtaining additional education. Since the returning veterans without additional education were at a competitive disadvantage with those having more education, it was felt that the federal government should subsidize the education of returning veterans.

KOREAN PROGRAMS

The Korean veterans were also provided with educational benefits, but the program differed in several respects. World War II veterans were permitted to obtain monthly benefits for one year plus the length of service but not to exceed four years. Korean veterans were permitted to remain in school one and a half times the period of active service, with a limit of 36 months. Instead of providing tuition plus an allowance as World War II veterans received, Korean veterans obtained only subsistence payments varying from $110 to $160 per month depending on the number of dependents. Out of this income the veteran was required to pay for his own tuition and other expenses such as books.

Several problems were encountered under the World War II and Korean educational programs. A number of profit-making organizations sprang up to obtain the educational money. Payments were even made for recreational or avocational courses, but these were outlawed in 1948. Strict regulations were adopted to prevent preying upon veterans. By and large the program was quite successful. Almost 8 million World War II veterans received training at a cost of almost $14 billion. After the Korean War almost 2.4 million received training. About half the Korean money went for college training, and smaller amounts were provided for on-the-job training, primary and secondary school education, and on-the-farm training. Of the Korean college veterans, the largest number majored in business administration, followed by engineering, teaching, medical and premedical studies, and the sciences. The success of providing more education for veterans through government subsidies has influenced a number of people to suggest that the

[2] *Annual Report of the Administrator of Veterans Affairs, 1961*, pp. 103-108; *The Historical Development of Veterans' Benefits*, pp. 101-106.

same system be adopted to educate all those who are willing to further their education regardless of whether they are veterans.

LOANS TO VETERANS

A number of other programs have been adopted for veterans to better enable them to earn a living in civilian society. In 1944 an important section of the Servicemen's Readjustment Act provided for a loan guarantee program for veterans. The federal government guarantees up to 60 percent of a home ownership loan and less on real estate and non–real estate loans. Most of the loans under this program went to construct new homes. From 1944 through June 30, 1965, the Veterans Administration guaranteed more than 6.6 million home, farm, and business loans made by private lenders. More than 6.3 million were home loans amounting to more than $60 billion. The federal government has had to pay claims on less than 3 percent of these loans because of default. Owing to the relatively low interest rate, many creditors were unwilling to lend money to veterans even with the loan guarantee. To alleviate this situation, in 1950 the federal government provided for a system of direct loans to veterans. From 1950 through June 30, 1965, a total of 256,367 loans have been made from $2.9 billion in loanable funds.

VETERANS HOSPITALS

World War II caused a large expansion in the number of Veterans Hospitals. In 1931, 54 VA hospitals were in existence with a bed capacity of slightly over 26,000 beds. At the end of fiscal year 1965 there were 168 VA hospitals with a bed capacity of 120,509. Hospital service is not only provided for those with service-connected disabilities but for all veterans who state they are unable to pay for medical care. During fiscal year 1965, 754,876 patients were treated in Veterans Hospitals. Over half of the patients had no service-connected disabilities. Over half were psychiatric patients, and almost 40 percent were over 65 years of age. Even with the expansion of facilities, a waiting list still exists for VA hospital treatment. On June 30, 1965, the waiting list was 13,195, almost all of whom were patients seeking care for psychiatric conditions.[3]

MENTAL ILLNESS TREATMENT

The Veterans Administration has received citations for its advanced treatment of patients with mental illness and neurological disorders. In 1961 the Joint Commission on Mental Illness and Health cited the Veterans Administration as a leader in development of new trends and ideas for the treatment

[3] *Annual Report of the Administrator of Veterans Affairs, 1965*, pp. 17-30.

of mental illness. The concept of the "psychiatric team" has been developed in which the mentally ill are aided by a number of people such as physicians, dentists, nurses, psychologists, social workers, physical medicine and rehabilitation personnel, and others. Most of those returning home on a trial basis were under social work supervision. Sixteen half-way houses were provided for those finding it difficult to leave the hospital. At such houses the patient is on his own and may come and go as he pleases, but supervision is still provided by social workers and psychiatrists.[4]

COST OF VETERANS' PROGRAMS

Table 21-1 shows that pension and other payments to veterans in fiscal year 1965 were made to over 4.5 million veterans and cost the government $4.1 billion, and that about three-fourths of the payments go to living veterans, about 62 percent of whom have service-connected disabilities. Those disabled in the service receive a pension which varies from $17 per month for a 10 percent disability to $240 for total disability (peacetime rates). Those with a more serious injury, such as blindness or loss of arms and legs, may obtain more than $800 per month.[5] Those veterans who are permanently and totally disabled and who are in need may also obtain a pension even though the disability was not service-connected.

TABLE 21–1.   PAYMENTS TO VETERANS, FISCAL YEAR 1965

Class of Beneficiary	Number of Beneficiaries	Total Amount Spent	Average Monthly Payments
Living veterans:			
Service-connected	1,992,234	$1,688,454,000	$ 70.63
Non–service-connected	1,223,529	1,284,821,000	87.51
Deceased veterans:			
Service-connected	365,422	469,049,000	106.97
Non–service-connected	928,885	654,914,000	54.84
Total	4,510,070	4,097,238,000	. . . . .

Source: *Annual Report, 1965*, Administrator of Veterans Affairs, Table 44, p. 270; Table 45, p. 272; Table 51, p. 278; and Table 53, p. 283.

Payments are also made to dependents of deceased veterans. Survivors of those whose death was due to service receive $112 per month plus 12

[4] *Ibid.*, *1961*, pp. 36-37.
[5] "Legislation Affecting Veterans and Servicemen, 1965," *Social Security Bulletin*, Vol. 29, No. 3 (March, 1966), pp. 17-18.

percent of the current basic military pay for the same rank, with a minimum pension of $122. Additional amounts are payable if there are dependent children. Parents of deceased veterans who are needy may also receive government payments, provided that the death was service connected. In 1960 the law was changed to permit payments to wives and children of those veterans of a war or the Korean conflict who have died as a result of a non–service-connected cause. Here payments go only to needy unmarried widows (income under $1,800) and unmarried minor children, if their unearned income does not exceed $1,800. Payments vary from $25 to a widow without a child to as much as $75 to a widow with one child, depending on the current income of the widow. Fifteen dollars is paid for each additional child.[6]

EVALUATION OF VETERANS' PROGRAMS

In addition to federal aid to veterans, most of the states have provided generous aid and bonuses to veterans. This brief summary of veterans' programs shows that veterans have been treated more generously than other groups in our society. Veterans' groups have had enough political power and influence in Congress that security measures are provided for them. Since veterans and their dependents constitute about one-half of our society, this half has much more adequate protection against insecurity than the other half. An important question to be faced in the future is whether these security measures should be applied to all members of our society or only to veterans and their dependents.

SECURITY PROGRAMS IN THE RAILROAD INDUSTRY

Labor unions in the railroad industry for a number of years have engaged in more political activity than most other unions. When they were unable to obtain concessions from management at the bargaining table, they went to Washington to ask for special legislation from the Congress.

PENSION PROGRAM

By 1934 almost 90 railroads had private pension plans for their employees.[7] These pensions typically provided for a benefit of 1 percent of the workers' salary during the last ten years for each year of service. Most of the plans were self-insured. The onslaught of the Great Depression made it doubtful if pension obligations would be met, for the plans were not fully funded. In order to guarantee payments of pensions, the railway labor unions were

---

[6] *Annual Report of the Administrator of Veterans Affairs, 1965,* pp. 57-69.
[7] *Annual Report of the Railroad Retirement Board, 1965,* pp. 3-7, 27-36.

successful in 1934 in having Congress pass a liberal compulsory retirement plan underwritten by the federal government. Both the 1934 law and a subsequent one in 1935 were declared unconstitutional, but another law in 1937 has remained the law of the land. In 1966 a tax of 7.95 percent of earnings up to $550 a month is assessed on both employers and employees. Current scheduling provides that the tax rate will increase to 10.15 percent in 1987 and thereafter. This percent includes the new 1965 taxes assessed to finance a Medicare program for aged railroaders. Additional income is obtained from interest on invested money since the railroad retirement fund over the years has collected more than it has paid out. The balance as of June 30, 1965, was $4.2 billion, which is invested in government bonds.

Income is also obtained from the financial interchange provision of the Railroad Retirement Act. Under this arrangement, the OASDHI trust fund is to be placed in the same position in which it would have been if railroad employment had been covered by the Social Security Act. That is, the railroad retirement account is credited with the additional benefits and administrative expenses that OASDHI would have had to pay on the basis of railroad earnings, and the OASDHI trust fund is credited with the payroll taxes which would have accrued to them with respect to railroad earnings. During the early years of the law some small transfers were made from the Railroad Retirement fund to the OASDHI trust fund. More recently, relatively larger sums have been transferred from the OASDHI trust fund to the Railroad Retirement fund.

To be eligible for a railroad pension, the employee must have worked for the railroad ten or more years. Those not having worked that long receive OASDHI benefits. The formula for a retirement benefit is based on earnings and years of service. In 1964 the average annuity paid was $150 per month. Payments are also made to an annuitant's spouse if she is aged 65. A reduced payment is permitted her if she has reached the age of 62. Disability payments are also granted railroad employees. Survivor's benefits are paid to widows aged 60 and over, or who have children under 18. They are also paid to children under 18 and dependent parents over 60.

The latest actuarial estimate shows an annual deficit of $29.8 million in the Railroad Retirement fund. The actuary concluded that the system was in a reasonably sound condition, since the deficiency was small in relation to the $1.25 billion annual cost.[8]

UNEMPLOYMENT INSURANCE

Labor unions were also successful in having a separate unemployment insurance law passed for railroad employees in 1938. The payments under this

[8] *Ibid.*, pp. 18-19.

program have been large, because the railroad industry has been a declining industry for a number of years. Freight traffic dropped 12 percent from 1951 to 1960 and passenger traffic declined 39 percent. Average employment in the industry declined from 2,093,000 in 1951 to 720,100 in January, 1966, a decline of 66 percent. Technological improvement accounted for part of the decrease in employment.

Unemployment benefits to railroad workers vary according to past wages, but currently 90 percent of the workers are drawing the maximum of $10.20 per day. Forty-three percent qualified for the maximum, because they had wages of $4,000 or more. An additional 47 percent qualified for the maximum under a section which provides that 60 percent of the last daily rate of pay will be paid. The benefits last for a duration of 130 days. Temporary extended benefits were provided in 1961, but these have now been discontinued. In 1963–1964, beneficiaries drew compensation for an average of 88 days. About 17 percent of the beneficiaries exhausted all their benefits.

Because of the heavy amount of unemployment on the railroads, drains on the unemployment fund have been exceptionally heavy. Funds had to be borrowed from the railroad retirement system to pay for unemployment insurance. By June of 1963 the deficit of the railroad unemployment insurance account was $307 million. Owing to regularly incurred deficits, the tax rate was raised from 3.75 to 4 percent on the first $4,000 of payrolls. Eligibility requirements were made more strict, and restrictions on the payments of benefits to employees who voluntarily leave their jobs was made more severe. Actuarial estimates after these changes showed that income should be sufficient to meet all expenses and permit a gradual retirement of the debt.[9] In fiscal year 1965, total expenditures were $127 million, compared with receipts of $145 million.

DISABILITY INSURANCE

The railroad industry also provides for payments when employees are ill. Illness payments averaged $8.97 per day and were paid to 100,600 persons at a total cost of $44 million (fiscal year ending June, 1965). Since 1958–1959 there has been a drop in beneficiaries owing to declining employment in the industry. The average duration of sickness was 80 days. The maximum duration paid is for 130 days, but even with this relatively long payment 5 percent exhausted their sickness benefits. The sickness fund is financed from the same payroll tax as the unemployment insurance system. Payments for sickness amount to 38 percent of the amounts paid out in the joint unemployment-disability program.[10]

[9] *Ibid.*, 1963, pp. 33-40.
[10] *Ibid.*, 1965, p. 7.

ACCIDENT INSURANCE

It has already been commented on in Chapter 7 that the railroads have an employers' liability law dealing with industrial accidents. As was indicated in that chapter, most employers' liability laws have been superseded by workmen's compensation laws, but awards have been sufficiently favorable under the railroad employers' liability system that the railway labor unions prefer to keep their present system.

GOVERNMENT EMPLOYEES

PENSION PROGRAM

The federal government has provided its employees with a number of security benefits for many years. As early as 1896 labor unions in government recommended that a pension system be set up for federal employees. In 1917 a number of labor unions joined together to form the Joint Conference on Retirement in the hope that by united strength they would be able to obtain a pension bill. Three years later in 1920 their efforts culminated in success. More recently there has been a controversy between labor unions in government as to whether a separate pension system is desirable. Some unions, as the National Federation of Federal Employees, have suggested that the present separate system be continued whereas other groups such as the United Public Workers of America recommended that the Social Security Act absorb federal employees into one pension plan.[11]

From fiscal 1921 through 1965 a total of 852,817 federal employees have received retirement or disability pay from the federal government. During fiscal year 1965, 508,731 retired federal employees or their survivors were receiving such pensions.[12] Persons may retire under a number of different circumstances. Five years of service is required to qualify for a pension. Persons may choose to retire at age 50 with a reduced benefit if they have 20 years of service. The average pension on June 30, 1965, for those retiring under provisions in effect prior to amendments by Public Law 854 was $50 monthly and $248 a month for those retiring under provisions of Public Law 854, as amended. Survivors also receive payments. In 1966, benefits were raised from 6.1 to 11.1 percent, depending on the effective opening date of the annuity. This program also has the unique feature of raising benefits when the cost of living goes up. Whenever the consumers' price

---

[11] Morton Robert Godine, *The Labor Problem in the Public Service* (Cambridge, Harvard, 1951), pp. 134-136.

[12] *Report*, U.S. Civil Service Commission, Bureau of Retirement and Insurance (1965), Table A-2, p. 5.

index increases 3 percent or more and remains at this level for three consecutive months, the pension is increased proportionately. Pensions are also paid to those federal employees who are disabled. Almost a third of all pensions are paid to those who are disabled.

Federal employees contribute 6½ percent of their pay to the retirement fund by a payroll deduction and the government matches this amount. The total income of the retirement fund in fiscal 1965 came to $2.7 billion and expenditures were $1.4 billion. The program has been running a surplus for a number of years, and as of June, 1965, had a balance of $15.6 billion.[13] The unfunded accrued liability amounted to over $40 billion, but in this program, as under OASDHI, actuaries maintain that the fund is safe provided that the tax revenues plus interest on its bonds provide sufficient revenue to match expenditures. Actuaries estimate that the total normal cost is 13.83 percent of payrolls. Therefore the present tax plus interest on bonds should be more than sufficient to pay Civil Service pensions in the future.

MEDICAL BENEFITS

A recent program instituted by the Federal Employees Health Benefits Act of 1959 provides for medical benefits for federal government employees. A total of almost seven million persons, both employees and dependents, were covered under such plans as of June 30, 1965. A majority of government workers are covered under government-wide plans, which provide for basic hospital and surgical benefits and the option of major medical coverage. Most of the employees enroll for the more comprehensive coverage. Lesser numbers are enrolled by labor unions or in group or individual practice plans. Under the government-wide plans, the family charges are $23.83 per month with major medical coverage and $14.21 without it. The government contributed $2.82 per month for a single person and $6.76 for a family. The individual employee contributes the rest.[14]

In 1960 the Retired Federal Employees Health Benefits Act provided health benefits to retired federal personnel. The new law required that the Civil Service Commission implement the law with wide discretionary powers to set the eligibility requirements for annuitants, provide a monthly government payment contract for one Government-wide Uniform Plan open to all eligible annuitants, and permit annuitants to choose a private health plan of their own provided that the plan qualified. The Government-wide Uniform Plan was instituted with the Aetna Life Insurance Company as the prime carrier. This plan gives the annuitant the choice of basic coverage only, major medical coverage only, or both. As of fiscal year 1964–1965, of over 400,000 eligible annuitants, 200,575 persons chose to enroll and the remainder did not. Slightly more than half have enrolled under the Uniform Plan and the

13 *Ibid.*, Table C-5, p. 33.
14 *Ibid.*, Table C-6, pp. 36-37.

remainder under other plans, mostly of the Blue Cross–Blue Shield type or those fostered by employee organizations. Of those enrolling in the Uniform Plan, about half elected basic coverage only, and smaller numbers elected major medical coverage only or both basic and major medical coverage.[15] The government's monthly contribution comes to $3 for annuitants without dependents and $6 for family enrollments. Annuitants contribute the other half of the expenses.[16]

LIFE AND DISMEMBERMENT INSURANCE

The federal government also provides life and dismemberment insurance to its employees. The employees themselves pay for about 62 percent of the cost and the federal government contributes the rest. In fiscal year 1965, 23,390 death claims were paid totalling $129 million, or $5,500 per claim. Slightly larger amounts are paid for accidental deaths and lesser amounts for dismemberment. This fund also has been paying in more than it has been disbursing, so that in fiscal year 1965, this program had assets of $390 million.[17]

WORKMEN'S COMPENSATION

The federal government provided for protection against industrial injuries before any of the state workmen's compensation laws were passed. The federal law was passed in 1908 and covers employees of all branches of the federal government. In general the federal law is more liberal than state laws. Full medical benefits are provided, and the disabled may receive benefits for life rather than for limited periods, as many states provide. Federal workmen's compensation benefits are financed by Congressional appropriations. Since the federal government provides a liberal sick-leave policy for its employees, many employees simply elect to be compensated by receiving sick pay while recuperating. In a recent year, almost half elected to receive full pay under the sick-leave provisions.[18]

UNEMPLOYMENT INSURANCE

Although the federal government was a leader in introducing workmen's compensation legislation, it lagged in providing for unemployment benefits for its employees. It was not until 1955 that a permanent program of unemployment insurance was established for federal civilian employees. The most

[15] *Ibid.*, Table D-7, p. 48.

[16] *Annual Report of the U.S. Civil Service Commission, 1963*, p. 131.

[17] *Report*, U.S. Civil Service Commission, Bureau of Retirement and Insurance (1965), p. 14; Table B-1, p. 15.

[18] *Annual Report of the U.S. Department of Labor, 1960*, p. 46.

recent change in the law (1960) provides that rather than denying unemployment insurance benefits to those federal employees receiving terminal leave pay, the employees shall be subject to the laws of the state to which their wages were assigned. If a state, for example, permits both terminal pay and unemployment insurance, then the federal employee will receive both payments. Unemployment compensation is also paid military personnel who cannot find jobs after separation from the Armed Forces. This program was made permanent in 1958 although earlier legislation had covered World War II and Korean veterans. The servicemen are paid by and according to the benefits of their respective states. These states are reimbursed by the federal government.[19]

STATE AND LOCAL PROGRAMS

State and local governments also provide security benefits for their employees. In general, wages and other benefits of state and local governments are inferior to those of the federal government. The average federal wage in 1964 per full-time worker was $6,479, compared with $5,676 for state and local employees.[20] A total of 505,000 state and local annuitants received pensions averaging $1,544 in 1959. More contributions are paid by the governments concerned than by the employees. Table 21-2 shows the contributions and receipts from 1959 through 1964. Much more has been taken in than paid out so that the total assets in 1964 were $28.6 billion. Much larger sums will be needed in the future to pay for the increasing numbers who will become eligible for benefits. Policemen and firemen's pension funds generally provide for survivors benefits, but other state and local plans do not. Under the federal OASDHI program about one-third as many survivors receive benefits as those retiring, whereas under state and local plans only 11 percent as many survivors benefits are paid as retirement benefits.[21]

The Social Security Act was amended to permit coverage of state and local employees under the OASDHI program provided that the latter groups were willing to enroll in the system. When given the opportunity to vote, state and local government employees have voted overwhelmingly in favor of coverage (527 out of 535 elections). Today about 70 percent of all state and local government employees are covered under the Social Security Act. Of these over half are fortunate enough not only to receive Social Security benefits, but state and local benefits as well. On the other hand, many state and local employees receive neither Social Security benefits nor state and local pensions. Most states and cities do not have as comprehensive a medical program as the federal government does. Group life insurance is not

---

19 *Ibid.*, 1963, pp. 94-95.
20 *Statistical Abstract of the United States, 1965*, Washington, D.C., U.S. Department of Commerce, Bureau of the Census, Table 556, p. 410; Table 596, p. 442.
21 *Ibid.*, 1960, Table 356, p. 264.

TABLE 21–2. FINANCES OF STATE AND LOCAL PUBLIC-EMPLOYEE RETIREMENT SYSTEMS, 1959–1964
(IN MILLIONS)

Year	Receipts					Payments				Assets at End of Fiscal Year
	Employee Contributions	Government Contributions		Earnings on Investments	Total[a]	Benefits	Withdrawals	Other[a]	Total	
		State	Local							
1959	$1,073	$538	$866	$498	$2,974	$921	$234	$40	$1,184	$16,341
1960	1,140	693	959	601	3,393	1,010	255	35	1,300	18,539
1961	1,201	769	1,037	717	3,724	1,133	250	29	1,412	20,875
1962	1,288	801	1,082	827	3,997	1,259	308	..	1,567	23,294
1963	1,374	900	1,221	950	4,445	1,390	300	..	1,690	25,929
1964	1,466	949	1,307	1,065	4,787	1,518	326	..	1,844	28,639

[a] Figures do not necessarily add to totals because of rounding.
Source: Statistical Abstract of the United States, 1965, U.S. Department of Commerce, Bureau of the Census, Table 411, p. 298.

provided as frequently either. When workmen's compensation and unemployment insurance laws were first passed, the states frequently exempted themselves from coverage. More recently, however, more state and city employees are being covered under both programs.

Summary

Veterans have been provided with more security than most other groups in the United States. Programs today consist of pension payments, loans, hospital care, and vocational rehabilitation. Relatively large sums are now being spent by the federal government to aid veterans. An important question which society must decide is whether these programs are sufficiently worthwhile to be provided for all groups or just for selected groups.

Railway labor unions have been successful in lobbying for separate laws for railway employees. These laws provide pensions, unemployment, disability, and accident payments. The retirement plan has been on a much sounder financial footing than the unemployment and disability programs. Heavy unemployment in the railroad industry has placed the unemployment fund in a precarious situation. Recent changes in the law should help the program to be more sound financially.

The federal government has provided a number of security programs for its employees. It has an adequate pension program. Also provided are a medical benefit plan, life and dismemberment insurance, workmen's compensation, and unemployment insurance. State and local governments have fewer such programs.

Bibliography

Clark, Kenneth B., Dark Ghetto (New York, Harper & Row, 1965).

Glueck, Sheldon, and Eleanor Glueck, Family Environment and Delinquency (Boston, Houghton Mifflin, 1962).

Golden, Gertrude, The American Indian, Then and Now (San Antonio, Nayler, 1957).

Havighurst, Robert J., American Indian and White Children (Chicago, The University of Chicago Press, 1955).

King, Martin Luther, Why We Can't Wait (New York, Harper & Row, 1964).

National Manpower Council, Womanpower (New York, Columbia, 1957).

Northey, Sue, The American Indian (San Antonio, Nayler, 1954).

Northrup, Herbert R., and Richard L. Rowan, eds., The Negro and Employ-

ment Opportunity (Ann Arbor, Mich., Bureau of Industrial Relations, University of Michigan, 1965).

President's Committee on Migratory Labor, *Report to the President on Domestic Migratory Farm Labor* (Washington, D.C., Government Printing Office, 1960).

Rand, Christopher, *The Puerto Ricans* (New York, Oxford University Press, 1958).

Schultz, Theodore W., *Transforming Traditional Agriculture* (New Haven, Yale, 1964).

Schwitzgebel, Ralph, *Streetcorner Research: An Experimental Approach to Juvenile Delinquency* (Cambridge, Harvard, 1964).

Sexton, Patricia C., *Spanish Harlem* (New York, Harper & Row, 1965).

Shotwell, Louisa R., *The Harvesters: The Story of Migrant People* (Garden City, N.Y., Doubleday, 1961).

Smuts, Robert W., *Women and Work in America* (New York, Columbia, 1959).

Spergel, Irving, *Racketville, Slumtown, Haulburg: An Exploratory Study of Delinquent Subcultures* (Chicago, The University of Chicago Press, 1964).

United Nations, *Equal Pay for Equal Work* (New York, United Nations, 1960).

Wakefield, Dan, *Island in the City* (Boston, Houghton Mifflin, 1959).

SOLUTIONS TO INSECURITY

IMPROVED EDUCATION
AND HOUSING

IMPROVED EDUCATION

Professor Theodore Schultz has pointed out that our rate of economic growth has been three times as large as the rate of increase of capital and labor in this country. He hypothesizes that the greater growth of income has been mainly due to our large investment in human wealth.[1] All studies on the correlation of income with education show much larger amounts earned by those who are more highly educated.

Herman Miller found that in 1958 the annual income of men over 25 was $2,551 if they had less than an eighth-grade education, $3,769 with an eighth-grade education, $4,618 with 1 to 3 years of high school, $5,567 with four years of high school, $6,966 with 1 to 3 years of college, and $9,206 with a college degree or more. More recently the CED has found that at 1960 rates, those with less than 8 years of schooling will earn $143,000 in their lifetime. This figure will gradually increase with more education until a figure of $455,000 is reached with those having five or more years of college.[2]

Professor Gary Becker has attempted to measure the returns of investment in education as compared to investment in corporations. He found that white males earned 10 percent return on what they had privately invested in acquiring a high school and college education. When other costs not borne by the student and parents were included, such as government subsidies to education, the rate of return on education was 9 percent, not much different from the return on tangible capital goods. He maintained from these statistics that underinvestment in education was not particularly great if measured solely from the monetary viewpoint. He excluded the impact of education on such nonmonetary matters as effects on democratic government, equality of opportunity, culture, and the like. Professor Schultz, on the other hand, felt that in analyzing the returns on nonhuman capital such costs as land, residences, government structures, and the like should be

[1] Theodore W. Schultz, "Investment in Man: An Economist's View," *Social Service Review*, Vol. 33 (1959), p. 115.
[2] Herman P. Miller, "Income in Relation to Education," *American Economic Review*, Vol. 50 (1960), Table 1, p. 966; *Raising Low Incomes through Improved Education*, Committee for Economic Development (1965), Table 1, p. 45.

included. Once these are considered, the return on human capital greatly exceeds the rate of return on nonhuman wealth. He further maintained that excessive concentration of investment on capital goods in India, Iraq, and other underdeveloped countries compared with the paucity of investment on human resources was hampering development of these countries. In short, he contended that economists have missed seeing the important role played by the increasing stock of human capital.[3]

For the 1965–1966 school year almost $26 billion was the total expenditures of public schools, elementary and secondary.[4] Figures from prior years show that expenditures on education have been increasing rapidly and faster than most other state-local expenditures.[5] A large part of the increased cost of schools has come about because of increased numbers of children attending school. In the eight-year period between 1954 and 1965 enrollment in elementary and secondary schools increased from over 29 million to over 42 million.[6]

SHORTAGE OF TEACHERS AND CLASSROOM FACILITIES

A shortage of teachers presents a problem in American education. Specific types of teachers are particularly in short supply; for example, teachers of science. Also the large increase in college enrollment has resulted in a shortage of teachers at this level. The quality of teachers needs improving also. Today there are many teachers in elementary and secondary education that do not have a bachelor's degree. Another problem is that of providing adequate physical facilities for our school children. According to a recent study, far too many of our schools are too old to be adequate. Furthermore, a shortage of classrooms has resulted in overcrowding present facilities, even in half-day session. Government statistics in 1962 showed a shortage of 121,235 classrooms. About 1.7 million students were enrolled in classes of excess capacity and 418,000 were attending school for less than a full or normal day, based on incomplete data.[7] Fortunately our school population will grow less rapidly than in the past, so less expenditure will be necessary in the future at the elementary and the secondary school levels, but large additional capital expenditures will be needed at the college level.

QUALITY OF EDUCATION

Not only have there been shortages of teachers and classrooms, but the quality of our education has been under attack in the United States. Only one

[3] Schultz, op. cit., p. 117.

[4] Fall 1965 Statistics of Public Schools, Washington, D.C., U.S. Department of Health, Education, and Welfare, Office of Education, Table 12, p. 26.

[5] Wade S. Smith, ed., "School Conference Position Moderate," National Municipal Review, Vol. 45 (1956), p. 34.

[6] Fall 1965 Statistics of Public Schools, Table 5, p. 14.

[7] Circular No. 703, Fall 1962, Washington, D.C., U.S. Department of Health, Education, and Welfare, Office of Education (1963), pp. 3-7.

out of three high school graduates has taken a full year of chemistry, and only about the same percentage have had a year of algebra. An even smaller percentage, 25 percent, have had a year of physics. Only 15 percent of our college students study a modern foreign language, and less than this percentage study such languages in high school. Although language experts contend that language abilities develop easiest and best when children first enroll in the elementary grades, only 1 percent of elementary students have been exposed to a foreign language.[8] Many millions of Russians are studying English in their schools, whereas relatively few Americans are studying Russian.[9] In addition, the relatively short instructional periods in the United States have resulted in our children getting fewer instructional hours in 12 years than the Russians give their children in a 10-year program.[10] James B. Conant lists ten of the major problems facing public schools today, without attempting to place them in order of priority. These are:

1. The reform of instructional methods and materials including the new developments in foreign language instruction in the lower grades and the new courses in physics, chemistry, mathematics, and biology.
2. The advanced placement program.
3. The improvement in the instruction in English composition.
4. The introduction of new techniques including TV and programmed instruction.
5. The recruiting of more intellectually able young people into the teaching profession.
6. The education of students of limited ability in the high school.
7. Vocation education.
8. Teaching reading to the children of disadvantaged families.
9. The slum schools.
10. Segregated schools.[11]

One suggestion for improvement that Conant makes is that there should be a strong state board of education. He favors a powerful chief state school officer responsible to a high-quality lay board, as in New York State. On the college level he suggests that other states adopt a type of master plan similar to that developed by California. He also suggested that the 50 states enter into a compact to create an "Interstate Commission for Planning a Nationwide Educational Policy," to aid in the improvement of education everywhere in America.

[8] "Administration Proposal on Education," *State Government,* Vol. 31 (1958), p. 35.

[9] Charles A. Quattlebaum, *Federal Educational Policies, Programs, and Proposals,* Part 1, Legislative Reference Service of the Library of Commerce, Washington, D.C., Government Printing Office, p. 35.

[10] Senator Clifford P. Case, "A National Emergency," *American Federationist,* Vol. 75, No. 3 (1958), p. 3.

[11] James B. Conant, *Shaping Educational Policy* (New York, McGraw-Hill, 1964), p. 26.

QUANTITY OF EDUCATION

Another major educational problem is that too few students receive the maximum amount of education they are able to assimilate. Although illiteracy has been reduced significantly in this country, the latest data show that about 2.6 million persons 14 years of age and older (2.2 percent) were unable to read and write.[12] Not only has our country failed to educate some of its population at all, but it also permits a high rate of drop-out from high schools. Both for illiteracy and drop-outs, the statistics show a much poorer picture for nonwhites than whites. The latest illiteracy statistics are for 1959. They show a 1.6 percent rate among whites aged 14 and over compared with 7.5 percent for nonwhites. Concerning drop-outs, statistics as of October, 1964, show that 1 percent of whites aged 14 and 15 are not in school compared with 3 percent for nonwhites. For ages 16 and 17, 12 percent of whites are not in school compared with 18 percent for nonwhites.[13]

Although enrollment in colleges has increased greatly in recent years, large additional groups not now going to college could profit from higher education. Of those who finish in the upper one-fourth of their class, more than one out of three does not go to college. One study shows that college attendance is directly correlated with income of parents. The results are shown in Table 22-1.

TABLE 22–1. RELATION BETWEEN FAMILY INCOME AND COLLEGE
ATTENDANCE

1959 Family Income	Percentage of Children, Aged 20–29 in 1960, Who Have Attended or Are Attending College
Less than $3,000	12
$3,000 to $4,999	25
$5,000 to $7,499	28
$7,500 to $9,999	55
$10,000 and over	65

Source: John B. Lansing, Thomas Lorimer, and Chikashi Moriguchi, How People Pay for College (Ann Arbor, University of Michigan Survey Research Center, 1960), Table 41, p. 108. Reprinted by permission.

Still another study reported that 71 percent of those dropping out of college listed either their own or their families' financial difficulties as one of their reasons for dropping out of school. For students who stayed to graduate, the

[12] Current Population Reports, Series P-20, No. 99, Washington, D.C., U.S. Department of Commerce, Bureau of the Census (1959), Table 6, p. 17.
[13] Ibid., No. 148 (1966), Table 3, p. 10.

median family income was $1,000 higher than for students who dropped out by the end of the first term.[14]

TEACHERS' SALARIES

In attempting to improve education in the United States, many students of the problem have suggested that salaries of teachers be increased, perhaps doubled. The average pay of the school teacher in 1965 was $6,035 for elementary teachers and $6,503 for secondary school teachers. About 14 percent of our teachers received less than $4,500.[15] Beardsley Ruml and Sidney Tickton found that allowing for the effects of inflation, teachers now are obtaining about the same income that they made in 1904. If teachers' salaries had risen as fast as other comparable professional groups, their average salary today would be $9,400.[16] On the other hand, salaries of teachers have risen faster percentagewise than all wages from 1929 to 1957.[17]

FEDERAL AID TO EDUCATION

Since many of the suggestions for improving the school system involve increased expenditures of funds, one of the major public policy questions today is whether and to what degree the federal government should aid education. To place this problem in its proper historical perspective, the aid given to education by the federal government in the past will be briefly reviewed. Federal aid to education of one sort or another has been present since the founding of the country. The federal government assumed the authority of education in the territories before these areas became states. Upon their becoming states, Congress in 1802 began setting aside land for the support of public schools. During the first half of the nineteenth century, monetary grants were also provided the states for educational purposes. The Morrill Act of 1862 provided for establishment of state universities to be financed in part from land grants of the federal government. One student of school finance has pointed out that federal grants were the source of the first stable support for free schools in more than half of the states.[18]

In 1917, the federal government agreed to subsidize vocational educa-

14 Robert E. Iffert, *Retention and Withdrawal of College Students*, Bulletin 1958, No. 1, Washington, D.C., U.S. Department of Health, Education, and Welfare, Office of Education (1958), p. 91.

15 *Statistical Abstract of the United States, 1965*, Washington, D.C., U.S. Department of Commerce, Bureau of the Census, Table 168, p. 126.

16 Testimony of Congressman John R. Foley, *School Support Act of 1959*, Hearings before a Subcommittee of the Committee on Education and Labor, House of Representatives, 86th Congress, 1st Session, on H.R. 22 and related bills (1959), p. 228.

17 Testimony of K. Brantley Watson, U.S. Chamber of Commerce, *School Support Act of 1959*, p. 419.

18 F. H. Smith, *Federal and State Policies in Public School Finance in the United States* (New York, Ginn, 1931), p. 67.

tion. In 1946, localities were helped by federal subsidies for a school lunch program. In addition, the federal government contributed money to school systems where federal installations lead to an influx of students. In 1958, Congress passed the National Defense Education Act, which provided for a federal contribution of about 90 percent of matching funds to supply loan funds to enable students to go to college. Grants were made to strengthen science, mathematics, and modern foreign language instruction in public elementary and secondary schools and junior colleges.

ARGUMENTS FOR FEDERAL AID

Proponents of federal aid to education advocate increased federal participation for a number of reasons. For one thing, the federal government in fiscal year 1962 contributed only 4 percent to the total cost of education, compared with 39 percent by the states and 57 percent by local communities.[19] In other governmental functions such as highways, public welfare, natural resources, and others, the federal government participates to a much larger extent. Several billion dollar subsidies per year by the federal government would still leave most of the financing of education to be carried on by the states and local communities.

Proponents of federal aid to education also point out that certain regions of the country have more resources with which to finance education. The highest-income states have about three times the per capita income that the poorer states have. In addition, the poorer states generally have more children to support per family than the wealthier states. The wealthier states thus have about four times more income per child than the poorer states. An even stronger case can be made for federal aid by considering county income. County income figures are pertinent, since federal money would be channeled from the wealthiest counties in a state. It would be expected that a state receiving money would allocate it mainly to its poorest rather than its wealthiest counties. If the median income of the three wealthiest counties of New York State, Nassau, Queens, and Westchester counties, housing almost three million people, is compared with the median income of the ten poorest counties in Mississippi, the New York counties have 14 times more income per school age child than do the Mississippi counties.[20] Had mean rather than median incomes been available, they would have shown an even larger disparity of income.

Proponents of federal aid further point out that many rural people leave their poorer states to reside in wealthier states. Local financing simply means that the poorer states have to bear the heavy burden of educating youth, only

[19] *Statistics of State School Systems, 1961–62,* Washington, D.C., U.S. Department of Health, Education, and Welfare, Office of Education, Table 29, p. 54.
[20] Paul A. Brinker, "County Income and Federal Aid to Education," *Southwestern Social Science Quarterly,* Vol. 42 (1962), pp. 390-391.

to see them leave. The poorer states do spend a larger percentage of their income on education but still fall short of matching expenditures of the wealthier states. Only one of the ten states spending the largest percentage of their income for public schools was among the ten highest on money spent per pupil.[21]

Proponents of federal aid also point out that the use of the progressive income tax by the federal government is a more equitable tax than the more regressive state and local taxes. For every billion dollars collected by the federal government in taxes, only $81 million is collected from those with less than $3,000 income (omitting Social Security taxes) whereas for a billion dollars collected by state revenue, $155 million is obtained from those with less than $3,000 income. Vice versa, almost twice the revenue ($387 million) is obtained by the federal government from those earning over $10,000 per year, compared with only $220 million obtained by the states from the same group.[22]

Last, proponents of federal aid to education point out that property taxes provide an insufficient base on which to finance education. In 1940, the assessed value of all property was $144 billion compared with a national income of $81 billion. By 1956, the assessed value of property had increased to $277 billion, but national income had increased to $343 billion.[23] One result of using property taxes is that many localities have reached a limit to their bonded indebtedness. In Michigan, for example, the legal bonding limit is 15 percent of the state-assessed valuation of the school district. Most bonding companies, however, will not go beyond a 10 percent limit. In one study made by Congressman John Lesinski, of 19 school districts, 13 had about reached or overreached the limit of their bonded indebtedness.[24] The fact that state and local spending has increased much faster than federal spending in recent years has resulted in severe strain on the former groups. Also their debt has expanded more rapidly than federal debt. From 1950 through 1963, state and local direct expenditures have expanded by larger absolute amounts than federal expenditures. From 1955 through 1964 state and local debt more than doubled compared with an 18 percent increase in federal debt.

ARGUMENTS AGAINST FEDERAL AID

Opponents of federal aid to education discuss the fiscal capacity of states in the following manner.[25] They maintain that the states have not reached

[21] Quattlebaum, *op. cit.*, p. 40.

[22] Testimony of Victor G. Reuther, United Automobile Workers Union, *School Support Act of 1959*, p. 395.

[23] Testimony of Carl J. Megal, American Federation of Teachers, *School Support Act of 1959*, pp. 536-537.

[24] Testimony of Congressman John Lesinski, *School Support Act of 1959*, p. 329.

[25] Statement of K. Brantley Watson, U.S. Chamber of Commerce, *School Support Act of 1959*, pp. 421-428.

the proper limit of their taxation. In 1964, only 36 states had a personal income tax, 38 had a general sales tax, and only 24 had both. The cigarette taxes range from 2 to 8 cents per pack and beer taxes from 62 cents to $13 per barrel (1964). Some of the states with lower tax rates could raise them. A further argument is that the federal government has already incurred too large a deficit. In rebuttal, the increase in state debt has far exceeded the increase in federal debt in recent years.

According to the formula used in one of the federal aid to education bills, 15 states and the District of Columbia would have to redistribute income to the other 34 states. These 15 states reported 44 percent of the need for new classrooms and 54 percent of the substandard teachers. The drain of almost three-fourths of a billion dollars from these states under the bill would weaken rather than aid our educational system. Proponents of federal aid reply that statistics on income per child show that these states have much larger incomes than the poorer states, and that they can afford to channel money into the poorer sections of the country. The wealthier states are also the most populous, and this fact accounts for the statistics showing that they account for a large percentage of the need for new classrooms. Opponents of federal aid close their argument on fiscal ability by quoting from a study by the Committee on Federal Responsibility in the Field of Education of the Commission on Intergovernmental Relations. This group concluded: "We have not been able to find a state which cannot afford to make more money available to its schools or which is economically unable to support an adequate school system."

One of the major arguments against federal aid to education has been the fear of federal controls. Proponents of federal aid have attempted to write federal aid bills with as little federal control as possible, but these attempts have not allayed the fears of those opposed to federal aid.

RECENT FEDERAL LEGISLATION

In the halls of Congress, the proponents of federal aid have scored important victories recently over those opposed to federal aid. The Vocational Education Act of 1963 provided that increasing grants reaching $255 million in fiscal 1967 and thereafter shall be supplied for aiding vocational education in the various states. Smaller amounts were provided for a work-study program for part-time employment of students aged 15 to 21. The amounts allocated are based on age groups and per capita income. This act has resulted in a greatly expanded system of vocational education all over the country.

Another important act passed was the Elementary and Secondary Education Act of 1965. A basic part of this law has been to provide federal money to schools that have low-income children. One billion dollars was provided for fiscal 1966. Aid was also given to improve library resources, textbooks, and other instructional material. In addition, grants were provided for school services which were not available in sufficient quantity or quality. Sums were also allocated for educational research and for improving state departments of education. As a safeguard to the states, it was provided that no federal control shall be permitted over "the curriculum, program of instruction, administration, or personnel of any educational institution or school system, or over the selection of library resources, textbooks, or other printed or published instructional materials by any educational institution or school system."

Lastly a Higher Education Act of 1965 was passed to grant money for higher educational research, extension services, libraries, grants to raise the academic quality of colleges, national teaching fellowships, grants to low-income students attending college, aids to student loan funds, payments to reduce the interest cost of students who have borrowed money to go to college, construction grants, and grants to provide jobs for students at colleges where they can earn part of the costs of their education. Also a National Teachers Corps was organized to aid the teaching of students in low-income areas. The total cost of this program is over $1 billion a year plus creation of a $1 billion loan fund for students.

IMPROVED HOUSING

One of the major economic problems of the present and the future in the United States will be to properly integrate low income and minority groups into urban living. The rapid mobility of these groups to urban areas accentuates the assimilation problem. In 1860, only 3.5 million lived in communities of 2,500 or more people (about 20 percent of the population). By 1900, 30 million lived in such communities, and by 1960, the figure had climbed to over 125 million, or 70 percent of the population.[26] By 1975, one estimate shows that 168 million (75 percent) Americans will be living in urban areas. Since many cities are reaching the saturation point in the number of people they can house, about 85 percent of future urban growth will be in suburban areas.

ADEQUACY OF HOUSING

The statistics for housing from the 1960 census show that of a total number of 58.3 million units, three million (5 percent) were dilapidated and another 7.9 million (14 percent), although not dilapidated, lacked private toilet or bath or hot running water. The statistics show that rural areas were

[26] *Census of Population, 1960,* Vol. II, *Characteristics of the Population,* Part 1, *United States Summary,* Washington, D.C., U.S. Department of Commerce, Bureau of the Census, Table 4, pp. 1-5.

more deficient in housing than urban areas. Housing is also much poorer in the South than in the rest of the nation. In urban areas poor housing tends to be concentrated in certain areas of the city, called slums. In general, slums tend to exist in areas surrounding the downtown business district, but many suburban areas have deteriorated also. Slums complicate many of the problems of our society. More crime and juvenile delinquency come from these areas along with more disease and higher death rates. The costs of fire and police protection also are higher in these areas.

The slums or blighted areas usually exist where housing has become obsolescent, but there are other causes of blight as well. Poor city planning which permits incompatible land uses may cause some deterioration. Blight is also caused by a lack of municipal services such as drainage, public water supply, sewage disposal, and utilities. Overbuilding or improper street patterns, inadequate streets, and poor subdivision design may also cause blight. One student of the subject maintains that the basic factor behind all these causes of blight is uneconomic land use—that is, uneconomic in terms of human considerations, needs, and conveniences.[27]

A comprehensive index of blight has been developed by the American Public Health Association. Its index includes an analysis of 30 dwelling items and 24 environmental factors. Penalty points are recorded for failings of one sort or another. A score of 80 would designate first-priority clearance. A penalty score below 60 would justify rehabilitation rather than demolition. A number of cities have used the American Public Health Association Appraisal Method, and other cities have used a rating system of their own.[28]

A vivid description of slum housing is given by Nathan Strauss in a classic book on housing. Although the description is dated 1950, the Census figures of 1960 reveal that large numbers of people are still living under the same conditions that existed in the earlier period.

A committee of citizens making a tour of one section of the slums in the fall of 1950 found that at 1247 Park Avenue between 96th and 97th streets, eight Puerto Rican families were living in tiny rooms in the cellar . . . the rent was $30 per month. This was one block from Park Avenue wealth.

At 121 East 109th St., a man and his wife and their nine children were living in three small rooms for which they said they paid $60 per month. At 1786 Lexington Avenue the group climbed some dingy stairs and entered an apartment where eight families were each living in a small room. Some paid $11 a week and some paid $7. There was one kitchen for the eight families.

At 530 West 45th St. two families were living in a two-room apartment. There was neither gas nor electricity because the occupants couldn't pay for it. They used kerosene lamps and cooked on a kerosene stove.[29]

[27] Reuel Hemdahl, *Urban Renewal* (New York, The Scarecrow Press, 1959), p. 31.
[28] For a critical analysis of the American Public Health Association Appraisal Method, *see* Hemdahl, *op. cit.*, Chapter IV.
[29] Nathan Strauss, *Two-Thirds of a Nation* (New York, Knopf, 1952), pp. 11-12.

Slum problems are accentuated by overcrowding. Census data as of December, 1959, found that over 11 percent of occupied units had more than one person per room.[30] Not only is overcrowding a problem in blighted areas, but overbuilding is a serious problem as well. To complicate matters, it is expected that population will increase faster in the next decade than in the previous ones. In addition, migration into certain suburban areas is expected to be extremely heavy. All of these factors will make the housing problem a difficult one to solve in the decade of the 1960's.

HOUSING ABROAD

In many of the Western European countries it has been recognized that lower-income groups have insufficient income to purchase or pay rent for adequate housing. For this reason, the governments of some of these countries have subsidized housing on a much larger scale than the United States. In England from 1918 to 1939, about 38 percent of the housing was subsidized or otherwise aided by the government, so that by 1939, 15 percent of the English were living in government-subsidized homes built and owned by municipalities. There was no problem in England as in the United States as to what type of projects the unemployed should construct during the Great Depression of the 1930's. The English simply concentrated on housing. Most of their worst slums were cleared and rebuilt by World War II. Following the second World War, new public construction made up for the 218,000 houses totally destroyed and the million or so that were seriously damaged.

In England, housing management has become a respected profession. Candidates are trained under the staff of a local housing authority for two or three years before being certified. The trend in England is to plan for a development of an entire neighborhood. Reams of statistics have been prepared to determine the correct ratio of homes to each type of store, acceptable distances children should walk to school, and the number of churches, community centers, and other facilities that are needed. A more recent innovation is the planning of a number of entirely new towns. In England, both the Conservative and the Labour Parties have supported public housing, and there are few groups which have opposed it since its inauguration in 1918.[31]

In the past years either cooperatives or nonprofit organizations have been responsible for one-fifth of all housing in Norway, about one-third in Iceland, and almost half in Denmark, Finland, and Sweden.[32] In the latter

[30] *Census of Housing, 1960,* Components of Inventory Change, Washington, D.C., U.S. Department of Commerce, Bureau of the Census, Part IA, Table 1, p. 30.

[31] Strauss, *op. cit.,* pp. 171-173.

[32] George R. Nelson, ed., *Freedom and Welfare* (Denmark, Krohns Bogtrykkeri, 1953), p. 286.

country, government capital has been responsible for the construction of over 90 percent of all dwellings produced. In addition, state subsidies have been paid on the construction of housing for large families, for invalids, and for old persons living on government pension. Additional subsidies have been granted to families with three or more children who live in approved housing.[33]

PUBLIC HOUSING IN THE UNITED STATES

As early as 1908, President Theodore Roosevelt appointed an advisory committee to study slum problems. During World War I, public housing was constructed near shipyards and other defense industries.[34] During the depression of the 1930's such agencies as the Public Works Administration and others constructed about 40,000 houses. The program was enlarged in 1937 with the passage of the United States Housing Act. Between 1937 and 1941, about 170,000 units were constructed. Additional public housing was constructed during World War II to provide dwellings for those working in defense industries.

The 1949 Housing Act authorized the construction of not more than 135,000 units per year for five years, but Congressional appropriations limited actual starts from 36,000 to 71,000 from 1951 through 1953. The Housing Act of 1954 and successive years provided for continuation of the program on a small scale. Table 22-2 shows the number of public starts each year. This table also reveals that more two family units are being constructed than in the past. Also nonmetropolitan areas are constructing more homes now than in 1945–1947.

POLICIES UNDER PUBLIC HOUSING

The guiding policy under the federal housing acts has been for the federal government to approve projects owned and administered by local authorities. To obtain capital, the local authorities usually sell bonds and temporary notes to private investors. As of December 31, 1965, $5.32 billion obligations were outstanding, $5.25 billion of which was held by private investors and the remaining small amounts by the (federal) Public Housing Administration.[35] The federal government agrees to pay a maximum amount equivalent to the debt-service requirements over four (originally six) decades. The federal annual contributions may be reduced by residual receipts accumulated

[33] Leonard Silk, *Sweden Plans for Better Housing* (Durham, Duke, 1948), pp. 105-106.

[34] Robert M. Fisher, *20 Years of Public Housing* (New York, Harper & Row, 1959), pp. 73-74.

[35] Letter from Marie C. McGuire, Commissioner, U.S. Department of Housing and Urban Development (June 22, 1966).

TABLE 22–2. PUBLICLY OWNED PERMANENT NONFARM DWELLING UNITS
STARTED, BY STRUCTURE AND LOCATION, 1945–1964
(IN THOUSANDS)

Year	Total Public Starts	Type of Structure			Metro- politan	Non- metro- politan	Urban	Rural Nonfarm
		1- Family	2- Family	Multi- family				
1945	1	0	0	1	a	a	1	0
1946	8	0	0	8	a	a	8	0
1947	3	0	0	3	a	a	3	0
1948	18	3	1	14	a	a	15	3
1949	36	2	2	32	a	a	32	4
1950	44	3	2	38	35	9	42	2
1951	71	8	0	63	54	18	64	7
1952	58	3	0	55	44	14	55	4
1953	36	5	0	31	27	9	32	4
1954	19	1	b	18	18	1	a	a
1955	19	4	b	15	16	4	a	a
1956	24	9	b	15	13	11	a	a
1957	49	33	b	16	22	27	a	a
1958	68	43	0	25	38	30	a	a
1959	37	17	3	17	22	15	a	a
1960	44	14	7	23	25	19	a	a
1961	52	15	6	31	34	18	a	a
1962	30	5	7	18	20	10	a	a
1963	32	1	8	23	23	9	a	a
1964	33	1	8	24	19	14	a	a

a Not available.
b Less than 50 units.
Source: 18th Annual Report, 1964, Housing and Home Finance Agency, Table
B–20, p. 387.

by the local authority. In 1948, the federal payments amounted to only 16
percent of the total costs of projects. However, by fiscal 1965, the federal
payments comprised 89 percent of all debt-service costs. The larger federal
contribution required has resulted for a number of reasons. For one thing,
construction costs have increased considerably. Public Law 412 units completed for occupancy in 1944 cost only $4,621 per unit, compared with
$15,072 in fiscal 1965, though the latter housing units do contain more space.
Another cause was that in the earlier period there was a tighter real estate
market so that there was full occupancy in the public projects. Furthermore,
rising tenant incomes assured that rental payments would be forthcoming
from tenants. By 1948, 25 percent of the families residing in public housing
had increased their income to such an extent that they were no longer eligible to remain in public housing. Their replacement by lower-income fami-

lies has resulted in less income for the projects. By mid-1957 and continuing through 1959 less than 1 percent of public housing households were ineligible to remain in public housing because of too large an income.[36] Other causes for higher costs were higher turnover rates and increased maintenance and repair costs.[37]

As of December 31, 1964, 1,593 local housing authorities existed. Almost a third of these were located in the three states of Alabama, Georgia, and Texas. There has been a concentration of public housing in the South, particularly in the three states cited above, in all three of the Middle Atlantic states, and in several midwestern states (Ohio and Illinois). The states with the least amount of public housing have been Arizona, Idaho, Oklahoma, Utah, and Wyoming.[38] About 3,900 urban areas containing more than one-third of our continental urban population have not yet constructed any low-rent public housing.[39]

PROBLEMS UNDER PUBLIC HOUSING

A number of problems have arisen with public housing. Only low-income recipients are admitted to low-rent public housing. This means that large numbers of those living in such housing are on public assistance and many have no workers in the family. On December 31, 1965, 28 percent of the families in low-rent public housing were receiving public assistance and 25 percent of nonelderly families had no workers in the family. Large numbers also are nonwhites. Nonwhite families resided in 49.7 percent of the occupied buildings. Many of these had no workers in the family. Many of these lower-income families have presented assimilation problems to public housing administrators. As yet little has been done to obtain the help of the social work profession with the problem. Recently, a joint task force of 30 persons from the Housing and Home Finance Agency and the Department of Health, Education, and Welfare have been working on the problem of increasing the quality, range, and availability of services for residents of low-rent public housing. Over a million dollars of nonhousing funds has been spent on four public housing projects in St. Louis, Missouri; New Haven, Connecticut; Miami, Florida; and Pittsburg, California. On these projects special services have been provided such as health care, intensive family counseling and social services, literacy training, psychiatric services, vocational rehabilitation, day-care services, and the like.[40] All of these services should make assimilation into society easier.

Another problem that presents itself is where to locate the public hous-

36 Fisher, *op. cit.*, pp. 157-175.
37 *Ibid.*, pp. 170-171.
38 *Annual Report, 1964*, Housing and Home Finance Agency, Washington, D.C., p. 236.
39 Fisher, *op. cit.*, p. 250.
40 *Annual Report, 1964*, Housing and Home Finance Agency, pp. 243-244.

ing project—on cleared slums or in new communities. In general, owners of rental slum areas prefer that the construction be on the original slum locations so that they may be reimbursed for their dwellings. Various other citizens groups have opposed the spreading of minority groups to new areas. Locating in old areas does have the advantage of using the facilities that already exist—schools, churches, stores, transportation facilities, and the like. On the other hand, it may be that the area has degenerated so badly that new community facilities would be preferable.

Another problem in public housing has been overcrowding. Recently many local housing authorities have attempted to decentralize public housing so that too many of the poor are not crowded into a small area. Less concentration of public housing at any one site should aid in this regard.

Segregation has also presented a problem. With Negroes being so large a proportion of public housing residents, obviously the race issue must be faced. In certain towns and states, an integrated program has worked well. In the past a number of states and cities have outlawed segregation in public housing. An Executive Order of President Kennedy on Equal Opportunity in Housing forbade any discrimination on any of the federal housing programs. About 16 percent of all public housing projects are completely integrated. In one study of both segregated and integrated housing projects it was found that there was more visiting even among whites with whites in the integrated projects. The interpretation of the findings was that segregation was felt to be morally wrong, and thus inhibited visits even among those of the same race.[41] On the other hand, in the South little integrated housing has been constructed. Even in integrated public housing in the North, it has been found that when the Negro population rises to from 25 to 35 percent, all the whites move out.[42]

Another problem in the public housing program revolves around the equivalent elimination of substandard dwellings. From the standpoint of goals of the public housing program, not only can the program provide better housing than the low-income groups can afford, but slums can be cleared as well. Apparently the free market mechanism does not arrange for the clearance of blighted areas. Certain areas tend to degenerate and will tend to remain blighted unless the government steps in to promote clearance.

Administration of the United States Housing Act of 1937 provided that for every public housing unit constructed an equivalent dwelling must be demolished within two years. The 1949 act required that equivalent elimination was required only for urban housing constructed in nonslum areas. Rural housing and construction on slum sites was exempt from the equivalent elimination requirement. It was further provided that where more than one family was living in substandard housing, the number of

41 Morton Deutsch and Mary Collins, *Interracial Housing* (Minneapolis, Minn., University of Minnesota Press, 1951).
42 Fisher, *op. cit.*, pp. 257-258.

families rather than the structure itself would be counted as equivalent elimination. In addition, where an acute housing shortage existed for low-income groups, equivalent elimination may be waived. Lastly, the normal closing of substandard housing by private owners may be counted as part of equivalent elimination. With all of these limitations to equivalent elimination, only about one-half as many substandard houses have been demolished as public housing has been constructed. About 400,000 units have been demolished. This still leaves large numbers of substandard units.

Another problem with public housing has been that there has been little experimentation with constructing parks and playgrounds as part of the program. Also until 1956, no single or unrelated individual accommodations were provided. Such a restriction eliminated over a third of the householders who inhabited substandard housing in standard metropolitan areas. Last, considerable complaint has been made that federal controls have been too extensive. To avoid wasteful local spending, the federal government has handed down many and detailed requirements that the local authorities must meet. Local housing authorities have severely criticized the extensive federal controls. Recently the federal government has eliminated all controls not specifically required to implement the annual contributions contracts.[43]

EXTENT AND COST OF PUBLIC HOUSING

Since the beginning of the program in 1937, over 737,000 public dwelling units have been constructed. Annual contribution costs by the federal government in fiscal year 1964 came to $186 million, and these costs have been rising each year. Over half again as much has been paid out by the federal government for development, administrative expenses, and the like.[44] Local costs are more difficult to compute. On the one hand, the local authority must grant tax exemption to the properties, and thus tax income is lost. At the same time, local housing authorities are required under normal circumstances to pay to local governments an amount equivalent to 10 percent of the annual shelter rents charged in lieu of taxes. At some projects more money was collected by the city after the project was completed than before it was built, but at other projects this was not the case. Offsetting possible tax losses are savings such as lower fire, police, health, and other costs.

Several recent innovations in the public housing program may be noted. In the three cities of New Haven, Chicago, and St. Louis, government payments were paid directly to private landlords to cover the difference between market rent and what the low-income tenants can afford. This type of program has been in existence in Europe for a number of years. A program of this type has the advantage of enabling lower-income persons

---

[43] *Annual Report, 1959,* Housing and Home Finance Agency, p. 199.
[44] *Ibid.,* 1964, Table IV-4, p. 260, and Table IV-16, p. 267.

to live in more adequate neighborhoods with higher-income people. It has been contended that this type of mixing of socioeconomic groups should lead to a more democratic society. The experiment was evaluated as successful in the three American towns, and on the basis of its success, the Housing and Urban Development Act of 1965 was passed to expand the program to encompass the entire country. However, insufficient funds were allocated to effectively implement the act. Another experiment has been to permit tenants to purchase the public housing they have been living in. This experiment was put into operation in Tulsa, San Francisco, and Glassboro, New Jersey. Families were permitted to rent with an option to buy.[45] The success of this experiment resulted in an amendment to the U.S. Housing Act to permit any public housing agency to allow tenant families to purchase a detached or semidetached public housing unit.

ARGUMENTS FOR PUBLIC HOUSING

One argument in favor of low-rent public housing is that lower-income people cannot afford to pay for adequate housing. Using the rule of thumb that not over one-fifth of a family's income should be allocated to rent including utilities, a $50 rent and utility bill would require a monthly income of $250 per month. Statistics on income in 1964 show that about 17 percent of our families do not earn this large an income.[46] Recognizing that certain low-income groups cannot afford adequate housing, the public housing program in the United States calls for federal subsidies.

The median monthly payment of rent in public housing was only $46 in calendar year 1965. These charges are below the $51 monthly rent asked on all vacant nonfarm dwelling units several years prior.[47] Certain savings are possible on public projects, such as lower charges for land, low utility rates, and lower vacancy rates. On the other hand, management costs on public projects tend to be higher than for private projects. With cheap rents and higher costs of construction, some subsidy is needed to keep the program going. The poor, it is maintained, simply cannot afford adequate housing on their low incomes.

Another argument in favor of public housing is that slum clearance generally accompanies such public construction. For a number of reasons areas do become blighted, and without government intervention, deterioration does continue. Private realtors know that slum clearance costs money. Many are reluctant to provide better facilities for fear that the renters will be priced out of the market. Unfortunately the slow rate of demolition under the present program will mean that blighted areas will remain for a long time in the future.

[45] Robert C. Weaver, *The Urban Complex* (New York, Doubleday, 1964), pp. 281-283.
[46] *Current Population Reports*, Series P-60, No. 48 (1966), Table 1, p. 13.
[47] *Annual Report, 1959*, Housing and Home Finance Agency, p. 200, and Table A-14, p. 299; *Annual Report, 1962*, p. 211.

A third argument for public housing is that it could be used as a contracyclical device. Whenever private investment started dropping, the government could begin the construction of more public housing. Then less could be constructed during boom times. Although such contracyclical construction is feasible, the public housing program has never been operated to aid in smoothing the business cycle.

A fourth argument for public housing is that such a program will demonstrate to lower-income groups that society is willing to help them. Perhaps such a program will provide the very incentive needed to stimulate lower-income groups to become more self-reliant. This argument has been stated well by Rev. McLoughlin, a Catholic priest who headed the Phoenix Housing Authority:

How can a mother have the spirit to lift her children to the higher standard of conduct and health when her own environment is one of failure and despair? How can she preach cleanliness when the bathtub is a barrel and the sum total of sanitary facilities is a hole in the ground? How can a father instill pride in his son and encourage his ambitions when he feels that his own efforts have provided no better sanctuary for his family than a shack of which he is ashamed? The raising of human values is the greatest benefit of public low rent housing.

To me, one of the great thrills of my life was to walk through our project in the evening of the day when the families had settled down for their first night in their new homes. All was quiet, lights were burning, people were bustling about cooking their meals and arranging their furniture. There was a spirit of hustle in the peace of that evening. A dream had come true.

Early the next morning I came down to the project to visit some of the tenants. I found one man sitting in his living room and looking at the wall. I asked what he was doing, and he said, "Just sitting here thinking about what America means. I used to read about the American way of life—and I wondered. Now I know what it means—and I am happy."

Another man was walking down the driveway, and when I asked him how he liked it, he said, "When I woke up this morning, I pinched myself to make sure that I was still in Phoenix and not in Heaven." [48]

ARGUMENTS AGAINST PUBLIC HOUSING

A number of objections have been raised against public housing. A major objection is that slum dwellers create the slums. If this is so, then there would be little point in providing adequate housing only to have it wrecked within a few years. It has been difficult to measure accurately the number of problem families in public housing projects. A few projects have been notorious for the large number of such families living there. One of these was commonly called "The Jungle." At other projects there have been few problem families. In one study made in 1954 at a federally aided project,

[48] Reprinted by permission of Alfred A. Knopf, Inc. from *Seven Myths of Housing* by Nathan Strauss. Copyright, 1944. Page 164.

it was determined that about 7 percent of the families were badly damaged. While this may not seem like a large percentage, such families can stigmatize a housing project as undesirable. Only a few undesirable families can make a floor or building unsatisfactory.[49]

Adequate management of housing projects may aid considerably with this problem. Two towns located near each other both had housing projects. One was neat and orderly, the other was not. When asked to explain how he succeeded in keeping his project clean, the manager replied:

As the tenants moved into this project, I noticed that most of them attempted to make use of all of the facilities offered. This was made evident in various ways, but especially in their desire to make their back yards attractive. However, this was not true of all the tenants. Some of them acted as though they believed that the back yard was intended as a place to dump the family waste.

When I had observed conditions for a few days, I paid a visit to one of the tenants whose yard revealed complete indifference and neglect. I introduced myself by saying that I had noted that he had had difficulty in making his yard as attractive as some of the others, and that it was my job as manager of the project to try to help him. I offered him a few flower seeds of the type I knew were doing well in other back yards in the project and explained that he was welcome to them. I told him that fertilizer was for sale at wholesale prices through the management office and that, if he did not have any garden tools, we would be glad to lend him a spade, rake, and a hoe. The man thanked me cordially and called his wife to hear of the kind offer of the manager of the project. The next evening as I passed by, I saw him digging in the yard. The day after that I was swamped with requests from other tenants who had heard the good news that the project management would help them make the best use of their own back yards.[50]

For more difficult problem families, it may be that the social work profession could lend a helping hand.

Another argument against low cost housing is that housing can be rehabilitated at much lower costs than it would take to construct new housing. A study by the New York City Planning Commission in 1958 found that for a 20-block West Side area, remodeling selected tenements would come to $1,380 for tenements and $1,875 for brownstone residences. These costs are substantially below new public construction, but the costs would have been higher if more extensive rehabilitation were undertaken.[51] One large-scale rehabilitation project was instituted in Philadelphia. The cost came to $10,000 to $11,000 per unit. Rehabilitation does have the disadvantage of the structures not lasting as long, and the costs of maintaining older structures are higher.

Where structures are relatively good, and deterioration has occurred

---

[49] Fisher, *op. cit.*, p. 66.
[50] Strauss, *Seven Myths of Housing*, pp. 149-150.
[51] Fisher, *op. cit.*, p. 144.

because of mixed land use, poor zoning and other factors, perhaps rehabilitation would be the best and cheapest program. Adequate zoning along with inspection and enforcement of building, sanitary, and fire codes can go a long way in correcting the growth of slums. Spot rather than total demolition may be feasible, and may provide space for playground and other needed community facilities.[52] The criticism of too little rehabilitation has been taken seriously by the federal government, and the Housing Act of 1965 authorized direct loan assistance to low-income property owners in rehabilitation areas. On the other hand, certain areas may be too dilapidated for rehabilitation. Here clearance plus new housing may be the only solution. Ratings such as those of the American Public Health Appraisal Method may be used to determine whether total razing of certain areas is necessary.

Another complaint against the public housing program is that it is too socialistic in nature. Here proponents of public housing point out that the houses are planned by private architects and built by private contractors who use materials sold by private companies. In addition, the state must pass enabling legislation for such housing, and the program is locally administered. The program is a "grass roots" one even though sponsored by the government. One careful student of the subject has proposed that local governments be required to put up more money of their own, so that they themselves will watch costs. Otherwise strict federal controls may be necessary.

EVALUATION OF PUBLIC HOUSING

After weighing all the pros and cons of public housing and after evaluating the experience of many years of public housing, it is the contention of this author that the program should continue on an expanded basis. Most of the low-income groups today in the United States simply cannot afford adequate housing. In the mass movement of poor rural and minority groups to urban areas, one of the best ways of assimilating these groups would be to see that adequate housing is made available to them. Such a program probably has and will provide more rather than less incentive to this group of people. Also, blight does not seem correctable without some government intervention.

URBAN RENEWAL

A new agency within the Housing and Home Finance Agency, the Urban Renewal Administration, was created under the Housing Act of 1949. The

[52] Allan A. Twichell, "Measuring the Quality of Housing in Planning for Urban Development," in Coleman Woodbury, ed., *Urban Redevelopment: Problems and Practices* (Chicago: The University of Chicago Press, 1953), pp. 63-64.

guiding principle of this agency is that something more than public housing is needed for proper community development. The entire needs of the city must be analyzed before any program is adopted. When certain slums are cleared, perhaps more expensive middle-class apartments are needed in a town rather than housing for low-income groups. Planning advances are granted local authorities to make the necessary surveys and plans for their community. Repayments are made from any funds available to the local agency for financing the project. Capital grants up to two-thirds for the net project cost may be advanced by the federal government. Relocation payments are made up to $200 per family and individuals and $3000 for business concerns when their displacement is the result of any government program, code enforcement, or voluntary repair and rehabilitation. The Urban Renewal Administration also provides professional assistance as well as demonstration grants for the testing of means of eliminating blight. Last, grants are available to state and local government to aid them in solving problems resulting from increasing urban population. Information has been released on the types of urban renewal projects for 822 projects which had reached the stage where cost estimates could be made. These are shown in Table 22-3. Almost 60 percent of the federal portion of the program has been in the form of grants and the rest in loans.

TABLE 22–3.   COST ESTIMATES OF 822 URBAN RENEWAL PROJECTS,
EXCLUDING LAND COSTS, DECEMBER, 1966
(CUMULATIVE DATA—000,000 OMITTED)

Type of Project	Cost Estimate
Private	
Residential	$1,742
Non-residential	1,842
Public	
Streets, etc.	244
Other	1,320
Total	$5,148

Source: Land Acquisition, Disposition and Redevelopment Report, U.S. Department of Housing and Urban Development, Renewal Assistance Administration.

Although it is true that comprehensive city planning is necessary for the proper development of urban areas, the urban renewal program has not been without its critics. Some of the programs called for razing slums without providing for erection of housing for low-income groups. Under such circumstances, the available housing facilities for low-income families were less after the program than before. Sometimes minority groups referred to urban renewal as "Negro removal." Even though projects were not supposed to be undertaken unless adequate housing was available for those removed, in a number of instances adequate housing did not exist for those removed. Today, administrators of the program have been more careful that those forced to move will have more adequate facilities.[53] Better administration of the program should aid in solving this problem.

In view of the fact that neither the public housing program nor urban renewal has obliterated slums in most cities, a Demonstration Cities and Metropolitan Development Act was passed in 1966. Upon application to the federal government, 60 to 70 cities in America will be able to obtain up to 80 percent in grants to rebuild entire slum neighborhoods. The program will combine physical rehabilitation of areas with social rehabilitation of the people who live in them. The program is expected to provide for schools, parks, playgrounds, community centers, and access to all necessary community facilities. The program is supposed to demonstrate that complete abolition of slums is possible. For this part of the program $24 million in federal grants will be provided for planning the projects in fiscal years 1957 and 1958 and $900 million will be available for carrying out the plans in fiscal years 1958 and 1959. An important innovation of the program is that larger percentages of federal grants are provided than under urban renewal. An additional $250 million was authorized for urban renewal projects which were part of an approved demonstration program. Smaller additional sums were made available for planned metropolitan development for such projects as mass transit, water and sewer facilities, highway construction, airport development, open-space land acquisition, and development and acquisition of land and water for recreational purposes.

There are many other governmental programs to aid housing. The Federal Housing Administration insures mortgages and thus encourages more housing loans than would exist without the insurance. The Federal National Mortgage Association provides a secondary mortgage market for FHA and VA insured mortgages. These and many other government programs have helped stabilize and expand the housing industry.

Summary

Improved education is particularly important as an aid to low-income groups. Unfortunately shortage of tax dollars has resulted in low pay for teachers and a failure to attract the highest quality personnel. It has also resulted

[53] Weaver, op. cit., pp. 99-102.

in insufficient classrooms, both qualitatively and quantitatively. Weaknesses also exist in the quality of education given. More basic curricula have been suggested along with more counseling of students. Too few students receive all the education they are capable of assimilating. To eradicate these weaknesses a number of suggestions have been made. Strengthening state boards of education should aid along with improved planning for future college development. More research and planning on educational problems are needed. Channeling more money into education both from federal, state, and local sources should help.

Low-income groups are able to purchase or rent only substandard housing. The problem is a particularly acute one since many lower-income families congregate together in areas in which most of the housing is sub-standard. These areas are called slums. Abroad, Western European countries have attempted to solve the slum problem by engaging in low-rent public housing on a vast scale and subsidizing rents. The latter program has been tried only experimentally in the United States. Although some public housing has been constructed in the United States, it has been on a much smaller scale. In order to keep communities from deteriorating, and to improve them, more public housing and urban renewal projects will have to be inaugurated.

WAGE AND HOUR LEGISLATION

A number of countries have passed minimum wage laws for the purpose of raising the income of low-wage earners. In the United States the 1965 federal minimum wage of $1.25 per hour provided an annual income of $2,500 per year if the worker was fortunate enough to work 40 hours a week for 50 weeks. Under the 1967 minimum of $1.40 for workers already covered, the worker's income would rise to $2,800 under the same assumptions. Obviously such a small increment added to an inadequate base will not provide an adequate income, but the extra $300 will at least be of some value.

A controversy has raged within the field of economics as to the merits of minimum wage legislation. A main theory of wages in economics, the marginal productivity theory, maintains that under competitive conditions workers are paid the value of their marginal product. Given the assumptions of this theory, a raise in wages would cause unemployment, for if wages equaled the value of the marginal product before the increase, they would exceed the value of the marginal product after the wage increase. Following the marginal productivity theory, Professor George Stigler, among others, concludes that "the legal minimum wage will reduce aggregate output, and . . . the direct unemployment is substantial and certain." [1] On the other hand, a number of economists have defended minimum wage legislation. Marginal productivity assumes that competitive conditions prevail. Any form of monopoly elements in the economy may prevent wages from equaling the value of the marginal product. In the following example, a monopsonist (single buyer) adds to his work force. As he does so he is required to pay higher wages. His marginal cost rises faster than the average wage as shown in the following example. [2] In this example, before a minimum wage law is imposed the employer will hire nine workers (where MPV equals MC). After the imposition of the higher minimum wage, the new average and the marginal cost become the same since each worker added must be paid the minimum. In the above example 10 workers are now hired (where MPV equals MC). See Fig. 23-1.

The crucial question is whether industries affected by minimum wage laws are competitive or not. Professor Stigler maintains that affected industries have a large number of employers who are competitive. He there-

[1] George J. Stigler, "The Economics of Minimum Wage Legislation," *American Economic Review*, Vol. 36 (1946), p. 361.

[2] D. Hamberg, "Minimum Wages and the Level of Employment," *Southern Economic Journal*, Vol. 15 (1948–1949), Figure 4, p. 335.

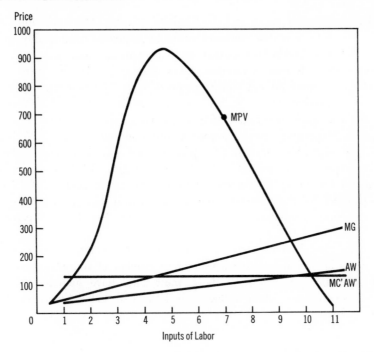

Source: D. Hamberg, "Minimum Wages and the Level of Employment," *Southern Economic Journal,* Vol. 15 (1948–49), Figure 4, p. 335. Reprinted by permission.

FIG. 23–1.

fore arrives at the conclusion that minimum wage laws simply throw people out of work. Implicit in his reasoning is the assumption that employers are already operating at maximum efficiency since they are attempting to maximize profits and are faced with a high degree of competition. On the other hand, some economists maintain that employers may be "shocked" into greater efficiency by minimum wage laws. In a study of 126 Oklahoma firms, it was found that almost one-fourth raised their efficiency when the federal government raised the minimum wage to one dollar an hour.[3] Additional evidence of firms operating inefficiently may be seen from Bureau of Labor Statistics studies on "Case Study Data on Productivity and Factory Performance."[4] Here it was found that in the shirt industry many more shirts were produced by the five most efficient firms than less efficient firms. Similar findings of much larger output for the most efficient firms were found in the canning of peas; the preserves, jams, and jellies industry; chair producing

[3] Paul A. Brinker, "The $1 Minimum Wage Impact on 15 Oklahoma Industries," *Monthly Labor Review,* Vol. 80 (1957), Table 2, p. 1094.

[4] *Case Study Data on Productivity and Factory Performance,* Washington, D.C., U.S. Department of Labor, Bureau of Labor Statistics, various issues (1951–1953).

plants; work jacket plants; and the fertilizer industry. The implication drawn from this study was that efficiency could be improved considerably in some firms. Solomon Barkin also pointed out that profits are sufficiently high to pay higher wages. He cited a number of low-wage industries that were earning 6 percent or more on net worth: confectionary, 7.82 percent; cotton cloth mills, 6.55 percent; furniture, 8.47 percent; knitted outerwear, 8.62 percent; overalls and work clothing, 7.16 percent; men's shirts, underwear and pajamas, 7.29 percent; men's, women's, and children's shoes, 7.26 percent; fruit and vegetable canners, 6.97 percent, and soft drink and carbonated water bottlers, 7.71 percent.[5] On the other hand, Dr. Emerson Schmidt, economist for the U.S. Chamber of Commerce, in an analysis of 19 industries showed that the 5 lowest profit industries paid the 5 lowest wages, with the exception of tobacco manufacturers (all made less than 2.4 percent on sales).[6]

Even though economists have not been able to agree unanimously on the merits of minimum wage legislation, a number of countries have passed such legislation. As was seen above, most states have such laws, and the federal government passed its law, called the Fair Labor Standards Act, in 1938.

THE FAIR LABOR STANDARDS ACT (1938)

Some government intervention to improve our wages, hours, and child labor has existed for many years. As early as 1840 President Martin Van Buren by executive order established a ten-hour day for workers in the federal navy yards. Congress in 1868 reduced the hours for the same group to eight hours. By 1892 all federal employees and all workers employed under contracts to which the federal government was a party enjoyed the benefits of an eight-hour day. Under the commerce clause of the Constitution, the Adamson Act of 1916 granted railroad employees the eight-hour day with time and a half for overtime. The passage of state minimum wage laws and child labor legislation has already been discussed in Chapter 20. In 1933 the National Industrial Recovery Act provided for the major sections included in the later Fair Labor Standards Act.[7] The National Industrial Recovery Act required that employers comply with the maximum hours of labor and minimum wages approved or prescribed by the President. Most of the NRA codes called for a 40-hour-week with overtime above 40 hours and a mini-

[5] Solomon Barkin, in Hearings before the Committee on Education and Labor, House of Representatives, 84th Congress, 1st Session, on *Proposed Legislation to Increase the Minimum Wage* (1955), p. 553.

[6] Emerson P. Schmidt, in *ibid.*, p. 745.

[7] Orme W. Phelps, *The Legislative Background of the Fair Labor Standards Act,* Studies in Business Administration, Vol. IX, No. 1 (Chicago, The University of Chicago Press, 1939), pp. 5-8.

mum wage of 40 cents in most industries, with a lower figure of 30 cents for a minority. After the National Industrial Recovery Act was declared unconstitutional in 1935, the Democratic Party in the Presidential election year of 1936 endorsed the enactment of a federal wage-and-hours law as an important plank in its platform. Because the United States Supreme Court had declared some of the New Deal legislation unconstitutional, President Roosevelt in 1937 held off introducing a wage-and-hours law until a decision had been made on his court reorganization plan. Shortly thereafter the Supreme Court approved several New Deal laws, and it was felt that a new federal wage-and-hours law would be approved also. Such a law, called the Fair Labor Standards Act, was passed in 1938.

COVERAGE

Coverage under the Fair Labor Standards Act was more narrowly subscribed than in most federal laws by the requirement that each individual employee had to be engaged in interstate commerce. Within any plant, some of the workers could be covered by the Fair Labor Standards Act while others might not be. Those engaged in interstate commerce were covered, and those who were not were exempt from the provisions of the law. As an example, most of the employees of a soft-drink manufacturer who sold solely in intrastate commerce would not be covered by the law. However, those specific employees who would unload sugar, syrup, bottles, caps, or other equipment from out of state would be covered by the law. The 1961 amendments of the law kept the individual employee coverage test, but an enterprise coverage test was added. Prior to the 1961 amendments about 24 million employees were covered under the act, and 21 million were not covered. The 1961 amendments added about 4 million new workers, and 1966 amendments added another 8.1 million.

Over half the newly covered workers in 1961 were in the retail and service trades. The 1966 amendments provided that coverage would be extended to the following industries if they had gross sales of $500,000 or more annually: retailing, transit and taxicab systems, almost all restaurants and food service establishments, farms using more than 500 man-days of labor in any calendar quarter of the previous year (roughly equivalent to the use of seven full-time workers), agricultural processing, hotels and motels, certain employees of the federal government, and federal service contract employees. The following industries were covered in 1966 regardless of their sales volume, provided they engaged in interstate commerce: laundries, dry cleaning establishments, clothing or fabric repair shops, construction firms, hospitals and related institutions, and nonprofessional elementary, secondary school, and college personnel. The largest groups still not covered are domestic service workers, government employees, professional personnel and the self-employed.

Several groups are still specifically exempt from both the wages and hours provisions of the law, others are covered only under the wage sections of the law, and several groups are partially exempt from the overtime provisions of the law. Canneries, for example, are provided one annual 14-week overtime exemption.

MINIMUM WAGES

One of the major sections of the Fair Labor Standards Act provides that certain minimum wages must be paid in covered industries. The following are the minimum wages that have been required, as amended:

1938—25 cents (per hour)
1939—30 cents
1945—40 cents
1950—75 cents
1956—$1.00
1961—$1.15 workers already covered)
        $1.00 (workers newly covered)
1963—$1.25 (workers already covered in 1961)
1964—$1.15 (workers newly covered in 1961)
1965—$1.25 (all covered workers)
1967—$1.40 (workers already covered, newly covered federal
        employees and federal service contract employees)
        $1.00 (all other newly covered workers in 1967)
1968—$1.60 (workers already covered, newly covered federal
        employees and federal service contract employees)
        $1.15 (all other newly covered workers in 1967)
1969—$1.30 (all other newly covered workers in 1967)
1970—$1.45 (all other newly covered workers in 1967 except agricultural
        workers who will remain at the $1.30 rate)
1971—$1.60 (all covered workers except agricultural workers
        who will remain at the $1.30 rate)

Owing to the heavy amount of unemployment that existed when the law was passed in 1938, it was decided not to raise the wage to 40 cents an hour in all industries until 1945. Industry committees were created to investigate and raise the wage to 40 cents an hour whenever the industry was able to absorb such increases without laying off workers. The improvement in economic conditions due to World War II enabled the 40-cent-an-hour wage to come into effect much earlier than the 1945 deadline. The industry committees were abolished in 1949 although they are still used in Puerto Rico, the Virgin Islands, and American Samoa.

IMPACT OF WAGE INCREASES

When the Fair Labor Standards Act was first passed in 1938, it was estimated that 300,000 of the 11 million covered workers were earning less than
25 cents an hour, and 1.4 million less than 40 cents an hour.[8] In 1939, when
the 30-cent minimum went into effect, 650,000 or 5.5 percent of the 12.3
million covered workers were earning below this amount. It was estimated
that from 2 to 4 percent of workers engaged in manufacturing, wholesale
trade, and motor carriers, the major industries covered under the law, were
below 30 cents an hour in the North compared with 30 percent of the
workers in the South, and very few workers in the West.[9] When the minimum wage was raised in 1950 from 40 cents an hour to 75 cents, it was
estimated that 1.3 million covered employees would be due increases.[10] An
estimate in April of 1954 showed that the wages of 1.8 million workers
would have to be raised (8.3 percent of those covered) if the minimum wage
was raised to $1.00 an hour.[11] A survey of the Department of Labor in the
fall of 1960 indicated that 1.9 million covered workers were receiving below
$1.15 and 3.0 million were below $1.25.[12] It was estimated that the increased
wages resulted in a $175 million increase in pay in 1961 and would eventu-
ally increase pay by $536 million.[13] Estimates in 1965 showed that raising
the minimum wage to $1.60 would affect over 2.5 million workers and in-
crease the wage bill by $2.3 billion.[14]

GEOGRAPHICAL DIFFERENTIALS

When the Fair Labor Standards Act was first passed, it was decided not to
provide for geographic differences in minimum wages, except that lower
minimums were permitted in Puerto Rico, the Virgin Islands, and American
Samoa. Professor John V. Van Sickle was extremely critical of not per-

[8] "Operation of the Wage and Hour Law, 1938," *Monthly Labor Review,* Vol. 48
(1939), p. 657.
[9] "Second Year of the Wage and Hour Act," *Monthly Labor Review,* Vol. 49, pp.
1439-1443.
[10] *Results of the Minimum-Wage Increase of 1950,* U.S. Department of Labor,
Wage and Hour and Public Contracts Division (Washington, D.C., Government Printing Office, 1954), p. 1.
[11] Statement of Solomon Barkin, *Amending the Fair Labor Standards Act of 1938,*
Hearings before the Subcommittee on Labor of the Committee on Labor and Public
Welfare, U.S. Senate, 84th Congress, 1st Session, on S. 18, S. 57, S. 662, S. 770,
S. 1127, S. 1288, S. 1437, S. 1447, Part I (April 14-22, 1955), Chart No. 1, p. 336.
[12] Statement of Senator Paul H. Douglas, *Amendments to the Fair Labor Standards
Act,* Hearings before Subcommittee on Labor, Committee on Labor and Public Welfare,
U.S. Senate, 87th Congress, 1st Session, on S. 256, S. 289 and S. 295 (Feb. 28–March
6, 1961), p. 13.
[13] U.S. Department of Labor, *Annual Report, 1961* (Washington, D.C., Government Printing Office, 1962), p. 6.
[14] Statement of Clarence T. Lundquist, *Minimum Wage-Hour Amendments, 1965,*
Hearings Before the General Subcommittee on Labor of the Committee on Education
and Labor, 89th Congress, 1st Session, on HR. 8259, Part I (May-June, 1965), p. 107.

mitting different minimums by regions. He maintained that wage differentials perform two functions: (1) They attract workers to areas of high pay where workers are needed, and (2) they attract capital into the low-wage areas. He feared that imposing a standard minimum wage throughout the country would tend to interfere with the proper functioning of geographic differentials. He did not oppose minimum wage legislation in its entirety. He pointed out that the W.P.A. had set differential rates of pay according to region. The country was divided into four regions, and Region I paid a maximum amount of $55 compared with $30 in Region IV. Furthermore, within regions differentials were paid according to the size of population. Professor Van Sickle thought that this scheme was economically sound, and should be adopted as a basic principle of the Fair Labor Standards Act. Until the passage of the Fair Labor Standards Act, prospects for the economic advancement of the South had been bright. He claimed that imposing too high minimums on the South would stagnate that entire region.[15] Fortunately, his prognostication has not been borne out. Even with the continuation of a minimum wage law, which has had its greatest impact in the South, this region has been able to advance at a faster pace than the rest of the nation.

WAGE REQUIREMENTS

The minimum wage of the Act must be paid regardless of whether the worker is paid by the hour, week, or on an incentive system. The wage must be recomputed in terms of hourly pay to determine whether the minimum hourly rate has been paid. The law does permit employers to deduct for board, lodging, or other facilities. The Wage-Hour Administrator determines what he considers to be a reasonable cost for such perquisites. Payment to workers must be made in cash or negotiable instruments. Payment in the form of scrip, token money, credit cards, and coupons is not permitted. On the other hand, it is permissible to deduct union dues, attachments and garnishments, and the like. However, the employer may not consider such items as Christmas bonuses, gifts, and payments made under profit sharing plans as a part of regular pay. In order that the minimum wage may not discourage the hiring of learners, apprentices, and handicapped workers, the Administrator may permit lower wages to be paid these groups as well as messengers and full-time students.

EMPIRICAL STUDIES—1950

In view of the allegation that minimum wage laws will cause unemployment, a number of studies have been made to measure the impact of the

---

[15] John V. Van Sickle, "Geographical Aspects of a Minimum Wage," *Harvard Business Review,* Vol. 24 (1946), pp. 277-294.

federal law. The following table shows the employment effects of the 1950 federal 75 cent minimum wage on 8 industries plus 41 individually surveyed plants. The first 5 industries listed in Table 23-1 were chosen at random from a number of low wage industries. Also investigations were made of every complaint about the 75 cent minimum wage. As a result studies were made in 3 other industries—Gulf Coast oysters, Louisiana raw sugar, and hand cigar manufacturing—plus 41 individually surveyed plants in various industries. The 3 industries and the 41 plants should not be considered representative of the impact of the minimum wage since these were the groups that complained the most.

Data were not available to determine whether the drop in employment in southern sawmilling and men's seamless hosiery industry was seasonal or not. Poor logging weather may have curtailed operations in the sawmilling industry. It is true that the Korean War occurred shortly after the new minimum wage law went into effect, and employment in men's seamless hosiery for 1950 was higher for the entire year than in 1949. The fertilizer industry showed a small decline in employment after the introduction of the minimum wage. The southeastern states and the Great Lakes area had equal proportionate drops in employment even though the southern wage averaged 74 cents in 1949 compared with $1.20 in the Great Lakes area. The smallest declines in employment were experienced in the Southwest, which paid lower wages and was more affected by the minimum wage than the Great Lakes area. For Gulf Coast oysters it was pointed out that some retrenchment had been occurring before the introduction of the higher minimum wage. Prices had been falling when the new minimum went into effect. It was concluded that the minimum wage was a contributing factor but not the sole cause of the retrenchment. The loss of employment in Louisiana raw sugar was negligible, because the Korean War intervened before the first grinding season after the new minimum wage went into effect, and sugar prices rose sufficiently to absorb the high wage scale. In general the findings for 1950 showed little adverse employment effects. One result that did occur was that there was a narrowing of the wage differential between high- and low-wage firms. The low-wage firms were forced to raise wages because of the minimum wage, and they drew closer to the wages paid by higher-wage firms in their industry.

FEDERAL STUDIES—1956

The federal government also made a study of 13 industries when the $1 minimum was imposed in March of 1956. Of the 13 industries, employment dropped in 12 and rose in 1. Employment decreased from 390,926 to 369,786. Not all of the decrease in employment could be attributed to the new minimum wage. Sawmill employment, for example, had been decreasing for a number of years. Some of the drop in employment in the seamless hosiery

TABLE 23–1. EMPLOYMENT EFFECTS OF THE 75-CENT MINIMUM WAGE, 1950

Industry	Average Hourly Earnings Before 75-Cent Minimum Wage Became Effective	Percentage of Workers Paid Below 75 Cents	Employment Before 75-Cent Minimum Wage (1949)[a]	Employment After 75-Cent Minimum Wage (1950)[b]
Southern sawmilling	69¢	69	180,000	176,000
Fertilizer	92¢	37	33,900	32,500
Men's dress shirts and nightwear	88¢	37	72,475	72,337
Men's seamless hosiery:				
Hickory-Statesville	90¢	40 ⎫		
Reading	88¢	31 ⎬	58,000[c]	51,000[c]
Winston-Salem–High Point	$1.00	13 ⎭		
Wood furniture:				
Winston-Salem	88¢	13 ⎫		
Martinsville, Va.	90¢	7 ⎬	110,000	119,000
Morganton-Lanoir, N.C.	92¢	6 ⎭		
Gulf Coast oysters	d	d	15,000	14,000
Louisiana raw sugar	d	d	10,000	10,000
Hand-made cigars	d	d	10,000	[e]
41 individually surveyed plants	d	d	3,000	2,890[f]

[a] Surveys were taken on specific dates from March to December, 1949.
[b] Surveys were taken on specific dates from March to April, 1950.
[c] Employment figures include the women's hose and women and children's anklet industry.
[d] Not available.
[e] Some job elimination at several mills.
[f] Excludes the impact of two plants that hired a combined force of nine employees. Both restricted sales in interstate commerce to avoid paying the minimum wage.

Source: Results of the Minimum Wage Increase of 1950, U.S. Department of Labor, Wage and Hour and Public Contracts Divisions, 1954.

industry was attributed to a previous overexpansion in the industry and the growth of stretch hose, a new major product which permitted wholesalers and retailers to carry less inventory. One of the main findings from a study of these industries was that geographical differentials narrowed as did the wages between firms within industries. The lower-wage firms had to raise wages because of the new minimum and thus narrowed the differential between what they were paying in relation to the higher-paying firms of the industry. Within firms the differential between the higher-paid workers and lower-paid workers was narrowed. The lower-paid workers received increases required by the new minimum, but many higher-paid workers received smaller increases than the lower-paid workers.[16]

OKLAHOMA STUDY—1956

To cite one other study, the effects of the $1 minimum were analyzed for 126 firms in 15 industries in Oklahoma. Of the 15 industries, two depended on agricultural products for their raw materials. Because of a drought in that year, less raw materials could be obtained, and employment was necessarily reduced. Of the other 13 industries, five increased employment, two hired the same number of workers, and six decreased employment. The increases in employment more than counterbalanced the decreases so that employment in the 13 industries increased from 5,044 to 5,093. This study found that firms could make a number of adjustments to the new minimum wage. Forty-four percent of the firms expanded sales after the introduction of the minimum wage to help provide for additional employment. Forty-five percent of the firms raised prices. Twenty-one percent of the firms reduced the amount of overtime worked and were able to absorb part of the higher minimum wage by this technique. Thirty-one percent of the firms added new machinery. Of the 34 firms doing this, 16 reduced employment, 11 increased it, and 7 maintained the same level. Lastly, 22 percent were able to improve efficiency to offset the added wage cost.[17]

FEDERAL STUDIES SINCE 1961

The conclusion arrived at on the effect of the 1961 minimum wage increase was that it "had no discernible effect on the nation-wide level of employ-

[16] Norman J. Samuels, "Effects of the $1 Minimum Wage in Seven Industries," *Monthly Labor Review,* Vol. 80 (1957), pp. 323-328; "Effects of the $1 Minimum Wage in Seven Industries," *Monthly Labor Review,* Vol. 80 (1957), pp. 441-446; "Effects of the $1 Minimum Wage in Three Seasonal Industries," *Monthly Labor Review,* Vol. 80 (1957), pp. 1087-1091; "Effect of the $1 Minimum Wage: Men's and Boys' Shirt Industry," *Monthly Labor Review,* Vol. 80 (1957), pp. 1339-1343; "Effects of the $1 Minimum Wage in Five Industries," *Monthly Labor Review,* Vol. 81 (1958), pp. 492-501.

[17] Paul A. Brinker, "The $1 Minimum Wage Impact on 15 Oklahoma Industries," *Monthly Labor Review,* Vol. 80 (1957), pp. 1092-1095.

ment in the industries affected. On an overall basis employment has risen in these industries since the 1961 amendments took effect." [18] Employment in retail trade increased for those firms covered from 2,422,000 in 1961 to 2,437,000 in 1962. The only groups within retail trade showing a decrease in employment were gasoline service stations and "other" retail stores. Since the impact on the South was greater than elsewhere, a study was made of 15 nonmetropolitan southern areas from October 1960 to March 1964. Here, for covered firms, it was found that employment increased in seven areas, decreased in seven and remained the same in one.[19]

EVALUATION OF MINIMUM WAGE LEGISLATION

On the theoretical level, it may be concluded that where competitive conditions do not prevail, wages may be raised without decreasing employment. Some employers can be and have been shocked into increasing efficiency sufficiently so that wage increases can be paid. There are, of course, limits to how much wages can be increased without having detrimental employment effects. The empirical studies have shown that wage increases must be limited in amount. When they are and if the economy is expanding rapidly enough, then dislocations caused by a minimum wage are minimal. Since so many persons living in poverty are full time workers earning low pay, it is expected that pressure will continue on low-wage industries to raise wages. Raising minimum wages in limited amounts should aid in small improvements in the standard of living of the poor.

OVERTIME PROVISIONS OF THE FAIR LABOR STANDARDS ACT

In 1938 when the Fair Labor Standards Act was first passed, large numbers of people were unemployed. At the same time, other people were working overtime. In an attempt to spread employment, it was provided that wages would have to be paid at a rate of not less than time and a half for any hours worked over 44. These were gradually reduced so that today, time and a half must be paid for all hours worked over 40 in any workweek.

PORTAL PAY ACT

Several knotty legal problems have arisen from the overtime provisions of the act. One question that arose was how to define "hours worked." In a coal mine, for example, should a coal miner be considered to have begun work as soon as he checked in at the employer's premises or only when he

[18] *Report Submitted to the Congress in Accordance with the Requirements of Section 4(d) of the Fair Labor Standards Act,* U.S. Department of Labor, Wage and Hour and Public Contracts Division (January, 1963), p. iii.

[19] *Ibid.,* January, 1965, p. 17.

was ready to begin digging coal? The United States Supreme Court ruled in 1944 and 1945 that hours worked must be counted from portal to portal, that is, from the time employees reach the employer's premises until they leave, in coal and iron mines.[20]

The same interpretation was applied to a manufacturing case in 1946 in the celebrated *Anderson v. Mr. Clemens Pottery Case*.[21] In that case the company had not paid for the time spent putting on aprons, turning on lights, sharpening tools and other tasks prior to their work. Many other suits were instituted for back pay, and the total of such claims reached $6 billion.[22] In order to ease the burden of employers, Congress in 1947 passed the Portal Pay Act. This act outlawed all claims prior to May 14, 1947, unless such activities were compensable by contract, custom, or practice. On or after May 14, an employer does not have to pay for walking, riding, or traveling to and from the place where the principal activity is worked nor for activities that are preliminary to or after his principal activity unless payment is called for by contract, custom or practice.

OVERTIME-ON-OVERTIME

Another question which arose was whether premium pay should be considered as part of regular pay upon which the time and a half premium would be paid or whether the premium could be considered as part of the time and a half. The Wages and Hours Administrator had ruled in 1938 that premium payments could be credited toward the overtime payment required. In 1948, however, the Supreme Court overruled the administrator and stated that premium payments could not be considered as part of the overtime payments.[23] The specific case involved longshoremen who had been paid premium rates of 50 percent for night work. These rates were not considered as part of their straight time pay upon which time and a half was paid. The Supreme Court ruled that the premium rates should have been considered as part of their regular pay. Numerous lawsuits were again filed by employees to recover past wages. To forestall such suits, Congress passed the "Overtime-on-Overtime" law (1949), which provided that premium pay of 150 percent could be excluded from the computation of regular rates.

EVALUATION OF OVERTIME

The overtime provisions of the law have withstood the test of time. When World War II broke out, there was some sentiment for abolishing the over-

[20] *Tennessee Coal, Iron, and Railroad Co. v. Muscoda Local No. 123* (1944), 321 U.S. 590; *Jewell Ridge Coal Corp. v. Local No. 6167 United Mine Workers of America* (1945), 325 U.S. 161.

[21] *Anderson v. Mt. Clemens Pottery Co.* (1946), 328 U.S. 630.

[22] *Prentice-Hall Labor Course, 1958* (Englewood Cliffs, N.J., Prentice-Hall, 1957), p. 7058.

[23] *Bay Ridge Operating Co. v. Aaron* (1948), 334 U.S. 446.

time provisions of the law since there was no longer any need for curtailing overtime work. If the overtime section had been deleted, however, there would have been even more intense pressure for increased wages. It was felt that it was better to keep the overtime provisions so as not to unduly distort the wage structure. Unemployment was at such relatively high levels from 1954 to 1964 that the AFL-CIO has pushed for a law paying overtime after 35 hours of work a week. However, the decline of unemployment since 1964 has weakened support for this proposal.

ADMINISTRATION

In administering the Fair Labor Standards Act, a Wage and Hour Division was created within the Department of Labor. This division is headed by an administrator who is appointed by the President. The administrator has been given authority to issue binding and authoritative regulations concerning specific provisions of the act. Regulations have been issued concerning such matters as record keeping, apprentices, and many other facets of the law. In addition, interpretative bulletins have been issued. These are not official but merely serve as guides to those who are covered by the act.

Records are required of covered employers although the administrator has not prescribed any particular form in which they must be kept. Data on payrolls must be kept for three years and supplementary basic records must be kept for two years. The Wage and Hour Division has authority to inspect employers' records, and has subpoena power to require them. The Wage and Hour Division does make regular inspections of covered firms, but relatively few firms are visited (56,370 in fiscal 1964). The failure to inspect more firms annually has resulted in much violation of the act, although most of it is unintentional. In fiscal year 1964, over 203,500 employees were illegally paid less than the minimum and slightly more than that number were not fully paid for overtime work.[24] About one-fourth of the investigations are made because reports of violation of the law have been made to the Wage and Hour Division.[25]

Payments agreed to by the employer are much less than that due employees. Prior to the 1961 amendments employees were required to authorize a court proceeding to enforce restitution. In many instances, employees were reluctant to institute suit for fear that they would lose their jobs. The 1961 amendments provide that the Department of Labor may bring suit to enforce restitution. It is hoped that this amendment will result in much larger amounts of back pay being given to employees.

At the present time enforcement of the Fair Labor Standards Act may take any one of five forms.[26] Criminal prosecution may be instituted only

[24] *Annual Report, 1964*, U.S. Department of Labor, Washington, D.C., p. 177.

[25] John Turnbull, C. Arthur Williams, and Earl F. Cheit, *Economic and Social Security* (New York, Ronald, 1962), pp. 476-478.

[26] *Labor Law Course, 1962* (Chicago, Commerce Clearing House, 1961), pp. 6160-6169.

against those deliberately or willfully violating the law, for example, by clearly falsifying payroll records. First offenders are subject to a fine of not more than $10,000. Repetition of the offense may result in both a fine and a maximum prison sentence of six months. Second, upon finding a violation, the Wage and Hour Division may seek an injunction restraining the employer from further violation. By the 1961 amendments these injunctions may include an order to pay any compensation due employees. Third, employees themselves may bring wage-damage suits in which they may receive double the unpaid wages plus costs and attorneys' fees. Fourth, since the 1949 amendments, the administrator may aid the employee in collecting back wages, presumably to avoid court proceedings. However, if the administrator does intervene, the employees are entitled only to the amount due them and must waive the liquidated damages. Last, the 1949 amendments conferred upon the Secretary of Labor the right to bring suit to recover past wages provided that the affected employees specifically request him to do so in writing. Here again only the amount of back pay may be paid without the liquidated damages. In all cases a two-year statute of limitations has been imposed so that suits are barred if the cause of action arose more than two years before the suits are filed.

PUBLIC WORKS—REQUIREMENTS

Several laws have been passed to protect workers employed on public construction projects. One of these, the Davis-Bacon Act, was passed in 1931 and amended in 1936 and 1940. This act provides that all employers having contracts of more than $2,000 on federal projects must pay at least the minimum wage prevailing in the community as determined by the Secretary of Labor. The purpose of the act is to prevent contractors from receiving the low bid on government contracts by paying substandard wages. The determination of the minimum wage is made in advance of the release of the request for bids. The minimum is based upon the prevailing wages paid in the area for the same types of workers on similar projects. The act covers only mechanics and laborers.

The Davis-Bacon Act requires that employees be paid at the site of construction at least once a week. One penalty of this act is that the contract may be terminated by the government. If the contract is terminated, the contractor and his surety are liable for any excess cost caused by the violation. Furthermore, contractors who violate this law may be blacklisted for three years from receiving further federal contracts. In case of violation the Comptroller General is authorized to withhold sums due to the contractor and to pay the amounts due the workers. If there is insufficient money with which to reimburse the workers, they may sue the contractor and his surety. To guarantee that payment will be made, the Miller Act, passed in 1935 and amended in

1959, requires that all contractors with contracts over $2,000 post surety bonds.

The Davis-Bacon Act says nothing about paying premium overtime rates. Hours of work on government projects had already been provided by the "Eight-Hour" laws, which were three laws passed in 1892, 1912, and 1948, as amended. Like the Davis-Bacon Act, these laws cover only mechanics and laborers, but unlike the Davis-Bacon Act they apply to all government projects, not just those in excess of $2,000. Another difference in the laws is that the Davis-Bacon Act applies to public works whereas the "eight-hour" laws cover all types of government contracts except for the purchase of those goods usually bought on the open market. Another law dealing with public work construction projects is the Copeland Act (1934). This law outlaws kickbacks to employers from employees on such projects. A prior investigation by the Senate Committee on Commerce found that as much as 25 percent of the money supposed to be paid out of federal funds to employees was actually repaid to employers in an improper manner. Accordingly, a bill was introduced and passed. A later court decision on this law held that it did not apply to kickbacks given union officials.[27]

PUBLIC CONTRACT REQUIREMENTS

The law regulating wages, hours, and working conditions on public contracts, as contrasted to public works, is the Walsh-Healey Act, which was passed in 1936 and amended in 1942. The Walsh-Healey Act provides that on public contracts a minimum wage determined by the secretary must be paid if the contract is for more than $10,000. Overtime at time and a half must be paid for all hours worked in excess of 8 in one day and 40 in one week. Convict and child labor are prohibited on such contracts. Coverage includes only the manufacture, fabrication, assembling, handling, supervision, or shipment of the items. Within the covered plant the employees must themselves be engaged directly in the manufacturing or shipping process or they are not covered. Exempt groups in this category are custodial employees, office employees, professional employees, and others. Also exempt are subcontractors and employees working on contracts dealing with advertising, rental contracts, and personal services. There are several penalties applied for the violation of the act. The government may cancel the contract and charge the contractor any extra cost which is involved in completing the project. The government may also withhold money due workers from amounts it owes on the contract. Employers are held liable to pay all amounts due employees plus liquidated damages of $10 per day for each person illegally employed.

Interesting problems have arisen under this law whether the minimum

[27] *U.S. v. Carbone* (1946), 327 U.S. 633.

wage may vary by geographic area or whether industry-wide wage minimums should be set. An industry-wide designation of the secretary was appealed to the courts, but was upheld as being legal.[28]

CONCLUSION

Laws regulating wages and hours in the United States have been on the statute books for a number of years. Apparently they have withstood the test of time. At any rate there has been little sentiment to repeal such laws. The major controversies that have arisen concern the questions of how much the minimum wage should be raised, if any, and what the coverage should be. The success of minimum wage legislation depends fundamentally on the expansion of our economy. The fact that the economy has been expanding almost continuously since the passage of the Fair Labor Standards Act in 1938 has resulted in little detrimental unemployment effects of the minimum. Since such large numbers living in poverty are able-bodied persons working full time at low pay, it is expected that continued pressure will be placed on these industries to improve productivity and increase wages. Limited minimum wage increases should provide a small improvement in the standard of living of the able-bodied poor.

The arguments over coverage have presented much controversy in recent years. As was indicated above, almost 28 million workers were covered under the law in 1961 and over 16 million were not covered. The AFL-CIO in 1961 recommended coverage for retail and service enterprises with an annual gross volume of sales of $500,000 rather than $1 million, the figure actually passed by Congress. Mr. Biemiller of the AFL-CIO pointed out that the figure had been raised from $500,000 to $1 million so that it would be easier to include certain other establishments as hotels and restaurants. Then when the figure of $1 million was accepted, hotels and restaurants were still excluded. The AFL-CIO stated that only 2 percent of retail employers would be covered under the $1 million cutoff, and only 5 percent would be covered under the $500,000 limit. The AFL-CIO in 1961 further requested that a figure of $250,000 should be adopted for laundering and dry cleaning establishments because a larger cutoff would exempt a disproportionate number of highly profitable firms who, in AFL-CIO terms, "flagrantly underpay" workers. Their suggestions were not adopted in the 1961 amendments, but many were followed in the 1966 amendments.

Many employer groups still oppose coverage for themselves. For example, the National Retail Merchants Association has vigorously opposed the extension of coverage of wage and hour controls to retail and service establishments. This organization has maintained that the extension of federal con-

[28] *Mitchell* v. *Covington Mills*, C.A., D.C. (December 1, 1955).

trols would have serious adverse effects on employment. Since many workers in retail trade are not primary breadwinners and since retailing provides steady employment throughout the years, unlike many industries, the association has felt that less hourly pay is needed for these workers.

In conclusion, it should be noted that most arguments today are on how much the minimum wage should be raised and on how far coverage should be extended rather than eliminating such laws altogether. Care does have to be taken that the minimum wage is not raised so high that large numbers of employees are thrown out of work. On the coverage question, exemptions in the past have been based mainly on lobbying considerations rather than economic analysis. The fact that the recent extensions of coverage have not resulted in excessive dislocation would indicate that coverage will be extended even further in the future. The demand for a living wage will probably outweigh the arguments of those opposed to further coverage.

A minimum wage of $1.50 an hour would raise a family to a $3,000 annual income if full-time work were available. This income, however, is still far below the minimum set for an adequate budget (rather than a poverty budget). It is expected that pressure will be placed on low-wage industries for a number of years to come to raise wages.

Summary

Although economists have not unanimously supported minimum wage legislation, many countries in the world have passed such legislation. In the United States, the federal government approved such legislation in 1938 with the passage of the Fair Labor Standards Act. This act had three major parts: minimum wages, penalties for overtime work, and limitation of child labor.

In order to test the merits of minimum wage legislation, a number of empirical studies have been made when minimum wages were raised. Although such studies have not settled the controversy conclusively, they have shown that small increases in minimums, when coupled with an expanding economy, have caused only minor dislocations in employment.

Due to the large scale unemployment of the 1930's, the Fair Labor Standards Act required that time and a half be paid for overtime work. When a dispute arose over whether overtime should be paid when the worker clocked in or sometime later when he began work, Congress, in 1947, passed the Portal Pay Act which outlawed all portal to portal claims prior to May 14, 1947, unless such activities were compensable by contract, custom, or practice. In 1949 the Overtime-on-Overtime law was passed to provide that premium pay up to 150 percent could be excluded from regular rates of pay when computing overtime rates of pay. During the past few years there has been little demand to change the overtime provisions of the Fair Labor Standards Act.

The Fair Labor Standards Act has been administered by the Wage and Hour Division of the U.S. Department of Labor. Over the years enforcement procedures have improved although criticism of lax enforcement of the law still exists. Laws like the Davis-Bacon Act and the Walsh-Healey Act exist to provide wage and hour regulation on public works and public contracts.

Today most of the arguments on wage and hour legislation deal with the problem of how fast minimum wages should be raised and coverage under the law.

CONCLUSION

CONSERVATISM AND WELFARE

Conservatives want to preserve the best elements that have been developed in society. Conserving the welfare state has not been a doctrine of this group since the welfare state has not been in existence long enough. Conservatives, however, do admit that change will occur in society. The question then becomes one of whether the change toward more welfare is beneficial to society. Some leading conservatives in the United States, like Peter Viereck and Clinton Rossiter, have espoused the principles of welfare; many, particularly with a more conservative view, have not. It is the views of this latter group which we will be analyzing in this section.

WORLD VIEW

Many conservatives have made a fetish of our religious tradition. Many of them believe that the universe has purpose, and that this purpose is a reflection of the Judeo-Christian God's will and creation. They then argue that his ways are mysterious, and that evil is a necessary part of his plan, including disease, poverty, inequality, and even bestiality of man toward man. Since man can not be trusted, creations of his, such as government, cannot be trusted either.

THE STATE

Much criticism of welfare by conservatives centers around the growth of government. Because man is evil, the state is evil also. The state is necessary simply to keep the peace among individual combatants. It can perform the useful function of protecting individual property rights, but this is about as far as it should go. The state is essentially artificial and evil, and because of the evil in man is also dangerous. The state should be drastically limited in function, and not even help the weak protect themselves from the strong. The fewer functions of government, the better. The conservative often argues that he believes in a republican form of government, American constitutionalism, and Western democracy; but historically, conservatives have usually opposed extension of suffrage, and sometimes have favored limitation of representation by race, property, or superior education. In the United States, conservatives place great stress upon a strict interpretation of the Constitution in terms of functions of government, upon separation of powers, a weak executive, and states' rights. All of these are favored in order to further a laissez-faire economic and social policy.

Conservatives voice several objections against involving government in welfare. Milton Friedman, economist, opposes public housing on the ground that the number of dwelling units destroyed in the course of erecting public housing projects has been far larger than the number of new dwelling units constructed. He opposes the old-age and survivor's insurance program on the ground that it involves a large-scale invasion into the lives of most people in the United States without any persuasive justification. He sees no reason why the young should subsidize the aged. Rather than requiring a compulsory purchase of old-age security through the government, Friedman would prefer that individuals be given the choice voluntarily as to whether they wish to purchase annuities or not.[1]

ABUSE OF WELFARE

Because man is evil, neither those dispensing welfare nor those receiving it can be trusted. A number of investigations of abuse have been undertaken in a number of cities, and in some of these abuse was found. Most publicity was received from complaints of abuse in Newburgh, N.Y., a small town on the Hudson River (1961). A "Citizens Committee" report, authorized largely by City Manager Joseph Mitchell of Newburgh, for a time a John Birch society organizer, complained that Newburgh's relief rolls were loaded with "undesirable newcomers," mainly Southern Negro migrants who were engaging in widespread fraud to remain on relief. In order to protect Newburgh from such alleged abuses, a Newburgh plan was adopted. This plan was composed of a 13-point Welfare Code. Some of the points of this code follow. All able-bodied adult males on relief were to be assigned relief jobs. Voucher payments were substituted for cash payments. All those who refused jobs regardless of the type of employment were to be denied relief as were those who quit a job voluntarily. Relief payments, except for the aged, blind, and disabled, were to be limited to three months in any one year. Payments were not to exceed that of the take-home pay of the lowest-paid city employeee with a family of comparable size. All applicants for relief who were new in the town were required to show evidence that their plans for coming to Newburgh involved a concrete offer of employment. Those on "general" relief and AFDC were required to pick up their vouchers in police courts, where they were photographed and threatened with publication of their names. The same treatment was promised for those on other types of relief. Any mothers on relief because of illegitimate children were to be

[1] Milton Friedman, *Capitalism and Freedom* (Chicago, University of Chicago Press, 1962), Chap. XI.

denied relief if they had any more illegitimate children. Foster-home care
was to be provided for children whose home environment was not satisfactory.[2]

Both support and criticism was received on the Newburgh Plan. Senator
Barry Goldwater described the plan "as refreshing as breathing fresh air of
my native Arizona." A number of newspapers praised the action of New-
burgh, whereas others criticized it. The *Richmond Times-Dispatch* editorial-
ized against the "shiftless, slothful parasites who make careers of milking
the public." On the other hand much criticism was directed at the Newburgh
Plan by the National Association of Social Workers, the Child Welfare
League of America, the American Public Welfare Association, the Citizens
Committee for Children of New York, Catholic Charities of New York, the
National Urban League, and the National Association for the Advancement
of Colored People. Forty percent of the people on Newburgh's relief roles
were nonwhites who had been largely agricultural workers, recruited in past
years and left stranded. However, the costs to the city were found to be 13
percent of the city budget rather than the 30–33 percent, which officials of
Newburgh had erroneously quoted. Furthermore, rather than 5 percent of
the population receiving assistance as reported by Newburgh officials, the
correct figure was 2.9 percent, which was the lowest percentage of people on
relief among five upstate New York cities of comparable size. Only one able-
bodied male could be found on relief, and not a single authenticated case of
fraud had been uncovered in Newburgh.[3]

A temporary injunction was issued against the city of Newburgh, prohibiting it from putting into effect 12 of the 13 points of their code. The
code was criticized by the National Association of Social Workers on a number of grounds. The use of vouchers was criticized because it identified the
recipient as being inferior. During the depression years, such vouchers had
been abused by merchants who would cash them at a discount and pocket
the difference. Cash payments have been used for years, because voucher
payments have been viewed as unnecessary, punitive, and destructive to morale. The three-month limitation on relief payments was viewed as punitive
and restrictive and not a solution to people without means of self-support
who still must eat, be clothed, and have shelter. The requirement that to be
eligible for relief the newcomer must have a bona-fide offer of employment
was viewed as decreasing the mobility of labor, which would stunt our economic and social growth. The National Association of Social Workers identified the cause of many on relief as failure of Newburgh and other towns to
solve the problem of hard-core unemployment. Its needle trades, resort employment, and function as a regional economic center had dwindled. It was

[2] *Will the Newburgh Plan Work in Your City?* (New York, National Association
of Social Workers, 1961), pp. 2-3.
[3] "What Happened in Newburgh?" *National Association of Social Workers News,*
Vol. 70, No. 1 (November, 1961), pp. 1, 7-9.

recommended that Newburgh engage in a program of economic and social reawakening rather than a "crackdown" on its relief population. Attraction of industries, slum clearance, and public housing were suggested. It was further recommended that Newburgh adopt some of the more advanced welfare practices of Washington, D.C., San Francisco, and other towns which have attempted physical, social, and moral rehabilitation of those welfare recipients who need and can respond to such services.[4]

If and when abuse of welfare is found, improved administration should be able to eradicate it. Improved social services should be and have been able to reduce the numbers on welfare in many towns. Such recommendations from professional social workers have not received unanimous support, as may be seen from a statement issued by City Manager Mitchell of Newburgh. He maintained that he planned to use some "thought control" on social workers employed by the city and that in the future he would hire only workers without social work training.[5] Although abuses of relief have been found on a larger scale in towns other than Newburgh, the remedy suggested by liberals is improved administration rather than abolition of the program. An investigation in Washington, D.C. by a Senate committee found that 59.7 percent of Aid to Families with Dependent Children cases should have been ruled ineligible for relief.[6] A more recent finding in 1963 from a nationwide study found about 5 percent who should not have been receiving AFDC payments. Many conservatives who have criticized welfare programs are really opposed to the entire welfare program. Having been outvoted on the welfare programs themselves, they devote their efforts to pointing out abuse of the programs. Abuse there has been and will be, but efficient administration should be able to reduce it to a minimum.

THE ELITE

A number of conservatives have departed from Judeo-Christian thought, and insist that the universe has no necessary meaning of a rational character, but is a struggle of all life for survival. The Nazi philosopher Rosenberg, the German philosopher Nietzsche, who argued that "God is dead," the social Darwinism of Herbert Spencer, and the notions of Stirner all reflect this attitude. Man is on his own as an individual because the universe makes no sense. Struggle is the essence not only of survival but the good life, and only strong or lucky men win. Selfishness and competition are the essence of the person. Success only goes to the cunning and strong. The good life and society comes about by the contributions of the elite, the successful, and the strong. This group, exemplified in the writings of John Cowper Powys (*In Defense of Sensuality*) and Ayn Rand, insist that environment is not so important as heredity and sheer will, hard work, and "guts." Welfare

[4] *Will the Newburgh Plan Work in Your City?*, p. 4.
[5] "What Happened in Newburgh?" p. 8.
[6] *U. S. News and World Report* (November 5, 1962), p. 84.

is feared as a burden on the successful. Some conservatives assert that the high costs of welfare will result in such heavy taxation of private property as to eventually result in confiscation.[7]

INDIVIDUAL RESPONSIBILITY

Conservatives are particularly fearful of the harmful effects of welfare upon the individual. Handouts by the government may destroy the incentive to work. An example is cited [8] in which a boy's incentive to go to college is destroyed simply because he gets along so well without it. There is little use in going to college, for without it the boy can earn $150 a week as an electrician. He works the 40-hour week, has paid vacations, has light work, and a union to protect him against discrimination. He has sufficient money to provide him a home, a car, the necessities of life and some luxuries for his family. Group insurance protects him against the problems of sickness and premature death, and his old age is taken care of by Social Security. Although a better position could be obtained by going to college, he would be less secure in this position. He would have to work longer hours and put in more effort as a professional worker. High taxes greatly reduce the extra income that he earns. In short, the advantages of college are not worth the effort.

Speaking of the effects of the welfare state on Britain, Charles Curran [9] points out that the welfare state there is built to working-class specifications. The British worker has demanded and obtained a noncompetitive society where "nobody need struggle to survive, where there is an assured livelihood for the weak, the slow, and the ungifted." [10] Although British workers are not dissatisfied with their lot, they don't show much enthusiasm for anything except mass amusements. Public housing is criticized by Curran on the ground that few meeting places have been erected to provide intellectual stimulation. The handouts of the welfare state have resulted in docility. Furthermore, freedom from responsibility creates an appetite for fantasy among the working class. The fantasy is shown in the worker's leisure-time tastes, his obsessional interest in television, and his appetite for football-pool gambling. The working man's newspapers are particularly deficient, for they stress personalities, entertainment, spectacle, sensual relations, and luxury. The basic criticism against the welfare state is that it has not generated an ethic. Christianity has been replaced by materialistic hedonism. About the only moral mortar of the welfare state is fear of the police. Although all the stock causes of crime have been removed—poverty, squalor, and illiteracy

[7] Barry Goldwater, *The Conscience of a Conservative* (Shepherdsville, Ky., Victor, 1960), p. 62.

[8] Jesse Raley "Economic Puzzle," *American Mercury,* Vol. 88 (March, 1959), p. 91.

[9] Charles Curran, "The Old Order Cometh," *The Reporter* (May 28, 1959), pp. 28-31.

[10] *Ibid.,* p. 28.

—the crime rate has soared to a record-breaking height. Like so many other conservatives, Curran suggests that the solution to the problem is moral regeneration. A basic question to be faced, however, is how this moral regeneration is to be effected.

Not only do welfare benefits have the disadvantage of conceding to the government the power to grant or withhold from the individual the necessities of life as the government sees fit, but also the responsibility of the individual to provide for his own needs and those of his family and neighbors is taken away.[11] The results are that the individual is transferred from "a dignified, self-reliant spiritual being into a dependent animal creature without his knowing it. There is no avoiding this damage to character under the Welfare State." [12] In private charity, on the other hand, both donor and recipient know that charity is the product of humanitarian impulses, not something due to the receiver. Furthermore, the granting of private charity uplifts the donor whereas there is no merit in forcing people to make a compulsory contribution through government programs when they may not want to do so.

Along similar lines, La Piere argues that the drive for security is malfunctional and that if continued may lead to disaster.[13] Rather than placing the blame on welfarism per se, La Piere criticizes the acceptance of the Freudian ethic. According to Freud, man is not born free; rather he is shackled with biological urges that in many instances must be suppressed to such an extent that the individual is in constant and grievous conflict with his society. The solution, according to Freudians, is to provide more security for individuals. But providing such security through psychoanalysts, permissive parents, progressive teachers, welfare workers, and others catering to the needs of individuals takes away individual striving. Like many other conservatives, La Piere contends that all social progress is initiated by a few enterprising individuals who appear among the masses as evolutionary mutants, with inordinate faith in their own inborn ideas. If these individuals are suppressed and society destroys the individual will to succeed, society will stagnate.[14]

LIBERALISM AND WELFARE

WORLD VIEW

Liberals in general take a hopeful view of life and the universe. They see the universe as having meaning, significance, and purpose, especially as

11 Goldwater, op. cit., pp. 68-75.

12 Ibid., p. 73.

13 Richard La Piere, "The Apathetic Ethic," Saturday Review of Literature (August 1, 1959), pp. 40-45.

14 Richard La Piere, The Freudian Ethic (New York, Duell, Sloan & Pierce, 1959).

related to the life of man. Sometimes, liberals follow the ideas of the Greeks and Roman Stoics; others follow in the Judeo-Christian religious tradition. Of immediate logical importance is the liberal position regarding man. Here it is maintained that man is significant, as a unique creature in the universe. The individual worth and dignity of man is affirmed. Man's character, behavior, and good or poor life are dependent in large measure upon both physical nature and social environment. Liberals are not pure "environmentalists," but they do argue that man's personality is affected drastically by weather, food, and his social-institutional life. Some go further than others in this emphasis, but most claim that society cannot have good men, healthy men, or the good life under natural or social conditions of disease, poverty, and brutality. These conditions are dependent upon group or social action for continuance or removal. Liberals maintain that one man can rarely by himself overcome deserts, floods, slums, unemployment, malarial swamps, and the like. Especially do they argue that, in a highly industrialized society, the individual is influenced by a dependence upon social action to make for the good life.

Furthermore, liberals generally believe that man *qua* man is by nature sufficiently altruistic, generous, and compassionate enough to want to overcome bad conditions for others as well as himself, and is aesthetically motivated to dislike filth, disease, and disorder around him. And of more importance, men are sufficiently rational to see that they need to act together to accomplish these desired objectives even at the cost of individual effort and some sacrifice of immediate fulfillment of individual satisfaction.

This view of man is generally called the social or corporate and rational or benevolent view of man. It nowhere denies that men are not also individually fearful, selfish, capricious. It simply insists that the constructive aspects of personality can be fulfilled and utilized through mutual aid and cooperation, and that negative or destructive personal and social influences of the situation can be reduced or even channeled to constructive ends.

THE STATE

Relative to the state, the liberal sees it not as an artificial or evil institution reflecting merely man's goodness or selfishness and tendency to violence but as a natural institution like business or the family by which many social aims are accomplished beyond the capacity of the individual or other institutions. It is an institution that helps to integrate and create conditions of cooperation between the other institutions of society. The liberal does admit that the state is unique in monopolizing the violence power of life (or insists that it should), but claims that this is desirable to bring justice, order, and peace to society. Individual violence is reduced by channeling the violence through orderly processes under regular procedures. Thus state action reduces the sum total of violence that might exist if each person and group acted through primitive self-help.

The liberal argues, furthermore, that the functions of government are not of necessity limited to police and military protection. The liberal insists that in a highly complicated society the state function must extend to the integration of institutional life, because only the state can secure overall effective results in certain areas. Most liberals in democratic countries with a social view of man do not believe that the state must "take on everything" and "own all property." When it comes to forms of government, most liberals are ardent democrats or parliamentarians who insist upon representative government, limitation of government under constitutional law, intellectual freedom, and one man–one vote with universal adult suffrage, or government of and by as well as for the people.

The "liberal" tradition, then, rests upon a long line of thinkers from the Stoics, the Judeo-Christian religionists, the modern movement for republican government as exemplified in Great Britain, the United States, and other such countries, of present British and U.S. Constitutions, upon the Magna Charta, Petition of Rights, Declaration of Independence, Locke, Jefferson, Madison, Paine, the Chartists, Robert Owen, the two Mills, the Protestant social gospel movement of Rauschenbusch, Niebuhr, William Temple (the late Archbishop of York, who originated the term "welfare state"), the union movements in Great Britain and the United States, Dewey, Pound, the Progressive political movement in America, the speeches of Wilson and Franklin Roosevelt, and the bulk of sociological investigation in this day.

In dealing with the problem of increasing governmental intervention for welfare, liberals point out that the increases have not been as Gargantuan as has been supposed. Expenditures on social welfare benefits including health and education now total over $100.2 billion (fiscal year 1966–1967). From Table 24-1 it can be seen that these expenditures are only slightly higher as a percentage of gross national product than they were in 1935–1936. Public assistance programs have decreased as a percentage of GNP due to the termination of W.P.A., P.W.A., and the like. Expenditures for health, education, "other welfare services," and veterans' programs have increased slightly. The largest gain has come in the social insurance programs. These programs by and large are financed through payroll taxes, so that much of the increased welfare program involves people transferring their own income from when they are young to when they are older or disabled. Even though social welfare expenditures as a percentage of GNP have generally been increasing since 1952–1953, the increases have been of small magnitude. The largest increases have gone to education and social insurance. It is not expected that these programs will be overexpanded or that the costs of these programs will be beyond the capacity to pay.

TABLE 24–1. CIVILIAN PUBLIC SOCIAL WELFARE PROGRAMS IN RELATION TO GROSS NATIONAL PRODUCT, FISCAL YEARS, 1935–1966

Fiscal Year	Social Welfare Expenditures (in Billions)	Social Welfare Expenditures as Percentage of Gross National Product						
		Social Insurance	Public Aid	Health and Medical Services	Education	Other Welfare Services	Veterans' Programs	Total
1935–1936	7.4	0.5	4.4	0.9	3.1	0.1	0.6	9.6
1940–1941	9.1	1.1	3.2	0.7	2.6	0.1	0.5	8.2
1945–1946	11.8	1.3	0.6	0.5	1.8	0.1	1.5	5.8
1950–1951	23.6	1.5	0.8	0.8	2.5	0.2	1.8	7.6
1955–1956	34.6	2.6	0.8	0.7	3.0	0.2	1.1	8.4
1960–1961	57.9	4.4	0.9	0.9	3.9	0.2	1.0	11.5
1965–1966	87.6	4.5	1.0	1.0	4.5	0.4	0.9	12.3
1966–1967	100.2	4.9	1.2	1.1	4.7	0.4	0.9	13.1

Sources: Social Security Bulletin, Vol. 18, No. 10 (October, 1955), Tables 1, 2, pp. 6, 9; Vol. 25, No. 11 (November, 1962), Tables 1, 2, pp. 4, 7; Vol. 15, No. 12 (December, 1966), Tables 1, 2, pp. 10, 14.

JUSTIFICATION FOR INCREASED GOVERNMENT INTERVENTION

Historically, classical liberalism has opposed the intervention of the state into the life of the nation. Abuses of government, typified by such monarchs as the Bourbons and Stuarts, certainly were apparent and needed rectifying. On the other hand, as the complexities of life have increased, the need for more rather than less government intervention has become necessary. To cite an example from Professor Calvin Hoover that he describes as a well-worn cliché, municipal ordinances against keeping pigs were needed as soon as enough citizens congregated in one place to constitute a municipality. The curtailment of individual liberty of the swinekeepers was more than offset by the reduction of unpleasant odors to other citizens. Also, the state may perform some functions better than individuals. This was recognized long before Adam Smith, who listed national defense, justice, road, bridge and harbor construction, expansion of foreign trade, and education as proper functions of government. Since Smith's time the list of functions that government can do more efficiently than individuals has expanded considerably. Professor Hoover mentions that it is now commonplace to accept the proposition that social security inevitably provides more protection for the individual than he could obtain through his individual efforts. State intervention is also necessary to prevent economic depressions and inflation. The state has also been used to lessen the uninhibited conflict of the countervailing powers of labor and management to prevent injury to the public. Here state intervention may even go so far as to regulate both the internal and external affairs of corporations and labor unions. Increases in the costs of national defense and the fighting of wars have also expanded the powers of government.[15] Few would accept either the universal proposition that no government intervention (complete anarchism) would provide the best system for mankind, nor the opposite universal proposition that government is always superior to individual effort. Since no universals are available to us, the use of additional government intervention must be decided on a case-by-case basis.

In many instances in the past government spending has been too little. In 1943 heart disease killed more than half a million and disabled some 8½ million persons in the United States. Yet in 1944 only $615,000 was spent for research on heart disease compared with the private expenditure of $31 million on advertising cigarettes. At the same time we spent almost nothing on cancer research, although it afflicted about 7 million people at that time. One company, on the other hand, spent $19 million to advertise soap.[16] The solution should not be to force people to consume what an enlightened person or group of persons believes they ought to, but rather conditions should be made available under which people may find out what

[15] Calvin E. Hoover, *The Economy, Liberty and the State* (Garden City, N.Y., Doubleday, 1961), pp. 356-359.
[16] Harry K. Girvetz, *From Wealth to Welfare* (Stanford, Stanford, 1950), p. 208.

they themselves want and recognize clearly the things which satisfy these wants.[17] Increased governmental expenditures on heart, cancer, and other research have indicated a growing awareness of the needs in this direction.

EXCESSIVE GOVERNMENT CENTRALIZATION

In determining which level of government should administer welfare functions, most people would contend that the local government should be given preference provided that the more decentralized agency can ably perform the function. In an interesting book entitled, *Beyond the Welfare State*, Gunnar Myrdal writes of the future of welfare in the countries already having the welfare state. He points out that a more responsible citizenship will result in eventually changing the welfare state from a rather shallow, bureaucratic, strongly centralized, institutional machinery, manipulated by crafty organizational entrepreneurs and vested interests, into a more decentralized society in which individuals will take over functions formerly handled by the state. As an example, he states that a law was passed in Sweden a little more than twenty years ago which forbade employers to discharge a woman for family reasons: because she became engaged, married, or had a child. The purpose of such a law was to prevent employers from substituting cheap, inexperienced help for more experienced, higher-paid women who had more seniority. Myrdal felt that the law was necessary then in order to force a change in an unwholesome prevailing mores of the time. At the present time, though, Myrdal believes that such a law could be repealed without risk, for public opinion is now more enlightened, and would not condone the firing of a woman for the reasons given above. He foresees that a "welfare culture" more locally administered will come into existence within the structure of the welfare state.

For the United States, which has much less of a welfare state than Western European countries, Myrdal points out that the process of national integration has still a considerable distance to go before it reaches the levels common to other Western countries. Far more federal government legislation is needed. The weaker local and sectional community controls call for more direct state control through the courts and administration to enforce the general mores. In the long run, though, he feels that even in America, as more active citizen participation occurs on the local level, less centralized government control would be necessary.[18]

MORE RESPONSIBLE GOVERNMENT

Professor Girvetz has analyzed methods by which governments, although expanding in function, may be made more responsive to the needs of the

[17] *Ibid.*, pp. 154-155.
[18] Gunnar Myrdal, *Beyond the Welfare State* (New Haven, Yale, 1960), Chap. VI.

people. First he lists the party system as necessary so that protest can be informed and organized. A multiparty system obviously is necessary for such protest rather than a single-party system. He also looks with favor upon such groups as the League of Women Voters, Americans for Democratic Action, the Committee for Economic Development, and the British Fabian Society to provide leadership in making the party system work and to make government more responsible to the people. He maintains that independent and powerful organization of workers is indispensable to democratic government. Labor needs protection not only against private managers but public supervisors as well. Those seeking monopoly power such as totalitarian governments dislike labor unions. Private groups who seek a monopoly of power, either covertly or openly, despise labor unions also. He thinks also that strong consumers' organizations are necessary to make governments responsible to the needs of the people, although he recognizes that in the United States consumer groups have been particularly weak and unorganized. Last but not least he lists private enterprise as necessary to provide responsiveness of government. Such enterprise places a check on public enterprise. With the proper countervailing power, more rather than less freedom will result even though the power of the government increases.[19]

DANGERS OF INCREASED TAXATION

Some conservatives fear that increased taxes to cover the expanding government sector may prove the downfall of our society. A number of studies have been made on the effect of taxes on incentives. One study on the relation between the income tax and the relation to work concluded that high progressive income taxes have not reduced incentives to work.[20] This study found that wage and salary employees have little choice in the amount of work they do. About the only choice available is whether to work at another job after working hours. Another study analyzed the impact of the federal income tax on labor force participation. The conclusion of this study was that the income tax has no effect on the size and composition of the labor force.[21]

Several studies have been made of the impact of taxes upon the work incentives of executives. Professor T. H. Sanders found that the economy has not lost a serious amount of executives' services due to taxes. He concluded that nonfinancial incentives outweigh financial incentives in motivating executives to work. The nonfinancial incentives of doing a good job,

[19] Girvetz, op. cit., pp. 226-229.

[20] George F. Break, "Income Taxes and Incentives to Work: An Empirical Study," American Economic Review, Vol. 47 (1957), pp. 529-549.

[21] Clarence D. Long, "Impact of the Federal Income Tax on Labor Force Participation," Federal Tax Policy for Economic Growth and Stability (Washington, D.C., Joint Economic Committee, 1955), pp. 153-166.

power, prestige, the sense of satisfaction of a responsible position, the sense of loyalty to an organization, and the organizational disciplines of the group outweigh any negative incentives to reduce the amount of work due to high taxes.[22] Professor Dan Throop Smith concluded that executives' "day-to-day efforts and activities are in general not lessened by taxation." [23] Another study of the effects of high taxes on savings and investment shows little impairment from taxes. A number of ways are provided by which upper-income recipients avoid the full impact of the upper-bracket tax rates and are able to save large sums of money. Investment has not been unduly affected either. Some investors place their money in risky ventures to obtain capital gains, which are taxed much less than regular income. Owners and managers of business enterprises have continued to invest heavily also. A final conclusion from a number of studies by Harvard's Graduate School of Business was that current levels of tax rates will not cause serious long-run damage to the economy. The viewpoint that expenditures and taxes must be greatly reduced to preserve economic strength at home was not "substantiated by the facts." [24]

Much of our welfare program is financed through payroll taxes. These taxes are regressive rather than progressive. Their use should not hurt incentives to invest. In a more pessimistic vein, Professor Colin Clark contended that the critical point of taxation was 25 percent of national income. When taxation approached that level, various pressure groups will insist on deficits and other devices, which will result in inflation and an impairment of incentives. He cited statistical data, mainly from France, to support his position.[25] Few economists today would support the position of Professor Colin Clark. Even with high taxes, investment has been high, and taxation has already exceeded the critical 25 percent level without disastrous results. It is true, however, that the many suggestions for expanding welfare would tend to increase taxes even more. Ways and means will be needed to finance an even larger amount of government participation. Some have suggested that additional revenue could be obtained by closing some of the loopholes in our present laws. Some of the increases of government could be paid out of our increasing gross national product. Some of the countries of Western Europe have substantially higher payroll taxes than we have. These countries have shown no ill effects from the higher taxes, and it would be expected that we could assimilate higher payroll taxes into our system without ill effects.

[22] Thomas H. Sanders, *Effects of Taxation on Executives* (Cambridge, Harvard Business School, 1951).

[23] Dan Throop Smith, "Taxation and Executives," *Proceedings of the National Tax Association, 1951* (Sacramento, Calif., 1952), p. 235.

[24] J. Keith Butters, "Taxation, Incentives and Financial Capacity," *American Economic Review,* Supplement (May, 1954), p. 519.

[25] Colin Clark, "Public Finance and Changes in the Value of Money," *Economic Journal* (December, 1945), pp. 371-389.

LIBERTY AND WELFARE

An important question to be answered is whether increased government intervention will result in the elimination of liberty. In Calvin Hoover's provocative book, *The Economy, Liberty, and the State,* he carefully analyzes the relation between the growth of the state and liberty. He concludes that for Western Europe and the United States there has been no close correlation between the increasing amount of state intervention and the net limitation upon personal liberty. His findings, he says, seem to contradict the theory that extension of the power of the state is incompatible with the maintenance of personal liberty. He agrees that the expanding state did result in a serious curtailment of liberty under Nazi, Fascist, and Soviet regimes, but he sees no diminution of personal liberty in Western Europe and the United States. He offers several reasons why personal liberty has not decreased in the latter countries. Of importance is his distinction between business liberty and personal liberty. A minimum wage law, for example, does limit the business liberty of an employer to pay less than the minimum, and acreage restrictions do limit the right of the farmer to plant as much as he wishes; yet such limitations are not considered as a loss of personal freedom of the type protected by the Constitution, such as freedom of the press, speech, religion, protection against self-incrimination, and the like. Second, the intervention of the state generally appeared only after the prior growth of power by some group. The purpose of the state intervention is to restrict too much power in the hands of one group. The National Labor Relations Act, for example, was passed primarily to give workers more power against the dominant corporate group. State intervention, then, was felt to provide more individual liberty in protecting against corporations rather than restricting such liberty. Third, the state may intervene primarily to avoid a crisis. The intervention of the state during war to curtail wage or price increases may be viewed primarily as a protection against inflation rather than as an extension of state power.[26]

Hoover recognizes that the growth of the government in Russia has severely limited personal freedom. Furthermore, Hoover doubts that a fully statized economy can be operated by a bureaucracy without the loss of personal liberty and representative government. In Western Europe and the United States he thinks that it will be possible to maintain personal liberty even with some further expansion of government functions. He states that the further extension of state control is inevitable to ameliorate the economic status of lower-income groups and to keep our modern complex economy functioning at a tolerable level. Whether personal liberty will be maintained will depend on the restriction of government functions to those truly necessary, and to the maintenance of continuing popular control through elected

[26] Hoover, *op. cit.,* pp. 330-337.

representatives. The success of our economic system itself will be important in determining how much government intervention is necessary. The proper evolution of our institutions to maintain both high per capita income and liberty will depend fundamentally on the contradictory traits of tough-mindedness, goodwill, and responsibleness by those who supply the guidance to our system.[27]

INDIVIDUAL RESPONSIBILITY

Proponents of increased welfare have attempted to refute the argument that cradle-to-grave security will result in destroying individual responsibility. They maintain that improved and expanded welfare programs should increase rather than decrease responsibility. If a young person's opportunity to attend school is conditioned on the merit of his own work rather than the economic and social status of his parents, his responsibility should increase. Furthermore, forcing a child to grow up in a slum environment may seriously hinder the growth of a sense of responsibility. Clearing slum areas may provide a more conducive environment in which the person may assume more responsibility. Increased expenditures for education, housing, aging, and other welfare measures should also provide increased responsibility. Professor Girvetz maintains that the number of shiftless and lazy in our society has been grossly overexaggerated mainly to relieve the remaining population of assuming responsibility for their care.[28] For those relatively few who are lazy or shiftless, the causes of such behavior are primarily due to lack of opportunity and a poor environment. Improving the environment through welfare measures should activate most persons to assume more of their responsibilities toward society. In short, welfare measures should increase responsibility rather than reduce it.

RADICALISM AND WELFARE

Not only has our modern welfare legislation been criticized as involving too much government intervention in society (the conservative viewpoint), but it also has been criticized as not accomplishing nearly enough. Statistics show that even with increased welfare, the lower-income groups receive no larger a share of national income than before the advent of large-scale welfare. In 1910 the bottom 10 percent received 3 percent of the national income in the United States, and by 1958 the figure was 2 percent.

Apparently welfare payments have not even kept the lower-income groups from falling further behind. For those who prefer a more egalitarian society, the welfare state has simply not got the job done. Further-

[27] *Ibid.*, pp. 341-377.
[28] Girvetz, *op. cit.*, p. 233.

more, Gordon K. Lewis points out that England is still the class-ridden
society it has always been. His criticism of this aspect of the welfare state
is as follows:

The welfare state is not the socialist commonwealth. England is still at
bottom a class-ridden society, a Dickensian mixture of aristocratic remnants, pluto-
cratic influence and middle-class sentiment. Professions such as the law and
medicine, although not closed castes, still carry the marks of hereditary occupations. Institutions such as the Anglican Church continue to be bastions of social
privilege and bishops, as a class, come overwhelmingly from a single social stratum
trained in select schools like Marlborough and Merchant Taylors. The Diplo-
matic Service, despite the Eden reforms of 1943 and despite their proof, in the
figure of Mr. Bevin, that a trade-union leader can become an outstanding Foreign
Secretary, still resists effective democratization, and since 1945 only the occasional
ambassador, Lord Halifax or Sir Oliver Franks, has been drawn from outside
the ranks of the traditional career men. The sociology of the peerage shows that
in its present state, approximately three-quarters of its members come from the
"public schools" and that, the creation of some one hundred new peers by Labor
Cabinets since 1945 notwithstanding, an ennobled individual very rapidly ac-
quires the conservative instincts of "noblesse oblige" and, in addition, sends his
sons to Eton or Harrow and himself will seek out a business position rarely below
the board-room level. It is also of interest to note that two of the major occupational sources of the class are ex-Army regular officers (39 percent of all peers)
and lawyers (25 percent of new peers). Behind all this there lies the common
source of a privileged educational system that has been substantially untouched
by reform. For apart from the grotesque exclusiveness of the "public school," recent investigations of educational opportunity at both the grammar-school and
university level suggest that, in the first place, a boy coming from a middle-class
home has a greater chance of entering a grammar school than a boy from a
working-class home and, secondly, the growing democratization of "Oxbridge"
has meant, in terms of social attitudes, an assimilation of the working-class student into the value system of the traditional upper-class influence. The conse-
quence, as Professor Pear has displayed in his fascinating study, is that English
life is still pretty well dominated by a set of social prejudices and class differen-
tiations based not so much upon graduations of income as upon the more subtle
differences of speech, manners, dress, leisure pursuits, even modes of eating and
drinking; and all of them defended in terms of a vague ideology of "Character"
calculated to sustain the national habits of class separatism. Nor has this been
seriously changed by the advent of new elites that, in themselves, are doing much
to break down the more comic aspects of that separatism and to challenge the
conservative spirit of the older professions, for although they are more hospitable
to talent and ability they have not seriously challenged the basic society values
and, indeed, themselves constitute covert elites profoundly disturbing to the principle of national community. The group-novel of C. P. Snow is a vast fictional
footnote to that truth.

The welfare state has done little more than to enable the working classes
to hold their own and thereby to keep just about in step with the general rise
in wealth. It follows from this, as the third point, that the welfare state has not

so much radically revised British social relationships as permitted the rise of a relatively larger minority of talented lower-class individuals into the strata above them. Public taxation has done little to eliminate the unearned income of the functionless shareholders of public companies, on the one hand, or the capital gains that have generated a new style of conspicuous consumption on the English rich, on the other, nor, even more important as a source of inegalitarianism, has it done much to reform a social value system wherein long and arduous work is often meanly rewarded and easy and satisfying work is generally well-paid.[29]

Gordon Lewis further points out that despite New Deal reforms, which he characterizes as basically the outcome of the distrust of the American gentleman class for a vulgar business society, the basic decisions of the American economy are still controlled by the corporate managerial class. It is they who determine the scale of operations, plant location, the commodities to be produced, the rate of capital expansion, and the amounts expended for research. The large powers held in the hands of the traditional rich and chief corporation executives are not affected by welfare legislation.

Some recent Fabians such as R. A. Crosland, in his recent *The Future of Socialism,* are less enamored with nationalization than previous socialist thought. Crosland contends that the supersession of the shareholder by managerial personnel and the enlarged power of labor unions have solved the important question of the ownership of production. Although Gordon Lewis agrees with Crosland that the technique of the public corporation is not entirely satisfactory, he would still favor nationalization. He suggests improving its weaknesses by such devices as a modernization of parliamentary controls, a new concept of the role of the prime minister, a widening of opportunity in promotions on the boards of control of industry, and an increasing role of labor unions in new administrative bodies such as Development Councils.

Professor Richard Titmuss in evaluating the last 15 years of experience with the welfare state in Britain states that larger gains have gone to the middle than lower classes. In view of the fact that lower-income persons move more frequently than upper-class persons, many of them become ineligible for private pensions. If the view is taken that all society pays for such pensions, as Titmuss does, then the pensions of the rich are subsidized more heavily by the community than the pensions of the poor. For tax purposes, an upper-class person may deduct all of his ex-wives' maintenance allowances without any loss, but relief for mothers and children may be stopped if cohabitation is taking place. The lower classes are penalized for so-called immoral behavior, but the upper class is not. Also it has been found that higher-income groups make more use of the health service than lower-income groups. The former receive more specialist attention, occupy more

[29] Gordon K. Lewis, "Twentieth-Century Capitalism and Socialism: The Present State of the Anglo-American Debate," *Western Political Quarterly,* vol. 12, 1959, pp. 101-103. Reprinted by permission of University of Utah, copyright owners.

of the beds in the better hospitals, and are more apt to obtain psychiatric care. Furthermore, the welfare state has not expanded the percentage of male undergraduates who are the sons of manual workers. Rather the percentage has dropped one percent. If subsidies to education are included, the father earning $60,000 a year receives 13 times more from the state than another father earning $1,500 in recognition of the dependent needs of childhood. Middle-class families are also more heavily subsidized in housing. In conclusion. Titmuss feels that we should now concentrate on the problem of "Ways of Extending the Welfare State to the Poor." [30]

A further criticism of simply limiting reform to welfare legislation is that the goals of our present society are deficient. C. Wright Mills has pointed out in *The Power Elite* that our society has narrowed the meaning of "success" to big money and condemns failure as the chief vice. The emphasis on money inevitably produces the sharp operator and the shady deal. Furthermore, the goal of money does not produce men of conscience.

In the United States it has also been alleged that the welfare state has been directed mainly toward aiding the middle rather than lower classes.[31] Michael Harrington points out that agricultural parity payments have gone mainly to upper-income farmers. Much of the money for urban renewal has not provided housing for lower-income groups. The poorest groups in our society, such as agricultural workers and domestic servants, are exempt from much of our social legislation. They are not covered under unemployment insurance laws and workmen's compensation laws, nor do they have collective bargaining rights under the National Labor Relations Act, as most other workers have. These observations by Mr. Harrington are irrefutable although it is also true that some welfare payments such as OAA, AFDC, and others do go to low-income families. Nevertheless, Mr. Harrington is correct in maintaining that coverage under most of our welfare programs needs to be broadened to include some of the low-income groups not now covered.

WAR ON POVERTY

Owing to the fact that the many and varied social welfare programs had not eradicated poverty in the United States, and possibly to create a "liberal" image, the Johnson Administration in 1964 inaugurated a new agency, the Office of Economic Opportunity, to lead in the war against poverty. This agency was created by the Economic Opportunity Act of 1964. About $1 billion was allocated for fighting the war on poverty, and the sum was increased to almost $2 billion by fiscal 1968.

The Economic Opportunity Act (EOA) created a number of new

[30] Richard Titmuss, "The Role of Redistribution in Social Policy," *Social Security Bulletin,* Vol. 28, No. 6 (June, 1965), pp. 14-20.
[31] Michael Harrington, *The Other America* (New York, Macmillan, 1962).

programs. About 44 percent of the poverty money in fiscal 1968 was channeled into Title I, consisting mainly of youth programs. One major program under Title I is the Job Corps, which provides training and education for disadvantaged youths in residential centers. On June 30, 1967, 42,032 youths, predominantly men, were enrolled in 90 conservation centers, 34 urban centers which had the largest total enrollment, and 5 demonstration centers. The male enrollees had completed an average of 8.8 years of schooling and the females 9.8, but the reading levels for the young men and women were grades 4 and 6 respectively. Eighty percent of the enrollees had not seen a doctor or dentist in the last ten years, 60 percent were from broken homes, 63 percent came from families in which the head of the household was unemployed, and 30 percent could neither read nor write.[32] Over half the group were Negroes.

At the conservation centers youths are trained in basic education, prevocational subjects, and citizenship. These youths spend about half of their time on work projects that preserve, expand, and beautify our natural resources and public recreational facilities. In the urban centers, more advanced training is given in such subjects as auto mechanics, welding, machine shop, electronics, data processing, and other trades. The cost of training youths under the Job Corps is quite high—about $6,900 in direct operating costs plus capital costs averaging $600 per enrollee (fiscal 1967). Prior to entering the Job Corps, the graduates earned $1.14 per hour; after training the wages earned were $1.48 (August, 1966). For those enrolling but never attending classes, wages increased from $1.17 to $1.31.[33] From this and other data, in a benefit/cost study, Glen C. Cain of the Institute for Research on Poverty at the University of Wisconsin concluded that increased earnings of Job Corps enrollees would be larger than the costs involved in their training. Later data for May, 1967, show a wage of $1.19 before entering, while the average wage of former Corpsmen was $1.58. For those who remained in the Job Corps for fifteen or more months the wage was $1.79.[34] Unfortunately, the dropout rate is quite high. More than 40 percent of the enrollees terminated in less than three months and another 24 percent terminated in less than six months.[35] In addition to the criticisms of high costs and a high dropout rate, isolated cases of delinquent behavior have been reported.

Also, the Office of Economic Opportunity (OEO) has been criticized for neglecting to experiment with other types of training such as combined residential and nonresidential facilities, centers located in or near ghetto

[32] *Economic Opportunity Amendments of 1967*, House of Representatives Committee on Education and Labor, Report No. 866 (October 27, 1967), p. 5.

[33] Glen G. Cain, *Benefit/Cost Study of Job Corps: Final Version*, Memorandum submitted to the Office of Economic Opportunity (May 22, 1967), Table 9, p. 40.

[34] *Economic Opportunity Amendments of 1967*, U.S. Senate Committee on Labor and Public Welfare, 90th Congress, 1st Session, S 2388 (September 12, 1967), p. 13.

[35] *Economic Opportunity Amendments of 1967*, House of Representatives, *op. cit.*, p. 148.

areas, smaller centers located closer to enrollees' homes, and centers which are run in conjunction with similar activities under the Manpower Development and Training Act and the Vocational Education Act of 1963.[36] In spite of the criticisms it should be remembered that the Job Corps is taking an extremely disadvantaged group of youths, and is showing some improvement in upgrading their skills and earnings.

The largest program under Title I is the Neighborhood Youth Corps, which is sponsored about equally among community action agencies, public schools, and other public and private nonprofit agencies. The three programs here are a work program for those in high school, a summer program geared to those attending school prior to enrolling, and a work program for out-of-school youth. As of June, 1966, about 527,725 youths were served by this program. There has been little criticism of the in-school program, but the out-of-school program has been criticized for providing only work and not training for the school dropout. Furthermore, in many instances the work with public or private nonprofit-making organizations is such that no permanent jobs are developed. Fortunately about 40 percent of the out-of-school group are receiving some type of remedial education and one-fourth receive occupational training, mainly on the job. Recently, a 1966 amendment has been implemented to provide job training opportunities in private industry. According to the Neighborhood Youth Corps, of the 12,500 who left during the fall of 1966, 31 percent took jobs, 2 percent entered the armed services, 20 percent returned to school, 2 percent joined the Job Corps, 1 percent entered into manpower development and training programs, 27 percent left for adjustment problems (poor attendance, dislike of staff or job content, could not get along), and 17 percent quit for other reasons or for whereabouts unknown. Having received little training in this program, this group was still inadequately equipped for most jobs.[37]

Under part D of Title I, a Special Impact Program has channeled money into nineteen cities and two rural areas (June 30, 1967), which have high concentrations of unemployment. In a Department of Labor study (November, 1966) of ten urban slums, it was found that the rate of unemployment was 10 percent compared to 3.8 percent for the nation. However, there was a large amount of hidden unemployment in the slum area, of persons working part-time even though they wanted full-time work, of persons earning so little at full-time work that they were not meeting the minimum subsistence needs of their families, and those who were so discouraged about job prospects that they had stopped looking. When all these groups were added together, the "subemployment" rate in the slum areas, including the 10 percent unemployed, came to 34 percent. It is these urban groups, plus the rural depressed areas of the Mississippi Delta and northern Michigan, to which this part of the program is directed. Individual counseling is provided, and prospects are

[36] *Economic Opportunity Amendments of 1967*, U.S. Senate, *op. cit.*, p. 203.
[37] *Ibid.*, pp. 18-20.

then referred to jobs, training, school, or a combination of the three. A serious effort is being made to work with private employers and labor unions to obtain jobs for the hard-core jobless, such as those with police records.

The largest sums appropriated to the OEO, about half in fiscal 1968, went in Title II to Community Action Programs (CAP). Over 1,000 local community action agencies have been created, either on a local, county, or multicounty basis, to service about five million persons in about 5,000 communities. The local community action groups, which must represent all segments of the community including the poor themselves, submit plans to the OEO after approval by local and state officials. About half of the money under CAP has gone for education and child development, including Project Headstart which Sargent Shriver, the Director of OEO, has felt was the "greatest single measurable success" of the entire War on Poverty. Project Headstart provides kindergarten training for underprivileged children either in an eight week summer program or, less frequently, a nine month regular school term. Recently, a new project of Follow Through was instituted to aid Project Headstart children through the first three grades. Another educational program is Project Upward Bound in which, in the summer of 1966, 19,000 students were enrolled in 216 separate programs. The enrollment figure increased to 22,000 students in 1967. The purpose of this program is to interest underprivileged high school students in college, where the summer programs are held. Tutorial work is then provided on an individual basis in the twelfth grade. Although the summer program in 1966 reported a 4 percent dropout rate, and 75 to 80 percent of Upward Bound enrollees entered college, reports indicate that the dropout rate in college is high. It is hoped that remedies to this dropout problem will be provided.[38]

An important part of CAP has been the creation of over 500 multipurpose neighborhood centers. As an example of what has been done at such centers, Detroit's program is cited here. Twenty-two subcenters were set up throughout the low-income sections of the city. Services offered included general counseling, job counseling and placement, training programs, marriage and family counseling, immunizations, and many other programs. Classes were arranged in food purchasing, credit buying, home management, and various other subjects. Thirty women were given an eight week training course in homemaking. They will be employed to care for children and older persons. They will also provide personal services for the sick and carry on general home management duties such as housekeeping, meal preparation, shopping, and similar responsibilities. In other centers and community action programs such services as medical care, legal aid, day care services, family planning, and other services are provided.

One requirement of a community action agency is that one-third of its members must be "chosen in accordance with democratic selection procedures adequate to assure that they are representative of the poor." The direct involvement of the poor in their problems is cited as a strength of the OEO program. One of the most controversial of the 1967 amendments to the EOA

[38] *Ibid.,* p. 42.

was granting to state or local government officials the power to create the community action agencies, which previously had been autonomous. Proponents of the change pointed out that without proper local government support, Community Action Agencies (CAA) could not operate effectively. Those opposed to the amendment feared too much governmental involvement and possible political chicanery in the OEO program. Under the 1967 amendments, the director of OEO may designate the appropriate CAA if such an agency has failed to function, or a governmental agency has failed to create such an agency.

The remaining sections of the EOA are smaller in scope. Title III, administered by the Farmer's Home Administration, provides loans to low-income farmers or cooperatives. This part of the program has been criticized on the ground that the average loan of $1,707 is not large enough to substantially raise farm income. However, over half of the 17,073 borrowers did raise their income by $300 or more annually, and 24 percent raised their income by $1,000 or more. Almost half the loans to individuals under this Title went for nonagricultural purposes, such as the purchase of machinery and equipment in nonagricultural pursuits. A number of loans have been made to cooperatives, which have used the money mainly for the purpose of buying machinery and equipment and engaging in construction and development.

Title IV provides for small business loans, and is administered by the Small Business Administration. From December, 1966 to June, 1967, 2,678 loans were made for a total value of $25 million. About half the loans enabled the borrower to open or expand a retail establishment, and one-fourth of the loans went to the service industry. About another fourth of the money went to provide working capital for the purchase of land, buildings, and equipment.

Title V, the Work Experience program, provides training for those on welfare. This title is administered by the Department of Health, Education and Welfare. In fiscal 1966, 84,820 workers were trained on 274 projects. Much of the training was in basic education or for work in the service industry. Fewer workers have been trained for skilled, semi-skilled, or technical work.

Title VIII is the VISTA program (Volunteers in Service to America), patterned after the Peace Corps. Under this program 3,592 volunteers (June, 1966) have been sent to poor urban and rural areas, Indian reservations, migrant labor and Job Corps camps, and mental health projects. The volunteers aid in providing community services, literacy training, and servicing the poor in a number of ways.

EVALUATION

The War on Poverty has aroused much interest and discussion in the United States. Extreme conservatives have seen no merit in the program. Conservatives on the Senate Committee on Labor and Public Welfare claim that the program has the single objective of securing votes. Patty Newman, a former journalism major, and Joyce Wenger, Vice-President of the Los Angeles County Federation of Republican Women, have written a book about the

War on Poverty in which they can find little merit in any of the many programs. Chapter One, entitled, "The Greatest Snow on Earth" has the following to say:

The greatest show on earth! The curtain has risen on a federal show the like of which you've never seen. Your tax money is being used to tell the poor how badly they are being treated, how much they must organize and "demand" that which everyone else has, and how they needn't worry if they get thrown in jail in the process because tax money will be used to get them out and to hire lawyers in their defense. School boycotts, rent strikes, and demonstrations (plus baby-sitting costs while all of this is going on) are being financed with tax dollars. Taxpayers are paying for the poor to go to expensive theaters, to have dinners in fine restaurants, to at long last live as the "other half"—all with no worries about paying for it. And if enough poor can not be found to participate, high-salaried "directors" are hired to go out and find them.[39]

Some conservatives find some merit in some of the programs, but they would prefer that the OEO be abolished and the programs handled by other agencies. For example, it is suggested that Project Headstart be administered by the local school system rather than a local CAA. Those defending the present arrangement contend that a single agency is necessary to coordinate and analyze the merits of the various programs and concentrate attention on problems of poverty. The multiplicity of federal, state, and local government agencies dealing with one aspect or another of poverty has made the coordination function of the OEO an extremely difficult one. A recurrent criticism of the OEO has been its failure to adequately coordinate the attack on the War on Poverty. The 1967 amendments to the EOA have attempted to improve coordination, but whether they will be successful remains to be seen. Critics of the program maintain that the OEO has merely added one more agency to the many in existence rather than having served in a coordinating capacity.

In general, those of liberal persuasion have supported the War on Poverty. This group believes that an expenditure of less than $2 billion is inadequate to immediately eradicate poverty since it has been estimated that about $11.5 billion would be necessary to eliminate poverty in the United States.[40] Furthermore, given the type of program that exists, much of the money now spent for the War on Poverty does not go directly to the poor but is paid to teachers, counselors, and others servicing the program. The fact that inadequate amounts are spent means that many living in poverty are not reached by the program. The lack of coverage was highlighted in a recent television news short in which Senator Robert Kennedy of New York interviewed a Mississippi sharecropper. In reply to two questions by Senator Kennedy on whether he had ever heard of the War on Poverty or Project Headstart, the answer to both was "No." Liberals have also tended to discount the criticism

[39] Patty Newman and Joyce Wenger, *Pass the Poverty Please* (Whittier, Calif., Constructive Action, Inc., 1966), pp. 5-6. Reprinted by permission.

[40] Mollie Orshansky, "Counting the Poor: Another Look at the Poverty Profile," *Social Security Bulletin,* Vol. 28 (Jan., 1965), pp. 9, 13.

that too many War on Poverty programs have incited the poor to engage in violence and riots. In thirty-two cities in which disorders broke out in the summer of 1967, of nearly 12,000 persons arrested, only sixteen were known to be paid poverty workers, nine of whom were temporary summer employees. Even though the less than $2 billion program has not abolished poverty, at least, according to liberals, the program has been a step in the right direction.

The War on Poverty has been criticized also by those of a more leftist persuasion. David Komatsu has described the program as "a mockery," "a deliberate fraud," and a "conservative embracing of the status quo." Richard Titmuss fears the program as a dangerous gimmick which is attempting to show that poverty can be eliminated without changing the structure of society. S. M. Miller and Martin Rein are less critical of the program, but they maintain that the absence of a strong, organized, and well-directed movement has resulted in a weak bill, which was further weakened by Congress. They fear that the War on Poverty may be merely a sop to the poor that possibly could discourage them from asking for a more effective program. They criticize the program for making no assault on the problem of inequality of income. In the program's attempt to change the poor and not their social situation, structural changes in our society are ignored and neglected. Miller and Rein point out, for example, that the textile industry may be organized so poorly that an overhauling of this industry may be necessary rather than reeducating and retraining the poor for work in it. Furthermore, they maintain that the poverty program is not comprehensive enough. The initial thrust of the program has been those who are disaffected from work, but many of the poor do not suffer from a lack of job motivation. Rather the problem of the stable poor is that of inadequate provisions of jobs. They further point out that while the tax cut has been beneficial it has been inadequate for the task of adequate job creation. They also maintain that the War on Poverty has not aided the vast numbers of aged and those on welfare living in poverty. In the program's emphasis on training youth, Miller and Rein wonder whether more concentration on raising the income of families in poverty would aid youth more than training them. Several specific programs of the War on Poverty have been criticized by Miller and Rein. In the Job Corps, youths with physical handicaps or serious delinquency records will not be accepted. A failure to help the rejected group may have serious consequences, for it may imply final rejection to this group. The Neighborhood Youth Corps has been criticized for not providing training for youth. In spite of these and other criticisms of the War on Poverty, Miller and Rein feel that the program does have the advantage of providing a public commitment to help the poor. The program may make its major contribution in legitimatizing the grievances of the poor. Organization of the poor may result in an enlarged and better program.[41]

[41] S. M. Miller and Martin Rein, "The War on Poverty: Perspectives and Prospects," in Ben S. Seligman, ed., *Poverty as a Public Issue* (New York, Free Press, 1965), pp. 272-320.

GUARANTEED INCOME PROPOSALS

The fact that the War on Poverty has not reached many of the people in poverty has caused a number of students of the problem to propose guaranteeing a minimum income to each family or individual. The fact that it would only cost about $11.5 billion to eliminate poverty seems well within reach of our economy which now has a GNP of over $800 billion. At the present writing, however, the costs of the Vietnam war preclude larger expenditures for the War on Poverty.

The problem of providing work incentives is obviously important in guaranteed income proposals. Lady Rhys Williams in her guaranteed-income proposal suggests that a new social contract be made whereby the state would assure all of the necessities to its citizens in return for the individual's promise to put forth his best efforts in the production of wealth.[42] Others favoring the minimum guarantee think that the state should make an unqualified guarantee to everyone. Clarence Ayres, for example, feels that only by an absolute guarantee could the prudent citizen trust the program. He feels that such a program would motivate most of the victims of poverty to reorient themselves in the industrial economy.[43]

A proposal similar to cash dividends is that of a negative income tax. Professor Milton Friedman has proposed a negative tax rate of 50 percent on unused tax exemptions and standard deductions.[44] If a family has total exemptions and deductions of $3,000 but has only $2,000 in income, 50 percent negative tax on the unused exemptions and deductions of $1,000 would result in a government subsidy of $500 to the family. Christopher Green has estimated the costs of a number of negative income tax proposals.[45] Of five such plans analyzed the costs ranged from $4.4 billion to $6.9 billion. In these plans about 50 percent negative tax rates were applied rather than guaranteeing a full 100 percent of income.

One of the criticisms leveled at the negative income tax is that no work test is provided to qualify for the subsidy. However, some minimum incentive is provided. For two men with $3,000 in exemptions and deductions, one who earned no income would receive an income of $1,500 (with a 50 percent negative tax rate). Another person who earned $1,000 in income would have $2,000 remaining in exemptions and deductions and thus receive a subsidy of $1,000. His total income would be $2,000. Nevertheless, a major objection to the negative income tax is that it might permit some people to draw income without making any effort to work.

[42] Lady Rhys Williams, *Something to Look Forward To* (London, MacDonald and Co., 1943), p. 145.

[43] Clarence E. Ayres, "Guaranteed Income: An Institutional View," in Robert Theobald, ed., *The Guaranteed Income* (New York, Doubleday, 1966), pp. 161-174.

[44] Milton Friedman, *Capitalism and Freedom* (Chicago, University of Chicago Press, 1962), pp. 191-195.

[45] Christopher Green, *Negative Taxes and the Poverty Program* (Washington, Brookings Institute, 1967), Table 9-1, p. 141.

A program of family allowances may be considered one form of a guaranteed income. Under this type of program, the government pays each family according to the number of children. Evidence does show that poverty exists more frequently when there are many children in the family. Family allowances should aid in improving the income of families with large numbers of children. Some thirty nations have instituted family allowance programs (1957), and the United States is the only western industrialized nation without such a system. Like most other welfare programs, family allowance programs have had their share of critics. It has been contended that family allowances will tend to increase the birth rate, but there is little statistical evidence to support this contention. A more valid criticism is that payments to all families with children results in large sums of money going to many families that do not need governmental support. This problem can be solved, as Denmark has done, by varying the family allowance payments inversely with income, and discontinuing them altogether after a certain level of income is reached.[46] Another criticism of such programs is that they fail to reach single adults living in poverty. Other programs in addition to family allowances would have to supplement a program of family allowances if poverty is to be totally eradicated.[47]

LONG-TERM TRENDS ON TYPES OF POVERTY

In a recently published book Professor John Turnbull has made a valuable contribution in tracing the changing trends in poverty from 1910 to 1960.[48] He points out that fewer people are dying prematurely today. Furthermore, the OASDHI program plus private insurance is much more adequately taking care of the problems caused by premature death in 1960 than in 1910. Although more people are living longer and retiring more frequently today than in 1910, Turnbull felt that the problem of the aged should be lessened in the future due to the OASDHI program. He also pointed out that the aggregate risk of unemployment is less today than 25 years ago and about the same as in 1910, although special risks, such as loss of skills, may be greater. Measured by the extent of coverage and the level of income restoration, society has taken care of the risk of unemployment much less successfully than for the risks of premature death and old age. Turnbull states that between 1955 and 1960 illness decreased by one-half to two-thirds in the aggregate. Fewer public programs exist to protect against illness, but private insurance is providing about as much protection for this risk as our public programs for unemployment insurance and workmen's compensation.

In 1910 Turnbull estimated that two-thirds of our poverty was due to the four causes of premature death, old age, economic unemployment, and illness.

---

[46] *Ibid.*, p. 49.

[47] For a more detailed analysis of family allowances, *see* James Vadakin, *Family Allowances* (Miami, University of Miami Press, 1958).

[48] John G. Turnbull, *The Changing Faces of Economic Insecurity* (Minneapolis, Minn., University of Minnesota Press, 1966).

In 1960 he estimated that these four accounted for about 50 percent of poverty. In the future the reduction in the risks of premature death, unemployment, and illness should more than balance the increasing risks of old age. He concluded that improvements are still necessary in fighting the four mentioned risks. Since the risks in three of the four are declining, attention will have to be directed to other causes of poverty, which percentagewise are becoming more important.

UNMET NEEDS

In the immediate future, it does not appear that the minimum guaranteed-income proposal will be put into operation, although it is gaining more and more adherents. Instead, attempts probably will be made to attack the problem of poverty on a number of fronts by older, piecemeal methods. For the poor in this country who are not in the work force, much still remains to be done. As was indicated earlier, many aged are still living in poverty. For those injured industrially, payments to those severely injured are particularly inadequate. Although programs for the ill have improved over the years, much still remains to be done to advance our programs in this area. We are particularly lacking in temporary disability insurance at the state level, for only four states and the railroads have such legislation. Fortunately, some of the problem is solved through private industry making provision for illness, but for those individuals not fortunate enough to work for a firm which provides for such payments, poverty may result. Hospital and medical care is still not comprehensive in this country, but at least improvements are being made.

A majority of people living in poverty today are able-bodied poor. Although World War II reduced the heavy unemployment of the 1930's to a minimum, there was a secular increase in unemployment during the 1950's and into the 1960's. The new laws of the 1960's of Aid to Depressed Areas and Retraining laws along with the tax cut have helped to reduce unemployment, but unemployment is still higher than necessary. Our unemployment insurance laws also need improvement in coverage and benefits.

Per capita income in the United States in the future should rise sufficiently high that most families will not experience poverty. The major economic problem in the next 25 years will be the assimilation of minority and lower-income groups into our urban society. Little has been done as yet to properly assimilate our subsistence farmers and hired farm labor into urban life, but the beginnings made by our Rural Areas Development Program should help. Improved training and guidance for our rural youth should aid also. Minority groups are in a particularly disadvantageous position in our society, but here too beginnings have been made to help such groups through Fair Employment Practice Laws, improved housing, and the like.

Of particular importance in eliminating poverty would be an improvement of our educational system. Depressed rural areas are simply too poor to provide an adequate education for their youth. Aid must be forthcoming both from the state and federal level. An upgrading of the educational curriculum is necessary as is the quality of our teaching and teachers. More counseling is desperately needed. Weaknesses of our schools in slum areas particularly need alleviating. Sometime in the not too distant future higher education should be made available to all those who are able to profit from it.

With more and more people moving to cities, and with the blight that results as cities deteriorate, more effort will have to be expended to eradicate blighted and slum areas. Providing a more adequate environment for our lower-income groups should aid them in becoming better assimilated into our American society.

Minimum wages aid in at least providing a minimum floor below which income may not fall. Coverage problems are particularly important, for vast numbers of lower-income people are exempt from our minimum wage laws. Lastly, a rapidly expanding economy is needed to eradicate poverty. Here all of the tools of society, including those of the physical and social scientist, are needed.

This book has shown that there has been improvement in the standard of living of American people over the years; yet much remains to be done to eradicate poverty in this country. The costs should not be excessively high. An additional $10 to $20 billions going to lower-income groups would aid these groups considerably. In the past, welfare has been improved primarily by expansion of our economy and improvement in our social welfare programs. This improvement has been made without affecting our distribution of income. Welfare measures have not resulted in a larger percentage of income going to lower-income groups although without such payments, the share going to the poorest groups would have decreased even further.

Additional effort is needed to eradicate poverty in the United States. Reliance on both improved private and public programs is an absolute necessity. By proceeding on both fronts, the worst problems of poverty should be eradicated within several decades. Additional effort will be needed for many, many years to aid underdeveloped countries raise their extremely low incomes. In closing, a few words from the late Professor Edwin E. Witte may be of value. In speaking on the topic of "The Bug-a-Boo" of the welfare state, he pointed out that the American concept has never been one of viewing the government as an agency of oppression, far removed from the people. Rather, in quoting Abraham Lincoln's famous words, it is a "government of the people, by the people, and for the people." With government viewed as a servant of the people, not their master, it can aid them and serve their purposes.[49] Improved governmental programs along with improved private measures should go a long way toward solving the problem of economic insecurity.

[49] Edwin E. Witte, *Social Security Perspectives* (Madison, Wisc., University of Wisconsin Press, 1962), p. 41.

Bibliography

Abrams, Charles, *Man's Struggle for Shelter in an Urbanizing World* (Cambridge, Mass., M. I. T., 1964).

Brameld, Theodore, *Education as Power* (New York, Holt, Rinehart, and Winston, 1965).

Conant, James B., *Shaping Educational Policy* (New York, McGraw-Hill, 1964).

———, *Slums and Suburbs: A Commentary on Schools in Metropolitan Areas* (New York, McGraw-Hill, 1961).

Friedman, Milton, *Capitalism and Freedom* (Chicago, University of Chicago Press, 1962).

Goldwater, Barry, *The Conscience of a Conservative* (Shepherdsville, Ky., Victor, 1960).

Hemdahl, Reuel, *Urban Renewal* (New York, Scarecrow Press, 1959).

Hook, Sidney, *Education for Modern Man: A New Perspective* (New York, Knopf, 1963).

Hoover, Calvin E., *The Economy, Liberty and the State* (New York, Doubleday, 1961).

Millspaugh, Martin, and Gurney Breckenfeld, *The Human Side of Urban Renewal* (New York, Washburn, 1960).

Myrdal, Gunnar, *Beyond the Welfare State* (New Haven, Conn., Yale, 1960).

Reid, Margaret G., *Housing and Income* (Chicago, University of Chicago Press, 1962).

Schorr, Alvin L., *Slums and Social Insecurity: An Appraisal of the Effectiveness of Housing Policies in Helping to Eliminate Poverty in the United States* (Washington, D.C., Government Printing Office, 1963).

Schultz, Theodore W., *The Economic Value of Education* (New York, Columbia, 1963).

Theobald, Robert, *The Guaranteed Income* (New York, Doubleday, 1966).

Titmuss, Richard M., *Essays on the Welfare State* (London, G. Allen, 1959).

Turnbull, John G., *The Changing Faces of Economic Insecurity* (Minneapolis, Minn., University of Minnesota Press, 1966).

Weaver, Robert C., *The Urban Complex* (New York, Doubleday, 1964).

Wendt, Paul Francis, *Housing Policy—A Search for Solutions: A Comparison of the United Kingdom, Sweden, West Germany, and the United States Since World War II* (Berkeley, University of California Press, 1963).

Witte, Edwin E., *Social Security Perspectives* (Madison, Wisc., University of Wisconsin Press, 1962).

INDEX